BIBLIOGRAPHIES AND GUIDES IN
AFRICAN STUDIES
James C. Armstrong, *Advisory Editor*

# Land Tenure and Agrarian Reform in Africa and the Near East: An Annotated Bibliography

*Compiled by the Staff*
*of the Land Tenure Center Library*
under the direction of
Teresa J. Anderson, Librarian

G. K. HALL & CO., 70 LINCOLN STREET, BOSTON, MASS.

Library of Congress Cataloging in Publication Data

Wisconsin. University--Madison. Land Tenure Center.
    Library.
    Land tenure and agrarian reform in Africa and the
Near East.
    *Bibliographies and guides in African studies*
    Includes indexes.
    1. Land tenure--Africa--Bibliography. 2. Land
reform--Africa--Bibliography. 3. Land tenure--Near East
--Bibliography. 4. Land reform--Near East--Bibliography.
I. Anderson, Teresa J. II. Title. *III. Series.*
Z7164.L3W56 1976 [HD963] 016.3333'2'096 76-3652
ISBN 0-8161-7921-2

*This publication is printed on permanent/durable acid-free paper.*
MANUFACTURED IN THE UNITED STATES OF AMERICA

# Contents

# Foreword

Since the founding of the Land Tenure Center in 1962, under the leadership of all three of its directors--Raymond J. Penn, Peter Dorner, and myself--the importance of a specialized Library to the work of the Center has been understood. The Library has always been viewed as an essential and integral part of the Center.

This recognition has led to the Library becoming one of the world's largest collection of book, journal, and pamphlet materials on the subjects of land tenure, land reform, problems of the small-acreage farmer, and related topics in the Third World countries. While other university and agency libraries do have larger holdings on Latin America, Africa, or Asia, there is no other place where a researcher can visit and actually use all of the material that has been collected on the subjects under discussion in these areas of the world.

The Library's staff has long worked to extend the use of this unique facility beyond the limits of the University of Wisconsin-Madison campus by means of the bibliographies in its Training and Methods series. Now it has gone a step further to create this anno-tated guide to a major portion of its holdings. It is a companion volume to the previously issued Agrarian Reform in Latin America:  An Annotated Bibliography (Land Economics Monograph, no. 5, 1974).  A volume on Asia will follow.

It is the hope of all of us associated with the Land Tenure Center that this bibliography will be of real assistance to all those con-cerned with the increasingly crucial problems of agrarian reform and rural development.

William C. Thiesenhusen, Director                Madison, Wisconsin
Land Tenure Center                               November 1975

# Introduction

It has long been clear to the staff of the Land Tenure Center Library that there is a demand for reference tools of the sort this volume represents. We receive requests daily for one or more of the individual country bibliographies in our Training and Methods series; our bibliography on colonization and settlement is now in its third printing; and we still receive requests for a 1965 bibliography on agrarian reform which long ago went out of print because of the difficulty in locating much of the material cited in it.

The bibliography in hand is intended to serve as a guide to literature in the field through its annotations. Locations have been designated for every item listed. If an item is not available for consultation on the University of Wisconsin-Madison campus, it has not been included in the bibliography. Thus interested persons, if unable to obtain an item included elsewhere, can be assured of being able to borrow or use the material here in Madison.

Persons wishing to borrow material listed in this bibliography on Inter-Library Loan should contact the appropriate library on the University of Wisconsin-Madison campus, as indicated by the Library symbol in the call number. All books and file items (pamphlets, reports, etc.) in the Land Tenure Center Library may be borrowed for four weeks and renewed for an additional four weeks providing no other request for the material has been received. LTC Library reference material may be borrowed for two weeks and renewed for an additional two weeks providing no other request for the material has been received. Use of the reference material is restricted to the premises of the borrowing library. LTC Library periodicals do not circulate. Photocopies of journal articles are available at a cost of $.10 per page plus postage. LTC Library microfilms do not circulate. Positive enlarged copies are available at a cost of $.15 per page plus postage. Special arrangements may be made in the case of international requests. Except for very unusual cases, requests from individuals will not be honored.

The countries included in this bibliography are listed alphabetically in the "Key to Symbols." Not included are Cape Verde Islands; Comoro Islands; Equatorial Guinea; French Territory of the Afars and

# INTRODUCTION

Issas; Guinea-Bissau; Namibia; São Tomé and Príncipe; Spanish Sahara; and Seychelles. Included under the section "Arabian Peninsula" are general works on the area as a whole and works on Saudi Arabia. None of the other countries on the Peninsula are covered individually. The annotators were unable to locate materials of any substance on the countries or territories excluded.

Numerous citations of materials not held by the University of Wisconsin library system were turned up in the process of compiling the bibliography. These citations have now been compiled into a desiderata list to be acquired for the Land Tenure Center collection in the future. Researchers and librarians will be able to contact the LTC Library for information on materials on agrarian reform and stand a better than average chance of obtaining them, even if they do not appear in this bibliography.

## GUIDE TO THE USE OF THE BIBLIOGRAPHY

The bibliography includes individual and corporate author and subject indexes. The author indexes are alphabetical listings of all personal and corporate authors, followed by the numbers of the items for which they are responsible.

Users interested in general information on a particular country's land tenure can go directly to the country division of the bibliography and scan the items in that section. Within each country, items are arranged alphabetically by author according to Library of Congress filing rules and numbered consecutively. Every effort has been made to ascertain the correct form of name, but in some cases the Arabic names could not be verified.

Users wishing only to see items on a specific aspect of land tenure in a given country should refer to the classified outline at the front of the subject index. For example, works on nationalization and expropriation of land in Algeria would be found under 311 in the subject index and consultation of that number would lead the user to fifteen entries in the Algeria section, including ALG-1, 12, 18, and 35.

Once the desired entry is located by turning to the Algeria section and finding the item number on the left hand side of the page, the user must interpret the citation.

The citation for published materials consists of:

1) the author, separated from the title by a period;
2) the title, in capital letters;
3) a series statement;
4) place of publication, publisher, and date of publication;
5) number of pages;

6) indication of the presence of a substantial bibliography;
7) call number,
    a) preceded by library code if in a collection other than
       LTC (See Key to Symbols for library codes);
    b) consisting only of Library of Congress or File number,
       if held by the LTC Library.

AFR-35. Coissoró, Narana.[1] / THE CUSTOMARY LAW OF SUCCESSION IN
        CENTRAL AFRICA.[2] / Estudos de Ciencias Políticos' e Sociais,
        78.[3] / Lisboa (Junta de Investigações do Ultramar) 1966.[4] /
        li, 492 p.[5] / Bibl.[6]             Mem JX 6510 A35 C6[7a]

The citation for journal articles and unpublished material consists of:

1) the author;
2) the title in lower case letters and quotation marks;
3) information relevant to the journal or other issuance,
    a) journal abbreviation, volume number, issue number, date
       and page numbers;
    b) place of writing if known, date of issue if known,
       number of pages, occasion or format of issue if known;
4) Call number, unless the citation is for an article in a
    journal in the LTC Library, in which case there is no call
    number at all.

AFR-57. Gershenberg, Irving.[1] / "Customary land tenure as constraint
        on agricultural development: a re-evaluation."[2] / (In
        EAJRD, 4:1, 1971. p. 51-62)[3a]           Ag Per[4]

AFR-81. Letnev, A. B.[1] / "Estimation of agricultural produce market-
        ing systems in connection with agrarian reforms; the case of
        West Africa."[2] / Moscow, 1967. 14 p. Bibl.[3b] /
                          Files Afr 63 L28[4]

The compilers' object has been to provide as many points of
access to each individual item as possible. Often, an article which
originally appeared in a journal not in the LTC collection is
actually available as a reprint, photocopy, detached copy or in
another form. In such cases, the citation to the original journal
will appear first, followed by information on other copies available
on the University of Wisconsin-Madison campus. For example:

AFR-110. Potekhin, Ivan I. "Land relations in African countries."
        (In JMAS, 1:1, 1963. p. 39-59)        Mem AP J83 M683
        Also available in Item AFR-3, p. 9.194-9.204
                          Files Afr 4 A37

In the case of detached copies or photocopies, the citation will
simply read "Also available as a separate," followed by the call
number.

# Introduction

To save space and labor, complete individual citations and annotations appear in the bibliography only once. Any further references to the item appear·in an abbreviated form consisting of author, title, date of publication, and call number with a reference to the original citation for complete bibliographical information.

AFR-32 Chambers, Robert.  SETTLEMENT SCHEMES IN TROPICAL AFRICA: A STUDY OF ORGANIZATIONS AND DEVELOPMENT.  New York, Praeger (1969).  xxv, 294 p.  Bibl.        HD 1516 A34 C5

This is the citation as it appears in the general African section followed by an annotation.  In the individual country sections it appears in the following form:

Chambers, Robert.  SETTLEMENT SCHEMES IN TROPICAL AFRICA: A STUDY OF ORGANIZATIONS AND DEVELOPMENT.  1969.

HD 1516 A34 C5

See Item AFR-32 for citation and annotation.

Items added to the bibliography after the annotating was completed are distinguished by the addition of a letter to the item number; e.g., SYRIA-3a and SYRIA-14a.  These additional citations are primarily to materials added to the LTC Library catalog between June 1, 1975 and October 31, 1975.

# Acknowledgments

In the four years it has taken to complete this bibliography, several staff members have contributed time and talent to it. Some of them did not comprehend exactly what it was to which they were contributing, nor what the final product would be like. But they worked, and, in spite of everyone's occasional doubts, the African ARB (as it is affectionately called) is seeing the light of day. I cannot recall every individual who had a hand in its completion, but several stand out as being instrumental.

William Thiesenhusen, director of the Land Tenure Center, has supported this project from the very beginning, has granted financing for it, and has prompted other faculty members to participate. I thank him especially for his recognition of the importance of a growing, vital library to a research program such as that of the Land Tenure Center.

David J. King, assistant professor in the Land Tenure Center, has been a driving force behind the completion of the Africa-Near East ARB. It was his support and conviction that the publication must be completed that really kept it going at times. I thank him for that support and for his tolerance of my way of "getting things done."

Jane Knowles, in her editorial capacity, guided me through the intricacies of preparing a book for publication. Faculty members of the Land Tenure Center--namely, David King, Kemal Karpat, and Marvin Miracle--read all or portions of the annotations and suggested changes, additions, etc. Julia Schwenn and Don Esser assisted in many ways, primarily by being at hand when we needed encouragement and advice on routines, regulations, etc.

Stephen Baier and Harold Lemel labored long and tediously at writing annotations for the African and Near Eastern sections respectively. They also created the outline for the subject index, and Harry assigned the classification numbers to the individual entries. Their expertise and cooperation were indispensable and greatly appreciated.

# ACKNOWLEDGEMENTS

Gerry Strey has been indispensable to me for the past three years in her capacity as "right-hand person" (officially, library publications assistant). I didn't realize how indispensable until she left to take a new position a few months before the completion of the manuscript. Jane Dennis and Pat Frye did superb jobs of typing the manuscript from all manner of illegible copy, and Helaine Kriegel compiled and typed the author index.

I also must mention the cooperation and hard work of my library staff who, when not actually involved in the production of this book, took on many extra duties in order that my time would be free to work on it: Charlotte Lott, Rick Puhek, Pat Frye, Shirley Van Sluys, and Shaukat Naeem.


Teresa J. Anderson                                    Madison, Wisconsin
Librarian                                             November 1975

# Key to Symbols

1.  SECTION ABBREVIATIONS

| | |
|---|---|
| AFR - AFRICA | MALAW - MALAWI |
| ALG - ALGERIA | MALI - MALI |
| ANG - ANGOLA | MAURITA - MAURITANIA |
| ARAB - ARABIAN PENINSULA | MAURITI - MAURITIUS |
| BOTS - BOTSWANA | MOR - MOROCCO |
| BURU - BURUNDI | MOZ - MOZAMBIQUE |
| CAF - CENTRAL AFRICAN REPUBLIC | MR - MALAGASY REPUBLIC |
| CAM - CAMEROON | NE - NEAR EAST AND NORTH |
| CHAD - CHAD | AFRICA |
| CONGO - CONGO | NIG - NIGERIA |
| CYP - CYPRUS | NIGER - NIGER |
| DAHOM - DAHOMEY | RHOD - RHODESIA |
| EGY - EGYPT | RWA - RWANDA |
| ETH - ETHIOPIA | SA - SOUTH AFRICA |
| GAB - GABON | SEN - SENEGAL |
| GAM - GAMBIA | SL - SIERRA LEONE |
| GHA - GHANA | SOM - SOMALIA |
| GUIN - GUINEA | SUD - SUDAN |
| IC - IVORY COAST | SWAZ - SWAZILAND |
| IRAN - IRAN | SYRIA - SYRIA |
| IRAQ - IRAQ | TANZ - TANZANIA |
| ISRAEL - ISRAEL | TOGO - TOGO |
| JORD - JORDAN | TUNIS - TUNISIA |
| KEN - KENYA | TURK - TURKEY |
| LEB - LEBANON | UGA - UGANDA |
| LESO - LESOTHO | UV - UPPER VOLTA |
| LIBE - LIBERIA | ZAI - ZAIRE |
| LIBY - LIBYA | ZAM - ZAMBIA |

2.  n.d.   NO DATE OF PUBLICATION

3.  n.p.   NO PLACE OF PUBLICATION

4.  l,   LEAVES

5.  v.   VOLUME(S)

# KEY TO SYMBOLS

6. Files.   IDENTIFICATION FOR ITEMS KEPT IN VERTICAL FILE
            CABINETS AT LTC LIBRARY

7. LIBRARY CODES INCLUDED IN CALL NUMBER

   Ag - STEENBOCK AGRICULTURAL LIBRARY BOOK COLLECTION
   Ag Doc - STEENBOCK AGRICULTURAL LIBRARY DOCUMENTS COLLECTION
   Ag Per - STEENBOCK AGRICULTURAL LIBRARY PERIODICAL COLLECTION
   Art - ART LIBRARY
   Geol - GEOLOGY LIBRARY COLLECTION
   Hist - WISCONSIN STATE HISTORICAL SOCIETY COLLECTION
   Law - LAW LIBRARY COLLECTION
   Mem - MEMORIAL LIBRARY COLLECTION
   (No Code - LTC LIBRARY COLLECTION)

8. REF.   LTC LIBRARY REFERENCE COLLECTION

9. Microfilm; Microfiche.   LTC LIBRARY MICROFORM COLLECTION

10. Separate; Also available as a separate - ADDITIONAL COPY OF ITEM
            AVAILABLE AS A REPRINT, PHOTOCOPY OR DETACHED COPY

11. Item.   INDIVIDUAL, INDEPENDENTLY CITED WORK

12. Bibl.   BIBLIOGRAPHY INCLUDED

# Acronyms and Abbreviations

| | |
|---|---|
| CADU | CHILALO AGRICULTURAL DEVELOPMENT UNIT (Asella, Ethiopia) |
| CERES | CENTRE D'ETUDES ET DE RECHERCHES ECONOMIQUES ET SOCIALES, UNIVERSITE TUNIS |
| CMS | CHURCH MISSIONARY SOCIETY |
| EPTA | EXPANDED PROGRAM OF TECHNICAL ASSISTANCE |
| FAO | FOOD AND AGRICULTURE ORGANIZATION OF THE UNITED NATIONS (Rome) |
| HCAR | HIGHER COMMITTEE FOR AGRARIAN REFORM (Egypt) |
| HMSO | HER MAJESTY'S STATIONERY OFFICE (Great Britain) |
| IAEA | INSTITUTE OF ASIAN ECONOMIC AFFAIRS (Tokyo) |
| IBRD | INTERNATIONAL BANK FOR RECONSTRUCTION AND DEVELOPMENT (Washington, D.C.) |
| IITA | INTERNATIONAL INSTITUTE OF TROPICAL AGRICULTURE (Ibadan, Nigeria) |
| ILO | INTERNATIONAL LABOUR ORGANISATION (Geneva) |
| INCIDI | INSTITUT INTERNATIONAL DES CIVILISATIONS DIFFERENTES (Bruxelles) |
| INSEE | INSTITUT NATIONAL DE LA STATISTIQUE ET DES ETUDES ECONOMIQUES (France) |
| IRAT | INSTITUT DE RECHERCHES D'AGRONOMIE TROPICAL ET DE CULTURE VIVRIERES |
| ISS | INSTITUTE OF SOCIAL STUDIES (The Hague) |
| MIT | MASSACHUSETTS INSTITUTE FOR TECHNOLOGY (Cambridge, Mass.) |
| NASA | NATIONAL AGRICULTURAL SETTLEMENT AUTHORITY (Libya) |
| NISER | NIGERIAN INSTITUTE OF SOCIAL AND ECONOMIC RESEARCH (Ibadan) |
| NOAS | NATIONAL ORGANIZATION FOR AGRICULTURAL SETTLING (Libya) |
| ORSTOM | OFFICE DE LA RECHERCHE SCIENTIFIQUE ET TECHNIQUE OUTRE MER (Paris) |
| PAU | PAN AMERICAN UNION (Washington, D.C.) |
| SEDES | SOCIETE D'ETUDES POUR LE DEVELOPPEMENT ECONOMIQUE ET SOCIAL (Paris) |
| SOMALAC | SOCIETE MALGACHE D'AMENAGEMENT DU LAC ALAOTRA |
| UAR | UNITED ARAB REPUBLIC |
| UN | UNITED NATIONS (New York) |
| UNDP | UNITED NATIONS DEVELOPMENT PROGRAMME |
| UNECA | UNITED NATIONS ECONOMIC COMMISSION FOR AFRICA (Addis Ababa) |
| UNESCO | UNITED NATIONS UCATIONAL, SCIENTIFIC AND CULTURAL ORGANIZATION (Paris) |

# Acronyms and Abbreviations

| | |
|---|---|
| UNRISD | UNITED NATIONS RESEARCH INSTITUTE FOR SOCIAL DEVELOPMENT (Geneva) |
| USAID | UNITED STATES AGENCY FOR INTERNATIONAL DEVELOPMENT (Washington, D.C.) |
| USDA | UNITED STATES DEPARTMENT OF AGRICULTURE (Washington, D.C.) |
| WADU | WOLLAMO AGRICULTURAL DEVELOPMENT UNIT (Ethiopia) |

# Journal Abbreviations

| | |
|---|---|
| AA | AFRICAN AFFAIRS; JOURNAL OF THE ROYAL AFRICAN SOCIETY (London) |
| AAGA | Association of American Geographers. ANNALS (Washington) |
| AB | AFRICANA BULLETIN (Warsaw) |
| AEBA | AGRICULTURAL ECONOMICS BULLETIN FOR AFRICA (Addis Ababa) |
| AEQUA | AEQUATORIA; MISSION CATHOLIQUE (Coquilhatville) |
| AFAS | AFRIQUE ET L'ASIE; REVUE POLITIQUE SOCIALE ET ECONOMIQUE ET BULLETIN DES ANCIENS DU C.H.E.A.M. (Paris) |
| AFD | AFRICAN DEVELOPMENT (London) |
| AFH | AFRIKA HEUTE (Bonn) |
| AFS | AFRICAN STUDIES (Johannesburg) |
| AFS/K | AFRICAN STUDIES (Kyoto) |
| AFSPEC | AFRIKA SPECTRUM (Hamburg) |
| AG | ANNALES DE GEOGRAPHIE (Paris) |
| A/GB | AGRICULTURE (Great Britain) |
| A/IAI | AFRICA (London) |
| AJCL | AMERICAN JOURNAL OF COMPARATIVE LAW (Berkeley) |
| AJES | AMERICAN JOURNAL OF ECONOMICS AND SOCIOLOGY (New York) |
| ALS | AFRICAN LAW STUDIES (New York) |
| AMS | ANNALES MAROCAINES DE SOCIOLOGIE (Rabat) |
| ANFRIDI | ANNUAIRE FRANCAISE DE DROIT INTERNATIONAL (Paris) |
| ANNALES | ANNALES; ECONOMIES, SOCIETES, CIVILISATIONS (Paris) |
| ANTH | ANTHROPOLOGICA (Ottowa) |
| AQ | ANTHROPOLOGICAL QUARTERLY (Washington) |
| ARBSD | AFRICA; RIVISTA BIMESTRALE DI STUDI E DOCUMENTAZIONE (Rome) |
| ARSCBS | Académie Royale des Sciences Coloniales. BULLETIN DES SEANCES (Brussels) |
| ASN/P | Agricultural Society of Nigeria. PROCEEDINGS (Nsukka) |
| ASR | AFRICAN STUDIES REVIEW (New York) |
| AUSBFD | Ankara. Université. Siyasal Bilgiler Fakültesi. SIYASAL BILGILER FAKULTESI DERGISI (Ankara) |
| AUTO | AUTOGESTION (Paris) |
| AW | AFRICAN WORLD (London) |
| BACBRU | BULLETIN AGRICOLE DU CONGO BELGE ET DU RUANDA-URUNDI (Brussels) |
| BESM | BULLETIN ECONOMIQUE ET SOCIAL DU MAROC (Rabat) |
| BJIDCC | BULLETIN DES JURIDICTIONS INDIGINES ET DU DROIT COUTUMIER CONGOLAISE (Elisabethville) |

# Journal Abbreviations

| | |
|---|---|
| BMIB | Bank-i-Markazi-i Iran. BULLETIN (Teheran) |
| BNR | BOTSWANA NOTES AND RECORDS (Gaberone) |
| BO/M | BULLETIN OFFICIEL, MOROCCO (Rabat) |
| BRES | BULLETIN OF RURAL ECONOMICS AND SOCIOLOGY (Ibadan) |
| BULIS/R | Brussels. Université Libre. Institut de Sociologie. REVUE DE L'INSTITUT DE SOCIOLOGIE (Brussels) |
| C&D | CULTURES ET DEVELOPPEMENT (Louvain) |
| CAIS | COMMUNAUTES; ARCHIVES INTERNATIONALES DE SOCIOLOGIE DE LA COOPERATION ET DU DEVELOPPEMENT (Paris) |
| CBEMR | Commercial Bank of Ethiopia. MARKET REPORT (Addis Ababa) |
| CD | COOPERATION ET DEVELOPPEMENT (Paris) |
| CE | COMERCIO EXTERIOR (Mexico) |
| CEA | CAHIERS D'ETUDES AFRICAINES (Paris) |
| CERES | CERES: THE FAO REVIEW ON DEVELOPMENT (Rome) |
| CES | CAHIERS ECONOMIQUES ET SOCIAUX (Kinshasa) |
| CGA/GC | Cyprus Geographical Association. GEOGRAPHICAL CHRONICLES (Nicosia) |
| CIV | CIVILISATIONS (Brussels) |
| CJAS | CANADIAN JOURNAL OF AFRICAN STUDIES (Montreal) |
| CJTL | COLUMBIA JOURNAL OF TRANSNATIONAL LAW (New York) |
| CLR | COLUMBIA LAW REVIEW (New York) |
| COLD | COLONIAL DEVELOPMENT (London) |
| COM/B | CAHIERS D'OUTRE-MER. REVUE DE GEOGRAPHIE DE BORDEAUX ET DE L'ATLANTIQUE (Bordeaux) |
| COMD | COMMONWEALTH DEVELOPMENT (London) |
| COR | CORONA (London) |
| CRAS | CENTENNIAL REVIEW OF ARTS AND SCIENCE (East Lansing, Mich.) |
| CRISP | Centre de Recherche et d'Information Socio-Politiques. ETUDES AFRICAINES (Brussels) |
| DA | DEUTSCHE AUSSENPOLITIK (Berlin) |
| DCI | DEVELOPPEMENT ET CIVILISATIONS (Paris) |
| DD | DEVELOPMENT DIGEST (Washington) |
| DEC | DEVELOPING ECONOMIES (Tokyo) |
| DUAA | Dakar. Université. Faculté de Droit et des Sciences Economiques. ANNALES AFRICAINES (Paris) |
| EAAJ | EAST AFRICAN AGRICULTURAL AND FORESTRY JOURNAL (Nairobi) |
| EAER | EASTERN AFRICA ECONOMIC REVIEW (Nairobi) |
| EAGR | EAST AFRICAN GEOGRAPHICAL REVIEW (Kampala) |
| EAJRD | EAST AFRICAN JOURNAL OF RURAL DEVELOPMENT (Kampala) |
| EALJ | EAST AFRICAN LAW JOURNAL (Nairobi) |
| EANHS/J | East African Natural History Society. JOURNAL (Nairobi) |
| EAR | EAST AFRICA & RHODESIA (London) |
| ECB | ENCYCLOPEDIE DU CONGO BELGE (Brussels) |
| ECON | ECONOMIST (London) |
| EDAH | ETUDES DAHOMEENNES (Porto-Novo) |
| EDCC | ECONOMIC DEVELOPMENT AND CULTURAL CHANGE (Chicago) |
| EGEOG | ECONOMIC GEOGRAPHY (Worcester, Mass.) |
| EJEA | EMPIRE JOURNAL OF EXPERIMENTAL AGRICULTURE (Oxford) |

# Journal Abbreviations

| | |
|---|---|
| EOB | ETHIOPIA OBSERVER (Addis Ababa) |
| EP | ECONOMIC PLANNING: JOURNAL FOR AGRICULTURE AND RELATED INDUSTRIES (Montreal) |
| ERDE | ERDE (Berlin) |
| ESR | EMPIRE SURVEY REVIEW (London) |
| ETR | ETUDES RURALES; REVUE TRIMESTRELLE D'HISTOIRE, GEOGRAPHIE, SOCIOLOGIE, ET ECONOMIE DES CAMPAGNES (The Hague) |
| EVOL | ETUDES VOLTAIQUES (Ouagadougou) |
| FA | FOREIGN AGRICULTURE (INCLUDING CROPS AND MARKETS) (Washington) |
| FAF | FOREIGN AFFAIRS; AN AMERICAN QUARTERLY REVIEW (New York) |
| FAL | FOOD AND AGRICULTURE LEGISLATION (Rome) |
| FRIS | FOOD RESEARCH INSTITUTE STUDIES (Stanford) |
| GBAE | GHANAIAN BULLETIN OF AGRICULTURAL ECONOMICS (Accra) |
| GEOG/N | GEOGRAPHY (Nanking) |
| GGAB | Ghana Geographical Association. BULLETIN (Legon) |
| GG/Z | GOVERNMENT GAZETTE, ZAMBIA (Lusaka) |
| GJL | GEOGRAPHICAL JOURNAL (London) |
| GJS | GHANA JOURNAL OF SOCIOLOGY (Accra) |
| GM | GEOGRAPHICAL MAGAZINE (London) |
| GR | GEOGRAPHICAL REVIEW (New York) |
| GRU | GEOGRAPHISCHE RUNDSCHAU; ZEITSCHRIFT FUR SCHULGEOGRAPHIE (Braunschweig, W. Germany) |
| HOMS | HOMME ET LA SOCIETE (Paris) |
| IAF | INTERNATIONALES AFRIKA FORUM (Munich) |
| IA/L | INTERNATIONAL AFFAIRS (London) |
| IASRR | Institute of African Studies. RESEARCH REVIEW (Legon) |
| IBADAN | IBADAN; A JOURNAL PUBLISHED AT UNIVERSITY COLLEGE (Ibadan) |
| IBGT | Institute of British Geographers. TRANSACTIONS AND PAPERS (London) |
| ICR | INDIAN COOPERATIVE REVIEW (New Delhi) |
| IER | INTERMOUNTAIN ECONOMIC REVIEW (Salt Lake City) |
| IJAE | INDIAN JOURNAL OF AGRICULTURAL ECONOMICS (Bombay) |
| ILR | INTERNATIONAL LABOUR REVIEW (Geneva) |
| ILRLSC | INFORMATION ON LAND REFORM, LAND SETTLEMENT, AND COOPERATIVES (Rome) |
| IR | INTERNATIONAL RELATIONS (Prague) |
| ISEAC | Institut de Science Economique Appliquée. CAHIERS (Paris) |
| IUR | Istanbul. Üniversite. Iktisat Fakultesi. ISTANBUL UNIVERSITESI IKTISAT FAKULTESI MECMUASI (Istanbul) |
| JA | JEUNE AFRIQUE (Tunis) |
| JAA | JOURNAL OF AFRICAN ADMINISTRATION (London) |
| JAE | JOURNAL OF AGRICULTURAL ECONOMICS (Reading) |
| JAH | JOURNAL OF AFRICAN HISTORY (London) |
| JAL | JOURNAL OF AFRICAN LAW (London) |
| JAO | JOURNAL OF ADMINISTRATION OVERSEAS (London) |
| JCLIL | JOURNAL OF COMPARATIVE LEGISLATION & INTERNATIONAL LAW (London) |

# JOURNAL ABBREVIATIONS

| | |
|---|---|
| JCR | JOURNAL OF CONFLICT RESOLUTION; A QUARTERLY FOR RESEARCH RELATED TO WAR AND PEACE (Ann Arbor, Mich.) |
| JDA | JOURNAL OF DEVELOPING AREAS (Macomb, Ill.) |
| JDS | JOURNAL OF DEVELOPMENT STUDIES; DEVOTED TO ECONOMIC, POLITICAL AND SOCIAL DEVELOPMENT (London) |
| JEARD | JOURNAL OF EASTERN AFRICAN RESEARCH AND DEVELOPMENT (Nairobi) |
| JETHL | JOURNAL OF ETHIOPIAN LAW (Addis Ababa) |
| JFE | JOURNAL OF FARM ECONOMICS (Lexington, Ky.) |
| JILE | JOURNAL OF INTERNATIONAL LAW AND ECONOMICS (Washington) |
| JLAO | JOURNAL OF LOCAL ADMINISTRATION OVERSEAS (London) |
| JMAS | JOURNAL OF MODERN AFRICAN STUDIES (London) |
| JNH | JOURNAL OF NEGRO HISTORY (Washington) |
| JO/RT | JOURNAL OFFICIEL DE LA REPUBLIQUE TUNISIENNE (Tunis) |
| JPS | JOURNAL OF PEASANT STUDIES (London) |
| JTG | JOURNAL OF TROPICAL GEOGRAPHY (Singapore) |
| KO | KONGO-OVERZEE; TIJDSCHRIFT VOOR EN OVER BELGISCH KONGO RUANDA-URUNDI EN AANPALANDE GEWESTEN (Antwerp) |
| LE | LAND ECONOMICS; A QUARTERLY JOURNAL DEVOTED TO THE STUDY OF ECONOMIC AND SOCIAL INSTITUTIONS (Madison) |
| LIS | LAW IN SOCIETY (Zaria, Nigeria) |
| LOASB | London. University. School of Oriental and African Studies. BULLETIN (London) |
| LQR | LAW QUARTERLY REVIEW (Toronto) |
| LRE | LOUISIANA RURAL ECONOMIST (University, La.) |
| LRLSC | LAND REFORM, LAND SETTLEMENT, AND COOPERATIVES (Rome) |
| LTC/N | Land Tenure Center. NEWSLETTER (Madison) |
| MAGHREB | MAGHREB; DOCUMENTS ALGERIE, MAROC, TUNISIA (Paris) |
| MAN | MAN; THE JOURNAL OF THE ROYAL ANTHROPOLOGICAL INSTITUTE (London) |
| MBI | MBIONI (Dar es Salaam) |
| MEA | MIDDLE EASTERN AFFAIRS (London) |
| MEEP | MIDDLE EAST ECONOMIC PAPERS (Beirut) |
| MEF | MIDDLE EAST FORUM (Beirut) |
| MEJ | MIDDLE EAST JOURNAL (Washington) |
| MR | MONTHLY REVIEW; AN INDEPENDENT SOCIALIST MAGAZINE (New York) |
| MT | MIGRATION TODAY (Geneva) |
| MW | MUSLIM WORLD; A QUARTERLY REVIEW OF HISTORY, CULTURE, RELIGIOUS AND THE CHRISTIAN MISSION IN ISLAMDOM (Hartford) |
| NA | NEUES AFRIKA; MONATSSCHRIFT FUER POLITIK, WIRTSCHAFT UND KULTUR IM NEUEN AFRIKA (Munich) |
| NAF | NOTES AFRICAINES (Dakar) |
| NBE/EB | National Bank of Egypt, Cairo. ECONOMIC BULLETIN (Cairo) |
| NGJ | NIGERIAN GEOGRAPHICAL JOURNAL (Ibadan) |
| NGRB | NEW GUINEA RESEARCH BULLETIN (Canberra) |

# Journal Abbreviations

| | |
|---|---|
| NGT | NORSK GEOGRAFISK TIDSSKRIFT; UTGITT AV DET NORSKE GEOGRAFISKE SELSKAB...(Oslo) |
| NJESS | NIGERIAN JOURNAL OF ECONOMIC AND SOCIAL STUDIES (Ibadan) |
| NLJ | NIGERIAN LAW JOURNAL (Lagos) |
| NLQ | NIGERIA LAWYERS' QUARTERLY (Lagos) |
| NM | NIGERIA MAGAZINE (Lagos) |
| NO | NEW OUTLOOK; MIDDLE EAST MONTHLY (Tel Aviv) |
| NRI | NOUVELLE REVUE INTERNATIONALE; PROBLEMES DE LA PAIX ET DU SOCIALISME (Paris) |
| NT | NEW TIMES (Moscow) |
| OAS | OXFORD AGRARIAN STUDIES (Oxford) |
| ODU | ODU (Ibadan, Nigeria) |
| OM | OPTIONS MEDITERANEENNES; REVUE DES PROBLEMES AGRICOLES MEDITERANEENNES (Paris) |
| ORBIS | ORBIS (Philadelphia) |
| PA | PRESENCE AFRICAINE (Paris) |
| PENSEE | PENSEE, REVUE DU RATIONALISME MODERNE, ARTS, SCIENCES, PHILOSOPHIE (Paris) |
| PETR | POLITIQUE ETRANGERE (Paris) |
| PG | PROFESSIONAL GEOGRAPHER (Washington) |
| PU/MP | Padua. Università. Istituto di Economia e Politica Agraria. Centro de Geografia Agraria. MISCELLANEOUS PAPERS (Padua) |
| QJER | QUARTERLY JOURNAL OF ECONOMIC RESEARCH (Teheran) |
| RA | RURAL AFRICANA: A NEWSLETTER OF RESEARCH NOTES ON RURAL POLITICS AND POLITICAL ANTHROPOLOGY (East Lansing, Mich.) |
| RAF | RECHERCHES AFRICAINES (Conakry) |
| RAIGBI/J | Royal Anthropological Institute of Great Britain and Ireland. JOURNAL (London) |
| RAN | RESEARCH ABSTRACTS AND NEWSLETTER (Kampala) |
| RAS/J | Royal African Society. JOURNAL (London) |
| RCA/J | Royal Central Asian Society. JOURNAL (London) |
| RDEC | REVUE DES ETUDES COOPERATIVES (Paris) |
| REA | RIVISTA DI ECONOMIA AGRARIA (Rome) |
| REC | REVUE ECONOMIQUE (Paris) |
| REM | REVUE ECONOMIQUE DE MADAGASCAR (Tananarive) |
| REP | RURAL ECONOMIC PROBLEMS (Tokyo) |
| RGL | REVIEW OF GHANA LAW (Accra) |
| RGM | REVUE DE GEOGRAPHIE DU MAROC (Rabat) |
| RH | REVUE HISTORIQUE (Paris) |
| RIDC | REVUE INTERNATIONALE DE DROIT COMPARE (Paris) |
| RJE | RHODESIAN JOURNAL OF ECONOMICS (Salisbury) |
| RJPOM | REVUE JURIDIQUE ET POLITIQUE D'OUTRE-MER (Paris) |
| RJPUF | REVUE JURIDIQUE ET POLITIQUE DE L'UNION FRANCAISE (Paris) |
| RJRB | REVUE JURIDIQUE DE DROIT ECRIT ET COUTUMIER DU RWANDA ET DU BURUNDI (Usumbura, Ruanda-Urundi) |
| RLJ | RHODES-LIVINGSTONE JOURNAL (Livingstone, Northern Rhodesia) |

# Journal Abbreviations

RPEN        RECUIEL PENANT (Paris)
RR          RAUMFORSCHUNG UND RAUMORDNUNG; ORGAN DER AKADEMIE FUR
            RAUMFORSCHUNG UND LANDESPLANUNG (Bremen-Horn)
RSAJ        Royal Society of Arts, London.  JOURNAL (London)
RTSS        REVUE TUNISIENNE DE SCIENCES SOCIALES (Tunis)
RURS        RURAL SOCIOLOGY; DEVOTED TO SCIENTIFIC STUDY OF RURAL AND
            SMALL-TOWN LIFE (University Park, Penn.)
SA          SOLS AFRICAINS (London)
SAGJ        SOUTH AFRICAN GEOGRAPHICAL JOURNAL, BEING A RECORD OF THE
            PROCEEDINGS OF THE S.A. GEOGRAPHICAL SOCIETY
            (Johannesburg)
SAJAA       SOUTH AFRICAN JOURNAL OF AFRICAN AFFAIRS (Pretoria)
SAJE        SOUTH AFRICAN JOURNAL OF ECONOMICS...(Johannesburg)
SAV         SAVANNA (Zaria)
SGM         SCOTTISH GEOGRAPHICAL MAGAZINE; pub. by the Royal Scottish
            Geographical Society (Edinburgh)
SJA         SOUTHWESTERN JOURNAL OF ANTHROPOLOGY (Albuquerque)
SLGJ        SIERRA LEONE GEOGRAPHICAL JOURNAL (Freetown, Sierra Leone)
SLS         SIERRA LEONE STUDIES (Freetown)
SMJ         Society of Malawi.  JOURNAL (Blantyre, Malawi)
SNR         SUDAN NOTES AND RECORDS...(London)
SRWA        SWISS REVIEW OF WORLD AFFAIRS (Zurich)
SYN         SYNTHESES; REVUE MENSUELLE INTERNATIONALE (Brussels)
TBCR        TIMES BRITISH COLONIES REVIEW (London)
TM          TERRE MALGACHE (Tananarive)
TROP        TROPICAL AGRICULTURE (Guildford, Surrey, Eng.)
TROPM       TROPICAL MAN (Leiden)
TVESG       TIJDSCHRIFT VOOR ECONOMISCHE EN SOCIALE GEOGRAPHIE (Leiden)
UCLALR      UCLA LAW REVIEW (Los Angeles)
UJ          UGANDA JOURNAL (London)
VEN         VENTURE (London)
VRU         VERFASSUNG UND RECHT IN UBERSEE (Hamburg)
WLR         WISCONSIN LAW REVIEW (Madison)
WPQ         WESTERN POLITICAL QUARTERLY (Salt Lake City)
WT          WORLD TODAY; CHATHAM HOUSE REVIEW (London)
YLJ         YALE LAW JOURNAL (New Haven)
ZAIRE       ZAIRE:  REVUE CONGOLAISE (Brussels; Antwerp)
ZAL         ZEITSCHRIFT FUR AUSLANDISCHE LANDWIRTSCHAFT (Frankfurt)
ZGG         ZEITSCHRIFT FUR DAS GESAMTE GENOSSENSCHAFTSWESEN
            (Göttingen)

# AFRICA: GENERAL

1. Adegboye, Rufus O. "A Study of the customary land tenure system and alternative methods of its improvement for accelerated agricultural development in selected African countries." n.p., (197-). (57) 1.                     Files Afr 58 A22

2. "African land tenure." (In JAA, October 1956. Special supplement. 44 p.)                     Mem AP J83 A258

   The report of the Conference on African Land Tenure in East and Central Africa, February 1956. It includes a review of patterns of landholding in British colonial possessions; policy recommendations, with emphasis on a suggestion for the use of negotiable titles; practical recommendations on how to go about issuing titles; and a comprehensive blueprint for a system of registering holdings.

3. "Agricultural development, land tenures, farm settlement, cooperatives, state farms" n.p., n.d. 347 p.
                     Files Afr 4 A37

   A collection of articles focusing on the ways in which Africans have addressed themselves to the problem of raising agricultural output. Five different approaches are discussed in detail: (1) the Kenyan solution, based on individual ownership; (2) land settlement schemes; (3) Ghanaian efforts to control land tenure systems; (4) cooperatives; and (5) Ghanaian State Farm experience. See Items AFR-27; AFR-69; AFR-110; GHA-4; GHA-41; KEN-100; KEN-114; SUD-12; and TANZ-68 for citations and annotations of individual articles.

4. Akabane, Hiroshi. "Traditional pattern of land occupancy in black Africa." (In DEC, 8:2, 1970. p. 161-179)

   According to the author, all forms of traditional land occupancy in sub-Saharan Africa have the following common characteristics: the basic land-occupying unit is the patriarchal family, called the "family-community," which uses land but may not dispose of it; larger kinship organizations, called

1

AFR 4-8

(Akabane, Hiroshi)
"tribe-communities," actually own the land and assure all of
their members access to it.

5.    Allan, William. THE AFRICAN HUSBANDMAN. New York, Barnes
      and Noble (1965). xii, 505 p. Bibl.    Ag HD 2117 A4 1965

A comprehensive survey of African agrarian systems, land use,
and land tenure. Includes case studies of environments and
land use studies emphasizing East Africa. Useful definitions
provide the basis for estimating the carrying capacities of
different systems, that is, the point of critical population
density beyond which the land begins to deteriorate. In
Chapter 20, "Land-Holding," Allan observes that "where money
income is obtained by labour migration the hierarchical system or some remnant of it survives and the sale of land is
resisted; but where cash cropping provides an adequate income
the intermediate rights in land are eliminated and sale of
land has become, or is in the process of becoming, common and
generally accepted practice."

6.    _____. "Changing patterns of African land use." (In RSAJ,
      July 1960.  p. 612-629)                      Art AP R889 A78
      Also available as a separate.        Files Afr 57.5 A55

A brief historical survey of African land use which includes
a section on tenure systems.

7.    Allott, Antony N. "Legal development and economic growth in
      Africa." (In Anderson, James Norman Dalrymple, ed. CHANGING
      LAW IN DEVELOPING COUNTRIES. London, Allen & Unwin, 1963.
      p. 194-209)                          Law S.AF SURV AND3c

In African countries most land law is dualistic, with elements
of customary African law existing side by side with out-of-
date European statutes. The author reviews the remedies to
this situation recommended by the East African Royal Commission
of 1955, which favored the individualization of tenure as a
means of providing collateral for loans so that farmers would
now be able to make productive investments in their land.

8.    _____. "Modern change in African land tenure." (In Cotran,
      Eugene; and Rubin, N. N., eds. READINGS IN AFRICAN LAW, VOL.
      1. London, Cass, 1970, c 1969.  p. 236-242)
                                          Law S.AF 6 SURV C82

African customary law evolves spontaneously as institutions
respond to changes in the economic environment. An example

2

AFR 8-11

(Allott, Antony N.)
of this kind of evolution is the response to population pressure. Changes in the law take the form of increasing security
of title, individualizing tenure, registering titles, increasing transfer of interests in land through market mechanisms,
and a declining influence of religious sanctions on use of
land. Change in land law can also come from above by means of
legislation, the introduction of new agricultural techniques,
and the decisions of appeal courts. The general trend of
these changes is almost always in the direction of European
law.

9.      . "Towards a definition of 'absolute ownership'." (In
JAL, 5:2, 1961. p. 99-102)                           Law Per
Also available as a separate.           Files Afr 59 A55

The dualistic nature of most African land law often creates
a problem of determining ownership, especially where questions
of title registration are concerned. The article posits a
tentative legal definition of "absolute ownership" which
includes three parts: indicators of ownership, the right of
alienation, and the interests of government authorities.

10.    Anton, Günther Kurt. LE REGIME FONCIER AUX COLONIES: RAPPORTS
PRESENTES A L'INSTITUT COLONIAL INTERNATIONAL. 2 ed.
Précédée d'une préface de M. J. Chailley-Bert et publiée sous
les auspices de l'institut. Bruxelles, Ve A. Martens et fils,
1904. 415 p.                              Mem HD 588 A6

Reports presented at a conference in 1899 reveal the viewpoint
of colonial administrators in an era of unabashed exploitation. Together the reports present the history of French
policy with regard to indigenous land tenure in Algeria and
Tunisia in the nineteenth century. The utilization of traditional structures in Tunisia for the benefit of the mother
country is contrasted to the attempt to impose French forms
upon local ones in Algeria. Touches upon these issues in
other French colonies, and in the Dutch East Indies, the Congo,
and British colonies in Africa and the Pacific as well.

11.    Apthorpe, Raymond. "Land law and land policy in Eastern
Africa." (In Item KEN-121, p. 115-125)          HD 982 016

The failure of rural reform to achieve desired goals should be
attributed to mistakes in planning or weaknesses in the policies themselves rather than to pre-existing conditions in the
societies to be reformed. The myth of the reactionary rural

3

AFR 11-14

(Apthorpe, Raymond)
social structure as a barrier to change and development should
not be allowed to stand.  The article concludes with a short
discussion of East African land reform.

12.    _____.  "Planned social change and land settlement."  (In
Item KEN-83, p. 5-13)                        Files Afr 17 L15

Divides planned social change into that which necessitates
population selection, relocation, and control, and that which
does not.  Focusing on the latter, the author presents a
typology of settlement schemes based on economic and organizational variables.

13.    Aydalot, P.  "Comportement économique, structures agraires et
développement."  (In REC, 17:2, 1966, p. 288-306)
                                              Mem AP R452 E18

Examines underdevelopment as a "psycho-sociological" problem.
A concise summary of structural barriers to development in
North Africa includes a discussion of a land tenure system
marked by inequality of access to land, a problem exacerbated
by Muslim laws of succession and inheritance.  Traces the
inability of small-scale farmers to see beyond their short-
term subsistence needs to these and other economic factors,
such as lack of access to capital and ignorance of modern
techniques.  Sees institutional change (including the limited
use of small cooperatives) as the key to the solution of the
problem.

14.    Bachelet, Michel.  SYSTEMES FONCIERS ET REFORMES AGRAIRES EN
AFRIQUE NOIRE.  Paris, Libraire Générale de Droit et de
Jurisprudence, 1968.  xxiii, 677 p.  Bibl.          HD 963 B12

A massive two-part socio-economic study of land tenure and
agrarian reform, with primary emphasis on Francophone Africa.
The first part contains a discussion of land tenure from an
anthropological viewpoint, emphasizing the interrelatedness of
African myth, indigenous world views, and customary forms of
land tenure.  A section on colonial land policy traces the
history of land legislation in British, French, Portugese,
Belgian, and German colonies.  The second part treats African
agrarian reform and includes material on land law, settlement
schemes, landholding and land use by pastoral nomads, crops,
planning, cooperatives, and a brief discussion of the possibility of transferring communal forms of land tenure from
Israel and the U.S.S.R. to Africa.

# LAND TENURE AND AGRARIAN REFORM

15.  Badouin, Robert.  "Regime foncier et développement économique
     en Afrique intertropicale."  (In CIV, 20:1, 1970.  p. 50-65)

     Criticizes indigenous African land tenure systems as obstacles
     to development.  Usufruct, because of its "instability," is
     seen as a hindrance to the introduction of tree crops.  Land
     taxes and agricultural credit, both seen as indispensable to
     development, are not functional in a system which does not
     guarantee individual and stable property rights.  The author
     favors the creation of a market in land as a means of encour-
     aging an economic environment more conducive to development.

16.  Barrows, Richard L.  INDIVIDUALIZED LAND TENURE AND AFRICAN
     AGRICULTURAL DEVELOPMENT:  ALTERNATIVES FOR POLICY.  Paper
     no. 85.  Madison, Land Tenure Center, 1973.  30 p. Bibl.
                                          Files Afr 82.5 B17

     The author uses the agricultural systems and tenure rules of
     the Mende and Limba of Sierra Leone as examples for his argu-
     ment that tenure systems define opportunities to earn income
     in agriculture.  Advocates and uses cost-benefit analysis to
     evaluate the effects of individualization of tenure rights and
     alternative measures.

17.  Bentsi-Enchill, Kwamena.  "Do African systems of land tenure
     require a special terminology?"  (In JAL, 9:2, 1965.  p. 114-139)
     Also available as a separate.                       Law Per
                                          Files Afr 58 B25

     Although actual systems differ from region to region, certain
     uniformities in patterns of landholding lend thenselves to a
     common analytical scheme.  Argues that writers on African
     land tenure fail to recognize these uniformities and use
     confusing terminology which suggests differences where none
     exist.  Posits a conceptual framework for general comparative
     analysis of tenure systems based upon the question:  "who
     holds what interest in what land?"

18.  Biebuyck, Daniel.  "Introduction."  (In Item AFR-67, p. 1-51)
                                          HD 966 I5 1960

     A list of the general features of African customary tenure
     systems, an overview of the historical evolution of land
     tenure systems, an analysis of the effect of religious belief
     on the use of the land, and a survey of land reform in tropical
     Africa.

19.  _____.  "Land holdings and social organization."  (In
     Herskovits, Melville Jean; and Harwitz, Mitchell, eds.

5

AFR 19-21

(Biebuyck, Daniel)
ECONOMIC TRANSITION IN AFRICA. Evanston, Ill., Northwestern
University Press, 1964. p. 99-112)                     HC 502 H43

Relates differential systems of land tenure to a number of
variables, including social organization, availability of
land, and religion. The end of the colonial period ushered
in new factors affecting patterns of landholding: new legal
systems, the development of cash and export crops, a demand
for increased food production, and a greater scarcity of
arable land. The effects of these new factors are varied; in
some areas they have caused changes in the inheritance system,
and in others changes in the status of women. Concludes that
there are almost no instances of spontaneous development
toward a "Euroamerican" type of landholding or land law.

20.   Bohannan, Paul. "Africa's land." (In CRAS, 4:4, 1960.
      p. 439-449)                                    Mem AP C3966

Western concepts of land tenure assume a notion of land as a
measurable entity divisible into thing-like "parcels" by
means of technical processes. While some African societies
did divide up the earth's surface into pieces, most did not.
Instead they visualized maps of land primarily "in terms of
social relationships in space. Thus they axiomized, so to
speak, the spatial aspect of their social groups and provided themselves with a social map, so that they were left
free to question the ways in which they attached either
social groups or individuals to exploitational rights in
the earth."

21.   _____. "'Land,' 'Tenure,' and 'Land Tenure'." (In Item
      AFR-67, p. 101-115)                          HD 966 I5 1960
      Also available as a separate.              Files Afr 58 B63

In African societies, the meanings of the concepts "land" and
"tenure" differ radically from Western usages. The most
important aspects of land occupancy in black Africa are relationships among men, not of men to the land, as the English
terms imply. A brief examination of tenure systems among the
Tiv, Plateau Tonga, and Kikuyu leads to the conclusion that
Africans are moving toward the Western concept of bounded
parcels of land; that new forms of relationships between men
and land, such as individual ownership of land, are evolving;
and that "social groups which in the past had merely a spatial
dimension are now being turned into territorial groups,
because they are assumed by European-dominated legal systems
to be 'juridical persons'."

6

# LAND TENURE AND AGRARIAN REFORM

22. _____. "Land use, land tenure and land reform." (In Herskovits, Melville Jean; and Harwitz, Mitchell, eds. ECONOMIC TRANSITION IN AFRICA. Evanston, Ill., Northwestern University Press, 1964. p. 133-149)          HC 502 H43

     A slightly modified version of the presentation in Items AFR-20 and AFR-21 using the tenure systems of the Tiv and Yoruba of Nigeria and the Kikuyu of Kenya as examples. See Item NIG-22 for additional annotation.

23. Branney, L. "Towards the systematic individualization of African land tenure." (In JAA, 11:4, 1959. p. 208-214)
                                                  Mem AP J83 A258

     Brief historical background of British administrative policy regarding the individualization of land tenure in Africa. Serves as a preface to Item KEN-74.

24. Bridger, G. A. "Planning land settlement schemes (with special reference to East Africa)." (In AEBA, 7, 1962. p. 21-54)                                Mem JX 1977 +A22

     A review of land settlement schemes in Kenya, Tanzania, and Uganda emphasizing the capital requirements of these projects. Since African countries are short of capital and trained personnel, it is wise to initiate settlement schemes only where serious population pressure on land cannot be alleviated by increased production brought about by less costly methods such as the use of fertilizer and improved seed.

25. Brokensha, David; and Pearsall, Marion, eds. THE ANTHOPOLOGY OF DEVELOPMENT IN SUB-SAHARAN AFRICA. The Society for Applied Anthropology, Monograph no. 10. Lexington, University Press of Kentucky, 1969. 100 p.                     HD 2117 B7

     Ten articles, nine of which focus on a particular region, describe recent research relating to African development. Three contributions (Victor Uchendu, Archie Mafeje, and Sandra Wallman) stress the role of agriculture (and, indirectly, of patterns of land use) in development. Articles by Thayer Scudder and David R. Smock deal with land settlement programs. See Items AFR-118; NIG-116; and UGA-44 for additional annotations.

26. Caroe, Olaf. "Land tenure and the franchise: a basis for partnership in African plural societies." (In JAA, 6:4, 1954. p. 152-160)                                Mem AP J83 A258

AFR 26-30

(Caroe, Olaf)
Writing before independence, the author envisions a situation in which the voting rolls of the African colonies would be swamped with uneducated people who owned no property. He proposes that the enfranchisement of new voters proceed only if they agree to register their landholdings, trading off something they want from the administration in return for something the administration wants from them.

27.   Carroll, Thomas F. "Appraising the adequacy of land tenure systems for agricultural production." (In Item AFR-3, p. 9-23 to 9-29)                                    Files Afr 4 A37

Land tenure systems are among the basic determinants of increased farm production efficiency, especially if they contribute to optimal farm size and layout, provide opportunities for sustained and economically efficient production, and encourage capital formation and productive investment.

28.   Chabas, Jean. "De la transformation des droits fonciers coutumiers et droit de propriéte." (In DUAA, 1959, p. 83-107)
                                                      Mem AP D138

The land law of 1932 in French West Africa declared that registration of land holdings was required when property held under customary law was the object of a transaction covered by a written contract. The article explores the record of how the courts, in particular the supreme court of Dakar, have interpreted this section of the law.

29.   _____. "La Réforme foncière et le régime des concessions en Afrique Occidentale Française." (In DUAA, 1958. p. 37-52)
                                                      Mem AP D138

An examination of the provisions of the laws of French West Africa, especially those of 1955 and 1956, regarding concessions, defined here as grants to groups or individuals of land or other property in the public domain.

30.   _____. "Le Réforme judiciare et le droit coutumier dans les états africaines qui formaient les anciennes féderations de l'AOF et l'AEF." 1965. (In Item AFR-109, p. 267-279)
                                                      Mem K 0.1 P755

A description of procedures for the integration of French law and local customary law in the states of former French West Africa and French Equatorial Africa.

# Land Tenure and Agrarian Reform

31. _____. "Le Régime foncier coutumier en A.O.F. (Afrique Occidentale Française)." (In DUAA, 1957. p. 53-78)

Mem AP D138

Similar to Item AFR-28 except that the emphasis is on the provisions of the laws of 1955 and 1956 governing the registration of land holdings.

32. Chambers, Robert. SETTLEMENT SCHEMES IN TROPICAL AFRICA: A STUDY OF ORGANIZATIONS AND DEVELOPMENT. New York, Praeger (1969). xxv, 294 p. Bibl. HD 1516 A34 C5

A comparative study of settlement schemes in eight Anglophone countries: Ghana, Kenya, Nigeria, Rhodesia, the Sudan, Tanzania, Uganda, and Zambia. The Mwea Irrigation Settlement in Kenya is examined in detail as an administrative case history and then used as a model to compare the achievements and failures of other schemes. The author concludes by warning that those who make developmental decisions must avoid succumbing to the strong psychological attraction of large-scale settlement schemes without understanding the risks they entail and the benefits which might accrue from alternate deployment of the resources involved. See Item KEN-22 for additional annotation.

33. Chodak, Szymon. "Social classes in sub-saharan Africa." (In AB, 4, 1966. p. 7-47)

A Marxist examination of the question of social classes in Africa which concludes: that there were no social classes in traditional African societies, since a large proportion of the population lived in an economy based on the common ownership of the means of production, including land; and that growing private ownership of land and the rise of wage labor are increasing the likelihood of class divisions occurring in the future.

34. Christodoulou, D. BASIC AGRARIAN STRUCTURAL ISSUES IN THE ADJUSTMENT OF AFRICAN CUSTOMARY TENURES TO THE NEEDS OF AGRICULTURAL DEVELOPMENT. Rome, FAO, 1966. 32 p.

Files Afr 3 C37

Also available in U.S. Agency for International Development. LAND REFORM: REGIONAL SURVEYS. RU:WLR/66/C. Rome, 1966. p. B1-B32. Files 3 U555

Post-independence Africa has a unique opportunity for creative institution building in efforts to overcome the constraints of customary systems of land tenure. Institutions adapted to

AFR 34-37

(Christodoulou, D.)
African societies should replace those borrowed from Europe.
Concludes that rapid modernization will depend upon the creation of new tenure arrangements accompanied by an organized
system of common services.

35.   Coissoró, Narana.  THE CUSTOMARY LAW OF SUCCESSION IN CENTRAL
      AFRICA.  Estudos de Ciencias Políticos e Sociais, 78.  Lisboa
      (Junta de Investigações do Ultramar) 1966.  li, 492 p.  Bibl.
      Mem JX 6510 A35 C6

      A reference work primarily for jurists, this is a highly
      technical handbook of judicial rulings and legal norms of
      succession among the Plateau Tonga, Bemba, Ngoni, Nyakyusa,
      Cewa, and Yao.  A chapter is devoted to each separately
      (except for the Yao and Cewa, treated together), following
      roughly the same lines:  general background, funeral rites,
      administration of estates, property left by the deceased,
      intestate succession, succession to women, and testate
      succession.  See Items MALAW-6 and ZAM-4 for additional
      annotations.

36.   Colonial Office Summer Conference on African Administration.
      7th, King's College, Cambridge, 1956.  AFRICAN LAND TENURE.
      African No. 1186.  London, 1956.  67 p.        Mem HD 1169 A3

      Includes discussions of individualization of tenure, adjudica-
      tion and registration, the recording of rights and cadastral
      surveys, consolidation of holdings, and land tenure in urban
      areas.

37.   Colson, Elizabeth.  "The Impact of the colonial period on the
      definition of land rights."  (In Gann, Lewis H., comp.
      COLONIALISM IN AFRICA, 1870-1960.  VOL. 3:  PROFILES OF CHANGE:
      AFRICAN SOCIETY AND COLONIAL RULE.  Cambridge, Eng., Cambridge
      University Press, 1971.  p. 193-215)          DT 31 G35

      Over most of Africa during the precolonial period, men and
      women conceived of themselves as linked to the land through
      membership in kinship groups.  With changes ushered in by
      colonial rule, the majority of African communities became
      aware of a conflict between the old political obligation to
      maintain general access to adequate resources for all citizens,
      and the possibility of extracting an individual profit from
      areas pre-empted under the rule that a man may enjoy the
      fruits of his labor.  Land has become a commodity which can be
      bought, sold, leased, and subdivided.

38. Congrès de l'Institut International de Droit d'Expression
Française tenu à Libreville du 16 au 28 octobre 1970 sur le
Régime du Sol. "(Documents)." 1970. (In Item AFR-112,
p. 560-1330)

Articles annotated individually. See Item AFR-112 for article
references.

39. CO-OPERATIVES AND RURAL DEVELOPMENT IN EAST AFRICA. Edited by
Carl Gösta Widstrand. New York, Africana (1970). 271 p.
HD 3561 A6 E22

A collection of articles examining the role of cooperatives in
East African rural development. Among the subjects treated
are marketing cooperatives, producer cooperatives, and the
relationship between cooperatives and the law. Several chapters deal indirectly with land tenure in the course of discussions of the role of producer cooperatives in alleviating
population pressure on land. See Item KEN-94a for individually
cited article.

40. Datoo, B. "Dynamics of tropical land use systems." (In
Conference of the Provisional Council for the Social Sciences
in East Africa, 1st, Dar es Salaam, 1970. PROCEEDINGS: VOL.
6. Dar es Salaam, University of Dar es Salaam, 1970.
p. 392-416) HC 517 E2 C6 1970

Establishes a typology of African land use systems based on
the frequency with which a given tract of land is cropped, or
conversely, the length of the fallow period. The author
emphasizes the need to recognize the aspects of land use systems which create disequilibrium, requiring change and adjustment in the system as a whole.

41. Deko, C. Akin. "Fundamental problems of agrarian structure
and reform in Africa, south of the Sahara." An address given
at the International Conference organized by the German
Institute for Developing Countries and FAO in Berlin, May 12,
1962. Berlin, 1962. 17 p. Files Afr 3 D24
Also available in FUNDAMENTAL PROBLEMS OF AGRARIAN STRUCTURE
AND REFORM IN DEVELOPING COUNTRIES. Berlin, German Foundation
for Developing Countries, n.d. p. 64-74. HD 105 F85

The former Minister of Agriculture of Western Nigeria outlines
weaknesses in Africa's agrarian structure and asserts that
land settlement schemes represent the best way to modernize
agricultural production.

# Land Tenure and Agrarian Reform

42. Demaison, D. "Le Régime foncier coutumier des autochtones en
Afrique Occidentale Française." (In RJPUF, 10:1, 1956.
p. 257-298)                                      Mem AP R454 J986

    A legal scholar presents a general description of customary
    land tenure systems, attempts to embody the provisions of
    customary systems in written law, and examines closely legis-
    lation and judicial decisions applying to conflicts between
    customary land law and that introduced by the colonizers.

43. Development Center on Land Policy for West African Countries,
Fourah Bay College, Freetown, Sierra Leone, 1964. REPORT.
EPTA report no. 1860. Organized by the FAO of the U.N. in co-
operation with the Economic Commission for Africa, Fourah Bay
College, Freetown, Sierra Leone, 28 Dec. 1963-9 Jan. 1964.
Rome, FAO, 1964. 48 p.                          Files Afr 58 D29

    Syntheses of discussions during a meeting in 1964 about the
    following land-related issues:  conflicts between customary
    and statutory law, land administration, the registration of
    landholdings, land reform, land settlement, cooperatives, and
    state farms.

44. De Wilde, John C. EXPERIENCES WITH AGRICULTURAL DEVELOPMENT
IN TROPICAL AFRICA. Baltimore, Published for the Interna-
tional Bank for Reconstruction and Development by the Johns
Hopkins Press (c1967). 2 v. (254, 466 p.)          HD 2117 D4

    The first volume is a general survey of agricultural develop-
    ment, with a chapter on land tenure (p. 132-156). A major
    conclusion is that land registration and consolidation are
    likely to prove most useful in areas where the relative den-
    sity of population and ecological conditions are favorable to
    development and the utilization of good land has been severely
    inhibited by fragmentation. Volume two presents case studies
    of four areas in Kenya, two in Mali, two in Uganda, and one
    each in Tanzania, Upper Volta, Chad, and the Ivory Coast.
    Issues related to land tenure are peripheral in all but the
    East African cases. See Items KEN-35 and TANZ-12 for annota-
    tions of individual parts.

45. Doublier, Roger. LA PROPRIETE FONCIERE EN A. O. F.; REGIME EN
DROIT PRIVE. Rufisque, Imprimerie du Gouvernement General,
1957. 257 p.                                        HD 992 D68

    The first part of the book deals with the dual nature of land
    law in French West Africa, with influences from French law
    and from local customary law. The second section concentrates

(Doublier, Roger)
on the provisions of the civil code for the registration of
title to land. The third presents an overview of land law at
the time of writing and calls for simplification and rationalization of land law.

46.   Dumont, René. DEVELOPPEMENT AGRICOLE AFRICAIN; ESSAI SUR LES
LIGNES PRINCIPALES DU DEVELOPPEMENT AFRICAIN ET LES OBSTACLES
QUI FREINENT. Etude presentée a la Commission Economique pour
Afrique des Nations Unis, Nairobi, février 1965. 1. ed.
Paris, Presses Universitaires de France, 1965.   223 p.
Mem HD 2117 D82

A series of essays on the obstacles to development in Africa.
Several chapters discuss agricultural production by ecological
zones (the Sahel, the West African forest), while others deal
with topics pertaining to a broad range of geographical conditions (animal husbandry, forestry, fishing, and cooperatives).  A brief section on land tenure (p. 57-63) recommends
that governments assume control of all land and grant farmers
use rights, renewable provided that they follow the advice of
extension agents and make an effort to increase their crop
yields.

47.   _____. FALSE START IN AFRICA.  Translated by Phyllis Nauts
Ott.  Introduction by Thomas Balogh.  With an additional chap-
ter by John Hatch.  New York, Praeger (1966).   320 p.
HC 502 D8413 1966

This survey of the prospects for agricultural development in
Africa includes a short section (p. 125-131) summarizing the
problems involved in reforming customary land tenure systems.
Dumont argues that governments should nationalize land so that
they have the power to revoke the use rights of anyone whose
activities permanently harm the productive qualities of the
soil.

48.   Dunning, Harrison C.  "Law and economic development in Africa:
the law of eminent domain."  (In CLR, 68, 1968.  p. 1286-1315)
Law Per

Examines the uses of eminent domain and the "public purpose"
doctrine, rules on compensation, and the procedure for exer-
cising the power of eminent domain in Ghana, Tanzania, and
Ethiopia to determine their effects on economic development.
Concludes that the right of eminent domain needs to be
broadened in African nations.

13

# LAND TENURE AND AGRARIAN REFORM

49. Elias, Taslim Olawale. "Some current problems of African land tenure." (In TROP, 33:4, 1956. p. 287-296)          Ag Per

    Notes the decline of the traditional authority of the chief and the trend toward individualization of rights in land. Elias examines several agrarian planning projects and appeals for increased experimentation with cooperative farming.

50. Flores, Xavier A. "Institutional problems in the modernization of African agriculture." (In United Nations Research Institute for Social Development. A REVIEW OF RURAL CO-OPERATION IN DEVELOPING AREAS. Geneva, UNRISD, 1969. p. 199-275)          HD 2951.5 U54

    Points out that while many organizational forms of the developed countries, from trade unions to cooperatives, have been transplanted to sub-Saharan Africa, they have had a minimal impact on development. Includes a short section on customary African tenure systems (p. 207-210), part of the socio-economic structure resisting change from the outside.

51. Food and Agriculture Organization. EAST AFRICAN LIVESTOCK SURVEY: REGIONAL--KENYA, TANZANIA, UGANDA. Rome, UNDP (and) FAO, 1967. 3 v.          HD 9427 E1 F6

    In a chapter on land tenure (chapter four of the first volume), the authors argue that modification of tenure arrangements is an important precondition for improving livestock production. In fragmented areas, consolidated individual holdings should be substituted for pre-existing tenure patterns. In good land which is not heavily fragmented, a more gradual development of individual enclosure should take place. In semi-arid lands, group tenure of large blocks of land should be recognized and registered as such. In extremely arid conditions, no change is warranted.

52. _____. Land Tenure and Agrarian Reform Branch. BIBLIOGRAPHY ON LAND TENURE IN AFRICA. BIBLIOGRAPHIE DES REGIMES FONCIER EN AFRIQUE. BIBLIOGRAFIA SOBRE TENENCIA DE LA TIERRA EN AFRICA. ESR/MISC:70/23. Rome, FAO, 1970. vi, 57 p.
          Files Afr 58 F66

    Contains about 800 references from the years 1958 to 1970 on land tenure systems and agrarian reform programs in Africa.

53. _____. Regional Office for Africa. AGRARIAN REFORM IN AFRICA. An analytical background document prepared for the Regional Meeting of the FAO Special Committee on Agrarian Reform, Accra, 1971. n.p., n.d. vi, 51 p.          Files Afr 3 F66

LAND TENURE AND AGRARIAN REFORM

(Food and Agriculture)
Contends that rural reform in Africa is necessitated by the
increasing monetization of many rural economies, the breakdown of pre-existing structures of authority, and accelerated
soil deterioration. The recommendations of the Special Committee include the transformation of traditional land tenure
laws, balanced programs of agrarian reform, and the infusion
of financial and technical assistance from world organizations.

54.   Frank, Michael. COOPERATIVE LAND SETTLEMENTS IN ISRAEL AND
      THEIR RELEVANCE TO AFRICAN COUNTRIES. Veröffentlichungen der
      List Gesellschaft, 53. Basel, Kyklos-Verlag, 1968. xii,
      168 p. Bibl.                                    HD 1491 P3 F72

      Examination of Israeli kibbutz and moshav forms of cooperative
      leads to the conclusion that Israeli experience is applicable
      in Africa. Contends that the cooperative (moshav) model,
      rather than private or collective (kibbutz) models, is most
      suitable for Africa. Concludes with a survey of the evolution
      of cooperatives and experimentation with cooperative farm
      settlements in Africa.

55.   Franklin, A. de Sousa. "The Portuguese system of protecting
      native landed property." (In JAA, 9, 1957. p. 16-22)
                                                    Mem AP J83 A258

      The expression of a paternalistic point of view by a Portu-
      guese colonial official who believes that the "pattern of
      indigenous landholding may vary according to the degree of
      civilization of the human group under consideration" (p. 16).
      That is, the more civilized the group, the closer its land
      tenure system will be to European systems. To aid in the
      "development" of its African colonies, Portuguese law provided
      for the expropriation of land belonging to Africans and its
      subsequent allotment to Europeans.

55a.  Gaitskell, Arthur. "Problems of policy in planning agricul-
      tural development in Africa south of the Sahara." (In Mac-
      Pherson, W. W., ed. ECONOMIC DEVELOPMENT OF TROPICAL AGRI-
      CULTURE: THEORY, POLICY, STRATEGY AND ORGANIZATION.
      Gainesville, University of Florida Press, 1968. p. 214-239)
                                                        HD 1417 E23

56.   Gasse, Victor. LES REGIMES FONCIERS AFRICAINS ET MALGACHE;
      EVOLUTION DEPUIS L'INDEPENDANCE. Bibliotheque africaine et
      malgache, Droit et sociologie politique, no. 12. Paris,
      Librairie générale de droit et de jurisprudence, 1971. 332 p.
      Bibl.                                              HD 1169 G3

AFR 56-59

(Gasse, Victor)
An extremely detailed and legalistic presentation of land law
governing property registration procedures in former French
colonies before and since independence. Local country differences are elaborated. See Item MR-7 for additional annotation.

57.   Gershenberg, Irving. "Customary land tenure as a constraint
      on agricultural development: a re-evaluation." (In EAJRD,
      4:1, 1971. p. 51-62)
                                                          Ag Per

A short article presenting the argument that the inability,
under customary land tenure arrangements, to use land as security for loans, and the diseconomies of scale associated with
fragmented landholdings, do not seriously impede agricultural
development. African governments would be well advised to use
customary land law to the fullest extent possible.

58.   Gluckman, Max. "Property rights and status in African tra-
      ditional law." (In International African Seminar. 8th,
      Haile Sellassie I University, 1966. IDEAS & PROCEDURES IN
      AFRICAN CUSTOMARY LAW; STUDIES PRESENTED & DISCUSSED. Edited
      by Max Gluckman, with an introduction by A. N. Allott, A. L.
      Epstein, and M. Gluckman. London, Published for the Inter-
      national African Institute by the Oxford University Press,
      1969. p. 252-266)
                                               Mem DT 23 I55 2/8

Focusing on the land tenure system of the Lozi of Zambia, the
author works out a terminology which emphasizes the relationship between hierarchical rights to land and the status hierarchy of African societies. He emphasizes that "ownership"
does not imply an exclusive right; it simply indicates that a
person has a stronger claim to a piece of land or other property than someone else in a particular dispute. In customary
law, "ownership cannot be absolute, for the crucial thing
about property is the role that it plays in a nexus of specific
relationships. . . . Property law in tribal society defines
not so much rights of persons over things, as obligations owed
between persons in respect of things."

58a.  Goody, Jack. TECHNOLOGY, TRADITION, AND THE STATE IN AFRICA.
      London, published for the International African Institute by
      Oxford University Press, 1971. 88 p.          HC 502 G63

59.   Gopalakrishnan, P. K. "Land relations and social change in
      Africa." (In Prasad, Bisheshwar, ed. CONTEMPORARY AFRICA.
      London, Asia Publishing House, 1960. p. 108-121)
                                                  Mem DT 30 P7

AFR 59–63

(Gopalakrishnan, P. K.)
A cursory and ethnocentric view of agricultural development
and land reform.

60.     Gosselin, G.  DEVELOPPEMENT ET TRADITION DANS LES SOCIETES
        RURALES AFRICAINES.  Etudes et Documents, Nouvelle Série,
        76.  Geneve, ILO, 1970.  343 p.          HN 773.5 G67

        A study of the reform of the institutional framework for agri-
        cultural production in eight African countries:  Cameroon,
        Dahomey, Upper Volta, Mali, Nigeria, Senegal, Tanzania, and
        the Central African Republic.  The author establishes a typol-
        ogy of rural reform projects and uses it to explore the suc-
        cesses and failures of undertakings in each of the eight
        countries.  See Items DAHOM-6; MALI-1; SEN-9; TANZ-24; and
        UV-4 for additional annotations.

61.     Great Britain.  East Africa Royal Commission.  THE FUTURE OF
        EAST AFRICA; A SUMMARY OF THE REPORT OF THE ROYAL COMMISSION,
        WITH AN INDEX TO THE REPORT.  Prepared by Ethel Wix.  London,
        Africa Bureau (1956).  47 p.          Mem HN 792.5 A552

        Summary of Item AFR-62.

62.     _____.  _____.  REPORT.  Cmnd.  9475.  London, H.M.S.O. (1955).
        xiv, 482 p.                          Mem HN 792.5 A55
        Also available in Great Britain.  Parliament.  House of Com-
        mons.  PARLIAMENTARY PAPERS:  REPORTS FROM COMMISSIONERS,
        ETC., 13, 1955/56.                   Mem Docs

        An economic and social survey of East Africa.  Part five is
        an extensive discussion of patterns of land tenure, customary
        land use, the implementation of land policy, and the potential
        for agricultural production.

63.     _____.  _____.  REPORT, 1924–1925.  Cmnd. 2387.  London,
        H.M.S.O., 1925.  195 p.  (In Great Britain.  Parliament.
        House of Commons.  PARLIAMENTARY PAPERS:  REPORTS FROM COMMIS-
        SIONERS, ETC., 9, 1924/25)           Mem Docs

        A brief section on land tenure (p. 23–32) emphasizes the need
        for administrative safeguards to assure that colonial govern-
        ments do not appropriate land already being used by African
        farmers.

LAND TENURE AND AGRARIAN REFORM

AFR 63a-66

63a.  Herskovits, Melville Jean. "Some problems of land tenure in
      contemporary Africa." (In Conference on World Land Tenure
      Problems, University of Wisconsin, 1951. LAND TENURE: PRO-
      CEEDINGS OF THE INTERNATIONAL CONFERENCE ON LAND TENURE AND
      RELATED PROBLEMS IN WORLD AGRICULTURE HELD AT MADISON, WISCON-
      SIN, 1951. Edited by Kenneth H. Parsons, Ray J. Penn, and
      Philip M. Raup. Madison, University of Wisconsin Press, 1956.
      p. 231-239)                                    HD 105 C67 1951

64.   Heseltine, Nigel. OBSTACLES TO AGRICULTURAL DEVELOPMENT IN
      UNDERDEVELOPED COUNTRIES IN AFRICA. Rehovot, Israel, Centre
      for Comparative Studies on Rural Development at the National
      and University Institute of Agriculture, 1964. 28 p.
                                                  Files Afr 4 H29

      Obstacles to agricultural development can be divided into two
      categories: technical and economic. The former includes such
      factors as soil fertility, irrigation, poor relationship be-
      tween agriculture and animal husbandry, and lack of crop diver-
      sification. The latter encompasses land tenure systems, lack
      of alternative employment, and the marketing system. Land-
      holding systems present obstacles not only because plot size
      is usually too small, but because, at present, land use is not
      amenable to regulation.

65.   Heyse, Théodore. PROBLEMES FONCIERS ET REGIME DES TERRES
      (ASPECTS ECONOMIQUES, JURIDIQUES, ET SOCIAUX): AFRIQUE,
      CONGO BELGE, RUANDA-URUNDI. Enquêtes bibliographiques, 4.
      Bruxelles, Centre de Documentation Economique et Sociale
      Africaine, 1960. iv, 163 p.              Mem Z 7164 L3 H4

      An exhaustive bibliography of works on the economic, social,
      and legal aspects of land tenure systems in Rwanda, Burundi,
      and the Belgian Congo, with some coverage of other regions of
      Africa.

66.   Hirschfeld, A. "Les Problemes agraires en Afrique Noire."
      (In RDEC, 138, 1964. p. 357-369)        Mem AP R449 E851

      Author believes in the necessity of transforming communal
      forms of property into more individualized ones in order to
      facilitate economic and technical progress. Cooperatives are
      envisaged as mediators in this process, helping the newly
      independent small African farmer to achieve entrepreneurial
      skills. Cooperatives are also seen as modern viable, market-
      oriented replacements for older communal (non-market-oriented)
      forms.

18

# Land Tenure and Agrarian Reform

66a.    Ijere, M. O.  "A Positive approach to the African land tenure
        question."  n.p. (197-).  17 l.                    Files Afr 58 I42

66b.    _____.  SOURCE MATERIALS FOR THE STUDY OF AFRICAN LAND TENURE.
        Departmental research notes, no. 2.  Nsukka, Nigeria, Dept.
        of Agricultural Management, University of Nigeria, 1974.  18 l.
                                                            Files Afr 58 I424

67.     International African Seminar.  2d, Leopoldville, Congo, 1960.
        AFRICAN AGRARIAN SYSTEMS.  Edited with an introduction by
        Daniel Biebuyck.  London, published for the International
        African Institute by the Oxford University Press, 1963.
        xiii, 407 p.                                        HD 966 I5 1960

        Collection of papers which "analyse case studies illustrating
        the various basic factors and problems connected with the land
        in tropical Africa today.  Indigenous systems of tenure and
        their adaptation to commercial agriculture, the balance be-
        tween rights and obligations of groups and individuals, and
        the authority and duties of chiefs and headmen are discussed
        in detail for many different areas.  Against this background
        important contributions are made toward better understanding
        of current problems raised by economic and political develop-
        ment, increase of populations, migration and scarcity of
        land."  See Items AFR-18; AFR-21; CONGO-3; DAHOM-12; IC-4;
        KEN-65; MALI-6; NIG-18; RHOD-9; RWA-10; SEN-1; SEN-20;
        TANZ-80; UGA-61; ZAI-4; ZAI-11; ZAI-14; ZAI-37; ZAI-40; and
        ZAM-21 for annotations of individual articles.

68.     International Labour Conference.  AGRARIAN REFORM, WITH PAR-
        TICULAR REFERENCE TO EMPLOYMENT AND SOCIAL ASPECTS.  Report 6.
        Geneva, ILO, 1964.  128 p.                          Files 3 I51

        Report prepared for the 49th session of the International
        Labour Conference at Geneva, 1965.  Summarizes national mea-
        sures (principally legislation) in the field of agrarian re-
        form in Asia, Europe, Latin America, Africa (p. 14-16), and
        the Near East (p. 12-14); UN, FAO, and ILO activities; and a
        number of specific problems of agrarian reform, along with
        measures adopted by national governments and international
        organizations to solve them.

69.     Kamarck, Andrew M.  "African agriculture:  problems and solu-
        tions."  (In his THE ECONOMICS OF AFRICAN DEVELOPMENT.  Rev.
        ed. New York, Praeger, 1971.  p. 125-169)          HC 502 K3 1971
        Also available in Item AFR-3, p. 9.1-9.22.         Files Afr 4 A37

# Land Tenure and Agrarian Reform

AFR 69-72

(Kamarck, Andrew M.)
Because agriculture is the mainstay of African development,
the author argues, its improvement must be the central feature
of any development program. After reviewing some of the impediments to agricultural development, notably poor soil and an
unfavorable climate, the article examines traditional agricultural systems and some recent programs and policies for
increasing the output of African farms--such as the individualization of tenure, consolidation of boundaries, organization of extension services, and establishment of cooperatives
and marketing boards.

70.    Kato, L. L.  "Has customary law in English-speaking Africa
       recognized long possession of land as a basis of title?"
       (In EALJ, 1:4, 1965.  p. 243-260)                    Law Per

       An article intended for legal practitioners arguing that local
       public opinion has afforded security of tenure even though
       customary law has not recognized long possession of land as a
       basis for title.  Formal legal recognition of title is now
       required.

71.    King, David J.  LAND REFORM AND PARTICIPATION OF THE RURAL
       POOR IN THE DEVELOPMENT PROCESS OF AFRICAN COUNTRIES.  Paper
       no. 101.  Madison, Land Tenure Center, 1974.  66 p.
                                                   Files Afr 3 K45

       Development must involve the willing economic and political
       participation of the rural populace.  Participation can be
       induced through the provision of structures that generate
       economic incentives and opportunities; land tenure systems
       provide one such structure.  Government efforts at land re-
       form, however, should not specify wholly new tenurial insti-
       tutions:  "only those elements of the customary arrangements
       that constrain opportunities to participate in the development
       process [should be] transformed."

72.    Kouassigan, Guy-Adjété.  L'HOMME ET LA TERRE; DROITS FONCIERS
       COUTUMIERS ET DROIT ET PROPRIETE EN AFRIQUE OCCIDENTALE.
       L'Homme d'outre-mer, Nouvelle series no. 8.  Paris, Editions
       Berger-Levrault, 1966.  283 p.  Bibl.            HD 1169 K68

       A scholarly study of West Africa's customary land law and
       property rights.  Part one deals with customary land law and
       the conception of land as collectively owned, inalienable,
       sacred property, with complementary individual rights.  Part
       two is concerned with the profound and rapid transformation
       of these laws and property rights induced by contact with
       Europeans.

20

# LAND TENURE AND AGRARIAN REFORM

73. Kuper, Hilda; and Kuper, Leo, eds. AFRICAN LAW: ADAPTATION
AND DEVELOPMENT. Berkeley, University of California Press,
1965. vii, 275 p. Bibl.        Coll K 0.1 K966

A collection of articles by anthropologists on the evolution
of African customary and statutory law and the interplay of
African and European concepts of law. Sections on land law
are found on p. 51-78 for the Gusii of Kenya and on p. 76-77
for the Kikuyu. See Item KEN-108 for annotation of one
article.

74. La Anyane, Seth. "Economic aspects of land tenure systems of
Western Africa." (In International Seminar on Land Taxation,
Land Tenure and Land Reform in Developing Countries, Univer-
sity of Hartford, 1966. INTERNATIONAL SEMINAR ON LAND TAXA-
TION, LAND TENURE, AND LAND REFORM IN DEVELOPING COUNTRIES.
Editors: Archibald M. Woodruff, James R. Brown, Sein Lin.
West Hartford, John C. Lincoln Institute, University of
Hartford, 1966. p. 445-477)       HD 105 I68 1966

La Anyane sees the following deficiencies in most tenure systems found in West Africa: a tendency toward fragmentation
of holdings, the inability to ensure security of tenure, the
failure to prevent inequalities of income and wealth, and
difficulties involved when farmers attempt to acquire additional land or settle new land.

75. Land Administration and the Development of African Resources
Seminar, University of Ibadan, Nigeria, 1972. REPORT OF PRO-
CEEDINGS. (London) 1972. 1 v. (various pagings). Sponsored
by UNECA and the Commonwealth Association of Surveying and
Land Economy.       Files Afr 57.4 L15

A collection of papers on national land policy, solutions to
the problems associated with land resource development, land
use, and relationships between land tenure systems and economic development. See Items AFR-77; AFR-100; AFR-101;
AFR-125; GHA-56; KEN-79; and NIG-95 for annotations of individual papers.

76. "Land tenure." Special supplement to JAA. London, Published
for the Secretary of State for the Colonies by H.M.S.O., 1952.
36 p.       Mem AP J83 A258

A series of articles focusing on land tenure and land utilization. Topics discussed include farming systems and land
tenure, factors affecting changes in land tenure, and the impact of public opinion on changes in tenure systems.

# LAND TENURE AND AGRARIAN REFORM

77.   Lawrance, J. C. D. "Land systems and land reform." 1972.
      (In Item AFR-75, 5.1. 14 p.)                    Files Afr 57.4 L15

      A concise overview of the main legal issues associated with
      the study of land tenure systems and land reform. Much of
      what is referred to as customary land law is not customary at
      all, "but case law, statute, or a mixture of customary and
      unofficially applied law. Its origin may be customary, but
      its customary character has everywhere been changed." Exist-
      ing forms of land tenure often prove inadequate to the needs
      of development and should be replaced by a statutory system
      of land tenure. Includes a commentary by B. C. Murage.

78.   _____. THE ROLE OF REGISTRATION OF TITLE IN THE EVOLUTION OF
      CUSTOMARY TENURES AND ITS EFFECT ON SOCIETIES IN AFRICA.
      E/CN.14/CART/253. n.p., UNECA, 1970. 15 p. Paper for UNECA
      Seminar on Cadastre, Addis Ababa, 1970.        Files Afr 58 L19

      Argues that registration of title is, at present, the best
      method of remedying the uncertainty of customary land law.
      It is, however, an expensive and highly technical operation
      and should be undertaken only when the potential economic
      advantages warrant it. Registration of title also has the
      effect of diminishing the influence of the traditional com-
      munity, "but these changes are sooner or later inevitable and
      it is only their timing that is affected by the introduction
      of registration of title."

79.   Leake, Hugh Martin. "Some thoughts on land tenure in tropical
      Africa." (In his LAND TENURE AND AGRICULTURAL PRODUCTION IN
      THE TROPICS. Cambridge, W. Heffer & Sons, 1927. p. 92-110)
                                                      Ag REWJ L47

      Writing in the 1920s, Leake predicted an inevitable growth in
      the value of African lands in response to worldwide demand
      for African agricultural exports. The development of a "land-
      lord class," who would make productive investments in agricul-
      ture, should be encouraged.

80.   _____. "Studies in tropical land tenure." (In TROP, various
      issues, 1932-1933. various pagings)              Ag Per
      Also available as a reprint. Port-of-Spain, Trinidad, Govt.
      Print. Off., 1933. 56 p.                        Files 58 L22

      Brief histories of land policies in the British African colo-
      nies to the early 1930s. See Items GHA-36; KEN-89; MAURITI-3;
      NIG-73; SL-9; SUD-15; TANZ-40; and UGA-37 for annotations of
      contents.

# LAND TENURE AND AGRARIAN REFORM

81. Letnev, A. B. "Estimation of agricultural produce marketing systems in connection with agrarian reforms; the case of West Africa." Moscow, 1967. 14 p. Bibl.    Files Afr 63 L28

An argument based on an ideological position; one of the reasons why African agriculture cannot overcome its present state of stagnation lies in the absence of a "rationally-organized, all-embracing and democratically controlled network of purchase organizations, mostly state-owned ones."

82. Luedtke, Roger Alfred. "Land tenure: a means of modernization in western Africa." 1969.    Thesis HD 986 N5 L82

See Item NIG-76 for citation and annotation.

83. Lugard, Frederick D. THE DUAL MANDATE IN BRITISH TROPICAL AFRICA. With a new introduction by Margery Perham. (5th ed. Hamden, Conn.) Archon Books, 1965. xlix, 643 p.
Mem DT 32.5 L8 1965

Three chapters on land tenure (14-16) summarize early knowledge of the traditional systems of tenure in East and West Africa, with special reference to Tanzania and Nigeria; delineate the respective rights of government and local people; and cover the special problems presented by settlers and leases for building, agriculture, and mining. See Item NIG-77 for additional annotation.

83a. Machyo, B. Chango. AFRICAN LAND TENURE CONCEPT AND DEVELOPMENT. Paper no. 94. (Kampala) 1971. 46 p. Paper for 7th Conference of the University of East Africa Social Sciences Council, Makerere, 1971.    Files Afr 58 M118

84. _____. LAND OWNERSHIP AND ECONOMIC PROGRESS. London, Africana Study Group, 1963. 36 p.    Files Afr 58 M12

This is a popularization of arguments first advanced by proponents of policies which have come to be known as "African Socialism." Village-based producer cooperatives are the units of production best suited to the social conditions of sub-Saharan Africa. Reforms involving individualization of tenure are unacceptable because they would tend to create social classes and inequalities of income where none existed before.

85. McLoughlin, Peter F. M. "The Policy relationship between individual rights to land and migrant labour systems in Africa." (In CIV, 14:1/2, 1964. p. 12-16)    Mem AP C5825

23

AFR 85-89

(McLoughlin, Peter F. M.)
Problems associated with land tenure and labor migration in
Africa are interrelated. Individualization of tenure under-
mines labor mobility by taking land away from local African
authorities who formerly allocated land, thus increasing the
chances that migrants returning home will be landless. Agriculture will no longer be able to subsidize the industrial
sector, which will have to pay higher wages to laborers who
have lost their access to land and need to be supported
entirely by wage employment.

86.    Mair, Lucy P. "Agrarian policy in British African colonies."
       (In Land Tenure Symposium, Amsterdam, 1950. TROPICAL AFRICA,
       NETHERLANDS, EAST INDIES BEFORE THE SECOND WORLD WAR. Leiden,
       1951. p. 41-56)                               Ag HD 965 L3

       A comparison of land policy in eight former British colonial
       territories. In East and Central Africa, expatriate agricul-
       tural enterprise was actively encouraged, while in West Africa
       it was discouraged.

87.    _____. "Native rights in land in British African territories."
       (Ibid., p. 57-60)                             Ag HD 965 L3

       Compares land policy in Uganda, Kenya, Nigeria, and Ghana.
       Increased litigation arising from disputes over land rights
       can be dealt with by amending customary law or by establishing
       a system of registration of holdings and issuance of title.

88.    Makings, S. M. AGRICULTURAL PROBLEMS OF DEVELOPING COUNTRIES
       IN AFRICA. Nairobi, Oxford University Press, 1967. viii,
       184 p.                                         HD 2117 M35

       Writing from an East African perspective, Makings argues for a
       modified traditional tenure system, incorporating the best
       features of group interest in land with safeguards and incen-
       tives for individual holders. The key element in the new sys-
       tem would be local land authorities with sole rights of
       purchase and sale, and hence able to prevent fragmentation of
       holdings.

89.    Masefield, B. G. "Farming systems and land tenure." (In JAA,
       4:4, 1952. Special supplement, p. 8-14)      Mem AP J83 A258

       Aspects of land tenure systems which have a negative impact on
       agricultural production fall under five broad headings: ex-
       cessive fragmentation of holdings, failure of the tenure sys-
       tem to give incentives to the occupier to preserve the

# Land Tenure and Agrarian Reform

(Masefield, B. G.)
fertility of the soil or to invest in its productive capacity,
share tenancy, tenure systems giving rights only to land under
cultivation with no provision for rotation or fallow, and
tenure systems encouraging speculation in land values.

90.  Meek, Charles Kingsley.  COLONIAL LAW; A BIBLIOGRAPHY WITH
SPECIAL REFERENCE TO NATIVE AFRICAN SYSTEMS OF LAW AND LAND
TENURE.  London, Published for Nuffield College by Oxford
University Press, 1948.  xiii, 58 p.        Mem Z 6458 G7 M45

91.  _____.  LAND LAW AND CUSTOM IN THE COLONIES.  (2nd ed.)
London, New York, Oxford University Press, 1949.  xxvi, 337 p.
HD 599 Z5 M4

A compendium of rural land tenure in British colonies in Africa
and Asia.  Meek describes customary land tenure systems and
the legal postures of colonial governments with respect to
land administration and land control.  He also includes material on factors influencing tenure systems, such as climate,
land use, marketing systems, religion, and social organization.
See Items CYP-9; GHA-39; KEN-110; MALAW-14; MAURITI-5; NIG-88;
SL-13; TANZ-48; TANZ-49; UGA-50; and ZAM-14 for annotations
of separate sections.

92.  _____.  "A Note on Crown lands in the colonies."  (In JCLIL,
3:3/4, 1946.  p. 87-91)                              Law Per

Reviews the position of the British Crown with respect to
ownership of land in various colonies.  Notes that in some
areas, like Barbados, the Crown owns almost no land, while in
others, like British Honduras, most of the land is Crown land.
The situation is less clear in most African colonies.

93.  Mifsud, Frank M.  CUSTOMARY LAND LAW IN AFRICA, WITH REFERENCE
TO LEGISLATION AIMED AT ADJUSTING CUSTOMARY TENURES TO THE
NEEDS OF DEVELOPMENT.  FAO legislative series, no. 7.  Rome,
FAO, 1967.  vi, 96 p.  Bibl.                    HD 1169 A3 M5

This useful and authoritative study by a legal scholar summarizes the basic elements of African land law and explores the
relationship between law and the economic exploitation of the
land.  Includes chapters on the legal basis of customary law,
ways of assigning land rights to individuals, types of legislation for instituting new land systems, and descriptions of
succession and inheritance among the Bakigo, Ibo, Yoruba, and
Akan--all peoples of West Africa.  The author emphasizes
judicial and administrative procedures in order to provide a
practical guide for lawyers and civil servants.

# Land Tenure and Agrarian Reform

94. Mifsud, Frank M. "Some legal aspects of African land reform."
(In International Seminar on Land Taxation, Land Tenure and
Land Reform in Developing Countries, University of Hartford,
1966. INTERNATIONAL SEMINAR ON LAND TAXATION, LAND TENURE
AND LAND REFORM IN DEVELOPING COUNTRIES. Editors: Archibald
M. Woodruff, James R. Brown, Sein Lin. 1967. p. 413-438)
HD 105 I68 1966

    Reviews the shortcomings of African land tenure systems,
    focusing on uncertainty of title and unexploited land. Dis-
    cusses examples of registration, legislation, and other reme-
    dies, but cautions that legal practitioners working in African
    countries should be fully aware of the social and economic
    implications of changes in land law.

95. Mitchell, Nicolas P. LAND PROBLEMS AND POLICIES IN THE AFRI-
CAN MANDATES OF THE BRITISH COMMONWEALTH. Louisiana State
University Studies, no. 2. Baton Rouge, Louisiana State Uni-
versity Press, 1931. xvi, 155 p. Bibl.          Mem HD 1003 M5

    Outdated treatment of land tenure systems in Togo, Cameroon,
    Tanzania, and South West Africa. Discusses alienation,
    "native segregation," surveys, and registration of land.

96. Müller, Peter. "Über die Formen des Bodenrechts und
Betriebstypen in der afrikanischen Landwirtschaft." (In ZAL,
4:3, 1965. p. 261-277)
Also available as a separate.              Files Afr 58 M85

    A general analysis of the obstacles to development in the
    agrarian structure. Discusses various forms of communal
    ownership, reforms of land law, changes in land use patterns,
    the individualization of tenure, the process of dissolution
    of traditional patterns, and the alternatives of large-scale
    farming enterprises or small holdings.

97. Müller-Praefke, Dieter; und Polster, Dietrich. ZUR FRAGE DER
BODENREFORM IN ENTWICKLUNGSLANDERN LATEINAMERIKAS UND AFRIKAS:
EINE LITERATURSTUDIE. Heidelberg, Forschungstelle für
Agrarstruktur und Agrargenossenschaften der Entwicklungsländer,
1966. 2 v.                                    HD 1251 M85

    Focuses on the problems of individual and communal ownership
    of land, demographic conditions, land law, and colonization.
    Based on agrarian reform literature in Kenya, Tanzania, and
    Uganda.

# LAND TENURE AND AGRARIAN REFORM

98.    Muralt, Jürgen von. "Rural institutions and planned change in
       the Middle East and North Africa." 1969.        HD 2951.5 U54

       See Item NE-27 for citation and annotation.

99.    Murray, J. S. "Rapporteur's review of traditional systems of
       land tenure and soil utilization." (In SA, 7:3, 1962.
       p. 341-346)                                                Ag Per

       Following a discussion and categorization of African land
       tenure systems, this conference report describes the change
       from shifting cultivation to small-scale farming.

100.   Nisbet, James. "The Quantity surveyor." 1972. (In Item
       AFR-75, 2.3   16 p.)                         Files Afr 57.4 L15

       Land tenure and land reform seen from the point of view of the
       quantity surveyor, whose profession is concerned with the cost
       factor of land acquisition in building and civil engineering
       projects. Includes a commentary by D. Kayagulanyi-Ntwatwa.

101.   Oludemi, S. B. "Land administration functions in developing
       countries." 1972. (In Item AFR-75, 2.2.   8 p.)
                                                    Files Afr 57.4 L15

       A brief survey of the main features of African systems of cus-
       tomary land tenure and the principles of state and community
       ownership of land. Includes a commentary by E. R. Redwood-
       Sawyerr.

102.   Ormsby-Gore, W. G. A.  REPORT . . .ON HIS VISIT TO WEST AFRICA
       DURING THE YEAR 1926.  Cmnd. 2744.  London, 1926.  188 p.
       (In Great Britain. Parliament. House of Commons.  REPORTS
       FROM COMMISSIONERS, ETC., 9, 1926)                    Mem Docs

       A comprehensive report on economic conditions in Gambia,
       Sierra Leone, Nigeria, and the Gold Coast. In a short section
       on land tenure in the Gold Coast, the author recommends no
       change in existing practice but notes the proliferation of
       litigation arising from disputes over land.

103.   Parsons, Kenneth H.  CUSTOMARY LAND TENURE AND THE DEVELOPMENT
       OF AFRICAN AGRICULTURE.  Paper no. 77.  Madison, Land Tenure
       Center, 1971.  82 p.                         Files Afr 58 P17

       A consideration of the "possibilities and limitations of tenure
       policies for stimulating and supporting agricultural develop-
       ment in tropical Africa." Parsons examines the issue of

# LAND TENURE AND AGRARIAN REFORM

(Parsons, Kenneth H.)
public and private ownership of land, problems of customary
tenure, attempts at organizational innovation including nationalization of land with long-term leases, group farming, and
farm settlement schemes. Reform of land tenure systems will
probably necessitate extensive government intervention. "In
simple fact, traditional agriculture and customary tenure in
tropical Africa have no future. New systems of agriculture
will be devised. It is this necessity...which gives significance to the bold attempts at organizational innovation now
under way."

104. Paulme, Denise. "Régimes fonciers traditionnels en Afrique
     Noire." (In PA, 48, 1963. p. 109-132)          Mem AP P929

     The installment of a juridically clear private property system
     is not a necessary precondition for economic development in
     black Africa. In fact, social upheaval attendant on such a
     change often has disastrous repercussions on the volume of
     agricultural production. The author criticizes current litera-
     ture on the topic as being too dependent on European legal
     notions, and she cites examples of practices from various Afri-
     can societies regarding land tenure and distribution of income
     as proof that considerations of the social and political
     effects of policies must take precedence over purely economic
     ones if social chaos and increased poverty is to be avoided.

105. Pelissier, Paul. "Effects of land tenure on migration, labor
     mobility and employment in West Africa." n.p. (1972). 9 p.
                                                   Files Afr 58 P25

     Dispossession from the land and population pressure on land
     must be ruled out as the causes of seasonal or long-term migra-
     tion from the savanna to the forest in West Africa. But land
     tenure systems come into play as instruments of social strati-
     fication in the areas where migrants arrive, since immigrants
     usually become landless agricultural laborers.

106. Pim, Sir Alan W. COLONIAL AGRICULTURAL PRODUCTION; THE CONTRI-
     BUTION MADE BY NATIVE PEASANTS AND BY FOREIGN ENTERPRISE.
     Issued under the auspices of the Royal Institute of Interna-
     tional Affairs. London, New York, Oxford University Press,
     1946. ix, 190 p.                            Mem HD 1930 A3 P5

     A review of agriculture in British colonial Africa is followed
     by a short section on land tenure (p. 171-175). The argument
     is that security of tenure is necessary for agricultural
     advancement, but nations must guard against the harmful conse-
     quences of unrestricted individual tenure.

# LAND TENURE AND AGRARIAN REFORM

107.  Podedworny, H. "The Customary land tenure; selected problems
      of agrarian reform and agricultural development in countries
      of Africa south of the Sahara." (In AB, 15, 1971. p. 95-122)
      Also available as a separate.          Files Afr 58 P62

      The first section of this article lists the following as the
      characteristic features of African land tenure systems:  col-
      lective ownership of land and individual use rights controlled
      by the community; a division of use and ownership rights
      corresponding to the hierarchy of the traditional political
      system; a preponderance of mystic-religious premises within
      the traditional customary rules and regulations concerning
      land tenure; and a lack of security of tenure which inhibits
      investment.  The second part treats the role of agrarian
      reform in agricultural development.  Even the best possible
      legislative measures cannot alter traditional land tenure
      systems without parallel and far-reaching changes in agricul-
      tural techniques, particularly a change from shifting cultiva-
      tion to commercialized agriculture.  Agrarian reform inevitably
      involves high investment costs, cadastral surveys, and the
      registration of holdings.  If agrarian reform can be achieved
      in African countries, pronounced inequality of income and the
      formation of antagonistic social classes can be avoided.

108.  Pohoryles, Samuel; and Szeskin, A. LAND TENURE IN AFRICA AND
      ITS EFFECT ON ECONOMIC GROWTH.  Paper no. 3.  Tel Aviv, David
      Horowitz Institute for the Research of Developing Countries,
      University of Tel Aviv, 1973.  85 p.  Bibl.    Files Afr 58 P63

      After a thorough discussion of the relationship between agri-
      cultural production and economic growth, the paper reviews
      the socio-economic and legal framework of land tenure in
      Africa, including traditional ownership patterns, European
      agriculture, and the effects of agrarian reform.  Concluding
      chapter discusses land tenure and agricultural development,
      and posits a quantified model that attempts to evaluate the
      impact of land on economic development through a determination
      of the relative value of land.

109.  Poirier, Jean, ed.  ETUDES DE DROIT AFRICAIN ET DE DROIT
      MALGACHE.  Etudes malgaches, 16.  (Paris, Editions Cujas, 1965).
      11, 529 p.  Bibl.                       Mem K 0.1 P755

      See Items AFR-30; AFR-133; and GUIN-3 for annotations of
      individual articles.

110.  Potekhin, Ivan I.  "Land relations in African countries."  (In
      JMAS, 1:1, 1963.  p. 39-59)              Mem AP J83 M683
      Also available in Item AFR-3, p. 9.194-9.204.  Files Afr 4 A37

# Land Tenure and Agrarian Reform

(Potekhin, Ivan I.)
In describing patterns of land use throughout Africa, this
Marxist scholar emphasizes expropriation of land by European
settlers and the solidification of "feudal" relationships
between landowners and tenants under colonial rule.  Communal
forms of land tenure once prevailed in large areas of Africa.
In general these tenure arrangements are evolving toward
individual ownership.

111.    Prothero, Ralph Mansell, comp.  PEOPLE AND LAND IN AFRICA
SOUTH OF THE SAHARA; READINGS IN SOCIAL GEOGRAPHY.  New York,
Oxford University Press, 1972.  iv, 344 p.  Bibl.

HD 969 S8 P7

Papers in this collection of essays by geographers are arranged
in six sections.  Those in the first treat the physical environment as a determinant of relationships between population
and land, and show the need for adjustment and adaptation to
the environment.  Those in the second section illustrate
successful adjustments to unusual and particularly difficult
environmental conditions, to increasing population, and to
economic change resulting from expanded production for overseas export.  The third section takes up examples of malad-
justment and its consequences.  The fourth group of papers
examines European influences.  Those in the fifth consider
readjustments and resettlement on land formerly belonging to
Europeans.  The last section illustrates prediction and
measurement in population-land relationships and posits a
model for interpreting these relationships.  See Items GHA-28;
KEN-21; KEN-113; RHOD-8; and ZAM-11 for annotations of individual articles.

111a.   Regional Symposium on Traditional Systems of Land Tenure,
Salisbury, Rhodesia, 1968.  (REPORT).  n.p., n.d.  xii, 65 p.

Files Afr 58 R23

112.    REVUE JURIDIQUE ET POLITIQUE, INDEPENDANCE ET COOPERATION,
no. 4, 1970.  Paris, Librairie Générale de Droit et de Jurisprudence, 1970.  32, 560-1344 p.

Papers of the 1970 Congress of the Institut International de
Droit d'Expression Française, dealing with African land tenure
systems.  See Items AFR-38; ALG-2; BURU-2; BURU-3; BURU-8;
CAM-1; CAM-2; CHAD-1; CHAD-2; CHAD-3; DAHOM-13; GAB-1; GAB-3;
GAB-4; GAB-6; GAB-7; IC-6; IC-7; LIBY-18b; MR-9; MR-14;
MAURITA-1; MAURITA-2; MOR-1; MOR-3; MOR-14a; RWA-8; SEN-6;
TOGO-3; TUNIS-6; TUNIS-7; UV-11; ZAI-22; ZAI-23; and ZAI-30
for citations and annotations of individual articles.

# LAND TENURE AND AGRARIAN REFORM

113.    Ringer, Karlernst. AGRARVERFASSUNGEN IM TROPISCHEN AFRIKA.
        ZUR LEHRE VON DER AGRARVERFASSUNG: VERANDERUNGEN ZUR HEBUNG
        DER AGRARTECHNIK (1.Aufl.). Freiburg im Breisgau, Rombach
        (1963). 236 p.                              Mem HD 966 R5

        A discussion of legal, economic, and social foundations of
        agrarian societies as they affect agrarian technology and
        attempts to change it. Means of bringing about change--
        individual, cooperative or state--are considered, and the
        importance of the individual in all change is underlined.

114.    Runowicz, Adam Z. "Some problems of agricultural development
        in Africa (South of the Sahara)." (In AB, 14, 1971.
        p. 95-118)

        Runowicz challenges some widely held views on the development
        of African agriculture. Most African agrarian economies are
        not characterized by disguised unemployment, and all but the
        most marginal land is already in use. Systems of land use
        based on bush fallow are probably more appropriate in African
        environments than mechanized techniques. The author catego-
        rizes approaches to land tenure problems as negative, opti-
        mistic, pessimistic, and "agnostic," and finds none
        satisfactory. As long as existing agricultural practices can
        be improved, radical changes in systems of land tenure are
        not necessary. Planners must have faith in the ability of
        African farmers to recognize and accept profitable innovations.
        Education and extension programs should play a large role in
        the gradual transformation of African agriculture.

115.    Sabry, O. A. "Starting settlements in Africa." (In LRLSC,
        1970:1. p. 52-61)                    REF HD 1261 A1 L1 1970 v.1
        Also available in Item ETH-61, p. 173-189.    HD 1026 E8 S25

        Recommendations on procedures for implementing land settlement
        projects include considerations of such economic factors as
        profitability, such social dimensions as the recruitment of
        farmers, and such administrative factors as planning and the
        training of personnel to oversee settlement programs.

116.    Sautter, Gilles. LES STRUCTURES AGRAIRES EN AFRIQUE TROPICALE.
        Paris, Centre de Documentation Universitaire, 1968. 267 p.
        Bibl.                                         HD 2117 S18

        Complete lecture notes of a Sorbonne course on African agrar-
        ian systems, including sections on village settings, techniques
        of cultivation, land use, and case studies of land tenure sys-
        tems and attempts at reform. Particularly useful are maps of
        land use patterns and charts of social structure.

# LAND TENURE AND AGRARIAN REFORM

117.    Schlippé, Pierre de.  SHIFTING CULTIVATION IN AFRICA:  THE
        ZANDE SYSTEM OF AGRICULTURE.  1956.          Mem S 471 A365 S4

        See Item ZAI-34 for citation and annotation.

118.    Scudder, Thayer.  "Relocation, agricultural intensification,
        and anthropological research."  1969.  (In Item AFR-25,
        p. 31-39)                                          HD 2117 B7

        Probably over one percent of the total rural African population
        has been relocated during the past 15 years.  Relocation proj-
        ects are an ideal laboratory in which to test theories of
        social change, and they provide an opportunity to prove that
        anthropology can make a contribution to African aspirations.

119.    Seidman, Ann.  PLANNING FOR DEVELOPMENT IN SUB-SAHARAN AFRICA.
        New York, Praeger (1974).  xvii, 260 p.            HC 502 S45

        Current efforts at planning for economic growth in Africa are
        likely to fail; what is needed is "a fundamental alteration
        of the institutional structures inherited from the colonial
        past."  It is necessary to create a new pattern of industrial
        growth balanced by the development of the agricultural sector.
        In a chapter on land tenure, an evaluation of the problems
        associated with individualization of tenure and the creation
        of large-scale producer cooperatives follows an overview of
        customary tenure systems.

120.    Seidman, Robert B.  "Land and economic development in indepen-
        dent English-speaking, sub-Saharan Africa."  (In AFRICA AND
        LAW; DEVELOPING LEGAL SYSTEMS IN AFRICAN COMMONWEALTH NATIONS.
        Madison, University of Wisconsin Press, 1968.  p. 3-74)
                                                 Law S.AF 6 SURV Afr8d

        In a section on land tenure (p. 50-55), Seidman points out
        that agricultural development may be envisaged as coming about
        through public sector investment in cooperatives and state
        farms, or through the efforts of the private sector.  If the
        latter is stressed, "clarity of title, alienability, and
        relief from fragmentation seem to be the principal demands."
        But if the direction of development is towards large-scale
        resettlement or state farms, the emphasis must be on assur-
        ances that governments have adequate powers of eminent domain.

121.    _____.  "Law and social change in Africa:  statutes, cases,
        and materials."  Draft.  n.p., 1970.  1 v. (various pagings)
                                                       Files Afr 60 S26

32

# LAND TENURE AND AGRARIAN REFORM

(Seidman, Robert B.)
A wide-ranging collection of readings on the legacy of colonial law in English-speaking African countries. Sections 1
(B), 4(C), 4(D), and 7(A) contain material on land tenure
systems.

122.   Sheira, A. Z.  "Credit aspects of land reform in Africa."
       (In AEBA, 7, 1965.  p. 36-53)            Mem JX 1977 +A22

       A paper on the use of agricultural credit to initiate and
       implement land reform.  The extension of loans to tenants for
       the purchase of land and to small farmers for the enlargement
       of holdings is an effective way of altering tenure arrange-
       ments.  If major land settlement schemes or efforts at redis-
       tribution of land are to be successful, they must be
       accompanied by an ongoing program of agricultural credit.

123.   Simpson, S. Rowton.  "Land tenure:  some explanations and
       definitions."  (In JAA, 6:2, 1954.  p. 50-64) Mem AP J83 A258

       Practical suggestions for the provision of legislation neces-
       sary for the individualization of tenure rights in British
       colonial Africa include the granting of title, land registra-
       tion, cadastral surveys, the prevention of fragmentation upon
       succession, and the provision of agricultural credit.

124.   Sonius, H. W. J.  INTRODUCTION TO ASPECTS OF CUSTOMARY LAND
       LAW IN AFRICA, AS COMPARED WITH SOME INDONESIAN ASPECTS.
       Leiden, Universitaire Pers Leiden, 1963.  47 p.
                                                Mem K 0.1 S6984

       Analyzes various concepts of land law (ownership, building
       rights, standing crops, and customary law) in the two regions.

125.   Steel, Robert.  "Surveying and land economy in the development
       of resources."  1972.  (In Item AFR-75, 2.1.  10 p.)
                                                Files Afr 57.4 L15

       An explanation of the main divisions within the profession of
       surveying and the general issues with which surveyors are
       concerned, including land tenure systems, land reform, land
       settlement, land management, and the acquisition of land by
       public authorities for building and civil engineering projects.
       Includes a commentary by K. R. Quist.

126.   Swynnerton, R. J. M.  "Agricultural advances in Eastern
       Africa."  (In AA, 61, 1962.  p. 201-215)    Mem AP A258 A256

AFR 126-130

(Swynnerton, R. J. M.)
When this address was delivered, Swynnerton had 27 years of
experience in colonial administration.  In a short section on
land tenure, he notes that among the Kikuyu of Kenya a system
of individual land ownership has developed largely as the
result of population pressure on land.

127.    Thomas, M. F.; and Wittington, G. W., eds.  ENVIRONMENT AND
LAND USE IN AFRICA.  London, Methuen, 1969.  x, 554 p.
HD 966 T36

Relates natural as well as social environment to patterns of
land use in Africa.  Parts 1 and 2 review general principles
and methodology in the study of African land-related environments.  Part 3 includes case studies of specific countries
from a geoenvironmental perspective.  See Items KEN-153;
SUD-10; SWAZ-7; and ZAM-9 for annotations of individual
articles.

128.    Uchendu, Victor C.  "Changing patterns of land tenure affect-
ing African agricultural development."  (Stanford) 1968.  11 1.
Paper read at the 11th annual meeting of the African Studies
Association, Los Angeles, Oct. 16-19, 1968.   Files Afr 58 U13

Same content as Item AFR-130.

129.    _____.  THE CONFLICT BETWEEN NATIONAL LAND POLICIES AND LOCAL
SOVEREIGNTY OVER LAND IN TROPICAL AFRICA.  Leiden, Afrika-
Studiecentrum, 1971.  19 p.  Bibl.  Paper presented at the
Seminar on Problems of Land Tenure in African Development,
Leiden, 1971.                               Files Afr 57.4 U13

The greatest contribution which national land policy can make
to agricultural development is to provide and police an institutional structure which increases the mobility and accessi-
bility of interests in land.  The development of agricultural
exports has often taken place in areas where the institutional
structure provided for the sale of land.  By eliminating local
restrictions on the sale of land, national land policy can
reverse the present trends of migration--from rural-urban
migration to intra-rural.

130.    _____.  "The impact of changing agricultural technology in
African land tenure."  (In JDA, 4:4, 1970.  p. 477-486)
Also available as a separate.               Files Afr 58 U23

Certain technological changes in agriculture--particularly the
introduction of tree crops, enclosure, and large capital

(Uchendu, Victor C.)
investments--tend to bring about changes in tenure systems
such that fewer people can claim the right to use any given
parcel of land.

131.    ____. "Some issues in African land tenure." (In TROP, 44:2,
1967. p. 91-101)                                           Ag Per

Because agricultural development necessitates the transformation of African economies from subsistence to market economies,
and because market economies treat inputs as well as products
as marketable commodities, land must be treated as a commodity.
Land tenure arrangements should guarantee security of title to
the cultivator and should make for easy transfer of interest
in the land.

132.    Vanderlinden, J. "Réflexions sur l'existence du concept de
propriété immobilière individuelle dans les droits africains
traditionnels." (In International African Seminar. 8th,
Haile Sellassie I University, 1966. IDEAS & PROCEDURES IN
AFRICAN CUSTOMARY LAW; STUDIES PRESENTED AND DISCUSSED.
Edited by Max Gluckman. New York, London, Oxford University
Press, 1969. p. 236-251)                    Mem DT 23 I55 2/8

Close readings of the legal definitions of "ownership" and
"property," together with an examination of the ethnographic
literature on various African societies, lead Vanderlinden to
the conclusion that differences between African and European
notions of land ownership are neither so pronounced nor so
widespread as many Africanists claim.

133.    Verdier, R. "'Chef de terre' et 'terre du lignage': contribution à l'étude des systèmes de droit foncier négro-africains."
1965. (In Item AFR-109, p. 333-359)            Mem K 0.1 P755

Dealing with African tenure systems in law involves numerous
semantic difficulties. This study defines the key terms in
juridical use in most African legal systems--chef de terre
("land chief") and terre du lignage ("ancestral land")--by
giving their full religious and social context, with extensive
reference to black African mythology and oral literature.

134.    ____. "Civilisations agraires et droits fonciers négro-
africains." (In PA, 31, 1960. p. 24-33)         Mem AP P929

An article criticizing Western jurists who apply European
legal concepts to African societies, "ignoring the humanist
teaching of Montaigne, who denounced the ethnocentric attitude

# Land Tenure and Agrarian Reform

(Verdier, R.)
of those who call everything opposed to their own custom
barbarism."

135. \_\_\_\_. "Essai de socio-économie juridique de la terre dans
les sociétés paysannes négro-africaines traditionnelles."
(In ISEAC, 95, 1959 (5:1). p. 137-154)   Mem H 31 I53
Also available as a separate.   Files Afr 94 V27

Certain French anthropologists, Verdier among them, stress the
importance of the mythology and cosmology of a people in understanding how their society works. Referring to studies of
West African peoples, Verdier writes of mystical links between
people and land, of ties between ancestors and the living, of
land as the source of life, and of inheritance as a symbolic
expression of the interests of the dead in the well-being of
the living and those yet unborn.

136. \_\_\_\_. "Evolution et réformes foncieres de l'Afrique noire
francophone." (In JAL, 15:1, 1971. p. 85-101)   Law Per
Also available as a separate.   Files Afr 58 V26

A summary history of land reform in French-speaking West
Africa, with special reference to the Ivory Coast, Cameroon,
and Senegal. See Items CAM-15; IC-10; and SEN-22 for additional annotations.

137. \_\_\_\_. "Féodalités et collectivismes africains: étude
critique." (In PA, 39, 1961. p. 79-99)   Mem AP P929

A wide-ranging review of literature on land tenure undertaken
to show that parallels drawn from European feudal relationships or from individual or collective ownership of land in
developed countries do not adequately describe African land
tenure systems. In Africa the control of land by groups and
the rights of individuals to use land complement each other,
and descriptions must take account of this interplay.

138. Verhelst, Thierry G. "Customary land tenure as a constraint
on agricultural development: a re-evaluation." (In C&D,
2:3/4, 1969/70. p. 627-656)   Mem AP C9687 E84
Also available as a separate.   Files Afr 58 V27

Many who criticize land tenure systems as impediments to agricultural development fail to make a distinction between land
use and land law. Insecurity of tenure, deterioration of
natural resources, fragmentation, and subdivision are due not
to legal deficiencies but to land use patterns, population

# Land Tenure and Agrarian Reform

AFR 138-142

(Verhelst, Thierry G.)
pressure, or lack of skills, and therefore require changes in
the social, cultural, or economic fields for their solution,
rather than changes in the legal structure.

139. _____. MATERIALS ON LAND LAW AND ECONOMIC DEVELOPMENT IN
AFRICA. Prelim. ed. (Los Angeles, University of California,
African Studies Center) 1968. iv, 605 p.          HD 962 V27

A collection of materials which is "intended to provide the
basis for seminar work on the topic of land law and economic
development in Africa." Consists of extracts from books and
articles, legal opinions, and statutes arranged in three categories: economic and sociological background to reforms and
changes in land law; land and land law reform for agricultural
development; and legislation to promote individual land tenure.
Countries discussed include Nigeria, Senegal, Cameroon,
Ethiopia, Kenya, Rhodesia, and Guinea.

139a. Vraný, Jan. "Economic behavior of Africans and transformation
of traditional structures." (In IR, 1971. p. 84-92)

140. Whetham, Edith H. COOPERATION, LAND REFORM AND LAND SETTLE-
MENT. Report on a survey in Kenya, Uganda, Sudan, Ghana,
Nigeria, and Iran. London, the Plunkett Foundation for Co-
operative Studies, 1968. xi, 79 p.          Ag HD 1491 A52 W4

A chapter analyzing the role of cooperatives in land reform
and land settlement schemes is followed by chapters examining
how the objectives of agrarian reform have been met in Kenya,
Uganda, the Sudan, Iran, Tanzania, Ghana, and Nigeria. In the
last chapter is a short section (p. 69-73) on cooperatives as
land holders. See Items GHA-58; IRAN-80; KEN-158; NIG-126;
SUD-28; and UGA-79 for additional annotations.

141. White, C. M. N. "African customary law: the problem of concept and definition." (In JAL, 9:2, 1965. p. 86-89) Law Per

Rejects either exclusively anthropological or exclusively legal
definition of customary law. Argues that because of blend of
African and European concepts, customary law can best be viewed
as a "diachronic process of development," ranging from traditional systems of social control to the introduction of courts
of law.

142. _____. "Aspects and problems of land tenure in Africa." (In
EALJ, 1:4, 1965. p. 276-283)          Law Per

37

AFR 142-ANG 2

(White, C. M. N.)
A brief review intended to illustrate the broad range of topics
related to land tenure problems.  The author stresses the need
for more information and factual documentation upon which land
reform legislation can be based.

143. _____. "Terminological confusion in African land tenure."
(In JAA, 10:3, 1958.  p. 124-130)              Mem AP J83 A258

An article drawing attention to incorrect usages of terms such
as "land tenure," "communal tenure," and "inheritance" of land
rights. Concludes that the best approach to describing customary African tenure systems is to analyze the types of land
rights enjoyed by individuals and groups.

144. Yudelman, Montague.  AFRICANS ON THE LAND; ECONOMIC PROBLEMS OF
AFRICAN AGRICULTURAL DEVELOPMENT IN SOUTHERN, CENTRAL, AND EAST
AFRICA, WITH SPECIAL REFERENCE TO SOUTHERN RHODESIA.
Cambridge, Mass., Harvard University Press, 1964.  xiv, 288 p.
HD 2130 R6 Y8 1964

Focusing principally on Rhodesia, the author notes that one of
the central problems of economic development in low-income,
predominantly agricultural societies is that of increasing
marketable surplus.  See Item RHO-21 for additional annotation.

145. Zimmer-Vorhaus, E.  "Planning of land tenure."  (In Joint
Seminar on Problems and Approaches to Planning Agricultural
Development, Addis Ababa, 1967.  PROCEEDINGS.  (Berlin, 1968).
p. 183-192)                                    HD 2118 1968 J6

The article outlines two measures to deal with the two main
shortcomings of land tenure systems in Africa:  the redistribution of rights to use land in cases where land could be made
available; and the individualization of ownership or rights to
use land in cases where the old social order is breaking down.

## ANGOLA

1. Jannettone, G.  "Il Regime fondiario in Angola."  (In ARBSD,
19:4/5, 1964.  p. 133-140)                     Mem AP A2573

2. Niemeier, G.  "Die modern Bauernkolonisation in Angola und
Mocambique und das portugiesische Kolonialproblem."  (In GRU,
18:10, 1966.  p. 367-376)                      Geol MC G28 R87

# LAND TENURE AND AGRARIAN REFORM

(Niemeier, G.)
By 1964 the Portuguese government had established about 2,900
modern family farms in 38 <u>colonatos</u>. According to the author,
black and white farmers have the same rights and duties and
are not allowed to employ anyone outside their own family.
See item MOZ-5 for additional annotation.

3. Pössinger, Hermann. LANDWIRTSCHAFTLICHE ENTWICKLUNG IN ANGOLA
   UND MOCAMBIQUE. Afrika-studien, nr. 31. München, Weltforum
   Verlag, 1968. 284 p.                                    S 472 P6

   An overview of agricultural development in these two Portuguese
   colonies. For Angola, emphasis is on plantations and large-
   scale European enterprises, and on the development policies of
   the Portuguese administration. See Item MOZ-6 for additional
   annotation.

4. Tschirschky, O. von. DIE ENTWICKLUNG DER LAND-UND
   FORSTWIRTSCHAFT IN ANGOLA. Materiel-Sammlung, 60. Göttingen,
   Agrarsoziale Gesellschaft, 1967. 86 p.          Files Ang 4 T71

   A study of the policies of the Portuguese administration for
   the development of agriculture and forestry. A key factor is
   the settlement of European farmers from the mother country
   and the provision of infrastructure and services for the immigrants, which the article describes in detail.


## BOTSWANA


1. Roberts, Simon. "Mmatlhong's field." (In RA, 22, 1973.
   p. 1-13)

2. Shapera, Isaac. "The Native land problem in the Tati district."
   (In BNR, 3, 1971. p. 219-268)              Mem DT 790 B67
   Also available as a separate.          Files Bots 58 S13

   Recommendations for the improvement of conditions on reserves
   in the Tati District, where the original African inhabitants
   lost title to land in the late nineteenth century as European
   mining interests moved in. The author states that the land
   area of the reserves should be increased.

3. _____. NATIVE LAND TENURE IN THE BECHUANALAND PROTECTORATE.
   (Lovedale, South Africa) The Lovedale Press, 1943. xiv,
   (2) 283 p.                                    Ag REWJ SCH13

# Land Tenure and Agrarian Reform

(Shapera, Isaac)
A detailed description of customary land tenure systems and systems of land use in Botswana at the time of writing. The book includes sections on rights to residential land, the migration of settlements, rights to pastoral land, as well as hunting and water rights.

4. Smit, P. BOTSWANA: RESOURCES AND DEVELOPMENT. Communications of the Africa Institute, no. 13. Pretoria, Africa Institute (of South Africa) 1970. 256 p.                    HC 517 B6 S54

    A survey of land, population, and economic resources in Botswana. A chapter on land tenure (p. 35-44) concentrates on the historical antecedents of the present system.

5. U.S. Foreign Agricultural Service. "Botswana - situation." Pretoria, 1969. 5 1. Unclassified memo from William R. Hatch, Agricultural Attaché, to USDA, Washington, Nov. 3, 1969.
                                                      Files Bots 7 U54

    This brief survey of Botswana's agricultural economy includes three paragraphs on land tenure: descriptions of freehold, customary tenure, and state ownership of land.

6. Werbner, Richard P. "Local adaptation and the transformation of an imperial concession in north-eastern Botswana." (In A/IAI, 41:1, 1971. p. 32-41)

    This article traces the evolution of economic and political relationships between a large-scale commercial landlord, a company whose principal interests lie in the fields of mining and commerce, and the local people in the area where the company has its concession.

## BURUNDI

1. BLOCAGES ET FREINAGES S'OPPOSANT A LA REUSSITE DES REFORMES AGRAIRES ET A L'INTRODUCTION DE LA REVOLUTION VERTE EN MILIEU RURAL DU BURUNDI. Bruxelles, Institut International des Civilisations Différentes, 1973. 13 1. Paper for INCIDI Study Session on Obstacles and Restraints Impeding the Success of Land Reform in Developing Countries, Brussels, 1973.
                                                      Files Buru 4 B56

# LAND TENURE AND AGRARIAN REFORM

2. Bukera, J. "Les Droits fonciers coutumiers au Burundi." 1970. (In Item AFR-112, p. 1207-1214)

   Customary land rights in Burundi derive from the occupation of the land and permit farmers to lease or sell their land and to pass it on to heirs. These rights thus fulfill all the conditions of the definition of rights of ownership.

3. Clerck, L. de. "Le Domaine des collectivités publiques au Burundi." 1970. (In Item AFR-112, p. 801-814)

   Defines the concepts of public and private domain of the state in Burundi's land law. The private domain of the state consists of occupied land which cannot be alienated from its occupants as long as they hold valid rights to the land according to customary law.

4. _____. "Note sur le droit foncier coutumier au Burundi." (In RJRB, 5:11, 1965. p. 38-42)        Mem AP R454 J97

   Customary land law has evolved rapidly since the beginning of the Belgian administration of the Congo. The powers of traditional political authorities to allocate land and control its use have been progressively limited, and the rights of individuals have become more and more secure.

5. Heyse, Théodore. GRANDES LIGNES DU REGIME DES TERRES DU CONGO BELGE ET DU RUANDI-URUNDI ET LEURS APPLICATIONS (1940-1946). Académie Royale des Sciences d'Outre-mer, Classe des Sciences Morales et Politiques. MEMOIRES. Collection in-8°, t. 15, fasc. 1. Bruxelles, Libraries Falk fils, 1947. 191 p.
                                        Mem DT 641 A27 15/1

   A descriptive study of the land law of the Belgian Congo and Ruanda-Urundi. Two sections deal with law governing concessions, and another presents a bibliography classified by subject headings.

6. _____. PROBLEMES FONCIERS ET REGIME DES TERRES (ASPECTS ECONOMIQUES, JURIDIQUES ET SOCIAUX): AFRIQUE, CONGO BELGE, RUANDA-URUNDI. 1960.                Mem Z 7164 L3 H4

   See Item AFR-65 for citation and annotation.

7. Raeck, H. de. "Le Régime des terres au Congo Belge et au Ruanda-Urundi; terres domaniales et terres indigènes, régime des cessions et concessions." 1953.        Files Zai 58 R12

   See Item ZAI-33 for citation and annotation.

# Land Tenure and Agrarian Reform

8. Verbrugghe, A. "L'Evolution de la propriété foncière coutumière au Burundi." 1970. (In Item AFR-112, p. 1201-1206)

   The land law of 1961 permits those who hold land under customary tenure to register their property and obtain title to it under written law.

9. _____. "Le Régime foncier coutumier au Burundi." (In RJRB, 5:2, 1965. p. 59-82)                                      Mem AP R454 J97

   An outline of the main features of the customary system of land tenure in Burundi including sections on the powers of chiefs, the powers of the Mwami or ruler, the evolution of the system in the direction of individual property rights, the acquisition and transfer of land rights, and taxes associated with control of land. Also included is a useful chart of the order of succession according to customary law and a glossary of terminology.

## CAMEROON

1. Aka'a Owoundi, L. "Les Droits fonciers coutumiers au Cameroun." 1970. (In Item AFR-112, p. 1163-1174)

   Traces the evolution of the government's approach to customary land law. The law of 1963 declared that occupied land--defined as land cultivated, needed for fallow, or used for pasture--belonged to its traditional users. Unused land belongs to the state, though individuals can use it for hunting or gathering until the state decides to develop it.

2. _____. "L'Expropriation pour cause d'utilité publique au Cameroun." 1970. (In Item AFR-112, p. 971-978)

   Traces the history of the legal framework for the acquisition of land by the state. The law of 1922 proved to be inadequate because it applied only to registered land, and it was supplanted in 1959 by a law which provided for the expropriation of communally held lands. The law of 1966 simplified and rationalized the procedures outlined in its predecessor.

3. Ardener, E.; Ardener, S.; and Warmington, W. A. PLANTATION AND VILLAGE IN THE CAMEROONS: SOME ECONOMIC AND SOCIAL STUDIES. London, Published for the Nigerian Institute of Social and Economic Research by the Oxford University Press, 1960. xxxvi, 435 p. Bibl.                         Mem HD 1538 C15 A75

# Land Tenure and Agrarian Reform

(Ardener, E.; Ardener, S.; and Warmington, W. A.)
Includes a chapter on the history of land policy and land
tenure in the Victoria Division (p. 309-335). The land
policy of the German protectorate subordinated the interests
of local people to those of the plantation owners. Among the
Bakweri land belongs to the lineage, and each adult male of
this kinship group enjoys rights to use land.

4. Dikoumé, Cosmé; et Lippens, Philippe. LES HOMMES ET LA TERRE;
ELEMENTS SUR LES PROBLEMES FONCIERS AU CAMEROUN ORIENTAL.
Douala, Cameroon, Institut Panafricain pour de Développement,
1972. 41 p.          Files Cam 58 D438

A slightly revised version of Item CAM-5.

5. _____; _____. LES PROBLEMES FONCIERS AU CAMEROUN ORIENTAL.
Douala, Institut Panafricain pour le Développement, 1970.
35 p.          Files Cam 58 D44

A description of land tenure systems among ethnic groups in
West Cameroon, with emphasis on systems of belief and religious
values applying to land. Since land belongs to the ancestors,
it is inalienable and use rights cannot be transferred outside
the group which owns it. The second part of the study outlines
the history of land law designed to accomodate customary land
tenure systems, ownership of land by the state, and ownership
of land by individuals.

6. Gosselin, G. DEVELOPPEMENT ET TRADITION DANS LES SOCIETES
RURALES AFRICAINES. 1970.          HN 773.5 G67

See Item AFR-60 for citation and annotation.

7. Hallaire, Antoinette. HODOGWAY (CAMEROUN NORD): UN VILLAGE
DE MONTAGNE EN BORDURE DE PLAINE. Atlas de structures
agraires au sud du Sahara, no. 6. Paris, Mouton, 1971. 79 p.
Publiée sous le patronage de la Maison des Sciences de l'Homme.
         S 473 C15 H15

A microstudy of a rural mountain village of northern Cameroon
characterized by extreme conditions: dense population, poor
soil, intense cultivation, and geographical and social isolation. A section on the land tenure system (p. 45-57) concludes that the buying and selling of land tends to allow those
whose families have the capacity to farm to acquire land.
Rents and sale prices are low in any case, but village authorities sometimes intervene in bargaining on the side of the
weak or impoverished who are in need of land. Includes a detailed map (scale 1:3,000) of landholding patterns in the village.

# Land Tenure and Agrarian Reform

8. Jouhaud, Yves. "La Notion de domaine ou patrimoine collectif national dans les nouvelles législations du Sénégal et du Cameroun: essai de synthèse entre le droit foncier coutumier et le droit foncier moderne." (In RJPOM, 20:1, 1966. p. 30-53)                                     Mem AP R454 J986
   Also available as a separate.                     Files Afr 57.4 J58

   The author views the notion of "national collective domain" as an important legal innovation capable of accommodating both customary notions of land ownership and the need of the state and individuals for exclusive rights of ownership.

9. Kaberry, P. M. "Some problems of land tenure in Nsaw, Southern Cameroons." (In JAA, 12:1, 1960. p. 21-28)   Mem AP J83 A258

   An article dealing with two specific areas of the land tenure system of the Nsaw: the granting of grazing rights to semi-nomadic Fulani herdsmen, and the need for assurances of security of tenure which arose with the introduction of coffee cultivation.

9a. Krauss, Heinrich. DIE MODERNE BODENGESETZGEBUNG IN KAMERUN 1884-1964. Afrika-studien, nr. 12. New York, Berlin, Springer-Verlag, 1966. xii, 156 p.          Mem HC 501 A32/12

10. Leupolt, M.; and Hage, K. "Land settlement and training center, Wum, West Cameroon." (In LRLSC, 1970:2, p. 70-76)
                                           REF HD 1261 A1 L1 1970 v.2

    Concise description of an integrated rural development project in an isolated and economically stagnant area of Cameroon. The project will combine a commercial farm, training and extension services, and land settlement.

11. Meek, Charles Kingsley. LAND TENURE AND LAND ADMINISTRATION IN NIGERIA AND THE CAMEROONS. Colonial Office, colonial research studies no. 22. London, H. M. S. O., 1957. vi, 420 p. Bibl.                            Mem JV 33 G7 A48/22

    The second section of the book (p. 343-410) treats land tenure and land administration in the British Cameroons, emphasizing the evolution of land policy under the German Protectorate and the United Kingdom Trusteeship. See Item NIG-87 for additional annotation.

12. Mitchell, Nicolas P. LAND PROBLEMS AND POLICIES IN THE AFRICAN MANDATES OF THE BRITISH COMMONWEALTH. 1931.
                                                   Mem HD 1003 M3
    See Item AFR-95 for citation and annotation.

# Land Tenure and Agrarian Reform

13. Tardits, Claude. CONTRIBUTION A L'ETUDE DES POPULATIONS BAMILEKE DE L'OUEST-CAMEROUN. L'Homme d'Outre-mer; nouvelle série, no. 4. Paris, Berger-Levrault, 1960. 135 p. Bibl.
Mem DT 570 T3

A short section on land tenure (p. 69-72) concludes that the tenure system of the Bamiléké assures adequate security of tenure to encourage investment in the productive capacity of the land, and that the tenure system can adapt to the pressures of population growth.

14. Vene, M. "Yabassi-Bafang: une opération intégrée de colonisation." (In CD, 26, 1969. p. 33-41) Mem AP C7767 E84

A brief description of the Yabassi-Bafang settlement project. This operation organized and controlled a pre-existing seasonal migration of Bamiléké resulting from population pressure. The government built an access road, helped settlers clear land, built housing, offered technical assistance to the immigrants, and set up marketing cooperatives.

15. Verdier, R. "Evolution et réformes foncières de l'Afrique noire francophone." 1971.

See Item AFR-136 for citation. Land policy under French colonial rule vacillated between the contrary impulses of preserving customary systems of land tenure and introducing western concepts such as registration for the purpose of recognizing full ownership rights. Since independence, legislation in Cameroon has substituted the notion of "collective national property" for the concept of "vacant and unowned lands" which, under the old system, belonged to the state. The new concept covers all lands except those subject to individual title.

16. Verhelst, Thierry G. MATERIALS ON LAND LAW AND ECONOMIC DEVELOPMENT IN AFRICA. 1968. HD 962 V27

See Item AFR-139 for citation and annotation.

16a. West Cameroon. Commission of Inquiry into the Affairs of the West Cameroon Department of Lands and Surveys. REPORT, 1ST APRIL TO 23RD JUNE, 1967. Buea, Govt. Printer, n.d. 182, (6) p. HD 1004 C3 A3

# Land Tenure and Agrarian Reform

## CENTRAL AFRICAN REPUBLIC

1.  Georges, M. "La Vie rurale chez les Banda (République Centrafricaine)." (In COM/B, 16:64, 1963. p. 321-359)
    Mem AP C132 D108

    Land use in this area of the Central African Republic is characterized by crop rotation for four years followed by a period of fallow ranging from seven to ten years. Village chiefs or earth priests assign rights to use land, and individuals do not have the right to sell or inherit land.

2.  Gosselin, G. DEVELOPPEMENT ET TRADITION DANS LES SOCIETES RURALES AFRICAINES. 1973 HN 773.5 G67

    See Item AFR-60 for citation and annotation.

## CHAD

1.  Amady, G. "Le Domaine des collectivités publiques tchadiennes." 1970. (In Item AFR-112, p. 783-796)

    Describes Chad's post-independence efforts to adapt the land laws of French Equatorial Africa to the particular national situation. The definition of land ownership includes both a public sector, from which land cannot be alienated, and a private sector, in which individuals or collectivities may lease or buy concessions in urban or rural areas.

2.  Brahim Seid, Joseph. "Les Droits fonciers coutumiers au Tchad." 1970. (In Item AFR-112, p. 1161-1162)

    Customary land rights in Chad have been voided by the laws of 1967 and 1968 which declared all nonregistered land legally vacant unless proof to the contrary is presented. All customary rights are nullified if they are not exercised for 10 years, and they may also be rescinded by procedures to take land into the public domain.

3.  _____. "L'Expropriation au Tchad." 1970. (In Item AFR-112, p. 959-970)

    A description of the provisions of laws pertaining to the expropriation of land into the public domain.

# LAND TENURE AND AGRARIAN REFORM

4. Marnay, P. "Les Paysannats du Tchad." (In Société d'Etudes pour le Développement Economique et Social, Paris. LE DEVELOPPEMENT RURAL DANS LES PAYS D'AFRIQUE NOIRE D'EXPRESSION FRANÇAISE, 3. Paris, SEDES, 1965. p. 90-135)    HN 803.5 S62

A discussion of efforts at rural modernization in Chad, focusing on the legal and administrative aspects of the establishment of paysannats (rural producer cooperatives). The final chapter presents a micro-study of the paysannats of Torrock, a village in the district of Pala.

5. Romba, Elie. BRIEF NOTES ON THE SYSTEM OF LAND TENURE IN THE REPUBLIC OF CHAD. E/CN.14/CART/273. n.p., United Nations, Economic and Social Council, 1971. 4 p. Presented at UNECA Seminar on Cadastre, Addis Ababa, 25 November-9 December 1970.
Files Chad 58 R65

This short article includes an explanation of the purposes of land registration within Chad's legal system and a brief survey of other aspects of land tenure and land administration.


## CONGO

1. Guillot, B. "Structures agraires koukouya (Congo-Brazzaville)." (In ETR, 37/38/39, 1970. p. 312-325)

Describes an area where relatively infertile soil supports a large population due to sophisticated farm management. Each crop corresponds to a certain soil type and degree of fertility, each has a certain place in the agricultural calendar, and crop rotations permit high productivity of land. But in the case of commercial crops, with which the people have had little experience, techniques are less sophisticated and the potential for damage to the soil and fragile environment is much greater.

2. Soret, Marcel. "Problèmes fonciers chez les Konga Nord-Ouest. Problèmes de terre ou problèmes démographiques?" (In ISEAC, 166, 1965 (5:9). p. 141-167)    Mem H 31 I53
Also available as a separate.    Files Congo 58 S67

Population pressure on land in the central zone of the area studied is not so much the result of an absolute shortage of land as a consequence of uneven population distribution. The solution to the problem lies in land reform, which the author

# LAND TENURE AND AGRARIAN REFORM

CONGO 2-DAHOM 3

(Soret, Marcel)
fails to discuss specifically, and in measures to reverse
migrations which have created the present pattern of population distribution.

3. _____. "La propriété foncière chez les Kongo du Nord-
Ouest: caractéristiques générales et évolution." (In Item
AFR-67, p. 281-296)                                    HD 966 I5 1960

A description of the customary land tenure system of the northwestern Congo focusing on historical changes. The author compares present land rights to those described by a sixteenth-
century Portuguese traveler.


## DAHOMEY

1. Beynel, Jean. "Revue des différents solutions dahoméennes du
problème du développement de l'agriculture." (In RPEN, 736,
1972. p. 209-245)                                    Mem JV 1853 R42

A lengthy article on the legal structure for agrarian reform
in Dahomey. The author considers the périmetres d'amenage-
ment rural to be a creative solution to the problems of form-
ing cooperatives in Africa because people living within the
boundaries of these designated areas are free to join or stay
away from communal economic activities.

2. Costa, E. "Back to the land: the campaign against unemployment in Dahomey." (In ILR, 93:1, 1966. p. 29-49)
                                                    Mem AP I616 L135

As part of an effort to attack high rates of urban unemployment, the government of Dahomey sponsored resettlement projects and agricultural development to encourage a "back to the
land" movement. Poor coordination and a failure to take
account of pre-existing social and economic institutions in
rural areas characterize all these efforts and explain many
failures.

3. Dissou, Machioudi Idriss. "Aspects of land tenure in the
rural areas of lower Dahomey." n.p., 1972. 12 1. Paper
prepared for the Seminar on Agricultural Research in West
Africa, "Aspects of land tenure," University of Ibadan, 1972.
                                                    Files Dahom 58 D47

# Land Tenure and Agrarian Reform

(Dissou, Machioudi Idriss)
Examines conflicts between customary land law and the laws of 1961 and 1965 which provided for the establishment of producer cooperatives. Special attention is given to customary law governing the leasing and pledging of land.

4. _____. "Structures et coutumes foncières dans la région d'Agonvy." (In EDAH, 8, 1966. p. 75-94)     Mem AP E85 D131

Interviews with Goun and Yoruba farmers revealed the mechanisms for the transfer and acquisition of rights to land by gifts, sale, lease, loan from relatives, pledge, and inheritance. The general conclusion is that most people, with the exception of a few Yoruba living in remote areas, see nothing wrong in the sale of land once thought to be inalienable because it belonged to the ancestors and those yet unborn.

5. Food and Agriculture Organization. Committee on Agrarian Reform. "Note sur la réforme agraire au Dahomey." (Porto-Novo?) n.d. 17, 30 p.     Files Dahom 3 F66

The impetus for agrarian reform in Dahomey stems from government-imposed economic goals rather than from a demand for land among the peasantry. Dahomey's innovative land reform program set up large tracts of land as public domain on which all landholders must subscribe to one of two basic cooperative forms, with fuller benefits accruing to the more communal organizations. An appendix to the article presents the complete texts of the law of 1961 as modified by laws of 1963 and 1966 pertaining to the establishment of producer cooperatives.

6. Gosselin, G. DEVELOPPEMENT ET TRADITION DANS LES SOCIETES RURALES AFRICAINES. 1970.     HN 773.5 G67

See Item AFR-60 for citation. Chapter 6 (p. 175-219) summarizes the Dahomean experience with land reform in the southern part of the country, where much land is devoted to palm products. Mandatory membership in producer cooperatives is designed to modernize production. The author views the Dahomean experience as an example of the benefits of intervention by the state in a traditional society undergoing rapid change. He minimizes problems posed by the lack of enthusiasm and cooperation from members forced to join the cooperatives.

# Land Tenure and Agrarian Reform

7.  Hurault, Jean; et Vallet, Jacques. MISSION D'ETUDE DES
    STRUCTURES AGRAIRES DANS LE SUD DAHOMEY; FEVRIER A NOVEMBRE
    1961. Paris, Institut Géographique National, Ministère des
    Travaux Publics et des Transports, 1963. 2 v.
    HD 2135 D32 S83

    This socio-economic study of agriculture in southern Dahomey
    presents a case study of the village of Fanvi as well as back-
    ground information. A chapter on land tenure (p. 23-30)
    discusses the pledging of land in Fanvi in detail. A survey
    revealed that 35 percent of the sample pledged land to obtain
    money for marriages, 23 percent for funerals, 13 percent be-
    cause of sickness in the family, and the rest for assorted
    other reasons. Thirty-five percent of the total number of
    parcels of land in Fanvi were pledged when the study was
    conducted.

8.  Magnes, B. "Les Champs collectifs au Dahomey." (In CD, 5,
    1965. p. 44-51)                                Mem AP C7767 E84

    In the early 1960s the Dahomean government experimented with
    having farmers from each village grow crops on small areas of
    land owned and worked collectively by the village. The experi-
    ment was unquestionably a failure, with average output on
    these champs collectifs averaging only about one-third the
    level attainable under pre-existing systems. Among the reasons
    for the failure of the plan was its complete and abrupt de-
    parture from customary tenure systems and existing patterns
    of land use.

9.  Mensah, M. "L'Expérience dahoméenne en matière de coopératives
    de production dans le cadre des périmètres d'aménagement
    rural." (In EDAH, 6/7, 1966. p. 73-80)        Mem AP E85 D131

    A discussion of the advantages of forcing farmers to form
    producer cooperatives: the removal of obstacles to development
    inherent in pre-existing land tenure systems, and the creation
    of opportunities for employment in the rural sector to stem
    the tide of rural-urban migration.

10. Quirino Lanhoumey, J. "Le Développement communautaire en
    Afrique noire: leçons d'une expérience au Dahomey." (In
    PETR, 2, 1964. p. 161-180)                     Mem AP P7712

    The author contends that cooperative farms established in
    Dahomey have been successful and will eventually provide a
    strong agricultural base for industrialization. Experiments
    with other forms of government-sponsored community agricultural

# LAND TENURE AND AGRARIAN REFORM

(Quirino Lanhoumey, J.)
effort, such as the champs collectifs, have been less
successful. The reason for this contrast is that the highly
organized structure of the cooperative farms replaced pre-
existing institutions, whereas more loosely organized projects
simply clashed with indigenous forms.

11.  Serreau, Jean.  LE DEVELOPPEMENT A LA BASE AU DAHOMEY ET AU
     SENEGAL.  Bibliotheque d'économie politique, 7.  Paris,
     Librairie Générale de Droit et de Jurisprudence, 1966.
     358 p.  Bibl.                                 Mem HC 547 D3 S4

     An analysis of the economic situation of Dahomey and Senegal
     in 1960 which focuses on the development of rural cooperatives
     and effective agricultural extension programs.  Includes a
     brief and very general section on land tenure in the two
     countries.

12.  Tardits, Claude.  "Développement du régime d'appropriation
     privée des terres de la palmeraie du Sud-Dahomey."  (In Item
     AFR-67, p. 297-313)                         HD 966 I5 1960

     A brief discussion of three systems of landholding in southern
     Dahomey:  land held as lineage property, private property,
     and a third system whereby individuals behave as private
     owners of land over which ancestors originally held usufruct
     rights.  A detailed micro-study of this third system in a
     single village is presented.

13.  Toko, Michel.  "L'Action des pouvoirs publics dans la
     répartition et l'affectation du sol en vue de l'aménagement et
     du développement au Dahomey."  1970.  (In Item AFR-112,
     p. 1243-1254)

     Describes the provisions of legislation establishing producer
     cooperatives as instruments of agrarian reform.  Owners of
     land in areas designated by the government must form coopera-
     tives.  If they are unable to work the consolidated holdings,
     the government can force them to lease land to tenants.
     Dahomean legislation provides for technical assistance, credit,
     and the services of auditors to aid these cooperatives.

## ETHIOPIA

1. "Agrarian reform and economic development: the Ethiopian case." (In CBEMR, January/February 1974. p. 1-29) Also available as a separate.     Files Eth 3 A37

1a. Alemante Gebre-Selassie. "Property relationships in Ethiopia and their implications for development." (Madison) 1972. iii, 82 l. Bibl. M. S. thesis, University of Wisconsin.     Files Eth 58 A52

2. Alemseged Tesfai. COMMUNAL LAND OWNERSHIP IN NORTHERN ETHIOPIA AND ITS IMPLICATIONS FOR GOVERNMENT DEVELOPMENT POLICIES. Paper no. 88. Madison, Land Tenure Center, 1973. 30 p. Bibl.     Files Eth 55.5 A52

The author distinguishes land ownership in the northern highlands, where land is mostly communally owned, from land tenure in the rest of the country, where private ownership prevails. The pressing problem in the south is the reform of tenancy relations, but national programs of land reform must recognize the differences between north and south. To show why individualization of tenure cannot be a common solution, the author describes ownership of land by villages and by extended families in the north, and stresses that reform must respect the egalitarian traditions of the peoples of the northern highlands.

2a. _____. "General background and theoretical framework for an evaluation of communal land tenure systems in Eritrea and their significance for economic development." n.p. (197-). 66 l.     Files Eth 55.5 A523

2b. Ambaye Zekarias. "Land tenure in Eritrea, Ethiopia." Addis Ababa, 1966. xi, 80 p.     HD 1021 E83 E73

2c. Aschenaki Tafere. "Maderia land rights in Wello Province: their consequences for the tenant cultivators." (Madison, 1974). 29 l.     Files Eth 58 A71

3. Assafe Dula. "Land tenure in Chercher Province." (In EOB, 12:2, 1969. p. 137-139)     Mem AP E8435 Also available as a separate.     Files Eth 58 A77

# Land Tenure and Agrarian Reform

(Assafe Dula)
A brief historical description of land tenure and land ownership in Chercher Awraja in Harar Province. Large areas of
land were given to soldiers, civil servants, and church offi-
cials as rewards for loyal service.

4. Assefa Bequele; and Eshetu Chole. "Agriculture and agrarian
   structure." (In their A PROFILE OF THE ETHIOPIAN ECONOMY.
   Addis Ababa, Oxford University Press, 1969. p. 27-49)
                                                   HC 591 A3 B26

   Backward technology, small holdings, and an archaic and confused system of land tenure hinder Ethiopian agricultural development. Tenancy reform, improved transport, credit
   institutions, and marketing facilities are all needed to
   rectify the situation. In the author's opinion, the government has shown little concern for any of Ethiopia's agricultural problems.

5. Bell, Pamela, comp. LAND TENURE IN ETHIOPIA: BIBLIOGRAPHY.
   Ethiopian bibliographical series no. 1. Addis Ababa, Haile
   Sellassie I University Library, 1968. 25 1. Files Eth 58 B25

   Contains over 300 references, many historical, to Ethiopian
   history, economics, travel, and land tenure.

6. Berhanou Abbebe. EVOLUTION DE LA PROPRIETE FONCIERE AU CHOA
   (ETHIOPIE) DU REGNE DE MENELIK A LA CONSTITUTION DE 1931.
   Bibliothèque de l'Ecole des Langues Orientales Vivantes, 23.
   Paris, Imprimerie Nationale, Librairie Orientaliste Paul
   Geuthner, 1971. xxiv, 270 p.                 HD 1023 E8 B27

   An historical study by a legal scholar on the evolution of the
   concept of property from 1867 to 1931. Land law applying to
   estates required that holders of estates give military or
   administrative services to the central government, whereas
   parcels were subject to payments in kind or services, or,
   more recently, money. Separate sections deal with state,
   church, and privately held estates as well as the law governing
   smallholders.

7. Bilillign Mandefro. "Agricultural communities and the Civil
   Code: a commentary." (In JETHL, 6:1, 1969. p. 145-199)
                                                       Law Per
   Also available as a separate.          Files Eth 58 B45

   A commentary on the provisions of the civil code governing
   what the author refers to as family (rist) and village (shihena)

# LAND TENURE AND AGRARIAN REFORM

ETH 7-10

(Bilillign Mandefro)
ownership and ownership by groups of pastoralists. According
to the author, these provisions make little sense. To demonstrate this, he describes the land tenure systems of both
pastoral and sedentary Ethiopian communities.

8.  Chilalo Agricultural Development Unit. Asella, Ethiopia.
    PRELIMINARY INVESTIGATIONS ON MECHANIZED FARMING AND ITS
    EFFECTS ON PEASANT AGRICULTURE. (By) Planning and Evaluation
    Section. (Asella) 1970. 16, (7) 1.        Files Eth 93.5 C34

In Chilalo in the Northern Project Area of CADU, the use of
machinery with improved seed and fertilizer has increased agricultural production. But it has also led to the eviction of
tenants, increased land values, and a reduction in the amount
of pasture land available.

9.  Cohen, John Michael. "Ethiopia after Haile Selassie: the
    government land factor." (In AA, 72:289, 1973. p. 365-382)

The author concludes that whatever the makeup of the regime
which follows Haile Sellassie, little basic change in Ethiopia
can be expected. Extensive grants of government land have
been used "to bind administrators, military men, local gentry
and even intellectuals to the support of the present land
tenure system. And the extent of government holdings is still
sufficient to allow this practice to be extended into the
future".

9a. _____. "Land reform in Ethiopia: the effects of an uncommit-
    ted center on the rural periphery." n.p., 1973. 31 1. Paper
    for 16th Annual Conference of the African Studies Association,
    Syracuse University, 1973.                Files Eth 3 C63

10. _____. "Rural change in Ethiopia: a study of land, elites,
    power and values in Chilalo Awraja." Boulder, 1973. 2 v.
    Bibl. Ph. D. dissertation. Univ. of Colorado. Photocopy.
    Ann Arbor, Mich., University Microfilms, 1974. HN 831 E83 C33

This thesis presents a micro-level study of political power in
the Chilalo region of the south-central Ethiopian highlands.
Local elites have the capacity to maintain the established
system and to preclude any significant change on the part of
the great mass of peasants. These elites are aided by a
national center which is not committed to agrarian reform because its own survival is dependent on the maintenance of the
traditional rural system. The central subject of the thesis
is how the traditional system is threatened by economic change
and how elites use their power to control the direction of change.

54

# Land Tenure and Agrarian Reform

10a.  "Comments on the general policy paper on land reform."  (By
Tamrat Kebede and others).  n.p.  (1971).  3 1.
                                            Files Eth 3 C65

10b.  Conti Rossini, Carlo.  "La Proprietà immobiliare."  (In his
PRINCIPI DI DIRITTO CONSUETUDINARIO DELL'ERITREA.  Roma,
Tipografia dell'Unione Editrice, 1916.  p. 97-163)
Also available as a separate.              Files Eth 58 C65

11.  Demissie Gebre Michael.  "Agrarian reform:  a proposal to
contribute to economic development in Ethiopia."  (Columbus)
1964.  iv, 152 1.  Bibl.  M. S. thesis, Ohio State University.
                                            Files Eth 3 D25

This thesis presents a brief history of the most common forms
of land tenure, focusing specifically on three major institutions:  the church, the army, and the sovereign.  The author's
proposals for land reform include registration of title, the
improvement of tenancy relations; settlement programs to redistribute population, and limitations on the size of holdings
which individuals may acquire.

12.  _____.  LAND TENURE IN BATE, ALEMAYA, MIKITIL-WOREDA, HARAR.
Experiment station bulletin no. 49.  Dire Dawa, Imperial
Ethiopian College of Agricultural and Mechanical Arts, Haile
Sellassie I University, 1966.  31 p.  Ethiopia-United States
Cooperative Agricultural Education Program, Oklahoma State
University-USAID contract.                 Files Eth 58 D25

This survey included interviews with sixty farmers and yielded
information on land tenure systems, landlord-tenant relationships, and the average size of holdings.

12a.  Dorner, Peter.  "Administrative matters in land reform."
(Addis Ababa) 1971.  6 1.                   Files Eth 3 D67

12b.  _____.  "Suggested additions and reorganization of the draft
paper on general policy."  n.p., 1971.  5 1.  Files Eth 3 D673

13.  Dunning, Harrison C.  "Land reform in Ethiopia:  a case study
in non-development."  (In UCLALR, 18:2, 1970.  p. 271-307)
                                                      Law Per
Also available as a separate.               Files Eth 3 D85

Haile Sellassie's government stated broad goals for land reform
but failed to implement them.  The article examines land tenure
systems, states the case for the necessity of reform, and discusses some of the political factors which are obstacles to
land reform.

ETH 14-18

14. Dunning, Harrison C. "Law and economic development in Africa:
the law of eminent domain." 1968.                           Law Per

See Item AFR-48 for citation and annotation.

15. Ellis, Gene. "Land reform in Ethiopia: whither, whether, and
why." Draft. n.p., 1974. 35 1. Paper presented to the
Annual Meeting of the Canadian African Studies Association,
Dalhousie University, 1974.                        Files Eth 3 E55

Legislation under consideration in Ethiopia in 1974 was designed to increase tenants' incomes by regulating rents, to
force landlords to give at least two-years' notice in the
event that they evict tenants, and to require landlords to pay
from two-to five-years' rent as a penalty for eviction. The
author concludes that the legislation would fail to protect
tenants because the bill raises the cost of labor but leaves
the cost of an alternative--tractorization--the same.

15a. Enguehart, François; et Verhelst, Thierry. ETHIOPIE.
Bruxelles, Institut International des Civilisations
Différentes, 1973. 19 1. Paper for INCIDI Study Session on
Obstacles and Restraints Impeding the Success of Land Reform
in Developing Countries, Brussels, 1973.        Files Eth 58 E33

16. Ethiopia. ETHIOPIA: CADASTRAL SURVEY AND REGISTRATION.
E/CN.14/CART/270. Addis Ababa, UNECA, 1970. 7 p. Paper for
Seminar on Cadastre, 25 Nov.-9 Dec. 1970.      Files Eth 59 E83

A modern cadastral survey will overcome the main obstacles to
the realization of Ethiopia's agricultural potential, namely
the lack of knowledge about land resources and insecurity of
tenure. But a cadastral survey can only recognize existing
land rights, not redistribute these rights.

17. _____. LAND REFORM AND ADMINISTRATION IN ETHIOPIA. RU:WLR-
C/66/33. (Rome) FAO, 1966. 4 p. Country paper for World Land
Reform Conference, Rome, 1966.                   Files Eth 3 E83

A brief outline of the economic objectives of land reform in
Ethiopia.

18. _____. "Report of the Review Committee on Progressive Tax of
Unutilized Land Proclamation." n.p. (1971). 6 1.
                                                 Files Eth 93 E83

A critique of proposed legislation for a progressive land tax.
The argument is that the proposed tax would fail to promote

# LAND TENURE AND AGRARIAN REFORM

ETH 18-21

(Ethiopia)
the objectives of land reform and would probably fail to
generate enough added revenue to offset increased administrative costs.

19.  _____. Central Statistical Office. REPORT ON SURVEY OF . . .
Addis Ababa, 1966-1968. 17 v.                  Mem HA 1961 A29

A concise statistical compilation of information on population
and agriculture for seventeen Ethiopian provinces and towns.
The section on agriculture, based on limited sample surveys,
includes material on holdings, the size of parcels, and land
tenure.

20.  _____. Livestock and Meat Board. "Highland sheep development
project; project identification report." n.p., 1973. iv, 56,
(3) 1.                                          SF 375.5 E8 A3

The objective of the misssion was to select areas as focal
points for the first phase of a development project for sheep
husbandry in the central highlands, and to collect information
to facilitate this task. A section on land tenure (p. 10-18)
notes that the absence of all but the smallest parcels of
privately owned grazing land and the multiplicity of rights
to common grazing land present serious obstacles to the implementation of plans for development projects.

20a. _____. Ministry of Agriculture. Extension and Project Implementation Department. RESULTS FROM SURVEYS OF BASIC FARM
CONDITIONS IN 48 AGRICULTURAL EXTENSION AGENT AREAS IN 11
PROVINCES OF ETHIOPIA. Publication no. 9. n.p., 1973. 2 v.
(287, 20 1.)                                    HD 2146 E8 A57

21.  _____. Ministry of Land Reform and Administration. "Policy of
the Imperial Ethiopian Government on agricultural land tenure."
Draft. n.p., 1972. iii, 61 1.                  Files Eth 58 E4

This report reviews land tenure problems in Ethiopia, the need
for measures to redistribute rural incomes as modern technology is introduced, and the continuing need for agriculture
to absorb the rural labor force. The report also presents
specific measures of land reform to be laid before parliament.
These include land registration, ceilings on land holdings,
provisions for the allocation of government land, and tenancy
reform designed to raise tenants' incomes and to force landlords to pay from two- to five-years' rent as a penalty for the
eviction of tenants.

# LAND TENURE AND AGRARIAN REFORM

22. Ethiopia. Ministry of Land Reform and Administration. A
    POLICY ORIENTATED STUDY OF LAND SETTLEMENT. Report prepared
    by V. E. M. Burke and F. Thornley. (Addis Ababa) 1969. 2 v.
    HD 1516 E8 A3

    This report explores the possibility of developing government
    lands in Ethiopia by instituting settlement schemes. It
    begins by making an inventory of the resources necessary for
    such projects, including land, settlers, and an institutional
    framework within the government capable of planning and
    implementing settlement schemes. The report recommends the
    creation of a Central Agricultural Project Development Board
    to coordinate agricultural development projects.

23. _____. _____. Dept. of Land Tenure. THE MAJOR FEATURES OF
    THE PREVAILING LAND TENURE SYSTEM IN ETHIOPIA. I. THE COMPI-
    LATION OF THE GENERAL LAND TENURE SURVEY REPORTS OF TEN NON-
    COMMUNAL PROVINCES. Draft. Addis Ababa, 1971. iv, 57 l.
    Files Eth 58 E52

    A summary of the data presented for non-communal areas covered
    in Item ETH-24. One conclusion is that 90 percent of the
    land on tax rolls is held under one of the following three
    types of tenure systems: gebbar, which is roughly equivalent
    to fee simple; semon and church gult tenures, which relate to
    the interests of the church in land; and mengist, gebretel,
    galla, waregenu, huddad, and maderia, all various types of
    tenures on government land.

24. _____. _____. _____. REPORT ON LAND TENURE SURVEY. Addis
    Ababa, 1967. 13 v.                          Files Eth 58 E527

    These reports, consisting of summaries of data taken from tax
    rolls with some additional material from interviews, include
    information on various land tenure systems, landlord-tenant
    relationships, and the extent of fragmentation in the following
    provinces: Shoa, Sidamo, Tigre, Welega, Welo, Arussi, Bale,
    Begemdir, Simien, Keffa, Gemu Gofa, Gojam, Illubabor, and
    Eritrea.

24a. _____. _____. _____. Communal and Nomadic Section. "First
    pilot study of nomadic regions: Awash Valley." n.p. (1972).
    12 l.                                         Files Eth 58 E6

24b. "Ethiopia: cropped area by tenure." n.p., n.d. (11) l.
                                                 Files Eth 58 E95

25. Foblets, Maurits. LAND TAXATION AND LAND CLASSIFICATION IN THEORY AND IN THE ETHIOPIAN PRACTICE: AN INTRODUCTORY PAPER. Addis Ababa, Land Classification and Land Taxation Section, Land Tenure and Administration Dept., Ministry of Land Reform and Administration, 1971. 46 1.      Files Eth 93 F62

The major obstacle to agricultural development in Ethiopia is the failure of the government to carry out the institutional reform. The land grant policy in practice at the time of writing promoted absentee landlordism. A program of land classification and reform of the system of taxation are prerequisites for development.

26. Food and Agriculture Organization. AGRICULTURE IN ETHIOPIA. Compiled by H. P. Huffnagel. Rome, 1961. 484 p.      Ag Docs

A comprehensive though dated survey of the agrarian structure of Ethiopia. Two chapters on land tenure (p. 97-129) present customary tenure systems on measured and unmeasured land, in nomad areas, and in regions paying a fixed tribute. Includes sections on land law reform in the twentieth century.

27. Gebre-Wold Ingida Worq. "Ethiopia's traditional system of land tenure and taxation." (In EOB, 5:4, 1962. p. 42, 302-339)      Mem AP E8435
Also available as a separate.      Files Eth 58 G22

A translation of Ya Ityopia Marethna Gibir Sim consisting mainly of an exhaustive listing of types of customary land tenure with no analysis or interpretation.

27a. Haile Sellassie. "(Emperor's speeches)." n.p. (197-). 23 1.
Files Eth 3 H14

28. Haileluel Getahun. "Tax policy and land reform in the development of Ethiopia." (Madison) 1967. 120 1. Bibl. M. S. thesis, University of Wisconsin.      Mem AWO G3941 H1512

Taking a broad view of economic development, the author recommends land reform, programs of agricultural extension and credit, decentralization of decision-making so that local bodies and even farmers themselves may have a voice in national policy, and tax reform.

# Land Tenure and Agrarian Reform

28a. Hailu W. Emmanuel. "Ethiopia: land tenure and reform programme." (In REPORT OF WORKING GROUP C. By K. Obayya and
others. n.p., 1973. p. 1-5) Paper for Study Seminar 35:
Land Tenure, Distribution and Reform, Institute of Development
Studies, University of Sussex, 1973.                    Files 3 R26

28b. _____. "Land tenure, land-use, and development in the Awash
Valley--Ethiopia." Draft. (Madison) 1973. 67 1. Bibl.
                                                     Files Eth 78 H14

29. Hoben, Allan. "Amhara land tenure; the dynamics of cognatic
descent in Ethiopia." (Addison, Me., 1971). vi, 296 1. Bibl.
                                                     Files Eth 58 H62

An early draft of Item ETH-30.

30. _____. LAND TENURE AMONG THE AMHARA OF ETHIOPIA: THE DYNAMICS
OF COGNATIVE DESCENT. Monographs in Ethiopian land tenure,
no. 4. Chicago, University of Chicago Press, 1973. xiv,
273 p.                                               HD 1021 E8 H63

A careful and detailed anthropological study of land rights
among the Amhara of Dega Damot and the basis of these rights
in territorially based cognatic descent groups. Men and women
may acquire land by inheriting it from either parent, through
marriage, or by pressing claims within the cognatic descent
group. Most men must actively strive against competition from
rival claimants to put together enough rist land to support
their household. Hoben advocates leaving the land tenure system unchanged, but encouraging the growth of agricultural output instead, thereby bringing about a gradual change in
farmers' attitudes toward land and creating a demand for
changes in the rules of tenure.

31. _____. "Social anthropology and development planning; a case
study in Ethiopian land reform policy." (In JMAS, 10:4, 1972.
p. 561-583)
Also available as a separate.                         Files Eth 3 H63

A study of the rist system of land tenure in several Amhara
villages in Dega Damot reveals that widely held assumptions
were incorrect: fragmentation of holdings was not a problem,
absentee landlordism was nonexistent, large holdings were
unusual, and tenure was secure enough to permit farmers to
make improvements in the productivity of the land. Hoben
agrees with what he describes as the majority opinion of the
local farming population; what is needed to spur economic
development is the construction of roads rather than a program
of land reform.

# LAND TENURE AND AGRARIAN REFORM

32. Huntingford, G. W. B. THE LAND CHARTERS OF NORTHERN ETHIOPIA.
    Monographs in Ethiopian land tenure, 1. Addis Ababa, Pub-
    lished by the Institute of Ethiopian Studies and the Faculty
    of Law, Haile Sellassie I University in association with Oxford
    University Press, 1965. xii, 132 p.         HD 1024 E8 H85

    A translation of 100 royal land charters dating from the four-
    teenth through the nineteenth centuries. Includes indices
    listing titles, grantors, grantees, chiefs, lands granted,
    and officials named in the land grants. In an introduction
    Huntingford comments on the sources of the documents and
    traces the evolution of land tenure systems in Ethiopia during
    the middle ages from early "communal" ownership of land to the
    gradual acquisition of land by the crown through confiscation
    and conquest, and the eventual establishment of two principal
    forms of land tenure: gult lands received by royal charter
    and rist land passed from father to son subject to the payment
    of tribute, though such land acquired a strictly hereditary
    character after long periods of occupation.

33. International Labour Office. REPORT TO THE GOVERNMENT OF
    ETHIOPIA ON INTEGRATED RURAL DEVELOPMENT. Geneva, 1970. 88 p.
                                          Mem HN 831 E84 C63

    A section on land settlement projects (p. 20-54) recommends
    the creation of a separate governmental agency to form the
    core of a composite sphere of specialists from other depart-
    ments and agencies concerned with all aspects of the settle-
    ment process. The document also recommends that Gemu Gofa
    province be selected as a planned integrated rural development
    project.

34. Jackson, Richard T. LAND USE AND SETTLEMENT IN GEMU GOFA,
    ETHIOPIA. Occasional paper, no. 17. Kampala, Uganda, Makerere
    University, Dept. of Geography, 1970. 25 p.
                                          Files Eth 57.5 J12

    A paper dealing with the overall patterns of land use and
    settlement in the area, based on a micro-level study and the
    analysis of aerial photographs.

35. Jacoby, Erich H. STRUCTURAL PROBLEMS IN ETHIOPIA IN RELATION
    TO AGRICULTURAL PROGRESS. Maddelande Frän Utredningsbyran,
    1973 02 20. (Stockholm) Swedish International Development
    Authority, 1973. 27 1.                  Files Eth 58 J11

    Divides Ethiopia into areas where communal tenure predominates
    and areas characterized by noncommunal forms of tenure. The

# Land Tenure and Agrarian Reform

ETH 35-39

(Jacoby, Erich H.)
author uses this division to organize his recommendations for
development policies.

36. Jandy, Edward C.  "Changing land tenure practice and land taxation in Ethiopia."  n.p., 1963.  25 1.  Paper presented at the
Conference on Land and Tax Reform in the Less Developed Countries, at the Alumni House, University of Wisconsin-Milwaukee,
Aug. 26-28, 1963.                                    Files Eth 58 J15

A discussion of patterns of land tenure, with background material on the structure of the Ethiopian economy.

37. "Justification on tax on unutilized land proclamation."  n.p.,
n.d.  32, 11 1.                                    Files Eth 93 J87

The draft of a proclamation for the taxation of unutilized land
follows a detailed commentary on the provisions of the proposed
legislation.

38. Lambton, Ann K. S.  "Ethiopia:  an approach to land reform."
(In LOASB, 34, pt. 2, 1971.  p. 221-240)    Mem AP L847 E587/B
Also available as a separate.                      Files Eth 3 L15

Land reform in Iran, which paid great attention to security of
tenure and the building of a cooperative movement, provides
a model for Ethiopia.  The article consists mainly of a review
of land tenure systems in Ethiopia and the modest efforts at
reform under way at the time of writing.

38a. "The Land system of Wello."  Rough translation by John Bruce.
n.p., n.d.  (3) 1.  Translation of "Il Regime delle terre nel
Uollo."  (Originally published in RIVISTA DI DIRITTO COLONIALE,
2, 1939.  p. 55-57)                                Files Eth 58 L145

38b. "Land tenure--Ethiopia."  n.p. (197-).  9 1.  Paper for Study
Seminar 35: Land Tenure, Distribution and Reform, Institute
of Development Studies, University of Sussex, 1973.
                                                   Files Eth 58 L15

39. Lawrance, J. C. D.; and Mann, H. S.  "FAO land policy project
(Ethiopia)."  (In EOB, 9:4, 1966.  p. 286-336)    Mem AP E8435

Policy recommendations from which the land reform provisions
of the Second Five-Year Development Plan were drawn.  Recommendations concentrate on the improvement of landlord-tenant
relationships, progressive taxation, the abolition of out-of-
date tenure systems, and cadastral survey as a prelude to land

(Lawrance, J. C. D.; and Mann, H. S.)
registration. The authors also recommend the establishment of
an autonomous government agency to handle land reform.

40. Lexander, Arne. THE CHANGING RURAL SOCIETY IN ARUSSI LAND:
SOME FINDINGS FROM A FIELD STUDY 1966-1967. CADU publication
no. 7. (Asella, Chilalo Agricultural Development Unit) 1968.
ii, 79 l.                                              HN 831 E83 A75

A socio-economic survey of the Chilalo Awraja in Arussi Province which gives historical background on the peoples of the
district and describes their institutions. A section on land
tenure (p. 44-51) describes patterns of inheritance, fragmentation of holdings, the principal customary land tenure
systems of the area, and forms of tenancy.

41. _____. LAND OWNERSHIP, TENANCY AND SOCIAL ORGANIZATION IN THE
WAJJI AREA. CADU publication no. 50. (Asella) Chilalo Agricultural Development Unit, 1970. 92, (13) l.   HD 1026 E8 L29

An intensive study of landholding patterns in an area covering
roughly 1,000 hectares located 15 kilometers south of the
capital of Arussi Province. The study determined the area of
properties and land tenancies, the percentages of holdings
under cultivation, the extent of fragmentation, the systems
of land tenure prevailing in the area, the extent of absentee
ownership, boundary features, the extent of disputes over
ownership and boundaries, and the nature, terms, and duration
of agreements between landlords and tenants.

41a. Lulseged Asfaw. THE ROLE OF STATE DOMAIN LANDS IN ETHIOPIA'S
AGRICULTURAL DEVELOPMENT. Paper no. 106. (Madison) Land
Tenure Center, 1973. 36 p.                    Files Eth 76 L85

42. MacArthur, J. D. "A Note on some aspects of the CADU project,
and their implications to land policy." n.p., n.d. 13 l
                                              Files Eth 82 M12

The introduction of better seed, fertilizer, new agricultural
techniques, the provision of extension services, and the
development of credit and marketing facilities have led to the
eviction of tenants and sharp increases in land rents.

43. _____. REPORT TO THE MINISTRY OF LAND REFORM AND ADMINISTRA-
TION, IMPERIAL ETHIOPIAN GOVERNMENT, ON SOME ASPECTS OF LAND
POLICIES IN ETHIOPIA. Bangor, Wales, U. K., Dept. of Agriculture, University College of North Wales, 1971. 1 v.
(various pagings)                             HD 1026 E8 M12

# Land Tenure and Agrarian Reform

ETH 43-47

(MacArthur, J. D.)
This report of the author's mission to Ethiopia to advise the
government on land policy touches on a wide variety of topics;
the possible consequences of proposed legislation on land
registration and progressive taxation, an evaluation of CADU
and WADU projects, and notes on other large-scale farming and
settlement schemes.

44. Mahteme Sellassie Wolde Maskal. "The land system of Ethiopia."
(In EOB, 1:9, 1957. p. 283-301)             Mem AP E8435

A description of customary systems of land tenure and land
taxation organized under the following headings: regions
where the land has been measured, regions where taxes were
calculated according to the number of houses or families,
regions paying a fixed head tax, and regions where individual
property rights derived from ancient traditions.

45. Mann, H. S. FIELD STUDY IN SYSTEMS OF LAND TENURE AND LAND-
LORD TENANT RELATIONSHIPS, TABOR WOREDA, SIDAMO. Addis Ababa,
Ministry of Land Reform and Administration, Dept. of Land
Tenure, 1966 (cover 1967). 46, (12) l.        Files Eth 58 M15

The principal objectives of the survey were to determine the
size and degree of fragmentation of landlords' and tenants'
holdings, the extent of absentee ownership, and the nature of
tenancy arrangements. A cadastral survey and a program of
land registration are necessary to prevent co-sharers from
being reduced to the status of tenants.

46. _____. LAND TENURE IN CHORE (SHOA): A PILOT STUDY. Monographs
in Ethiopian land tenure, no. 2. Addis Ababa, Published by
the Institute of Ethiopian Studies and the Faculty of Law,
Haile Sellassie I University in association with Oxford University Press, 1965. 78 p.                      HD 1026 E8 M15

A pilot study undertaken to develop a suitable methodology for
field research on landlord-tenant relationships. In Choré the
modal size of farms is about one gasha (40 hectares). About
nine-tenths of the farms are in one parcel; about 25 percent
of the farms are cultivated by the owners; more than half of
the landowners are absentee; the prevailing rental arrangement
is one-third share tenancy; and tenancies are typically of
long duration.

47. _____. REPORT TO THE GOVERNMENT OF ETHIOPIA ON LAND TENURE
AND LANDLORD-TENANT RELATIONSHIPS. UNDP reports, no.
TA2651. Rome, FAO, 1969. 24 p.               Files Eth 58 M157

64

# Land Tenure and Agrarian Reform

(Mann, H. S.)
A report by the FAO Rural Institutions Officer on Land Tenure,
who held the post in Ethiopia from 1962 to 1968, recommending
the abolition of systems of land tenure incompatible with
social and economic development, advocating further intensive
field studies, and urging legislation to regulate landlord-
tenant relationships.

47a. Mesfin Kassu. "Report of a field trip to the Province of
Arussi, Sidamo and Gemu Gofa." n.p., n.d.  5 1.
Files Eth 58 M27

48. Mesfin Kinfu. ANALYSIS OF CULTIVATED HOLDINGS IN ETHIOPIA.
Addis Ababa, Land Classification and Taxation Section,
Ministry of Land Reform and Administration, 1970.  16, (6) 1.
Files Eth 58 M32

The prevalence of absentee landlordism, excessive areas of
unutilized holdings, declining returns to scale on small and
fragmented holdings, and inadequate institutions for agricultural credit are all factors inhibiting agricultural development in Ethiopia.

49. _____. LAND MEASUREMENT AND LAND CLASSIFICATION IN ETHIOPIA.
Addis Ababa, Land Classification and Taxation Section, Ministry
of Land Reform and Administration, 1971.  28, 3 1.
Files Eth 57.5 M27

The fact that a large proportion of Ethiopia's land remains
unmeasured for the purposes of taxation results in substantial
losses in government revenue.  A new system of land classification should help in planning for efficient land use and
revising the present structure of land taxation.

50. _____. THE POSSIBILITIES OF DEVELOPING AGRICULTURALLY GOVERN-
MENT LAND IN ETHIOPIA. (Addis Ababa) Ministry of Land Reform
and Administration, 1970.  13 1.          Files Eth 4 M27

In order to increase Ethiopia's agricultural production, it is
necessary to bring into cultivation vast tracts of potentially
productive land in the lowlands.

51. _____. THE PROS AND CONS OF THE PROPOSED DRAFT PROCLAMATION
ON UNUTILIZED LAND VIS A VIS A BLANKET IMPOSITION OF A PROGRES-
SIVE TAX ON ALL LANDS--THE CASE OF ETHIOPIA. Addis Ababa,
Ministry of Land Reform and Administration, Land Classification
and Taxation Section, 1971.  9 1.          Files Eth 93 M27

LAND TENURE AND AGRARIAN REFORM

(Mesfin Kinfu)
An analysis of the relative merits of a progressive tax on
land irrespective of its utilization and a progressive tax on
unutilized land.  The conclusion is that a tax on all land
would more effectively reduce the size of large landholdings.

52.  Mulugeta Taye.  "The Impact of land ownership systems on the
     development patterns of Shashemene and Ada districts."
     (Madison) 1972.  19 1.  Bibl.  A paper for Economics 983,
     University of Wisconsin.                    Files Eth 4 M85

     Contrasts the land tenure systems of Shashemene and Ada dis-
     tricts and states that differing systems of landholding require
     different development strategies.

53.  Nadel, S. F.  "Land tenure on the Eritrean plateau."  (In
     A/IAI, 16:1, 1946.  p. 1-21; 16:2, 1946.  p. 99-109)
                                               Mem AP A257

     A description of the land tenure systems of Eritrea:  resti,
     or family holdings; individual property and village ownership
     called shehena.  Ways of acquiring temporary rights to use
     land include short- or long-term lease and various forms of
     share tenancy.  The second part of the article contains a de-
     tailed discussion of the operation of Eritrean customary courts
     emphasizing the total absence of procedures or governmental
     institutions to enforce the decisions of the courts regarding
     land disputes.

53a. Nicolas, Gildad.  "Peasant rebellions in the socio-political
     context of today's Ethiopia."  Paper no. 72-114.  n.p., 1972.
     33 p.  Bibl.  Paper for 15th Annual Meeting of the African
     Studies Association, Philadelphia, 1972.  Files Eth 69.75 N41

54.  Pankhurst, Richard Keir Pethick.  ECONOMIC HISTORY OF
     ETHIOPIA, 1800-1935.  1st ed.  Addis Ababa, Haile Sellassie I
     University Press, 1968.  772 p.  Bibl.          HC 591 A3 P24

     A chapter on land tenure (p. 135-183) views Ethiopian land
     policy in historical perspective.  Opening with information on
     the land policies of various rulers in the eighteenth and
     nineteenth centuries, the chapter traces the opposing themes
     of the concentration of rights to land in the hands of a few
     under the auspices of governments and the efforts of the
     government to carry out programs of reform.

55. _____. STATE AND LAND IN ETHIOPIAN HISTORY. Monographs in Ethiopian land tenure, no. 3. Addis Ababa, The Institute of Ethiopian Studies and the Faculty of Law, Haile Sellassie I University, in association with Oxford University Press, 1966. vii, 211 p. HD 1023 E8 P15

This historical study traces the role of the state in controlling and allocating rights in land. It shows that land reform in Ethiopia has a long history, but that earlier reforms were largely motivated by political considerations, not a desire to raise the standard of living of those working the soil.

56. Pankhurst, Sylvia. "Land distribution and farm financing." (In EOB, 4:12, 1961. p. 404-405) Mem AP E8435

A report of the Emperor's announcement of a new program of land distribution and development, broadcast in 1959, in which he promised that Ethiopians who had no land would be granted land; that those who had no capital would be able to obtain loans with easy terms for repayment; that expert advice would be given to assist farmers; and that the establishment of cooperatives would be pressed. Contains aggregate data on loans to smallholders in each province.

57. Pausewang, Siegfried. "The History of land tenure and social personality development in Ethiopia." (In RA, 11, 1970. p. 82-89)

The rist system of land tenure, which gives the individual inalienable rights in land, places the burden on him to defend these rights against all rival claimants. The author contends that the personality traits of the Amhara--variously described as suspicious, skeptical, and pessimistic--are the result of child-rearing practices which evolved as an adaptive response to the highly competitive system of land tenure which prevails in the area of Amhara settlement.

57a. Perrini, Ruffido. "Sulla proprieta fondiaria nel Seraè." Summary and free translation by Alemseged Tesfai. (Madison, 1973). 15 l. Article originally published in NUOVA ANTOLOGIA, 129, 1893. p. 663-693. Files Eth 94 P27

58. Sabry, O. A. "Report to the Imperial Ethiopian Government, Ministry of Land Reform and Administration, on land tenure and settlement problems in the nomadic areas of Ethiopia." Addis Ababa, 1970. (11) l. Files Eth 95.13 S12

# Land Tenure and Agrarian Reform

ETH 58-62

(Sabry, O. A.)
In a section on land tenure (p. 6-8), the author states that
one of the principal obstacles to the development of the
pastoral areas of Ethiopia is the existence of overlapping
claims to grazing and water rights and the lack of any institutional apparatus for sorting out these claims.

59. Schiller, A. Arthur. "Customary land tenure among the high-
land people of northern Ethiopia: a bibliographical essay."
(In ALS, 1, 1969. p. 1-22)                          Law Per
Also available as a separate.            Files Eth 58 S1

An attempt "to record, in chronological sequence, the more
extensive treatments of customary land tenure among the highland people of Ethiopia from the earliest essays to the
present day." Annotated.

60. Schwab, Peter. "Emperor still struggling to achieve land
reform." (In AFD, November 1972. p. 11)

The three draft proclamations sent to the Parliament to limit
the power of landlords and the church have not been passed because members of Parliament are also land owners. The abuses
of the land tenure system remain.

61. SEMINAR PROCEEDINGS ON AGRARIAN REFORM, 25TH NOVEMBER-5TH
DECEMBER 1969. Organized by the Ministry of Land Reform and
Administration, Addis Ababa, Ethiopia. Addis Ababa, 1970.
485 1.                                       HD 1026 E8 S25

Contains 41 seminar papers on land tenure systems, land law,
and land reform in Ethiopia. The seminar was organized in
the hope that discussions would suggest approaches to land
reform which would bring social justice in tenure patterns and
increased agricultural production. Authors include Richard
Pankhurst, T. C. Varghese, Stanislaw Stanley, Eshetu Chole,
John Bruce, Gebre-Egziabher Degou, Lulseged Asfaw, Aberra
Moltot, Hailesilassie Belay, D. T. R. Elsmore, Awgichew Kassa,
George C. Savard, Allan Hoben, and Taye Reta. See Item
AFR-115 for annotation of individual article.

62. Sileshi Wolde-Tsadik. LAND OWNERSHIP IN HARARGE PROVINCE.
Experiment station bulletin no. 47. Dire Dawa, Ethiopia,
Imperial Ethiopian College of Agricultural and Mechanical Arts,
Haile Sellassie I University, 1966. 27 p. Ethiopia-United
States Cooperative Agricultural Education Program: Oklahoma
State University-USAID contract.            Files Eth 58 S45

# Land Tenure and Agrarian Reform

(Sileshi Wolde-Tsadik)
This study relies on tax records to determine the sizes of
holdings and types of tenure in Hararge Province. The average
size of holdings of "measured land" is roughly 40 hectares in
all sub-provinces except Harar. Ownership is skewed, with a
very small proportion of the population owning most of the
land.

62a.    _____. LAND TAXATION IN HARARGE PROVINCE. Experiment station
bulletin, no. 48. Dire Dawa, Ethiopia, Imperial Ethiopian
Government College of Agricultural and Mechanical Arts, 1966.
24 p.                                         Files Eth 93 S45

62b.    "Sub-Committee formed to study and prepare recommendation on
the land reform; second working paper." (Addis Ababa, 1961).
4 l.                                          Files Eth 3 S91

62c.    Tamrat Kebede. "Will family planning ever eliminate the need
for land reform?" (In Ethiopian Nutrition Institute. ON
FAMILY PLANNING IN ETHIOPIA, 2. Addis Ababa, 1972. p. 30-38)
                                              Files Eth 37.3 E83

62d.    Taye Gurmu. AGRARIAN STRUCTURE IN ETHIOPIA AND ITS EFFECT ON
ECONOMIC DEVELOPMENT. IDEP/ET/M/2382. Dakar, United Nations
African Institute for Economic Development and Planning, 1971.
39 p.  Bibl.                                  Files Eth 58 T19

63.     Teame Beyene. "The Communal land tenure problem in Ethiopia
and the requirements for its solution." (Madison) 1971. iv,
110 l.  Bibl.  Thesis (Master of Legal Institutions), University of Wisconsin.                            Files Eth 58 T22

An examination of the deficiencies of land tenure systems in
Ethiopia leads the author to the conclusion that the formation
of cooperative farms is preferable to the promotion of individual tenure. Cooperative farming as envisioned by the author
cannot be introduced without extensive legal reform.

63a.    Tesfaye Shenkute. "An Evaluation of the significance for
development of the Imperial Ethiopian government policies in
agrarian reform." Madison, 1974. 91 l. M.S. thesis, University of Wisconsin.                         HD 1021 E8 T27

64.     _____. "The Need for a special machinery for implementing the
proposed tenancy legislation." (Addis Ababa) n.d. 3 l.
                                              Files Eth 81 T27

# LAND TENURE AND AGRARIAN REFORM

ETH 64-68

(Tesfaye Shenkute)
Judges are not likely to enforce the legislation being proposed at the time of writing to regulate landlord-tenant
relationships. The problems are the judges' lack of legal
training and their sympathies with landlords.

64a.    _____. "The Systems of land tenure in Ethiopia." n.p., 1970.
        7 l.                                        Files Eth 58 T27

64b.    Tucovic, Miodrag. "The Problems of agrarian reform in
        Ethiopia." (Addis Ababa, 1961). 8 l.       Files Eth 3 T81

65.     Varghese, T. C. "The need for inclusion of certain provisions
        in the draft proclamation on tenancy to make it an enforceable
        law." n.p., 1971. 5 l.                      Files Eth 81 V17

        A discussion of the difficulties involved in the regulation of
        landlord-tenant relationships followed by a list of exclusions
        and amendments in the original draft of legislation designed
        to regulate these relationships.

66.     _____. "A Preliminary study of landlord-tenant relationships
        in Ada Woreda." Addis Ababa, Dept. of Land Tenure, Ministry
        of Land Reform and Administration, 1970. 39 l.
                                                    Files Eth 81 V172

        This study found that landlords gave almost no help to tenants
        in the form of seed, housing, tools, or services. The author
        recommends measures to assure tenants security of tenure--
        long-term leases, the abolishment of fees for the renewal of
        tenancies, and the replacement of share tenancies with fixed
        rents.

67.     _____. "The Prevailing land tenure structure in Ethiopia;
        problems and policies." n.p., 1970. 50 p. Country paper
        prepared for the use of FAO Special Committee on Agrarian
        Reform.                                     Files Eth 58 V17

        An overview of patterns of land tenure in Ethiopia is followed
        by an appraisal of the major problems associated with the
        tenure system and government land policy.

68.     Verhelst, Thierry G. MATERIALS ON LAND LAW AND ECONOMIC
        DEVELOPMENT IN AFRICA. 1968.                 HD 962 V27

        See Item AFR-139 for citation and annotation.

LAND TENURE AND AGRARIAN REFORM

## GABON

1. Agondjo-Okawe, Pierre-Louis. "Les Droits fonciers coutumiers au Gabon (Société Nkomi, groupe Myene)." 1970. (In Item AFR-112. p. 1135-1152)
   Also available in RA, 22, 1973. p. 15-29.

   Describes the customary land tenure system of the Nkomi sub-group of the Myene. Includes sections on mythology about land, the acquisition and exercise of land rights, and the evolution of new types of plantations which accompanied the development of markets for cocoa and coffee during the colonial period.

2. Gabon. Ministère du Plan et de la Coopération. Service de Statistique Générale. RESULTATS DE L'ENQUETE AGRICOLE AU GABON, 1960-1961. RESULTATS DEFINITIFS. Paris, Secrétariat d'Etat aux Affaires Étrangères, I.N.S.E.E., Dépt. de la Coopération, 1969. 139 p.      REF HD 999 G3 A2 1960/61

   A statistical presentation of agriculture in Gabon based on sample surveys conducted in 1960 and 1961. Includes data on land tenure, the size of holdings, fragmentation, crop rotation, and land use.

3. Minko, Henri. "Le Régime domanial de la République gabonaise." 1970. (In Item AFR-112, p. 775-782)

   A brief survey of the land law of 1963 and two subsequent amendments.

4. _____. "Le Régime foncier de la République gabonaise: l'immatriculation." 1970. (In Item AFR-112, p. 695-698)

   Describes administrative and judicial procedures for the registration of title to land under the ordinance of 1970. Title to rural land can be obtained if the applicant can prove that he has occupied land continuously for five years.

5. Mouity, Albert. REPORT ON CADASTRE IN GABON. E/CN.14/CART/271. Addis Ababa, UNECA, 1971. 3 p. Paper for Seminar on Cadastre, 25 Nov.-9 Dec. 1970.      Files Gab 12.5 M68

   A very brief review of the purpose, history, methods of work, and organization of the Cadastral Department of Gabon. Concludes that the major problem facing the department is the lack of local staff.

# LAND TENURE AND AGRARIAN REFORM

6.  Nguema, Isaac. "La Terre dans le droit traditionnel ntumu (Gabon)." 1970. (In Item AFR-112, p. 1119-1134)

    A short essay on the place of land in the cosmology and ideology of the Ntumu subgroup of the Fang.

7.  Rogombe, Francine-Rose. "L'Expropriation pour cause d'utilité publique au Gabon." 1970. (In Item AFR-112, p. 953-958)

    Describes procedures set forth in the law of 1961 for the acquisition of land for public purposes, the payment of idemnities, and appeal in the event of disagreements about remuneration.

## GAMBIA

1.  Curtin, Philip D. ECONOMIC CHANGE IN PRECOLONIAL AFRICA: SENEGAMBIA IN THE ERA OF THE SLAVE TRADE. 1975.

    Mem HC 503 W4 C87

    See Item SEN-4 for citation and annotation.

2.  Gambia. Laws, statutes, etc. LANDS (BATHURST AND KOMBO SAINT MARY) ACT. Bathurst, Govt. Printer, 1965. (32) p.

    Files Gam 58 G15

    This Gambian statute consolidates and amends the law governing tenure and control of land use in the city of Bathurst and the Kombo Saint Mary Division. It sets forth law on grants (defined as any sale, lease, or license to use land) as well as acquisition of land for public purposes.

3.  _____. _____. LANDS (PROVINCES) ACT. Bathurst, Govt. Printer, 1965. (30) p.

    Files Gam 58 G16

    This law applies to land tenure and the control of land use in Gambia's provinces. States that customary law shall govern the use of provincial land by indigenous inhabitants and regulates the granting of leases to non-indigenes. Also gives the rules for public acquisition of land in the provinces.

4.  Noble, B. P. "Mémoire sur quelques aspects du régime foncier au Sénégal, en Angleterre et en Gambie." 1965. Mem AP D138

# Land Tenure and Agrarian Reform

(Noble, B. P.)
See Item SEN-13 for citation. The English colonial adminis-
tration of Gambia was content to let most land disputes be
settled according to customary law. The importation of
English common law was generally limited to the capital,
Bathurst. The article compares customary law in Senegal with
English common law and compares these in turn to land law in
Gambia. See Item SEN-13 for additional annotation.


## GHANA


1.  Adegboye, Rufus O. "Ghana." n.p., n.d. 12 1.

    Files Gha 58 A22

    A general discussion of land tenure systems in Ghana with
    recommendations for reform. The author argues that the govern-
    ment should acquire land and lease it to individuals or groups.

2.  Allott, Antony N. ESSAYS IN AFRICAN LAW WITH SPECIAL REFER-
    ENCE TO THE LAW OF GHANA. Butterworth's African Law series,
    no. 1. London, Butterworth's, 1960. 323 p. Mem K 0.1 A4413

    A collection of essays dealing with the impact of English law
    and legal institutions on indigenous systems in former British
    African colonies. Chapters ten and eleven deal specifically
    with land tenure in Ghana. The former concentrates on the
    introduction of written titles to land in societies where the
    notion that writing can be legally binding is a foreign one.
    The latter deals with questions raised by claims to the owner-
    ship of land based on long possession.

3.  Arhin, Kwame, ed. PAPERS ON AHAFO LANDHOLDING. Research
    review, supplement no. 3. Legon, Institute of African Studies,
    University of Ghana, 1970. xxi, 30 p. Bibl.

    Files Gha 58 A73

    A collection of letters and records of court cases on Ahafo
    landholding from the Kumasi branch of the Ghana National
    Archives. Includes an introduction by the editor summarizing
    Ahafo history and presenting the main features of Ahafo land
    tenure viewed against patterns of land tenure in the rest of
    Ashanti.

# Land Tenure and Agrarian Reform

4.    Asante, Samuel K. B. "Interests in land in the customary law
      of Ghana: a new appraisal." (In YLJ, 74, 1965. p. 848-885)
                                                          Law Per
      Also available in Item AFR-3, p. 9.177-9.184. Files Afr 4 A37

      The article includes an outline of the customary system of
      interests in land, an analysis of the social and economic
      pressures impinging upon the customary scheme, a consideration
      of the reactions of the courts to these forces, and a review
      of the involvement of the central government in the adminis-
      tration and regulation of land. One conclusion is that "No-
      where is the cleavage between textbook law and social reality
      more glaring than in the customary land law of Ghana."

5.    Bartels, Jonathan E. "Land tenure in northern Ghana."
      Madison, 1964. v, 83 1. Bibl. M.S. thesis, University of
      Wisconsin.                                  Mem AWO B2853 J763

      A discussion of the main problems associated with reforming
      customary tenure systems in northern Ghana, including histor-
      ical and geographical background, a review of past efforts at
      changing customary tenure, and a recommendation that the
      individualization of tenure be encouraged.

6.    Becher, H. J. "Bodenrecht in Ghana." (In NA, 4:5, 1962.
      p. 186-189)                                Mem AP N481 A258

      A brief review of Ghanaian customary land law and the rules
      governing the inheritance of property.

7.    Beckett, W. H.  AKOKOASO - A SURVEY OF A GOLD COAST VILLAGE.
      Monographs on social anthropology, no. 10. London, Published
      for the London School of Economics and Political Science by
      P. Lund, Humphries and Co. Ltd., 1947. 95 p.
                                                  Mem HN 800 G6 A53

      A socio-economic survey of a small village in the Central
      Province of Ghana done in the 1930s. A chapter on land tenure
      (p. 56-59) notes that the inhabitants of the village have
      free access to lands controlled by the chief and can establish
      farms without his consent. Land rights are passed from one
      generation to the next according to the principles of matri-
      lineal inheritance. Strangers may acquire land rights by
      purchase or by agreeing to give the owner a one-third share
      of cocoa produced on the land.

# LAND TENURE AND AGRARIAN REFORM

8.  Benneh, George. "Land tenure and farming system in Nkrankwanta: a village in the pioneer-cocoa area of Ghana." (In GGAB, 10:2, 1965. p. 6-15)
    Also available as a separate.                    Files Gha 58 B248

    While the influx of migrant cocoa farmers into the Nkrankwanta area has resulted in an increase in the demand for and value of agricultural land, the forces of conservatism and long-held ideas about land have prevented the outright sale of virgin land to strangers. Unrestrained by high land prices and spurred on by the money incentives which accessible markets and the reasonably high prices of cocoa, coffee, and food crops provide, both local and stranger farmers have embarked on a scramble for the control of the rest of the unclaimed land.

9.  _____. LAND TENURE AND LAND REFORM IN GHANA. FAO special committee on agrarian reform background paper. Legon, 1970. 32 1. Bibl.                    Files Gha 58 B25

    A comprehensive review of factors influencing the evolution of land tenure systems in Ghana. Customary tenure systems are being modified at critical points under pressure for change; for example, in areas committed to production for overseas export, where individual tenure is evolving. But the proliferation of land disputes and the fragmentation of holdings are problems requiring the attention of the government.

10. _____. "Land tenure and land use systems in the first savannah contact zone in Ghana: a case study." n.p., n.d. 10, (3) 1.
                                          Files Gha 57.5 B25

    The forest-savannah contact zone, rapidly becoming an important agricultural region of the country, shows the same evolution of the land tenure system which occurred in the forest region with the introduction of cocoa. Since the early 1950s, when tobacco and yam production increased dramatically, land in the Mampong-Ejura district was no longer given free to strangers.

11. _____. "Land tenure and Sabala farming system in the Anlo area of Ghana: a case study." (In IASRR, 7:2, 1971. p. 74-94)
                                          Mem AP G4115 C855
    Also available as a separate.         Files Gha 58 B255

    An analysis of the Anlo system of shallot farming along the Ghanaian coast, one of the most intensive systems of farming in Ghana. Individual ownership of land permits productive investment such as irrigation, manuring, crop rotation, and the maintenance of drainage systems. The author believes this case study disproves the assertion that resistance to change on the part of African farmers is the primary obstacle to agricultural development, since Anlo farmers have evolved a highly efficient use of resources, and a land tenure system to match largely on their own.

# Land Tenure and Agrarian Reform

12.  Benneh, George. "Small-scale farming systems in Ghana." (In A/IAI, 43:2, 1973. p. 134-146)

The well known generalization that farmers in tropical Africa practice shifting cultivation persists even though changes have occurred in many regions. This article classifies the agrarian system of Ghana into bush fallow, cash tree cropping, compound farming, mixed farming, and specialized horticulture.

13.  Bentsi-Enchill, Kwamena. GHANA LAND LAW; AN EXPOSITION, ANALYSIS, AND CRITIQUE. Law in Africa, no. 10. London, Sweet & Maxwell, 1964. xxv, 408 p.          HD 1169 G6 B4

A comprehensive treatment of Ghanaian land law. Part one views land law in the perspective of other social and political institutions. Part two focuses on original interests in land, relationships within landowning groups, intestate succession, and testamentary inheritance. Part three surveys the ways in which the modern state affects traditional land law systems by controlling land use and by providing mechanisms to assure security of tenure.

14.  Birmingham, Walter Barr; Neustadt, I.; and Omaboe, E. N., eds. A STUDY OF CONTEMPORARY GHANA. Evanston, Northwestern University Press, 1966-1967. 2 v. Bibl.          HC 517 G6 B52

Volume one focuses on Ghana's economy. Volume two, which deals with Ghanaian social structure, contains a chapter (p. 251-265) giving a general but concise picture of Ghana's customary land tenure systems and a short history of land policy.

15.  Cardinall, Allen Wolsey. THE NATIVES OF THE NORTHERN TERRITORIES OF THE GOLD COAST; THEIR CUSTOMS, RELIGION AND FOLKLORE. London, G. Routledge & Sons, Ltd.; New York, E. P. Dutton & Co. (1920). 158 p.          Mem DT 511 C3

An early work on the history, customs, and language of the peoples of northern Ghana. Includes a chapter on land tenure which observes that communal patterns of landholding have given way to individual or familiar systems.

16.  Chambers, Robert. SETTLEMENT SCHEMES IN TROPICAL AFRICA: A STUDY OF ORGANIZATIONS AND DEVELOPMENT. (1969).
          HD 1516 A34 C5

See Item AFR-32 for citation and annotation.

# LAND TENURE AND AGRARIAN REFORM

17.  Chambers, Robert, ed. THE VOLTA RESETTLEMENT EXPERIENCE.
     London, Pall Mall, 1970.  286 p.              HD 1516 G5 C32

     A collection of articles presented at the Volta Resettlement
     Symposium in 1965.  Discussion centers on the compensation and
     resettlement of some 80,000 persons displaced by the Volta
     River Project.  Papers describe social surveys conducted
     before and after resettlement, planning processes, and case
     studies of resettlement sites.

18.  Dunning, Harrison C.  "Law and economic development in Africa:
     the law of eminent domain."  1968.                    Law Per

     See Item AFR-48 for citation and annotation.

19.  Fortes, Meyer. THE DYNAMICS OF CLANSHIP AMONG THE TALLENSI.
     London, New York, published for the International African
     Institute by Oxford University Press, 1945.  270 p.
                                                      Mem GN 492 F6

     A comprehensive study of the social structure of the Tallensi
     of northern Ghana.  A section on land tenure (p. 171-190)
     notes that land ownership and use rights are strictly regu-
     lated by clan and kinship ties and by the moral and ritual
     values of the ancestor cult and earth cult.  Relationships
     between men and land are spatial aspects of the social system:
     "every unit of farm land corresponds to a unit of the social
     structure."

20.  Gildea, R. Y.  "Culture and land tenure in Ghana."  (In LE,
     40:1, 1964.  p. 102-104)                             Ag Per

     Argues that government efforts to control land ownership and
     leasing violate traditional cultural patterns.  If efforts at
     changing customary tenure systems are to succeed, then new
     structures must replace traditional social and political sys-
     tems in areas resisting national initiatives.

21.  Gold Coast (Colony). Lands Dept. GOLD COAST LAND TENURE.
     By R. J. H. Pogucki.  Accra, Ghana Publishing Corp., 1955-1956.
     4 v.  Bibl.  Reissued in 1968 by the Lands Dept.  Library has:
     vols. 1, 2, 5, 6,                                  HD 990 G7 A33
     Also available as 4 v. in 1.                   Mem HD 990 G7 A33

     Volume one contains a survey of customary land tenure systems
     in the former protectorate of the Northern Territories.  The
     second volume reports on customary land law in the area of
     Adangme settlement northeast of Accra.  Volume five is a

GHA 21-25

(Gold Coast)
handbook of the main principles of land tenure in Ghana, with
emphasis on administrative land policy and taxation. The
sixth volume is an expanded version of the fifth.

22. Gordon, J. "State farms in Ghana: the political defamation
of agricultural development." (In International Seminar on
Change in Agriculture. CHANGE IN AGRICULTURE. London,
Duckworth, 1970. p. 577-583)                    S 401 I68 1968

Experiments with state farms in Ghana underline the enormous
scale on which crash programs of mechanization can waste
financial and human resources. State farms were created for
political reasons and occasioned "a calculated and ostenta-
tious waste of resources...." The absence of records or
accounts makes it impossible even to draw lessons for future
action or to assess the suitability of various makes and
types of tractors to Ghanaian conditions.

23. Hayford, J. E. Casely. GOLD COAST NATIVE INSTITUTIONS.
London, 1903. 16, 418 p.                      Mem DT 511 H41

This pioneering work by a Ghanaian lawyer trained in Britain
vehemently opposed British legislation which assumed that
unoccupied land rightfully belonged to the state. He notes
that all land in Ghana is owned by individuals or by chiefs
representing the groups they govern.

24. _____. THE TRUTH ABOUT THE WEST AFRICAN LAND QUESTION. 2d.
ed. (London) Frank Cass and Co., Ltd., 1971. 203 p.
                                               HD 981 H3 1969

A reprint of a book first published in 1913 by an African
jurist, newspaperman, and early critic of British land policy.
The book was a pioneering attempt to counter the attempts of
the British to assume ownership and control of all unused land
in Ghana.

25. Hill, Polly. "Ghanaian capitalist cocoa-farmers." (In her
STUDIES IN RURAL CAPITALISM IN WEST AFRICA. Cambridge, Eng.,
University Press, 1970. p. 21-29)             HD 2130 W5 H54

A short summary of material presented in Item GHA-26, with
emphasis on the innovative aspects of the migration of cocoa
farmers to the Akwapim ridge, and subsequent development of
cocoa farming.

# Land Tenure and Agrarian Reform

GHA 26-29

26.    _____.  THE MIGRANT COCOA-FARMERS OF SOUTHERN GHANA; A STUDY
IN RURAL CAPITALISM.  (Cambridge, Eng.)  University Press,
1963.  xv, 265 p.                              Mem HD 9200 G62 H53

This important study by an economic anthropologist traces the
early twentieth century movement of farmers to the Akwapim
ridge northeast of Accra, where they bought land and established cocoa farms.  Individuals from matrilineal societies
tended to band together with non-kin when they bought land in
order to offset the bargaining power of the corporate groups,
represented by chiefs, from whom they bought land.  These
groups were called "companies."  Migrant farmers from patrilineal societies tended to form associations with their
consanguineal and affinal relatives when they bought land.
The price paid for land depended on the size of the area purchased, as measured by a local system of reckoning, and the
unit price.

27.    Hilton, T. E.  "The Volta resettlement project."  (In JTG, 24,
1967.  p. 12-21)                              Geol MC J83 T74

Briefly reviews the spatial aspects of the Volta Resettlement
Scheme, the geophysical characteristics of the land settled
and the prospects for improved agricultural practices among
the resettled population.

28.    Hunter, John M.  "Cocoa migration and patterns of land ownership in the Densu valley near Suhum, Ghana."  (In IBGT, 33,
1963.  p. 61-87)                              Geol MC IN71/1
Also available in Item AFR-111, p. 85-109.        HD 969 S8 P7

The author surveyed and mapped 5,605 farms in the area of
Suhum, a village located in southeastern Ghana.  The article
presents a listing of the areas of origin of migrant cocoa
farmers, a spatial analysis of patterns of landholding among
the immigrants, as well as descriptions of local methods of
surveying and customs governing the subdivision of land
among both matrilineal and patrilineal cocoa farmers.

29.    _____.  "The Social roots of dispersed settlement in northern
Ghana."  (In AAGA, 57:2, 1967.  p. 338-349)       Geol MC A56

A study of the bases and consequences of settlement patterns
in northern Ghana.  Circular farms surround the household and
are subdivided into radial strips, diminishing in size over
the generations.  If development is to occur, it is necessary
to concentrate settlement, since the lack of a cash crop and
ingrained social predisposition for dispersed settlement
present major obstacles.

79

30. Kotey, R. A. COMPETITION BETWEEN COCOA AND COFFEE: A CASE
    STUDY. Technical publication series no. 29. Legon, Univer-
    sity of Ghana, Institute of Statistics, 1972. vi, 42 p.
    Bibl.                                        Files Gha 15.7 K68

    A socio-economic study of the village of Kute near the border
    with Togo. In contrast to other regions of Ghana, land here
    can be alienated to strangers. Consequently emigrants can
    obtain land and eventually play an important role in the local
    economy.

31. Kumekpor, Tom K.; and Banini, W. K. "Land tenure and inheri-
    tance in Anlo." (In GJS, 6:2, 1970; and 7:1, 1971. p. 31-55)
                                              Mem AP G4115 J815

    A study of the land tenure system of the Anlo, who practice
    intensive farming on a narrow strip of land between the sea
    and the coastal lagoon east of Accra. A detailed examination
    of land rights, ways in which ownership can be alienated or
    use rights transferred, and provisions for share tenancy leads
    the authors to conclude that the land tenure system provides
    for effective and efficient use of the narrow coastal belt.
    The success of farming in this area is largely due to the
    constant modification and improvement of the institutions and
    rules governing the use of land.

32. La Anyane, Seth. "Effects of land tenure on migration, labour
    mobility and employment in Ghana." (Legon) Ghana, 1972.
    17 1.                                        Files Gha 58 L11

    Specific features of Ghanaian land tenure systems which con-
    stitute barriers to development are their failure to ensure
    that those who will obtain the greatest economic returns from
    the land will have use of sufficient land, that the fertility
    of the land is conserved, that large farm size is realized,
    and that disputes over land are discouraged. These limitations
    of the land tenure systems have prevented labor mobility in
    agriculture.

33. _____. GHANA AGRICULTURE: ITS ECONOMIC DEVELOPMENT FROM
    EARLY TIMES TO THE MIDDLE OF THE 20TH CENTURY. London,
    Oxford University Press, 1963. 228 p. Bibl.
                                              Ag HD 2130 G5 A47

    An historical survey of agricultural development in Ghana,
    with emphasis on the policies and programs of the colonial
    government. This work treats issues associated with land
    tenure systems and their change or reform only in passing.

# LAND TENURE AND AGRARIAN REFORM

34.     _____. "The Oil-palm belt of Ghana."  (In GBAE, 1:1, 1961.
        43 p.)
        Also available as a separate.           Files Gha 44 L12

        This description of the palm oil industry of Ghana includes
        a short section (p. 11-16) on land tenure.  Existing land
        tenure systems allow little flexibility in the size of hold-
        ings, encourage inequality of income, and prevent investment
        to improve the productivity of land.

35.     Lawson, Rowena.  "The Volta resettlement scheme."  (In AA, 67:
        267, 1968.  p. 124-129)              Mem AP A258 A256

        A brief review of the Volta resettlement project, focusing on
        problems associated with implementing agricultural schemes.
        Approves of the government's emphasis on projects to aid indi-
        vidual farmers instead of large-scale cooperative farms.

36.     Leake, Hugh Martin.  "Studies in tropical land tenure:  West
        Africa (the Gold Coast)."  (In TROP, 10:1, 1933.  p. 13-17)
                                                      Ag Per
        Also available as a separate.           Files 58 L22

        Two themes emerge in the history of British land policy in
        Ghana:  the desire of the government to exclude foreign owner-
        ship or use of land in the south, and in the north the appli-
        cation of the principles of indirect rule which had been
        worked out in northern Nigeria.

37.     Loveridge, A. J.  "A Note on the development of land tenure
        in the Gold Coast."  (In AA, 42, 1943.  p. 31-33)
                                                Mem AP A258 A256

        Contends that the authority of chiefs is derived from their
        control of land use and that economic development is under-
        mining chiefly authority by encouraging the individualization
        of land tenure.

37a.    Mair, Lucy P.  "Native rights in land in British African
        territories."  1951.                      Ag HD 965 L3

        See Item AFR-87 for citation and annotation.

38.     Manshard, Walther.  DIE GEOGRAPHISCHEN GRUNDLAGEN DER
        WIRTSCHAFT GHANAS UNTER BESONDERER BERUCKSICHTIGUNG DER
        AGRARISCHEN ENTWICKLUNG.  Wiesbaden, F. Steiner, 1961.  xvi,
        308 p.  Bibl.                           Mem HC 517 G6 M2

# Land Tenure and Agrarian Reform

(Manshard, Walther)
This survey of Ghana's agricultural economy includes concise
sections on customary land tenure in each of the three geographical regions: the coastal plain (p. 40-43), the forest
(p. 122-130), and the savannah (p. 225-227).

39.   Meek, Charles Kingsley. "The Gold Coast (including a note on
the West African Land Committee of 1912 and a note on litigation and registration)." 1949. (In Item AFR-91, p. 169-194)
                                                  HD 599 Z5 M4

Two distinct systems of land tenure prevailed under British
colonial rule in Ghana. In the north the crown asserted
general rights over land, but in the south the crown waived
control over land at the time of the Ashanti conquest, leaving
absolute ownership with African communities. Having been
waived, the claim could not subsequently be reasserted.

40.   Mifsud, Frank M. CUSTOMARY LAND LAW IN AFRICA, WITH REFERENCE
TO LEGISLATION AIMED AT ADJUSTING CUSTOMARY TENURES TO THE
NEEDS OF DEVELOPMENT. 1967.                        HD 1169 A3 M4

See Item AFR-93 for citation and annotation.

41.   Miracle, Marvin P.; and Seidman, Ann. STATE FARMS IN GHANA.
LTC paper 43. Madison, Land Tenure Center, University of
Wisconsin, 1968. 54 p.                       Files Gha 58 M47
Also available in Item AFR-3, p. 9.298-9.347. Files Afr 4 A37

Ghana's State Farm Corporation ran up huge losses because it
"attempted to expand far too rapidly for the country's
limited technical personnel." This survey of the history of
Ghana's state farms concludes that they have been unable to
compete with smallholder farmers who have little or no
overhead.

42.   Moore, Franklin C. "Land tenure in the Ashanti region of
Ghana." Madison, 1975. 89 1. Bibl. M. S. thesis, University of Wisconsin.                         Mem AWO M823 F736

A review of the economic history of the Ashanti region of
Ghana provides background for this study of social relationships determining land tenure systems. The study also analyzes the interaction of land tenure systems with other institutions important in agricultural production. The thesis
describes in detail systems of share and cash tenancy which
have evolved in response to rapid growth in the exports of
cocoa during the colonial period.

LAND TENURE AND AGRARIAN REFORM

42a.   Murphy, M. C.; and Acquaye, E.  LAND TENURE, LAND USE AND
       AGRICULTURAL PRODUCTIVITY IN GHANA; A CASE STUDY IN KUMBUNGU/
       TAMALE IN THE NORTHERN REGION OF GHANA.  Research paper no.
       1.  Kumasi, Land Administration Research Centre, University of
       Science and Technology, 1972.  iv, 104 p.  Bibl.
                                                    Files Gha 7 M87

43.    Nukunya, G. K.  "Land tenure and agricultural development in
       the Anloga area of the Volta region."  n.p., n.d.  13 1.
                                                    Files Gha 78 N84

       An analysis of the land tenure systems of the Anlo, who prac-
       tice intensive farming along a narrow coastal belt.  Most
       rights to land are vested in individuals, who acquire land by
       inheritance, gift, purchase, or pledge.  Descent groups retain
       nominal ownership of land but have no control over the aliena-
       tion of land to outsiders.

44.    _____.  LAND TENURE AND INHERITANCE IN ANLOGA.  Technical
       publications series no. 30.  Legon, University of Ghana,
       Institute of Statistics, 1972.  v, 34 p.      Files Gha 58 N84

       This report presents the major principles governing Anlo land
       tenure and inheritance and new elements introduced into the
       system as a result of the introduction of shallots as a cash
       crop.  Innovations include share-cropping, tenancies, pledging,
       and purchase of land.  The Anlo inheritance system, although
       patrilineal, allows for the acquisition of land and other
       property by maternal relatives.

45.    Ofori, I. M.  "Land tenure interactions and land use patterns
       in Ghanaian agriculture:  some basic theoretical considera-
       tions."  n.p., n.d. 31 1.                     Files Gha 58 O36

       Land tenure systems can hinder agricultural development if
       they promote excessively high rents or costly share cropping
       arrangements, cause uncertainty about the cost of entry to
       productive activities in agriculture, or lead to uncertainty
       of expectations as a result of defective titles or the absence
       of a system of registration.

46.    _____.  "Reflections on land reform in Ghana."  (In LRLSC,
       1972:2, p. 69-74)                     REF HD 1261 A1 L1 1972 no.2

       The determination of the Ghanaian government to make the
       country self-sufficient in agricultural production is based
       on a desire to save foreign exchange by substituting locally
       grown foodstuffs for imports, to make raw materials available

GHA 46-51

(Ofori, I. M.)
for agriculturally based processing industries, to improve
money incomes in rural areas, and to arrest the drift of
population from rural to urban areas.  The success of the program depends on overall agricultural planning, including a
policy of land reform.

47.   Okali, C.; and Kotey, R. A.  AKOKOASO: A RESURVEY.  Technical
      publication series no. 15.  Legon, Institute of Statistical,
      Social and Economic Research, University of Ghana, 1971.
      54 1.                                    Files Gha 7 042

      A socio-economic survey of a village first studied by W. H.
      Beckett in the early 1930s (see Item GHA-7).  The local
      people complain of a land shortage which prevents them from
      planting cocoa, while stranger farmers who acquired large
      tracts of land earlier still have land to plant.

48.   Ollennu, Nii Amaa.  PRINCIPLES OF CUSTOMARY LAND LAW IN GHANA.
      Law in Africa, no. 2.  London, Sweet & Maxwell, 1962.  272 p.
                                                       K 0.1 0505

      A distinguished Ghanaian jurist describes the main features
      of the customary laws of Ghana, drawing upon case law and
      statutory law amending local custom.  The book includes a
      lengthy appendix (p. 167-260) outlining benchmark cases and
      decisions of Ghana's courts regarding land law.  Also of
      interest to legal scholars are tables of cases and statutes
      referred to in the text.

49.   Ormsby-Gore, W. G. A.  REPORT. . . ON HIS VISIT TO WEST AFRICA
      DURING THE YEAR 1926.  1926.                    Mem Docs

      See Item AFR-102 for citation and annotation.

50.   Osei, A. H.  THE SYSTEM OF REGISTRATION IN GHANA.  E/CN.14/
      CART/265.  n.p., UNECA, 1970.  9 p.  Paper for Seminar on
      Cadastre, Addis Ababa, 1970.              Files Gha 59 072

      Briefly reviews the main features of land tenure systems in
      Ghana and details procedures for the registration of title.
      Defects in the existing system of registration include the
      absence of a cadastral survey or any other means of verifying
      boundaries.

51.   Pogucki, R. J. H.  "The Main principles of rural land tenure."
      (In Item GHA-59, p. 179-191)              Ag S 338 G6 W5

# LAND TENURE AND AGRARIAN REFORM

GHA 51-55

(Pogucki, R. J. H.)
A review of the main principles in state control of the
exercise of rights in rural land as they emerge from the law
in force in 1957. Emphasis is on the prerogatives of the
state, the powers of local governments, and land taxation.

52.    _____.  REPORT ON LAND TENURE IN CUSTOMARY LAW OF THE NON-
AKAN AREAS OF THE GOLD COAST COLONY, NOW EASTERN REGION OF
GHANA.  Accra, Lands Dept., 1952-54 (Re-issued 1968).  2 v.
Bibl.                                           HD 989 G32 P63

A survey of the customary land law of the Ga (volume 1) and
Adangme (volume 2) of eastern Ghana.  Reviews allodial and
nonallodial rights in land, land transactions, customs regarding succession and inheritance, and conflicts between English
and customary or Islamic law.

53.    _____.  REPORT ON LAND TENURE IN NATIVE CUSTOMARY LAW OF THE
PROTECTORATE OF THE NORTHERN TERRITORIES OF THE GOLD COAST,
NOW NORTHERN AND UPPER REGIONS OF GHANA.  PART 2.  Accra,
Lands Dept., 1951 (Re-issued 1968).  33 1.      HD 989 G35 P63

A survey of customary land law with a classification and
description of rights in land in Ghana.  The discussion centers on the Native Lands and Rights Ordinance and on state
control of the exercise of rights in land.  Recommends reten-
tion of the Governor's prerogatives in the control of land,
the codification of customary land law, and the establishment
of a system of title registration linked to a real property
code.

54.   Quraishy, B. B.  "Land tenure and economic development in
Ghana."  (In PA, 77, 1971.  p. 24-35)        Mem AP P929
Also available as a separate.              Files Gha 58 Q87

Concludes that traditional forms of land tenure are at the
heart of the problems of what the author considers to be
irrational behavior on the part of Ghana's farmers.  Existing
tenure systems are not conducive to economic development
because they rank social obligations ahead of economic welfare, fail to assure conservation of the soil, and discourage
innovative agricultural techniques.

55.   Rattray, Robert S.  ASHANTI LAW AND CONSTITUTION.  Oxford,
Clarendon Press (1969).  xix, 420 p.  Reprint of 1929 ed.
                                 Law GN 493.4 A9 R3 1969

85

# LAND TENURE AND AGRARIAN REFORM

(Rattray, Robert S.)
An early survey of the customary land law of the Ashanti. A
chapter on land tenure (p. 340-366) discusses the religious
aspects of tenure, the effects of changing agricultural practices on the land tenure system, and the transition from
family control to individual usufruct. The author decried the
growing tendency of African farmers to sell land because he
felt that they might not be able to withstand the temptation
of "immediate pecuniary gain."

56.    Sagoe, K. A. "Land problems in urbanisation programmes in
       Ghana." 1972. (In Item AFR-75, 5.3. 10 p.)
                                                Files Afr 57.4 L15

An exposition of the problems associated with public acquisition of land for urban development schemes in Ghana. Includes
a commentary by N. S. Lamba.

57.    Sarbah, John M. FANTI CUSTOMARY LAWS. A BRIEF INTRODUCTION
       TO THE PRINCIPLES OF THE NATIVE LAWS AND CUSTOMS OF THE FANTI
       AND AKAN DISTRICTS OF THE GOLD COAST, WITH A REPORT OF SOME
       CASES THEREON DECIDED IN THE LAW COURTS. 3rd ed. Africana
       modern library no. 5. London, Cass, 1968. xiii, iii-xxxv,
       317 p.                                   Mem K 0.1 S243

This pioneer legal and sociological study by Ghana's first
indigenous barrister was first published in 1897. It contains
a short chapter on land tenure (p. 65-74) summarizing the
main aspects of customary tenure systems. Other chapters
detail customary provisions for the alienation and inheritance
of property.

58.    Whetham, Edith H. COOPERATION, LAND REFORM, AND LAND SETTLE-
       MENT. 1968.                              Ag HD 1491 A52 W4

See Item AFR-140 for citation. The cooperative movement in
Ghana was virtually destroyed during Nkrumah's rule, but
after his overthrow, at the time of the author's visit, it was
in the process of being rebuilt. None of the so-called cooperative farms survived into the growing season after Nkrumah
was ousted.

59.    Wills, J. Brian, ed. AGRICULTURE AND LAND USE IN GHANA.
       London, New York, Published for the Ghana Ministry of Food and
       Agriculture by the Oxford University Press, 1962. xviii,
       503 p. Bibl.                             Ag S 338 G6 W5

GHA 59-63

(Wills, J. Brian, ed.)
A comprehensive survey of agriculture in Ghana. Part one
provides background information about environment and land use.
The second part treats plant and animal husbandry. See Item
GHA-51 for a separately annotated article.

60. Woodman, Gordon R. "Acquiescence in English law and the customary land law of Ghana and Nigeria." (In JAL, 15:1, 1971.
p. 41-59)                                              Law Per
Also available as a separate.           Files Afr 59 W66

In English law the doctrine of "acquiescence" is applicable
when a person leads another to believe that a certain situation
exists, though in reality it does not, and accordingly causes
him to act against his own best interests. In Ghana and
Nigeria the doctrine has been applied in litigation arising because of uncertainty of title to land, especially when strangers attempt to buy or use land and misunderstand the nature of
their own or another's interest in land. The article analyzes
in detail how and why the courts of Ghana and Nigeria have
departed from the rules in English law governing the application of this doctrine. See Item NIG-128 for an additional
annotation.

61. _____. "The Acquisition of family land in Ghana." (In JAL,
7:3, 1963. p. 136-151)                                Law Per

Reviews the circumstances under which a family may acquire
land according to customary laws in Ghana. These include
succession, acquisition with family resources, redemption of
family property by a member, building by a member of the
family on family land, acquisition by virtue of political
authority, gift, and the severance of family ties.

62. _____. "The Constitution and land--addenda." (In RGL, 2:3,
1970. p. 235-253)                                     Law Per
Also available as a separate.           Files Gha 59 W66

Woodman offers his interpretation of the articles of Ghana's
constitution pertaining to rights in land held by noncitizens.

63. _____. "Developments in pledges of land in Ghanaian customary
law." (In JAL, 11:1, 1967. p. 8-26)                   Law Per

Pledging is a procedure sanctioned by the customary law of
southern Ghana and elsewhere, whereby a landowner conveys land
to a creditor as security for a loan which the landowner receives and will almost certainly repay in due course. The law

GHA 63-GUIN 2

(Woodman, Gordon R.)
of pledges has developed considerably in southern Ghana; for
example, the law imposes limits on the profit which the
pledgee may make.  The article is concerned only with developments in the law administered in the courts.

64.     Woodman, Gordon R.  "The Scheme of subordinate tenures of
        land in Ghana."  (In AJCL, 15:3, 1968.  p. 457-477)    Law Per

The law of Ghana has for more than a century consisted of
three types of law:  Ghanaian and English statutory enactments,
Ghanaian customary law, and common law.  This article summarizes the present position of the law with respect to subordinate tenures:  usufruct, interests in land held by one person
through another according to customary law, and common law
subordinate tenures.  There are, in addition, systems which
combine elements of these forms.


## GUINEA


1.      Diallo, Ousmane Poréko.  "Evolution sociale chez les Peuls du
        Fouta-Djalon."  (In RAF, 4, 1961.  p. 73-94)    Mem AP R297 A47

This description of change in political, economic, and social
life in Fouta-Djalon includes a brief note on land tenure
(p. 77-80).  Among the topics treated are the Islamization
of land administration during the eighteenth century and the
adjudication of rights to land near Labe, one of the principal
towns of the region.

2.      Fréchou, H.  "Le Régime foncier chez les Soussous de Moyen-
        Konkouré (Guinée)."  (In ISEAC, 129, 1962 (5:4).  p. 109-198)
                                                      Mem H 31 I53

Detailed description combined with thoughtful analysis make
this a valuable work.  Landholding follows the articulations
of Sousou social structure, especially in the relationship
between the conjugal family and the group of families called
fokhe.  Rules governing land tenure are not fixed, and their
fluidity permits constant adjustment to changing social situations.  External factors such as recent economic growth have
had little effect on the land tenure system.  Rich soil in
low-lying areas, prized for its productivity, is divided
according to rules both more flexible and more precise than
those applying to other land.

3. _____. "Le Régime foncier dans la region di Timbi (Fouta-
Dialon)." 1965. (In Item AFR-109, p. 407-502)

Mem K 0.1 P755

An analysis of the customary land tenure systems of the area concentrating on the functions of the conjugal family as the basic landholding unit, a description of transfers of land rights among these
basic units, historical background on the formation of village
sites, and the interplay of various factors--chief among them demographic pressure--on the evolution of individual property rights.

4. Hazard, John H. "Guinea's 'non-capitalist' way." (In CJTL,
5:231, 1966. p. 231-262)

Law Per

A short section on land (p. 242-244) focuses on the law of
1960, which provides a legal framework for the founding of
agricultural producer cooperatives.

5. Verhelst, Thierry G. MATERIALS ON LAND LAW AND ECONOMIC
DEVELOPMENT IN AFRICA. 1968.

HD 962 V27

See Item AFR-139 for citation and annotation.

## IVORY COAST

1. Augé, M. "Tradition et conservatisme, essai de lecture d'un
terroir: pays Alladian (Basse Côte-d'Ivoire)." (In ETR,
37/38/39, 1970. p. 281-298)

Ag Per

Among the Alladian, the author found a surprisingly large
difference between the popular ideology on land tenure, which
claimed that every adult male had equal access to land, and
the facts: seven men, or less than one-eighth of the planters
of a village, held use rights for 61 percent of the cultivated
land. The land tenure system reflects various aspects of
social organization: the relative importance of land in the
local economy, an emphasis which changes over time; the differential role of individuals in developing the land according
to age, sex, and chance; and memberships in groups such as
lineages or moitiés, the bipartite division of society.

2. Boni, Dian. LE PAYS AKYE (COTE D'IVOIRE): ETUDE DE L'ECONOMIE
AGRICOLE. Annales de l'Université d'Abidjan, 1970, Série G,
tome 2, fascicule 1. (Abidjan) Université d'Abidjan (1970).
206 p.

HN 810 I82 B65

IC 2-6

(Boni, Dian)
A study of the rural economy of the Akyé, who live in the
forest north of Abidjan. The first part gives background on
the physical setting and history of the area; the second
treats the social structure; the third is about the agrarian
system; and the fourth is about development. A chapter on
land tenure (p. 107-116) points out that land rights are
vested in the person who clears the bush and that a national
law has replaced matrilineal inheritance, which bypassed sons
and widows, with a patrilineal system.

3. Ivory Coast. Service de la Statistique Générale et de la
Mécanographie. ENQUÊTE AGRICOLE DU 1$^{er}$ SECTEUR DE LA COTE-
D'IVOIRE 1957-58. Par Jean Causse et Jacques Gauthier.
(Paris, Impr. Servant-Crouzet, 1959). 88 p. Mem S 354 I9 A3

Includes data on population size and distribution, average
size of holdings, and aggregate statistics on crop yields.

4. Köbben, A. J. F. "Land as an object of gain in a non-literate
society: land tenure among the Bete and Dida (Ivory Coast,
West Africa)." (In Item AFR-67, p. 245-266)   HD 966 I5 1960

Among the Bete and Dida of the forest zone of the Ivory Coast, the
eldest male of a lineage segment exercises control over cultivation
on the lineage land. At the death of a lineage member, land tradi-
tionally reverted to the elder, but recently many farmers have
given their sons land as a gift inter vivos.

5. Ley, Albert. LE REGIME DOMANIAL ET FONCIER ET LE DEVELOPPE-
MENT ECONOMIQUE DE LA COTE-D'IVOIRE. Bibliothèque Africaine
et Malgache, tome 18. Paris, Librairie Générale de Droit et
de Jurisprudence, R. Pichon et R. Durant-Auzias, 1972. vi,
746 p. Bibl.                                    HD 999 I8 L29

A massive study of land administration and economic development in the Ivory Coast. The first part treats the establishment of a legal framework for land control under French
rule and its subsequent evolution after independence. The
second part deals with customary land tenure systems, land
tenure under the French-inspired civil code, and the registration of title. The final section of the book examines
land taxation, public acquisition of land, and other aspects
of land law in the light of contributions to an institutional
framework conducive to economic development.

6. _____. "Le Régime domanial et foncier et le développement
économique de la Côte-d'Ivoire." 1970. (In Item AFR-112,
p. 713-718)

IC 6-9

(Ley, Albert)
Reform of the land tenure system is necessary to promote
capital investment.  Three conditions must be fulfilled if
the land tenure system is not to be an obstacle to economic
development:  the legal structure must be such that the state
or other investors can acquire land rapidly; investors must
be able to determine who owns the land they intend to acquire;
and the state must have a cadastral survey to permit land use
planning.

7.    Ley, Albert; et Subsol, Henri.  "Conservation foncière et
      ordinateur."  1970.  (In Item AFR-112, p. 718-722)

      Proposes the creation of a rapid and technologically advanced
      method of recording property rights and transactions in order
      to aid development planners and economists.

8.    Meillassoux, Claude.  ANTHROPOLOGIE ECONOMIQUE DES GOURO DE
      COTE-D'IVOIRE:  DE L'ECONOMIE DE SUBSISTANCE A L'AGRICULTURE
      COMMERCIALE.  Le Monde d'outre-mer passé et présent; 1 sér.
      Études, 27.  Paris, Mouton, 1964.  382 p.  Bibl.
                                          Mem HC 547 I8 M4

      A study of the Gouro by one of the most respected economic
      anthropologists in France.  A chapter on land tenure
      (p. 245-262) points out that no formal land law exists,
      since cases are sometimes decided one way, sometimes another.
      The underlying principles in land cases are considerations of
      personal position and the relationships between lineages or
      between villages upon which the society is based.  Outsiders
      are able to obtain land by being accepted by the elders of a
      village, who determine the exact nature of the social rela-
      tionships to be initiated with the newcomer, sometimes offer-
      ing him one of the unmarried women of the village as a bride.
      Once satisfactory social ties have been created, the gift of
      land to farm is automatic.

8a.   Raulin, Henri.  PROBLEMES FONCIERS DANS LES REGIONS DE GAGNOA
      ET DALOA.  Documents du Conseil Superieur des Recherches
      Sociologiques Outre-Mer; Mission d'Etude des Groupements
      Immigrés in Côte d'Ivoire, fascicule 3.  Paris, Office de la
      Recherche Scientifique et Technique Outre-Mer, 1957.  139 1.
                                          HD 999 I8 R18

9.    Schatzberg, Michael Gordon.  "Residual politics and political
      integration:  the Agni region of the Ivory Coast."  (Madison)
      1972.  34 1.  Bibl.  Paper for Anthropology 983, University
      of Wisconsin.                       Files IC 72 S13

# LAND TENURE AND AGRARIAN REFORM

IC 9-KEN 1

(Schatzberg, Michael Gordon)
The paper examines how the political system of the Agni has
resisted pressures for change. Describes the impact of
modern commercial agriculture on social stratification, the
indigenous political system, and important social values,
including those embodied in the land tenure system. Under the
traditional tenure system each Agni, regardless of status, had
the right to use enough land to assure sufficient food for
himself and his family. But the alienation of land to non-
Agni immigrants poses a threat to traditional attitudes toward
land.

10.    Verdier, R.  "Evolution et réformes foncières de l'Afrique
       noire francophone." 1971.                   Files Afr 58 V26

       See Item AFR-136 for citation. According to a land law en-
       acted in 1963 but never promulgated, the government of the
       Ivory Coast became the proprietor of all unregistered lands
       which were not effectively occupied. Registration became the
       only way to acquire full ownership rights. Customary rents
       and payments were suppressed, and the government claimed sole
       power to allocate vacant lands.

11.    Wurtz, Jacqueline. ADIAMPRIKOFIKRO-DOUAKANKRO:  ETUDE
       GEOGRAPHIQUE D'UN TERROIR BAOULE DE COTE D'IVOIRE.  Atlas des
       structures agraires au sud du Sahara, 5.  Paris, Mouton, 1971.
       68 p.                                            S 473 I8 W8

       A study of an area noted for its unusual capacity to support a
       relatively dense population, in part a result of an extremely
       flexible land tenure system characterized by extensive frag-
       mentation and a remarkably even distribution of income from
       the land. The government has chosen this area as a rural
       development model, supplementing the traditional yam-based
       agriculture with commercial crops and promoting the consoli-
       dation of fragmented holdings.

## KENYA

1.    Adegboye, Rufus O.  "Kenya."  n.p., n.d.  21 1.
                                                   Files Ken 58 A22

      A review of the main advantages and disadvantages of customary
      land tenure systems followed by a survey of land consolidation
      and resettlement schemes in Kenya.

# Land Tenure and Agrarian Reform

2. AFRICAN LAND DEVELOPMENT IN KENYA, 1946-1962. Nairobi? Govt.
Printer, 1962. xi, 312 p.                     Mem HD 990 K4 A33

   This book was published by the Ministry of Agriculture under
   the colonial government and includes an exhaustive, district-
   by-district accounting of all rural development schemes,
   though little detail is given.  A short chapter on land tenure
   (p. 233-242) gives an overview of land consolidation and
   registration from the government's perspective.

3. "African land settlement at Makueni."  (In COLD, 14, 1953.
   p. 40-41)                                    Mem AP C7335

   A very brief description of the settlement schemes at Makueni
   for Kamba from an overcrowded reserve nearby.

4. "Agrarian revolution at work in Kikuyuland."  (In TBCR, 26,
   1957.  p. 12)                                Mem AP T5835

   Consolidation of holdings and registration of title to land has
   permitted economic progress in Kikuyuland.

5. Ali, M.  POLITICAL IMPLICATIONS OF LAND REGISTRATION:  A CASE
   STUDY FROM NYERI DISTRICT IN KENYA.  Political science paper
   no. 7.  Dar es Salaam, University College, 1970.  42 p.
                                                Files Ken 59 A54

   The government policy of issuing secure individual rights to
   land has allowed farmers to use land as collateral for loans.
   But increased productivity resulting from the availability of
   credit has been offset by increasing population pressure on
   the land.

6. Apthorpe, Raymond; and MacArthur, J. D.  "Land settlement
   policies in Kenya."  1968.  (In Item KEN-83, p. 29-32)
                                                Files Afr 17 L15

   An historical survey of land settlement in the White Highlands,
   divided into the periods 1902-1930, 1945-1960, 1960-1965,
   and post-1965.  Emphasis is on developments after 1945 and on
   the institutional framework of government agencies responsible
   for the settlement schemes.

7. Ayiro, A. A.  THE EFFECTS OF THE MAUTUMA SETTLEMENT SCHEME
   ON ITS SETTLERS.  Political science paper 7a.  Dar es Salaam,
   University College, 1971.  33 p.  Bibl.      Files Ken 17 A94

LAND TENURE AND AGRARIAN REFORM

KEN 7-12

(Ayiro, A. A.)
This paper contains a very general discussion of change in the
agricultural techniques and economic situations of the settlers at Mautuma Settlement Scheme.

8.  Barber, W. J.  "Land reform and economic change among African
farmers in Kenya."  (In EDCC, 19:1, 1970.  p. 6-24)

Programs granting freehold title to individual farmers jeopar-
dize the sytem of peasant proprietorship dependent on customary
land tenure systems, and these programs offer little assurance
that the pattern superceding it will be superior.  The danger
is that wealthy farmers may prefer to acquire land titles
rather than to accumulate modern forms of capital, so that
individualization of title may eventually lead to the prevalence of some form of tenancy.

9.  Barlow, A. R.  "Kikuyu land-tenure and inheritance."  (In
EANHS/J, 11:45/46, 1932.  p. 56-66)        Mem AP E13 A259 J

An historical account of traditional land ownership, a system
whereby individuals held rights to land within the parcel of
land controlled by the sub-clan.  The author notes that custom
was adaptable and flexible, so that local problems could be
settled on a basis of mutual accommodation and conciliation.

10.  Beech, Mervyn H.  "Kikuyu system of land tenure."  (In RAS/J,
17:45, 1917.  p. 46-59)              Mem AP A258 A256

An article which recreates the original acquisition of land
by Kikuyu migrating to their present homeland and describes
the Kikuyu customary land tenure system based on the githaka
or estate.

11.  Belshaw, Deryke G. R.  "Agricultural settlement schemes on the
Kenya Highlands."  (In EAGR, 2, 1964.  p. 30-36)
Also available as a separate.              Files Ken 17 B25

A note describing the location of major agricultural settlement schemes in Kenya in 1964 and indicating the relationship
between these areas and the former reserves.

12.  Bernard, Frank Edward.  EAST OF MOUNT KENYA:  MERU AGRICULTURE
IN TRANSITION.  Afrika-Studien, nr. 75.  München, Weltforum
Verlag (1972).  176 p.  Bibl.              HD 2130 K44 M43

Traces agricultural change in the Meru district from 1890 to
the present.  A section on land tenure (p. 101-118) stresses

# LAND TENURE AND AGRARIAN REFORM

(Bernard, Frank Edward)
the spatial aspects of land consolidation and resettlement.
The change from communal to individual tenure leads to the
disintegration of traditional settlement patterns.  Government-
sponsored resettlement programs have introduced and encouraged
the spread of agricultural innovation.  The author anticipates
difficulties in the future, despite land reform, if the population continues to grow rapidly.

13.      _____.  RECENT AGRICULTURAL CHANGES EAST OF MOUNT KENYA.
Papers in international studies, Africa series no. 4.
(Athens) Ohio University, Center for International Studies,
1969.  36 1.                                 HD 2130 K4 B27

A discussion of the spatial aspects of agricultural change
among the Meru of the eastern slopes of Mount Kenya.

13a.    Bohannan, Paul.  "Land use, land tenure, and land reform."
1964.                                          HC 502 H43

See Item AFR-22 for citation and annotation.

13b.    Bolstad, Paul Raymond.  "Land consolidation and culture in
Kenya:  the Kikuyu and Luo."  (Stillwater) 1973.  vii, 106 1.
M. S. thesis, Oklahoma State University.      HD 1481 K4 B65

14.     Branney, L.  "Commentary on the report of the working party
on African land tenure in Kenya, 1957-58."  (In JAA, 11:4,
1959.  p. 215-224)                          Mem AP J83 A258

An explanation of the proposals of the working party (Item
KEN-74) to formally recognize de facto rights in land.  The
proposals contained a practical guide to administrative procedures required for the ascertainment and adjudication of
rights in land.

14a.    Bridger, G. A.  "Planning land settlement schemes (with special
reference to East Africa)."  1962.        Mem JX 1977 A22

See Item AFR-24 for citation and annotation.

14b.    Briey, Pierre de.  KENYA:  RAPPORT SUR LA REFORME AGRAIRE ET
LES MESURES D'APPLICATION DE CELLE-CI.  Bruxelles, Institut
International des Civilisations Différentes, 1973.  14 1.
Paper for INCIDI Study Session on Obstacles and Restraints
Impeding the Success of Land Reform in Developing Countries,
Brussels, 1973.                              Files Ken 3 B74

# Land Tenure and Agrarian Reform

15.  Brokensha, David. MBERE CLANS AND LAND ADJUDICATION. Staff
     paper no. 96. Nairobi, University College, Institute for
     Development Studies, 1971. 21 p.          Files Ken 58 B76

     Among the Mbere, the social units controlling land rights are
     clans and lineages. The article outlines plans for allowing
     clans to participate in the adjudication of land claims aris-
     ing from the implantation of a land reform program. It also
     predicts the probable direction of change in Mbere social
     institutions as settlement patterns and tenure systems evolve.
     The author argues that a class of landless laborers will
     emerge.

16.  Brokensha, David; and Glazier, Jack. "Land reform among the Mbere
     of Central Kenya." (In A/IAI, 43:3, 1973. p. 182-206)

     An analysis of the probable effect of land consolidation on
     the Mbere of central Kenya. Social institutions such as the
     parish, dispute settlement by lineage and age-set elders,
     and the oath will disappear or take on new functions. Pat-
     terns of land use and even the division of labor between men
     and women will change.

17.  Brown, Brack. TWO VARIABLES AFFECTING RURAL TRANSFORMATION IN
     KENYA: THE SETTLEMENT CASE. Occasional paper no. 30. Syra-
     cuse, Syracuse University, Maxwell Graduate School of Citizen-
     ship and Public Affairs, Program of Eastern African Studies,
     1967. 29 1.                               Files Ken 17 B76

     A political scientist examines bureaucratic traditions inher-
     ited from colonial rule as well as attitudes toward the use of
     information and research in the selection, implementation,
     and evaluation of development projects. Disciplinary bias
     may be a factor in his conclusion that planners are too pre-
     occupied with economic considerations.

17a. Brown, L. H. AGRARIAN STRUCTURE AND LAND SETTLEMENT. E/CONF.
     39/C/92. n.p., United Nations Conference on the Application
     of Science and Technology for the Benefit of the Less
     Developed Areas, 1962. 6 p.              Files Ken 58 B765

18.  _____. "Agricultural change in Kenya, 1945-1960." (In FRIS,
     8:1, 1968. p. 33-90)

     A history of agriculture in Kenya emphasizing economic factors.
     A short section on land tenure (p. 76-78) concentrates on
     programs aiming at granting secure individual title to land
     in order to promote intensive development of holdings.

# Land Tenure and Agrarian Reform

19.  _____. "Land consolidation and better farming in Kenya."
(In EJEA, 30:120, 1962.  p. 277-285)                    Ag Per

Land consolidation is a means of promoting agricultural development rather than an end in itself.  Development depends on
follow-up to assure that farm layouts are optimal for soil
conservation and promote the fullest possible usage of every
available square yard of the holding.  Other preconditions for
development are that credit be made available and that farmers
be shown how to best use loans.

20.  Bunche, Ralph J.  "The Land question in Kenya as seen by a
Kikuyu chief."  (In JNH, 24:1, 1939.  p. 33-35)
Coll AP J82 OF164

A brief background to the land policy of the British colonial
government and the hardships it has created for Africans,
followed by excerpts from the biography of Chief Koinange of
Krombu District.  Details the conditions which eventually led
to the Mau Mau rebellion.

21.  Carey-Jones, N. S.  "The Decolonisation of the White Highlands
of Kenya."  (In GJL, 131:2, 1965.  p. 186-201)
Geol MC G273 J82
Also available in Item AFR-111, p. 268-283.      HD 969 S8 P7

The European hold on the White Highlands began to weaken
following the Mau Mau rebellion in the 1950s, setting the
stage for the resettlement of the land by Africans.  Following
independence radical readjustments in population-land relationships took place, as many Kikuyu farmers were settled according
to a number of schemes, all of which involved consideration of
the needs of the people.  The article traces the planning and
execution of these schemes, concentrating on the problems
associated with determining boundaries between Kikuyu and non-
Kikuyu areas.

22.  Chambers, Robert.  SETTLEMENT SCHEMES IN TROPICAL AFRICA:  A
STUDY OF ORGANIZATIONS AND DEVELOPMENT.  (1969)
HD 1516 A34 C5

See Item AFR-32 for citation.  Chapters three to six (p. 43-
136) are devoted to a case history of the administration of
the resettlement scheme in the area of Kenya known as the
Mwea.  The author emphasizes that the planning of resettlement
schemes should take into consideration the probable motivations
and behavior of the actors involved.  He also argues that the
simplest possible organizational structure be adopted for any

KEN 22-26

(Chambers, Robert)
given scheme: "If the beginning is ambitious, a complex
organization may collapse...; but if the beginning is modest,
a more complex technology and organization can grow up organ-
ically and gradually."

23.   Chambers, Robert; and Moris, Jon, eds. MWEA: AN INTEGRATED
      RICE SETTLEMENT IN KENYA. Afrika-Studien, nr. 83. München,
      Weltforum Verlag (c1973). 539 p.              Mem HC 501 A32/83

      Contributions to this collection cover the natural environment
      and history of Mwea, technical questions, the organization
      of production, administration, the lives of the tenants, co-
      operatives, health, household life, and an economic evaluation
      of the scheme.

24.   Charnley, E. F. SOME ASPECTS OF LAND ADMINISTRATION IN KENYA.
      [and] LAND SETTLEMENT IN KENYA, by J. W. Maina. RU:WLR-C/66/
      20. Rome, FAO, 1966. 27 p. Country paper for World Land
      Reform Conference, Rome, 1966.              Files Ken 57.4 C32

      An historical overview of the formulation of national land
      policy. An appendix on land control concludes that resettle-
      ment has been successful considering the speed and scope of
      the undertaking and the fact that staff and settlers were
      hastily recruited. See Item KEN-100 for annotation of Maina
      paper.

25.   Clayton, Eric S. AGRARIAN DEVELOPMENT IN PEASANT ECONOMIES:
      SOME LESSONS FROM KENYA. Oxford, Pergamon Press, 1964.
      vi, 154 p.                                   HD 2130 K4 C55

      Concentrates on shifts in agricultural policy in Kenya after
      the 1950s: land consolidation, farm planning, and the rapid
      introduction of smallholder export crops. Concludes that a
      high labor-to-land ratio is a precursor of economic develop-
      ment because most of Kenya's cash crops are labor intensive.

26.   _____. "Agrarian reform, agricultural planning and employment
      in Kenya." (In ILR, 102:5, 1970. p. 431-453)
      Also available in International Labour Office. AGRARIAN
      REFORM AND EMPLOYMENT. Geneva, 1971. p. 119-141.
                                                   HD 111 I57

      A study of the employment and income-generating effects of
      Kenya's agrarian reforms. By calling for the intensification
      of cultivation on private small holdings, planners correctly
      selected the agricultural sector which will absorb the most
      labor, given limited expenditure.

# Land Tenure and Agrarian Reform

27. _____. "Safeguarding agrarian development in Kenya." (In
JAA, 11:3, 1959. p. 144-150)                Mem AP J82 A258

Reviews progress in Kenya's agricultural sector and suggests
that research be done in plant disease to lessen the danger of
a serious setback in production, that government policy obviate
the effects of fluctuations in the prices of agricultural produce, and that an efficient processing and transportation system be built up to encourage commercialized agriculture.

28. Clough, R. C. "Land settlement in Kenya." (In ILRLSC,
1965:2. p. 33-38)               REF HD 1261 Al I5 1963/7

The resettlement of African farmers on land formerly held by
Europeans was carried out on both high density schemes,
designed to give land to the landless, and low density schemes,
which gave larger tracts of land to experienced farmers.
Settlers have not always been able to reach target incomes
envisioned by planners, but settlement in Kenya "contrasts
vividly with the disorderly transfer of expropriated land that
has often occurred in other countries in similar circumstances."

29. _____. SOME ECONOMIC ASPECTS OF LAND SETTLEMENT IN KENYA. A
REPORT ON AN ECONOMIC SURVEY IN FOUR DISTRICTS OF LAND SETTLE-
MENT IN WESTERN KENYA, 1963-1964. Njoro, Egerton College
(1965). v, 110 p.                         Files Ken 17 C56

Settlers' incomes were on average lower than those expected in
the settlement plans, although income varied greatly from farm
to farm. Settlers could have been expected to have difficulty
repaying loans because they were allowed to borrow 90 percent
of the capital needed for initial outlays. On economic
grounds, land settlement has been a success, but little effort
has been made to identify and help farmers who perform poorly.
This should be done before they are too deeply in debt.

30. Cosnow, J. E. "A High density scheme." 1968. (In Item
KEN-83, p. 65-78)                        Files Afr 17 L15

A paper reviewing the Bandek Land Settlement Scheme, a project
designed to place land which formerly belonged to Europeans in
the hands of Kipsigis farmers, as an experiment in social
change. The paper shows that plot holders have been willing
to accept innovations, such as artificial insemination or the
keeping of European breeds of cattle, to the extent that
such innovations are economically profitable and do not inter-
fere with traditional farming methods.

# Land Tenure and Agrarian Reform

31.  Davidson, B. R. "The Economics of arable land and labour use
     in African and European areas of Kenya." (In EAER, 7:1, 1960.
     p. 5-12)                                              Mem AP E13 A265

     The author uses economic data to suggest a model of the land
     use system which will yield the maximum net output and the
     highest standard of living. He concludes that dividing large
     estates into small holdings would lead to a higher overall
     standard of living for agricultural employees because of a
     more even distribution of income.

32.  Davidson, B. R.; and Yates, R. J. "Relationship between population
     and potential arable land in the African reserves and the European
     highlands." (In EAER, 6:2, 1959, p. 133-138) Mem AP E13 A265

     If all arable land held by Europeans were to be evenly distri-
     buted among all African males, the net increase in the size
     of holdings of Africans would be only 8.4 percent larger than
     the average size of holdings in the reserves. This argument
     disregards differences in the quality of land and the fact
     that Europeans had most of the best land.

33.  Davis, Robert K. "Some issues in the evolution, organization,
     and operation of group ranches in Kenya." (In EAJRD, 4:1,
     1971. p. 22-33)                                              Ag Per
     Also available as a separate.              Files Ken 55.5 D19

     A discussion of the key issues involved in the formation of
     group ranches among Kenya's pastoral peoples and the granting
     of title to grazing land. Recent legislation provides for
     evolutionary change toward an increased emphasis on the
     commercialization of livestock. The author describes the
     management of group ranches, the possibilities for the sale
     or leasing of grazing rights from one group ranch to another,
     and the ways in which the redistribution of income within pas-
     toral groups is likely to occur, with the young and the pro-
     gressive being the winners.

34.  DESPATCHES FROM THE GOVERNORS OF KENYA, UGANDA AND TANGANYIKA
     AND FROM THE ADMINISTRATOR, EAST AFRICA HIGH COMMISSION
     COMMENTING ON THE EAST AFRICA ROYAL COMMISSION 1953-1955
     REPORT. Cmd. 9801. London, H.M.S.O., 1956. 196 p. (In
     Great Britain. Parliament. PARLIAMENTARY PAPERS. HOUSE OF
     COMMONS ACCOUNTS AND PAPERS, 35, 1955/56)              Mem Docs

     Comprehensive reports on economic conditions and administrative
     policies in Kenya, Uganda, and Tanzania. Short sections on
     land tenure (p. 83-97, 145-152, and 157-161) stress the

(DESPATCHES FROM THE GOVERNORS)
importance of providing for individual ownership of land in
Kenya and Tanzania and regulating the system of individual
ownership of land which had already evolved in Uganda.

35. De Wilde, John C. "Kenya." 1967. (In Item AFR-44, 2, p. 3-
241)                                                    HD 2117 D4

An analysis of agricultural development in four areas representing the principal types of ecological and human environmental conditions in Kenya: the Nyeri District, the Machakos
District, Central Nyanza, and the Baringo and Elgeyo-Marakwet
District. In each land reform is examined within the context
of an overall plan for development of African agriculture. A
chapter on settlement schemes (p. 188-220) concludes that an
increase in overall output above the pre-settlement levels is
likely. Another chapter (p. 221-241) surveys the Perkerra
and Mwea irrigation schemes.

35a. Dundas, Charles. "Native laws of some Bantu tribes of East
Africa." 1921.                                    Mem AP M26602

See Item TANZ-16 for citation and annotation.

36. "The East Africa Royal Commission and African land tenure."
(In JAA, 8:2, 1956. p. 69-74)              Mem AP J82 A258

The Royal Commission recommended a land policy encouraging
individualization of tenure.

37. East African Institute of Social Research Conference, Kampala,
Uganda, 1963. PROCEEDINGS OF THE EAISR CONFERENCE, HELD AT
THE INSTITUTE, JUNE 1963. Kampala, 1963. 1 v. (various
pagings)                                      Files Afr 3 E17

See Items KEN-42; KEN-146; and UGA-5 for individually cited
and annotated articles.

38. Etherington, D. M. "Land resettlement in Kenya: policy and
practice." (In EAER, 10:1, 1963. p. 22-34)    Mem AP E13 A265

A list of recommendations for measures to assure that the
activities of farmers participating in settlement schemes are
economically viable. Categories of suggestions include the
choice of site for the settlement scheme, the recruitment of
settlers, the size of holdings, preparation of the site,
provision of capital to settlers, and security of land tenure.

# Land Tenure and Agrarian Reform

39. Fabian Society, London. Colonial Bureau. OPPORTUNITY IN
    KENYA: A REPORT TO THE FABIAN COLONIAL BUREAU. Research
    series no. 162. (London) Fabian Publications (1953). 48 p.
    Mem AP F1185/162

    Calls for "controlled African settlement on unallocated or
    unused land in the White Highlands." But the report stops
    short of recommending the settlement of Africans on land held
    by Europeans.

40. Fearn, Hugh. "Population as a factor in land usage in Nyanza
    Province of Kenya Colony." (In EAAJ, 20:3, 1955. p. 198-201)
    Ag Per

    Emphasizes the importance of information on the distribution
    and density of the African population. This information would
    make it possible to understand land use and land tenure prob-
    lems and would be extremely helpful in determining agricul-
    tural policy in the future.

41. Fliedner, Hanfried. DIE BODENRECHTSREFORM IN KENYA; STUDIE
    UBER DIE ANDERUNG DER BODENRECHTSVERHALTNISSE IM ZUGE DER
    AGRARREFORM, UNTER BESONDERER BERUCKSICHTIGUNG DES KIKUYU-
    STAMMESGEBIETES. Afrika-Studien, nr. 7. Berlin, New York,
    Springer-Verlag, 1965. xiv, 114 p. Bibl.     Mem HC 501 A32/7

    An account of land reform begun in 1954, preceded by a detailed
    examination of the customary system of land tenure among the
    Kikuyu, based on the communal ownership of the githaka or
    estate. Also examined is land administration under the colo-
    nial government. Land reform is described as aiming at the
    individualization of ownership and control over subdivision of
    holdings below a minimum efficient size. The author concludes
    that one effect of reform will be the emergence of two
    sharply divided classes, the landless and the landowners.

42. _____. "Some legal aspects of land reform in Kenya." 1963.
    (In Item KEN-37. 10 p.)                          Files Afr 3 E17

    An important article pointing out that ownership of land con-
    sists not of a single indivisible right but of a bundle of
    many different rights. Kenya's programs of land consolidation
    and registration of title failed to recognize some lesser
    rights such as the rights of tenants or the rights of inheri-
    tance. In practice many holdings registered to individuals are
    not being worked as a single unit but have already been sub-
    divided among heirs or among joint holders. Thousands of
    holdings are registered in the names of people who are no
    longer alive.

# LAND TENURE AND AGRARIAN REFORM

43.    _____. "Die Wandlung der Agrarstruktur in Kenia. (In GRU, 20:3, 1968. p. 81-86)                        Geol MC G28 R87

A description of the agrarian structure of Kenyan peoples in the pre-colonial era and of changes in social and economic institutions, including land tenure systems, following the introduction of cash crops in the colonial period. A discussion of recent agrarian reforms concentrates on attempts to change land tenure patterns in the former reservations and in the White Highlands.

44.    Food and Agriculture Organization.  EAST AFRICAN LIVESTOCK SURVEY:  REGIONAL--KENYA, TANZANIA, UGANDA.  1967.
                                               HD 9427 E1 F6

See Item AFR-51 for citation and annotation.

45.    Giglioli, E. C.  "Staff organization and tenant discipline on an irrigated land settlement."  (In EAAJ, 30:3, 1965.  p. 202-205)                                              Ag Per

Background information of the Mwea Irrigation Settlement is followed by a description of the organizational structure of the scheme and procedures for disciplining settlers.

46.    Golkowsky, R.  BEWASSERUNGSLANDWIRTSCHAFT IN KENYA: DARSTELLUNG GRUNDSATZLICHER ZUSAMMENHANGE AM BEISPIEL DES MWEA IRRIGATION SETTLEMENT.  Afrika-Studien, nr. 39.  München, Weltforum (for IFO-Institut, München) 1969.  141 p.
                                               HD 1741 K4 G65

An account of the irrigation agriculture of the Mwea Irrigation Settlement discussing the organization of this rice-growing scheme and technical, social, administrative, and economic aspects of its operation.

47.    Great Britain.  Colonial Office.  MEMORANDUM ON INDIANS IN KENYA.  Cmd.  1922.  London, 1923.  19 p.  (In Great Britain. Parliament.  PARLIAMENTARY PAPERS.  HOUSE OF COMMONS REPORTS AND PAPERS, 18, 1923)                        Mem Docs

Contains a section (p. 15-17) detailing the exclusion of Indian immigrants from the Highlands.  The Crown Lands Ordinance of 1915 gave the governor of the protectorate the power of veto over transactions in land between persons of different races.

# LAND TENURE AND AGRARIAN REFORM

48.  Great Britain. Kenya Land Commission. KENYA LAND COMMISSION
     REPORT. Summary of conclusions reached by His Majesty's
     government, presented by the Secretary of State for the
     colonies to Parliament by command of His Majesty, May, 1934.
     London, H.M.S.O., 1934.  8 p.          Mem HD 990 K4 A5 1935

     A summary of Item KEN-49.

49.  _____. _____. REPORT OF THE KENYA LAND COMMISSION, SEPTEMBER
     1933. Cmd. 4556. London, 1934.  618 p.  (In Great Britain.
     Parliament. PARLIAMENTARY PAPERS. HOUSE OF COMMONS SESSION
     REPORTS FROM COMMISSIONERS, ETC., 10, 1933/34)        Mem Docs

     Often called the Carter Commission Report, this document sets
     forth in great detail the nature of Kikuyu land grievances,
     conditions in Kikuyuland before the colonial occupation, the
     precolonial boundaries of Kikuyuland, and suggestions for the
     settlement of claims. The commission recommended creation
     of "native reserves" outside the areas already occupied by
     Africans, to allow for population growth; the creation of
     areas where Africans would be allowed to hold leased land; and
     the demarcation of land areas where Indians, Africans, and
     Europeans would all be able to lease or purchase land.  The
     commission also ruled on claims by the Meru, the Masai, and
     other ethnic groups. See Items KEN-48; KEN-88; and KEN-157
     for summaries of this report.

50.  _____. Parliament. CORRESPONDENCE RELATING TO THE TENURE OF
     LAND IN THE EAST AFRICA PROTECTORATE. Cmd. 4117. London,
     1908. 34 p.  (In Great Britain. Parliament. PARLIAMENTARY
     PAPERS. HOUSE OF COMMONS ACCOUNTS AND PAPERS, 71, 1908)
                                                           Mem Docs

     Correspondence between the Governor of Kenya and the Secretary
     of State presents the British policy supporting racial segre-
     gation in the White Highlands.

51.  Hamilton, Robert W.  "Land tenure among the Bantu Wanyika of
     East Africa." (In RAS/J, 20:77, 1920.  p. 13-18)
                                                  Mem AP A258 A256

     This excellent anthropological study of land rights among the
     Wanyika presents the case history of a Wanyika who became a
     Muslim, was ostracized, and lost his rights to land. The fear
     was that he would introduce individual freehold tenure as
     sanctioned by Islamic law, a form of land tenure fundamentally
     opposed to Wanyika notions of communal control over land.

# LAND TENURE AND AGRARIAN REFORM

52.  Harbeson, John W.  "Land reforms and politics in Kenya,
     1954-70."  (In JMAS, 9:2, 1971.  p. 231-251)

     The article analyzes the political impact of major land reform
     programs undertaken in Kenya in the last 15 years.  It con-
     cludes, "Nation building since independence has shown little
     recognition of the historical objectives of African national-
     ism with respect to land, so that those without land have few
     economic means, and the landed and landless alike have few
     political avenues, for participatory identification with the
     new Kenya nation."

53.  _____.  NATION BUILDING IN KENYA:  THE ROLE OF LAND REFORM.
     Evanston (Ill.) Northwestern University Press, 1973.  xxi,
     367 p.  Bibl.                                     HD 989 K4 H16

     Kenya's land reform programs set forth individual freehold
     tenure as a model because "the objective was in fact to
     establish the economic basis for the emergence of a new Afri-
     can political leadership cadre, one which would cooperate with
     Europeans in opposing African nationalist leaders when they
     were freed and would cooperate in furthering economic develop-
     ment in the spirit of multiracialism rather than pressing for
     more rapid African political advancement."  African resettle-
     ment in the White Highlands was supported by Europeans before
     independence because they feared an African government would
     seize their land to redistribute without compensating them.
     The independent government considers the resettlement program
     more a European creation than an African one, and the govern-
     ment's legitimacy, insofar as it is based on the tenets of
     African nationalism, is thereby weakened.

54.  _____.  "Nationalism and nation-building in Kenya:  the role
     of land reform."  Madison, 1970.  viii, 703 1.  Bibl.  Ph. D.
     dissertation, University of Wisconsin.  Photocopy.  Ann Arbor,
     Mich., University Microfilms, 1972.              HD 989 K4 H17

     Early version of Item KEN-53.

55.  Haugwitz, Hans-Wilhelm von; and Thorwart, Hermann.  SOME
     EXPERIENCES WITH SMALLHOLDER SETTLEMENT IN KENYA, 1963/64 TO
     1966/67.  Afrika-Studien, nr. 72.  München, Weltforum Verlag,
     (c1972).  104 p.  Bibl.                          HD 1516 K4 H38

     After independence Kenya subdivided plantations formerly owned
     by Europeans into smallholder settlements.  This study uses
     farm management surveys to investigate the economic situation
     of small farms and to determine reasons for successes and
     failures.

# Land Tenure and Agrarian Reform

56. Hay, Margaret Jean. "Economic change in Luoland, Kowe, 1890-1945." Madison, 1972. 278 1. Bibl. Ph. D. dissertation, University of Wisconsin.                    Mem AWB H413 M375

    A section on the acquisition of land rights (p. 99-105) notes that Luo obtained use rights through inheritance, from friends, clansmen, maternal uncles, the family of their brides, by becoming someone's client, or by simply clearing the land. Once acquired, land was allotted to each of a man's wives. The size of the holdings allotted to each depended on her abilities and the size of her family.

57. Healy, A. M. "Land problems and land policies in Kenya and Papua-New Guinea: a comparative historical perspective to 1963." (In NGRB, 40, 1971. p. 65-124)

    Kenya's program of agrarian reform is considered as a possible model for change in Papua-New Guinea. One of the lessons of the Kenyan example was that the reform of land tenure has to be linked with a comprehensive program to promote better farming. This in turn has to be based on research and agriculture extension. The Kenyan experience shows that a revolution in landholding and an increase in agricultural production can be achieved among similar societies without disastrous social strains.

58. Hecklau, H. "Die agrarlandschaftlichen Auswirkungen der Bodenbesitzreform in den ehemaligen White Highlands von Kenya." (In ERDE, 99:3, 1968. p. 236-264)                    Geol MC ER25

    The author discusses the influence of the Million-Acre Settlement Scheme on land use patterns in the former White Highlands. Includes a detailed description of the Lietego Settlement Scheme in Kisii District and survey of other similar projects.

59. Hennings, R. O. "Some trends and problems of African land tenure in Kenya." (In JAA, 4:4, 1952. p. 122-134)
                    Mem AP J83 A258

    A detailed presentation of the process of adjudication, demarcation, and registration required by Kenya's program of land consolidation as set forth in the Land Registration Ordinance of 1951.

60. Herz, Barbara K. LAND REFORM IN KENYA. SR/LR/C-16. Washington, USAID, 1970. iv, 68,(7) p. Country paper for Spring Review of Land Reform.                    Files Ken 3 H27

(Herz, Barbara K.)
A generally favorable evaluation of the Kenyan land reform
experience. The reform has involved two major efforts--the
Swynnerton plan for consolidation and enclosure of African
land, and the Million-Acre Scheme of African resettlement on
formerly European lands. Results of these programs have been
good in terms of increased production and in social benefits
to African farmers. However, the author recognizes that not
all farmers have benefitted equally from land reform, and that
expanding population offers a continuing threat to the continued success of the land reform program.

61.    Heyer, Judith. THE ECONOMICS OF SMALL-SCALE FARMING IN LOW-
       LAND MACHAKOS. Occasional paper no. 1. Nairobi, University
       College, Institute for Development Studies, 1967. 82 p.
                                                Files Ken 7 H29

A summary of the results of research on agricultural production
in the Masii location. The most important constraint identified was managerial skill; better farmers could make about
four times as much as poorer ones with the same labor and
resources. The project also found cotton to be only marginally
superior in terms of return and risk avoidance to the food
crops grown at present, but Katumani maize was slightly more
promising.

62.    Holmquist, Frank. MATUNWA FARMERS COOPERATIVE SOCIETY AND
       THE COOPERATIVE FARMING EXPERIMENT IN KISII DISTRICT. Staff
       paper no. 106. Nairobi, University College, Institute for
       Development Studies, 1971. (16) p.        Files Ken 55.5 H65

Eighty-seven Matunwa landowners, acting entirely on their own
initiative, separated out valley bottom portions of their own
plots and designated this largely contiguous lower area as
communal land. The Matunwa Farmers Cooperative Society governs
the farming of this land, and the cooperative has received
generous assistance for capital development.

63.    Homan, F. D. "Consolidation, enclosure and registration of
       title in Kenya." (In JLAO, 1:1, 1962. p. 4-14)
                                                Mem AP J83 L811

Describes procedures for adjudication and registration of
title under the Land Registration (Special Areas) Ordinance,
1959, and measures to prevent subsequent subdivision of
holdings under the Land Control (Native Rights) Ordinance.

# LAND TENURE AND AGRARIAN REFORM

64. Homan, F. D. "Inheritance in the Kenya native land units."
(In JAA, 10:3, 1958. p. 131-135)            Mem AP J83 A258

   Customary land law encourages fragmentation of holdings by
   distributing land equally among heirs. One solution is to
   amend local and national law to allow testamentary succession.
   Others include empowering provincial boards to prescribe the
   minimum size of parcels which can be registered as separate
   holdings.

65. _____. "Land consolidation and redistribution of population
   in the Imenti sub-tribe of the Meru (Kenya)." (In Item AFR-
   67, p. 224-244)                            HD 966 I5 1960

   The Imenti, the subject of this study, form one of the five
   sub-groups of the Meru. The introduction of the cultivation
   of coffee caused stress in the land tenure system because it
   exacerbated fragmentation of holdings and because Imenti
   custom concerning land sales did not take into consideration
   economic improvements to the land such as fertilizer and
   standing crops. The article concentrates on measures to move
   some people from crowded land suitable for coffee into contiguous areas, and the author makes suggestions for a program of
   land consolidation which would respect Imenti tradition and
   provide for a fair redistribution of land.

66. _____. "Succession to registered land in the African areas
   of Kenya." (In JLAO, 2:1, 1963. p. 49-54)     Mem AP J83 L811

   Details changes in statutory procedures for registering a
   transmission from the original landholder to an heir. The
   importance of this article is that these are procedures which
   have proven to be ineffective, since thousands of holdings
   have been subdivided after the death of the original holder
   but remain officially registered in the name of the person
   who is no longer alive.

67. Huxley, Elspeth; and Perham, Margery. RACE AND POLITICS IN
   KENYA, A CORRESPONDENCE BETWEEN ELSPETH HUXLEY AND MARGERY
   PERHAM. 2d rev. ed. London, Faber and Faber, 1956. 247 p.
                                            Mem DT 434 E2 H78

   An informal interchange of opinions between the authors in
   the form of correspondence covering a wide range of issues
   in Kenya. The discussion of land policy (p. 42-83) concentrates on European settlement and the failure of the Carter
   Commission Report to generate action to redress the deep
   sense of grievance among the Kikuyu.

# LAND TENURE AND AGRARIAN REFORM

68.  "Important statement on land policy in Kenya:  desperately
     urgent problems to be vigorously tackled."  (In EAR, 22:1107,
     1945.  p. 340-343, 354; 22:1108, 1945.  p. 368-369; 22:1117,
     1946.  p. 598-599; and 22:1119, 1946.  p. 656)
                                              Mem AP R4773 A543

     An example of the colonialist point of view on land policy.
     Implied here is that European settlement should continue be-
     cause Europeans put the land to better use than do African
     farmers.

69.  Karuga, James G.  LAND TRANSACTIONS IN KIAMBU.  Working paper
     no. 58.  Nairobi, University College, Institute for Develop-
     ment Studies, 1972.  39, (1) 1.            Files Ken 58 K17

     An economist examines land transactions in Kiambu District
     from 1956 to 1971 against a background of classical land
     value theory.  The second part of the article focuses on land
     tenure and the way in which the monetization of transactions
     has resulted in fragmentation.

70.  Kenya.  Central Land Board.  FINAL REPORT, 1964-1965.  Nairobi,
     Govt. Printer, 1965.  20 p.               Mem D24798 control

     A review of the activities of the Central Land Board in 1964
     and 1965.  This body, made up of Kenyan politicians and
     government officials, was created to supervise the purchase of
     land in the White Highlands and the subsequent settlement of
     African farmers so as to assure that no African ethnic group
     made gains at the expense of another.

71.  _____.  Ministry of Lands and Settlement.  "Recent land reforms
     in Kenya."  (1969)  (In Item KEN-121, p. 233-254)   HD 982 016

     A summary of the most important directions which land law re-
     form has taken in the field of general land administration,
     reform through land adjudication and consolidation, reform
     through programs of land settlement, and the reform of land
     registration.

72.  _____.  Mission on Land Consolidation and Registration.
     REPORT, 1965-1966.  (n.p., n.d.).  192 p.    HD 990 K4 A4 1966

     A comprehensive report recommending ways to accelerate land
     consolidation and registration as a means of increasing pro-
     ductivity in smallholder farming.  The report includes a pro-
     posed land adjudication act and recommendations for amendments
     to existing statutes.  Recommendations cover all phases of
     adjudication, land measurement, registration, and administration.

# Land Tenure and Agrarian Reform

73. Kenya (Colony and Protectorate). LAND TENURE AND CONTROL
    OUTSIDE THE NATIVE LANDS. Sessional paper no. 6 of 1959/60.
    Nairobi, Printed by the Govt. Printer, 1960.  8 p.
    Mem HD 990 K4 A32

    A sessional paper proposing modifications of legislation
    covering land tenure outside the reserves.

74. _____. Working Party on African Land Tenure, 1957-58.  REPORT.
    Nairobi, 1958.  161 p.                  Mem HD 990 K4 A4

    The report examines and makes recommendations about measures
    needed to introduce a system of land tenure applicable to all
    land held by Africans.  The report covers a wide range of
    issues associated with the transformation of traditional
    tenure systems, including registration, control of land trans-
    actions, consolidation, and inheritance.  See Item KEN-14 for
    commentary.

75. Kibaki, Mwai.  "The Political economy of land in Kenya."
    (In VEN, 11, 1959.  p. 6-7)                 Mem AP V468

    African elected representatives criticized land consolidation
    on the following grounds:  the lack of planning for the conse-
    quences of a major agrarian reform meant that the landless
    suffered; many legitimate claims to land were not satisfacto-
    rily dealt with; the legal machinery for control of land
    rights enhanced the already considerable power of British
    colonial officials; the granting of freehold title to Africans
    was seen as the possible predecessor to a similar move in the
    White Highlands, one which would have given the Europeans a
    tighter hold on land Africans claimed as their own.

76. Kilson, Martin.  "Land and politics in Kenya:  an analysis of
    African politics in a plural society."  (In WPQ, 10, 1957.
    p. 559-581)                                 Mem AP W527 P769

    A detailed analysis of the forces which shaped Kikuyu political
    movements.  Europeans settled on land the Kikuyu claimed as
    their ancestral home.  Unable to redress their grievance
    through political channels, the Kikuyu finally resorted to
    armed rebellion.

77. _____.  "Land and the Kikuyu:  a study of the relationship
    between land and the Kikuyu political movements."  (In JNH,
    40:2, 1955.  p. 103-153)                 Coll AP J82 OF164

# LAND TENURE AND AGRARIAN REFORM

(Kilson, Martin)
An examination of the effect of British land policy on the
customary land tenure system of the Kikuyu. The alienation
of land to Europeans and population pressure on remaining
land was the principal cause of the Mau Mau rebellion.

78. Kimani, S. M. "The Structure of land ownership in Nairobi."
(In CJAS, 6:3, 1972. p. 379-402)
Also available in JEARD, 2:2, 1972. p. 101-124.

An analysis of patterns of land ownership and the spatial
distribution of various classes of owners—Asians, Africans,
Europeans, the Kenyan government, the city government,
foreign governments, and businesses. Disproportionately large
amounts of highly valued land are in the hands of Asians and
businesses.

79. Kinyanjui, J. K. "The Adjudication and registration of
rights and interests in rural land in Kenya." 1972. (In
Item AFR-75, 5.2. 8 p.)                    Files Afr 57.4 L15

Sections of this paper treat adjudication of rights and land
consolidation, land settlement, land legislation, and control
of transactions in land. Includes a commentary by E. C. Sowe.

80. _____. "Land reform in Kenya." (In NGRB, 40, 1971. p. 124-
136)

On the whole, Kenya's land reform program works well: "individual tenure has resulted in increased productivity, a
greater investment in land, and increased social stability."

81. Lambert, H. E. "Land tenure among the Akamba." (In AFS, 6:3,
1947. p. 131-147; and 6:4, 1947. p. 157-175)
                                          Mem AP A258 S933

A comprehensive survey of the land tenure system of the Kamba
of Machakos District, prefaced by information on their kinship
system and political organization. Includes sections on
acquisition of land, permanence of rights, inheritance, testa-
ments, sale, mortgages, water rights, and public land.

82. _____. THE SYSTEM OF LAND TENURE IN THE KIKUYU LAND UNIT;
PART I. HISTORY OF THE TRIBAL OCCUPATION OF THE LAND. Commu-
nications from the School of African Studies, University of
Cape Town, new ser. no. 22. (Capetown) 1963 (c1949). 183 p.
                                          Mem GN 489.1 L3/1

(Lambert, H. E. )
A detailed presentation of oral traditions pertaining to early migrations and settlement followed by a discussion of the customary land tenure systems of the Kiyuyu, Meru, Mwimbi, Muthambi, Tharaka, Chuka, Embu, Mbere, Gichugu, and Ndia. Of particular interest are pre-colonial social relationships which transcended ethnic boundaries and permitted newcomers to acquire rights in land from the original occupiers.

83. LAND SETTLEMENT AND RURAL DEVELOPMENT IN EASTERN AFRICA. Edited by Raymond Apthorpe. Nkanga editions, no. 3. (Kampala, Uganda, Transition Books, 1968). 102 p.    Files Afr 17 L15

A volume which includes histories of land settlement schemes in Kenya and Uganda, a proposal for an approach to the problem of settling refugees, case histories of the Bandek and Nyakashaka settlement schemes, and an exhortation for more applied research on Kenyan and Tanzanian resettlement projects. See Items AFR-12; KEN-6; KEN-30; UGA-5; UGA-14; UGA-26; and UGA-80 for annotations of individual articles.

84. "Land titles in native land units: a report to the Kenya African Affairs Committee." (In JAA, 2:2, 1950. p. 19-24)
Mem AP J83 A258

A proposal for granting title to recognize the holder's rights in land, as set out in customary law, and for restrictions on the sale and subdivision of holdings.

85. Langley, Michael. "Agrarian revolution in Africa." (In COMD, 9:2, 1962. p. 13-16)    Mem AP C7335

A brief article pointing out contrasts in programs to reapportion land to Africans in Kenya and Rhodesia.

86. Lawrance, J. C. D. "Land consolidation and registration in Kenya." (In International Seminar on Change in Agriculture, University of Reading, 1968. CHANGE IN AGRICULTURE. (London) Gerald Duckworth and Co., 1970. p. 451-460)    S 401 I68 1968

Traces the progress of the land consolidation program, which began in 1954 as the Swynnerton Plan. The author suggests that agricultural development was not the original objective of the program, since social, political, and security considerations weighed heavily at its inception. Nevertheless, land consolidation has undoubtedly had a beneficial effect on agricultural productivity.

# LAND TENURE AND AGRARIAN REFORM

87.   _____. THE ROLE OF REGISTRATION OF TITLE IN FRAGMENTATION
AND MULTIPLE OWNERSHIP OF LAND. E/CN.14/CART/261. n.p.,
UNECA, 1970. 13 p. Paper for Seminar on Cadastre, Addis
Ababa, 1970.                                        Files 58 L19

A discussion of fragmentation and multiple ownership of land
in Kenya, under the headings of causes, cures, and prevention.
Both conditions hinder the negotiability of land and prevent
its proper use.

88.   Leake, Hugh Martin. "Further studies in tropical land tenure:
Kenya." (In TROP, 15:9, 1938. p. 195-198)          Ag Per

Includes a discussion of the Carter Commission Report of 1934
(Item KEN-49) and a description of leasehold tenure in the
Highlands.

89.   _____. "Studies in tropical land tenure: East Africa (Kenya)."
(In TROP, 9:11, 1932. p. 346-350)                  Ag Per

An historical account of land administration in Kenya. The
administration allowed land to be alienated to settlers in
part because of ignorance of customary African land tenure
systems.

89a.  Link, Heinrich. DIE BESITZREFORM VON GROSSFARMEN IM HOCHLAND
VON KENYA: ANALYSE UND ERFOLGSBEURTEILUNG. Forschungsberichte
der Afrika-Studienstelle, no. 43. München, Ifo-Institut für
Wirtschaftsforschung, Weltforum Verlag, 1973. ix, 206 p.
Bibl.                                            HD 989 K4 L55

90.   MacArthur, J. D. "Agricultural settlement in Kenya." (In
Helleiner, G. K., ed. AGRICULTURAL PLANNING IN EAST AFRICA.
Nairobi, East African Pub. House, 1968. p. 117-135)
                                                 HD 2130 E2 H45

The author discusses planning and evaluation of settlement
schemes undertaken by the Department of Settlement and the
Ministry of Economic Planning.

91.   _____. "The Economic study of African small farms: some
Kenya experiences." (In JAE, 19:2, 1968. p. 193-205) Ag Per

Better planning in developing economies depends on improved
statistical information on the peasant sectors. The article
discusses various methodological approaches tried in Kenya
since 1960: the study of small farms, full farm business
studies, enterprise studies, and the collection of agricultural statistics.

# Land Tenure and Agrarian Reform

92. MacArthur, J. D. THE EVALUATION OF LAND REFORM IN KENYA.
RU:WLR/66/L. Rome, FAO, 1966. 9 p. Paper for World Land
Reform Conference, Rome, 1966.          Files Ken 3 M11

Author's preliminary evaluation of the consequences of land
registration is that it is beneficial, particularly if credit
can be made available to small farmers. Land settlement led
to declining agricultural production in all but the low density
schemes, where experienced farmers worked relatively large
plots.

93. _____. "Land tenure reform and economic research into African
farming in Kenya." (In EAER, 8:2, 1961. p. 79-91)
                                        Mem AP E13 A265

This survey of the deficiencies of customary tenure concludes
with a note on pilot studies undertaken to gather information
on the economics of smallholder farming in Kenya.

94. McAuslan, J. P. W. B. "Control of land and agricultural
development in Kenya and Tanzania." (In Seminar on Law and
Social Change in East Africa, University College, Dar es
Salaam, 1966. EAST AFRICAN LAW AND SOCIAL CHANGE. Nairobi,
East African Publishing House, 1967. p. 172-257)
                                        HN 800 E2 S25

Agricultural development requires changes in land use and
land tenure systems which in turn depend on increased governmental control of land. But this has certain dangers. Tanzania has failed to deal with the pressing problem of customary
land law, while Kenya may be creating a small but potentially
powerful landowning class. Land law reform must not lose
sight of the economic ends it is intended to serve. See Item
TANZ-42 for additional annotation.

94a. _____. "Co-operatives and the law in East Africa." 1970.
(In Item AFR-39, p. 81-120)          HD 3561 E2 C6

95. McEntee, P. D. "Improved farming in the Central Nyanza District, Kenya Colony." (In JAA, 12:1, 1960. p. 68-73)
                                        Mem AP J83 A258
Also available as a separate.           Files Ken 58 M112

A brief report on land consolidation in Central Nyanza. Opposition to the scheme was overcome by having the people themselves oversee the procedures for consolidation.

# Land Tenure and Agrarian Reform

96. McGlashen, N. D. "Consolidation of land holdings in Kenya." (In GEOG/N, 45:4, 1960. p. 105-106)          Geol MC G287

    A brief note on land consolidation schemes in progress at the time of writing.

97. _____. "Resettlement in the Meru District in Kenya." (In GEOG/N, 43:4, 1958. p. 209-210)          Geol MC G287

    A brief evaluation of resettlement schemes in Meru District. Landless persons from the overpopulated coffee belt and others selected locally were given land.

98. McKenzie, B. R. "Agricultural development in Kenya." (In COMD, 8:3, 1961. p. 25-28)          Mem AP C7335

    States that "sound farming is important to Kenya's future and the recent agrarian reforms are designed to encourage the farmer, European or African, to improve his farming methods and consequently his production."

99. Madiman, S. G. "Land reform in East Africa." Rome, FAO, n.d. 23 1.          Files Afr 3 M12

    Three types of land tenure systems can be delineated in East Africa: modern, transformed, and traditional. While each type of tenure system requires different reform measures, planners should conceive of reform as part of an overall national land policy, which must take into account the organization of local self-government, modes of production, the need for land distribution, and planned change in the structure of production.

100. Maina, J. W. "Land settlement in Kenya." n.d. (In Item AFR-3, p. 9.107-9.115)          Files Afr 4 A37
     Also available in Item KEN-24, p. 19-27.     Files Ken 57.4 C32

    Kenya's director of settlement concludes that land settlement has been successful considering the speed and scope of the undertaking, and the fact that both staff and settlers were hastily recruited.

101. Maini, Krishan M. A GUIDE TO REGISTRATION OF TITLE PRACTICE. Nairobi, East African Literature Bureau (1969). 72 p.
                              HD 1186 K4 M14

    A practical guide for legal practitioners on the procedures to be followed concerning transactions in land registered

# LAND TENURE AND AGRARIAN REFORM

(Maini, Krishan M.)
under the Registered Land Act of 1963 and the Registered Land
Rules of the same year. The book includes examples of how
some of the most commonly used forms should be filled out.

102.    _____. LAND LAW IN EAST AFRICA. Nairobi, Oxford University
Press, 1967. xvii, 270 p.                          HD 1169 M14

Includes chapters on the historical development of land law
in Kenya; the registration of land holdings; juridical provisions for sale, lease, mortgage, trusts, restraints on disposition, and rights in land owned by another person. The
book also contains a table of cases cited and a chronological
table of the land laws of Kenya, Tanzania, and Uganda. See
Items TANZ-45 and UGA-45 for additional annotations.

103.    _____. "The Problems of the unification of Kenya land laws."
1969. (In Item KEN-121, p. 223-232)              HD 982 016

Provides succinct background on important land laws, outlines
steps taken to unify and rationalize branches of the law,
and suggests that closely related subjects should be treated
under unified headings as the law is further amended.

104.    Mair, Lucy P. "Agrarian policy in British African colonies."
1951.                                          Ag HD 965 L3

See Item AFR-86 for citation and annotation.

105.    _____. "Mise en valeur de terres pour Africaines au Kenya."
(In BULIS/R, 1, 1960. p. 45-53)              Mem AP B9134 R

Pre-independence plans such as the Swynnerton Plan conceived
of rural development as a combination of land settlement projects and investment in infrastructure. This brief note
traces the history of certain of these projects and outlines
various recommendations for legal measures to secure land
rights for Africans in Kenya.

106.    _____. "Native land tenure in East Africa." (In A/IAI, 4:3,
1931. p. 314-329)                            Mem AP A257

A short survey of anthropological sources on East Africa
extant at the time of writing. The author criticizes the lack
of a clear definition on the social groups referred to in the
official Report on Native Land Tenure in the Kikuyu Province.

# LAND TENURE AND AGRARIAN REFORM

106a.    _____. "Native rights in land in British African territories."
1951.                                          Ag HD 965 L3

See Item AFR-87 for citation and annotation.

107.    Manners, R. A. "Colonialism and native land tenure:  a case
study in ordained accommodation." (In his PROCESS AND PATTERN
IN CULTURE. Chicago, Aldine Press, 1964.  p. 266-280)
                                          Mem HM 101 M257

A description of the process of change from communal to individual tenure among the Kipsigis.  The article is flawed by a
paternalistic approach.

108.    Mayer, P.; and Mayer, I.  "Land law in the making." (In Item
AFR-73, p. 51-78)                          Coll K 0.1 K966

A study of the evolution of land law among the Gusii of
western Kenya between 1925 and 1950 as a response to population pressure on land.  The British introduced native tribunals
empowered to decide land cases, and these new judicial authorities were instrumental in the development of Gusii land law.
By 1950 the whole of Gusii land had been divided into parcels
with definite boundaries, a division reflecting a tenure system
which was in marked contrast to the former basis for access
to land through clan membership.

109.    Meadows, S. J.  THE SCENE IN KENYA.  Rome, FAO, 1971.  22 1.
At head of title:  FAO Consultation on the Settlement of
Nomads in Africa and the Near East, Cairo, 1971.
                                          Files Ken 57.4 M21

An account of how the Range Management Division identified
groups of pastoral peoples willing to join together in corporate organizations for the development and management of
their own or adjacent range lands.  One of the many problems
encountered is that of issuing title to land to pastoral
peoples living in Trust Lands.  Multiple ownership of roughly
defined land units was a partial solution to the problem of
increasing the size of the group responsible for range management in a given area.

110.    Meek, Charles Kingsley.  "Kenya."  1949.  (In Item AFR-91,
p. 76-99)                                  HD 599 Z5 M4

A survey of conflicting interests in land in Kenya:  European
claims to land they settled in the Highlands and the presence
of African squatters; settlers' attempts to forge land policy

# Land Tenure and Agrarian Reform

KEN 110-114

(Meek, Charles Kingsley)
in their own interest; and land administration in areas
reserved to Africans.

111. Moody, R. W. LAND TENURE IN SAMIA. Conference paper no. 140.
(Kampala) Makerere Institute of Social Research (196-). 12 p.
Files Afr 58 M66

Concise account of land tenure among the Samia, who occupy
approximately 200 square miles of land in Kenya and Uganda.
Material covered includes settlement patterns, land use, and
customary rights in land, which are based principally on
lineage groupings.

112. Morgan, W. T. W. "Agricultural land use." (In NAIROBI; CITY
AND REGION. Edited by W. T. W. Morgan. New York, Oxford
University Press (1967). p. 78-89) Mem DT 434 N3 N3

A geographer analyzes population-land relationships and land
use patterns near Nairobi.

113. _____. "The 'White Highlands' of Kenya." (In GJL, 129:2,
1963. p. 140-155) Geol MC G273 J82
Also available in Item AFR-111, p. 208-224. HD 969 S8 P7

This article provides historical perspective on the origins
and spread of white settlement in the Highlands. The British
allowed settlement in order to establish an economic base for
a colony which could pay its own way. The author contends that
white settlement was necessary because Africans lacked the
knowledge and capital to be able to develop their own
resources.

114. Mugerwa, P. J. Nkambo. "Land tenure in East Africa: some
contrasts." (In EAST AFRICAN LAW TODAY. Commonwealth law
series no. 5. London, British Institute of International
and Comparative Law, 1966. p. 101-114) Law JX 31 I5/5
Also available in Item AFR-3, p. 9.52-9.65 Files Afr 4 A37

Problems of land tenure in East Africa are discussed chrono-
logically: under customary law, under colonial rule, and
after independence. Within each heading, Kenya, Tanzania, and
Uganda are treated separately. Territorial contrasts in
approaches to tenure problems during the colonial era have
solidified and continue to exercise a determining influence
on the direction of evolution of tenure systems in each of
these East African countries.

115.    Müller-Praefke, Dieter; und Polster, Dietrich.    ZUR FRAGE
        DER BODENREFORM IN ENTWICKLUNGSLANDERN LATEINAMERIKAS UND
        AFRIKAS:   EINE LITERATURSTUDIE.   1966.              HD 1251 M85

        See Item AFR-97 for citation and annotation.

116.    Munro, Ann P.   "Land law in Kenya."   (In WLR, 4, 1966.
        p. 1071-1095)                                         Law Per

        In Kenya as elsewhere in Africa, two or more legal systems
        existed side by side during the colonial period.  The article
        discusses the effect of disparate legal systems on social
        change in post-independence Kenya.

117.    Newiger, Nikolaus J.   COOPERATIVE FARMING IN KENYA AND TAN-
        ZANIA.   München, Ifo-Institut für Wirtschaftsforschung,
        Afrika-Studienstelle, 1967.   157 p.            Ag HD 1486 K4 N4

        Compares and contrasts experience with producer cooperatives
        in Kenya and Tanzania.  The objective in both countries was
        the resettlement of poor farmers in order to increase both
        individual incomes and aggregate production.  In Kenya, Farm
        Purchasing Cooperative Societies first developed without
        government supervision and have been given little encourage-
        ment, since members are required to have 50 percent of the
        purchase price of the land to be bought by the producer co-
        operative and must borrow the rest at a rate of six and one-
        half percent.  In Tanzania the government was involved in
        planning and support from the beginning.  Both countries face
        serious problems stemming from the lack of trained personnel,
        overcapitalization, and operating losses.  See Item TANZ-56
        for an additional annotation.

118.    Nguyo, Wilson.   "Some socio-economic aspects of land settle-
        ment in Kenya."   (In Makerere Institute of Social Research.
        CONFERENCE PAPERS.  Kampala, 1967.  20 p.)
                                            HC 517 E2 M14 1967 pt. D

        A farm management survey of 26 of the 321 plots comprising the
        Mweiga Settlement Scheme as of 1964.  Input-output data
        revealed a considerable increase in production over presettle-
        ment levels, but the cost to the nation in terms of capital
        and manpower resources must also be considered.

119.    Njao, Njuguna.   "The Economics of African smallholdings in
        Kenya."   Madison, 1959.  167 1.  Bibl.  M. S. thesis, Univer-
        sity of Wisconsin, 1959.                          Mem AWM N655

(Njao, Njuguna)
Kenyan smallholder farming is beset with the problems of low
productivity per acre and per man.  The author of this thesis
surveys a variety of remedies and devotes a brief section
(p. 63-65) to land tenure.  He argues that fragmentation of
holdings is a serious problem but questions whether individualization of tenure is the answer.

120.    Nottidge, C. P. R.; and Goldsack, J. R.  THE MILLION-ACRE
        SETTLEMENT SCHEME, 1962-1966.  Nairobi, Dept. of Settlement
        (1966?).  44, (26) p.                        Files Ken 17 N68

        An historical account of the organization and administration
        of the scheme, including sections on land valuation, settler
        selection, marketing, and the drafting of settlement rules.

121.    Obol-Ochola, James Yonason, ed.  LAND LAW REFORM IN EAST
        AFRICA.  Papers delivered to a Seminar organised by the Milton
        Obote Foundation, Adult Education Centre.  Edited by James
        Obol-Ochola.  (Kampala)  Milton Obote Foundation, Adult Edu-
        cation Centre (1969).  320 p.                    HD 982 016

        A collection of articles organized around the theme of the
        need for reform in the prevailing systems of land law in East
        Africa as a precondition for political, economic, and social
        change.  Treats the following main subject areas:  background
        of the extant system, problems and needs for reform, present
        land reform efforts, and proposals for future land reform.
        See Items AFR-11; KEN-71; KEN-103; TANZ-33; TANZ-63; UGA-10;
        UGA-28; UGA-39; and UGA-58 for annotations of individual
        articles.

122.    Odingo, R. S.  "Cooperatives in the Kenya highland settlement
        schemes."  (In Conference of the University of East Africa
        Social Sciences Council, 1968/69.  PAPERS (GEOGRAPHY).
        Kampala, Makerere University College, 1969.  p. 111-117)
                                        HC 517 E2 C6 1968/69 G

        The author criticizes the cooperative movement in the Highlands
        settlement schemes for its failure to encourage the emergence
        of local cooperative leaders and for an unwarranted emphasis
        on size, so that most cooperatives are too large to
        encourage enthusiastic participation.

123.    _____.  "Land settlement in the Kenya Highlands."  (In EDUCA-
        TION, EMPLOYMENT AND RURAL DEVELOPMENT.  Proceedings of a
        conference held at Kericho, Kenya in September 1966.  (Nairobi)

120

KEN 123-127

(Odingo, R. S.)
East African Publishing House (1967).  p. 141-161)
Mem HD 1538 K4 E3

A very brief survey of land settlement in Kenya, including
historical background, a discussion of the costs of settlement programs, and an appraisal of their capacity to generate
income and employment opportunities.

124.    Ominde, Simeon H.  LAND AND POPULATION MOVEMENTS IN KENYA.
        Evanston, (Ill.) Northwestern University Press (1968).  ix,
        204 p.  Bibl.                                    HB 2126 K4 047

        A geographical study divided into three parts:  the evolution
        of the boundaries of modern Kenya, spatial aspects of
        economic development, and the spatial distribution of popula-
        tion with particular emphasis on both rural-to-rural and
        rural-to-urban migration.

125.    _____.  "Problems of land and population in Western Districts
        of Kenya."  (In East African Academy.  PROCEEDINGS OF THE
        FIRST SYMPOSIUM.  Nairobi, Oxford University Press, 1963.
        p. 23-36)                                        Mem AS 625 E17

        A survey of the physical geography and the spatial distribu-
        tion of population in western Kenya.

126.    Orchardson, I. Q.  "Future development of the Kipsigis with
        special reference to land tenure."  (In EANHS/J, 12:5/6,
        1935.  p. 200-210)                               Mem AP E13 A259 J

        Advocates the following approach to the formulation of land
        law applicable to the Kipsigis:  control of access to land
        should be left with the social unit known as the kokwet, and
        some temporary and permanent fencing should be allowed subject
        to the approval of the kokwet.

127.    Oser, Jacob.  PROMOTING ECONOMIC DEVELOPMENT WITH ILLUSTRA-
        TIONS FROM KENYA.  (Nairobi) East African Publishing House
        (1967).  ix, 242 p.                              HC 517 K4 D7

        A short section on land tenure (p. 185-195) contains a survey
        of Kenyan land policy with particular emphasis on land values,
        the African resettlement of the White Highlands, and problems
        associated with the administration of improved land use
        practices.

# LAND TENURE AND AGRARIAN REFORM

128.   Palmer, Gary Bradford.  "The Shimba Hills Settlement Scheme:
the administration of large-scale innovation in Kenya."
(Minneapolis) 1971.  vii, 286 l.  Ph. D.  dissertation, University of Minnesota.  Photocopy.  Ann Arbor, Mich., University Microfilms, 1972.                        HD 1516 K4 P15

An analysis of the history, growth, administration, and social
organization of this resettlement scheme based on interviews
and attendance at public meetings.  Concludes that most
settlement schemes have been expensive failures and that
communication between planners and settlers should be improved.

129.   Pedraza, G. J. W.  "Land consolidation in the Kikuyu areas of
Kenya."  (In JAA, 8:2, 1956.  p. 82-87)      Mem AP J83 A258

Discusses major obstacles to progress in dealing with land
problems among the Kikuyu:  the suspicion with which the
Kikuyu regard any government move affecting the land, the
innate conservatism of farmers accustomed to traditional
farming methods, and the land tenure system.  A description
of the customary tenure system is followed by a summary of
procedures for consolidation and registration.

130.   Penwill, D. S. O.  "A Pilot scheme for two Kikuyu improved
villages near Nairobi."  (In JAA, 12:2, 1960.  p. 61-67)
                                              Mem AP J83 A258

A description of improved villages established near Nairobi
after land consolidation.  The government supervised the construction of housing and provided low interest loans, so that
housing was both good and inexpensive.

131.   Pilgrim, J. W.  LAND OWNERSHIP IN THE KIPSIGIS RESERVE.
Conference paper no. 110.  (Kampala) Makerere Institute of
Social Research, 1959.  32 p.                 Files Ken 58 P45

Discusses various aspects of case histories of land inheritance
among the Kipsigis and the relevance of these cases to social
and economic change.  Most of the land of the Kipsigis has
been enclosed in the last two decades.

132.   Pollock, N. C.  "Agrarian revolution in Kikuyuland (Kenya)."
(In SAGJ, 41, 1959.  p. 53-58)                Geol MC S08 AF87

A brief note based on the author's visit to Kiambu and Fort
Hall Districts in 1957.

# LAND TENURE AND AGRARIAN REFORM

133. Ratzerburg, F. H. CADASTRAL SURVEY AND REGISTRATION IN KENYA.
E/CN.14/CART/257. n.p., UNECA, 1970. 15 p. Paper for
Seminar on Cadastre, Addis Ababa, 1970.     Files Ken 59 R18

   A summary of procedures adopted by Kenya for consolidating and
   registering land, preceded by a discussion of two model systems of land registration--the guaranteed boundaries system
   for which Australia is the model, and the general boundaries
   system, for which England is normally considered the model.

134. Rodewald, James M. "Land reform in Kenya." (Madison) 1965.
42 1. Paper for Economics and Agricultural Economics 474,
University of Wisconsin, summer session, 1965. Files Ken 3 R62

   A review of the literature on land reform by the British
   colonial administration and the independent Kenyan government.

135. Rogers, Margaret. "The Kenya land law reform programme; a
model for modern Africa?" (In VRU, 6:1, 1973. p. 49-63)
                                            Mem AP V494 U54
Also available as a separate.             Files Ken 58 R63

   The author concludes that Kenya's program of adjudication,
   consolidation, and registration of land rights provides a
   model of land reform applicable in countries where the goal is
   to register title to communal ownership of land as well as to
   individual ownership. The only problems with the program are
   the failure to set a fixed limit on the amount of land which
   can be held by one person, and the cost of the program.

136. Ruigu, George M.; and Ascroft, Joe. LAND POLICY AND THE
SMALL-SCALE FARMER. Working paper no. 35. Nairobi, Univer-
sity College, Institute for Development Studies, 1972. 14 1.
Bibl.                                      Files Ken 38 R84

   A proposal for research designed to investigate the causes
   for the failure of small farmers in Tetu District to produce
   for export markets.

137. Ruthenberg, Hans. AFRICAN AGRICULTURAL PRODUCTION DEVELOPMENT
POLICY IN KENYA 1952-1965. Afrika-Studien, nr. 10. New
York, Berlin, Springer-Verlag, 1966. xv, 164 p. Bibl.
                                            Mem HC 501 A32/10

   A cost-benefit analysis of different approaches to agricultural
   development tried between 1952 and 1965 in Kenya: agricultural
   extension programs, smallholder tea development schemes,
   settlement on areas formerly reserved to whites, settlement

KEN 137-141

(Ruthenberg, Hans)
of new areas, and grazing schemes. All of these programs
incorporate heavy public subsidies to smallholder agriculture,
and the author doubts whether the economy can support subsidies of the magnitude involved in the last decade and a half
for very much longer.

138. Saltman, M. "The Status of Kipsigis customary law." (In
Conference of the University of East Africa Social Science
Council. 5th, Nairobi, 1969. PROCEEDINGS, VOL. 3. Nairobi,
University of East Africa, 1969. p. 1230-1236)
HC 517 E2 C6 1969

An examination of the customary land law of the Kipsigis led
to the conclusion that its fundamental aim was to re-establish
equilibrium in a situation of conflict. Although laws exist,
they are subject to broad interpretation and may even be
ignored if by doing so a pragmatic solution can be reached.

139. Segal, Aaron. "The Politics of land in East Africa." (In
EDCC, 16:2(1), 1968. p. 275-296)

Each of the East African countries has adopted its own approach
to land tenure because the political elites of each country
conceive of political stability in different terms and envision
different means to achieve these ends. According to the
author the resettlement of Africans on land formerly held by
Europeans was a prerequisite for Kenya's political stability.
See Item TANZ-65 for additional annotation.

140. Seymour, John. "Good from evil: Kikuyuland builds anew
(factors and nature of the agricultural revolution): some
effects of the 'emergency'; the agricultural revolution."
(In GM, 27:1, 1955. p. 431-442; and 27:2, 1955. p. 485-495)
Geol MC G273 M27

An informal article by a former colonial official with photo-
graphs of Kikuyu fortified villages and agricultural
activities.

141. Shannon, Mary L. "Land consolidation in Kenya: helping Africans to make the best use of their land." (In AW, June 1957.
p. 11+)                                        Mem AP A258 W927

A brief description of the Kikuyu land grievances which led
to the Mau Mau rebellion. The article also outlines the land
consolidation policy and other measures taken to enable Africans to make the best use of their land.

142.    Sillitoe, K. K.  "Land and community in Nyeri, Kenya."  (In
        Kampala, Uganda.  Makerere University College.  East African
        Institute of Social Research.  CONFERENCE PAPERS, 1963.
        14 p.)                                            Mem AP K148

        A discussion of the social role of land in Nyeri.  The sub-
        division of land upon inheritance leads to uneconomically
        small holdings and adversely affects the level of agricultural
        production.

143.    _____.  PRELIMINARY NOTES ON THE SOCIOLOGICAL AND ECONOMIC
        ASPECTS OF LAND TENURE AND USAGE IN MERU DISTRICT, KENYA.
        Conference paper no 134.  (Kampala) Makerere Institute of
        Social Research, 1962.  10 p.              Files Ken 58 S45

        This proposal contains historical background material and an
        outline of research to be undertaken on land tenure and its
        relationship with social and economic institutions.

144.    Simmance, A. J. F.  "Land redemption among the Fort Hall
        Kikuyu."  (In JAL, 5:2, 1961.· p. 75-82)            Law Per

        "A 'redeemable purchase' was the only form of landholding from
        another individual which the traditional Fort Hall system
        acknowledged."  After World War II opinion in Fort Hall began
        to turn against the seller's retention or rights of redemption.
        Land consolidation after 1954 finally swept away this right
        so that sales became final.

145.    Sonius, H. W. J.  HET RECHT OP DE GROND IN KENYA; EEN KORTE
        BESCHOUWING EN ENIGE VERGELIJKINGEN MET INDONESIE, VOL. I.
        Leiden, Afrika-Studiecentrum, 1960.  96 1.  Text in Dutch.
                                                    Mem HD 1169 K4 S6

        A comparison of the land law of Kenya and Indonesia.  The
        discussion covers Kenyan customary law, Islamic law, and
        English law; as well as the land policies which permitted
        settlement to Europeans.

146.    Sorrenson, M. P. K.  "Counter revolution to Mau-Mau:  land
        consolidation in Kikuyuland, 1952-1960."  1963.  (In Item
        KEN-37, 13 p.)                               Files Afr 3 E17

        Land consolidation and the development of cash crops have
        enabled a large number of Kikuyu landowners to produce in
        excess of their needs for self sufficiency.  But consolidation
        failed to aid landowners with small holdings who continue to
        cling to their land and do not work for wages on larger farms,

LAND TENURE AND AGRARIAN REFORM

(Sorrenson, M. P. K.)
as the government had hoped.  The real test of the policy will
come in the next generation, when landowners may follow the
Kikuyu custom of dividing their holdings among all male heirs
rather than handing them over as holdings of an economically
efficient size to a single heir.

147.    Sorrenson, M. P. K.  LAND REFORM IN THE KIKUYU COUNTRY:  A
STUDY IN GOVERNMENT POLICY.  Nairobi, published on behalf of
the East African Institute of Social Research, Makerere University College by Oxford University Press (1967).  ix, 266 p.
Bibl.                                              HD 990 K42 K55

A well documented analysis of land reform in Kenya based
largely on official records.  The study places Kikuyu land
problems in the context of the expropriation of their land
under colonial rule and other aspects of Kenyan history.  It
traces the first movement for land consolidation in Nyeri
District, where the need to prevent further litigation over
titles and the desire to improve farming methods induced local
people to consolidate their holdings independently of government pressure or intervention.  The chapter on Nyeri concludes
with an analysis of why village settlements failed.  In
Kiambu District, land consolidation began with a close association between a District Commissioner and a prominent
loyalist chief, and village settlements almost all remained
occupied, in contrast to Nyeri, because most villages in
Kiambu included some commuters.  The early stages of land
consolidation in Fort Hall were especially slow because of
inaccuracies in surveying plots, a problem which the author
traces to poor organization, which was largely corrected by
about 1958.  But there are signs that the slower tactics
adopted in Fort Hall since 1960 are proving a more suitable
model for other parts of Kenya than the heavy handed methods
of Kiambu.

148.    _____.  ORIGINS OF EUROPEAN SETTLEMENT IN KENYA.  British
Institute of History and Archaeology in East Africa, Memoir
no. 2.  Nairobi, Oxford University Press, 1968.  xii, 320 p.
Bibl.                                          Mem HD 990 K4 S67

This history of European settlement in Kenya to 1915 concentrates on the land policies of the British Foreign Office and
Colonial Office which permitted overseas settlement, the
attempts of the settlers to force the administration to heed
their demands, and the society which was the end product of
collaboration between settlers and administration.  The
settlers and the Colonial Office looked back to the history

126

(Sorrenson, M. P. K.)
of Australia, New Zealand, and South Africa for precedents
with which to justify their causes in Kenya.

149.    Speller, Charles.  "Land policy and economic development in
Kenya."  (In RAS/J, 30:121, 1931.  p. 377-385)
Mem AP A258 A256

The absence of planned land policies has hindered Kenya's
economic development.  Research must be undertaken on soils,
rainfall, water supplies, and climate in order to have adequate
information to be able to plan agricultural development
projects.

150.    Storrar, A.  "A Guide to the principles and practices of
land settlement in Kenya."  (In JLAO, 3:1, 1964.  p. 14-19)
Mem AP J83 L811

The planning of settlement schemes should provide for funds
to finance schemes, for a means of recovering loans from
settlers, for the purchase and pre-settlement development of
land of high agricultural potential, and for the establishment
of settlers on their holdings.

151.    Sytek, William L.  "A History of land consolidation in Central
Nyanza."  (In Makerere Institute of Social Research.
CONFERENCE PAPERS, 1966.  PART D:  AGRICULTURE.  Kampala,
1966.  24 p.)                          HC 517 E2 M14 1966 D

The author undertook an intensive study of government documents to determine the direction taken by the land consolidation program in Central Nyanza between 1956 and 1962.  He
found that the scheme was too large, under-staffed, and
tradition-bound.  In addition, the administration failed to
make an effort to understand the needs and customs of the Luo
people among whom they were working.

152.    _____.  "Social factors in Luo land consolidation."  (In
Makerere Institute of Social Research.  CONFERENCE PAPERS,
1965.  PART C:  SOCIOLOGY.  Kampala, 1966.  1 p.)
HC 517 E2 M14 1965 C

This one-page note concludes that lack of capital, a shortage
of young educated males, and tendencies promoting the fragmentation of land holdings have hampered land consolidation
programs and agricultural development among the Luo.

# Land Tenure and Agrarian Reform

153.    Taylor, D. R. F.  "Agricultural change in Kikuyuland."  1969.
        (In Item AFR-127, p. 463-493)                    HD 966 T36

        A discussion of the traditional agricultural system of the
        Kikuyu, population pressure on land and fragmentation of
        holdings during the colonial period, the Swynnerton Plan for
        land consolidation, the resulting rise in agriculturally
        based incomes, and the marketing of agricultural products in
        Kenya.

153a.   _____.  "Land reform in Kenya:  a reappraisal."  (In RA, 23,
        1974.  p. 79-90)

154.    _____.  "Land tenure and settlement patterns in Kenya."
        (In LE, 40:2, 1964.  p. 234-237)                    Ag Per

        A short note on land consolidation and land use planning in
        the Fort Hall District.

155.    Verhelst, Thierry G.  MATERIALS ON LAND LAW AND ECONOMIC
        DEVELOPMENT IN AFRICA.  1968.                       HD 962 V27

        See Item AFR-139 for citation and annotation.

156.    Wasserman, Gary.  "Continuity and counter-insurgency:  the
        role of land reform in decolonizing Kenya, 1962-70."  (In
        CJAS, 7:1, 1973.  p. 133-148)

        In 1962 the major objective of land reform schemes in Kenya
        was to meet the threat of rural insurgency by satisfying
        Kikuyu land hunger.  After 1964 planners could be more flex-
        ible, but the value of continued emphasis on private small-
        holder farming was never questioned.

157.    Watkins, O. F.  "Kenya Land Commission report."  (In RAS/J,
        33:132, 1934.  p. 207-216)               Mem AP A258 A256

        A useful summary of Item KEN-49 and its recommendations for
        policy on land consolidation.

158.    Whetham, Edith H.  COOPERATION, LAND REFORM AND LAND SETTLE-
        MENT.  1968.                            Ag HD 1491 A52 W4

        See Item AFR-140 for citation.  A chapter on Kenya (p. 11-22)
        focuses on settlement schemes in the highlands and on coopera-
        tives on these settlements.  At the time Whetham wrote,
        farmers had little understanding of the principles of coopera-
        tion and regarded cooperatives as an unnecessary complication

# Land Tenure and Agrarian Reform

(Whetham, Edith)
thrust upon them by the government. The central problem is
that membership in the cooperatives is compulsory for those
participating in the settlement schemes.

159.    _____. "Land reform and resettlement in Kenya." (In EAJRD,
1:1, 1968. p. 18-29)                              Mem AP E13 A2654
Also available as a separate.                     Files Ken 3 W3

A review of the literature on the purchase of more than one
million acres of land in the highlands from European owners
and its conversion into smallholder farms. The article also
assesses the prospects for making these farms into commercially
successful enterprises. The outlook is good as long as the
government retains control over land use and follows up to
make sure that efficient farming techniques are being used.

160.    Wilson, Gordon M. LUO CUSTOMARY LAW AND MARRIAGE LAWS CUS-
TOMS. Nairobi, Govt. Printer, 1961. 153 p.      Mem GN 650 W5

The first section of the book presents Luo land law in great
detail by referring to court decisions which reflect various
aspects of custom and establish precedents in the settlement
of conflicting claims to land rights.

161.    Wilson, R. G. "Land consolidation in the Fort Hall District
of Kenya." (In JAA, 8:3, 1956, p. 144-151)    Mem AP J83 A258

The demand for land consolidation is widespread and emanates
from the Kikuyu themselves. The initial experiment in consolidation in Fort Hall was undertaken within the territory of a
progressive chief who had been taken to Nyeri to see how land
adjudication and consolidation worked there.

162.    Wilson, Rodney J. A. THE ECONOMIC IMPLICATIONS OF LAND
REGISTRATION IN KENYA'S SMALLHOLDER AREAS. Staff paper no.
91. Nairobi, University College, Institute for Development
Studies, 1971. 25 p.                           Files Ken 59 W45

The author concludes that land registration had little effect
on transfers of interests in land and failed to reduce litigation arising from land disputes. Registration increased
security of tenure, but no correlation between security of
tenure and incentives to invest in the productive capacity of
land existed.

# LAND TENURE AND AGRARIAN REFORM

163. Wilson, Rodney J. A. "Land control in Kenya's smallholder farming areas." (In EAJRD, 5:1/2, 1972. p. 123-148)  Ag Per

Modified and shortened version of Item KEN-164.

164. _____. LAND CONTROL IN KENYA'S SMALLHOLDER FARMING AREAS. Staff paper no. 89. Nairobi, University of Nairobi, Institute for Development Studies, 1971. 36 p.    Files Ken 58 W45

The author contends that certain types of governmental control over land transactions can create an egalitarian society, encourage private initiative, and remove obstacles to the economic development of rural Kisu District by encouraging the evolution of holdings large enough to permit efficient exploitation.

165. _____. PROPOSAL FOR RESEARCH IN KENYA LAND TENURE AND ECONOMIC DEVELOPMENT. Staff paper no. 76. Nairobi, University College, Institute for Development Studies, 1970.  9 1.
                                            Files Ken 57.7 W45

A proposal for research to evaluate the short- and long-term effects of land consolidation and registration programs on the economy of the Central Province. Of particular interest is the hypothesis that these programs increased incentives to invest in improvements in the productive capacity of the land, an hypothesis to be tested with an empirical study.


## LESOTHO

1. Cowen, D. V. "Land tenure and economic development in Lesotho." (In SAJE, 35:1, 1967. p. 57-74)  Mem AP S724 A264

Over-population and land shortage are as much to blame for the low level of productivity as the land tenure system. The author sees only one solution to the problem--the development of industries in Lesotho to employ the Basotho.

2. Duncan, Patrick. SOTHO LAWS AND CUSTOMS; A HANDBOOK BASED ON DECIDED CASES IN BASUTOLAND TOGETHER WITH THE LAWS OF LEROTHOLI. Capetown, Oxford University Press, 1960. xiv, 169 p.                                    Files Leso 60 085

A section on land tenure (p. 74-102) cites decisions of the Judicial Commissioner's Court on diverse aspects of Lesotho's customary land law.

# Land Tenure and Agrarian Reform

3. Hamnett, T. G. Ian. "Some problems in the assessment of land shortage: a case study in Lesotho." (In AA, 72:286, 1973. p. 37-45)
   Also available as a separate.                Files Leso 58 H15

   This re-evaluation of Sheddick's study (see Item LESO-5) twenty years after the original fieldwork was done, discounts Sheddick's optimism about the size of population in relation to usable land. The author claims that Sheddick overlooked the physical condition of the land, which has continued to deteriorate since the original study was completed.

3a. _____. "Sotho law and custom in Basutoland." Edinburgh, 1970. 463 p. Bibl. Thesis, University of Edinburgh.
                                                          Microfilm

4. Pim, Sir Alan W. REPORT ON THE FINANCIAL AND ECONOMIC POSITION OF BASUTOLAND. Cmd. 4907. London, 1935. viii, 225 p. (In Great Britain. Parliament. House of Commons. PARLIAMENTARY PAPERS: REPORTS FROM COMMISSIONERS, 7, 1934/1935)   Mem Docs

   Included in this comprehensive report is a general description of the tenure systems of Lesotho (p. 45-46) and recommendations for reform in the direction of private ownership of land (p. 177-180).

5. Sheddick, Vernon. LAND TENURE IN BASUTOLAND. Commonwealth Relations Office, Colonial research studies no. 13. London, H.M.S.O., 1954. New York, Johnson Reprint, 1970. xvi, 196 p.
                                                     HD 989 L47 S34

   A systematic study of land tenure systems and land administration, based on field research done in 1947-1949. Separate chapters treat the nature of land ownership in general, the elements of the social system related to land tenure, settlement patterns, tenure for arable farming, and rights to pastoral land.

6. Wallman, Sandra. "The Farmech scheme: Basutoland (Lesotho)." (In AA, 67:267, 1968. p. 112-117)          Mem AP A258 A256

   A description of the Farmech scheme for a central tractor and threshing service. A new manager came to the scheme shortly after it began operation and made innovations in administration and changed the allocation of funds so that the responsibilities of participating farmers were clearly understood. Local opposition then dissolved.

7.   Williams, John Cox. LESOTHO: LAND TENURE AND ECONOMIC
     DEVELOPMENT. Communications no. 19. Pretoria, Africa Insti-
     tute of South Africa, 1972. 52 p.          Files Leso 58 W45

     The first part of this pamphlet describes customary systems of
     land tenure in Lesotho. The second part examines the economic
     implications of the land tenure system; for example, the lack
     of incentive for productive investment in land. Part 3 deals
     with farm size, fragmentation, and sharecropping. The final
     section recommends the formation of producer cooperatives and
     improved methods for controlling the use of grazing land.


## LIBERIA

1.   Curry, R. L.  "Agricultural land development in Liberia."
     (In JILE, 6:1, 1971.  p. 125-137)                    Law Per

     The author identifies four distinct land use subsectors within
     agriculture:  foreign rubber concessions, independent rubber
     plantations, farms producing foodstuffs for domestic and ex-
     port sale, and farms producing primarily for family consump-
     tion needs. The author briefly analyzes each subsector and
     recommends export diversification and the substitution of
     locally produced foodstuffs for food which is now imported.

2.   GROWTH WITHOUT DEVELOPMENT:  AN ECONOMIC SURVEY OF LIBERIA.
     By Robert W. Clower (and others). Evanston, Ill., North-
     western University Press, 1966. xv, 385 p.       HC 591 L6 G7

     An appendix on land and mineral ownership (p. 248-258) outlines
     Liberian land law, especially law governing sales and trans-
     fers of rights in land.

2a.  Liberia. Ministry of Planning and Economic Affairs. CENSUS
     OF AGRICULTURE, 1971; SUMMARY REPORT FOR LIBERIA. Preliminary
     (version). Series AC-B. Monrovia, 1973. v, 70 p.
                                            Files Libe 90.5 L44

3.   McBorrough, M. W. J. REGLEMENTATION CONCERNANT LES LEVES
     CADASTRAUX ET L'ENREGISTREMENT FONCIER AU LIBERIA. E/CN.14/
     CART/275. n.p., Nations Unies, Commission Economique pour
     l'Afrique, 1971. 7 p.                      Files Libe 59 M12

     Briefly describes Liberian land law applying to private,
     communal, and jointly owned land. The functions of the

# Land Tenure and Agrarian Reform

(McBorrough, M. W. J.)
cadastral service and procedures for the registration of title
are also touched upon.

4.  Parnall, T.  "Aliens and real property in Liberia."  (In JAL,
    12:2, 1968.  p. 64-80)
                                                          Law Per

Liberian law prohibits the ownership of real property by
aliens, but the law is unclear, especially as it applies to
alien-owned corporations.  Amendments to the law under consideration at the time of writing are also ambiguous.  The article enumerates the quite extensive interests, aside from
fee-simple ownership, which aliens hold in Liberian property
in the form of leaseholds, concessions, and mortgages.

5.  Tarpeh, Dominic Nmah; and Mueller, James V.  "A Study of
    Liberia's traditional and modern land tenure systems."
    n.p., 1970.  29, 12 1.  An abbreviated version of Tarpeh's
    senior thesis, edited by J. V. Mueller.
                                            Files Libe 58 T17

Traces the history of customary land tenure systems in rural
Liberia and discusses social and economic change resulting
from the introduction of the contemporary national land tenure
system.

## MALAGASY REPUBLIC

1.  Berthelot, Jacques.  "Bilan et perspectives de la coopération
    agricole à Madasgascar."  (In CAIS, 32, 1972.  p. 61-111)

In-depth analysis of the failure of the Malagasy Republic's
marketing cooperatives, presented under the headings of endog-
enous causes, such as the fact that cooperatives in developing
countries cannot evoke voluntary participation from their
members, and exogenous reasons why cooperatives continue to be
supported by developing countries despite manifest failure to
generate returns commensurate with costs.

2.  Blanc-Jouvan, Xavier.  "Les Droits fonciers collectifs dans
    les coutumes malgaches."  (In RIDC, 16:2, 1964.  p. 333-368)
                                                          Law Per
    Also available as a separate.            Files MR 94 B51

# Land Tenure and Agrarian Reform

3.  Bonnemaison, J. "Des Riziculteurs d'altitude: Tsarahonenana, village de l'Ankaratra (Madagascar)." (In ETR, 37/39, 1970. p. 326-344)

    A study of a village noting that 14 percent of the villagers hold 41 percent of the land. Exogamous marriage patterns permit outsiders to press claims to village land and for those who have moved away to retain claims.

4.  Charmes, Jacques. "De la rente foncière au capitalisme: transformation des structures sociales sur les perimètres d'Anony et Sahamaloto (SOMALAC)." (In TM, 15, 1973. p. 127-149)

    A study of the impact of land reform on socio-economic structures near Lake Alaotra. The main conclusion is that sharecroppers now constitute only about 25 percent of the population, a decline from a figure of about 50 percent before reform was undertaken.

5.  Delenne, M. "Terroirs en gestation dans le Moyen-Ouest malgache." (In ETR, 37/39, 1970. p. 410-448)

    Studies the problem of agricultural development in the highlands of central Madagascar, where increasing poverty is the result of inability to adopt new agricultural techniques. The article treats land use, social organization, and agricultural techniques, and contrasts patterns of land tenure among immigrants and the local people.

6.  Gasse, Victor. LE REGIME FONCIER A MADAGASCAR ET EN AFRIQUE. Paris, Librairie Autonome (1959). 351 p.      Mem HD 999 M3 G3

    An earlier version of Item MR-7.

7.  _____. LES REGIMES FONCIERS AFRICAINS ET MALGACHE: EVOLUTION DEPUIS L'INDEPENDANCE. 1971.      HD 1169 G3

    See Item AFR-56 for citation and additional annotation. An extremely detailed presentation of the provisions of the land law governing property registration before and after independence. Sections on the Malagasy Republic, scattered throughout the book, can be located by using the geographical index (p. 316-317 for the Malagasy Republic).

8.  Hamicotte, Guy. "Les Fermes d'etat." (In TM, 15, 1973. p. 151-165)

(Hamicotte, Guy)
An historical survey of state farms in the Malagasy Republic
in the light of experience elsewhere, followed by an examination of economic aspects of this form of direct intervention
by the state in rural production.

9.  Jarison, J. F.  "L'Action des pouvoirs publics dans la
répartition et l'affectation du sol en vue de l'aménagement
et du développement à Madasgascar." 1970.  (In Item AFR-112,
p. 1255-1278)

Under Malagasy law, the state is empowered to take possession
of land which has been abandoned or insufficiently developed,
but the state also guarantees the rights of land holders who
show good faith.

10.  Koerner, Francis.  "Décolonisation et économie de plantations
dans les régions cotières du nord et de l'ouest Malgache."
(In REM, 5, 1970.  p. 317-331)

About 30 or 40 percent of the land ceded to Europeans during
the colonial period had been given up when this article was
written.  The reason is not that the independent Malagasy
government has asserted political pressure, but rather that
commercial agriculture has had difficulty finding cheap labor
and ready markets.  The author stresses that unused land should
be reclaimed and redistributed to Malagasy farmers.

11.  _____.  "Les Types de sociétés agricoles privées à Madagascar:
formation, structure, et propriétés."  (In COM/B, 21:83, 1968.
p. 276-297)                              Mem AP C132 D108

An article about the role of large-scale commercial companies
in the agricultural economy of Madasgascar.  Includes historical information on the nature and extent of land concessions
to each of the principal companies during the colonial period.

12.  Louzoun, G.  "Le Remembrement au Lac Alaotra."  (In TM, 2,
1967.  p. 101-127)

A detailed report on a land consolidation project near Lake
Alaotra.  Included is information on the average size of
holdings before and after consolidation, the problems involved
in re-establishing terraces for rice cultivation, legal provisions for adjudication, problems encountered in establishing
land inventories for each family, and the need to constantly
explain operating procedures to farmers who had been disturbed
by rumors that their own best interests were not being served.

# LAND TENURE AND AGRARIAN REFORM

13. Marchal, J. Y. "Un Exemple de colonisation agricole à Madagascar: Antanety-Ambohidava (sous-préfecture de Betafo)." (In ETR, 37/39, 1970. p. 397-409)

    A study of spontaneous land colonization which occurred over the last seventy years. Immigrants settled land in a frontier area and were joined by others as the frontier of settlement advanced. The article describes the way in which newly arrived settlers obtained land from those who had already established themselves. The principle of individual ownership, once reserved for low lying rice land, has recently made gains on upland pastures as well.

14. Rabemanda, André. "L'Evolution du régime de la propriété immobilière à Madasgascar." (In Item AFR-112. p. 723-734)

    An historical review of Malagasy land law. The colonial government used the principle of eminent domain to redistribute land to colonial interests. When the nation became independent in 1959, national political leaders judged it not wise to return to the system of communally held land and property rights which applied before colonial rule.

15. Raison, J. P. "Paysage rural et demographie Leimavo (nord du Betsileo, Madagascar)." (In ETR, 37/39, 1970. p. 345-377)

    An article on how a group beset by population pressure and a highly restricted water base have evolved a satisfactory and original agricultural technology which has discouraged the out-migration characteristic of other groups in the region.

16. Rarijaona, René. LE CONCEPT DE PROPRIETE EN DROIT FONCIER DE MADAGASCAR; ETUDE DE SOCIOLOGIE JURIDIQUE. Université de Madagascar, Faculté de Droit et des Sciences Economiques; Etudes Malgaches no. 18. Paris, Editions Cujas, 1967. 306 p.
    HD 1169 M15 R17

    A philosophical treatise by a jurist on the nature, evolution, and probable future development of land law in the Malagasy Republic.

17. Wurtz, Jacqueline. "Evolution des structures foncières entre 1900 et 1968 à Ambohiboanjo (Madagascar)." (In ETR, 37/39, 1970. p. 449-479)

    An analysis of the impact of commercialization of agriculture on a relatively isolated community characterized by a high degree of social cohesiveness. The land tenure system is the

# LAND TENURE AND AGRARIAN REFORM

(Wurtz, Jacqueline)
key to understanding the social organization and ways in which
agricultural practices can be altered. The market economy has
tended to augment the economic independence of the slave
caste, but extreme fragmentation of land holdings has also
occurred as this caste adopted inheritance patterns formerly
limited to the upper echelons of society.


## MALAWI


1.  Agnew, Swanzie. "The History of the Nkata family's land in
    the domain of Nkosi ya Makosi, Edingeni." (In RA, 20, 1973.
    p. 47-51)

    The history of the Nkata family and the manner in which they
    have acquired and have had to surrender land illustrates the
    complexity of land tenure arrangements under Ngoni customary
    law.

2.  Benda-Beckmann, F. von. "Einige Gedanken zur Bodenrechtsreform
    in Malawi." (In IAF, 6:1, 1970. p. 58-63)  Mem AP I6188 A258

    A fundamental problem of a political nature confronts the
    question of land reform in Malawi. Most farmers do not want
    the government to confirm individual rights in land because
    they prefer the present system, which in theory at least
    leaves them free to migrate to areas where land is abundant.
    The article also describes the customary land tenure system,
    the Customary Land Development Act, and experiments with the
    granting of land rights to matrilineal families in Lilongwe
    District.

3.  Brietzke, Paul H. "Rural development and modifications of
    Malawi's land tenure system." (In RA, 20, 1973. p. 53-68)

    A tentative assessment of the scheme to replace Malawi's
    customary land tenure system with statutory land tenure.
    Concludes that the contemplated modifications will not pro-
    mote rural development because the new statutes are too nega-
    tive in character and contain too few rewards to farmers to
    encourage them to comply with development goals.

4.  Chilivumbo, Alifeyo. "On labor and Alomwe immigration."
    (In RA, 24, 1974. p. 49-57)

# LAND TENURE AND AGRARIAN REFORM

(Chilivumbo, Alifeyo)
Malawi has received large numbers of Alomwe laborers from
Mozambique throughout the colonial period to recent times.
European tea planters gave immigrants small plots of land on
which to settle in return for labor.  They had no permanent
rights to land but were able to stay as long as they provided
labor to the planters.

5. Chipeta, W.  "Land tenure and problems in Malawi."  (In SMJ,
   24:1, 1971.  p. 25-34)                   Mem AP S677 M239 J
   Also available as a separate.           Files Malaw 58 C34

   The Malawian land law of 1965 divides the country into areas
   of customary land, public land, and privately owned freehold
   land.  The author argues that the individualization of tenure
   alone would not significantly alter incentives to put land to
   commercial use.

6. Coissoró, Narana.  THE CUSTOMARY LAW OF SUCCESSION IN CENTRAL
   AFRICA.  1966.                          Mem JX 6510 A35 C6

   See Item AFR-35 for citation.  The book contains a discussion
   of the African Wills and Succession Ordinance of Nyasaland,
   according to which an African can draw up a will and still have
   it challenged if it is not in accord with the customary law
   of the testator's ethnic group.  The author adds that Africans
   are not aware of this legal distinction and think that admis-
   sion to probate makes the will unchallengable as a legal
   instrument.

6a. Mair, Lucy P.  "Agrarian policy in British African colonies."
    1951.                                    Ag HD 965 L3

    See Item AFR-86 for citation and annotation.

7. Malawi.  LAND IN MALAWI.  RU:WLR-C/66/34.  (Rome) FAO, 1966.
   3 p.  Paper for World Land Reform Conference, Rome, 1966.
                                           Files Malaw 58 M14

   A three-page outline of categories of land ownership, customary
   systems of land tenure, and government land policy.

7a. _____.  Dept. of Lands.  ANNUAL REPORT, 1966.  Zomba, Govt.
    Printer, 1967.  6 p.                   Files Malaw 57.4 M15

8. _____.  Laws, statutes, etc.  ACT NO. 5 OF 1967.  (Zomba)
   1967.  14 p.                            Files Malaw 58 M15
   Also available in FAL, 16:3, v/1e, 1968.            Ag Docs

LAND TENURE AND AGRARIAN REFORM

(Malawi. Laws, Statutes, etc.)
The Customary Land Development Act of 1967 provides for the
formation of land committees to assist the development officer
in the allocation of land within development areas.

9. _____. _____. "Act no. 6 of 1967." (Zomba) 1967. 68 p.
Files Malaw 59 M15

Text of the Registered Land Act of 1967, covering organization
and administration, formation of a Land Register, maps, boundaries, leases, transfers, restraints, and disposition of land.

10. _____. _____. ACT NO. 25 OF 1965. (Zomba) 1965. 12 p.
At head of title: Malawi Land. Files Malaw 58 M16

The text of the Malawi Land Act of 1965 which sets forth rules
for the administration of public, private, and customary land.

11. _____. National Statistical Office. A SAMPLE SURVEY OF
AGRICULTURAL SMALL HOLDINGS IN CENTRAL REGION, MALAWI, APRIL-
JUNE, 1967. Zomba, Govt. Printer, 1967. 50 p.
Files Malaw 90.5 M14

The results of a sample survey conducted in Lilongwe and
Salima Districts. A section on land tenure includes data on
boundary changes, transfers among relatives, and patterns of
inheritance.

12. _____. _____. A SAMPLE SURVEY OF AGRICULTURAL SMALL HOLDINGS
IN CHIKWAWA DISTRICT, MALAWI, SEPTEMBER-NOVEMBER, 1965. Zomba,
1966. 25 1. Files Malaw 90.5 M143

A report presenting data from a sample survey of patterns of
agricultural land use. The high points of a section on land
tenure (p. 6-11) are that payment is seldom made for the
transfer of rights to small plots of land and that village
headsmen apparently control only the new land.

13. _____. _____. A SAMPLE SURVEY OF AGRICULTURAL SMALL HOLDINGS
IN SOUTHERN REGION, MALAWI, SEPTEMBER-NOVEMBER, 1965. Zomba,
1965. 31, 8 p. Files Malaw 90.5 M145

A report incorporating the results of MALAW-12 and giving a
slightly wider geographical coverage.

14. Meek, Charles Kingsley. "Nyasaland." 1949. (In Item AFR-91,
p. 115-119) HD 599 Z5 M4

MALAW 14-18

(Meek, Charles Kingsley)
Describes the land policy of the protectorate in the 1930s,
when land was divided into crown land and native trust land.
Freehold estates alienated to Europeans were included under
reserved lands. Native trust land constituted 95 percent of
the total area, so that the alienation of land to Europeans
was not of the magnitude of the settler problem in Kenya.

15.  Nyasaland. Dept. of Lands. REPORT. Zomba, 1961. 1 v.
                                              Mem HD 990 N8 A32

     A report on the activities of the Department of Lands in 1961.
     The department was chiefly concerned with the administration
     of leases, tenancies, conveyances, and the like on public
     lands and African trust lands.

16.  Page, Melvin E. "Land and labour in rural Malawi:  an over-
     view." (In RA, 20, 1973.  p. 3-9)

     An overview of the efforts of the Malawian government to pro-
     mote rural development.  The author notes that these efforts
     have concentrated on improving smallholder agriculture and
     that the greatest efforts to transform agrarian systems have
     been through agricultural extension.

17.  Reader, R. A. "The Structure of small-holder agriculture."
     n.p., 1971.  viii, 53, 33 1.            Files Malaw 7 R21

     This socio-economic survey includes a section on land tenure
     (p. 19-25).  The author surveyed garden holders and found that
     most received permission to use land from a consanguineal
     relative and that most intended to pass usufructuary rights
     along to consanguineal heirs.

18.  Simpson, R. "New land law in Malawi." (In JLAO, 6:4, 1967.
     p. 221-228)                              Mem AP J83 L811

     A description of the origins and purposes of legislation being
     considered in Malawi in 1967 for the purposes of introducing
     individual title to land:  the Customary Land (Development)
     Bill, the Registered Land Bill, the Local Land Boards Bill,
     and the Malawi Land (Amendment) Bill.

## MALI

1.  Gosselin, G. DEVELOPPEMENT ET TRADITION DANS LES SOCIETES
    RURALES AFRICAINES. 1970.                    HN 773.5 G67

    See Item AFR-60 for citation. Includes an analysis of the
    problems encountered in recruiting settlers for the Office
    du Niger project, a massive irrigation scheme on the interior
    delta of the Niger in Mali, the planning of which dates back
    to 1919. The scheme has been able to bring only a very poor
    return on capital invested. Chief among the problems was a
    failure to elicit a permanent comittment from the settlers to
    their new way of life.

2.  Idiart, P. "Métayage et régimes fonciers dans la région du
    Faguibine (Cercle de Goundam, Soudan)." (In ETR, 2, 1961.
    p. 37-59; and 3, 1961. p. 21-44)                    Ag Per

    A two-part article on customary tenure systems in a desert-
    edge region of Mali characterized by extreme diversity of
    ethnic composition and differing adaptations to the semi-arid
    environment. The author presents case studies of four widely
    divergent tenure systems, emphasizing the different functions
    of tenancy within each of the societies. Of particular
    interest are studies of two sections of the nomadic Tuareg,
    Berber-speaking desert people whose control of land derives
    from their military superiority over sedentary peoples in
    pre-colonial times.

3.  Pollet, E.; and Winter, G. "L'Organisation sociale du travail
    agricole des Soninke (Dyalumu, Mali)." (In CEA, 8:32, 1968.
    p. 509-534)                               Mem AP C132 D1043

    Land rights among the Soninke of Dyalumu follow a pattern
    common among peoples of the Mande family. Land ownership was
    vested in certain clans whose elders allocated land rights to
    heads of families in return for a small payment of grain. The
    privilege of allocating land rights remains with these clans,
    though payments are no longer made. Renting land is rare
    and sale nonexistent.

4.  Skotnicki, Maksymilian. "Une Etude de terroir au Mali.
    Remarques méthodologiques et techniques." (In AB, 9, 1968.
    p. 57-66)

    The author describes the methodology he applied in his study
    of patterns of land use in a Malian village. Topics covered

MALI 4–MAURITA 2

(Skotnicki, Maksymilian)
include the choice of a representative village, mapping techniques, and the kinds of survey questions which elicited usable
information from respondents.

5.   United Nations. Economic Commission for Africa. REPORT OF A
     MISSION FOR THE STUDY OF PROBLEMS AND PROSPECTS IN RURAL
     DEVELOPMENT OF MALI, NIGER, AND UPPER VOLTA. By A. C. Bessis,
     et al. E/CN.14/SWCD/29. n.p., 1966. v, 246 p.
                                                   HN 803.5 U58

     A compilation of economic and demographic data followed by
     recommendations for development, including "sedentarization
     of the nomads," increased security of land tenure, and a study
     of land use. See Item UV-12 for additional annotation.

6.   Zahan, Dominique. "Problèmes sociaux posés par la transplanta-
     tion des Mossi sur les terres irriguées de l'Office du Niger."
     (In Item AFR-67, p. 392-403)                 HD 966 I5 1960

     The resettlement of Mossi from overpopulated areas of Upper
     Volta, in this case the kingdom of Yatenga, on the irrigated
     land of the Office du Niger in Mali was complicated by social
     factors:  settlers retained strong ties with their homeland,
     returning to find marriage partners and sending money to rela-
     tives who remained behind.  In the early years, the population
     movement more closely resembled seasonal labor migration than
     resettlement, but recently settlers have developed a more
     lasting committment to their new homes.


                            **MAURITANIA**


1.   Mohamed Fall, Ould Ahmed. "Le Domaine en droit mauritanien."
     1970. (In Item AFR-112, p. 797-800)

     A brief summary of a 1960 law regulating the disposition of
     lands "vacant and without owner" or "unused and unoccupied
     for ten years or more."  The law respects customary systems of
     land tenure except when land is clearly not permanently
     occupied.

2.   _____. La Réforme mauritanienne du droit foncier." 1970.
     (In Item AFR-112, p. 735-740)

## Land Tenure and Agrarian Reform

MAURITA 2-MAURITI 3

(Mohamed Fall, Ould Ahmed)
Describes the provisions of a 1960 land law designed to
encourage modern development and at the same time to protect
certain features of customary land tenure systems.  Property
registration is encouraged in order to provide collateral for
loans to foster development goals.


## MAURITIUS


1.  Barclays Bank (Dominion, Colonial and Overseas).  MAURITIUS:
    AN ECONOMIC SURVEY.  Port Louis, Office of Mauritius Manager,
    1971.  43 p.                                    Files Mauriti 1 B17

    A general overview of economic conditions in Mauritius,
    including information on the principal agricultural exports
    and a paragraph (p. 8) on patterns of landholding in the sugar
    industry.

2.  King, John.  MAURITIUS, MALTHUS AND PROFESSOR MEADE.  Communi-
    cations series no. 49.  Brighton, Eng., Institute of Develop-
    ment Studies, University of Sussex, 1970.  14, 4 p.
                                                    Files Mauriti 31 K45

    This paper questions the appropriateness of the neo-classical
    economic model applied to the economy of Mauritius by J. E.
    Meade and recommends an alternative analytical framework.  The
    author mentions patterns of land tenure in passing:  the land
    area of the island is divided about equally between large-
    scale sugar estates and smaller plantations of up to about
    500 acres each.  Although the number of large estates had
    decreased over the years, they still occupy about the same
    area of land because their average size has grown.

3.  Leake, Hugh Martin.  "Studies in tropical land tenure:
    Mauritius."  (In TROP, 10:4, 1933.  p. 111-113)        Ag Per

    The foundation of land tenure upon which the agriculture of
    Mauritius has been built up is one of relatively small planta-
    tions owned by settlers of European ancestry and worked by
    hired labor.  Land acquisition and alienation is tightly
    regulated by local ordinances based on the French civil code
    and dating, for the most part, to the nineteenth century.

143

# LAND TENURE AND AGRARIAN REFORM

4.  Mauritius. Ministry of Housing, Lands and Town and Country
    Planning. ANNUAL REPORT FOR THE YEAR ENDED 30TH JUNE, 1970.
    No. 3 of 1971. Port Louis, Govt. Printer, 1971. 9 p.
    Files Mauriti 52 M18 1970

    A brief report on the organization and main features of the
    ministry in 1970.

5.  Meek, Charles Kingsley. "Mauritius and Fiji." 1949. (In
    Item AFR-91, p. 201-211)
    HD 599 Z5 M4

    A short section (p. 201-203) notes the importance of large
    estates in patterns of landholding and the dominance of the
    sugar industry in the economy.

## MOZAMBIQUE

1.  Coissoró, Naraná. O REGIME DAS TERRAS EM MOÇAMBIQUE. Lisboa,
    Instituto Superior de Ciências Sociais e Política Ultramarina,
    1965. 73 p.
    Mem C80581

2.  Issacman, Allan F. MOZAMBIQUE: THE AFRICANIZATION OF A
    EUROPEAN INSTITUTION; THE ZAMBESI PRAZOS, 1750-1902. Madison,
    University of Wisconsin Press (1972). xviii, 260 p. Bibl.
    HD 1019 M68 I8

    During the early part of the seventeenth century, the Portu-
    guese government established several crown estates, or prazos
    da coroa, in the lower Zambezi Valley. This book seeks to
    correct the Euro-centric bias of previous histories of the
    Zambezi which viewed the prazos as an alien institution. The
    author's approach, which relies heavily on oral testimonies
    recorded during field research, is to examine the prazos as
    African institutions and to concentrate on the relations of
    the estate holders with indigenous African chiefs. As with
    most institutions on the frontier of European settlement, the
    prazos were absorbed into the local culture.

2a. Missiaen, Edmond. MOZAMBIQUE'S AGRICULTURAL ECONOMY IN BRIEF.
    Washington, USDA, 1969. 12 p.
    Files Moz 5 M4

3.  Newitt, M. D. D. "The Portuguese on the Zambesi: an histori-
    cal interpretation of the prazo system." (In JAH, 10:1, 1969.
    p. 67-85)
    Mem AP J83 A262

(Newitt, M. D. D.)
From the seventeenth century to the coming of the Salazar
regime, Portuguese control of the Zambezi basin rested on the
prazos da coroa (grants of crown land).  Private titles became common in the seventeenth century, when conquistadores
sought official recognition of their position.  In the nineteenth century the dependence of the prazo holders on their
African clients and followers, as well as intermarriage,
greatly accentuated their African characteristics.  The prazos
survived into the twentieth century as units of fiscal and
administrative policy.

4.      _____.  PORTUGUESE SETTLEMENT ON THE ZAMBESI; EXPLORATION,
LAND TENURE, AND COLONIAL RULE IN EAST AFRICA.  New York,
Africana Publishing Co.  (1973)  434 p.  Bibl.
                                          DT 463 N49 1973

An expansion of Item MOZ-3.  Includes an analysis of the
prazos da coroa as a system of land tenure, relations between
the government and the prazo-holders, prazo society, and the
evolution of the institution over three centuries.

5.   Niemeier, G.  "Die moderne Bauerkolonisation in Angola und
Moçambique und das portugiesische Kolonialproblem."  1966.
                                          Geol MC G28 R87

See Item ANG-2 for citation.  On the right bank of the Limpopo
about 1,000 white and black families lived in 14 villages at
the time of writing.  According to the author, black and white
farmers have the same rights and duties and are not allowed
to employ anyone outside their own family.

6.   Pössinger, Hermann.  LANDWIRTSCHAFTLICHE ENTWICKLUNG IN
ANGOLA UND MOÇAMBIQUE.  1968.                      S 472 P6

See Item ANG-3 for citation and additional annotation.  A
cross-sectional analysis of the trends of agricultural development in Angola and Mozambique along with a review of Portuguese
development policy.  A section on traditional agricultural
systems (p. 183-204) in Mozambique focuses on market and subsistence sectors as well as cooperatives for African farmers.

7.   Torres, J. L.  "Rural development schemes in southern
Mozambique."  (In SAJAA, 3:2, 1973.  p. 60-69)
                                          Mem AP S724 A262

The first settlement scheme at Guija was originally planned to
channel to Mozambique the thousands of Portuguese who found

# LAND TENURE AND AGRARIAN REFORM

(Torres, J. L.)
their way to Brazil in the 1920s and 1930s. By the time it
was implemented these potential white settlers were no longer
available, and the Portuguese opened the settlement project to
Africans. The scheme at Guija has been inordinately expensive.

8. _____. "Some settlement schemes in the Gaza District of
southern Mozambique." (In SAJE, 35:3, 1967. p. 244-255)
Mem AP S724 A264

A brief discussion of the economic aspects of the Limpopo
Valley Settlement and the Inhamissa Settlement Scheme in
southern Mozambique.

9. Weber, P. "Agrarkolonisation in Mittel Moçambique." (In
RR, 28:3, 1970. p. 118-126)
Mem AP R246

Historical background followed by a report on the operation of
three settlement projects concentrating on growing tobacco,
cotton, and sugar, respectively.

## NIGER

1. Baier, Stephen; and King, David J. "Drought and the development of Sahelian economies: a case study of Hausa-Tuareg
interdependence." (In LTC/N, 45, 1974. p. 11-22)

Access to pasture in the Sahel and savanna formed the basis
for the survival of the pastoral peoples of the southern
Sahara during droughts in the pre-colonial period. Since the
present land tenure system of Niger and northern Nigeria
largely excludes the nomads from southern pasture, an alternative survival mechanism must be found. The authors suggest
that during droughts nomads be allowed to bring herds to fat-
tening ranches far enough south that they are not adversely
affected by shortages of pasture and water.

2. Bernus, E. "Espace géographique et champs sociaux chez les
Touareg Illabakan (République du Niger)." (In ETR, 37/39,
1970. p. 46-64)

The colonial administration and the government of independent
Niger sought to create among the nomadic Tuareg of the Sahel
a political organization parallel to that of neighboring
sedentary people: groupes nomades corresponding to cantons

# LAND TENURE AND AGRARIAN REFORM

(Bernus, E.)
and nomadic sections equivalent to villages. As a result,
present administrative groupings do not necessarily correspond
to traditional fractions, but this has presented no particular
problem to the Illabakan, who have managed to preserve their
unity despite geographical dispersion by means of holding to
their custom of endogamous marriages. The article details
the patterns of seasonal transhumant migration which characterize Tuareg land use.

3.  Niger. ENQUETE AGRICOLE AU NIGER. Ce rapport a été redigé
    par M. Louis Marciniak. (Paris), I.N.S.E.E., Service de
    Coopération, Secrétariat d'Etat aux Affaires Etrangers, n. d.
    199 p.                                                    S 473 N5 A3

    Statistics on area cultivated, crops grown, fragmentation,
    population distribution, and animal ownership, most frequently
    aggregated to the level of one of five regions of the country.
    Preceding the data is a word of caution about their use be-
    cause of internal inconsistencies and serious problems in the
    way the information was gathered.

3a.  _____. NOTE SUR: LE REGIME FONCIER AU NIGER, LES DROITS
    COUTUMIERS, LES DOMAINES PUBLIC ET PRIVE. Presente par le
    Gouvernement de la République du Niger. E/CN.14/CART/267.
    n.p., UNECA, 1970. (47) p.                      Files Niger 58 N43

4.  Raulin, Henri. "Cadastre et terroirs au Niger." (In ETR, 9,
    1963. p. 58-79)                                           Ag Per

    A cadastral survey in Niger would have major legal, social,
    and economic implications and would contribute greatly to a
    better knowledge of the country from every point of view.
    Economic development has in general led to a tendency toward
    individualization of rights in land. In certain regions, such
    as on islands in the Niger, disputes over land have reached
    a point where only a cadastral survey could disentangle con-
    flicting and overlapping claims. In other regions, a cadastral
    survey can be justified by its contribution to a knowledge
    of land use. The article presents three examples of different
    kinds of village settings and details the kinds of questions
    which a survey would help resolve.

5.  _____. "Communautés d'entraide et développément agricole au
    Niger: l'exemple de la Majya." (In ETR, 33, 1969. p. 5-26)

    The introduction of cotton cultivation in the Majya valley
    in south-central Niger created a new economic situation which

# Land Tenure and Agrarian Reform

(Raulin, Henri)
had an impact on the land tenure system. Land was previously
abundant enough that leasing it was rare and sale almost nonexistent. Recently, however, leasing has tended to replace
the rent-free loans of land once common.

6. _____. "Public acquisition of land." n.p. (1972). 4 1.
Files Niger 76 R18

A short paper summarizing experience with irrigation projects
in the Ader-Doutchi, where egalitarian forms of social organization in Hausa villages facilitated the redistribution of
irrigated land, and in the Niger valley, where pronounced
social stratification led to a complete failure.

7. _____. "Travail et régimes fonciers au Niger." (In ISEAC,
166, 1965 (5:9). p. 119-139) Mem H 31 I53

Briefly traces the evolution of tenure systems among various
peoples of Niger. In western Niger a tendency toward the
concentration of landholding in the hands of a few was taking
place in 1960. In the center and east, most heads of families
had more land than they could farm, and they often rented excess land to neighbors whose families could provide the labor
needed to work the fields.

8. Seminar on Cadastre, Addis Ababa, 1970. NOTE ON THE LAND
TENURE SYSTEM IN THE NIGER; CUSTOMARY RIGHTS, PUBLIC AND
PRIVATE DOMAIN. E/CN.14/CART/267. Addis Ababa, UNECA, 1972.
10 p. Files Niger 12.5 S25

An outline of the history and present state of Nigérien land
law.

9. United Nations. Economic Commission for Africa. REPORT OF A
MISSION FOR THE STUDY OF PROBLEMS AND PROSPECTS IN RURAL
DEVELOPMENT IN MALI, NIGER, AND UPPER VOLTA. 1966.
HN 803.5 U58

See Item MALI-5 for citation and annotation.

## NIGERIA

1. Adalemo, I. A. "The Kainji Dam: a resettlement." (In NM,
99, 1968. p. 265-279) Mem AP N685

# Land Tenure and Agrarian Reform

(Adalemo, I. A.)
The construction of the Kainji dam on the Niger and the subsequent inundation of a large area of land necessitated the resettlement of 50,000 people. This article briefly describes the
physical setting, patterns of land use, and modes of settlement
in the region before and after the flooding.

2.  Adegboye, Rufus O. "Analysis of land tenure structure in some
    isolated areas in Nigeria." (In NJESS, 8:2, 1966. p. 259-268)
                                                Mem AP N6882 J84
    Also available as a separate.              Files Nig 58 A217

    Field research in eight isolated Nigerian villages led
    Adegboye to conclude that the sale of land is rare; that all
    members of the land-owning group must give their consent if
    sale is to take place; that equal division of land among heirs
    is not encouraged to the same degree in all regions of Nigeria;
    and that equal division of land into parcels corresponding to
    the number of wives who bore sons is more widely practiced
    than either primogeniture or equal division among all male
    heirs.

3.  _____. "Farm tenancy in Western Nigeria." (In NJESS 8:3,
    1966. p. 441-453)                           Mem AP N6882 J84
    Also available as a separate.              Files Nig 58 A22

    The results of a survey of tenants in 36 towns and villages
    show that the terms of lease are usually verbal; that the
    landlord often helps the tenant get started by loaning tools
    and providing housing; that rents are determined not by the
    fertility and location of the land but by the closeness of
    kinship ties between landlord and tenant; and that landlords
    sometimes absorb tenants into their families by arranging
    marriages between their daughters and their tenants.

4.  _____. "Incorporating communally-owned farmlands in Nigeria."
    (Ames, Iowa, 1962. 10 1.) Paper for Economics 512, Iowa
    State University, 1961-62.                  Files Nig 58 A23

    Examines the extent to which the land tenure system in Nupeland
    inhibits agricultural development. Both communal ownership
    and freehold family ownership exist. This dual system gives
    security of title and mobility to the farming population, but
    reduces production.

5.  _____. "Land tenure in Uboma," (In Oluwasanmi, H. A., et al.
    UBOMA: A SOCIO-ECONOMIC AND NUTRITIONAL SURVEY OF A RURAL
    COMMUNITY IN EASTERN NIGERIA. (Bude (Eng.) Geographical
    Publications, 1966. p. 71-81)               HD 2130 N52 O58

LAND TENURE AND AGRARIAN REFORM

(Adegboye, Rufus O.)
A study based on a sample of 33 families in the region shows
that land may be acquired or disposed of in any of the following ways:  through inheritance, lease, pledge, gift, purchase,
sale, or exchange.  Most farmers have less than five acres of
land, and most land is already in use.

6.    _____.  "Need for land reform in Nigeria."  (In NJESS 9:3,
1967.  p. 339-350)                         Mem AP N6882 J84

The need for land resettlement schemes in Nigeria arises from
the concentration of population in the north and along the
southern coast, leaving the Middle Belt relatively sparsely
populated.  The experience of Kenya, Egypt, Sudan, India,
and Turkey with resettlement schemes illustrate the importance
of setting up a Lands Commission and of enacting laws to give
the government rights of disposal over all unoccupied land.

7.    _____.  "Procuring loan through pledging of cocoa trees."
Reprint no. 94.  Madison, Land Tenure Center, n.d. (14) p.
Reprinted from JOURNAL OF THE GEOGRAPHICAL ASSOCIATION OF
NIGERIA, 12, 1969.  p. 63-76.              Files Nig 23 A22

A description of the pledging of rights to cocoa trees in
Western Nigeria to creditors in return for which the pledgor
receives a loan.  Included are sections on the reasons for
pledging to obtain loans, rights and risks of pledgor and
pledgee, the terms and conditions of signing of contracts, and
suggestions for the regulation of contracts by the government.

8.    _____.  "Public acquisition of land."  n.p. (197-).  14.1
                                           Files Nig 76 A22

Analyzing the welfare problems associated with public acquisition of land, the author recommends that local elders and
notable persons be placed on land committees.

9.    _____.  "Redemption of pledged property through rural credit."
(In RURAL DEVELOPMENT IN NIGERIA:  PROCEEDINGS OF THE 1972
ANNUAL CONFERENCE OF THE NIGERIAN ECONOMIC SOCIETY.  Idaban,
Nigerian Economic Society (1973).  p. 181-189)   HN 800 N5 R87

The author advocates a program of government-financed credit to
extend loans to people who have had to pledge their land--that
is, to give up usufruct rights to a creditor in order to be
able to procure a loan.  A scheme of this kind would restore
a sense of ownership and responsibility to the pledgor, put
money in the hands of the lender, and correct the situation

(Adegboye, Rufus O.)
whereby the owner (and debtor in this case) is being taxed
instead of the user.

10.     Adegeye, A. J.  "Re-examination of issues involved in the
farm settlement scheme of the Western State of Nigeria."
(In OAS, 3:2, 1974.  p. 79-88)

The Farm Settlement Scheme of the Western State of Nigeria
has failed to achieve any of its main objectives:  to provide
employment for school leavers, to arrest rural migration to
towns, to increase agricultural productivity, to demonstrate
modern techniques of farming, and to solve the land tenure
problem.  The last objective was based on false premises,
since insufficient research has been done on the relationship
between agricultural productivity and local land tenure systems.  The author conducted a survey which shows that about
80 percent of the farmers in his sample were owner occupiers
and that only 27 percent had no extra land available.  Both
these findings run counter to commonly held views on land
tenure problems in Nigeria.

11.     Adejuwon, O.  "Agricultural colonization in twentieth century
Western Nigeria."  (In JTG, 33, 1971.  p. 1-8)
                                                Geol MC J83 T74

This paper describes the colonization of the former forest
lands of Western Nigeria during the first half of the twentieth
century, focusing on the Ife division.  The purpose of the
colonization was mainly to acquire land to grow cocoa, and
colonization is largely a completed process.  Villages frequently engage in boundary disputes with their neighbors.

12.     Adeniyi, Eniola Oloruntobi.  "Land tenure and agricultural
development in Nupeland."  (In NGJ, 15:1, 1972.  p. 49-57)
                                                Mem AP N687 G245
Also available as Reprint no. 78.  Ibadan, Nigerian Institute
of Social and Economic Research, 1972. (9) p.  Files Nig 58 A24

Land tenure systems in Nupeland can be conveniently divided
into two categories:  communal ownership of land, with the
authority of allocation vested in the village head; and fief-
holds or individual family ownership of land.  The latter is
gradually leading to the development of a class of absentee
landlords and a landless proletariat at the other end of the
scale.  Communal ownership also has its disadvantages, namely
a severe restriction of labor mobility and insufficient security of tenure to permit long-term investment.

NIG 13-16

13.    Adeniyi, Eniola Oloruntobi.  "Land tenure as a socio-cultural
       factor in rural development in the middle belt of Nigeria."
       (In RURAL DEVELOPMENT IN NIGERIA:  PROCEEDINGS OF THE 1972
       ANNUAL CONFERENCE OF THE NIGERIAN ECONOMIC SOCIETY.  Ibadan,
       Nigerian Economic Society (1973) p. 281-294)      HN 800 N5 R87
       Also available as Reprint no. 81.  Ibadan, Nigerian Institute
       of Social and Economic Research (1973).  (20) p.
                                                    Files Nig 58 A25

       Both of the two main tenure systems of Nupeland, communal
       tenure and fiefholds embodying individual tenure, have advan-
       tages for agricultural development.  The principal disadvan-
       tages, however, are the inability to mortgage land, the
       immobility of rural labor caused by these tenure systems,
       and excessive rents paid to fiefholders.

14.    Akinwolemiwa, J. O.  THE FARM SETTLEMENT SCHEME IN WESTERN
       NIGERIA:  AN ASSESSMENT OF THE PROBLEMS INVOLVED AND EVALUATION
       OF THE RESULTS ACHIEVED TO DATE.  RU:WLR-C/66/27.  Rome, FAO,
       1966.  7 p.  Paper for World Land Reform Conference, Rome,
       1966.                                         Files Nig 17 A44

       A survey of the problems associated with the farm settlement
       scheme begun in Western Nigeria in 1959.  According to the
       author, customary land tenure systems represent one of the
       major obstacles to agricultural development which the scheme
       was meant to overcome.

15.    Alao, J. Alde.  "Relationship between land tenure and adoption
       of agricultural innovations."  Ife, Nigeria (197-).  21 1.
       Bibl.                                          Files Nig 58 A51

       The paper focuses on the interaction effects between land
       and agricultural innovations.  It suggests that changes in
       land tenure practices should be backed by such things as
       supervised credit and effective farmers' cooperatives.

16.    Anthonio, Q. B. O.  "Towards an agrarian reform in Nigeria."
       (In ASN/P, 3, 1964.  p. 20-26)                         Ag Per
       Also available as a separate.                  Files Nig 3 A58

       Labor productivity in Nigerian agriculture is low and the price
       of food is high.  To solve these problems, it is not necessary
       to change existing systems of land tenure, since "communal
       ownership of land is very nearly ideal for the extensive improve-
       ment of agriculture."  What is needed instead is a central
       planning agency for agriculture, the local processing of agri-
       cultural products, an agricultural credit bank, the creation

(Anthonio, Q. B. O.)
of labor-intensive nonagricultural industries in Nigeria, and
programs of research and extension.

17.   Baier, Stephen; and King, David J.  "Drought and development
      of Sahelian economies:  a case study of Hausa-Tuareg inter-
      dependence."  1974.

      See Item NIGER-1 for citation and annotation.

18.   Baldwin, Kenneth David Sutherland.  "Land tenure problems in
      relation to agricultural development in the Northern Region
      of Nigeria."  (In Item AFR-67, p. 65-82)        HD 966 I5 1960

      After a general description of agriculture in the region,
      including information on the average size of holdings and the
      labor requirements of major crops, Baldwin considers the costs
      and benefits of resettlement schemes and cautions that changes
      in land tenure systems alone are not enough to improve the
      productivity of land and labor in agriculture.

19.   _____.  THE NIGER AGRICULTURAL PROJECT; AN EXPERIMENT IN
      AFRICAN DEVELOPMENT.  Cambridge, Mass., Harvard University
      Press, 1957.  xvi, 221 p.                       HD 1516 N4 B2

      An analysis of the failure of the mechanized farming scheme at
      Mokwa.  The problems which arose were largely the result of
      inadequate knowledge about tropical soils, the appropriateness
      of mechanized techniques, and the customary land tenure systems
      of those recruited to be settlers.

20.   Berry, Sara S.  "Cocoa and economic development in Western
      Nigeria."  (In Eicher, Carl K; and Liedholm, Carl, eds.
      GROWTH AND DEVELOPMENT OF THE NIGERIAN ECONOMY.  (East Lansing)
      Michigan State University Press, 1970.  p. 16-29)
                                                        HC 517 N48 E4

      As more and more people became involved in growing cocoa in
      Western Nigeria in the 1930s and 1940s, various organizational
      problems arose which had to be solved by altering established
      systems of economic activity.  Old methods of acquiring labor
      services and land changed, and traditional forms of credit
      were adapted to new conditions.  These changes in the organiza-
      tion of productive activity underline a weakness in the vent-
      for-surplus model of development, the theoretical construct
      most often used to explain historical growth in export produc-
      tion in Nigeria.

# Land Tenure and Agrarian Reform

21.  Berry, Sara S.  MIGRANT FARMERS AND LAND TENURE IN THE NIGERIAN
     COCOA BELT.  Paper no. 79.  Madison, Land Tenure Center, 1972.
     25, (7) 1.                                      Files Nig 15.7 B27

     Migration into Ife by persons seeking land for growing cocoa
     in the 1940s and 1950s led to the development of a system of
     tenancy quite different from the older relationship between
     the head of a lineage or community.  The new system of tenancy
     was more exclusively economic in character and retained fewer
     of the social and personal aspects of the traditional relation-
     ship between lineage head and stranger.

22.  Bohannan, Paul.  "Land use, land tenure, and land reform."
     1964.                                            HC 502 H43

     See Item AFR-22 for citation.  Case studies of the Tiv and
     Yoruba of Nigeria form the basis for Bohannan's argument
     that Africans conceive of relationships between men and land
     as social relationships expressed in spatial terms.  Both Tiv
     and Yoruba allocate rights to use land by virtue of membership
     in descent groups.

23.  _____.  TIV FARM AND SETTLEMENT.  Colonial research studies no.
     15.  London, H.M.S.O., 1954.  New York, Johnson Reprint Corpora-
     tion, 1970.  iv, 87 p.  Bibl.              HD 989 N5 B6 1970

     Chapters seven and eight contain an analysis of rights to land,
     with emphasis on relationships among people arising from
     these rights, not on the jural rights which may be held in
     any particular piece of land.  Among the Tiv, groups may be
     said to hold title to land, but most important rights to land
     are vested in individuals.  Rights may be transferred by in-
     heritance or gift, but not by rental or sale.

24.  Branney, L.  "Registration of title to land in Lagos."  (In
     JAA, 10:3; 1958.  p. 136-143)              Mem AP J83 A258

     An analysis of why registration of title was necessary in
     Lagos at the end of the colonial era:  to solve problems
     created by the survival of an unwritten customary law and the
     uncertain application of nineteenth-century English law, with
     its cumbersome procedures for ascertaining the validity of
     title.

24a. Chambers, Robert.  SETTLEMENT SCHEMES IN TROPICAL AFRICA:  A
     STUDY OF ORGANIZATIONS AND DEVELOPMENT.  (1969).
                                                  HD 1516 A34 C5

     See Item AFR-32 for citation and annotation.

# Land Tenure and Agrarian Reform

25.    Chima, Christopher. ANDERUNGEN DER AGRARSTRUKTUR UND DER
       AGRARVERFASSUNG ALS VORAUSSETZUNG DER ENTWICKLUNG DER
       LANDWIRTSCHAFT IN NIGERIA. Freiburg (Institut für
       Entwicklungspolitik) 1969. 147, (8) p. Bibl. Thesis,
       Albert-Ludwigs Universität, Freiburg im Breisgau.
                                          HD 2130 N5 C34

       After a description of existing systems of land tenure among
       the Hausa, Yoruba, and Ibo, the author examines alternative
       ways of reforming the agrarian structure—large-scale resettle-
       ment schemes, and individualization of tenure through
       legislation. Agriculture can contribute to Nigeria's economic
       development only if extensive change takes place—land reform,
       the integration of crop cultivation and animal husbandry, the
       modernization of techniques, and enlargement of the internal
       market.

26.    Chubb, L. T. IBO LAND TENURE. 2nd ed. Ibadan, Ibadan
       University Press, 1961. vii, 115 p. Bibl.    HD 1265 N63 C38

       Among the Ibo, land is held corporately by patrilineal, exoga-
       mous lineages or lineage segments, and it is allocated
       according to principles of seniority and need. Land may also
       be owned by individuals, in which case it is usually inherited
       by sons. Sale of land to people of the same or neighboring
       villages is common, but sale to outsiders is rare. The
       author recommends the relocation of people from densely popu-
       lated areas, the encouragement of security of tenure by the
       introduction of long-term leaseholds, and various other
       measures.

27.    Coker, George Baptisa Yodola. FAMILY PROPERTY AMONG THE
       YORUBAS. With a foreword by Maxine de Comarmond. London,
       Sweet and Maxwell, 1958. 314 p. Bibl.    Mem HD 990 N5 C6

       This book, intended primarily for lawyers, treats land as the
       most important form of "family property." It traces the
       impact of English law on Nigerian land tenure systems, outlines
       the concepts underlying the notion of family property in
       customary law, and presents a survey of the rules and prin-
       ciples of Yoruba law and custom pertaining to communally held
       property. Tables of statutes, ordinances, and cases cited are
       included.

27a.   Comhaire, J. "Droit foncier et propriété familiale à Lagos."
       (In ISEAC, 166, 1965 (5:9). p. 91-100)         Mem H 31 I53

# LAND TENURE AND AGRARIAN REFORM

28. Consortium for the Study of Nigerian Rural Development.
STRATEGIES AND RECOMMENDATIONS FOR NIGERIAN RURAL DEVELOPMENT,
1969/1985. By Glenn L. Johnson (and others). CSNRD 33.
Lagos, 1969. ii, 158 p.                                   HD 2130 N5 C618

A short section on land tenure (p. 27-30) concludes that programs of land reform are unnecessary. What is required are
policies to facilitate optimal resource use in agriculture. These
would include "more favorable price policies which would raise
the equity value of land, thus making it easier to raise credit
and strengthen the desire of farmers to increase the productivity of land from available but currently largely unused
technologies and management practices."

29. Dennett, Richard E. NIGERIAN STUDIES, OR, THE RELIGIOUS AND
POLITICAL SYSTEMS OF THE YORUBA. London, Macmillan, 1910.
xiii, 235 p.                                     Mem G764 D41 Cutter

In this early work a short section on land law (p. 195-208)
contains a hypothetical model of the historical evolution of
customary land tenure systems and long quotations from
Yoruba informants describing customary land law.

30. Dennison, E. B. "The Possible effects of changes in land
tenure on farming and soil fertility in Northern Nigeria."
(In EJEA, 28:110, 1960. p. 94-98)                          Ag Per

Briefly describes the prevailing systems of land tenure in
Northern Nigeria and discusses their advantages and disadvantages in relation to the level of husbandry and soil fertility.
Concludes that the trend from communal ownership, through
tenancy, towards freehold possession is, on the whole, beneficial in spite of the concomitant tendency towards
fragmentation.

31. Eicher, Carl K. "The Dynamics of long-term agricultural
development in Nigeria." (In Eicher, Carl K.; and Liedholm,
Carl, eds. GROWTH AND DEVELOPMENT OF THE NIGERIAN ECONOMY.
(East Lansing) Michigan State University Press, 1970. p. 6-
15)                                              HC 517 N48 E4

"The long-term growth process of Nigeria has been aided by
the complementarity between government infrastructure
development. . . and private investment by millions of small
Nigerian bush farmers." The colonial government acted with
foresight in developing a land policy which prevented the
formation of an enclave of foreign investors in agriculture
and which induced investment by small farmers. See Item
NIG-109 for a discussion of this article.

156

# LAND TENURE AND AGRARIAN REFORM

32.  Elias, Taslim Olawale. NIGERIAN LAND LAW. 4th ed. London,
     Sweet and Maxwell, 1971. xxix, 393 p.
                              Law S.Af. Nig. 16 PROP ELI 4r 1971

     A comprehensive survey of Nigerian land law for lawyers.
     Following chapters presenting historical background and general
     descriptions of customary systems of land tenure are chapters
     on alienation of land, servitudes and easements, inheritance,
     the law of landlord and tenant, and the registration of title.
     The general conclusion is that land law remains subject to
     institutions of group or family ownership, but that individ-
     ualization of tenure is occurring, especially where rapid
     economic change is taking place.

33.  _____. PUBLIC ACQUISITION OF LAND. Ibadan, International
     Institute of Tropical Agriculture, 1972. 15 l. Paper deliv-
     ered at an international seminar sponsored by IITA, Ford
     Foundation, and IRAT, University of Ibadan, 1972.
                                              Files Nig 76 E54

     By making extensive references to Nigeria's land laws and
     benchmark judicial decisions, Elias discusses the modes of
     acquisition of land for the public purpose, the definition of
     "public purpose" in the law, assessment of compensation,
     procedures for payment outlined in the law, and the question
     of to whom payment should be made in the event of communal
     ownership.

34.  Eri, Ali Umaru. "A problem of land ownership in Nigeria."
     (In LIS, 4, 1970. p. 49-53)         Files Nig 60 L19

     Relying heavily on Item AFR-83, this brief article focuses on
     the British claim to land in Nigeria by virtue of conquest.

35.  Essang, S. M. "Effects of land tenure on labor mobility and
     employment." n.p., 1972. 24 l. Paper presented at the
     International Seminar on Aspects of Land Tenure in Tropical
     Africa, University of Ibadan, 1972.      Files Nig 58 E77

     The main conclusion here is that existing patterns of land
     tenure in Nigeria should not be singled out as the crucial
     variables in attempts to explain problems associated with
     inadequate land utilization and the failure of the agricul-
     tural sector to generate growing opportunities for employment.

36.  Fabiyi, Yakub Layiwola. "Land tenure innovations in rural
     development: the problems in Western Nigeria with some
     Tanzanian comparisons." Madison, 1974. xi, 287 p. Ph. D.
     dissertation, University of Wisconsin.    Thesis HD 986 F12

# Land Tenure and Agrarian Reform

(Fabiyi, Yakub Layiwola)
One major objective of this study is to identify points of
innovation and change in the customary land tenure system
which can serve as foci for the modernization of traditional
agriculture. On the basis of the evaluation of information
collected in field research in Western Nigeria, the author
proposes the introduction of family- or lineage-based producer
cooperatives. See Item TANZ-19 for additional annotation.

37.  Famoriyo, Segun. "Land tenure institution and food production:
an analytical exposition." n.p., n.d. 24 l. Bibl. Paper
prepared for the First Conference of West African Association
of Agricultural Economists, University of Ibadan, 1972.
                                                    Files Nig 58 F15

The author argues that the exigencies of agricultural development require that the government guide the direction of development of the market in land rights, provide for the
registration of title, regulate landlord-tenant relationships,
integrate and rationalize land law, and promote the mobility
of rural labor.

38.  _____. "Land transactions and agricultural development in
Nigeria." (In EAJRD, 7:1/2, 1974.  p. 177-188)        Ag Per

The author advocates various governmental measures to control
land transactions:  in the north, the projected development
of large-scale farming necessitates measures for fully compensating farmers whose land is expropriated; in the south,
registration of all rights in land should be made compulsory;
and all land transactions should go to land committees for
thorough examination in the light of the needs of economic
development.

39.  _____. "A Panorama on aspects of the agrarian structure."
n.p., 1973.  10 p.  A paper given at the Joint NISER/Depart-
ment of Economics Seminar, 1973.          Files Afr 3 F15

Includes general overview of the agrarian structure, defined
as the institutional framework within which agricultural
production takes place.  The author divides this structure
into four principal segments, one of which is the land tenure
system.  In Nigeria efforts are being directed at understanding and gradually changing backward elements in each segment
of the agrarian structure rather that carrying out a sweeping
program of agrarian reform.

# Land Tenure and Agrarian Reform

40. _____. "Some crucial issues in the land tenure system: bases for an agricultural land tenure policy in Nigeria." n.p., 1972. 22 p.                                    Files Nig 57.4 F15

    Argues that the institutional framework provided by customary land tenure systems is outmoded and that the government should take an active role in providing a new structure. Land tenure policy should begin with comprehensive research and should include registration of title, rationalization of land law, and the regulation of tenancy relationships.

41. Field, J. O. "Sale of land in the Ibo community, Nigeria." (In MAN, 45:47, 1945.  p. 70-71)                Mem AP M266

    Farmland could be sold to strangers, in which case the land became an individual holding for all practical purposes. The interest of the owner in his land is more than a heritable usufruct, "for he may alienate it temporarily by letting it out at a rental or by pledging it."

42. Floyd, Barry. "Terrace agriculture in Eastern Nigeria:  the case of Maku." (In NGJ, 7:2, 1964.  p. 91-108)
                                                    Mem AP N687 G245
    Also available as a separate.                   Files Nig 24 F56

    A detailed study of terrace agriculture in a small area of Eastern Nigeria, with an overview of the distribution of the practice in Nigeria and throughout Africa.  In Maku land rights are vested in individuals, permitting farmers to undertake and maintain terracing, a form of permanent investment to improve the productivity of the land.

43. Floyd, Barry; and Adinde, Monica. "Farm settlements in Eastern Nigeria:  a geographical appraisal." (In EGEOG, 43:3, 1967.  p. 189-230)                              Ag Per

    An article presenting farm settlements in Eastern Nigeria in an extremely favorable light.  The analysis is marred by a simplistic view of customary land tenure and land use systems which exaggerates their potential to harm the environment and natural resource base and overlooks the historical record of adaptation and change on the part of smallholders reacting to economic opportunity and incentive.

44. Food and Agriculture Organization. "Land tenure and related social problems." (In Its AGRICULTURAL DEVELOPMENT IN NIGERIA; 1965-1980. Rome, 1966.  p. 331-347)              Ag Docs

NIG 44-48

(Food and Agriculture Organization)
A brief description of customary land tenure systems is followed by recommendations for change, including the establishment of a national commission on land policy, experimentation
with pilot schemes designed to test the viability of various
approaches to altering existing tenure systems, and a call for
further research.

45. Forde, Daryll. "Land and labour in a cross river village."
(In GJL, 90:1, 1937. p. 24-59)           Geol MC G273 J82

A socio-economic study of the village of Umor, where the
patrilineal kinship group called kepun allocates land for use
by its members. If a man's own kin group is short of land, he
may obtain land to use from another group. The land is made
productive principally by an investment of labor to clear the
very dense vegetation.

46. Gleave, M. B. "The Changing frontiers of settlement in the
uplands of Northern Nigeria." (In NGJ, 8:2, 1965. p. 127-141)
Mem AP N687 G245

In the precolonial era raiding and warfare pushed settlement
in many areas of Nigeria's Middle Belt to hill and hill-top
sites. Examination of local sites in Zaria Province reveals
that the frontier of settlement reversed direction in the
late colonial period, with whole villages relocating in the
plains below the hills. The impetus came partially from a
government-sponsored resettlement scheme, but scattered ham-
lets and isolated homesteads have grown up not far from
officially designated resettlement areas, in marked contrast
to the highly nucleated settlement of the hill-top sites.

47. Goddard, A. D. "Changing family structures among the rural
Hausa." (In A/IAI, 43:3, 1973. p. 207-218)

48. _____. "Land tenure, land holding and agricultural develop-
ment in the Central Sokoto close-settled zone, Nigeria." (In
SAV, 1:1, 1972. p. 29-41)                  Mem AP S265
Also available as a separate.             Files Nig 58 G62

A survey of land tenure in three villages shows that communal
rights to land are giving way to rights vested in nuclear
families and individuals. Two factors important in this
change are Islamic law, which recognizes individual tenure,
and population pressure. Laws of inheritance encourage fragmentation of holdings, but with capital a farmer may increase
the size of his holdings by purchase or consolidate fragmented
holdings.

LAND TENURE AND AGRARIAN REFORM

NIG 49-53

49.    Goddard, A. D.; Fine, J. C.; and Norman, D. W.  A SOCIO-
ECONOMIC STUDY OF THREE VILLAGES IN THE SOKOTO CLOSE-SETTLED
ZONE.  Samaru miscellaneous papers, nos. 33 and 34.  Zaria,
Nigeria, Ahmadu Bello University, Institute for Agricultural
Research, 1971.  2 v.                         Files Nig 81.9 G62

A section on land tenure in the villages studied concludes
that farmers have a large degree of security of tenure, that
land has become a transferable economic commodity, and that
tenurial rights approach those of freeholders in practice if
not in law.  But the tenure system does inhibit agricultural
development in two important ways:  land cannot be used as
collateral for loans, and inheritance laws encourage the subdivision of plots.

50.    Gosselin, G.  DEVELOPPEMENT ET TRADITION DANS LES SOCIETES
RURALES AFRICAINES.  1970.                        HN 773.5 G67

See Item AFR-60 for citation and annotation.

51.    Great Britain.  MINUTES OF EVIDENCE AND APPENDICES.  Cmd. 5103.
London, 1910.  140 p.  (In Great Britain.  Parliament.  House
of Commons.  HOUSE OF COMMONS ACCOUNTS AND PAPERS, 44, 1910)
                                                      Mem Docs

Reports of governors of Northern Nigeria and minutes of evidence presented to the Northern Nigerian Lands Committee.  See
Item NIG-52 for the report of the Committee.

52.    _____.  REPORT OF THE NORTHERN NIGERIA LANDS COMMITTEE.
Cmd.  5102.  London, 1910.  (31) p.  (In Great Britain.
Parliament.  House of Commons.  HOUSE OF COMMONS ACCOUNTS AND
PAPERS, 44, 1910)                                 Mem Docs

The report recommends that all land in Northern Nigeria be
placed under the control and dominion of the government in
order to facilitate the collection of a land tax, and that no
title to use, occupation, or enjoyment of land be valid without the assent of the government.

53.    Grossman, David.  "Migratory tenant farming in northern
Iboland in relation to resource use."  New York, 1968.  xii,
379 1.  Ph. D. dissertation, Columbia University, 1968.  Photocopy.  Ann Arbor, Mich., University Microfilms, 1973.
                                            HD 1511 N62 I23

A thesis on migrant farmers who grow food crops on land they
rent outside their home area.  They establish temporary camps

161

NIG 53-57

(Grossman, David)
or permanent settlements in their host areas. A chapter on
land tenure (p. 250-294) stresses arrangements permitting
hosts to collect rent from tenant farmers.

54.   _____. "The Roots of the practice of migratory tenant farming: the case of Nikeland in Eastern Nigeria." (In JDA,
1:2, 1972. p. 163-183)

Present-day patterns of migration by tenant farmers resemble
pre-colonial population movements which came about when people from over-populated areas where soil was exhausted sold
members of their family into slavery to purchase grain. The
former slave-owning class in Nikeland, where soils are fertile and population relatively sparse, now derives most of its
income from leasing land to tenants from neighboring areas.

55.   Helleiner, Gerald K. PEASANT AGRICULTURE, GOVERNMENT, AND
ECONOMIC GROWTH IN NIGERIA. Homewood (Ill.), Irwin, 1966.
xx, 600 p. Bibl.                          HC 517 N48 H43

An historical analysis of Nigeria's economic growth since
1900, emphasizing peasant export agriculture, the structure of
the government, and the influence on economic growth of such
governmental institutions as marketing boards. Land tenure is
discussed briefly along with other characteristics of peasant
agriculture. Tenure is usually communal, but recently there
has been a shift towards individual land ownership and the
assignment of a market value to land. The author argues that
communal land tenure has not restrained the development of
cash crop agriculture but presents no supporting evidence. He
also speculates that the tenure system may become a severe
hindrance to growth in the future. The appendix contains
much useful production data in the form of tables.

56.   Hill, Polly. "Farms and farmers in a Hausa village." (In
her STUDIES IN RURAL CAPITALISM IN WEST AFRICA. African
studies, 2. Cambridge, Eng., Cambridge University Press,
1970. p. 146-159)                          HD 2130 W5 H54

In a rural Hausa village near Katsina, much land is under continuous cultivation and farmland is often sold. For a more
complete discussion, see Item NIG-57.

57.   _____. RURAL HAUSA: A VILLAGE AND A SETTING. Cambridge,
Eng., Cambridge University Press, 1972. xv, 368 p. Bibl.
                                          DT 515.42 H54

(Hill, Polly)
Fourteen chapters analyze the socio-economic affairs of a
single Hausa village near Katsina, while a long alphabetical
glossary gives general background material on rural Hausaland.
The most important finding is that the village is characterized
by marked economic inequality. Chapter six (p. 84-95) examines
interaction between rich and poor farmers in the form of selling and pledging of land. The glossary contains a concise
presentation of the Hausa land tenure system (p. 240-241).
Since land was plentiful in most areas, the payment of taxes
to a chief guaranteed farmers the right to use land, but
chiefs could and did evict farmers for various reasons,
forcing them to emigrate.

58.   Huth, William Powers. "Traditional institutions and land
      tenure as related to agricultural development among the Ibo
      of Eastern Nigeria." Madison, 1969. 520 1. Bibl. Ph. D.
      dissertation, University of Wisconsin.          Mem AWB H949 W716

A thesis applying the theoretical framework elaborated by
John R. Commons for the analysis of the ways in which society
and social groups control individual actions by means of collective action. Includes chapters on Ibo agriculture, Ibo
land tenure, Ibo traditional society, and changes during
colonial rule.

59.   _____. TRADITIONAL INSTITUTIONS AND LAND TENURE AS RELATED TO
      AGRICULTURAL DEVELOPMENT AMONG THE IBO OF EASTERN NIGERIA.
      Research paper no. 36. Madison, Land Tenure Center, 1969. v,
      161 p. Bibl.                                    HD 1265 N6 H88

An abbreviated version of Item NIG-58.

60.   Igbozurike, M. Uzo. "Land tenure relations, social relations,
      and the analysis of spatial discontinuity." n.p., n.d. 8 1.
                                                      Files Nig 58 I31

Proposes a mathematical index for the degree of fragmentation
of land holdings which takes into account the distances between an individual's holdings and the size of the outlying
parcels of land.

61.   Igwe, D. C. "The Need for enclosure and land resettlement in
      Nigerian agriculture." (In TROP, 31:1, 1954. p. 57-68)
                                                      Ag Per

Economic and social change has promoted the individualization
of land tenure in Nigeria just as it did in Tudor England.

LAND TENURE AND AGRARIAN REFORM

NIG 61-66

(Igwe, D. C.)
The author advocates the adoption of a 20-year plan for the
registration of title to land.

62.  Ijaodola, J. O.  "The Creation of states in Nigeria:  an
opportunity for amending the law of land tenure in the former
Northern Region."  (In LIS, 4, 1970.  p. 1-12)
Files Nig 60 L19

An examination of Nigerian and European concepts of property
and sovereignty leads the author to the conclusion that the
land law of the former Northern Region should be applied
throughout the Nigerian federation.

63.  James, Roden William.  "The Changing role of land in Southern
Nigeria."  (In ODU, 1:2, 1965.  p. 3-23)      Mem AP 0271

Economic growth over the past hundred years in Yorubaland has
brought about significant change in land law.  Alienation of
land outside the group which controls its use, once rare, is
now frequent.  Courts have stepped in to protect the rights
of those who invest time and money in enhancing the value of
the land.

64.  _____.  MODERN LAND LAW OF NIGERIA.  Ile-Ife, University of
Ife Press (1973).  lxvi, 285 p.              HD 1169 N6 J15

A handbook on Nigerian land law presented in six parts; introductory material on the basic principles of Nigerian law as
well as an introduction to terminology; a section on customary
land tenure; a section on noncustomary land tenure; a section
on the interaction of these two forms; a section on legal
machinery for enforcing land rights; and a conclusion on land
tenure and development.  This final section contends that the
government has not provided an adequate legal framework for
the settlement of disputes over land and the enforcement of
statutory law, and that time lost in disputes and uncertain-
ties over land rights impedes development.

65.  James, Roden William; and Kasunmu, A. B.  ALIENATION OF FAMILY
PROPERTY IN SOUTHERN NIGERIA.  Ibadan, Ibadan University Press,
1966.  xvii, 117 p.                          HD 1186 N6 J15

A handbook for lawyers and jurists on problems associated with
the alienation of family property.

66.  Jones, G. I.  "Ibo land tenure."  (In A/IAI, 19:4, 1949.
p. 309-323)                                  Mem AP A257

164

(Jones, G. I.)
Land belonging to groups of villages, the landholding unit in
Iboland, is divided into farmland and household land. The
village group allocates land and controls its use and transfer. Formerly few restrictions were placed on the transfer
and sale of land, but population pressure on land has resulted
in an interdiction on sale. The land tenure system is not
well suited to present conditions because it prevents agricultural development by inhibiting the movement of people from
overcrowded areas to those where surplus land is available.

67. Kemmis, Ernest L. LAND MANAGEMENT STUDY OF NORTHERN NIGERIA.
(Washington) U.S. Dept. of the Interior, Bureau of Land
Management, 1967. 1 v. (various pagings) Files Nig 57.5 K25

A detailed analysis of the technical and economic aspects of
five existing range management projects. Optimistic cost-
benefit analysis shows these programs in an extremely favorable light.

68. King, David J. "A Critique of approaches to agricultural
development in Western Nigeria." Madison, 1969. 249 1.
Bibl. Ph. D. dissertation, University of Wisconsin.

Mem AWB K53 K249

An analysis of the main features of Nigeria's agricultural
development with special emphasis on the importance of relationships between men and land. Includes historical background. The thesis concludes with a proposal that communities
holding excess land relinquish it to allow for the settlement
of those who previously had no access to land. Local governments would hold title to such land and grant long-term leases
to settlers. Rental payments would be funneled back to the
communities having given up land, in the form of funds to be
used for agricultural development.

69. Kreinin, M. E. "The Introduction of Israel's land settlement
plan to Nigeria." (In JFE, 45:3, 1963. p. 535-546) Ag Per

A discussion of the establishment of farm settlements based
on the model of the Israeli moshav.

70. Kuhn, Johannes. AGRARVERFASSUNG UND LANDWIRTSCHAFTLICHE
SIEDLUNGSPROJEKTE IN NIGERIA. Marburger Schriften zum
Genossenschaftswessen. Reihe B, Veröffentlichung des Instituts
für Genossenschaftswessen in Entwicklungsländern der Phillips-
Universität Marburg (Lahn), Bd. 4. Marburg/Lahn, 1967. 102 p.
Bibl.
Mem HD 981 Z8 N54

(Kuhn, Johannes)
Part one contains a general discussion of land tenure systems
in southern Nigeria and a caution that much further research
is needed before changes in existing systems designed to promote economic development can be recommended. The second part
describes farm settlement projects based on Israeli models.
Despite the drawbacks inherent in capital-intensive production
in a labor-surplus economy, the author feels that these projects represent a promising alternative to customary systems
of land tenure.

71.   THE LAND RESOURCES OF NORTHEAST NIGERIA. P. Tuley, editor.
      Land resource study, no. 9. Tolworth Tower, Eng., Land
      Resources Division, Overseas Development Administration,
      Foreign and Commonwealth Office, 1972. 5 v.   GF 721 N52 L15

A detailed study of the hydrology, climate, geology, topography,
landform, soil, land use, distribution of tsetse, and agricultural potential of the area centering on Maiduguri. Volume
four contains a description of present land use and recommendations for improvements in farming techniques, the livestock
industry, tree cropping, and rural health.

72.   Leake, Hugh Martin. "Further studies in tropical land tenure:
      Nigeria." (In TROP, 15:12, 1938. p. 273-275)      Ag Per

A brief history of the land policy of the British colonial
government.

73.   _____. "Studies in tropical land tenure:  West Africa
      (Nigeria)." (In TROP, 10:2, 1933. p. 48-52)      Ag Per
      Also available in Item AFR-80, p. 30-34.      Files 58 L22

A brief historical description of British colonial land policy
in Lagos. The article points out that the customary law was
neglected and English law was imposed in matters concerning
land tenure.

74.   Lloyd, Peter Cutt. "Some modern developments in Yoruba cus-
      tomary land law." (In JAA, 12:1, 1960. p. 11-20)
                                                Mem AP J83 A258

Customary land law and British law remain separate. The High
Court fails to take cognizance of the mass of case law
enshrined in the records of customary courts, and customary
courts continue to work in almost total ignorance of the principles of English law. The article explores this legal duality by examining the principles of Yoruba land law with

# Land Tenure and Agrarian Reform

(Lloyd, Peter Cutt)
respect to ownership, occupancy, and the settlement of disputes, and by studying the procedures of customary courts and
the manner in which the judges of these courts arrive at
decisions.

75.    ____. YORUBA LAND LAW. London, New York, Published for the
Nigerian Institute of Social and Economic Research, Ibadan, by
The Oxford University Press, 1962. xii, 378 p. Bibl.

Mem HD 1169 N6 L5

This valuable work was written by an anthropologist and based
on field work which included interviewing and reading the
records of the customary courts. The first part of the book
contains a general description of Yoruba customary law, with
background information on the social and political structure
and definitions of legal concepts. The second part examines
regional differences in land law by presenting case studies
of four Yoruba kingdoms. In the final section the author
discusses succession, credit, and the decisions of local
government councils.

76.    Luedtke, Roger Alfred. "Land tenure; a means of modernization
in Western Africa." Madison, 1969. 93 1. Bibl. M. S.
thesis, University of Wisconsin.        Thesis HD 986 N5 L82

A thesis applying the theory of John R. Commons to the problem
of reforming customary land tenure systems in Western Nigeria,
where a dual legal system, in which rules are based on funda-
mentally different precepts, is seen as a major obstacle to
development. Recommends the establishment of a commission
responsible for "the formation and planned evolution of modern
land management."

77.    Lugard, Frederick D. THE DUAL MANDATE IN BRITISH TROPICAL
AFRICA. 1965.                           Mem DT 32.5 L8 1965

See Item AFR-83 for citation. Chapters on land tenure
(p. 280-353) make frequent references to the situation in
northern Nigeria, emphasizing the rights of the colonial
government to land by virtue of the British conquest of the
region.

78.    Luning, H. A. AN AGRO-ECONOMIC SURVEY IN KATSINA PROVINCE.
(Kaduna, Nigeria, Govt. Printer, 1963). v, 154 p.

HD 2130 N4 L8

A thorough and useful study of environment, land use, agricultural techniques, and economic variables in agricultural

(Luning, H. A.)
production, based on surveys conducted in villages near
Katsina. Numerous tables and charts give information on crop
returns, labor requirements, size of holdings, land use,
sources and uses of credit, the volume of trade in foodstuffs,
and similar data. Chapter nine, on land tenure, notes a
tendency to view what was a right of usufruct over land as a
right of freehold, with a concomitant high incidence of purchase, pledge, loan, lease, sharecropping, and sale of land.

79. _____. "The Impact of socio-economic factors on the land
tenure pattern in Northern Nigeria." (In JLAO, 4:3, 1965.
p. 173-182)                                          Mem AP J83 L811

An article on the market for land in Sokoto and Katsina Provinces. A survey revealed that the density of population in an
area and production for export or domestic markets has an
effect on the price of land; that land prices have risen
rapidly; and that the buying and selling of land had been
taking place for thirty years when the article was written.

80. Mabogunje, A. L. "Some comments on land tenure in Egba
division, Western Nigeria." (In A/IAI, 31:3, 1961.
p. 258-269)                                          Mem AP A257

The sale of land near Abeokuta probably began before 1850,
long before exports of locally grown kola and cocoa began to
have an influence on the land tenure system. Two factors
explain this unusual situation. First, the Yoruba wars of
the early nineteenth century swept away customary land tenure
systems, and by 1850 most of the people living near Abeokuta
were immigrants from other Yoruba areas. Second, Egba returning from Sierra Leone, where they had been put ashore after
being freed from slave ships going to the New World, brought
new ideas about transfers of rights in land.

81. MacBride, D. F. H. "Land survey in Kano Emirate." (In AA,
37:146, 1938. p. 75-91)                              Mem AP A258 A256

The Kano close-settled zone, where a dense agricultural population worked defined holdings of limited size, was the only
region in Nigeria where the government taxed the farm, not the
farmer. After a brief historical background, the article
describes the simple methods used to make approximate measure-
ments of land areas--methods later combined with a more
orthodox cadastral survey.

# Land Tenure and Agrarian Reform

82. McDowell, Charles M. "The Breakdown of traditional land tenure in Northern Nigeria." (In International African Seminar. 8th, Haile Sellassie I University, 1966. IDEAS AND PROCEDURES IN AFRICAN CUSTOMARY LAW; STUDIES PRESENTED AND DISCUSSED. Edited by Max Gluckman. London, Published for the International African Institute by the Oxford University Press, 1969. p. 266-279)                Mem DT 23 I55 2/8

    An analysis of the historical foundations of the present land law of the former northern region of Nigeria, presented under the following headings: customary and Islamic law which was in force during the period of Fulani rule, 1804-1903; land law under the British; and the consequences of the land tenure law of 1962.

83. _____. "The Interpretation of the land tenure law of Northern Nigeria." (In JAL, 14:3, 1970. p. 155-177)        Law Per
    Also available as a separate.            Files Nig 58 M11

    An analysis of the land tenure law of 1962. McDowell argues that the courts ought not to rely on analogies between local situations and those covered by the English law of landlord and tenant, but should interpret the law in terms of its own language, seen against the background of the context of Nigerian law and custom.

84. _____. AN INTRODUCTION TO THE PROBLEMS OF OWNERSHIP OF LAND IN NORTHERN NIGERIA. Zaria, Institute of Administration in cooperation with the Graduate School of Public and International Affairs, University of Pittsburgh, and USAID, 1966. 35 p.                Files Nig 58 M12

    This is an expanded and slightly modified version of the presentation in Item NIG-82.

85. Mair, Lucy P. "Agrarian policy in British African colonies." 1951.                Ag HD 965 L3

    See Item AFR-86 for citation and annotation.

86. _____ "Native rights in land in the British African territories." 1951.                Ag HD 965 L3

    See Item AFR-87 for citation and annotation.

87. Meek, Charles Kingsley. LAND TENURE AND LAND ADMINISTRATION IN NIGERIA AND THE CAMEROONS. 1957.        Mem JV 33 G7 A48/22

# Land Tenure and Agrarian Reform

(Meek, Charles Kingsley)
See Item CAM-11 for citation. A comprehensive survey including historical background and chapters on land law in Southern
Nigeria, Northern Nigeria, and the colony of Lagos. The work
also contains chapters on customary tenure, the inheritance
of land rights, pledging, mortgaging, lease, sale, land registration, rights over tree crops, and rights to urban land.
The Cameroons referred to are the old British Cameroons which
became partly Nigeria and partly Cameroon.

88. _____. "Nigeria." 1949. (In Item AFR-91, p. 145-164)
                                                    HD 599 Z4 M4

A presentation of the main features of Nigerian customary
tenure systems with a supplementary note on the Land and
Native Rights Ordinance of Northern Nigeria.

89. Mifsud, Frank M. CUSTOMARY LAND LAW IN AFRICA, WITH REFER-
ENCE TO LEGISLATION AIMED AT ADJUSTING CUSTOMARY TENURES TO
THE NEEDS OF DEVELOPMENT. 1967.             HD 1169 A3 M5

See Item AFR-93 for citation and annotation.

90. Mortimore, M. J.; and Wilson, J. LAND AND PEOPLE IN THE KANO
CLOSE-SETTLED ZONE. A report to the Greater Kano Planning
Authority. Occasional paper no. 1. (Zaria) Ahmadu Bello
University, Dept. of Geography, 1965. vii, 120 p. Bibl.
                                            Files Nig 78 M67

Geographers analyze a region where most of the land is under
continuous cultivation. In a short section on land tenure
(p. 10-12), the authors report that land rights are vested in
individuals to a greater extent than in southern Nigeria,
that the breakdown of communal tenure has been accelerated by
commercial influences, that land is often bought and sold,
and that the fragmentation of holdings at the death of the
owner or user is counterbalanced by the consolidation of
holdings occurring as wealthy farmers buy additional land.

91. Nadel, Siegfried F. A BLACK BYZANTIUM, THE KINGDOM OF NUPE
IN NIGERIA. London, New York, published for the International
Institute of African Languages and Cultures by the Oxford
University Press, 1942. xiv, 420 p. Bibl.    Mem DT 515 N27

This excellent ethnographic work devotes most of a chapter
(p. 181-201) to a description of Nupe land tenure systems.
The author combines five methods of land acquisition into
two main categories: (1) acquisition by virtue of membership

170

(Nadel, Siegfried F.)
in a group, and (2) acquisition of land by virtue of a contract between individual land owners.

92. Netting, Robert McC.  HILL FARMERS OF NIGERIA; CULTURAL
ECOLOGY OF THE KOFYAR OF THE JOS PLATEAU.  American Ethno-
logical Society, Monograph 46.  Seattle, University of Washington Press (1968).  259 p.  Bibl.           GN 653 N28

An ethnographic study of the Kofyar with a brief discussion
of a land tenure system which is uncommon in sub-Saharan
Africa.  Most important rights to land inhere in individuals
rather than kinship groups or official personages, though no
permanent alienation of land is possible without the permis-
sion of the owner's lineage.  Rights to land are concentrated
in the individual by virtue of his investment of labor to
make the soil productive.

93. Nigeria.  Cocoa Marketing Board.  NIGERIAN COCOA FARMERS:  AN
ECONOMIC SURVEY OF YORUBA COCOA FARMING FAMILIES.  By
R. Galletti; K. D. S. Baldwin; and I. O. Dina.  Westport, Conn.,
Greenwood Press (1972).  xxxix, 744 p.  Bibl.  Reprint of 1956
edition.                                  SB 268 N6 A46 1972

An important conclusion of the section on land rights
(p. 107-131) is that "old systems of land rights . . . are
being modified into forms more suited to a commercial agriculture."  Farmers who intend to plant cocoa often have to go
somewhere where they are strangers to find vacant land.  They
are willing to pay for the privilege of making a profitable
investment, and payments to the group owning the land, whatever they are called, are equivalent to annual rents and
purchase prices.

94. Nwabara, Samuel Nwankwo.  "Ibo land:  a study in British
penetration and the problem of administration, 1860-1930."
Evanston, Ill., 1965.  ix, 277 l.  Bibl.  Ph. D. dissertation,
Northwestern University.  Photocopy.  Ann Arbor, Mich.,
University Microfilms, 1973.              DT 515.7 N91

A section on land tenure (p. 206-218) describes Ibo systems of
land tenure, ways in which rights in land could be transferred,
and legislation considered by the British.  The conclusion is
that the impact of the colonial government on land tenure was
very slight, since the British respected pre-existing forms
of individual, family, and communal ownership.

95.    Nwabueze, B. O.  "Reform of land tenure:  economic development
       and the reform of the land law."  1972.  (In Item AFR-75, 5.4.
       16 p.)                                        Files Afr 57.4 L15

       The author advocates the registration of title to land in
       Nigeria and reviews steps taken to institutionalize this
       process, noting the proposals of the Lloyd Commission, the
       Simpson Report for Lagos, and the provisions of the Registered
       Land Act of 1965.  He doubts that a policy of nationalizing
       land and granting use rights to farmers would promote economic
       development.  Includes a commentary by P. J. Wakelin.

96.    Obi, Samuel N. C.  IBO LAW OF PROPERTY.  London, Butterworths,
       1963.  239 p.  Bibl.                             Mem K 0.1 0125

       An excellent, detailed description of Ibo law and custom on
       personal property, viewed in the context of the social, eco-
       nomic, and political organization of Ibo society.  In a chap-
       ter on land tenure (p. 35-67), Obi examines the rights and
       interests in land vested in village groups, villages, local
       patrilineages, extended families, and individuals.  In follow-
       ing chapters he examines rules governing inheritance and
       other transfers of land and other forms of property.

97.    _____.  "Women's property and succession thereto in modern
       Ibo law."  (In JAL, 6:1, 1962.  p. 2-18)                Law Per

       A discussion of rights to land among matrilineal Ibo-speaking
       peoples.  Women's rights to land are classified as direct,
       meaning independent of their status as wives or wards, and
       derivative, meaning linked to their social and legal status
       as dependents.  Land acquired by a married woman is inherited
       in the following order of priority:  sons jointly or eldest
       son exclusively, husband, husband's sons by other wives,
       husband's brothers, or the nearest male relative.

98.    Ojo, G. J. A.  "The Changing patterns of traditional group
       farming in Ekiti, North Eastern Yoruba country."  (In NGJ,
       6:1, 1963.  p. 31-38)                          Mem AP N687 G245

       The northeastern Yoruba sometimes organized farming in large
       groups:  patrilineal kinship groups who worked together as a
       team throughout the farming season; farmers' mutual aid
       societies who traded labor services; and work parties whose
       labor was reimbursed at the end of the day by entertainment,
       food, and drink paid for by the person who benefited from the
       labor.  Such practices are on the wane, largely because of the
       growing importance of cash crops.

99.  Okediji, Oladejo O.  "Motivating youths to settle in rural
     areas."  (In IBADAN, 27, 1969.  p. 13-21)        Mem AP I117

     The author examines various reasons for dissatisfaction among
     participants in farm settlement schemes in the former Western
     Region.  He suggests that political pressure on those respon-
     sible for the management of the schemes prevents them from
     running them as profitable projects.

100.  _____.  "Some socio-cultural problems in the Western Nigeria
     land settlement scheme."  (In DD, 5:1, 1967.  p. 101-108)

     Chief among the reasons for settlers leaving the Ilora Farm
     Settlement are tensions between young and old, insufficient
     training, clashes between managers and settlers, a system of
     mandatory savings which is manipulated to discipline settlers,
     and the fact that settlers feel isolated from the urban roots
     of Yoruba culture.

101.  Olatunbosun, Dupe.  "Nigerian farm settlements and school
     leavers' farms--profitability, resource use and social-
     psychological considerations."  East Lansing, 1967.  303 p.
     Ph. D. dissertation, Michigan State University.  Microfilm.
     Ann Arbor, Mich., University Microfilms, 1968.       Microfilm

     This study analyzes the socio-psychological characteristics of
     farmers participating in farm settlement schemes and school-
     leaver farms, computes the rate of return on farmers' invest-
     ments under different technical and price assumptions for a
     33-year cycle, and recommends that the expansion of farm
     settlement schemes be halted until further research on the
     economics of food crop production and alternative forms of
     organization of production--especially projects to improve
     smallholder agriculture--can be conducted.

102.  Oluwasanmi, H. A.  AGRICULTURE AND NIGERIAN ECONOMIC DEVELOP-
     MENT.  (Ibadan)  Oxford University Press, 1966.  240 p.
                                                   HD 2130 N5 O42

     Chapters 3 and 4 (p. 22-57) pertain to land tenure.  A general
     discussion is followed by presentations on land tenure and
     the role of the central government in land administration in
     Northern and Southern Nigeria.  The fourth chapter underlines
     the importance of investment in agriculture and analyzes the
     prospects for agricultural development under existing land
     tenure arrangements.  This approach represents a shift from
     the author's earlier pessimism about the transformation of
     traditional agriculture (see Item NIG-103).

# LAND TENURE AND AGRARIAN REFORM

103. Oluwasanmi, H. A. "Agriculture in a developing economy."
(In JAE, 14:2, 1960. p. 234-241)                    Ag Per

Two approaches to the problem of low productivity in Nigerian
agriculture are possible: improvement of the existing technical framework, meaning a general improvement of the typical
three-acre farm through the use of fertilizer or high yield
seed, or modification of the existing institutional framework,
with particular reference to reform of the land tenure system
and changes in credit institutions.

104. _____. "Land tenure and agricultural improvement in tropical
Africa." (In JFE, 39:3 (Part 1), 1957. p. 731-738)   Ag Per

Concentrating on Nigeria, the author assesses the direction of
change in land tenure systems and land policies. He advocates
the adoption of the policy that nation states assume responsibility in land matters and be vested with authority over
uncultivated land in much the same manner as traditional African authorities disposed of virgin land in the past.

105. Orr, Charles W. J. THE MAKING OF NORTHERN NIGERIA. (2nd ed.).
New York, Barnes and Noble (1965). xxxviii, 306 p.
                                          Mem DT 515 08

The author devotes most of the third chapter to a description
of customary systems of land tenure and historical background
on the government land policy. In a later section (p. 193-
197), he advocates the control of unused land by local government in order to facilitate its distribution to farmers from
overcrowded areas, to prevent land from falling into the hands
of speculators and landlords, and to allow the government to
share in increasing land values by collecting increased taxes.

106. Osidipe, Wole. "Size and nature of estate and interest in
land; a problem of terminology." (In NLQ, 5:1/4, n.d.,
p. 48-58)                                          Law Per
Also available as a separate.          Files Nig 58 074

An article urging members of the legal profession in Nigeria
to stop misusing terminology borrowed from English law. An
analysis of the use of "fee simple" and "leasehold" in Nigerian
land law reveals that these terms do not accurately describe
the situations to which they are usually applied.

107. Park, Andrew E. W. "The Dual system of land tenure: the experience of Southern Nigeria." (In JAL, 9:1, 1965. p. 1-19)
                                                   Law Per

# Land Tenure and Agrarian Reform

(Park, Andrew E. W.)
The author discusses the complexities of land law created by
the joint operation of English and customary law in Nigeria.
He suggests that the duality of the system of land tenure
should be eliminated. Two distinct types of land tenure oper-
ate in Nigeria, since both English law and customary law apply
to the enjoyment and transfer of rights in land. A particular
piece of land may shift back and forth from one type of tenure
to the other with successive owners or in differing situations.
The enactment of legislation to eliminate this legal duality
would eliminate much unnecessary litigation.

108. Parsons, Kenneth H. THE LAND REFORM PROBLEM IN NIGERIA. SR/
LR/C-15. (Washington) USAID, 1970. 43, 3 p. Bibl. Country
paper for Spring Review of Land Reform.

Files Nig 3 P17

Population pressure on land and attempts to modernize agriculture place strain on existing systems of land tenure. Programs
initiated by the government to improve existing systems of
tenure have had little effect. Caution should be exercised
before any additional program of reform is attempted. The best
approach is to allow land law to evolve on its own, in conso-
nance with the English tradition of common law, whereby the
customary rules of the people formed the basis for rules of
law and economic organization.

109. _____. "Specification of the agricultural development process."
(In JFE, 49:5, 1967. p. 1183-1187)                    Ag Per

This discussion of Eicher's paper on agricultural development
(Item NIG-31) criticizes his optimism about the capacity of
agriculture to absorb population increases. Parsons' analysis
relies on a distinction between subsistence and modern sectors
in agriculture and focuses on the land tenure system as a
crucial institutional variable which can be changed to hasten
the transition to modern forms of agricultural production.

110. Perham, Margery. NATIVE ADMINISTRATION IN NIGERIA. London,
New York, Oxford University Press, 1937. xii, 404 p.

Mem DT 515 P45

A chapter on land tenure (p. 304-324) briefly reviews land
legislation in Nigeria and issues raised by the reform of
customary systems of land tenure. The author cautions against
hasty action without a firm basis in knowledge of existing
conditions and the likely consequences of change: "Freehold
tenure, in the hands of a poor and ignorant peasantry, is preg-
nant with the dangers of debt, mortgage, and eviction. . . ."

175

# Land Tenure and Agrarian Reform

111.    Posnett, N. W.; Reilly, P. M.; and Whitfield, P., comps.
        NIGERIA. Land resource bibliography, no. 2. Tolworth Tower,
        Eng., Land Resources Division, Overseas Development Administra-
        tion, Foreign and Commonwealth Office, 1971. 3 v.
                                          REF Z 3553 N5 P67

        Citations are concentrated generally in the environmental
        sciences, agriculture and forestry, with peripheral interest
        in the economic and cultural background of the country. Volume
        1 contains sections on "Agricultural systems," "Cooperatives,"
        "Farm settlement and resettlement schemes." Volume 3 contains
        a section on "Land tenure" (p. 35-37).

112.    Roider, Werner. "Nigerian farm settlement schemes." (In
        International Seminar on Change in Agriculture, University of
        Reading, 1968. CHANGE IN AGRICULTURE. London, Duckworth,
        1970. p. 421-426)                    S 401 I68 1968

        An abbreviated version of the material presented in Item NIG-
        113.

113.    _____. DIE ROLLE DES FARM SETTLEMENTS IN DER ENTWICKLUNG DER
        LANDWIRTSCHAFT WEST-NIGERIAS. Arbeit, D83, nr. 282. Berlin,
        Institut für Ausländische Landwirtschaft, Technischen Universi-
        tät, Berlin, 1969. 1 v. (various pagings)   HD 1516 N4 R64

        An analysis of the economic and social costs and benefits of
        the farm settlement program begun in Western Nigeria in 1959.
        The study is based on surveys and interviews conducted during
        field research in 1965-67. According to the author, the fail-
        ures of the program can all be traced to the heavy burdens
        placed on the relatively young and inexperienced staff assigned
        to plan and follow through on the projects.

114.    Rowling, C. W. LAND TENURE IN IJEBU PROVINCE. Ibadan, Govt.
        Printer, 1956. 67 p.                    Mem HD 990 N5 R6

        An examination of land tenure systems in this Yoruba province
        beginning with a categorization of land: state land, title
        land, common land, village land, quarter land, ebi (patrilin-
        eage) land, land held by a branch of an ebi, and individually
        owned land. The alienation of land and rights to tree crops
        are also discussed in detail. Includes long section (p. 36-50)
        on inheritance of rights to land in Ijebu.

114a.   Sertorio, Guido. STRUTTURA SOCIALE POLITICA E ORDINAMENTO
        FONDIARIO YORUBA DALL'EPOCA TRADIZIONALE ALL'ODIERNA. Como,
        P. Cairoli (1967). 572 p.               Mem DT 513 S4

LAND TENURE AND AGRARIAN REFORM

115. Smock, David R. AGRICULTURAL DEVELOPMENT AND COMMUNITY
PLANTATIONS IN EASTERN NIGERIA. Lagos, Rural Development
Project, Ford Foundation, 1965. ii, 63 1.    Files Nig 4 S56

The report combines four papers dealing with different aspects
of the "community plantation." One of the papers found conflicting advice given to the villagers by the Rural Development Officers and the Cooperative Officers. Part 3 describes
land tenure systems in Eastern Nigeria and points out that
fragmentation, difficulties involved in the acquisition of new
land, and the absence of registration and titles to land are
all barriers to agricultural development. Part 4 describes
the establishment of community plantations, where members of
producer cooperatives work consolidated holdings.

116. _____. "The Role of anthropology in a Western Nigerian
resettlement project." 1969. (In Item AFR-25, p. 40-47)
HD 2117 B7

The author directed a resettlement project undertaken jointly
by the Ford Foundation and the government of Western Nigeria.
He argues that the anthropologist's skills are an important
ingredient in the total pool of skills necessary for the
successful planning of resettlement projects.

117. Smock, David R.; and Smock, Audrey C. CULTURAL AND POLITICAL
ASPECTS OF RURAL TRANSFORMATION: A CASE STUDY OF EASTERN NIGERIA.
New York, Praeger Publishers (1972). xvii, 387 p.  HN 800 N52 S6

In this comprehensive and carefully presented study of rural
development in the former Eastern Region, a chapter on land
tenure (p. 147-155) argues that the government should take
an active role in promoting changes in existing tenure systems.
Among the drawbacks to such systems are the following: the
unwillingness of villagers to lease or pledge land to outsiders, the refusal of communities to allow individuals to
plant tree crops on communally owned land, and the way in
which the system of inheritance contributes to the fragmentation of land into tiny, scattered parcels which are difficult
to farm efficiently.

118. Temple, Charles L. NATIVE RACES AND THEIR RULERS: SKETCHES
OF OFFICIAL LIFE AND ADMINISTRATIVE PROBLEMS IN NIGERIA.
Cape Town, Argus Printing and Publishing Co., 1918. xi, 252 p.
Mem DT 515 T4

According to Temple, the arrival of the British probably
hastened the evolution of freehold tenure in the emirates of

# Land Tenure and Agrarian Reform

(Temple, Charles L.)
northern Nigeria by abolishing the military obligations of
farmers to chief and of chief to emir.  With these "feudal"
relationships out of the way, economic forces were seen as
likely to take over.  Temple questions whether the evolution
of freehold tenure under the pressure of economic forces
should be encouraged by administrative measures, using an
argument frequently heard in 1918 which is racist in essence:
the "mental condition" of African farmers is such that they
are likely to lose their land and a class of landlords will
emerge.

119.    Uchendu, Victor C.  "Livestock tenancy among Igbo of southern
        Nigeria."  (In AFS, 23:2, 1964.  p. 89-94)    Mem AP A258 S933

        The Igbo "contract of agistment," defined as an agreement
        according to which the owner of animals gives them to another
        person to tend or nurture, is the basis for a discussion of
        the nature of contracts in nonliterate societies--an issue of
        central importance in the study of land tenure systems in
        Africa.

120.    Udo, R. K.  "Characteristics of migrant tenant farmers of
        Nigeria."  (In NGJ, 14:2, 1971.  p. 121-140)  Mem AP N687 G245

        The survey examines patterns of migration, the age and sex
        composition of the migrant population, their occupations, and
        their reasons for migrating.  Includes survey data and a map
        of migration patterns.

121.    _____.  "Disintegration of nucleated settlement in Eastern
        Nigeria."  (In GR, 55:1, 1965.  p. 53-67)    Geol MC G273 R32

        Where individual tenure has displaced communal control over
        land, the dispersed household is the predominant pattern of
        settlement.  Nucleated settlements are the most common form
        where communal forms of land tenure still prevail.

122.    _____.  "The Migrant tenant farmer of Eastern Nigeria."  (In
        A/IAI, 34:4, 1964.  p. 326-339)                    Mem AP A257
        Also available as a separate.              Files Nig 64 U26

        In eastern Nigeria farmers periodically leave areas of high
        population density (over 800 per square kilometer) and migrate
        to areas of sparse population (less than 100 persons per square
        kilometer).  Migrant farmers rent land from local people; most
        collect palm products, thereby making a substantial contribu-
        tion to the economy of the region, since the palm fruit they
        harvest would otherwise be wasted.

# Land Tenure and Agrarian Reform

123. _____. "Sixty years of plantation agriculture in Southern Nigeria: 1902-1962." (In EGEOG, 41:4, 1965. p. 356-368)

Ag Per

Contends that the prejudice of the British colonial administration against the establishment of plantations retarded the economic growth of southern Nigeria. The fear that plantation agriculture would dispossess farmers from the land was groundless. The relatively high crop yields and high quality of produce characteristic of plantation agriculture justify the intensified interest of planners in this mode of production.

124. Vanden Driesen, I. H. "Patterns of land holding and land distribution in the Ife division of Western Nigeria." (In A/IAI, 41:1, 1971. p. 42-53)

The article describes three broad categories of land holding: (a) land owned; (b) land held on permanent lease, and (c) land held on impermanent lease. Data presented in tables show the extent of different types of landholding. Between 1952 and 1968, permanent leases increased at the expense of ownership in the Ife Division. In the future, temporary leases are likely to increase relative to the other two categories because of population pressure on land.

125. Verhelst, Thierry G. MATERIALS ON LAND LAW AND ECONOMIC DEVELOPMENT IN AFRICA. 1968.                       HD 962 V27

See Item AFR-139 for citation and annotation.

126. Whetham, Edith H. COOPERATION, LAND REFORM AND LAND SETTLEMENT. 1968.                       Ag HD 1491 A52 W4

See Item AFR-140 for citation. Sections on Nigeria (p. 43-55) discuss the efforts of the government to improve existing land tenure systems by promoting land settlement schemes and group farms.

127. Willoughby, P. G. "Land registration in Nigeria: past, present and future." (In NLJ, 1:2, 1965. p. 260-283)    Law Per

The Registered Land Act of 1965 introduced a new system for the registration of title to land in the Federal Territory of Lagos. The article presents a history of legislation on land registration in Nigeria, examines the main provisions of the 1965 Act, and discusses how the principles of the Act could be applied to Nigeria as a whole.

# LAND TENURE AND AGRARIAN REFORM

128.    Woodman, Gordon R.  "Acquiescence in English law and the
        customary land law of Ghana and Nigeria."  1971.
                                              Files Afr 59 W66

        See Item GHA-60 for citation and annotation.


## RHODESIA


1.    Brown, Ken.  LAND IN SOUTHERN RHODESIA.  Foreword by Clyde
      Sanger.  (London)  Africa Bureau, 1959.  32 p.
                                              Mem HD 990 R7 B7

      The present system of land apportionment in Rhodesia is
      disciminatory and unjust.  As a result, the African population
      is suffering great hardship; in the interests of racial har-
      mony and peace, widespread reforms are urgently needed.  The
      author concludes that the Land Husbandry Act officially sanc-
      tions continuous cultivation on soils completely unable to
      support such a practice.

2.    Chambers, Robert.  SETTLEMENT SCHEMES IN TROPICAL AFRICA:  A
      STUDY OF ORGANIZATIONS AND DEVELOPMENT.  (1969)
                                              HD 1516 A34 C5

      See Item AFR-32 for citation and annotation.

3.    Christopher, A. J.  "Recent trends in land tenure in Rhodesia
      1961-70."  (In GEOG/N, 56:3, 1971.  p. 140-144)   Geol MC G287
      Also available as a separate.            Files Rhod 58 C37

      The author contends that the process of dispossession of
      Africans slowed after 1961.  Legislation of 1969 ended the
      period of "unrestricted competition for land between the
      races," but left most good land in the hands of the European
      settlers.

4.    Clarke, D. G.  "Institutional wage-supply determinants of
      plantation labor in postwar Rhodesia."  (In RA, 24, 1974.
      p. 29-47)

      Institutional constraints, including land alienation, land
      segregation, and land tenure policies, have been instrumental
      in fostering a process of displacement of the peasant mode of
      production and the subsidizing of a plantation sector.  Devel-
      opment in the plantation center is thus closely related to
      underdevelopment in the peasant periphery.

# Land Tenure and Agrarian Reform

RHOD 5-8

5.  Dunlop, Harry. THE DEVELOPMENT OF EUROPEAN AGRICULTURE IN
    RHODESIA 1945-1965. Occasional paper no. 5. Salisbury,
    University of Rhodesia, Dept. of Economics, 1971. 73 p.
    Files Rhod 4 D85

    A chapter on land use policies (p. 2-12) points out how land
    apportionment cleared the way for the postwar growth of agri-
    cultural output from European-owned farms. Included is
    material on the size of farms and patterns of ownership; for
    example, about 54 percent of the total European farm area
    was occupied by owners in 1949-1950.

6.  _____. "Land and economic opportunity in Rhodesia." (In
    RJE, 6:1, 1972. p. 1-19)
    Also available as a separate.
    Mem HC 517 R4 R48
    Files Rhod 57.4 D85

    Among the conclusions reached here are the following: a
    settlement that fails to provide for the economic and social
    advancement of the African rural population will prove unwork-
    able; existing apportionment of land between Europeans and
    Africans cannot be justified on the grounds of equality or
    economic and social stability; the opening up for settlement
    of the balance of unused land, much of which is marginal to
    agricultural use, will do nothing to raise incomes; the exist-
    ing conservation policy will be very difficult to sustain in
    the absence of improved farming profitability; the safety
    margin of food supplies in the Tribal Trust Lands has fallen
    to a critical level and creates a real threat of famine.

7.  Floyd, Barry N. "Changing patterns of African land use in
    Southern Rhodesia." (In RLJ, 25, 1959. p. 20-39)
    Mem AP R477

    This analysis of the impact of the Native Land Husbandry Act
    concludes that the individualization of tenure cannot take place
    without a massive exodus of the rural population to towns.
    Instead the author recommends that the Rhodesian government
    encourage group systems of farming of the type which would
    allow mechanization.

8.  _____. "Land apportionment in Southern Rhodesia." (In GR,
    52:4, 1962. p. 566-582)
    Also available in Item AFR-111, p. 225-239.
    Geol MC G273 R32
    HD 969 S8 P7

    Examines the contemporary pattern of the division of land and
    traces its evolution through the so-called "land apportionment"
    legislation of the Rhodesian government.

181

# Land Tenure and Agrarian Reform

9.   Garbett, G. K.  "The Land Husbandry Act of Southern Rhodesia."
     (In Item AFR-67, p. 185-202)                    HD 966 I5 1960

     The Shona once occupied about 500,000 acres of land, but they
     lost a considerable proportion to Europeans.  The Land Appor-
     tionment Act of 1930 granted 50 million acres to Europeans and
     30 million to Africans.  Concern for preserving the productiv-
     ity of overcrowded land provided the impetus for the Land Hus-
     bandry Act of 1951, but the Shona kinship system resists
     outside pressure to arrest the fragmentation of land holdings.

10.  Gray, Richard.  THE TWO NATIONS:  ASPECTS OF THE DEVELOPMENT
     OF RACE RELATIONS IN THE RHODESIAS AND NYASALAND.  1960.
                                            Mem DT 856 G72

     See Item ZAM-8 for citation and annotation.

11.  Hellmeier, Rudolf.  "Ländliche Siedlungsformen und Sozialord-
     nung der Shona in Rhodesien."  (In FESTSCHRIFT L. G. SCHEIDL
     ZUM 60 GEBURTSTAG, 2.  Wien, F. Bergen, 1968.  p. 241-256)
                                            Mem HC 59 F475 2

     This article examines the influence of the Rhodesian government
     on settlement and land use patterns among the Shona.  Two sys-
     tems exist side by side:  dispersed settlement characterized
     by customary land tenure systems and nucleated settlement
     associated with individualized land tenure.  The latter pattern
     is a result of government efforts to concentrate settlement
     and control land use by classifying land into arable, pastoral,
     forest, and waste land.

12.  THE LAND TENURE ACT AND THE CHURCH.  (Gwelo)  Published on be-
     half of the Rhodesia Catholic Bishops' Conference (by) Mambo
     Press, 1970.  56 p.                    Files Rhod 58 L15

     A pamphlet reviewing the fundamental opposition between the
     government of Rhodesia, which committed itself to a policy of
     rural segregation with the Land Tenure Act of 1969, and the
     Catholic Church, which is "committed divinely to a policy of
     non-racial free development."

13.  Langley, Michael.  "Agrarian revolution in Africa."  1962.
                                            Mem AP C7335
     See Item KEN-85 for citation and annotation.

14.  M'tukudzi, Bonet.  "Land tenure in Rhodesia 1961-72."  (Madison)
     1973.  6 l.  Paper for Agricultural Economics 472, University
     of Wisconsin.                          Files Rhod 58 M88

# LAND TENURE AND AGRARIAN REFORM

(M'tukudzi, Bonet)
In 1961 the introduction of a new category of land--unreserved
land with no racial restriction on ownership--promised to
lessen inequalities in land allocation.  Transfer of land to
this category slowed after 1962.  The new policy became a dead
letter in 1969 when the possibility of a settlement with
Britain became remote, so that the need for ties of partnership between the races was no longer pressing.

15.    _____.  "Rhodesia--economic blockade and implications for land
tenure."  (Madison) 1973.  14 1.  Paper for Agricultural
Economics 472, University of Wisconsin.      Files Rhod 30 M88

Land tenure and land segregation policies prevent Rhodesia's
African population from participating in the development process.  The author feels that the policy of economic separation
will gradually become untenable, since the survival of the
country in the face of the blockade depends on the participation of the indigenous population.

16.    Nyoka, Justin V. J.  "Rhodesia's new land tenure act:  more
forced migration of southern Africans."  (In MT, 14, 1970.
p. 25-32)
Also available as a separate.              Files Rhod 58 N96

The Land Tenure Act of 1969 was an outgrowth of the Land
Apportionment Act of 1930, which provided the legal framework
for the dispossession of hundreds of thousands of African
farmers from their land.  The new law made it illegal for
families of African servants of white farmers to remain on
European-owned land or for Europeans to lease or sell land to
Africans.

16a.   Pendered, A.; and von Memerty, W.  "Native Land Husbandry Act
of Southern Rhodesia."  (In JAA, 7:3, 1955.  p. 99-109)
                                               Mem AP J83 A258
Also available as a separate.              Files Rhod 58 P25

16b.   Rhodesia.  Agricultural Land Settlement Board.  REPORT. . .
FOR THE YEAR ENDED 31ST DECEMBER, 1972.  Presented to the
Parliament of Rhodesia.  Salisbury, printed by the Govt.
Printer, 1973.  2 p.                       Files Rhod 17 R36

16c.   _____.  Laws, statutes, etc.  THE LAND APPORTIONMENT ACT,
CHAPTER 257.  Salisbury, Mardon Rhodesian Printers, n.d.,
(100) p.                                   HD 1169 R4 A3

# LAND TENURE AND AGRARIAN REFORM

17. Rhodesia. Laws, statutes, etc. LAND TENURE ACT: NO. 55, 1969. (Salisbury) 1969. (157) p.       Files Rhod 58 R36

    A complete text of legislation classifying land into European, African, and national areas, a division which makes possible the continued exclusion of Africans from the most fertile land.

17a. Rifkind, Malcolm L. "The Politics of land in Rhodesia; a study of land and politics in Southern Rhodesia with special reference to the period 1930-1969." Edinburgh, 1969. 236 p. Bibl. Thesis, University of Edinburgh.     Microfilm

18. Roder, W. "The Division of land resources in Southern Rhodesia." (In AAGA, 54:1, 1964. p. 41-58)     Geol MC A56

    Africans occupied some but not all of the land eventually ceded to European settlers. Africans did not cede the land in accordance with Western concepts of private property, and the land presently occupied by Africans is much less productive than the land used by Europeans. Following the article are commentaries by Robert Oliver, Philip Mason, and Barry Floyd.

19. Sonius, H. W. J. RHODESIA. EIN DILEMMA VAN RAS EN GROND. Leiden, Universitaire Pers, 1966. 100 p.     Mem HD 990 R7 S6

    A discussion of the land problem as complicated by the racial situation and the policies of the Rhodesian government. The colonization, land apportionment, and the Native Land Husbandry Act are discussed. The author concludes that the agrarian problem cannot be solved except through general socio-economic planning based on the premise that all workers (agricultural as well as others) be given equal work opportunity.

20. Verhelst, Thierry G. MATERIALS ON LAND LAW AND ECONOMIC DEVEL-OPMENT IN AFRICA. 1968.     HD 962 V27

    See Item AFR-139 for citation and annotation.

21. Yudelman, Montague. AFRICANS ON THE LAND: ECONOMIC PROBLEMS OF AFRICAN AGRICULTURAL DEVELOPMENT IN SOUTHERN, CENTRAL, AND EAST AFRICA, WITH SPECIAL REFERENCE TO SOUTHERN RHODESIA. 1964.     HD 2130 R6 Y8 1964

    See Item AFR-144 for citation. This book examines the problem of raising the productivity of African agriculture and discusses policies which would foster this development. The principal geographical focus is Rhodesia. The first part of the book examines African and European patterns of landholding and

# LAND TENURE AND AGRARIAN REFORM

(Yudelman, Montague)
agricultural production in the wider region. The second part emphasizes the political, social, and economic factors which have influenced the over-all use of resources in Rhodesia's dual economy. It includes material on land settlement, land apportionment, the creation of African reserves, and on European colonization through 1963. The principal contribution of the chapter on land tenure (p. 107-129) is its critique of the Native Land Husbandry Act, which was designed to force the rate and direction of change through massive intervention allocating individually owned holdings to Africans and fixing theoretical livestock-to-land and man-to-land ratios.

## RWANDA

1. Harroy, J. P.; et Willot, P. FREINAGES ET BLOCAGES S'OPPOSANT A LA REUSSITE DE LA REFORME AGRAIRE DANS LES PAYS EN VOIE DE DEVELOPPEMENT: RWANDA. Bruxelles, Institut International des Civilisations Différentes (1973). 15 1.     Files Rwa 3 H17

In the prefecture of Kibungo in eastern Rwanda, the aristocratic Tutsi, who constitute only a small proportion of the population, held feudal rights over arable land, pasture, and cattle. Even after the political reforms of 1959, development was effectively blocked because the once servile Hutu were unable to benefit from any increases in agricultural production which might occur.

2. Heyse, Théodore. GRANDES LIGNES DU REGIMES DES TERRES DU CONGO BELGE ET DU RUANDI-URUNDI ET LEURS APPLICATIONS (1940-1946). 1947.     Mem DT 641 A27 15/1

See Item BURU-5 for citation and annotation.

3. _____. PROBLEMES FONCIERS ET REGIME DES TERRES (ASPECTS ECONOMIQUES, JURIDIQUES ET SOCIAUX): AFRIQUE, CONGO BELGE, RUANDA-URUNDI. 1960.     Mem Z 7164 L3 H4

See Item AFR-65 for citation and annotation.

4. Lamy, E. "Le Problème foncier au Rwanda." (In RJRB, 2:3, 1962. p. 73-79)
Also available as a separate.     Mem AP R454 J97
                                    Files Rwa 3 L15

RWA 4-8

(Lamy, E.)
The insurrection of November 1959, in the Ruhengeri and
Kisemyi areas was largely the result of Hutu dissatisfaction
with the tenure system imposed by the ruling Tutsi group. The
article briefly reviews legislation of 1960 and 1961 designed
to curb the worst of the abuses.

5.   Leurquin, Philippe P. "Agricultural change in Ruanda-Urundi,
     1945-60." (In FRIS, 4:1, 1963. p. 38-89)
     Also available as a separate.                    Files Afr 4 L28

     A study of land use, cropping patterns, yields, and changing
     factors of production. Land tenure is still in the form of
     fragmented smallholdings, but an increased tendency toward
     private ownership has come into conflict with the traditional
     lord-vassal system of the dominant Tutsi tribe. Population
     pressure on land has led to spontaneous and government-sponsored
     colonization and migration.

6.   Maquet, Jacques. "La Tenure des terres dans l'état Rwanda
     traditionnel." (In CEA, 7:28, 1967. p. 624-626)
                                              Mem AP C132 D1043
     Also available as a separate.            Files Rwa 58 M16

     In the nineteenth century the power of the king to allocate
     rights to use pastoral and arable land permitted the central
     government to collect the considerable revenues necessary to
     maintain a large cadre of functionaries. More recently land
     rights have been a key element in the consolidation of Tutsi
     domination of the subordinate Hutu people. Preceding this
     analysis is a detailed description of the nineteenth-century
     system of royal land administration.

7.   Raeck, H. de. "Le Régime des terres au Congo Belge et au
     Ruanda-Urundi; terres domaniales et terres indigènes, régime
     des cessions et concessions." 1953.          Files Zai 58 R12

     See Item ZAI-33 for citation. Traces the historical evolution
     of the land law of the Belgian Congo from 1885 to 1947. With
     a few rare exceptions, this law applied to Rwanda and Burundi
     as well.

8.   Sebatwaré, André. "L'Evolution du droit foncier coutumier au
     Rwanda." 1970. (In Item AFR-112, p. 1181-1200)

     In the precolonial period all land rights were vested in the
     king. In each province one chief allocated rights to arable
     land and adjudicated conflicting claims, while another chief

# LAND TENURE AND AGRARIAN REFORM

RWA 8-SEN 1

(Sebatwaré, André)
performed the same functions with respect to pastoral rights.
Each province was divided into territorial sub-sections
presided over by sub-chiefs.  The article concludes with a
brief description of modern land law in Rwanda.

9.    Stetkiewicz, L.  "Genèse et devenir d'un terroir sur peuplé
      Kansérégé (Rwanda)."  (In ETR, 37/39, 1970.  p. 257-265)

      A study of the land tenure and land use systems of a village
      in an area of high population density.  Since agriculture is
      no longer capable of supporting all of the villagers, some
      have had to move away.  Because of land shortage most villagers
      are forced to rent land from five to fifteen kilometers away
      from their homes.

10.   Vansina, J.  "Les Régimes fonciers Ruanda et Kuba:  une
      comparaison."  (In Item AFR-67, p. 348-363)      HD 966 I5 1960

      The following variables account for differences between the
      Rwanda and Kuba systems of land tenure:  density of population,
      type of land use, mode of social organization, and political
      structure.  For example, differences in social structure ex-
      plain the contrast between the holding of land by lineages in
      Rwanda and by villages among the Kuba.  Patrilineal descent
      and patrilocal residence promote the formation of extensive
      residential lineages in Rwanda, whereas among the Kuba
      matrilineal descent and virilocal marriages discourage the
      formation of large residential kinship groups.


## SENEGAL

1.    Boutillier, Jean-Louis.  "Les Rapports du système foncier
      Toucouleur et de l'organisation sociale et économique
      traditionnelle--leur évolution actuelle."  (In Item AFR-67,
      p. 116-136)                                      HD 966 I5 1960

      The rules of the land tenure systems along the Senegal valley
      reflect the existence of two kinds of land:  seasonally
      flooded lands of limited extent and high fertility, and the
      upland flanks of the valley which are almost unlimited in
      area but require long periods of bush fallow in order to
      regenerate fertility.  Tenure rules, far more strict for the
      alluvial lands, reflect a long history and recognize rights
      of ownership based on first clearing, rights of cultivation,
      and use rights through the renting of land.  Since it is

SEN 1-5

(Boutillier, Jean-Louis)
virtually impossible to sell land under the customary system,
reform is necessary.

2.   Brochier, Jacques. LA DIFFUSION DE PROGRES TECHNIQUE EN
     MILIEU RURAL SENEGALAIS. Paris, Presses Universitaires de
     France, 1968. 396 p. Bibl.                    HD 2135 S4 B76

     The author evaluates the impact of agricultural extension on
     pre-existing techniques in the arondissement of Thiénaba. He
     concludes that the results of rural modernization projects
     failed to justify the high level of expenditures required.

3.   Chabas, J. "Le Domaine national du Sénégal: réforme foncière
     et agraire." (In DUAA, 1965, p. 33-70)          Mem AP D138

     A survey of the history of Senegalese land law. The law of
     the colonial period relied principally on European procedures
     for the registration of private property and was hostile on
     the traditional indigenous system of usufruct rights on col-
     lectively held lands. The law of 1964 is viewed as a success-
     ful reconciliation between the exigencies of modern development
     and the preservation of customary rights. The law uses the
     concept of "national domain," which sets up the state as the
     sole owner of lands not registered to individuals and thus
     guarantor of usufruct rights.

4.   Curtin, Philip D. ECONOMIC CHANGE IN PRECOLONIAL AFRICA:
     SENEGAMBIA IN THE ERA OF THE SLAVE TRADE. Madison, University
     of Wisconsin Press, 1975. xxix, 363 p.      Mem HC 503 W4 C87

     A section on Senegambian agriculture (p. 13-29) includes
     summaries of the main features of precolonial land tenure sys-
     tems in the regions of Fuuta Toro, Gajaaga, and Bimdu, and
     among the Wolof and Serer.

5.   Diarassouba, Valy-Charles. L'EVOLUTION DES STRUCTURES
     AGRICOLES DU SENEGAL: DESTRUCTURATION ET RESTRUCTURATION DE
     L'ECONOMIE RURALE. Série "Système et structures économiques"
     no. 2. Paris, Editions Cujas, 1968. 298 p. Bibl.
                                                   HD 2135 S4 D4

     The agrarian structure is defined as the interaction of two
     types of complex relationships--between man and nature as in
     the case of the techniques of agricultural production, and
     between man and man as in the case of land tenure systems.
     The topics covered include the customary tenure systems of
     various peoples, the effects of development projects on these

# Land Tenure and Agrarian Reform

(Diarassouba, Valy-Charles)
tenure systems, and the creation of new rural institutions
such as cooperatives.

6.  Diop, Abdoulaye. "L'Evolution de la propriété immobilière au
    Sénégal." 1970. (In Item AFR-112, p. 699-712)

    Land law during the colonial period failed to recognize cus-
    tomary law. For this reason it was poorly suited to the pro-
    motion of economic development. The law of 1964 remedied the
    situation by establishing the government as a guarantor of
    the rights of land use.

7.  _____. "La Tenure foncière en milieu rural Wolof (Sénégal):
    historique et actualité." (In NAF, 118, 1968. p. 48-52)
                                              Mem AP N911 A258

    A brief survey of the evolution of tenure structures among
    the Wolof and the effect of current government land reform
    policies, which make the state the guarantor of usufruct
    rights. The Senegalese land law of 1964 abolished land use
    fees paid to chiefs and vested in the national government
    ownership rights to all land not registered to individuals.

8.  France. Institut National de la Statistique et des Etudes
    Economiques. Service de Coopération. LA MOYENNE VALLEE DU
    SENEGAL: ETUDES SOCIO-ECONOMIQUES. Par Jean-Louis Boutillier,
    et al. Paris, Presses Universitaires de France, 1962. 368 p.
                                              Mem HC 547 S4 F8

9.  Gosselin, G. DEVELOPPEMENT ET TRADITION DANS LES SOCIETES
    RURALES AFRICAINES. 1970.                 HN 773.5 G67

    See Item AFR-60 for citation. A chapter (p. 221-262) presents
    experiences with polyvalent cooperatives and agricultural
    extension services in Sine-Saloum (west-central Senegal).

10. Goundiam, O. "Aspects du régime foncier sénégalais." (In
    CIV, 15:1, 1965. p. 82-90)                Mem AP C5825

    A brief survey of the main characteristics of customary land
    law and an appraisal of the land laws of 1955 and 1961. Con-
    cludes that Senegal is building a coherent body of land law
    solidly based on local economic, political, and social
    structures.

11. Jouhaud, Yves. "La Notion de domaine ou patrimoine collectif
    national dans les nouvelles législations du Sénégal et du

LAND TENURE AND AGRARIAN REFORM

SEN 11-14a

(Jouhaud, Yves)
Cameroun: essai de synthèse entre le droit foncier coutumier
et le droit foncier moderne." 1966.          Mem AP R454 J986

See Item CAM-8 for citation and annotation.

12.   Lericollais, André. "La Détérioration d'un terroir Sob, en
      pays Sérèr (Sénégal)." (In ETR, 37/39, 1970. p. 113-128)

A reconstruction of Serer land use in the past, when animal
husbandry and cultivation complemented each other, permits
the author to assess the impact of population growth, increased use of fertilizers, and the shift to the cultivation
of peanuts and animal-drawn plowing. All of these changes
have interfered with the traditional system of fallow and
crop rotation which maintained soil fertility.

12a.  Le Roy, Etienne. "Le Système contractuel du droit traditionnel
      Wolof (Sénégal)." (In RA, 22, 1973. p. 45-56)

13.   Noble, B. P. "Mémoire sur quelques aspects du régime foncier
      au Sénégal, en Angleterre et en Gambie." (In DUAA, 1965.
      p. 229-249)                              Mem AP D138

The first section of this article compares customary law in
Senegal with English common law and compares these in turn to
land law in Gambia, which was influenced by English law during
the colonial period. A second section takes up the Senegalese
land law of 1964, which transferred the ownership of land to
the state and made it the guarantor of use rights. See Item
GAM-4 for additional annotation.

14.   Pelissier, Paul. LES PAYSANS DU SENEGAL: LES CIVILISATIONS
      AGRAIRES DU CAYOR A LA CASAMANCE. Saint-Yrieix (Haute Vienne)
      Imp. Febrègue, 1966. 941 p. Bibl.          Mem HD 2135 S4 P4

A massive geographical study of land-use patterns and relationships between man and his environment. Emphasis is on agricultural techniques rather than on political, social, or
economic analysis.

14a.  Pheffer, Paul Edward. "Problems of land and labor in colonial
      Senegal: French colonial administrative action before 1930."
      Paper 72-129. n.p., 1972. 23, 6 p. Paper for 15th annual
      meeting, African Studies Association, Philadelphia, 1972.
                                              Files Sen 58 P32

190

LAND TENURE AND AGRARIAN REFORM

15.   Pocthier, G.   "Relationship between land tenure and agricul-
      tural innovations."  n.p., 1972.  11 1.          Files Sen 58 P61

      Efficient use of animal-drawn machinery in the Senegalese
      region of Sine-Saloum required the consolidation of fragmented
      holdings.  This paper reports on an experiment in consolidation
      and calls for more research on the land tenure system so that
      further reform can be undertaken.

16.   Ravault, F.  "Kanel:  l'exode rural dans un village de la
      vallée du Sénégal."  (In COM/B, 17:65, 1964.  p. 58-80)
                                                    Mem AP C132 D108

      Fertile alluvial land is underutilized because of a tenure
      system which excludes some members of the community from
      access to land and places a heavy burden of taxation on others.
      A pattern of seasonal migration has developed, with the people
      of Kanel leaving the village land during the rainy season to
      farm the almost limitless areas on the flanks of the Senegal
      valley.

17.   Reverdy, Jean-Claude.  UNE SOCIETE RURALE AU SENEGAL:  LES
      STRUCTURES FONCIERES FAMILIALES ET VILLAGEOISES DES SERER.
      Aix-en-Provence, Centre Africain des Sciences Humaines
      Appliquées (1967?).  115 p.                    Files Sen 81.9 R29

      One important innovation in the second development plan was a
      heavy emphasis on development projects at the village level.
      Sociologists must provide information on village societies
      and on the interaction of these societies with local-level
      government officials in order to allow central planners to
      work effectively.  A chapter on Serer land tenure (p. 17-39)
      details correspondences between the land tenure system and the
      social hierarchy, ways in which land can be transferred, and
      religious observances associated with land allocation.

18.   Serreau, Jean.  LE DEVELOPPEMENT A LA BASE AU DAHOMEY ET AU
      SENEGAL.  1966.                             Mem HC 547 D3 S4

      See Item DAHOM-11 for citation and annotation.

19.   Snyder, Francis G.  "Land transfers and land reform in
      Senegal."  Preliminary version.  n.p., 1973.  17 1.  Paper
      for 16th annual meeting, African Studies Association.
                                                    Files Sen 58 S59

      National legal reform, particularly the application of the
      Law on the National Domain of 1964, has been minimal outside

SEN 19-22

(Snyder, Francis G.)
the Thiès region. By examining one form of land transfer
among a Diola subgroup in the Casamance, this paper shows
that the question of controlling land transfers is considerably more complex than has been appreciated by the drafters
of Senegal's land reform legislation. At the heart of effective reform is the establishment of adequately functioning
rural councils.

20.   Thomas, Louis V. "Essai sur quelques problèmes relatifs au
régime foncier des Diola de Basse-Casamance (Sénégal)." (In
Item AFR-67, p. 314-330)                    HD 966 I5 1960

Under the pre-existing tenure structure, restricted lineages
were responsible for parceling out land in cooperation with
elders and chiefs. This system was dominated by traditional
religious beliefs, but Islamic influence has produced a
progressive individualization of landholding, fostering the
emergence of testamentary inheritance and patrilineal
succession.

21.   _____. "L'Organisation foncière des Diola (Basse-Casamance)."
(In DUAA, 1960. p. 199-223)                    Mem AP D138

Understanding of land tenure systems in Africa must be based
on interpretive as well as descriptive studies. The author
argues that land tenure systems are total social phenomena,
meaning that they are inextricably interwoven with many
aspects of society and cannot be studied in isolation. The
methodology for the study of tenure systems should include
the analysis of situations of conflict, study of historical
texts, direct observation, and linguistic analysis. The
author applies this theoretical framework and methodology to
a lengthy case study of the Diola.

22.   Verdier, R. "Evolution et réformes foncières de l'Afrique
noire francophone." 1971.                    Files Afr 58 V26

See Item AFR-136 for citation. This paper on the evolution
of land law since independence in francophone Africa includes
a section on the Senegalese land reform of June 17, 1964.
Inspired by the principles of "African Socialism," this
reform aimed to restore the communal aspect of customary
tenure, took all land into the national domain except that
which was held under individual title, and provided for the
creation of local councils to allocate land to farmers and to
oversee the use of the land.

23.   Verhelst, Thierry G.   MATERIALS ON LAND LAW AND ECONOMIC
      DEVELOPMENT IN AFRICA.   1968.                     HD 962 V27

      See Item AFR-139 for citation and annotation.


## SIERRA LEONE


1.    Barrows, Richard L.   "African land reform policies:   the case
      of Sierra Leone."   (In LE, 50:4, 1974.   p. 402-410)

      The individualization of land tenure is likely to be accom-
      panied by loss of economic security for individuals and
      severe distributional impacts with respect to landholding
      and employment.   In formulating land policy, planners in
      countries where customary tenure systems impede agricultural
      development should consider the costs and benefits of alter-
      native tenure systems and compare these policies with other
      means of overcoming development bottlenecks.   The paper gives
      examples of how government subsidies overcame constraints on
      investment in land, thereby surmounting one of the most
      salient defects of the existing land tenure system without
      resorting to radical reform.

2.    _____.   INDIVIDUALIZED LAND TENURE AND AFRICAN AGRICULTURAL
      DEVELOPMENT:   ALTERNATIVES FOR POLICY.   1973.
                                              Files Afr 82.5 B17

      See Item AFR-16 for citation and annotation.

2a.   _____.   "Issues in African land policy:   a case study of
      Sierra Leone."   (Madison) 1973.   18 1.   Paper for annual
      meeting, African Studies Association, Syracuse, 1973.
                                              Files SL 58 B17

      An earlier version of Item SL-1.

3.    _____.   "Land tenure and agricultural development in Sierra
      Leone."   Madison, 1970.   109 1.   Bibl.   M. A. thesis, Univer-
      sity of Wisconsin, 1970.            Mem AWO B2787 R639

      Farmers have little incentive to make productive investments
      in the land because the land tenure system fails to provide
      for security of tenure.   The author believes that individual-
      ization of tenure is not the answer, since the land tenure
      system will respond to changes in the structure of incentives

# LAND TENURE AND AGRARIAN REFORM

SL 3-7

(Barrows, Richard L.)
and opportunities: "If an innovation is profitable to the
small farmer..., then it will be adopted, and furthermore
the land tenure system will adjust to the new situation."

4. Dorjahn, V. R.; and Fyfe, C. "Landlord and stranger; change
in tenancy relations in Sierra Leone." (In JAH, 3:3, 1962.
p. 391-397)                                    Mem AP J83 A262

An historical description of relationships between immigrants
and landlords who grant them rights to farm, hunt, or follow
their trades in return for gifts. The landlord could revoke
the tenant's right to use land after the harvest and he
claimed any buildings or other improvements left behind by
the tenant.

5. Goddard, Thomas N. THE HANDBOOK OF SIERRA LEONE. London,
G. Richards, 1925. xvi, 335 p.                 Mem DT 516 G6

A chapter on land tenure (p. 81-93) describes the principles
underlying patterns of land tenure among the peoples of Sierra
Leone. Includes short sections on slaves' rights to land,
transfers of rights, land administration by chiefs, succession,
and hunting, fishing, and water rights.

6. Jedrej, M. C. "Sociological aspects of mechanical cultivation
in Southern Province, Sierra Leone: an introductory outline."
(Njala, 1967). 9 p.                            Files SL 93.5 J22

An outline of the salient features of the geography, economy,
and social organization in the region of the Sewa River where
the mechanical cultivation of deep water swamp rice takes
place on a large scale. Distinct systems of land tenure apply
to the fertile riverain grasslands and the less fertile uplands. The tenure system on land farmed by producer cooperatives using mechanical cultivation is analogous to the
pre-existing system found in the fertile riverain lands.

7. Johnson, Omotunde Evan George. "Contract costs and the
liability structure for stranger-tenant damages in Sierra
Leone's customary land law: an economic analysis." (In ASR,
17:3, 1974. p. 548-557)

In the Sierra Leone provinces, landlords are liable for
damages caused by their tenants to the property of neighbors.
The author applies economic theory to show that this arrangement minimizes collection costs.

8. _____. "Economic analysis and the structure of land rights
in the Sierra Leone provinces." Los Angeles, 1970. x, 121 1.
Bibl. Ph. D. dissertation, University of California, Los
Angeles. Photocopy. Ann Arbor, Mich., University Microfilms,
1971.                                                  HD 989 S5 J63

The author analyzes the economic costs and benefits of
individualization of tenure, the economic causes of fragmentation, the economic costs of restrictions on the sale of land,
the effects of a legal structure in which contracts are not
easily enforceable, and the economic effects of customs
whereby landlords are liable for tenants' damages.

9. Leake, Hugh Martin. "Studies in tropical land tenure: West
Africa (Sierra Leone)." (In TROP, 10:2, 1933. p. 52-53)
                                                           Ag Per

A brief history of land administration in Sierra Leone under
the British.

10. Little, Kenneth. THE MENDE OF SIERRA LEONE; A WEST AFRICAN
PEOPLE IN TRANSITION. (rev.). London, Routledge & Kegan
Paul (1967). 308 p.                           GN 655 M4 L48

Mende society recognizes two classes of persons in relation to
land and two types of land tenure. The descendants of original
settlers inherit a complete set of rights in land and trans-
mit them to their heirs. The rights of subsequent settlers,
strangers, and the descendants of domestic slaves are limited
to personal occupation and use. The chapter on land tenure
(p. 77-95) also explores leasing, pledging, and inheritance
of land, as well as the control of land exercised by paramount
chiefs and heads of kinship groups.

11. Mair, Lucy P. "Agrarian policy in British African colonies."
1951.                                        Ag HD 965 L3

See Item AFR-86 for citation and annotation.

12. May-Parker, I. I.; and Deen, S. S. "Land tenure and agricultural credit (the Sierra Leone case)." n.p., 1972. 13 1.
Paper prepared for the Seminar on Agricultural Research in
West Africa, "Aspects of land tenure," University of Ibadan,
1972.                                        Files SL 58 M19

An analysis of the flow of credit from institutional sources,
such as banks, and from noninstitutional sources, such as
private money lenders and pledgees, reveals that communal

SL 12-17

(May-Parker, I. I.; and Deen, S. S.)
forms of tenure are not necessarily obstacles to the expansion
of lending for agricultural development.

13.  Meek, Charles Kingsley. "Sierra Leone." 1949. (In Item
     AFR-91, p. 195-200)                               HD 599 Z4 M4

     Concise discussion of the Concessions Ordinance of 1931 and
     the Protectorate Land Ordinance of 1927, and of the indigenous
     system of land tenure, stressing transfer and lending of land.

14.  Njoku, Athanasius Onwusaka. "Labor utilization in traditional
     agriculture: the case of Sierra Leone rice farms." Urbana,
     Ill., 1971. xi, 194 l. Bibl. Ph. D. dissertation, Univer-
     sity of Illinois, Urbana-Champaign. Photocopy. Ann Arbor,
     Mich., University Microfilms, 1972.               HD 2130 S5 N4

     A study of farm wage labor rates, farm labor resources, and
     the structure of the population of Sierra Leone in relation
     to agricultural development. In a section on land tenure
     (p. 25-29), the author advocates "legislation to protect the
     investments of the land user without denying ownership to
     the land owner."

15.  Peace Corps in Country Training Programme. Chiefdom Develop-
     ment Group, Sierra Leone. LAND TENURE AND RURAL DEVELOPMENT
     IN SIERRA LEONE. Njala, 1967. 7 l.              Files SL 58 P21

     In Sierra Leone customary land tenure systems are based on the
     principles of membership in a landowning group and priority of
     access through first settlement. The article briefly out-
     lines recent changes in customary tenure and explores the
     relationship between land tenure systems and rural development.

16.  Pilgrim, J. W. "Social aspects of agricultural development in
     Sierra Leone: I, land tenure." (In SLS, 20, 1967. p. 191-200)
                                                        Mem AP S572
     Also available as a separate.                   Files SL 58 P45

     Land reform designed to create a uniform national land law and
     to strengthen central control should not pursue legal preci-
     sion for its own sake. Reform must maintain communal and
     family elements in land tenure systems, and it should increase
     security of tenure and encourage the transferability of land
     to whoever has the best resources to use it.

17.  Saylor, Ralph G. THE ECONOMIC SYSTEM OF SIERRA LEONE. Pub-
     lication no. 31. Durham, N. C., Published for the Duke

SL 17-SOM 1

(Saylor, Ralph G.)
University Commonwealth Studies Center (by) Duke University
Press, 1967.  xii, 231 p.  Bibl.                    HC 517 S53 S3

A short section on land tenure (p. 50-58) points out that the
residents of the former colony, which is now western Sierra
Leone, have more secure title to their land than the residents
of the former protectorate.  In the former colony, the crown
claimed ownership of land but granted title to people living
in undisturbed occupancy for twenty years.  Title to land in
the former protectorate remains in the hands of paramount
chiefs and their councils.

18.  Siddle, D. J.  "The Evolution of rural settlement forms in
     Sierra Leone circa 1400-1968."  (In SLGJ, 13, 1969.
     p. 33-44)                              Mem AP S5718 L2875

     A description of evolution in methods of house construction
     and settlement patterns in response to social and economic
     change.  The general trend has been away from the palisaded,
     defense-oriented village of round huts to a European grid
     pattern of rectangular houses aligned along motor roads.

19.  Sierra Leone.  Central Statistics Office.  AGRICULTURAL
     STATISTICAL SURVEY OF SIERRA LEONE, 1965/66.  Freetown, 1967.
     1 v. (various pagings).                    Files SL 90.5 S42

     The results of this survey show that family tenure accounts
     for nearly 80 percent of all holdings; that only about one-
     eighth of all holders made more than a token payment for the
     use of land; and that about 54 percent of holders had more
     than one field.

## SOMALIA

1.  Jorgenson, Harold T.  LAND TENURE PROBLEMS; REPUBLIC OF
    SOMALIA, 1960.  n.p., International Cooperation Administra-
    tion, 1960.  61 1.                        Files Som 58 J67

    Includes a discussion of legislation pending in 1960 to
    nationalize land and create facilities for surveying holdings,
    adjudication of rights, and registration of title; recommenda-
    tions for methods of cadastral survey suited to local condi-
    tions; a description of the economics of an irrigation project
    at Bulo Mereta; and recommendations for levels of assistance
    from the United States in these projects.

# LAND TENURE AND AGRARIAN REFORM

2.   Konczacki, Z. A. "Nomadism and economic development of
     Somalia." (In CJAS, 1:2, 1967. p. 163-175)

     Three-fourths of the Somali Republic's population is involved
     in nomadic herding, while only one-tenth of the country's
     arable land is cultivated. Consequently, much of the nation's
     food must be imported. The author believes that a large part
     of the nomadic population must be shifted to settled agricul-
     ture. Some nomadism will remain, since large areas of the
     country are unsuited to any other form of land use.

3.   Noor, Hassan Adan. "Toward a land policy in Somalia." (In
     Item NE-10, p. 267-272)              HD 850.8 Z63 D46 1965

     According to the author, land policy to promote agricultural
     development should include measures to provide for the regis-
     tration of land holdings, the consolidation of fragmented
     holdings, a cadastral survey, and the settlement of nomadic
     peoples.


## SOUTH AFRICA


1.   Behrmann, H. I. TECHNIQUE AND TENURE IN SOUTH AFRICAN
     AGRICULTURE. Pietermaritzburg, University of Natal Press,
     1965. 18 p.                              Files SA 7 B23

     This lecture includes a classification of land tenure systems
     according to their place in a process of evolutionary develop-
     ment. African forms of land tenure are placed at the low end
     of the evolutionary scale.

2.   Bundy, Colin. "The Emergence and decline of a South African
     peasantry." (In AA, 71:285, 1972. p. 369-388)

     A corrective to the liberal tradition of South African
     historiography which posits the fundamental, inherent weakness
     of the traditional African economy and the inability of Afri-
     cans either to adapt that economy or to forsake it for partic-
     ipation in the market economy. The paper emphasizes a period
     of early prosperity, in the late nineteenth and early twenti-
     eth centuries, in the reserve areas. It argues that there
     was a substantially more positive response by African agri-
     culturalists to market opportunities than has usually been
     indicated; that an adapted form of the traditional subsistence
     provided for hundreds of thousands of Africans a preferable

SA 2-5

(Bundy, Colin)
alternative to wage labor on white colonists' terms; that a
small group of Africans made considerable adaptations, depart-
ing entirely from the traditional agricultural economy, and
competing effectively with white farmers.

3.    Davenport, Rodney; and Hunt, S. K., eds. THE RIGHT TO THE
      LAND. Cape Town, D. Philip, 1974. v, 90 p. Bibl.
                                              HD 989 S7 D19

      A collection of extracts from government documents, books,
      articles, and memoirs arranged chronologically in four cate-
      gories: "The Imposition of European Tenures"; "The Expansion
      of White Settlement and the Establishment of Reserves";
      "African Land Tenure, Traditional and Transitional"; and
      "Ownership and Occupation of Land by Africans and Asians in
      Urban Areas."

3a.   Desmond, Cosmas. THE DISCARDED PEOPLE; AN ACCOUNT OF AFRICAN
      RESETTLEMENT IN SOUTH AFRICA. Preface by Lord Caradon. Fore-
      word by Nadine Gordimer. (Harmondsworth, Eng., Baltimore)
      Penguin Books (1971). xx, 264 p.        HD 989 A3 D4 1971

4.    Dison, L. R.; and Mohamed, I. GROUP AREAS AND THEIR DEVELOP-
      MENT, INCLUDING LAND TENURE AND OCCUPATION. Durban,
      Butterworths, 1960. xv, 310 p.            Mem DT 763 D6

      _____; _____.  _____. Cumulative supplement, 1962.
                                          Mem DT 763 D6 Supp.

      A legal scholar interprets and explains the Group Areas Act,
      one of the cornerstones of current apartheid policy. Intended
      primarily for lawyers, the book sets out the main provisions
      and definitions of the statute and its forbearers, and makes
      extensive reference to the case law which embodies judicial
      interpretation of the statute.

5.    Duly, Leslie C. BRITISH LAND POLICY AT THE CAPE, 1795-1844,
      A STUDY OF ADMINISTRATIVE PROCEDURES IN THE EMPIRE. Durham,
      N. C., Duke University Press, 1968. xiv, 226 p. Bibl.
                                              Mem HD 984 D8

      A study of the land policies framed and enforced in the Cape
      colony from 1795 to 1844. The principal focus is on the
      relationship between the Colonial Office in London and the
      local government. The conclusion is that both abrogated
      their power so that no effective administrative office con-
      trolled the alienation of land, leaving squatting a common

(Duly, Leslie C.)
form of tenure in the 1820s and failing to efficiently apply
a quitrent system of freehold tenure thereafter.

6.  Hiemstra, V. G.  THE GROUP AREAS ACT.  Cape Town, Juta, 1953.
    147 p.                                        Mem DT 763 H5

    A South African jurist interprets and explains the Group
    Areas Act, a key piece of legislation in the current policy
    of apartheid in the Republic of South Africa.

7.  Horrell, Muriel.  GROUP AREAS:  THE EMERGING PATTERN, WITH
    ILLUSTRATIVE EXAMPLES FROM THE TRANSVAAL.  Johannesburg,
    South African Institute of Race Relations, 1966.  v, 98 p.
                                                   Mem HD 983 H6

    A survey of the effects of apartheid legislation, organized
    along geographical lines.  The book catalogues all the areas
    where Africans, Indians, or Coloured (in South African termi-
    nology this means people of mixed European and African ances-
    try) have been driven from their land and homes.  The author
    lists one supposed beneficial effect of apartheid legislation,
    namely that rents in some areas have fallen.

8.  Houghton, D. H.  "Land reform in the Bantu areas and its
    effect upon the urban labor market."  (In SAJE, 29:3, 1961.
    p. 165-184)                                    Mem AP S724 A264

    In order to grant land holdings of adequate size to some
    Africans, the South African government has had to evict others.
    This latter group will have to earn wages which will cover
    their own living expenses as well as those of dependents left
    behind.  The author advocates dispersal of industry to areas
    where Africans are allowed to live, in order to provide em-
    ployment for some 300,000 persons removed from the land.

9.  Jones, B. M.  LAND TENURE IN SOUTH AFRICA:  PAST, PRESENT AND
    FUTURE, BEING THE APPORTIONMENT, TENURE, REGISTRATION AND
    SURVEY OF LAND IN SOUTHERN AFRICA AND PROPOSALS FOR THE
    ESTABLISHMENT OF A CADASTRAL SYSTEM FOR THE BANTU AREAS OF
    SOUTH AFRICA.  (Durban?  Reproduced by the Photoduplication
    Dept. of the University of Natal, 1964).  193 p.  Bibl.
                                                   HD 1169 S6 J65

    Represents the point of view of the white South African
    academic establishment.  According to the author, black South
    Africans on the "reserves" have been increasingly attracted
    to wage employment, so that less land is needed for Africans'

SA 9-12a

(Jones, B. M.)
attempts to feed themselves. Population pressure has contributed to a tendency for holdings in areas reserved to
Africans to be subdivided. The book includes lengthy historical material on the development of land law, land registration systems, and cadastral survey, as well as a long series
of recommendations for reorganizing cadastral survey in South
Africa.

10.    Kerr, Alastair J.  THE NATIVE LAW OF SUCCESSION IN SOUTH
       AFRICA, WITH SPECIAL REFERENCE TO THE NGUNI TRIBES OF THE
       ASKEIAN AND TRANSKEIAN TERRITORIES AND NATAL.  African law
       series, 21.  London, Butterworths, 1961.  xxviii, 131 p.
                                                    Mem GN 498.1 K4

The author describes the concept and nature of succession in
African customary law and in Roman-Dutch common law, and the
effect of the practice of polygamy on rules of succession,
intestate succession, and the administration of estates.

11.    Loudon, J. B.  WHITE FARMERS AND BLACK LABOUR-TENANTS:  A
       STUDY OF A FARMING COMMUNITY IN THE SOUTH AFRICAN PROVINCE OF
       NATAL.  African social research documents, 1.  Leiden,
       Netherlands, Afrika-Studiecentrum, 1970.  136 p.  Bibl.
                                                    HD 1511 S6 L68

An invaluable document on life in South Africa in the 1950s.
The author, who served as a doctor in an isolated community
of white farmers and their black "labor tenants," describes
the impoverishment and subservience of the Africans; the
court-ordered whipping of an African tenant under the Masters
and Servants Act; social interaction between the two groups;
terms of employment and tenancy; and the daily life and work
of provincial white farmers and their tenants and servants.

12.    MacMillan, William Miller.  THE SOUTH AFRICAN AGRARIAN PROB-
       LEM AND ITS HISTORICAL DEVELOPMENT.  Witwatersrand, Pub. by
       the Central News Agency, Ltd., for the Council of Education,
       1919.  104 p.                               Mem HD 983 M3

A series of lectures from the early twentieth century on rural
conditions in South Africa.  The central concern was the issue
of poverty among British and Boer, but information on population densities and land tenure systems is interwoven into
the main argument.

12a.   Pepler, L. A.  AGRARIAN STRUCTURES AND LAND SETTLEMENT.
       E/CONF.39/C/15.  n.p., United Nations Conference on the

LAND TENURE AND AGRARIAN REFORM

(Pepler, L. A.)
Application of Science and Technology for the Benefit of the
Less Developed Areas, 1962.  6 p.            Files SA 58 P26

13.   Plaatje, Solomon T.  NATIVE LIFE IN SOUTH AFRICA, BEFORE AND
      SINCE THE EUROPEAN WAR AND THE BOER REBELLION.  5th ed.  Lon-
      don (1915?).  382 p.            Mem F742 P69 Cutter

      A black South African journalist tells of race relations in
      the early twentieth century.  Several chapters explain how
      the Natives Land Act prohibited Africans from owning or
      leasing land in both rural and urban areas.

14.   Rogers, Howard.  NATIVE ADMINISTRATION IN THE UNION OF SOUTH
      AFRICA.  2nd ed. rev. on behalf of the Dept. by P. A.
      Linington.  Johannesburg, Union of South Africa (Dept. of
      Native Affairs) 1949.  267 p.            Mem DT 779.6 R6

      Sets forth in detail the policy of the South African govern-
      ment toward African peoples in the 1930s and 1940s.  A chapter
      on land administration (p. 96-166) provides historical back-
      ground on land law.  The principal focus is on the establish-
      ment of reserves and on restrictions on the ownership of land
      by Africans and their access to crown land.

15.   Rutman, Gilbert L.  "Innovation in the land tenure system of
      the Transkei, South Africa."  (In LE, 45:4, 1969.  p. 467-471)

      Recent changes in the land tenure system in the Transkei,
      namely the granting of individual titles to arable land, are
      not likely to encourage investment in agriculture.  Land
      shortage is extreme, a result of South Africa's policy of
      enforced territorial segregation of Africans.  The author is
      willing to overlook this larger issue and recommends the
      individualization of title to all land, not just arable land
      as provided for in current policy.

16.   South Africa.  Asiatic Inquiry Commission.  REPORT.  Cape
      Town, Cape Times, Govt. Printers, 1921.  64 p.
                                    Mem HC 517 S7 A6

      This commission represents a response to the growing pressure
      in the early 1920s to restrict the rights of Chinese and
      Indians to acquire agricultural and urban land.  The commis-
      sion recommended that "voluntary" rather than compulsory
      measures be implemented to segregate these races from whites.
      Municipalities were to set aside certain residential and
      business areas for "Asiatics."

17.  \_\_\_\_\_. Commission on Small-holdings in the Peri-Urban Areas.
REPORT. In collaboration with the Natural Resources Development Council. Pretoria, Govt. Printer, 1957. 81 p.
                                            Mem HD 983 A414

The commission notes the oversupply of smallholder plots near
cities, some 70 percent of which remain vacant, and recommends
legislation to control the subdivision of small plots of land.

18.  \_\_\_\_\_. Natives' Land Commission. REPORT. Cape Town, Cape
Times, Govt. Printers, 1916. 2 v.          Mem HD 983 A4

Minutes of evidence presented to the Natives' Land Commission
by white South Africans in 1913. Describes race relations
and the conditions of tenancy forced upon Africans.

19.  \_\_\_\_\_. Parliament. Senate. Select Committee on Concessions,
Expropriation of Property and Leasing of State Land. "Report
together with the proceedings of the Committee and minutes
of evidence." Pretoria, 1970. viii, 36 p.   Files SA 76 S68

Minutes of a meeting of a Select Committee to investigate
alleged improprieties in the leasing of state land in the late
1960s.

20.  Tatz, C. M. SHADOW AND SUBSTANCE IN SOUTH AFRICA: A STUDY
IN LAND AND FRANCHISE POLICIES AFFECTING AFRICANS, 1910-1960.
Pietermaritzburg (S. Africa) University of Natal Press, 1962.
238 p. Bibl.                                HD 989 S7 T18

A history of the implementation of the concept of territorial
segregation, as reflected in policies given different names
by successive governments, from 1910 to 1960. Land laws of
1913 and 1936 were cornerstones of government policy whereby
Africans have had to surrender real and established rights in
return for promises--all of which remain unfulfilled today--
of compensatory gains. This valuable work documents the process whereby black Africans have arrived at a situation in
which they have almost no rights at all.

21.  Van Reenen, T. H. LAND; ITS OWNERSHIP AND OCCUPATION IN SOUTH
AFRICA. A treatise on the Group Areas Act (No. 36 of 1966)
and the Community Development Act (No. 3 of 1966). Cape Town,
Juta and Co., 1962. 1 v. (loose-leaf)       HD 1169 S6 V3

A legal scholar interprets in detail the Group Areas Act and
the Group Areas Development Act. Included are indices and
tables of statutes and cases cited.

SUD 1-3

## SUDAN

1. Adam, Farah Hassan. "Agrarian reform and economic development in Southern Sudan." (Ames, Iowa), 1962. 15 1. Bibl. Mimeograph paper prepared for Economics 512, Iowa State University, May 1962.                                    Files Sud 3 A22

   Argues that economic development in the Sudan is contingent upon agrarian reform which would replace existing patterns of communal tenure with individual landholding.

2. _____. CONTRIBUTION OF LAND TENURE STRUCTURES TO AGRICULTURAL DEVELOPMENT IN SUDAN THROUGH INCENTIVES, KNOWLEDGE AND CAPITAL. Research bulletin no. 5. Khartoum, Dept. of Rural Economy, University of Khartoum, 1966. 157 p.          Files Sud 58 A21

   At the time of writing in the mid 1960s, the choice between alternative forms of land tenure had not been given serious consideration in the Sudan. The adoption of large-scale, capital-intensive projects is indicative of poor economic planning, according to the author. Instead, the government should have concentrated on the reform of existing tenure structures; the creation of producer cooperatives in the south; the establishment of minimum legal sizes for holdings in the Northern Province; and experimentation to find an ideal tenure structure in the Gezira.

3. _____. ECONOMIC APPRAISAL OF AGRARIAN REFORM IN THE PRIVATE COTTON ESTATES, SUDAN. Research bulletin no. 20. Khartoum, University of Khartoum, Dept. of Rural Economy, 1971. 49 1.
                                              Files Sud 3 A21

   Conflict between tenants and licensees of the Nile pump irrigation schemes endangered the success of these projects in the mid-1960s. In 1968 a government reform program revised regulations for landlord-tenant relationships, and the Agrarian Reform Corporation took over the management of about half of the area of privately grown cotton. The author recommends revising the scale of compensation for managers, consolidation of schemes to form larger units, increased investment in irrigation installations, and tenant participation in production decisions.

# LAND TENURE AND AGRARIAN REFORM

3a.      _____. "Socio-economic appraisal of agrarian reform in the private cotton estates of Sudan." n.p. (1973). 21 p. Paper for Study Seminar 35: Land Tenure, Distribution and Reform, Institute of Development Studies, University of Sussex, 1973.
                                                          Files Sud 3 A24

4.    Awad, Mohammed Hashim. "The Evolution of landownership in the Sudan." (In MEJ, 25:2, 1971. p. 212-228)      Mem AP M6272
      Also available as a separate.                   Files Sud 58 A92

      After describing the system of land tenure introduced in the Sudan by the Arabs, the author traces the development of the patterns adopted in turn by the Funj, the Turks, and the Mahdists, and explains how the rule of the Anglo-Egyptian Condominium restored the traditional system. Concludes by assessing the impact of the extant system on agricultural development.

5.    Bolton, Alexander R. C. "Land tenure in agricultural land in the Sudan." 1948. (In Item SUD-26, p. 187-197)
                                                          Ag S 338 S8 T6
      Also available as a separate. Training course document, no. 48. n.p., n.d. 11 p.                          Files Sud 58 B65

      A brief presentation of the main features of land tenure systems in rural areas of the Sudan. In the northern Sudan agricultural land is divided into three categories: government land not subject to use rights, government land subject to rights vested in a local community, and land owned individually. In the southern Sudan all land was held in trust by the government for the people. Because of the abundance of land, individual tenure did not exist.

5a.   Center on Land Problems in the Near East, Salahuddin, Iraq, 1955. COUNTRY INFORMATION REPORT: SUDAN. Country information report, no. CI-5. (Rome) FAO, 1955. 13 p.
                                                          Files Sud 58 C25

5b.   Chambers, Robert. SETTLEMENT SCHEMES IN TROPICAL AFRICA: A STUDY OF ORGANIZATIONS AND DEVELOPMENT. (1969).
                                                          HD 1516 A34 C5

      See Item AFR-32 for citation and annotation.

6.    Dishoni, Sharif Ahmed. "The Impact of development on three irrigated areas of Sudan." (Madison) 1966. 123 l. Bibl. Ph. D. dissertation, University of Wisconsin.
                                                          Thesis HD 1741 S73 D47

SUD 6-9

(Dishoni, Sharif Ahmed)
A study of the transformation of the traditional agricultural
economy of the Merowe-Dongola area of Sudan's Northern Province as a result of irrigation. The third chapter includes
a section on the legal framework for adjudication of claims
to land and the registration of title.

6a.    El Mahdi, Saeed M. A.  A GUIDE TO LAND SETTLEMENT AND
       REGISTRATION.  (Khartoum)  Khartoum University Press  (1971).
       (xii), 92 p.                              HD 1206 S73 E5

7.     Farah, El Mahadi Mohamed.  PAST AND PRESENT DIFFICULTIES IN
       CADASTRAL SURVEY AND LAND REGISTRATION.  Submitted by the
       Government of the Democratic Republic of the Sudan.
       E/CN.14/CART/269.  n.p., UNECA, 1970.  8 p.  Paper for
       Seminar on Cadastre, Addis Ababa, 1970.      Files Sud 59 F17

       States the case for the necessity of resurveying Sudan's
       registered land:  discrepancies in registration and mapping,
       the disappearance of physical boundaries in floods, multiple
       registrations, encroachment of persons not holding rights,
       and the opening up of new land on alluvial deposits.

8.     Food and Agriculture Organization.  LAND AND WATER RESOURCES
       SURVEY IN THE JEBEL MARRA AREA, THE SUDAN.  FINAL REPORT.
       Report prepared for the Government of Sudan by the FAO...for
       the United Nations Development Programme.  Rome, 1968.  70 p.
                                                 HD 1698 S73 F66

       An inventory of land and water resources in the Jebel Marra
       and Wadi Azum areas of western Sudan designed to obtain data
       upon which development planning can be based.  Recommends
       that the United Nations Development Programme be continued
       with emphasis shifted from survey to demonstration projects.
       A four-paragraph review of land tenure systems notes that
       land belongs to the state, as was the case in the old Dar Fur
       sultanate, but land use rights are vested in the descendants
       of those who first brought it under cultivation.

9.     Gaitskell, Arthur.  "The Development of the Gezira in the
       Sudan."  n.p., n.d.  31 1.                  Files Sud 4 G14
       Also available in Weitz, Raanan, ed.  RURAL DEVELOPMENT IN A
       CHANGING WORLD.  Cambridge, Mass., MIT Press (1971).
       p. 532-553                                 HD 17.5 W43

       A history of the Gezira irrigation project which concludes by
       spelling out the lessons for the planning of similar schemes
       elsewhere:  the need for simplicity and uniformity in crop

# LAND TENURE AND AGRARIAN REFORM

(Gaitskell, Arthur)
planning; the importance of securing control over land use;
and the importance of locating a research station in a project
area.

10.    Graham, Anne. "Man-water relations in the east central Sudan."
1969. (In Item AFR-127, p. 409-445)        HD 966 T36

A description of resettlement in an arid region made possible
by deep bore wells and the modernization of a previously known
technique for catching surface run-off.

11.    Guttman, E. "Land tenure among the Azande people of Equatoria
Province in the Sudan." (In SNR, 37, 1956. p. 48-55)
                                        Mem AP S943

Argues that while there may be a kind of political feudalism
among the Azande, there is no corresponding structure in terms
of land tenure. Indeed, the Azande seem to have no land tenure
system at all, as long as such a system is defined as legally
enforceable relationships according to which land is held.
Any obligations between land owner and land occupier are based
on a political relationship between them as chief and subject,
not the relationship of landlord and tenant. The author attributes the lack of a land tenure system to the abundance of
land.

12.    Hance, William. "The Gezira scheme: a study in agricultural
development." (In his AFRICAN ECONOMIC DEVELOPMENT. Rev. ed.
New York, published for the Council on Foreign Relations by
Praeger, 1967. p. 31-53)            HC 502 H33 1967
Also available in Item AFR-3, p. 9.158-9.169    Files Afr 4 A37

Discusses the Gezira scheme in the context of agricultural
development in Africa. A short section (p. 42-45) describes
the tenurial arrangements permitting the government to control
land use in the scheme and outlines the structure of the three-
way partnership between tenants, the government, and the
managing board.

13.    Issawi, Charles P., ed. THE ECONOMIC HISTORY OF THE MIDDLE
EAST. 1966.                        Mem HC 412 I787

See Item NE-19 for citation and annotation.

14.    Leake, Hugh Martin. "Further studies in tropical land tenure:
Sudan." (In TROP, 16:1, 1939. p. 13-14)        Ag Per

SUD 14-19

(Leake, Hugh Martin)
A summary of the early history of the Gezira scheme with a brief reference to other aspects of land administration in the southern Sudan in the 1930s.

15.     ____. "Studies in tropical land tenure:  the Sudan."  (In TROP, 10:5, 1933.  p. 126-131)                          Ag Per

An historical view of land administration in the Sudan followed by a discussion of the Gezira scheme from the perspective of the early 1930s.

16.  Mahgoub, Sayed Mirghani.  "Land policy and settlement in Sudan."  (In Item NE-10, p. 175-189)
                                    HD 850.8 Z63 D46 1965

A summary of Sudan's experience with irrigation schemes, mechanized farming, the introduction of coffee plantations among the Azande, and pilot projects to settle nomads.  At the beginning of the paper is a brief outline of land tenure systems in the widely divergent ecological zones of the country.

17.  Mueller, Peter.  "Some aspects of land tenure in the Sudan." Outline of a talk given to Land Tenure Center fellows, March 7, 1963.  (Madison, 1963).  3 l.      Files Sud 58 M82

Concise review of land tenure in the Sudan in outline form. Includes demographic, geographic, and economic background data, as well as a summary of government land policies.

18.  Roden, David.  "Changing patterns of land tenure amongst the Nuba of Central Sudan."  (In JAO, 10:4, 1971.  p. 294-309)
                                        Mem AP J83 L811
Also available as a separate.             Files Sud 58 R62

The expansion of Nuba settlement into lowland areas during the twentieth century left the fundamental aspects of the Nuba land tenure system intact, but the system has changed in detail.  The most important rights in land are still vested in individuals.  However, inheritance is less important as a means of obtaining land than 30 years ago, and it now operates in a more flexible way.

19.  Schlippé, Pierre de.  SHIFTING CULTIVATION IN AFRICA:  THE ZANDE SYSTEM OF AGRICULTURE.  1956.      Mem S 471 A365 S4

See Item ZAI-34 for citation and annotation.

# Land Tenure and Agrarian Reform

20. Schlippé, Pierre de; and Batwell, B. L. "Preliminary study of the Nyangwara system of agriculture." (In A/IAI, 25:4, 1955. p. 321-351)
    Mem AP A257

    This article is primarily concerned with the agricultural techniques of the Nyangwara, but the concluding recommendations include a call for land reform so that each family would have enough land to allow for crop rotations with intervening periods when the land lies fallow.

21. Simpson, S. Rowton. "Land law and registration in the Sudan." (In JAA, 7:1, 1955. p. 11-17)
    Mem AP J83 A258

    Outlines the history of land administration and land registration in the Sudan from the end of the nineteenth century to the 1930s, making extensive references to the relevant statutes and ordinances.

22. Sudan. LAND REFORM IN THE REPUBLIC OF THE SUDAN. RU:WLR-C/66/36. (Rome) FAO, 1966. Country paper for World Land Reform Conference, Rome, 1966.
    Files Sud 3 S82

    A brief and general review of the legal framework for land reform in the Sudan. Focuses on government control of land use and includes a brief discussion of the Gezira scheme.

23. _____. Dept of Statistics. A REPORT ON THE SAMPLE CENSUS OF AGRICULTURE FOR THE YEAR 1964-65. Khartoum, 1969. 2 v. Library has: Blue Nile Province. Northern and Khartoum Provinces.
    REF HD 2150 S8 A2 1964/5

    Statistics on agriculture in the Northern, Khartoum, and Blue Nile provinces of the Sudan. A section on land tenure reports on the size of holdings and on types of tenure. About 45 percent of the agricultural land in the area surveyed was leased.

24. Taha, Taha El Jack. LAND TENURE AND SIZE OF HOLDINGS; TOWARDS A NEW STRATEGY FOR ECONOMIC STUDIES IN TENANCY FARMING IN THE GEZIRA SCHEME. n.p., Sudan Gezira Board, Development Branch, 1972. 11 1. Paper presented at the Annual Agricultural Meeting, Agricultural Research Corporation, Wad Medani, Democratic Republic of the Sudan, 1972.
    Files Sud 38 T13

    Although the size of agricultural holdings is decreasing rapidly in the Gezira scheme, output can be boosted by intensifying land use, providing additional agricultural extension services, establishing credit schemes, and improving the administration of the project.

# LAND TENURE AND AGRARIAN REFORM

25.  Thornton, D. S.  "Agricultural development in the Sudan
     Gezira Scheme."  (In TROP, 49:2, 1972.  p. 105-114)      Ag Per

     Intensification and diversification of crop production patterns
     in the Gezira scheme are technically feasible but will bring
     about increased pressure on an organizational structure which
     is already in some respects inappropriate.  Increased inci-
     dences of tenants hiring laborers and of absentee tenants
     employing foremen run counter to the long-term dream of the
     architects of the scheme, namely the ultimate transformation
     of the tenants into a body of committed mixed farmers with
     considerable managerial and entrepreneurial skills.

26.  Tothill, John D., ed.  AGRICULTURE IN THE SUDAN, BEING A
     HANDBOOK OF AGRICULTURE AS PRACTISED IN THE ANGLO-EGYPTIAN
     SUDAN.  London, Oxford University Press, 1948.  xviii, 974 p.
     Bibl.                                             Ag S 338 S8 T6

     A comprehensive collection of articles covering climate, soils,
     vegetation, land tenure, irrigation, and animal husbandry.
     See Items SUD-5 and SUD-27 for annotation of individual
     sections.

27.  ____.  "The Problem of land fractionation."  1948.  (In Item
     SUD-26, p. 210-221)                               Ag S 338 S8 T6

     A sample survey of thirteen households documenting the process
     of impoverishment as a result of fragmentation of landholdings.

28.  Whetham, Edith H.  COOPERATION, LAND REFORM AND LAND SETTLE-
     MENT.  1968                                       Ag HD 1491 A52 W4

     See Item AFR-140 for citation.  A chapter on the Sudan
     (p. 32-37) focuses on the Gezira Scheme and the Khasim el
     Girba Resettlement Scheme.  The Gezira Scheme must have strong
     central control because of the organizational requirements of
     large-scale irrigation, but the author views the growth of
     credit cooperatives as a healthy sign.

29.  Witucki, Lawrence A.  "The Transformation of agriculture in
     the Merowe area of Northern Sudan."  Madison, 1967.  xvi,
     407 l.  Bibl.  Ph. D. dissertation, University of Wisconsin.
                                                  Mem AWB W8327 L419

     A lengthy analysis of agricultural development in Merowe based
     on the author's field research.  The author traces the impact
     of a major innovation--the introduction of pump irrigation--
     on patterns of crop production and the marketing system,

# Land Tenure and Agrarian Reform

SUD 29-SWAZ 4

(Witucki, Lawrence A.)
analyzing in detail data on the costs and returns which
influence individual farmer decisions.


## SWAZILAND


1.  Daniel, J. B. "Some government measures to improve African
    agriculture in Swaziland." (In GJL, 132:4, 1966. p. 506-515)
    Geol MC G273 J82

    Government efforts to improve agriculture include the funding
    of an all-encompassing rural development scheme, attempts to
    change patterns of land use, the Native Land Settlement Scheme,
    and several irrigation schemes. The study concludes that
    radical changes in the land tenure system should not be
    contemplated until a cash crop economy can be established.

2.  Hughes, Arthur John Brodie. LAND TENURE, LAND RIGHTS AND LAND
    COMMUNITIES ON SWAZI NATION LAND IN SWAZILAND: A DISCUSSION
    OF SOME INTERRELATIONSHIPS BETWEEN THE TRADITIONAL TENURIAL
    SYSTEM AND PROBLEMS OF DEVELOPMENT. Monograph no. 7. Durban
    (South Africa) Institute for Social Research, University of
    Natal, 1972. vi, 351 p. Bibl.                HD 989 S9 H83

    A description and discussion of Swazi land tenure, emphasizing
    the need to reconsider western assumptions about what sort of
    social and economic changes are "desirable" in the context of
    agricultural and economic development. Concludes with sugges-
    tions for bringing about development "through deliberate
    efforts to work with, or within the framework of, Swazi
    customary land law."

3.  _____. "Reflections on traditional and individual land
    tenure in Swaziland." (In JAO, 3:1, 1964. p. 3-13)
    Mem AP J83 L811

    Swazi students expressed strong objections to the replacement
    of customary forms of land tenure with individual freehold
    rights in land.

4.  _____. "Some Swazi views on land tenure." (In A/IAI, 32:3,
    1962. p. 253-278)                            Mem AP A257

    An expanded version of Item SWAZ-3.

211

# Land Tenure and Agrarian Reform

5.  Swaziland. Central Statistical Office. CENSUS OF INDIVIDUAL
    TENURE FARMS, 1969/70. (Mbabane) 1971. 19 p.
    Files Swaz 90.5 S92

    Statistics for all farms held individually; included are data
    on land use, size of holdings, levels of production, value of
    crop sales, as well as use of irrigation, pesticides, farm
    machinery, and hired labor.

6.  _____. _____. REGIONAL AGRICULTURAL SAMPLE CENSUS, 1971.
    Mbabane, 1972. 2 v. Contents--Part 1. Swazi Nation lands:
    RDA's and adjoining areas. Part 2. Individual tenure farms:
    adjoining RDA's. REF HD 2130 S9 A2

    A report setting out the methodology employed in the agricul-
    tural census of 1971. Also included are data on number, area,
    and type of agricultural holdings, land use, crop production,
    livestock, agricultural machinery, and average yield of
    principal crops.

7.  Wittington, G. W.; and Daniel, J. B. "Problems of land tenure
    and ownership in Swaziland." 1969. (In Item AFR-127,
    p. 447-461) HD 966 T36

    The law of Swaziland recognizes two basic categories of land:
    land available for exclusive occupation by the Swazi, and land
    held on a freehold or leasehold basis, most of which is held
    by European-owned companies. Concludes that the dualistic
    structure of the rural economy and the customary Swazi system
    of land tenure combine to inhibit agricultural development.

## TANZANIA

1.  Bantu, Kasella. "The Arusha declaration and its immediate
    effects on the agriculture of Tanzania." (In MBI, 3:11, 1967.
    p. 2-6) Mem AP M478

    A brief statement of the argument that the government must
    reorganize rural villages into producer cooperatives in order
    to encourage agricultural development.

2.  Baum, Eckhard. "Ujamaa: ein Konzept der Agrar- und
    Siedlungspolitik in Tanzania." (In ZAL, 10:2, 1971.
    p. 114-124)

# LAND TENURE AND AGRARIAN REFORM

(Baum, Eckhard)
The most important instruments of Tanzania's policy to
socialize agriculture are _ujamaa_ villages.  Common property
in the form of land and capital, voluntary membership, and
democratic self-administration are the principal features of
the organization of these villages.  Ujamaa has not been
successful in those parts of the country already heavily
committed to production for the market, or where population
pressure is great, or where land rights are predominantly
vested in individuals.

3.       .  "Ujamaa villages--an approach to rural development in
Tanzania."  (In SAJAA, 3:2, 1973.  p. 37-46)  Mem AP A724 A262

This article reviews the principal features of the organization
of _ujamaa_ villages in Tanzania.  The author contends that the
ujamaa village movement has been particularly successful in
sparsely populated areas.

4.  Belshaw, Deryke G. R.  "Land reform policy in Tanzania:  a
preliminary assessment."  Draft.  Rome, 1971.  30, iii l.
                                            Files Tanz 3 B25

Agricultural development in Tanzania since World War II has
been striking and has occurred largely through increased
plantings on existing small peasant farms and the extension
of the margin of cultivation into previously uncultivated
areas.  The article reviews customary land tenure systems,
leaseholds, and the role of policy in capital-intensive
agricultural development projects.

5.  Berry, Len; and Berry, Eileen.  LAND USE IN TANZANIA BY
DISTRICTS.  Research notes, 6.  Dar es Salaam, University
College, Bureau of Resource Assessment and Land Use Planning,
1969.  15 p.                          Files Tanz 57.5 B27

A preliminary map of land use in Tanzania accompanied by
tables showing the areas of land in each district according
to land in agricultural use and unused land.  The former
category is subdivided into smallholder cultivation, rough
grazing land, and large-scale agricultural enterprises.

5a.  Bridger, G. A.  "Planning land settlement schemes (with
special reference to East Africa)."  1962.     Mem JX 1977 A22

See Item AFR-24 for citation and annotation.

213

# LAND TENURE AND AGRARIAN REFORM

6.   Burke, Fred G. "Tanganyika: the search for Ujamaa." (In
     Friedland, William H.; and Rosberg, Carl G., eds. AFRICAN
     SOCIALISM. Stanford, Ca., Stanford University Press, 1964.
     p. 194-219)                                          Mem HX 439 F7

     According to Julius Nyerere, ujamaa, or African socialism,
     inheres in the very nature of African society and is an exten-
     sion of a belief in responsibility for one's neighbors. The
     author discusses how this concept has provided the basis for
     public policy in Tanzania: for cooperatives, self-help pro-
     grams, and land policy. Ujamaa-inspired land policy seeks to
     abolish freehold tenure and re-establish communal farms.

6a.  Chambers, Robert. SETTLEMENT SCHEMES IN TROPICAL AFRICA:  A
     STUDY OF ORGANIZATIONS AND DEVELOPMENT.  (1969).
                                                        HD 1516 A34 C5

     See Item AFR-32 for citation and annotation.

7.   Chidzero, B. T. G.  TANGANYIKA AND INTERNATIONAL TRUSTEESHIP.
     London, New York, Oxford University Press, 1961. x, 286 p.
     Bibl.                                        Mem JQ 3513 1961 C47

     Chapter 9 presents a general survey of land tenure in Tanzania
     and includes sections on customary land law, the alienation
     and transfer of land rights, and land law under British colo-
     nial rule.

8.   Cocking, W. P.; and Lord, R. F.  "The Tanganyika Agricultural
     Corporation's farming settlement scheme." (In TROP, 35:2,
     1958.  p. 85-101)                                          Ag Per

     A description of a settlement scheme begun in 1952 with the
     object of raising productivity and eventually the standard of
     living of African farmers.  The corporation provided tools and
     services to the farmers, the costs of which were deducted from
     the farmers' profits at the end of the year.  The problems
     associated with the project included a high turnover of tenants,
     high administrative costs, and problems of social organization
     stemming from the varied ethnic background of the participants.
     On the positive side, a range of viable crops was introduced
     and cash incomes of the farmers were raised above the average
     for nonparticipants.

9.   Cox, Paul.  "Recent changes in land tenure and rural develop-
     ment policies in Tanzania." (Madison) 1973. 35 1.  Paper
     for Agricultural Economics 472, University of Wisconsin-
     Madison.                                          Files Tanz 58 C69

# Land Tenure and Agrarian Reform

TANZ 9-13

(Cox, Paul)
This seminar paper examines the principles on which recent
Tanzanian land legislation has been based and evaluates current
land tenure policies in the light of national goals of development and integration.

10. Daniel, J. THE STATUS OF CADASTRAL SURVEYS AND LAND REGISTRA-
    TION SERVICES IN TANZANIA AND FUTURE DEVELOPMENT. E/CN.14/
    CART/260. Addis Ababa, UNECA, 1970. 7 p.   Files Tanz 59 D15

    An explanation of administrative procedures governing cadastral
    survey and of the organizational structure of the Land Registry
    Division.

11. DESPATCHES FROM THE GOVERNORS OF KENYA, UGANDA, AND TANGANYIKA
    AND FROM THE ADMINISTRATOR, EAST AFRICA HIGH COMMISSION COM-
    MENTING ON THE EAST AFRICA ROYAL COMMISSION 1953-1955 REPORT.
    1956.
                                                          Mem Docs

    See Item KEN-34 for citation and annotation.

12. De Wilde, John C. "Tanzania: agricultural development in
    Sukumaland." (In Item AFR-44, 2. p. 415-450)   HD 2117 D4

    Marked increases in agricultural production, especially of
    cotton, have taken place in Sukumaland, but they have come
    about in ways not anticipated or greatly influenced by the
    government. The Sukuma have taken advantage of opportunities
    to raise cotton production, but they have done it in their
    own way; for the most part they have raised output by patterns
    of extensive land use, rather than by the intensive methods
    advocated by the government.

13. Dobson, E. B. "Comparative land tenure of ten Tanganyikan
    tribes." (In JAA, 6:2, 1954. p. 80-89)   Mem AP J83 A258

    A typology of land tenure systems based on comparisons of the
    tenure systems of the Arusha, Samboa, Gogo, Arimi, Nyamwezi,
    Sukuma, Kerewe, Haya, Hangaza, and Kuria. The three variables
    in the classification scheme are the political system, the
    scarcity or abundance of land suitable for cultivation, and
    the type of crops grown. In all cases traditional political
    authorities derived much of their power from the control of
    land; as they lose this control, one of the main bases of
    their power will be undercut.

14.  Dumont, René. "The Strengthening of Tanzanian socialism
     through Julius Nyerere's Arusha Declaration." (In Dumont,
     René; and Mazoyer, Marcel. SOCIALISMS AND DEVELOPMENT. Trans-
     lated by Rupert Cunningham. New York, Praeger, 1973.  p. 143-
     172)                                            HC 59.7 D813 1973b

     This translated essay includes sections on the failure of
     settlement schemes, the weaknesses of cooperatives, and the
     political apparatus for establishing ujamaa villages.

15.  _____. TANZANIAN AGRICULTURE AFTER THE ARUSHA DECLARATION.
     Dar es Salaam, Ministry of Economic Affairs and Development
     Planning, 1969.  v, 62 l.                        HD 2136 T3 D95

     This survey of Tanzanian agriculture assesses the failure of
     the 1960 IBRD recommendations (Item TANZ-31) for emphasizing
     industrial development and suggests alternatives;  further
     extension work, the diversification of production through the
     adoption of new crops, and the gradual improvement of existing
     techniques of production.

16.  Dundas, Charles. "Native laws of some Bantu tribes of East
     Africa." (In RAIGBI/J, 51, 1921.  p. 217-278)   Mem AP M26602

     One of the architects of indirect rule in Tanganika reviews
     the customary law of the Wazeguka, Wapare, and Wachagga of
     Tanzania, as well as the Wakamba, Wakikuyu, Watheraka, and
     Wodigo of Kenya.  Includes a short section on land tenure
     which emphasizes that none of the peoples under discussion
     permitted the sale of land.

17.  Dunning, Harrison C. "Law and economic development in Africa:
     the law of eminent domain." 1968.                       Law Per

     See Item AFR-48 for citation.  This discussion of legal struc-
     tures providing for the public acquisition of land makes
     extensive reference to policies in Tanzania.

18.  Ellman, Antony O. "Kitete:  a land settlement in northern
     Tanzania." (In LRLSC, 1967: 1.  p. 12-21)
                                          REF HD 1261 A1 L1 1967 v. 1

     The former manager of the Kitete land settlement scheme makes
     recommendations for the improved planning of future projects:
     the selection of settlers, the introduction of technical
     innovations, the finance of settlement schemes, and the trans-
     fer of authority to settlers.

# LAND TENURE AND AGRARIAN REFORM

19.   Fabiyi, Yakub Layiwola.  "Land tenure innovations in rural
      development:  the problems of Western Nigeria with some
      Tanzanian comparisons."  1974.              Thesis HD 986 F12

      See Item NIG-36 for citation.  Chapters seven and eight (p.
      158-235) summarize Tanzanian land tenure systems and the crea-
      tion of ujamaa villages.  The author concludes that transla-
      ting the ideals of the Arusha Declaration into reality have
      been difficult, and that Tanzanian experience is not applicable
      to Nigeria.

19a.  Feldman, Rayah.  "Custom and capitalism:  changes in the basis
      of land tenure in Ismani, Tanzania."  (In JDS, 10:3/4, 1974.
      p. 305-320)

20.   Food and Agriculture Organization.  EAST AFRICAN LIVESTOCK
      SURVEY:  REGIONAL--KENYA, TANZANIA, UGANDA.  1967.
                                                    HD 9427 E1 F6

      See Item AFR-51 for citation and annotation.

21.   Fraser-Smith, S. W.  "Agricultural transformation through the
      Village Settlement Scheme."  1965.  (In Item TANZ-66, p. 32-
      37)
                                          Files Tanz 4 S54

      Discusses the background, objectives, accomplishments, and
      difficulties of village settlement schemes in Tanzania.  The
      two greatest obstacles to the implementation of the scheme are
      the shortage of trained staff and the tendency to establish
      settlements indiscriminately without prior research or
      planning.

22.   Fuggles-Couchman, N. R.  "Agricultural problems in Tanganyika."
      (In COR, 12:12, 1960.  p. 451-454)            Mem AP C8223

      One of the most intractable problems associated with increasing
      agricultural productivity lies in finding effective ways of
      approaching peasants and convincing them of the value of new
      techniques.  The author advocates encouraging agricultural
      extension officers to work closely with interested individuals,
      and he asserts that it is necessary to have an overall land
      use plan to regulate settlement and conserve soil resources.

23.   Gagern, Axel von.  DIE AFRIKANISCHEN SIEDLER IM PROJEKT
      URAMBO/TANZANIA.  Afrika-Studien, nr. 38.  München, Weltforum
      Verlag (1969).  130 p.  Bibl.              HD 1516 T3 G3

      Despite considerable economic progress, the settlers on the
      tobacco settlement at Urambo are discontented.  The author

TANZ 23-27

(Gagern, Axel von)
used survey techniques to trace the sources of their uneasi-
ness to problems they encountered and to poor planning at the
inception of the project.

24.  Gosselin, G. DEVELOPPEMENT ET TRADITION DANS LES SOCIETES
RURALES AFRICAINES. 1970.                HN 773.5 G67

See Item AFR-60 for citation. A chapter on the development of
Sukumaland (p. 263-306) reviews the introduction of plows and
tractors, settlement schemes, and cooperatives as well as the
traditional socio-political structure, land use, and land
tenure systems. Farmers freely loan to and borrow parcels of
land from each other.

25.  Gulliver, P. H. "Land shortage, social change, and social conflict in East Africa." (In JCR, 5:1, 1961. p. 16-26)
                                        Mem AP J83 C747

The growing scarcity of land in East Africa is largely the
result of rapidly increasing population, the demand for land
to produce cash crops, and the introduction of techniques
allowing individuals to work larger areas. This shortage has
engendered social conflicts. Among the Nyakyusa and Arusha,
there are four main foci of conflict: between brothers; between father and son; between members of the same village; and
between villages.

26.  _____. LAND TENURE AND SOCIAL CHANGE AMONG THE NYAKYUSA.
East African Studies, no. 11. Kampala, Uganda, East African
Institute of Social Research, 1958. 47 p.
                                        Mem HN 791 E2 E2/11

The essential feature of the land tenure system of the Nyakyusa,
a Bantu-speaking people of southern Tanzania, is an acute
shortage of land in relation to needs for arable farming under
current systems of agriculture. Land shortage is primarily a
result of increased production for export. Village unity and
the tendency to exclude strangers seeking land have become
more pronounced, as has the authority of the village headman.

27.  Gunza, J. K. F. RWAMKOMA PILOT VILLAGE SETTLEMENT SCHEME:  A
CASE STUDY. Political science paper 7a. Dar es Salaam, University College, 1971. 24 p. Bibl.          Files Tanz 17 G85

The Rwamkoma Pilot Village Settlement Scheme was an attempt to
provide land to help reduce population pressure in densely
settled areas and to relocate people living in arid regions.

(Gunza, J. K. F.)
The introduction of modern farming techniques was intended to
raise settlers' standards of living. The paper analyzes the
various social, political, and economic problems which led to
the failure of the scheme in 1969 and its transformation into
a state farm.

28.  Gutmann, Bruno. DAS RECHT DER DSCHAGGA, MIT EINEM NACHWORTE
DES HERAUSGEBERS ZUR ENTWICKLUNGSPSYCHOLOGIE DES RECHTS.
Arbeiten zur Enwicklungspsychologie, nr. 7. München, Beck,
1926. 777 p.
Mem BF 23 A7/7

Distinguishes three types of land—clan land, conquered land,
and newly opened land—and describes rights of ownership,
rules governing inheritance, and conditions of alienation,
as well as the place of land in the settlement of feuds.
Rights to water and forest land are also reviewed.

29.  Harty, W. J. REPORT TO THE GOVERNMENT OF TANZANIA ON VILLAGE
SETTLEMENT SCHEME AND FARMERS TRAINING CENTER AT MLALE.
(FFHC PROJECT). Freedom from Hunger Campaign, FAO 34. Rome,
FAO, 1968. iii, 19 p.
Files Tanz 17 H17

An evaluation of a village settlement scheme and farmer training center set up at Mlale in 1963. Among the recommendations
are a call for more research, better selection procedures for
settlers, less expensive housing, and planning a longer
period for starting up future settlements.

30.  Heijnen, J. D. THE MECHANIZED BLOCK CULTIVATION SCHEMES IN
MWANZA REGION, 1964-69. Research paper 9. Dar es Salaam,
Bureau of Resource Assessment and Land Use Planning, University
College, 1969. vii, 44 p.
Files Tanz 93.5 H24

A short history of the block cultivation schemes of Mara,
Shinyanga, and Mwanza Regions. The author's purpose is to
review the problems encountered and to draw attention to the
potential of these schemes for national development.

31.  International Bank for Reconstruction and Development. THE
ECONOMIC DEVELOPMENT OF TANGANYIKA. Report of a mission
organized by the IBRD at the request of the government of
Tanganyika and the United Kingdom. Baltimore, published for
IBRD by Johns Hopkins Press (1961). xxvii, 548 p.
HC 557 T3 I5

The report includes an assessment of resources available for
development, recommendations for practical measures to promote

(International Bank for Reconstruction)
development, and indications of the financial implications of
such recommendations. A section on land tenure (p. 91-100)
recommends the establishment of local land boards to reconcile
initiative for change, which comes largely from the central
government, with due consultation of local interests and the
securing of local consent.

32.  Jacob, Abel. "Foreign aid in agriculture: introducing
     Israel's land settlement scheme to Tanzania." (In AA, 71:
     283, 1972. p. 186-194)

A major part of Israel's aid program in the 1960s consisted of
technical assistance in land settlement schemes patterned
after the Moshav (cooperative village) and Lachish area (a
regional settlement concept). This paper examines the case
of the Mwanza project and analyzes problems encountered in
adapting a complex socio-economic structure to a foreign
environment.

33.  James, Roden William. "An Appraisal of post-independence
     Tanzanian land reforms." 1969. (In Item KEN-121, p. 265-296)
                                                        HD 982 016

The presupposition of post-independence Tanzanian land reform
programs is that conditions favorable for economic development
should be sought in directions other than the evolution of
individual private ownership. The article examines the conversion of freehold tenures into leaseholds by the Tanzanian
government, a change-over designed to facilitate range management and village settlement schemes.

34.  _____. LAND TENURE AND POLICY IN TANZANIA. Nairobi, East
     African Literature Bureau (1971). liv, 375 p.
                                                HD 1004 T35 J15

The purposes of this work are to explain the land law of
Tanzania--what the land tenure structure was, what it is, and
what it will be in the future--and to appraise changes in
land tenure in light of national needs for agricultural development. Parts 1 through 4 treat relationships between individuals and the state with respect to land. Part 5 examines
spontaneous reactions to changing land policies. Part 6 analyzes the law of secured credit transactions. In Part 7 the
author reiterates some of his major criticisms of policies
and principles embodied in the law.

# LAND TENURE AND AGRARIAN REFORM

35. James, Roden William; and Fimbo, G. M. CUSTOMARY LAND LAW OF TANZANIA; A SOURCE BOOK. Nairobi, East Africa Literature Bureau, 1973. xxv, 678 p.                    HD 1169 T2 J15

    A detailed presentation of the rules and principles of customary land tenure based on an analysis of the decisions of superior courts. Includes a survey of political and social change affecting the evolution of land law. Chapter three and part four provide background to the policies laid out in the Arusha Declaration by showing that the natural evolution of customary land tenure systems was toward individual ownership and away from communal control over land use.

36. Japhet, Kirilo; and Seaton, E. THE MERU LAND CASE. Nairobi, East Africa Publishing House, 1967. 92 p. Mem B99037 control

    This book recounts the eviction of the Meru people from their homelands at Engare Nanguki and their subsequent petition to the United Nations in 1952. Mr. Japhet argued the case before the UN and was an important participant in the struggle, as was Mr. Seaton, a lawyer who represented Meru interests.

37. Johnsen, Tom. SMALL-HOLDER ADAPTATION TO TECHNOLOGICAL AND ECONOMIC CHANGE; IMPLICATIONS FOR LOCAL LEVEL IMPLEMENTATION OF DEVELOPMENT PLANS: A CHAGGA CASE. Leiden, Afrika-Studiecentrum, 1970. 25 l. Paper for seminar on changes in Tanzanian rural society and their relevance for development planning, Leiden, 1970.                    Files Tanz 4 J63

    This paper on agricultural development among the Chagga includes a brief section on land tenure which describes the present situation. Smallholders have nearly full rights of disposition over their land. The author considers land values to be extremely high in relation to the value of output, a reflection of an acute shortage of arable land.

38. Kates, R. W.; McKay, J.; and Berry, L. "Twelve new settlement schemes in Tanzania, a comparative study of success." (In Conference of the University of East Africa Social Sciences Council, 1968/69. PAPERS (GEOGRAPHY). Kampala, Makerere University College, 1969. p. 63-100)       HC 517 E2 C6 1968/69 G

    The article classifies settlement schemes according to the degree to which they are communal or individual, planned or spontaneous. A comparative evaluation of the settlements in terms of the social and economic well-being of the settlers is unconvincing because the authors fail to explain how they obtained the data they present or how they worked out the scores for various criteria.

# LAND TENURE AND AGRARIAN REFORM

39.  LAND SETTLEMENT AND RURAL DEVELOPMENT IN EASTERN AFRICA.  1968.
     Files Afr 17 L15

     See Item KEN-83 for citation and annotation.

40.  Leake, Hugh Martin.  "Studies in tropical land tenure:  East
     Africa (Nyasaland and Tanganyika)."  (In TROP, 9:12, 1932.
     p. 375-376)
     Ag Per

     A one-paragraph review of changes in land administration when
     Great Britain assumed control of Tanganyika after the defeat
     of Germany in World War I.

41.  Lugard, Frederick D.  THE DUAL MANDATE IN BRITISH TROPICAL
     AFRICA.  1965.
     Mem DT 32.5 L8 1965

     See Item AFR-83 for citation and annotation.

42.  McAuslan, J. P. W. B.  "Control of land and agricultural devel-
     opment in Kenya and Tanzania."  1967.
     HN 800 E2 S25

     See Item KEN-94 for citation.  Government control of land has
     increased in Tanzania and Kenya during the 1960s.  The re-
     quirements of agricultural development, and especially of
     Tanzania's form of African socialism, may have prevented Tan-
     zania from grappling with the pressing problem of the reform
     of customary land law.  To arrive at these conclusions, this
     long essay reviews land law with reference to the economic
     ends which the law was originally designed to serve.

42a.  _____.  "Co-operatives and the law in East Africa."  1970.
     HD 3561 E2 C6

     See Item KEN-94a for citation.

43.  McKay, John.  PLANNING FOR DEVELOPMENT:  A REVIEW OF TRADI-
     TIONAL RURAL SETTLEMENT IN TANZANIA.  (Kampala, 1968).  25 p.
     Bibl.
     Files Tanz 17 M13

     The author raises a number of issues related to the planning
     of new and modified villages in Tanzania in order to determine
     which questions can be answered by referring to existing liter-
     ature and which require field investigation.  Includes a
     useful typology of land tenure systems based on forms of
     land ownership, the relative scarcities of land, and the types
     of crops grown.

# Land Tenure and Agrarian Reform

44.   Madiman, S. G.   "Land reform in East Africa."   n.d.
                                                        Files Afr 3 M12

See Item KEN-99 for citation and annotation.

45.   Maini, Krishan M.   LAND LAW IN EAST AFRICA.   1967.
                                                        HD 1169 M14

See Item KEN-102 for citation.   Includes chapters on the historical development of land law in Tanzania; the law of 1954
governing registration of holdings; legal procedures for sale,
lease, mortgage, trusts, restraints on disposition, and rights
in land held by another person.   The book also contains a
table of cases cited and a chronological table of the land
laws of Tanzania, Kenya, and Uganda.

46.   Mair, Lucy P.   "Agrarian policy in British African Colonies."
      1951.
                                                        Ag HD 965 L3

See Item AFR-86 for citation and annotation.

47.   Maro, M. A. M.   "A Note on progress in land tenure; the case
      for Tanzania."   Dar es Salaam, 1972.   6 1.   Paper given at
      IITA Land Tenure Seminar, Ibadan, Nigeria, 1972.
                                                        Files Tanz 58 M17

A brief statement of the case that the communal forms of land
tenure embodied in the application of the concept of ujamaa in
post-independence Tanzania will prevent the formation of
social classes.

48.   Meek, Charles Kingsley.   "Tanganyika (with a note on
      Nyarubanja tenure)."   1949.   (In Item AFR-91, p. 100-114)
                                                        HD 599 Z5 M4

The Land Tenure Ordinance of 1923, although a confused piece
of legislation, served the purpose of preventing the alienation
of African land to non-Africans and made it possible for
individuals to acquire private rights in land by obtaining
certificates of occupancy from the government.

49.   _____.   "Zanzibar."   1949.   (In Item AFR-91, p. 72-75)
                                                        HD 599 Z5 M4

A brief assessment of government efforts to deal with the
problem of indebtedness among the owners of clove plantations
in Zanzibar in the 1930s.

# LAND TENURE AND AGRARIAN REFORM

TANZ 50-54

50.  Middleton, John F. M.  "Land and settlement in Zanzibar."
     (In MAN, 60:232, 1960.  p. 181)                    Mem AP M266

     A short sketch of land tenure and settlement patterns on
     Zanzibar and Pemba.  Freehold tenure is common on Arab-owned
     clove plantations, and the idea of individual ownership is
     spreading into areas on the margins of the clove plantations.

51.  _____.  LAND TENURE IN ZANZIBAR.  Colonial research studies,
     no. 33.  London, H.M.S.O., 1961.  88 p.     Mem JV 33 G7 A48/33

     A detailed presentation of the various customary land tenure
     systems of the peoples of Zanzibar and Pemba.  One tenure
     system is found in areas where individually owned clove planta-
     tions are held by their owners under a system of freehold
     tenure and inherited according to Muslim law.  Another system
     applies to coral areas settled by Shirazi, where freehold
     tenure is generally not possible.

52.  Mitchell, Nicolas P.  LAND PROBLEMS AND POLICIES IN THE AFRICAN
     MANDATES OF THE BRITISH COMMONWEALTH.  1931.    Mem HD 1003 M5

     See Item AFR-95 for citation and annotation.

53.  Mugerwa, P. J. Nkambo.  "Land tenure in East Africa:  some
     contrasts."  1966.                          Law JX 31 I5/5

     See Item KEN-114 for citation and annotation.

53a. Müller-Praefke, Dieter; und Polster, Dietrich.  ZUR FRAGE DER
     BODENREFORM IN ENTWICKLUNGSLANDERN LATEINAMERIKAS UND AFRIKAS:
     EINE LITERATURSTUDIE.  1966.                    HD 1251 M85

     See Item AFR-97 for citation and annotation.

53b. Mutahaba, Gelase R.  THE IMPORTANCE OF PEASANT CONSCIOUSNESS
     FOR EFFECTIVE LAND TENURE REFORM; THE PROBLEM OF ABOLISHING
     NYARUBANJA LAND TENURE IN BUKOBA DISTRICT.  Political science
     paper 6:  dissertation.  Dar es Salaam, University College,
     1969.  49 p.                               Files Tanz 58 M88

54.  Nasser, S. F.  "Statutory and customary land tenure."  1965.
     (In Item TANZ-66, p. 56-59)                 Files Tanz 4 S54

     A very brief outline of the legal framework governing land
     tenure in Tanzania.

224

# Land Tenure and Agrarian Reform

55.  Nelson, Anton. THE FREEMEN OF MERU. Nairobi, New York,
     Oxford University Press, 1967. xii, 227 p. Bibl.
     Mem DT 443 N43

     A first person account of the forcible eviction of some 3,000
     Meru from their ancestral lands in order to form thirteen new
     ranches for European settlers, the subsequent development of
     Meru resources, and the return of the confiscated land.

56.  Newiger, Nikolaus J. COOPERATIVE FARMING IN KENYA AND TAN-
     ZANIA. 1967.                                       Ag HD 1486 K4 N4

     See Item KEN-117 for citation. Compares and contrasts pro-
     ducer cooperatives in Kenya and Tanzania. The objective in
     both countries has been the resettlement of poor farmers in
     order to increase individual incomes and aggregate production.
     Tanzania, unlike Kenya, had no problem with Africanizing an
     island of white settlement. The Tanzanian government is
     seeking to break the vicious circle of subsistence agriculture
     by establishing cooperative village settlements governed by
     new technical, social, and legal systems.

57.  Ntirukigwa, Esperius N. THE IMPACT OF TRADITIONAL LAND TENURE
     SYSTEM ON UJAMAA VILLAGES; A CASE STUDY OF KALEBEZO BUCHOSA,
     IN GEITA. Political science paper 7: dissertation. Dar es
     Salaam, University of East Africa, University College, 1970.
     34 p.                                            Files Tanz 58 N84

     Using the ward of Kalebezo as a case in point, the author
     argues that as long as customary land tenure systems prevail
     and use rights continue to be vested in individuals, the pros-
     pects for the establishment of ujamaa villages without coercion
     are dim.

58.  Obol-Ochola, James Yonason. LAND LAW REFORM IN EAST AFRICA.
     1969.                                               HD 982 016

     See Item KEN-121 for citation and annotation.

59.  Pitblado, J. Roger. A REVIEW OF AGRICULTURAL LAND USE AND
     LAND TENURE IN TANZANIA. Research notes no. 7. Dar es
     Salaam, Bureau of Resource Assessment and Land Use Planning,
     University of Dar es Salaam, 1970. iii, 41 p.
     Files Tanz 58 P48

     Reviews the history of legislation affecting land tenure from
     1884 to 1970 and analyzes four major areas of land holding:
     traditional systems, large rural holdings, new settlements,
     and ujamaa villages.

# Land Tenure and Agrarian Reform

59a. Pokorny, Dusan. "The Haya and their land tenures: property rights and the surplus problem." (In RA, 22, 1973. p. 93-123)

60. Reining, Priscilla C. "Haya land tenure: landholding and tenancy." (In AQ, 35:2, 1962. p. 58-73)      Mem AP A62794

An investigation of two forms of tenancy among the Haya of northwestern Tanzania. The first form treats land as the basis for political patron-client relationships, while the second more nearly resembles a contract for the use of land and has few ramifications in the Haya political system.

61. Ruthenberg, Hans, ed. AGRICULTURAL DEVELOPMENT IN TANGANYIKA. Afrika-Studien, nr. 2, Berlin, New York, Springer, 1964. xiv, 212 p. Bibl.      Mem HC 501 A32/2

A survey of the role of agriculture in Tanzania's economy which concludes that the most productive forms of aid to agriculture are the furtherance of local industrialization to boost urban purchasing power and investment in industries processing agricultural raw materials. Also important is the diffusion of knowledge of new techniques among smallholder farmers as the incentives of an expanding market begin to have an effect.

62. _____. SMALLHOLDER FARMING AND SMALLHOLDER DEVELOPMENT IN TANZANIA. TEN CASE STUDIES. Afrika-Studien, nr. 24. München, Weltforum Verlag (1968). 360 p. Bibl.      S 338 T3 R8

Ten case studies on land use systems, husbandry practices, and the productivity of smallholder farming in Tanzania. A conclusion by Hans Ruthenberg provides an overview, indicates the trends in the evolution of smallholder agriculture, and analyzes the underlying principles of the economic behavior of smallholders and their attitudes toward development measures.

63. Sawyerr, G. G. A. "Discriminatory restrictions on private dispositions of land in Tanganyika: a second look." 1969. (In Item KEN-121, p. 59-88)      HD 982 016

In the Tanganyika of the 1920s, legislation which made a distinction between exploiter and exploited was properly cast in racial terms, but the emergence of a privileged class of Africans makes this distinction less valid today, when it is necessary to protect the powerless from other Africans who are their potential exploiters. The article examines in detail section 2 of the Land Ordinance and calls for a thorough review of the policy objectives embodied in the ordinance.

# Land Tenure and Agrarian Reform

64. Sayers, Gerald F. THE HANDBOOK OF TANGANYIKA. London, Macmillan and Co., 1930. x, 636 p.                Mem DT 438 H3

    A short section on land tenure (p. 242-257) includes a brief
    history of land tenure systems under German and British colo-
    nial rule, customary land tenure systems, land registration,
    transfers, alienation, and land settlement.

65. Segal, Aaron. "The Politics of land in East Africa." 1968.

    See Item KEN-139 for citation. Kenya, Tanzania, and Uganda
    have adopted strikingly different policies toward land tenure,
    public investment in agriculture, and overall development
    strategies. The author notes that political leaders in Tan-
    zania are committed to forging a nation composed of "Swahili-
    speaking cooperative farmers living in multi-tribal, government
    and party controlled villages."

66. Smith, Hadley E., ed. AGRICULTURAL DEVELOPMENT IN TANZANIA.
    Study no. 2. Dar es Salaam, University College, Institute of
    Public Administration (1965). 119 p.        Files Tanz 4 S54

    A collection of brief papers presented at the Seminar for
    Agricultural Officers on Agricultural Development in 1964.
    Topics include marketing, credit, cooperatives, land settle-
    ment, land tenure, and land reform. See Items TANZ-21; TANZ-
    54; and TANZ-82 for annotations of individual papers.

67. Spry, J. F. "Some notes on land tenure, adjudication of
    rights, and registration of titles, with special reference to
    Tanganyika." (In JAA, 8:4, 1956. p. 175-179)
                                                Mem AP J83 A258

    An argument by a colonial official that all forms of land
    tenure in Tanganyika should be assimilated into one standard
    form of freehold so that both Africans and Europeans would have
    equal rights before the law. This should be done gradually,
    with the Governor empowered to convert into standard tenure
    any existing rights within specific areas on a piecemeal basis.
    The machinery for conversion would be the adjudication of
    existing rights and registration of title.

68. Tanganyika. "Land tenure reform." Text of 'Proposals of the
    Tanganyika Government for Land Tenure Reform, Government paper
    no. 2, 1962.' p. 1-13. (In Item AFR-3, p. 9.272-9.284)
                                                Files Afr 4 A37

TANZ 68-72

(Tanganyika)
An outline of proposals by the Tanzanian government for the
conversion of freehold titles to leasehold and for measures to
encourage the development of land for which rights of occupancy
had been granted.

69. _____. Legislative Council. THE MERU LAND PROBLEM. Dar es
Salaam, Govt. Printer, 1952. 8 p.      Mem HD 1004 T3 A54

A white paper circulated by the Legislative Council of Tanganyika in 1952 attempting to justify the seizure of lands of the
Meru, a small group living near the border with Kenya.

70. _____. _____. REVIEW OF LAND TENURE POLICY; PART I. Government paper, no. 6-1958. Dar es Salaam, Govt. Printer, 1958.
4 p.      Files Tanz 58 T14

Written in 1958, this report is a response to the recommendations of the East African Royal Commission of 1953-1955.
Following the lead of the commission report, at the heart of
these proposals are measures to encourage the evolution of
individual freehold tenure.

71. Tanner, R. E. S. "Land rights on the Tanganyika coast." (In
AFS, 19:1, 1960. p. 14-25)      Mem AP A258 S933

A study of three villages on the Tanzanian coast in an attempt
to determine the extent of changes in the systems of land tenure stemming from the presence of large sisal estates nearby.
Concludes that little change has taken place in the last fifty
years; inheritance and the opening up of new land remain the
predominant patterns of land acquisition, not sale and
purchase.

72. Tanzania. LAND SETTLEMENT IN TANZANIA. LAND TENURE IN RURAL
AREAS OF TANZANIA. RU:WLR-C/66/11. (Rome), FAO, 1966. 13 p.
Country paper for the 1966 World Land Reform Conference.
     Files Tanz 17 T15

The first part describes patterns of land use and settlement,
noting that cash crop production is concentrated in certain
areas of the country. The second part analyzes land tenure
systems and concludes that the government is attempting to
reconcile its program of land reform with traditional tenure
systems.

LAND TENURE AND AGRARIAN REFORM

73.   Temu, Peter. "Tanzanian experience with rural development
      schemes over the past decades." (In SAJAA, 3:2, 1973. p. 33-
      36)                                           Mem AP S724 A262

      This brief outline of the history of Tanzanian resettlement
      policy concludes that the authoritarian approach to agricul-
      tural development was largely ineffective, but that the ujamaa
      village movement represents a new and fruitful departure.

74.   _____. "The Ujamaa experiment." (In CERES, 6:4, 1973. p.
      71-75)

      A review of Tanzanian experience leading up to the Arusha
      declaration. In the five years which passed between the
      launching of the policy of socialism and self-reliance, over
      2 million people, or about 15 percent of Tanzania's population,
      chose to form ujamaa communities. What was once a foreign
      agricultural enclave has been nationalized, but there is still
      little integration between the plantation and smallholder
      sectors.

75.   Thomas, I. D. SOME NOTES ON POPULATION AND LAND USE IN THE
      MORE DENSELY POPULATED PARTS OF THE ULUGURU MOUNTAINS OF
      MOROGORO DISTRICT. Research note no. 8. Dar es Salaam, Bureau
      of Resource Assessment and Land Use Planning, University of
      Dar es Salaam, 1970. viii, 51 p.          Files Tanz 72.5 T36

      Maps and enumeration data from the 1967 population census are
      used in conjunction with land use surveys to describe popula-
      tion distribution and density in Morogoro District.

76.   _____. SOME NOTES ON POPULATION AND LAND USE IN THE NORTH
      PARE MOUNTAINS. Research note no. 9. Dar es Salaam, Bureau
      of Resource Assessment and Land Use Planning, University of
      Dar es Salaam, 1970. v, 61 p.             Files Tanz 72.5 T365

      A study similar to Item TANZ-75 for North Pare District.

77.   Van Hekken, Nel; and Thoden Van Velzen, Bonno. CONSEQUENCES
      OF RELATIVE LAND SCARCITY. Leiden, Afrika-Studiecentrum,
      1970. Paper for Seminar on Changes in Tanzanian Rural Society
      and their Relevance for Development Planning, Leiden, 1970.
                                                  Files Tanz 81.9 V15

      In Rungwe district inequalities of income and wealth among the
      rural populations stem from unequal access to land, the prin-
      cipal means of production. Rich peasants can be recruited to
      man development projects organized by the government, but

TANZ 77-81

(Van Hekken, Nel; and Thoden Van Velzen, Bonno)
their participation may arouse feelings of antagonism toward
government projects on the part of their poorer neighbors.
The second part of the study describes social processes whereby either the masses or the rich seek to prevent "social
climbers" from accumulating wealth and improving their position
relative to others.

78.    Van Hekken, P. M.; and Thoden Van Velzen, H. U. E.  LAND
       SCARCITY AND RURAL INEQUALITY IN TANZANIA.  SOME CASE STUDIES
       FROM RUNGWE DISTRICT.  Communications, no. 3.  The Hague,
       Mouton (1972).  127 p.  Bibl.                    HN 814 T35 R854

       Explores relationships between land scarcity and other social
       and micro-political variables in three villages in Rungwe
       District.  The article poses questions about the extent to
       which land scarcity exists, how it gives rise to inequalities
       of status and political power, and what forces are working to
       counter rural inequality.

79.    Wilson, Godfrey.  THE LAND RIGHTS OF INDIVIDUALS AMONG THE
       NYAKYUSA.  The Rhodes-Livingstone papers, no. 1.  (Manchester,
       Eng.)  Manchester University Press for the Institute for Social
       Research, University of Zambia (1968, c1938).  52 p.
                                                   Files Tanz 58 W45

       A description of land rights among the Nyakyusa of southern
       Tanzania during the years 1934-1938.  At this time many kinds
       of land were plentiful, so that the land tenure system was
       characterized by a lack of rigorous enforcement.

80.    Wilson, Monica.  "Effects on the Xhosa and Nyakyusa of scarcity
       of land."  (In Item AFR-67, p. 374-391)         HD 966 I5 1970

       Both the Xhosa of South Africa and the Nyakyusa of southern
       Tanzania are faced with the choice of subdividing plots beyond
       the point where they can support the families working them, or
       of creating a class of landless laborers.  For both the Xhosa
       and Nyakyusa land scarcity has necessitated migration to labor
       in nearby mines, farms, or factories.

81.    Winter, E. H.  "Some aspects of political organization and land
       tenure among the Iraqw."  (In AFS/K, 2, 1968.  p. 1-29)
       Also available as a separate.               Files Tanz 72 W45

       Every Iraqw household is concerned with both agriculture and
       stock management.  The growth of the herds and the human popu-
       lation have necessitated the movement of the Iraqw into new

# Land Tenure and Agrarian Reform

TANZ 81-TOGO 2

(Winter, E. H.)
lands. The article describes the acquisition of land rights
during this process of colonization, the transfer of rights,
and access to common grazing land.

82. Yonge, D. D. "Land tenure reform." 1965. (In Item TANZ-66.
p. 60-62)
Files Tanz 4 S54

Reform of customary forms of land tenure should aim at demar-
cation of boundaries to minimize the potential for dispute,
security of tenure, and ease of transferability.

83. Young, Roland; and Fosbrooke, Henry. LAND AND POLITICS AMONG
THE LUGURU OF TANGANYIKA. London, Routledge and Paul, 1960.
212 p.
Mem DT 449 M6 Y59

In Luguru society rights to land derive from membership in a
lineage. Outsiders may cultivate land belonging to a lineage
by making small annual payments to the lineage head. The colonial government initiated a terracing scheme to halt soil erosion, a program which necessitated strict control of land use
by outsiders. Widespread discontent erupted in riots in 1955,
and the program was abandoned.

# TOGO

1. Binet, J. "Le Droit foncier des Ewés de Tsévié." (In ISEAC,
166, 1965 (5:9). p. 101-118)
Mem H 31 I53

A study of the Ewe customary system of land tenure. The author enumerates persons who may hold rights in land, lists the
forms of property to which these rights apply, and examines
the nature of rights and interests in land. The tenure system
is complicated by the coexistence of matrilineal and patrilineal rights and by a growing tendency for land rights to be
vested in individuals.

2. Foli, Messanvi Léon. "Le Régime juridique des terres au Togo."
Paris, 1970. 423 1. Bibl. Thesis, University of Paris,
Faculté de Droit et des Sciences Economiques. HD 1004 T6 F65

This massive thesis covers nearly every aspect of land tenure
and agrarian reform in Togo. The first section treats land
legislation and customary land law under the headings of sale,
gift, succession, first occupation, and other modes of acquisition of land rights. The second section deals with land use

231

TOGO 2–UGA 2

(Foli, Messanvi Léon)
and agricultural development programs. The third section
presents the alternatives for Togolese land reform. The author
favors communal over individual forms of tenure because the
former would be less of a break with existing patterns of land
tenure.

3. Messavussu-Akue, H. "L'Expropriation por cause d'utilité
   publique au Togo." 1970. (In Item AFR-112, p. 979–1016)

   Gives a history of procedures for the public acquisition of
   land in Togo under the French administration and afterwards.
   Land held according to customary law was not initially subject
   to expropriation, but later this exemption was dropped.

4. Mitchell, Nicolas P. LAND PROBLEMS AND POLICIES IN THE AFRICAN
   MANDATES OF THE BRITISH COMMONWEALTH. 1931.    Mem HD 1003 M5

   See Item AFR-95 for citation and annotation.

5. Pauvert, J. C. "Migrations et droit foncier au Togo." (In
   ISEAC, 166, 1965 (5:9). p. 69–88)      Mem H 31 I53

   The first part of the study examines the relationship between
   migration and the use or ownership of land in the homeland of
   the Kabré of Togo. The second is about modes of acquisition
   of land in areas to which Kabré migrate. The author concludes
   that mobility is not provoked by problems in the land tenure
   system in the Kabré homeland and that migration is compatible
   with efficient modes of access to land in both the region of
   origin and in the region receiving migrants.


## UGANDA


1. Adegboye, Rufus O. "Customary land tenure systems in Uganda."
   (In LRLSC, 1971:1. p. 68–73)      REF HD 1261 A1 L1 1971 v.1

   A brief description of the evolution of the mailo system of
   land tenure, present legal provisions for the public acquisition of land, and ways in which individuals can obtain rights
   to use land. Concludes with a brief evaluation of land problems in Uganda.

2. _____. "Uganda." n.p., n.d. 12 l.      Files Uga 58 A22

UGA 2-5

(Adegboye, Rufus O.)
Outlines the main types of land rights and the methods of
acquiring land in Uganda. Points out some of the problems encountered by the British and later by the Uganda Government
when attempting to carry out land tenure reform without separate consideration of land ownership, land use, and land transfer. Recommends that planners should introduce and guarantee
farmers a higher degree of freedom in these three areas to
encourage each family to make improvements.

3.  Agrawal, G. D.; and Raja, A. G. "An Economic study of six
    settlers at Mubuku (Uganda)." (In AEBA, 11, 1969. p. 37-51)

Presents input-output data on the farming activities of six
settlers at the Mubuku irrigation settlement during the first
year of its operation. The conclusion is that settlements can
make an important contribution to the betterment of rural life.

4.  Beattie, J. THE KIBANJA SYSTEM OF LAND TENURE IN BUNYORO.
    Conference paper no. 44. (Kampala) Makerere Institute of
    Social Research, n.d. 11 p.                    Files Uga 58 B21
    Also available in East African Institute of Social Research
    Conference, Kampala, Uganda, 1953. PAPERS. Kampala, 1953.
    11 p.
                                                   Files Afr 86.6 E17

An account of the nature and distribution of rights in <u>kibanja</u>
estates, which have evolved from fiefs held under royal sanc-
tion to land characterized by the more strictly economic
relationships of landlord and tenant. Concludes with a description of the way this system of land tenure fits into the
wider social system of Bunyoro.

5.  Belshaw, Deryke G. R. "An Outline of resettlement policy in
    Uganda 1945-1963." 1963. (In Item KEN-37, 16 p., iii l.)
                                                   Files Afr 3 E17
    Also available in Item KEN-83, p. 14-23.       Files Afr 17 L15

An overview of resettlement policy in Uganda from 1945 to 1963.
The author estimates that 75,000 persons were resettled at an
estimated cost of £1,000,000. The planners' assumption that
the best way to boost agricultural production was to increase
the area under cultivation, rather than to raise productivity
per acre while holding acreage constant, was not well founded.
Planners of settlement schemes failed to investigate the
social backgrounds of the settlers and did not distinguish
scarce resources (capital and management) from abundant ones
(land and labor).

# LAND TENURE AND AGRARIAN REFORM

5a.   Bridger, G. A.  "Planning land settlement schemes (with special
      reference to East Africa)."                     Mem JX 1977 A22

      See Item AFR-24 for citation and annotation.

6.    Brock, Beverly.  "Customary land tenure, 'individualization'
      and agricultural development:  some comments on a conference."
      (In EAJRD, 2:2, 1969.  p. 1-27)
      Also available as a separate.              Files Uga 58 B76

      Criticizes the view that the granting of individual freehold
      rights to land is a major means of furthering agricultural
      development.  "Customary systems of land tenure are far more
      resilient and flexible than visiting Commissions, Missions,
      and experts have thought them to be.  But where government
      intervention does become necessary, a range of possible mea-
      sures is available, of which individual freehold title is only
      one."  (p. 22)

7.    _____.  "Land tenure and social change in Bugisu."  (In Rigby,
      Peter, ed.  SOCIETY AND SOCIAL CHANGE IN EASTERN AFRICA.
      Kampala, Makerere Institute of Social Research, n.d.  p. 13-23)
                                                  Files Afr 83 R43

      In the customary Gisu land tenure system, land was owned by
      the individual, subject to certain checks by the lineage group
      on the way he could dispose of it.  Land could be acquired
      through inheritance, gift, loan, lease, or purchase; and in
      the last case, permission from the lineage group was needed.
      At present the power of lineage groups to influence and control
      the disposition of land is waning.  This loss of control may
      lead to the concentration of larger amounts of land in the
      hands of fewer individuals with the resultant development of
      a landless class.  The author stresses that more information
      on the extent of the trend toward land concentration is
      needed before a land policy for the Bugisu can be formulated,
      but that it may be necessary to impose limitations on the
      size of land holdings or on absentee ownership.

8.    Brushfield, T. N. N.; and Relton, A. J.  "Land registration in
      Buganda."  (In ESR, 13:99, 1955/56.  p. 194-202; and 13:100,
      1955/56.  p. 243-252)                        Geol MC SU68

      An historical view of land registration in Buganda emphasizing
      survey and mapping.  According to the author, the government
      should have established adequate facilities for registration
      and survey with the enactment of the first important land
      ordinance in 1908.

# LAND TENURE AND AGRARIAN REFORM

9. Buell, Raymond L. "Land policy in Uganda." (In his THE
   NATIVE PROBLEM IN AFRICA, 1. New York, Macmillan, 1928 (repr.
   1965). p. 559-642)                          Mem DT 31 B8 1965 v.1

   A chapter on land policy (p. 590-601) focuses on the agreement
   of 1900 between the kabaka or ruler of Buganda and Sir Harry
   Johnston, the ramifications of this agreement, and subsequent
   acts and statutes governing rents and transfers of rights in
   land.

10. Butagira, F. K. "The Mailo tenure in Buganda." 1969. (In
    Item KEN-121, p. 44-58)                              HD 982 016

    The introduction of the mailo system of land tenure, which
    created an approximation of freehold rights in land, radically
    altered pre-existing tenure systems. The architects of the
    mailo system erroneously believed that they were merely con-
    firming existing rights in land. The article traces these
    changes in tenure systems and recommends a scheme for re-
    introducing communal ownership of land.

11. Byagagaire, J. M.; and Lawrance, J. C. D. "The Effect of
    customs of inheritance on sub-division and fragmentation of
    land in South Kigezi." 1957. (In Item UGA-33, p. 17-22)
                                             Files Uga 58 L15

    Subdivision and fragmentation of holdings have reached a
    stage in South Kigezi where they inhibit efficient agriculture.
    The article illustrates the operation of these processes in the
    life cycle of a typical farmer.

12. Carter, W. M. "The Clan system, land tenure and succession
    among the Baganda." (In LQR, 25, 1909. p. 158-177)   Law Per

    The author gives a brief overview of the political structure
    of precolonial Buganda and the organization of clans, and then
    describes butaka tenure on clan lands and the butongole tenure
    of estates awarded to court officials by the kabaka or king.

13. Chambers, Robert. SETTLEMENT SCHEMES IN TROPICAL AFRICA: A
    STUDY OF ORGANIZATIONS AND DEVELOPMENT. 1969. HD 1516 A34 C5

    See Item AFR-32 for citation and annotation.

14. Charsley, Simon. "The Group Farm Scheme in Uganda." 1968.
    (In Item KEN-83, p. 57-64)                      Files Afr 17 L15

UGA 14-19

(Charsley, Simon)
The author traces the origins of the Group Farm Scheme to
adaptations of the tractor hire service, which had been in
operation for fifteen years before the beginning of the Group
Farm Scheme, and the Cooperative Credit Scheme. Also included
is a discussion of the layout, management, and economic returns
of group farms.

15.   DESPATCHES FROM THE GOVERNORS OF KENYA, UGANDA, AND TANGANYIKA
      AND FROM THE ADMINISTRATOR, EAST AFRICA HIGH COMMISSION COM-
      MENTING ON THE EAST AFRICA ROYAL COMMISSION 1953-1955 REPORT.
      1956.                                                    Mem Docs

      See Item KEN-34 for citation and annotation.

16.   Fallers, A. L.  "The Politics of landholding in Busoga."  (In
      EDCC, 3:3, 1955.  p. 260-270)

      A description of Busoga customary land tenure focusing on the
      role of chiefs in the colonial administrative hierarchy.

17.   Food and Agriculture Organization.  EAST AFRICAN LIVESTOCK
      SURVEY:  REGIONAL--KENYA, TANZANIA, UGANDA.  1967.
                                                    HD 9427 E1 F6

      See Item AFR-51 for citation and annotation.

18.   _____.  IRRIGATION AND PILOT DEMONSTRATION PROJECT, MUBUKU,
      UGANDA; FARM MANAGEMENT, LAND TENURE AND SETTLEMENT.  AGL:SF/
      UGA 4 - Technical report 7.  Rome, 1971.  viii, 98 p.
                                                    Files Uga 17 F66

      A detailed study of the irrigation settlement at Mubuku.  A
      chapter on land tenure (p. 45-51) presents the terms of agree-
      ment between the settler and the settlement authority.  The
      agreement in fact goes beyond land tenure to specify conditions
      for the eviction of settlers, the formation of cooperatives,
      and the management of the scheme.

19.   Forbes Watt, D.  "Mechanized group farming in Uganda."  (In
      LRLSC, 1968:1.  p. 1-12)            REF HD 1261 A1 L1 1968 v.1

      The economic lessons of past efforts to mechanize agriculture
      in Uganda have largely been overlooked in the planning of new
      schemes.  Group farming schemes were discontinued because of
      disappointing crop yields, excessive repair and maintenance
      costs for machinery, and other problems.  The more recent ex-
      periments with tractor hire centers have been plagued by an

LAND TENURE AND AGRARIAN REFORM

UGA 19-24

(Forbes Watt, D.)
economically low ratio of revenue-earning hours to hours
spent going to and from jobs.

20.   Fortt, Jean M. "Land tenure and the emergence of large-scale
farming." (In Richards, Audrey I.; Sturrock, Ford; and
Fortt, Jean M., eds. SUBSISTENCE TO COMMERCIAL FARMING IN
PRESENT-DAY BUGANDA: AN ECONOMIC AND ANTHROPOLOGICAL SURVEY.
Cambridge, Eng., Cambridge University Press, 1973. p. 66-84)
HD 2130 U54 B87

An excellent summary of the development of land law in
Buganda, based largely on Item UGA-74, followed by a section
on the emergence of progressive farmers. As land became increasingly scarce after World War II, rising mailo prices, a
trend toward smaller holdings, and the decreasing value of
returns from land tenanted by bibanja holders resulted in a
growing emphasis on farming for profit.

21.   Gayer, C. M. A. "Report on land tenure in Bugisu." 1957.
(In Item UGA-33, p. 1-16)
Files Uga 58 L15

A report on Bugisu customary land law preceded by historical
background and a description of the political and economic
organization of Bugisu society.

22.   Great Britain. Colonial Office. UGANDA; REPORT OF THE UGANDA
CONSTITUTIONAL CONFERENCE, 1961, AND THE TEXT OF THE AGREED
DRAFT OF A NEW BUGANDA AGREEMENT INITIALLED IN LONDON ON 9th
OCTOBER 1961. Cmnd. 1523. London, H.M.S.O., 1961. iv, 72 p.
Files Uga 71 G72

The responsibilities of the Land Commission for Uganda are set
forth in chapter three (p. 25-27).

23.   Hall, Malcolm. REGIONAL ECONOMIC PLANNING IN UGANDA: THE
BUGANDA EXPERIENCE, 1963-66. No. 426. Kampala (Makerere
University College, 1968?). 18 p.
Files Uga 79 H15

A description of planning in Buganda with recommendations for
changes in the organization of governmental planning agencies.
Includes a summary of actions taken affecting land tenure.

24.   Harmsworth, Josephine. DYNAMICS OF KISOGA LAND TENURE. Con-
ference paper no. 128. (Kampala) Makerere Institute of Social
Research, n.d. 9 p.
Files Uga 58 H17

237

(Harmsworth, Josephine)
Data gathered in three villages in Busoga show that the land
tenure system is in reality a series of accommodations to
local circumstances and is changing rapidly.

25. Haydon, Edwin S. LAW AND JUSTICE IN BUGANDA. Butterworth's
    African Law Series no. 2. London, Butterworth, 1960. 342 p.
    Bibl.                                                Mem K 0.1 H4164

A lengthy section on land tenure (p. 127-168) details Buganda
tenure systems before the arrival of the British, the mailo
system, landlord-tenant relations, acquisition and transfer
of interests, and jurisdiction in land cases.

26. Hutton, Caroline. "Making modern farmers." 1968. (In Item
    KEN-83, p. 38-56)                         Files Afr 17 L15

An article on the origins and organization of the Nyakashaka
Settlement Scheme for Ugandan school leavers. It describes
in detail the characteristics of the settlers and their attitudes toward farming. Concludes that the scheme has been
successful in inculcating a positive attitude toward farming
among its participants.

27. _____. "Nyakashaka: a farm settlement scheme in Uganda."
    (In AA, 67:267, 1968. p. 118-123)       Mem AP A258 A256

The settlers on this scheme, school leavers for the most part,
were aware that their own education did not qualify them for
skilled or white collar employment. Their commitment to the
settlement scheme was therefore strong.

28. Kate, E. M. S. "The Relevance and implications of land tenure
    to urban development in Uganda." 1969. (In Item KEN-121,
    p. 297-302)                                       HD 982 016

The existence of urban slums indicates that the government has
insufficient control of land use in urban areas under the
existing system based on leases of 199 years.

29. Kato, L. L. "Government land policy in Uganda; 1889-1900."
    (In UJ, 35:2, 1971. p. 153-160)            Mem AP U26
    Also available as a separate.           Files Uga 94 K18

A discussion of land tenure in Uganda during the last decade
of the nineteenth century. The two main themes are religious
influences on the tenure system in Buganda and the difference
between the stated position of the protectorate government and
what actually happened as a result of the initiatives of local

(Kato, L. L.)
administrators seeking practical solutions to the problems
they faced.

30. Kunya, P. F.  THE GROUP FARMING SCHEME IN UGANDA.  RU:WLR-
    C/66/25.  (Rome) FAO, 1966.  16 p.  Paper for World Land
    Reform Conference, Rome, 1966.                Files Uga 58 K85

    A description of the organization and operation of the Group
    Farm schemes in Uganda covering the first three years of their
    operation.

31. Kururagire, A. R.  "Land fragmentation at Rugarama, Kigezi."
    (In UJ, 33:1, 1969.  p. 59-64)                   Mem AP U26
    Also available as a separate.               Files Uga 58 K87

    Fragmentation of holdings has permitted a breakdown of clan
    attachments to land, thereby paving the way for private land
    ownership.  But fragmentation also has disadvantages, chief
    among which is a disincentive for farmers to adopt new agri-
    cultural techniques because they would not bring an econom-
    ically justifiable return on small and scattered plots.

32. LAND SETTLEMENT AND RURAL DEVELOPMENT IN EASTERN AFRICA.
    1968.                                       Files Afr 17 L15

    See Item KEN-83 for citation and annotation.  See Items UGA-5;
    UGA-14; UGA-26; and UGA-80 for annotations of individual
    articles on Uganda.

33. LAND TENURE IN UGANDA.  (Entebbe, Govt. Printer, 1957).  30 p.
                                                Files Uga 58 L15

    Includes articles by Gayer and Byagagaire, an adaptation of a
    note in the C. M. S. archives written by a saza chief, and the
    text of the Ankole Landlord and Tenant Law of 1937.  See Items
    UGA-11 and UGA-21 for individually annotated articles.

34. Langlands, B. W.  A PRELIMINARY REVIEW OF LAND USE IN UGANDA.
    Occasional paper no. 43.  Kampala, Makerere University, Dept.
    of Geography, 1971.  219 p.                    HD 989 U2 L15

    A classification of land use in Uganda followed by an appendix
    of detailed information on land use in each county.

35. Lawrance, J. C. D.  FRAGMENTATION OF AGRICULTURAL LAND IN
    UGANDA.  Entebbe, Govt. Printer (1963).  7 p.
                                                Files Uga 58 L19

(Lawrance, J. C. D.)
Each year more and more farms in Uganda are fragmented, a
factor which leads to an ever-increasing loss of productivity.
The true extent of fragmentation remains unknown unless a
survey is undertaken or all land is registered.

36. _____. "A Pilot scheme for grant of land titles in Uganda."
(In JAA, 12:3, 1960. p. 135-143)          Mem AP J83 A258

Except for Buganda, Ankole, and Toro, land in Uganda was
declared to be crown land and held in trust for the African
population. In 1956 the Ugandan government proposed to con-
firm individual tenure on these crown lands by a process of
adjudication of rights and registration of title. The article
documents this process in Kigezi in the extreme southwest
corner of the country, where interest in the program has been
high since its inception.

37. Leake, Hugh Martin. "Studies in tropical land tenure: East
Africa (Uganda)." (In TROP, 9:12, 1932. p. 371-375)   Ag Per

Describes the evolution of the land tenure system in Buganda
to the early 1930s by presenting an outline of the legal
structure and the main features of British land administration.

38. Low, Graeme Campbell. REPORT OF THE COMMISSIONER APPOINTED TO
INQUIRE INTO THE OPERATION OF THE LAND TENURE SCHEME IN
ANKOLE. Entebbe, Govt. Printer (1962). 30 p.
                                        Mem HD 990 U3 L6

The Ankole land tenure scheme was established in 1958 to
register titles to land. The report of the commission which
investigated the scheme three years later found no serious
difficulties in the operation of the scheme.

39. Luswata, F. J. "The Implications of land tenure to agricultural development projects in Uganda." 1969. (In Item
KEN-121, p. 126-136)                      HD 982 016

An examination of the land tenure systems of Busoga and Lango
leads the author to the conclusion that communal ownership of
land retards capitalization and improvement of the land.

39a. McAuslan, J. P. W. B. "Co-operatives and the law in East
Africa." 1970.                          HD 3561 E2 C6

See Item KEN-94a for citation.

# LAND TENURE AND AGRARIAN REFORM

40. MacDonald, A. S. "Some aspects of land utilization in Uganda."
    (In EAAJ, 29:2, 1963. p. 147-156)                    Ag Per

    Aggregate land utilization in Uganda is in the neighborhood of
    1.3 acres per person, a statistic which has remained remark-
    ably constant over the years. Over-production of food is a
    necessary adjunct of a system where every family is respon-
    sible for its own sustenance, since losses in storage are
    common.

41. McIntyre, Paula. "Land tenure in Buganda." (Madison) 1972.
    20 1. Bibl. Paper for Anthropology 983, University of
    Wisconsin.
                                             Files Uga 58 M14

    A seminar paper in which land tenure in Buganda is viewed
    within an historical framework.

42. Madiman, S. G. "Land reform in East Africa." n.d.
                                             Files Afr 3 M12

    See Item KEN-99 for citation and annotation.

43. Mafeje, Archie. AGRARIAN REVOLUTION AND THE LAND QUESTION IN
    BUGANDA. I.S.S. occasional paper no. 32. The Hague, Insti-
    tute of Social Studies, 1973. 27 p. Bibl.   Files Uga 3 M13
    Also available in DUALISM AND RURAL DEVELOPMENT IN EAST AFRICA.
    Copenhagen, Institute for Development Research (1973).
    p. 127-156.                               HC 517 E2 D82

    A Marxist analysis of the history of Buganda from precolonial
    times to the present followed by a call for an all-encompassing
    program of land reform to sweep away the old order.

44. _____. "Large-scale farming in Buganda." 1969. (In Item
    AFR-25, p. 22-30)                         HD 2117 B7

    Most large-scale farmers who acquired land after World War II
    bought it piecemeal. Enterprising farmers tried to avoid land
    which already had tenants settled on it, and they overcame
    the problem of fragmentation of holdings by concentrating
    their efforts on one main plot.

45. Maini, Krishan M. LAND LAW IN EAST AFRICA. 1967.
                                             HD 1169 M14

    See Item KEN-102 for citation. Contains sections on the
    historical development of land law in Uganda; the Registration
    of Titles Act of 1922; and legal provisions for sale, lease,
    mortgage trusts, restraints on disposition, and rights in

UGA 45-51

(Maini, Krishan M.)
land owned by other persons. A table of cases cited and a chronological table of statutes pertaining to land enhance the work's value as a handbook for legal practitioners and scholars.

46. Mair, Lucy P. "Agrarian policy in British African colonies." 1951.                                                         Ag HD 965 L3

See Item AFR-86 for citation and annotation.

47. _____. "Buganda land tenure." (In A/IAI, 6:2, 1933.
p. 187-205)                                                      Mem AP A257
Also available in her AN AFRICAN PEOPLE IN THE TWENTIETH
CENTURY. London, 1934. p. 154-172.          Mem DT 434 U2 M3

A paper on the rights and duties of the peasants, the authority of chiefs, the status of clan lands, and changes in land policy under British rule, in particular the changing situation of the bataka or clan leaders, whose position was undercut by the introduction of individual freehold rights to land among their followers.

48. _____. "Native land tenure in East Africa." (In A/IAI, 4:3,
1931. p. 314-329)                                                Mem AP A257

A short survey of existing anthropological sources on land tenure in the East African countries as of 1930. The section on Uganda notes the neglect of the study of land tenure.

49. _____. "Native rights in land in the British African territories." 1951.                                                    Ag HD 965 L3

See Item AFR-87 for citation and annotation.

50. Meek, Charles Kingsley. "Uganda." 1949. (In Item AFR-91,
p. 131-144)                                                         HD 599 Z4 M4

From the point of view of the colonial administration, land tenure in Uganda fell into two main categories: crown lands and mailo lands. Crown land, defined as all land not subject to documentary title, was held in trust by the government for the African peoples who occupied it. Mailo land, which was subject to rights approximating freehold tenure, could be held only by people native to Buganda Province.

51. Moody, R. W. LAND TENURE IN SAMIA. (196-)   Files Afr 58 M66

See Item KEN-111 for citation and annotation.

# LAND TENURE AND AGRARIAN REFORM

51a.    Mugerwa, E. B.  THE POSITION OF THE MAILO-OWNERS IN THE PEAS-
        ANTRY SOCIETY OF BUGANDA; A CASE STUDY OF MUGE AND LUKAYA
        VILLAGES.  University examinations, 1973; political science
        paper 7(a):  dissertation.  Dar es Salaam, Dept. of Political
        Science, University of Dar es Salaam, 1973.  39 p.
                                                    Files Uga 58 M83

52.     Mugerwa, P. J. Nkambo.  "Land tenure in East Africa:  some
        contrasts."  1966.                          Law JX 31 I5/5

        See Item KEN-114 for citation and annotation.

53.     Mukwaya, A. B.  LAND TENURE IN BUGANDA:  PRESENT DAY TENDEN-
        CIES.  East African studies no. 1.  Kampala, Published for
        the East African Institute of Social Research by Eagle Press,
        1953.  79 p.                               Files Uga 58 M84

        A pamphlet on land tenure in Buganda focusing on refinements
        in the rules governing the rights of peasant landholders and
        the evolution of the political and usufructuary rights dele-
        gated by chiefs over the last seventy-odd years.

53a.    _____.  SOME OF THE PROBLEMS OF LAND TENURE IN BUGANDA.
        Conference paper no. 43.  (Kampala) Makerere Institute of
        Social Research (195-).  7 p.              Files Uga 58 M843

54.     Müller-Praefke, Dieter; und Polster, Dietrich.  ZUR FRAGE DER
        BODENREFORM IN ENTWICKLUNGSLANDERN LATEINAMERIKAS UND AFRIKAS:
        EINE LITERATURSTUDIE.  1966.                    HD 1251 M85

        See Item AFR-97 for citation and annotation.

55.     Nypan, Astrid.  SOCIOLOGICAL ASPECTS OF AGRICULTURAL DEVELOP-
        MENT:  A CASE STUDY OF TWO AREAS IN UGANDA.  Report no. 5.
        Oslo, University of Oslo, Institute of Sociology, Section for
        Development Studies, 1971.  58 l.           Files Uga 4 N96

        This study explores institutional and motivational factors
        related to development and concludes that there is little to
        be found in the rules of the communal land tenure systems of
        Acholi and West Nile to make them an obstacle to development.
        Opposition to the attempts of progressive farmers to expand
        their holdings arises not because the farmer breaks the rules
        of the communal tenure system, but because of the adverse
        effects of expansion on the traditional organization of pro-
        duction and on the family system.  The best approach is there-
        fore to focus development efforts on influential opinion
        leaders who will spread information to less innovative members
        of rural communities.

# LAND TENURE AND AGRARIAN REFORM

56. Obol-Ochola, James Yonason, ed.  LAND LAW REFORM IN EAST
    AFRICA.  1969.                                    HD 982 016

    See Item KEN-121 for citation and annotation.  See Items
    UGA-10; UGA-28; UGA-39; and UGA-58 for annotations of indivi-
    dual articles on Kenya.

57. Obol-Owit, L. E. C.  "The Changing pattern of settlement at
    Omia Anyima in East Acholi."  (In Makerere Institute of Social
    Research.  CONFERENCE PAPERS:  PART E, GEOGRAPHY.  (Kampala)
    1968.  20 p.)                      HC 517 E2 M14 1968 Pt. E

    In the precolonial past, settlement patterns were largely
    determined by the need for security, with population concen-
    trated in strategic sites on hills and high ground.  Recently,
    however, the availability of land and a desire to be close to
    roads and towns have resulted in migration down the slopes to
    low ground.

58. Okec, J.  "Pilot schemes for the registration of land titles
    in Uganda."  1969.  (In Item KEN-121, p. 255-264)   HD 982 016

    A summary of experience with adjudication and registration of
    rights to land in Kigezi and Ankole districts.  These pilot
    schemes were an outgrowth of the recommendations of the same
    Royal Commission of 1953 which laid the groundwork for sim-
    ilar projects in Kenya.

59. Perlman, M. L.  "Land tenure in Toro."  (In Kampala, Uganda.
    East African Institute of Social Research Conference, 1962.
    PAPERS.  Kampala, 1962.  16 p.)             Mem AP K148 1962
    Also available as a separate.              Files Uga 58 P27

    A description of customary land tenure in Toro on the basis
    of a content analysis of court cases in Mutenge and Burtuya
    counties.  Includes sections on the acquisition and transfer
    of land rights, the impact of changes in the land tenure sys-
    tem on marriage customs, and an assessment that individualiza-
    tion of tenure would be accepted by old people and actively
    sought by the young.

60. Richards, Audrey I.  THE CHANGING STRUCTURE OF A GANDA
    VILLAGE.  East African studies no. 24.  Nairobi, East African
    Publishing House (1970).  116 p.  Bibl.    Mem HN 791 E2 E2/24

    A section on land tenure (p. 96-104) outlines the main fea-
    tures of tenure systems of the area studied and classifies
    villages into those with no land owners, those with single
    owners, and those with multiple land owners.

# LAND TENURE AND AGRARIAN REFORM

61. _____. "Some effects of the introduction of individual free-hold into Buganda." (In Item AFR-67, p. 267-278)

HD 966 I5 1960

The principal focus here is the evolution of freehold tenure in Buganda in the context of the economic change of the last half century. The author considers a number of historical factors which have influenced the development of the land tenure system: the plentiful supply of migrant labor in the early twentieth century, the role of the traditional political system, the introduction of cotton and coffee, the fact that land was alienated in large parcels rather than in small ones, and the failure of large European-owned plantations to gain a foothold.

62. Segal, Aaron. "The Politics of land in East Africa." 1968.

See Item KEN-139 for citation and annotation.

63. Southwold, M. "The Inheritance of land in Buganda." (In UJ, 20:1, 1956. p. 88-96)

Mem AP U26

A description of a dispute between brothers over inherited land is used to illustrate the general principles governing succession to rights in land in Buganda.

63a. _____. "Land and leadership in a Ganda village." (In Kampala, Uganda. East African Institute of Social Research Conference, 1959. PAPERS. Kampala, 1958/59. 19 p.) Mem AP K148 1958/59

64. Thomas, Harold B. "An Experiment in African native land settlement." (In RAS/J, 27:107, 1927/8. p. 234-248)

Mem AP A258 A256

A review of British land policy in Buganda to the late 1920s. The author asserts that the two main forms of tenure in pre-colonial Buganda were characterized by individual ownership of land "but devoid of any conception of land as a negotiable possession."

65. Thomas, Harold B.; and Scott, Robert, comps. UGANDA. New York, Oxford University Press, 1949. xx, 559 p.

Mem DT 434 U2 T5

A chapter on land tenure (p. 98-111) outlines the main fea-tures of contrasting types of customary land tenure found in Uganda, tenure arrangements on _mailo_ land, rules governing acquisition of land by non-Africans, and registration of title.

# LAND TENURE AND AGRARIAN REFORM

66.  Tindituuza, R. J.; and Kateete, B. M.  ESSAYS ON LAND FRAG-
     MENTATION IN KIGEZI DISTRICT.  Occasional paper no. 22.
     Kampala, Dept. of Geography, Makerere University, 1971.  91 p.
     HD 989 U2 T45

     The size and distribution of the population of Nyarurambi is
     derived from a sample survey.  Concludes that population
     growth and traditional patterns of land inheritance have con-
     tributed to a shortage of cultivable land.  The second essay
     in this collection treats land use from the perspective of
     locational analysis.

67.  Uganda.  LAND TENURE PROPOSALS.  Published by Authority.
     Entebbe, Govt. Printer, 1955.  9 p.          Files Uga 58 U325

     Proposals intended to stimulate discussion on a new land
     policy having the following objectives:  to redefine the status
     of land in Uganda and to afford greater local control over
     land administration, to redefine the processes of law by which
     rights in land may be transferred, and to encourage individual
     land ownership by Africans in a manner which will not alienate
     the good will of traditional authorities.

68.  _____.  Agriculture Dept.  THE REPORT OF THE COMMITTEE ON THE
     ESTABLISHMENT OF STATE FARMS IN UGANDA.  Entebbe, Dept. of
     Agriculture, Ministry of Agriculture and Forestry, 1969.
     32 p.                                         Files Uga 7.5 U32

     Recommends the types of sites, cropping patterns, sources of
     finance, and modes of organization considered to be requisite
     for the success of state farms in Uganda.

69.  _____.  Constitution.  THE CONSTITUTION OF THE REPUBLIC OF
     UGANDA.  Entebbe, 1967.  v, 109 p.          JQ 2953 A5 1967

     Sections 108 and 109 provide for the creation of a commission
     on land tenure.

70.  _____.  Laws, statutes, etc.  THE PUBLIC LANDS ACT, 1969.
     Entebbe, Govt. Printer, 1969.  30 p.          Files Uga 76 U32

     An outline of legislation empowering the Land Commission and
     Land Committees to manage and control public lands.

71.  _____.  Ministry of Land Tenure.  BIBLIOGRAPHY OF LAND TENURE.
     (Entebbe, 1957).  57 p.                      Mem Z 7164 L3 U3

     A bibliography of 82 works and 109 laws and court rulings on
     land tenure in Uganda.

72.   _____. Uganda Relationships Commission. REPORT, 1961.
Entebbe, Govt. Printer (1961).  232 p.         JQ 2951 A53 A3

Report of a 1961 commission to consider the form of government
for an independent Uganda.  A chapter on land tenure (p. 80-84)
summarizes the history of the country's land tenure under
British rule and recommends that crown lands be administered
by district land boards, that limitations on acquisition of
land by non-Africans be retained, that pre-independence leases
be respected, and that provision be made for compulsory acquisition of land by the government when necessary.

73.   Watts, Susan J.  THE SOUTH BUSOGA RESETTLEMENT SCHEME.  Occa-
sional paper no. 17.  Syracuse, Syracuse University, Maxwell
School of Citizenship and Public Affairs, Program of Eastern
African Studies, 1966.  36 l.              Files Uga 17 W18

In 1956 the Uganda government sponsored a resettlement scheme
in south Busoga, an area which had been evacuated twice
because of epidemics of sleeping sickness.  By the end of
1961 the Protectorate Government had abandoned the entire
project.  The author concludes that most mistakes made in the
scheme could be attributed to poor planning and lack of control over agricultural activities.

74.   West, Henry W.  LAND POLICY IN BUGANDA.  African studies
series no. 3.  Cambridge (Eng.) Cambridge University Press,
1972.  xiv, 244 p.                         HD 989 U2 B868

The kingdom of Buganda, which forms a distinct administrative
unit within the state of Uganda, has been the scene of an
unusual experiment in the individualization of land tenure,
which led to a synthesis of English and Ganda notions of
property.  This book, based on the author's experience in the
service of the Uganda government and subsequent field research,
presents a detailed and well-researched study of the nature of
freehold and mailo tenure, the nature of derivative rights in
land, devolution upon death, the market in property rights,
and records of land rights.  The author concludes with recommendations for measures to rectify the more important faults
and weaknesses of the current situation.

75.   _____. THE MAILO SYSTEM IN BUGANDA: A PRELIMINARY CASE STUDY
IN AFRICAN LAND TENURE.  With a foreword by the Commissioner
of Lands and Surveys, Uganda.  Entebbe, Govt. Printer (1965).
xi, 179 p.                                 HD 989 U2 W26

(West, Henry W.)
A preliminary version of Item UGA-74 written before the author
completed his extensive field research. However, historical
background on the development and evolution of land policy in
Buganda is more complete here than in the later version.

76.  _____. "Reflections upon the problems of land registration in
Buganda." (Kampala, 1963). 8 p. Paper read to the Conference
of the East African Institute of Social Research, Makerere
University College, Kampala, December 1963.  Files Uga 59 W27

A brief article on difficulties encountered in the operation
of a land registry in Buganda over the last fifty years. The
ordinance of 1924, for example, failed to provide for the
decentralization of the land register, so that for thirty years
this was retained in a single office in Entebbe.

77.  _____. THE TRANSFORMATION OF LAND TENURE IN BUGANDA SINCE
1896. African social research documents, 2. (Leiden, Nether-
lands, Afrika-Studiecentrum, n.d.). 102 p. Bibl.
HD 989 U2 W27

Presents a series of documents tracing the interaction of English and Ganda notions of property over the last seventy-odd
years. Includes documents on each of the following subjects:
land grants prior to 1900, the Uganda Agreement of 1900, the
implementation of the agreement, and areas of difficulty in
the implementation of the new land policy.

78.  Weyel, Volker. "Land ownership in Nyakinengo, Ruzhumbura
(North Kigezi); a preliminary survey." (In RAN, 1:3, 1973.
p. 41-47)

A short note on field research in North Kigezi which showed
that land ownership was sharply skewed, with one-fifth of the
population owning one-half of the land. The author views this
situation as incontrovertible evidence of the emergence of
rural social classes.

79.  Whetham, Edith H.  COOPERATION, LAND REFORM AND LAND SETTLE-
MENT.  1968.                                   Ag HD 1491 A52 W4

See Item AFR-140 for citation. A chapter on Uganda (p. 23-31)
describes cooperative credit schemes and group farms, which
function as producer cooperatives to facilitate mechanized
cultivation of cotton. A particularly difficult aspect of the
organization is tension between the manager, an outsider, and
the members of the governing committee composed of members of
the cooperative.

# LAND TENURE AND AGRARIAN REFORM

79a.   Wintrob, Joseph W.  "The Importance of land tenure to political
and economic change in Buganda."  (Madison) 1966.  15 l.  Bibl.
Paper for Agricultural Economics 429, University of Wisconsin.
Files Uga 58 W45

80.   Yeld, Rachel.  "Land hunger in Kigezi, south-west Uganda."
1968.  (In Item KEN-83, p. 24-28)          Files Afr 17 L15

Population pressure on land in Kigezi dates to the 1930s when
natural increase in population and immigration from Rwanda
began to create serious problems.  Possible solutions include
resettlement elsewhere in Uganda, out-migration of surplus
labor, or the provision of local employment by developing light
industry in the area.


## UPPER VOLTA

1.   Barral, Henri.  TIOGO; ETUDE GEOGRAPHIQUE D'UN TERROIR LELA
(HAUTE-VOLTA).  Atlas des structures agraires au sud du
Sahara no. 2.  Paris, Mouton (1968).  72 p.  Bibl.  Publiée
sous le patronage de la Maison des Sciences de l'Homme.
S 473 U6 B17

A study of land tenure, land use, and the social structure of
a village in the central region of Upper Volta.  A section on
land tenure (p. 41-46) analyzes the distribution of land within
the kélé, or lineage segment residing within a fortress-like
group of buildings.  Rights to land outside the enclosure reflect kinship relationships and the spatial arrangement of
residences within.  Rights to cultivate fields in the bush, as
well as rights to those surrounding the enclosure, are obtained
from the head of the co-residential lineage segment.

2.   Boutillier, Jean-Louis.  "Relationships among land tenure,
village hierarchy, and family systems:  the situation in Upper
Volta."  n.p., 1972.  7 l.  Paper prepared for the Seminar on
Agricultural Research in West Africa, "Aspects of Land Tenure,"
University of Ibadan, 1972.          Files UV 58 B68

This excellent conference paper presents the main features of
customary land tenure in Upper Volta and sets forth a classification of different types of tenure.  The frequency with which
each type of tenure is found in the five regions of the country
is related to population density.  The author concludes that
more than anything else the conservative nature of relationships within village communities hinders individual initiative

249

UV 2-6

(Boutillier, Jean-Louis)
and prevents permanent improvement of the land. But land tenure is an area in which a number of interests and ideologies converge, and hence the question should be asked as to whether immediate radical reform would be compatible with the preservation of certain important values of West African civilization.

3. _____. "Les Structures foncières en Haute-Volta." (In EVOL, 5, 1964. p. 5-179) Mem AP E85 V935
Also available as a separate. Files UV 58 B67

This is the report of a project headed by Boutillier which the government of Upper Volta commissioned to do a comprehensive study of land tenure. Included are the principal characteristics of land tenure systems in the country, the influence of traditional economic and political systems on land ownership, and an analysis of the costs and benefits of agrarian reform in this context. In the second half of the report, separate chapters present the tenure systems of each of the ten largest ethnic groups of the country.

4. Gosselin, G. DEVELOPPEMENT ET TRADITION DANS LES SOCIETES RURALES AFRICAINES. 1970. HN 773.5 G67

See Item AFR-60 for citation. A chapter on Mossi migration to Mali contains sections describing the agrarian structure of the Yatenga region, which was a Mossi state in precolonial times.

4a. Hurault, Jean. "L'Organisation du terroir dans les groupements Bamiléké." (In ETR, 37/39, 1970. p. 232-256)

5. Kohler, Jean Marie. ACTIVITES AGRICOLES ET CHANGEMENTS SOCIAUX DANS L'OUEST-MOSSI (HAUTE-VOLTA). Mémoires ORSTOM no. 46. Paris, Office de la Recherche Scientifique et Technique Outre Mer, 1971. 248 p. HD 2135 U62 K64

A study of the agrarian systems and social structure of the western area of Mossi settlement. A chapter on land tenure (p. 139-164) analyzes the relationship between the social structure and land tenure systems, defines the nature of various rights to land as well as the rules of succession to these rights, and analyzes the distribution of land rights within and among lineage segments.

6. Lahuec, Jean Paul "Une Communauté évolutive mossi: Zaongho (Haute-Volta)." (In ETR, 37/39, 1970. p. 150-172)

UV 6-10

(Lahuec, Jean Paul)
The principal focus here is the evolution of land use in a
Mossi village in Upper Volta. Demographic pressure resulted in
dispersed settlement patterns and encouraged crop diversification as villagers began to cultivate rice, manioc, and other
crops on low-lying land.

7.  Pradeau, Christian. "Kokolibou (Haute-Volta) ou le pays
    Dagari à travers un terroir." (In ETR, 37/39, 1970. p. 85-
    112)

    An analysis of land use and the social structure in a Dagari
    village in Upper Volta. The principal focus of the article is
    population pressure on land and its effect upon the agrarian
    system.

8.  Remy, Gérard. YOBRI, ETUDE GEOGRAPHIQUE DU TERROIR D'UN VIL-
    LAGE GOURMANTCHE DE HAUTE-VOLTA. Atlas de structures agraires
    au sud du Sahara no. 1. Paris, Mouton (1967). 99 p.
                                                    S 473 U6 R25

    A study of land use, land tenure, and the spatial organization
    of a village economy, done by a geographer and based on his
    field research of 1962-1963. A chapter on land tenure (p. 55-
    63) presents the main features of the tenure system and de-
    scribes how land is distributed among family units and how
    family members distribute land among themselves.

9.  Rouamba, Paul T. "Terroirs en pays Mossi: à propos de
    Yaoghin (Haute-Volta)." (In ETR, 37/39, 1970. p. 129-149)

    An article on settlement patterns and land use in a densely
    populated area of Upper Volta about 40 km. south of Ouagadougou.

10. Savonnet, Georges. PINA: ETUDE D'UN TERROIR DE FRONT PIONNIER
    EN PAYS DAGARI (HAUTE-VOLTA). Atlas des structures agraires
    au sud du Sahara no. 4. Paris, Mouton, 1970. 63 p. Publiée
    sous le patronage de la Maison des Sciences de l'Homme.
                                                    S 473 U6 S19

    A socio-economic study of the village of Pina in south central
    Upper Volta, located on the frontier of northward expansion of
    Dagari settlement, where a vanguard of immigrants arrives and
    reclaims land from the bush. A section on land ownership
    (p. 36-41) notes that the tenure system is organized according
    to rights vested in an earth priest, with use rights conferred
    on village heads and delegated to heads of households and in
    turn to members of households.

LAND TENURE AND AGRARIAN REFORM

11.   Sawadogo, Maurice. "Le Chef de terres au Yatinga (Haute-
      Volta)." 1970. (In Item AFR-112, p. 1153-1160)

      An analysis of the role of the earth priest in Yatinga, one
      of the Mossi states of Upper Volta. The earth priest is a
      guardian of customary land rights rather than the owner of the
      land. His economic role is negligible, though he enjoys con-
      siderable prestige and a high social status in village life and
      exercises authority in customary courts.

12.   United Nations. Economic Commission for Africa. REPORT OF A
      MISSION FOR THE STUDY OF PROBLEMS AND PROSPECTS IN THE RURAL
      DEVELOPMENT OF MALI, NIGER, AND UPPER VOLTA. 1966.
                                                    HN 803.5 U58

      See Item MALI-5 for citation. A general survey of the pros-
      pects for development in the region. Recommends "the eradica-
      tion of illiteracy," increased security of land tenure
      (though no specific measures or in-depth analyses are given),
      and a study of land use.


                              ZAIRE

1.    Beguin, H. LA MISE EN VALEUR AGRICOLE DU SUD-EST DU KASAI.
      Série scientifique, 88. Brussels, Institut National pour
      l'Etude Agronomique du Congo Belge, 1960. 288 p.
                                              Mem S 19 I6524/88

      This survey of the agricultural economy of the southeast Kasai
      includes a chapter on land tenure (p. 59-77) which notes that
      land ownership rests with territorially based groups--villages,
      groups of villages, and wards of large villages.

2.    Biebuyck, Daniel P. "Le Problème des terres du Congo dans ses
      rapports avec les systèmes fonciers traditionnels." (In SYN,
      14:163/164, 1959/60.· p. 78-90)              Mem AP S995
      Also available as a separate.              Files Zai 58 B42

      An understanding of the impact of new legal, social, economic,
      political, and religious concepts on African societies pre-
      supposes a thorough knowledge of the African culture being
      affected. The author discusses the general principles of cus-
      tomary land tenure systems in Zaire.

# LAND TENURE AND AGRARIAN REFORM

3. _____. RIGHTS IN LAND AND ITS RESOURCES AMONG THE NYANGA (REPUBLIC CONGO-LEOPOLDVILLE). Classe des sciences morales et politiques, Nouv. sér., t. 34; fasc. 2. Brussels, Académie Royale des Sciences d'Outre-Mer, 1966. 45 p.

Mem DT 641 A27 Ser.2/34/2

A study of various principles underlying the system of rights, privileges, and obligations related to ownership of land and its resources. The nature and extent of these rights and obligations is examined in the wider context of Nyanga oral traditions, geographical concepts, moral and religious rules, relations between persons and between groups, the social and political structure, and economic activities.

4. _____. "Systèmes de tenure foncière et problèmes fonciers au Congo." (In Item AFR-67, p. 83-100)        HD 966 I5 1960

Systems of landholding in Zaire have many common features: the importance of lineage groups in land ownership; the influence of rules of residence, kinship, and marriage; and the maintenance of distinctions between hunting, fishing, gathering, and agricultural rights. The article, written by an anthropologist, compares lineage structures, internal segmentation, and degrees of lineage corporateness as factors determining the nature of land tenure systems.

5. _____; et Dufour, Jean. "Le Régime foncier du Congo belge: étude ethnologique et juridique." (In ZAIRE, 12, 1958. p. 365-382)
Mem AP Z21

Presents the methodology employed by a government-sponsored commission for the study of land tenure. The commission was composed of ethnographers and specialists on land law. The results, described only in a very general manner, include the establishment of a typology of land tenure systems and a call for deeper knowledge of the social principles underlying customary land tenure systems.

6. Boeckhout, J. van. "Le Droit foncier du groupement Bakwanga du secteur Baluba Bushimaie." (In BJIDCC, 26:10, 1958. p. 285-291)
Mem Microfilm 2021

A discussion of various rights in land as defined by Baluba customary law: ownership of immovable property on land, rights to the use of land, rights in forest and savannah land, rights in crops, and hunting rights.

# LAND TENURE AND AGRARIAN REFORM

7.  Boelaert, Edmond. L'ETAT INDEPENDANT ET LES TERRES INDIGENES.
    Class des sciences morales et politiques: Mémoires in 8°,
    Nouv. sér., t. 5; fasc. 4. (Bruxelles, 1956). 66 p. Bibl.
    Mem DT 641 A27 Ser.2/5/4

    Various interpretations of a law of 1885 governing African land
    tenure are possible. Two diametrically opposed views emerge:
    that of jurists, who recognized customary rights of land
    tenure; and that of the administrators, who allowed land alien-
    ation to Europeans on a massive scale. The interpretation of
    the administrators triumphed. Other legal questions in the
    early years of the Congo Free State are similarly analyzed to
    show a systematic policy of government subversion of laws
    protecting communal land rights.

8.  Buelens, K. "Analyse économique du problème de la propriété
    foncière au Congo." (In ZAIRE, 12, 1958. p. 227-249)
    Mem AP Z21

    An ethnocentric account which views the problems of economic
    development in agriculture as stemming from the weakness of
    African tenure systems, which fail to guarantee security of
    property. Another weakness, according to the author, lies in
    African judicial systems, which are characterized by "the
    absence of deeply-rooted Christian concepts of justice and
    respect for the human person, such as impregnate social rela-
    tions in the Occident."

8a. Coene, R. de. "Agricultural settlement schemes in the Belgian
    Congo." (In TROP, 33:1, 1956. p. 1-12)         Ag Per

9.  Collier, J. "Les Paysannats du Nord-Sankuru (territoire de
    Lodja et de Katako-Kombe)." (In BACBRU, 50:3, 1959. p. 569-
    648)                                            Mem S 339 A6

    A one-dimensional study of government-controlled paysannats
    (rural producer cooperatives) written by an agronomist more
    interested in technical aspects of production than in modes of
    social organization. Local cultivators are seen as "irrational"
    and backward because of their resistance to techniques forced
    on them by outsiders.

10. Congo (Democratic Republic). Ministère de l'Agriculture. LAND
    REFORM IN THE CONGO. RU:WLR-C/66/1. Rome, FAO, 1966. 12 p.
    Country paper for World Land Reform Conference, Rome, 1966.
    Files Zai 3 C65

    Describes several forms of paysannats and trends in legislation
    affecting rural life outside these development schemes. Also

# LAND TENURE AND AGRARIAN REFORM

ZAI 10-15

(Congo (Democratic Republic))
lists development projects planned or under way at the time
of writing.

11.　Crine, Fernand.　"Aspects politico-sociaux du système de tenure des terres des Luunda septentrionaux."　(In Item AFR-67,
p. 157-172)　　　　　　　　　　　　　　　　　　HD 966 I5 1960

The historical development of the Luunda state in the territory
of Kapanga determined the political and land-owning aspects of
the machinery of government.　Territorial chiefs and new political authorities were superimposed over the pre-existing landowners and political leaders.　The central government respected
the pre-existing distribution of the land among political
authorities, and it set up a delicate balance between the
rights of land ownership and the exercise of political
authority.

12.　Doutreloux, Albert.　"Note sur le domaine foncier au Mayumbe."
(In ZAIRE, 13, 1959.　p. 499-508)　　　　　　　　Mem AP Z21

The social organization of the Mayumbe is reflected in their
system of land tenure.　Litigation over disputed rights in
land has been a constant problem and has been exacerbated in
recent times by the introduction of a legal system of European
origin.

13.　_____.　"Tenure foncière et valeurs socio-culturelles dans un
groupe africain."　(In ANTH, 8:2, 1966.　p. 217-233)
　　　　　　　　　　　　　　　　　　　　　　　Hist E 78 C2 A53

Discusses aspects of land tenure among the Yombe, who view
land principally as a support for religious and socio-political
values and only secondarily as property or means of production.

14.　Dufour, Jean P.　"Quelques aspects juridiques du problème
foncièr au Congo."　(In Item AFR-67, p. 173-184)
　　　　　　　　　　　　　　　　　　　　　　HD 966 I5 1960

Land law in Zaire has the dualistic heritage of a system of
written law and local customary law.　The concept of "vacant"
land embodied in much colonial legislation is entirely foreign
to the African way of thinking about land.　On the other hand,
the author feels that customary law cannot fully meet the requirements of a modern African society.

15.　Dufrénoy, Paul.　LE REGIME FONCIER AU CONGO BELGE ET L'ACT
TORRENS.　Brussels, A. Hauchamps, 1934.　220 p.
　　　　　　　　　　　　　　　　　　　　　　Mem JQ 3608 D8

255

ZAI 15-19

(Dufrénoy, Paul)
A jurist's study of the land law of the Belgian Congo with
emphasis on the law of 1920 and its sources in Belgian law.

16.　"¿Existe un problema de reforma agraria en el Africa negra?"
(In CE, 15:6, 1965. p. 447-449)

An angry critique of colonial economic policy and the failure
of the newly independent Congolese government to formulate an
agricultural policy. Stresses that the country's problems
are largely rural. The author's concept of "agrarian reform"
is unclear.

16a.　Harms, Robert. "Indigenous land tenure systems in Zaire."
n.p., 1973. (9) l. Bibl. Paper for Agricultural Economics
472, University of Wisconsin.　　　　　Files Zai 58 H17

17.　_____. LAND TENURE AND AGRICULTURAL DEVELOPMENT IN ZAIRE,
1895-1961. LTC no. 99. Madison, Land Tenure Center, 1974.
26 p. Bibl.　　　　　　　　　　　　Files Zai 58 H173

An examination of the land tenure systems of the Zande, Kuba,
Mongo, and Nyunga of Zaire. The generalization that land is
held by corporate groups is confirmed in all four cases, but
the nature of these corporate groups varies widely. For example, among the Zande, it is the chiefdom which holds land
rights, but among the Kuba it is the village. The paper concludes with a summary of changes in land tenure systems during
the colonial period and includes a short section on the
paysannats.

18.　Hecq, J. "Le Système de culture des Bashi (Kivu, Territoire
de Kabare) et ses possibilités." (In BACBRU, 49:4, 1958.
p. 969-1000)　　　　　　　　　　　　　Mem S 339 A6

Projects the probable evolution of the customary system of land
tenure of the Bashi under the influence of newly introduced
intensive agricultural techniques. The article describes the
environment, land use, tenure structure, and cultivation practices, and proposes changes in the system to augment production. Includes a description of tenure reform on an
experimental paysannat at Mivendo.

19.　Heyse, Théodore. GRANDES LIGNES DU REGIME DES TERRES DU CONGO
BELGE ET DU RUANDI-URUNDI ET LEURS APPLICATIONS (1940-1946).
1947.　　　　　　　　　　　　　　　Mem DT 641 A27 15/1

See Item BURU-5 for citation and annotation.

256

20.    _____. PROBLEMES FONCIERS ET REGIME DES TERRES (ASPECTS
ECONOMIQUES, JURIDIQUES, ET SOCIAUX): AFRIQUE, CONGO BELGE,
RUANDA-URUNDI. 1960.
                                              Mem Z 7164 L3 H4

See Item AFR-65 for citation and annotation.

21.    _____; et Leonard, H.  REGIME DES CESSIONS ET CONCESSIONS DE
TERRES ET DU MINES AU CONGO BELGE.  Bruxelles, Weverburgh,
1929.  205 p.  Bibl.
                                              Mem HC 591 C6 H4

An analysis of the law pertaining to the granting of concessions for plantations and mining operations in the Congo under
colonial rule.  The book, which drew heavily on previously
published material, was intended to be a guide to the procedures and formalities required to obtain rights in land in the
colony.

22.    Kalambay, Gaston.  "Les Droits fonciers coutumiers à travers
la législation de la République démocratique du Congo."  1970.
(In Item AFR-112, p. 1175-1180)

Legislation has had an important impact on customary systems
of land tenure by reducing the extent of control over land
rights exercised by traditional authorities.

23.    _____. "L'Expropriation pour cause d'utilité publique en
République démocratique du Congo."  1970.  (In Item AFR-112,
p. 1017-1040)

The legal bases for public acquisition of land are derived
from colonial statutes and have been given a widened scope
under the Constitution of Zaire.  Expropriation is in the
domain of the executive branch of the government.

23a.   Kamanda, Lumpungu.  REGIME DES TERRES ET CRISE AGRICOLE AU
ZAIRE; PRESENTATION SYNTHETIQUE DU PROBLEME AGRAIRE ET SES
CONSEQUENCES SUR LE DEVELOPPEMENT AGRICOLE AU ZAIRE.
Bruxelles, Institut International des Civilisations
Differentes, 1973.  20 p.  Bibl.  Paper for INCIDI Study Ses-
sion on Obstacles and Restraints Impeding the Success of Land
Reform in Developing Countries, 1973.         Files Zai 4 K15

24.    Massitu, M. Jean Albert.  LE CADASTRE CONGOLAISE.  E/CN.14/
CART/266.  Addis Ababa, UNECA, 1970.  64 p.  Paper for Seminar
on Cadastre, Addis Ababa, 1970.               Files Zai 12.5 M17

A lengthy document including historical background on land
administration in Zaire, details on the organization and

# LAND TENURE AND AGRARIAN REFORM

ZAI 24-27

(Massitu, M. Jean Albert)
functions of the cadastral service, and a description of the
working relationship between the cadastral service and the
registry of deeds.

25. Miracle, Marvin P. AGRICULTURE IN THE CONGO BASIN: TRADITION
AND CHANGE IN AFRICAN RURAL ECONOMIES. Madison, University of
Wisconsin Press, 1967. xv, 355 p.          S 472 C75 M45

Agricultural production in the local economies of the Congo
Basin is both complex and diverse. It is common for a farmer
to grow 30 or more crops and to have several varieties of many
of them. Most types of cultivation involve efforts to restore
soil fertility, in contrast to the stereotype of shifting cultivation often found in the literature. Technical change in
agriculture has occurred frequently, and African farmers are
accustomed to choosing between alternative enterprises or
factor proportions.

26. Morel, Edmund Dene. GREAT BRITAIN AND THE CONGO; THE PILLAGE
OF THE CONGO BASIN. With an introduction by Sir A. Conan
Doyle. New York, H. Fertig, 1969. xxvi, 291 p. Bibl. Re-
print of the 1909 ed.                      HC 591 C6 M66 1969

An impassioned condemnation of early Belgian administration in
the Congo Basin, first published in 1909. Written with the
intent of provoking British intervention in the area, the book
exposes the brutal excesses permitted by administrative policy.
Sections on land tenure (p. 31-54 and 82-114) describe African
land use and land tenure systems to refute the principle of
"vacant land" which the colonial administration used to justify
the alienation of large tracts of African land to Europeans.
Contends that the intensification of rubber exports caused
social upheaval. Based on eyewitness accounts, correspondence,
and government documents.

27. Müller, Ernst W. LE DROIT DE PROPRIETE CHEZ MONGO BOKOTE.
Classe des sciences morales et politiques: Nouv. sér., t. 9,
fasc. 3. Bruxelles, Académie Royal des Sciences Coloniales,
1959. 79 p.                      Mem DT 641 A27 Ser.2/9/3

A work on the customary law of the Bokôté, a Mongo subgroup.
A section on land tenure (p. 9-34) consists of a review of the
writings of Malengreau, Possez, Boelaert, and Hulstaert.
Separate chapters cover custom governing succession and other
forms of property transfer.

# Land Tenure and Agrarian Reform

28. N'Dongala, E. "Développement rural et fonction coopérative dans l'agriculture congolaise avant la décolonisation." (In CES, 4:4, 1966. p. 387-434)     Mem AP C132 E21

According to the author, the essential function of agriculture in developing countries is to form savings in the rural sector in order to finance industrialization. Savings in the agricultural sector presupposes means to invest in the modernization of techniques in order to raise levels of production. The formation of rural cooperatives is the best way to achieve this. Part of the annual profit of cooperatives should be channeled into lending institutions, and ways should be found to encourage the investment of these funds in industry.

29. "Paysannat settlement in the Congo (Leopoldville)." (In AEBA, 1, 1962. p. 64-65)     Mem JX 1977 A22

A brief description of a pre-independence form of cooperative settlement involving individual peasant cultivators, jointly provided services, and scheduled land use. According to the author, these cooperatives were successful but collapsed after independence because the Zairois had never received training or been allowed to assume responsibility under the colonial regime.

30. Phanzu, Valentin. "L'Evolution du régime de la propriété immobilière en République Démocratique du Congo." 1970. (In Item AFR-112, p. 741-744)

Belgian law prevented Africans from holding title to immovable property, but after independence this discriminatory legislation was repealed. Now every change in the status of rights to immovable property must also be recorded with the registrar of titles.

31. Philippe, R. "L'Accession des Congolais à la propriété foncière individuelle." (In AEQUA, 21:1, 1958. p. 5-28)     Mem Microfilm 2716

Suggests that African civil servants and tradesmen be allowed to hold property under freehold tenure, that merchants be permitted to do likewise provided they could show proof of solvency and commercial ability, and that retired soldiers and workers be allowed to gradually acquire the legal status requisite for freehold title to land. The author feels that the best approach in rural areas is to promote various forms of collective ownership, such as producer cooperatives, rather than individual freehold tenure.

ZAI 32-36

32.    Philippe, R.  "Les Modes de propriété chez les Mongo."  (In
       KO, 25:1, 1959.  p. 17-72)                        Mem AP K822

       This lengthy descriptive study of the Ntombe Njale, a Mongo
       subgroup living on both sides of Lake Mayi-Ndombe (formerly
       Lake Leopold II), includes background on the economy as well
       as sections on rights in village, rural, river bank, and
       hunting land; collective and individual rights in land; acqui-
       sition, transfer, and inheritance of rights; the lack of
       interest in freehold tenure among farmers in the traditional
       sector; and the need for the introduction of freehold tenure
       among workers and civil servants.

33.    Raeck, H. de.  "Le Régime des terres au Congo Belge et au
       Ruanda-Urundi; terres domaniales et terres indigènes, régime
       des cessions et concessions."  (In ECB, 3, 1953.  p. 627-646)
                                              Mem G76 EN18 Cutter
       Also available as a separate.           Files Zai 58 R12

       Traces the historical evolution of the land law of the Belgian
       Congo from 1885 to 1947.  Emphasis is on law regulating the
       granting of concessions to Europeans for plantation agriculture
       or mining.  With rare exceptions, this law applied to Rwanda
       and Burundi as well.  See Item RWA-7 for another annotation.

34.    Schlippé, Pierre de.  SHIFTING CULTIVATION IN AFRICA:  THE
       ZANDE SYSTEM OF AGRICULTURE.  London, Routledge & Paul, 1956.
       304 p.                                      Mem S 471 A365 S4

       A descriptive study of an agricultural system in an area of
       uniformly poor soil.  Fields and households are moved from
       place to place as the soil in a given location loses its fer-
       tility.  Land rights are not normally contested because land
       is abundant and rights to its use are acquired by virtue of
       the labor to prepare the soil for cultivation.

35.    Sousberghe, Lide de.  "Régime foncier ou tenure des terres chez
       les Pende."  (In ARSCBS, 4:7, 1958.  p. 1346-1352)
                                                  Mem JV 2802 A2

       A note on Pendi belief and custom governing hunting rights and
       land tenure.

36.    Vanderlinden, Jacques.  "Principes de droit foncier Zande."
       (In BULIS/R, 3, 1960.  p. 557-610)          Mem AP B9134 R

       Argues that a land tenure system is defined by the interaction
       of people, land, and power, and uses this scheme to describe

# LAND TENURE AND AGRARIAN REFORM

(Vanderlinden, Jacques)
the tenure system of the Zande. The land law of the Zande consists of a minimum number of principles for the simple reason that land is abundant and infertile and therefore has little value in the eyes of potential holders of rights in land.

37. _____. "Problèmes posés par l'introduction de nouveaux modes d'usage des terres chez les Zande Vungara du Congo." (In Item AFR-67, p. 331-347)  HD 966 I5 1960

The major principles of the Zande land tenure system are the following: the pre-eminence of the chief over both persons and land, balance between the exercise of this power and the need for the chief to show restraint if he is to keep his following; the importance of relationships between rights in land and other rights and obligations in the society; and the balance of rights of chiefs against the rights of their subjects.

38. Van Hecke, Etienne. "Structure agraire et habitat au Bas-Congo." (In CRISP, 106/107, 1970. p. 1-63)  Mem DT 31 C43
Also available as a separate.  Files Zai 7 V15

This study of the agrarian economy, social structure, settlement patterns, and land use of the region includes a section on land tenure (p. 8-15) covering family and clan holdings, fallow land, and acquisition of land rights by strangers.

39. _____. "Le Village du Bas Congo en évolution." (In CIV, 20:2, 1970. p. 199-211)

Among the Bakongo ownership of land is becoming individualized because of land shortage and the commercialization of agriculture. The degree to which local chiefs choose to exercise authority and are able to do so also tends to define the process of individualization of rights in land.

40. Vansina, Jan. "Les Régimes fonciers Ruanda et Kuba: une comparaison." (In Item AFR-67, p. 348-363)  HD 966 I5 1960

The following variables account for differences between the Rwanda and Kuba systems of land tenure: density of population, type of land use, mode of social organization, and political structure. For example, differences in social structure explain the contrast between the holding of land by lineages in Rwanda and by villages among the Kuba. Patrilineal descent and patrilocal residence account for the formation of extensive

LAND TENURE AND AGRARIAN REFORM

ZAI 40-ZAM 4

(Vansina, Jan)
residential lineages in Rwanda, whereas among the Kuba matrilineal descent and virilocal marriage do not promote large
residential kin groups.

## ZAMBIA

1.  Allan, William.  LAND HOLDING AND LAND USAGE AMONG THE PLATEAU
    TONGA OF MAZABUKA DISTRICT:  A RECONNAISSANCE SURVEY, 1945.
    With additional sections by J. H. M. McNaughton (and) D. W.
    Conroy.  Westport, Conn., Negro Universities Press (1948,
    1970).  vii, 192 p.                          GN 489 A44 1970

    A study undertaken by the Native Land Tenure Committee to in-
    vestigate African land tenure systems and patterns of inheri-
    tance and succession.  Of particular concern is the failure of
    the Tonga to adopt methods of farming advocated by the Agricul-
    ture Department.  The conclusion is that the expansion of
    acreage without radical improvements in agricultural techniques
    actually hindered agricultural development.

2.  _____.  STUDIES IN AFRICAN LAND USAGE IN NORTHERN RHODESIA.
    The Rhodes-Livingstone papers no. 15.  Cape Town, New York,
    Published for the Rhodes-Livingstone Institute by Oxford
    University Press, 1949.  85 p.  Bibl.          Mem HD 990 R68 A6

    Discusses resettlement work in progress at the time of writing,
    land and soil requirements for agriculture, population densi-
    ties in relation to available land, and the population distri-
    bution in the Lamba-Lima Reserve and in Mkushi District.  The
    book also reviews the recommendations of the 1941 Land Commis-
    sion for the resettlement of people from overcrowded areas.

2a. Carpenter, Frances.  "The Introduction of commercial farming
    into Zambia and its effects, to 1940."  1973.  (In Item ZAM-16,
    p. 1-13)                                       HD 2130 Z3 P15

3.  Chambers, Robert.  SETTLEMENT SCHEMES IN TROPICAL AFRICA:  A
    STUDY OF ORGANIZATIONS AND DEVELOPMENT.  1969.  HD 1516 A34 C5

    See Item AFR-32 for citation and annotation.

4.  Coissoró, Narana.  THE CUSTOMARY LAW OF SUCCESSION IN CENTRAL
    AFRICA.  1966.                                Mem JX 6510 A35 C6

# Land Tenure and Agrarian Reform

(Coissoró, Narana)
See Item AFR-35 for citation. A reference work primarily for
jurists, this is a highly technical handbook of judicial rulings
and legal norms of succession among the Plateau Tonga, Bemba,
Ngoni, Nyakyusa, Cewa, and Yao. A separate chapter is devoted
to each (except for the Yao and Cewa, which are treated together), following roughly the same lines:  general background,
funeral rites, administration of estates, property left by the
deceased, intestate succession, succession to women, and
testate succession.

5.　Colson, Elizabeth. "Land law and land holdings among Valley
　　Tonga of Zambia." (In SJA, 22:1, 1966. p. 1-8)
　　　　　　　　　　　　　　　　　　　　　Mem AP S7283 J8301

Landholding among the Valley Tonga of Chezia changed drastically
between 1956-1957 and 1962-1963. The building of a dam in the
interim necessitated their movement into a sparsely populated
area. Although actual patterns of landholding changed significantly, the legal rules remained unchanged, creating a wide
gap between theory and practice.

5a.　＿＿＿＿. THE SOCIAL CONSEQUENCES OF RESETTLEMENT:  THE IMPACT
　　OF THE KARIBA RESETTLEMENT UPON THE GWEMBE TONGA. Kariba
　　studies, 4. (Manchester, Eng.) Published on behalf of the
　　Institute for African Studies, University of Zambia, by Man-
　　chester University Press (c1971). xi, 277 p. Bibl.
　　　　　　　　　　　　　　　　　　　　　HN 800 Z33 Z34

6.　Gluckman, Max. "African land tenure." (In RLJ, 3, 1945. p.
　　1-12)
　　　　　　　　　　　　　　　　　Mem Microfilm 4050

The concept of communal ownership of land as understood in
early writing on African land tenure systems must be refined.
In reality African land tenure systems consist of complicated
and delicately balanced clusters of rights held by individuals
and groups. The author refers in passing to the tenure systems of the peoples of Zambia.

7.　＿＿＿＿. "Property rights and status in African traditional law."
　　1969.
　　　　　　　　　　　　　　　　Mem DT 23 I55 2/8

See Item AFR-58 for citation and annotation.

8.　Gray, Richard. THE TWO NATIONS:  ASPECTS OF THE DEVELOPMENT OF
　　RACE RELATIONS IN THE RHODESIAS AND NYASALAND. London, Oxford
　　University Press, 1960. xvii, 373 p.　　Mem DT 856 G72

# LAND TENURE AND AGRARIAN REFORM

(Gray, Richard)
A short section (p. 84-88) gives the history of the alienation
of land to Europeans and the crowding of African peoples into
reserves, a trend which was partially reversed by the 1950s.

9.    Kay, George. "Agricultural progress in Zambia." 1969. (In
Item AFR-127, p. 495-524)                          HD 966 T36

An historical description of land use systems and their evolution, marred by a patronizing tone.

10.    _____. CHANGING PATTERNS OF SETTLEMENT AND LAND USE IN THE
EASTERN PROVINCE OF NORTHERN RHODESIA. Occasional papers in
geography no. 2. Hull, University of Hull, 1965. 108 p.
                                           Mem HD 2130 Z15 K3

An historical survey of land use which provides background information on the problem of population pressure on land. Includes a section on the resettlement schemes of the 1940s which
were designed to alleviate overcrowding.

11.    _____. "Resettlement and land use planning in Zambia:  the
Chipangali scheme." (In SGM, 81:3, 1965.  p. 163-177)
                                              Geol MC SC08
Also available in Item AFR-111, p. 284-297.       HD 969 S8 P7

This paper outlines the origin and nature of the problem of
overcrowding and the role of resettlement schemes in alleviating the situation. The second section describes work on the
Chipangali resettlement scheme from 1956 to 1962 and its place
in the regional plan for Chipangali.

11a.    _____. SOCIAL ASPECTS OF VILLAGE REGROUPING IN ZAMBIA.
(Lusaka) Institute for Social Research, University of Zambia,
1967. ix, 94 1. Bibl.                          HN 800 Z33 K19

12.    Mair, Lucy P. "Agrarian policy in British African colonies."
1951.                                            Ag HD 965 L3

See Item AFR-86 for citation and annotation.

13.    Makings, S. M. "Agricultural change in Northern Rhodesia/
Zambia:  1945-65." (In FRIS, 6:2, 1966.  p. 195-247)

A lengthy historical review of Zambian agricultural policy and
development projects with a short section (p. 243-245) on land
tenure. Warns against an early move to promote freehold tenure
until a clear picture of the future pattern of agricultural
development is possible.

14.    Meek, Charles Kingsley. "Northern Rhodesia (with a note on
       the taxation of undeveloped land)." 1949. (In Item AFR-91,
       p. 120-130)                                           HD 599 Z5 M4

       A brief description of a land policy which was new at the time
       of writing in 1944 and had not yet been implemented by legis-
       lation. All land was to be divided into crown land and native
       trust land.

14a.   Mutsau, R. J. "The Shona and Ndebele settlements in Kabwe
       Rural Area, 1953-1963." 1973. (In Item ZAM-16, p. 41-47)
                                                           HD 2130 Z3 P15

14b.   Muyangana, G. M. "A Survey of land tenure among the Ila of
       Chief Mungaila in the Namwala District." 1973. (In Item
       ZAM-16, p. 48-57)                                   HD 2130 Z3 P15

15.    Nzatamulilo, J. D. STATUS OF CADASTRAL SURVEYS AND LAND
       REGISTRATION SERVICES IN ZAMBIA. E/CN.14/CART/250. Addis
       Ababa, UNECA, 1970. 12 p. Paper for Seminar on Cadastre,
       25 Nov.-9 Dec. 1970.                              Files Zam 59 N92

       The law governing land registration and cadastral survey in
       Zambia, which is derived from pre-1911 English land law, is
       cumbersome and needs to be revised. A simplified system, not
       necessarily based on present English land law, would reduce
       costs associated with land surveys.

15a.   Palmer, Robin. "Land in Zambia." 1973. (In Item ZAM-16, p.
       56-66)                                              HD 2130 Z3 P15

16.    Palmer, Robin, ed. ZAMBIAN LAND AND LABOUR STUDIES. VOL. I.
       Occasional paper no. 2. Lusaka, National Archives of Zambia,
       1973. iii, 66 1.                                    HD 2130 Z3 P15

       Includes five essays on land tenure, colonization, commercial
       farming, and migration written by final year students at the
       University of Zambia for a course on land and labor in Central
       Africa, and a sixth chapter by the editor summarizing Zambia's
       land tenure history and problems. See Items ZAM-2a; ZAM-14a;
       ZAM-14b; and ZAM-15a for citations of individual articles.

17.    Peters, D. U. LAND USAGE IN SERENJE DISTRICT: A SURVEY OF
       LAND USAGE AND THE AGRICULTURAL SYSTEM OF THE LALA OF THE
       SERENJE PLATEAU. London, Oxford University Press, 1950. xvi,
       99 (1) p. Bibl.                                   Mem S 471 R48 A52

(Peters, D. U.)
A survey of the patterns of land use among the Lala. The mean
population density of the plateau at the time of writing was
7.3 persons per square mile, whereas the theoretical carrying
capacity of chitemene agriculture--which consists of chopping
down trees and brush, burning the refuse, and casting seeds in
the ashes--is only 6.1 to the square mile in the area being
studied. Chitemene agriculture permits the use of land uncul-
tivable with other indigenous technologies, but it requires
extremely long periods of regeneration for the replacement of
ground cover.

18.  Phillips, R. "Zambian settlement schemes; factors in their
     success." (In Conference of the University of East Africa
     Social Sciences Council 1968/69. PAPERS (GEOGRAPHY). Kampala,
     Makerere University College, 1969. p. 101-110)
                                        HC 517 E2 C6 1968/69 G

     The principal reasons for the lack of success of Zambian
     settlement schemes have been poor procedures for the selection
     of settlers and poor coordination between the various minis-
     tries in charge of planning and implementing the schemes.

19.  Richards, Audrey I. LAND, LABOUR AND DIET IN NORTHERN RHODESIA;
     AN ECONOMIC STUDY OF THE BEMBA TRIBE. (2nd ed. London)
     Published for the International African Institute by the Oxford
     University Press (1969). xviii, 425 p. Bibl.  GN 657 R4 R42

     First published in 1939, this book concentrates on aspects of
     the Bemba socio-economic system which determine levels of
     nutrition. A lengthy chapter on land tenure (p. 228-276) em-
     phasizes the relationship between the political system and the
     land tenure system and notes that each individual Bemba has the
     freedom to select land for cultivation and enjoys security of
     tenure. Individualization of tenure would not promote develop-
     ment but would be of interest to Africans seeking to protect
     their land from Europeans.

20.  Tuthill, Dean F.; Williams, John A.; and Foster, Phillips W.
     THE STRUCTURE OF SHIFTING AGRICULTURE IN TWO CHEWA VILLAGES.
     Miscellaneous publication no. 629. College Park, Md., Agri-
     cultural Experiment Station, University of Maryland, 1968.
     ix, 55 p. Bibl.                          Files Zam 7 T88

     The values and institutions which appeared to act as the most
     important constraints to increased agricultural production
     among the Chewa people of the two villages studied were those
     concerned with capital accumulation. Besides credit

(Tuthill, Dean F.; Williams, John A.; and Foster, Phillips W.) institutions, effective and practical demonstrations of technology were needed to improve the process of making decisions on the use of agricultural resources. The land tenure system ranked low as a constraint to the improvement of agricultural productivity.

21.   White, Charles M. N. "Factors determining the content of African land tenure systems in Northern Rhodesia." (In Item AFR-67, p. 364-373)                              HD 966 I5 1960

After listing common characteristics of customary land tenure systems in Zambia, the author examines the Bemba, Tonga, and Luvale systems in detail. Among the Bemba, land is abundant and has little economic value, in marked contrast to the Tonga situation, where land is scarce. The Luvale case differs from these two in that the lineage structure largely determines the nature of the tenure system.

22.   _____. A PRELIMINARY SURVEY OF THE LUVALE RURAL ECONOMY. Manchester (Eng.) Manchester University Press, 1959.  xii, 58 p.                                        Mem HC 517 R42 W5

A short section on land tenure (p. 31-33) notes that village matrilineages control access to land, but land, even when lying fallow, is usually passed on to heirs after the death of its user. Land is transferred freely by gift between matrilineal lineages.

23.   Zambia. Dept. of Lands. REPORT. Lusaka. 11 v. in 5. Library has:  1957-1963; 1964; 1967-1969.    Mem HD 990 Z3 A32

A brief survey of the activities of the Department of Lands in land settlement schemes, the registration of deeds, and other services.

24.   _____. Laws, statutes, etc. "Act no. 2 of 1970:  the Lands Acquisition Act, 1969 (an Act to make provision for the compulsory acquisition of land and other property; and to repeal and replace the Public Land Acquisition Ordinance)--9 January 1970." (In FAL, 19:2, 1970. V/1c) Taken from GG/Z, 6:5, 1970. Supplement, p. 27                              Ag Docs
Also available as a separate.              Files Zam 36 Z1

Sets forth procedures for the public acquisiton of land and for compensation.

LAND TENURE AND AGRARIAN REFORM

NE 1-5

## NEAR EAST AND NORTH AFRICA

1. Abd, Salah. THE DEVELOPMENT OF WELL-INTEGRATED RURAL COMMU-
   NITIES IN LAND SETTLEMENT AND LAND REFORM AREAS. Paper no. 3.
   (Rome) FAO, 1965. 8 p. Paper for Development Center on Land
   Policy and Settlement for the Near East, Tripoli, 1965.
   Files NE 17 A12
   Also available in microfiche. Zug, Switzerland, Inter Docu-
   mentation Co., n.d. 1 sheet. Microfiche NE 288 25
   Also available in Item NE-10, p. 81-86. HD 850.8 Z63 D46 1965

2. Ahmad, M. S.; and Roy, E. P. "Cooperation and land reform in
   the Middle East." (In LRE, 25:4, 1963. p. 14-16)
   Also available as a separate. Files Asia 3 A35

   Brief overview of common features of land reforms in Egypt,
   Iraq, and Syria. Future success of cooperatives depends on
   depoliticization, education, and a stable legal-institutional
   framework.

3. Al-Sa'ud, Mahmoud Abu. "The Exploitation of land and Islamic
   law; the leasing of land." Training course document no. 44.
   n.p., n.d. 13 p. Files 14 A57

   According to the author's interpretation of Islamic traditional
   law, private landownership is permissible only as long as the
   land is exploited for the good of society as a whole. Thus,
   expropriation and nationalization are possible. In addition,
   leasing of land, either for cash or for a share of the crop,
   is counter to Islamic traditions.

4. Ashford, D. E. "The Politics of rural mobilization in North
   Africa." (In JMAS, 7:2, 1969. p. 187-202) Mem AP J83 M686

   A comparison of rural land reform in Algeria, Morocco, and
   Tunisia. The framework for the study is each country's
   approach to the problem of mobilizing and integrating a large
   rural population into the political system.

5. Aydalot, P. "Comportement économique, structures agraires et
   développement." 1966. Mem AP R452 E18

   See Item AFR-13 for citation and annotation.

268

# Land Tenure and Agrarian Reform

6.   Berque, J. "Les Droits des terres au Maghreb." (In Sachs,
     Ignacy, ed. AGRICULTURE, LAND REFORMS, AND ECONOMIC DEVELOP-
     MENT. Warsaw, PWN, Polish Scientific Publishers, 1964.
     p. 211-232)
                                                Mem HD 1415 S2

     Islamic law recognizes individual landownership in the form of
     estates held by laymen or Muslim clerics.  In precolonial
     North Africa, the owners of large estates were members of the
     communities in which they held land, but during the colonial
     period, estates increasingly came to be held by outsiders.
     The introduction of French law led to a situation in which
     litigation was based on conflicting premises:  the essential
     features of Islamic legal argument were based on establishing
     proof of the right of usufruct, but European legal procedure
     emphasizes retracing the history of the property to prove
     ownership.

7.   Central Treaty Organization. SYMPOSIUM ON RURAL DEVELOPMENT.
     Held in Teheran, Iran, September 25-30, 1963.  Ankara, Office
     of U.S. Economic Coordinator for CENTO Affairs, 1963?  211 p.
                                                HT 395 A77 C25

     Situational reports and proposals dealing with land reform,
     credit, capital and resource development, and the role of
     government initiative in Iran, Turkey, and Pakistan.  See
     Items IRAN-17; IRAN-48; IRAN-67; TURK-34; and TURK-35 for
     individually cited and annotated articles.

8.   Crist, Raymond E.  LAND FOR THE FELLAHIN; LAND TENURE AND LAND
     USE IN THE NEAR EAST.  New York, Robert Schalkenbach Founda-
     tion (1962?).  134 p.
                                                Mem HD 850.8 C7

     Analyzes the interaction of physical-agronomic, historical,
     social, and cultural features of the agrarian scene.  Sees
     socio-economic constraints, most notably the land tenure sys-
     tem, as the principal reason for the agricultural underdevelop-
     ment of the region.

9.   Dajani, Nijmeddin.  PRACTICAL PROBLEMS IN CARRYING OUT PLANNED
     SETTLEMENT.  Paper no. P-3.  (Rome) FAO, 1955.  10 p.  Paper
     for Center on Land Problems in the Near East, Salahuddin, Iraq,
     1955.
                                                Files NE 17 D14

9a.  Despois, Jean.  "Les Paysages agraires traditionnels du
     Maghreb et du Sahara septentrional."  (In AG, 73:396, 1964.
     p. 129-171)
                                                Geol MC AN62
     Also available as a separate.           Files Afr 57.5 D27

10.     Development Center on Land Policy and Settlement for the Near
        East, Tripoli, 1965.  LAND POLICY IN THE NEAR EAST.  Pro-
        ceedings of the Development Center on Land Policy and Settle-
        ment for the Near East, held in Tripoli, Libya, from 16 to 28
        Oct. 1965, organized by the Food and Agriculture Organization
        of the United Nations.  Compiled by Mohamad Riad El-Ghonemy.
        Rome, published (for the Government of Libya) by the FAO,
        1967.  vii, 417 p.                          HD 850.8 Z63 D46 1965

        Describes agricultural development projects in seven Middle
        Eastern and African countries.  Examines the issue of land
        policy in relation to overall national economic planning,
        sedentarization, land settlement, community development,
        employment implications, and legal elements involved.  See
        Items ALG-26; ARAB-1; EGY-18; IRAN-65; JORD-7a; LIBY-2;
        MOR-14; NE-1; SOM-3; SUD-16; SYRIA-2a; TUNIS-9; and TURK-21
        for individually cited papers.

10a.    _____.  REPORT ON THE DEVELOPMENT CENTER ON LAND POLICY AND
        SETTLEMENT FOR THE NEAR EAST.  Prepared by M. Riad El Ghonemy.
        FAO report no. TA 2160.  Rome, FAO, 1966.  85 p.
                                                    HD 850.8 Z63 D46 1965a

11.     Dresch, Jean.  "Réforme agraire et sous-développement; Moyen-
        Orient Muselman."  (In Sachs, Ignacy, ed. AGRICULTURE, LAND
        REFORMS, AND ECONOMIC DEVELOPMENT.  Warsaw, PWN, Polish
        Scientific Publishers, 1964.  p. 175-190)      Mem HD 1415 S2

        This survey of Middle Eastern land reform efforts concludes
        that results have not been dramatic even in the case of Egypt,
        where reforms were most radical and comprehensive.  Advocates
        a multifaceted approach encompassing cooperativization, pro-
        vision of credit, etc., to increase potential for greater
        success.

11a.    El Ghonemy, Mohammed Riad.  INCOME DISTRIBUTION AND CAPITAL
        FORMATION IN RELATION TO LAND REFORM.  Paper no. P-11.  (Rome)
        FAO, 1955.  11 p.  Paper for Center on Land Problems in the
        Near East, Salahuddin, Iraq, 1955.              Files NE 3 E52

12.     _____.  LAND REFORM AND ECONOMIC DEVELOPMENT IN THE NEAR EAST.
        RU:WLR/66/E.  Rome, FAO, 1966.  19 p.  Paper for World Land
        Reform Conference, Rome, 1966.                  Files NE 3 E53

        Comparative analysis of land reform initiatives in the Near
        East after World War II, classifying them according to rela-
        tive emphases on changing landownership patterns, tenancy
        reform, and settlement.  Concludes that these measures had a

LAND TENURE AND AGRARIAN REFORM

(El Ghonemy, Mohammed Riad)
favorable impact on economic development and redistribution
of wealth.

13.      _____.  _____.  (In LE, 44:1, 1968.  p. 36-49)
Also available in U.S. Agency for International Development.
LAND REFORM:  REGIONAL SURVEYS.  SR/LR/C-32.  Washington,
1970.  14 p.  Country paper for Spring Review of Land Reform.
Files 3 U555

Based on Item NE-12.

13a.     _____.  "The Role of land policy in agricultural production
and income distribution in the Near East."  Tripoli, Libya,
1965.  Microfiche.  Zug, Switzerland, Inter Documentation Co.
Microfiche NE 288 31

13b.     _____.  THE WORK OF THE CENTER IN REVIEW; WHAT HAS BEEN
ACHIEVED AND WHAT REMAINS TO BE DONE?  Paper no. 10.  Tripoli,
FAO, Development Center on Land Policy and Settlement for the
Near East, 1965.
Files NE 58 E53

14.  Food and Agriculture Organization.  CENTER ON LAND PROBLEMS
IN THE NEAR EAST, SALAHUDDIN, IRAQ, 1955.  n.p., 1955?  1 v.
(various pagings)
Files NE 57.6 F66

Contains a general introduction by Kenneth Parsons on the
broad issues and particular approaches toward agrarian reform
and development in the Middle East, followed by a series of
workshop discussions.  Includes background documents on credit,
forestry programs, land tenure security, agricultural production problems, etc.

15.  Gibb, H. A. R.; and Bowen, Harold.  ISLAMIC SOCIETY AND THE
WEST:  A STUDY OF THE IMPACT OF WESTERN CIVILIZATION ON MOS-
LEM CUTURE IN THE NEAR EAST.  London, Oxford University Press,
1957.  386 p.
Mem DS 38 G485

Analysis of institutions prevailing in the Ottoman Empire at
the time of major western European impact.  Examines rural
tenure structures in the Turkish-Balkan areas and the Arab
provinces at some length, especially in the chapter entitled
"The Peasantry, Land Tenure, and Agriculture."

16.  Granott, Abraham.  THE LAND SYSTEM IN PALESTINE; HISTORY AND
STRUCTURE.  (Translated from the Hebrew by M. Simon).  London,
Eyre and Spottiswoode, 1952.  359 p.
HD 850.8 P1 G71

NE 16-18b

(Granott, Abraham)
Probes common Muslim influences on the land system and its
local variation under particular social, economic, political,
and legal pressures. Especially emphasizes the impact of
Ottoman legal developments during their hegemony. Ottoman
law remains an important source of land tenure rules in the
region. Outlines two major trends: the emergence of large
estates and the development of de facto private ownership by
the beginning of the twentieth century. This work has direct
relevance to the Fertile Crescent, including Turkey.

16a.    Guillaume, Albert. LES ASPECTS JURIDIQUES DE LA MODERNISATION
        RURALE EN AFRIQUE DU NORD RURALE. IDEP/ET/CS/2379-24. Dakar,
        Nations Unies, Institut Africain de Développement Economique
        et de Planification, 1972. 11 p.            Files Afr 58 G84

17.     Hakim, George. "Land tenure reform." (In MEEP, 1954.
        p. 76-90)                                    Mem AP M62707

        Maintains that the central problem of land tenure reform is
        that of enhancing incentives for higher production. Regards
        family-owned peasant proprietorship as the optimal framework
        for such improvement.

18.     Harik, Iliya F. THE IMPACT OF THE DOMESTIC MARKET ON RURAL-
        URBAN RELATIONS. Working paper no. 2. Bloomington, Inter-
        national Development Research Center, Indiana University,
        1971. 50 1. Bibl.                            HC 410.7 H17

        Views as fairly recent the domination of rural by urban areas
        in their capacity as credit, market, and landholding centers.
        Relates the impact of this development and the overall socio-
        economic transformation since the nineteenth century to agrar-
        ian structural changes.

18a.    Himadeh, Sa'id B. "Economic factors underlying social prob-
        lems in the Arab Middle East." (In MEJ, 5:3, 1951.
        p. 269-283)                                  Mem AP M6272

        Agrarian patterns discussed within context of other factors
        contributing to poverty.

18b.    _____. EFFECT OF LAND TENURE ON LAND USE AND PRODUCTION IN
        THE NEAR EAST. Paper no. P-4. (Rome) FAO, 1955. 13 p.
        Paper for Center on Land Problems in the Near East, Salahuddin,
        Iraq, 1955.                                  Files NE 58 H15

19. Issawi, Charles P., ed. THE ECONOMIC HISTORY OF THE MIDDLE EAST. Chicago, University of Chicago Press, 1966. xv, 543 p.
Mem HC 412 I787

Contains general statements on country-by-country as well as topical basis by Issawi, followed by excerpts from other authors' works. Includes analysis of the evolution of Mid-Eastern land tenure in general, with specific references to developments in Turkey, Egypt, Syria, Arabia, Iraq, and Sudan. Focuses on changes engendered under the impact of Western market demand and economic penetration into the region.

19a. _____. POPULATION AND LAND RESOURCES IN THE ECONOMIC DEVELOPMENT OF THE NEAR EAST. Paper no. P-1. (Rome) FAO, 1955. 14 p. Paper for Center on Land Problems in the Near East, Salahuddin, Iraq, 1955.
Files NE 72.5 I77

20. Kamal, Adel. "Feudalism and land reform." (In Adams, Michael, ed. THE MIDDLE EAST; A HANDBOOK. New York, Praeger, 1971. p. 493-503)
DS 44 A3 1971b

Traces historical development of large estates and attempts in Egypt, Syria, and Iraq to change this and other aspects of their agrarian structure. Reviews and assesses land reform efforts in these countries.

21. Kermani, Taghi T. ECONOMIC DEVELOPMENT IN ACTION: THEORIES, PROBLEMS AND PROCEDURES AS APPLIED TO THE MIDDLE EAST. Cleveland, World Pub. Co., 1967. xix, 236 p.
HC 410.7 K4

Insists on the need for a multidimensional development approach encompassing infrastructural development as well as institutional reform, particularly land reform. Urges coordination of land reform with appropriate credit and price policies. Discusses agrarian reform in Iran, Iraq, and Jordan.

22. Klat, Paul J. "Whither land tenure in the Arab world." (In MEEP, 1955. p. 47-61)
Mem AP M62707

Criticizes land tenure in this region for perpetuating gross social and political inequality as well as hindering improved agricultural production by promoting absentee ownership, high rents, and excessive land fragmentation. Stresses education as a means to lift peasants from the ignorance and apathy that have hindered the success of land reform efforts.

# LAND TENURE AND AGRARIAN REFORM

23.  "Land reform." n.p., n.d. (13) 1.                    Files 3 L15

Brief review of assistance provided by the International
Cooperative Association to effect agrarian reform in several
Asian and Middle Eastern countries, including Egypt and Iran.

24.  Lebanon. Institute of Rural Economics. A SERIES OF LECTURES
ON AGRARIAN TENURE AND AGRICULTURAL COOPERATION IN THE
MEDITERRANEAN BASIN. Beirut, n.d. 2 v.          HD 850.8 L21

Lectures delivered in 1962-63 and dealing primarily with
socio-economic aspects of agrarian problems and development
efforts in Lebanon and Syria. See Items LEB-5; LEB-6; LEB-11;
SYRIA-2; and SYRIA-16 for citations and annotations of
individual articles.

25.  Madiman, S. G. INDICATIVE WORLD PLAN: INSTITUTIONAL PLANNING
FOR INDICATIVE WORLD PLAN, NEAR EAST REGION. (Rome, reproduced
by FAO, 1966. 16 1.)                            Files 3 M12

Presents conceptual framework and research strategy, including
analytical categories and subdivisions regarding land tenure.
States the central theme of the Indicative World Plan as being
increased production. Advocates an agrarian framework of
cooperatively organized family farms. Stresses the need to
synchronize price, credit, and land reform policies.

26.  _____. LAND TENURE AND OTHER STRUCTURAL PROBLEMS IN THE NEAR
EAST AGRICULTURE. (Rome, FAO, 1966. 26 p.) Files NE 58 M12

Outlines major development constraints in the area's agrarian
structure and makes broad remedial proposals. Suggests consolidation of fragmented landholdings and crop diversification
to increase production. Generally advises coordinating land
reform with the overall economic development program.

27.  Marthelot, Pierre. "Les Poids des traditions communautaires
dans l'agriculture au Maghreb." (In OM, 6, 1971. p. 26-29)

A nontechnical review of the social structure and underlying
indigenous agrarian practices in both the dry and wetland
farming areas of North Africa. The communal cooperative
tradition is stressed.

# Land Tenure and Agrarian Reform

28.   Muralt, Jürgen von.  "Rural institutions and planned change
      in the Middle East and North Africa."  (In United Nations
      Research Institute for Social Development.  A REVIEW OF RURAL
      CO-OPERATION IN DEVELOPING AREAS.  Geneva, UNRISD, 1969.
      p. 277-340)
                                                    HD 2951.5 U54

      The modernization of rural life requires more than structural
      reforms of agriculture.  New behavior patterns must be intro-
      duced, and the mentality of the rural masses must change so
      that active participation in the development process is pos-
      sible.  In the countries of the Middle East and North Africa,
      cooperatives are used primarily for the implementation of
      rural reform; they are largely the "governments' institutional
      means of organizing the peasantry rather than genuine self-
      help organizations."  (p. 333)

28a.  Parsons, Kenneth H.  "Land problems survey of the Middle East;
      a preliminary report."  n.p. (1955).  18 p.     Files NE 58 P17

29.   ____.  "Land tenure in Asia."  (In FA, 24:4, 1960.  p. 4-6;
      and 24:5, 1960.  p. 16-18)
                                                          Ag Docs
      Also available as a separate.            Files Asia 58 P17

      Brief overview of land reform in the Near East, mentioning
      experiences in Egypt, Syria, Iraq, and Iran.  Regards the
      Egyptian reform as the outstanding one.  Views the issue in
      terms of a comparison between "Communist" and "Free World"
      approaches.

30.   Poliak, A. N.  "Agrarian problems in the Middle East."  (In
      MEA, 3:6/7, 1952.  p. 165-171)
                                                    Mem AP M6275

      A general survey of agrarian problems and measures required to
      increase production and modernize rural life.  Maintains that
      displacement of communal by private landownership has operated
      to freeze inequality in landholding and has accentuated the
      problem of peasant landlessness.

31.   Rosciszewski, Marcin M.  "Traditional sector of Maghreb
      agriculture:  character and development trends."  (In AB, 11,
      1970.  p. 25-58)

      French rule in Algeria, Tunisia, and Morocco encouraged the
      evolution of individual ownership of land.  Many merchants
      and other townsmen became landowners, but the concentration of
      holdings did not tend to increase the productivity of land
      because estates were often parcelled out to tenants.

32.    RURAL POLITICS AND SOCIAL CHANGE IN THE MIDDLE EAST.  Richard
       Antoun and Iliya F. Harik, eds.  International Development
       Research Center, Studies in development no. 5.  Bloomington,
       Indiana University Press (1972).  xiv, 498 p.  Bibl.  Based
       on the 1969 Conference on Rural Politics and Social Change,
       organized by the Center.                          DS 57 R87

       Emphasis is on the response of the rural Mid-East to the chal-
       lenge of modernization.  Includes a review of the "state of
       theory and literature" on this topic, followed by case studies
       of local political processes and economic change and reform.
       See Items EGY-28; IRAN-39; and LEB-8 for individually cited
       and annotated articles.

32a.   Schickele, Rainer.  LAND PROBLEMS IN REVIEW.  Paper no. P-13.
       (Rome) FAO, 1955.  8 p.  Paper for Center on Land Problems in
       the Near East, Salahuddin, Iraq, 1955.            Files NE 3 S13

32b.   _____; and Himadeh, Sa'id B.  LAND REFORM AND ECONOMIC DEVEL-
       OPMENT.  Workshop report no. 9.  (Rome) FAO, 1955.  (16) p.
       Paper for Center on Land Problems in the Near East,
       Salahuddin, Iraq, 1955.                           Files NE 3 S133

33.    Sicard, H.  "Problèmes fonciers au Maghreb."  (In AFAS, 72,
       1965.  p. 22-36)                                  Mem AP A2585 E83

       In the countries of the Maghreb, the French colonial govern-
       ments rescinded Islamic law and bypassed the administrative
       hierarchy, expropriating large areas of land from religious
       and political leaders.  Since the imposition of foreign law
       was ill-conceived and incomplete, the colonial legacy in this
       area is one of confusion and inconsistency.  North African
       leaders must find new solutions to the problems of land tenure,
       solutions which should be based on the following principles:
       in good lands, the notion of Islamic law which stresses own-
       ership deriving from the investment of labor in land should
       be strengthened; in marginal lands, the basic unit of land-
       ownership should be the extended family; and reforms must
       make use of local religious leaders and Islamic courts.

34.    Tannous, Afif F.  "Land ownership in the Middle East."  (In
       FA, 14:12, 1950.  10 p.)                          Ag Docs
       Also available in Conference on World Land Tenure Problems,
       University of Wisconsin, 1951.  PAPERS, 4.  Madison, 1951.
       10 p.                                             HD 105 C67 1951b

       Reviews common land tenure problems of the region with an
       overview of landownership patterns in Egypt, Iraq, Syria, and

(Tannous, Afif F.)
Saudi Arabia. Discusses remedial land reform measures
attempted, regarding such reforms as a basic prerequisite
for economic development.

35.    _____. "Land reform: key to the development and stability
of the Arab world." (In MEJ, 5:1, 1951. p. 1-20)

Mem AP M6272

A plea for the adoption of land reform as a central concern
of Point Four aid. Traces efforts to deal with problems of
ambiguous land titles, communal ownership, fragmentation, etc.
Economic development and socio-political stability depend on
attending to these issues.

35a.   Treydte, Klaus-Peter; and Ule, Wolfgang, comps. AGRICULTURE
IN THE NEAR EAST; ORGANIZATIONAL PATTERNS AND SOCIO-ECONOMIC
DEVELOPMENT. Research Centre for International Agrarian
Development, publication no. 2. Bonn-Bad Godesberg, Verlag
Neue Gesellschaft (1973). 150 p.            HD 2060.5 T72

36.    Tuma, Elias H. "Agrarian reform and urbanization in the
Middle East." 1970. (In MEJ, 24:2, 1970. p. 163-177)

Mem AP M6272

Also available as a separate.                Files NE 3 T85

Argues for emphasis on economic and production needs over
social and political considerations. Thus, agrarian reform
is not to be directed at reversing or suppressing rural-to-
urban migration if this movement contributes to greater
economic efficiency.

37.    Verdier, Jean M.; Desanti, Pierre; et Karila, Juliana.
STRUCTURES FONCIERS ET DEVELOPPEMENT RURAL AU MAGHREB.
Travaux et Recherches de la Faculté de Droit et des Sciences
Economiques de Paris; série Afrique, 4. Paris, Presses
Universitaires de France, 1969. 167 p.        Mem HD 1169 V4

A thorough study of the evolution of postindependence land
legislation in the three North African countries of the
Maghreb--Algeria, Morocco, and Tunisia. While the three
countries share similar goals with respect to social and
economic development and have similar problems, such as
conflicts between peasant aspirations and the need to promote
economic development, quite different juridical measures have
been taken to meet these goals and problems. For each of the
three nations the authors cite legal texts on decolonization,
land distribution, public domain, and refer to various rural
development projects.

38.  Warriner, Doreen.  "Employment and income aspects of recent
     agrarian reforms in the Middle East."  (In ILR, 101:6, 1970.
     p. 605-625)                                    Mem AP I616 L135
     Also available in International Labour Office.  AGRARIAN
     REFORM AND EMPLOYMENT.  Geneva, 1971.  p. 77-98.    HD 111 I57

     Examines environmental, social, and political influences
     either inhibiting or contributing to land reform success in
     improving production, farm income, and employment in Iraq,
     Iran, and the U.A.R.  Though land redistribution may have
     increased incomes, the impact on employment was minimal,
     requiring, in addition to land reform, improvement in methods
     of land use.

39.  _____.  LAND REFORM AND DEVELOPMENT IN THE MIDDLE EAST; A
     STUDY OF EGYPT, SYRIA AND IRAQ.  2nd ed.  London, Oxford
     University Press, 1962.  xi, 238 p.            HD 850.8 W3 1962

     Regarding agrarian reform as "a point of intersection between
     economic development and social change."  Warriner places her
     discussion within this broad context.  Avoids a comprehensive
     view of land reform, substituting a more restricted one con-
     fined to redistribution, so as not to cloud or dilute this
     primary issue.  See Items EGY-66 and IRAQ-44 for additional
     annotations.

40.  Wilson, Rodney J. A.  AGRICULTURAL DEVELOPMENT IN THE MIDDLE
     EAST, 1950-1970.  Economic research paper no. 1.  Durham (Eng.)
     Durham University, Centre for Middle Eastern and Islamic
     Studies, 1972.  35 1.  Bibl.                   Files NE 4 W45

     Concludes that "land reform has not provided a panacea for the
     Middle East's economic and food problems."  On balance, though
     neutralization of landlord influence was limited, reforms did
     provide greater tenurial security and therefore increased
     incentives for production.  Implementation of land reform was
     most successful in Egypt, less so in Syria and Iraq, and
     least successful in Turkey and Iran.

41.  Yacoub, Salah M.  THE ROLE OF LAND REFORM PROGRAMS IN COMMUNITY
     DEVELOPMENT AND OVERALL SOCIAL AND ECONOMIC DEVELOPMENT IN
     SELECTED NEAR EASTERN COUNTRIES.  Beirut, Lebanon, Faculty of
     Agricultural Sciences, American University of Beirut, 1970.
     36 1.                                          Files NE 3 Y12

     Evaluates land reforms in Jordan, Iraq, and Syria on their
     "actual contribution to and role in community development
     and overall social and economic development...."  Cites

# LAND TENURE AND AGRARIAN REFORM

NE 41-ALG 3

(Yacoub, Salah M.)
problems of implementation stemming from an inadequate consideration and knowledge of the practical, social-psychological
realities at the lower levels in the formulation of measures,
as in cooperatives, etc.

41a.   Zeid, A. M. Abou. SEDENTARIZATION AND LAND PROBLEMS. Back-
ground document no. 7 Tripoli, FAO, Development Center on
Land Policy and Settlement for the Near East, 1965. 10 p.
Files NE 17 Z24


## ALGERIA

1.   Ait-Mesbah, M. "L'Autogestion agricole et la réforme agraire
en Algérie." (In MAGHREB, 7, 1965. p. 48-54)   Mem AP M1938
Also available as a separate.   Files Alg 3 A48

Considers the weakest point of socialized ex-colonial estates
(autogestion farms) to be the inherent conflict between state
bureaucratic control and the desire to establish responsibility at the lower levels. Disorganization is blamed for the
incompleteness of initial agrarian reforms.

2.   _____. "Les Terres arch en Algérie." 1970. (In Item AFR-112,
p. 1105-1112)

Defines terres arch and their changing legal status since
1830. These collective lands were originally inalienable.
Successive statutes in 1830, 1863, 1873, 1897, and 1926
gradually transformed them into private property for the
most part. The fate of the remaining terres arch is still
uncertain, i.e., whether to include them in the national
agrarian reform, grant full property rights to usufruct oper-
ators, or reserve some other role for them.

3.   Algeria. Laws, statutes, etc. "Decree No. 56-691 relative
to agrarian reform in Algeria - 13 July 1956." (In FAL,
5:4, V.1/56.10) From JOURNAL OFFICIEL DE L'ALGERIE, 69,
1956. p. 1498.                                           Ag Docs
Also available as a separate.                  Files Alg 3 A5

Designates terms and procedures for the transference of various
categories of land to the Rural Estate and Holding Acquisition
Fund.

279

# LAND TENURE AND AGRARIAN REFORM

4.    Algeria. Laws, statutes, etc. "Ordinance No. 71-73 on the
      agrarian revolution: ordonnance No. 71-73 portant revolution
      agraire - 8 November 1971. (Extracts)" (In FAL, 21:1, 1972.
      p. 18-44) From JOURNAL OFFICIEL DE LA REPUBLIQUE ALGERIENNE
      DEMOCRATIQUE ET POPULAIRE, 97, 1971. p. 1281        Ag Docs
      Also available as a separate.              Files Alg 3 A53

      The ordinance sets forth the guiding principles of the
      "agrarian revolution" and provides for: establishment of the
      National Agrarian Revolution Fund (for nationalizing property);
      nationalization of and compensation for confiscated lands;
      allocation of state lands; rights and duties of beneficiaries;
      etc.

5.    _____. Ministère de l'Agriculture et de la Réforme Agraire.
      LA STATISTIQUE AGRICOLE. Algiers, 1966. 86 p. Numéro spécial
      L'ALGERIE AGRICOLE, mai 1966            Files Alg 90.5 A52

      Presents statistics on land use in the private and socialist
      sectors in 1964-65. Changes in land use between 1955 and 1964
      are monitored by viewing the shifting balance of cultivation
      and production within the modern and traditional branches,
      respectively.

5a.   _____. Ministère de l'Information. THE FACES OF ALGERIA;
      VOL. 23; THE AGRARIAN REVOLUTION. (Siracusa, 1970). 61 p.
                                                    HC 547 A4 A3

6.    "Algérie: la révolution agraire." (In JA, 618, 1972.
      p. 58-65)                              Mem AP J5929 A258
      Also available as a separate.             Files Alg 3 A55

      A journalistic report of the progress of Algeria's agrarian
      reform plans in the early 1970s. Includes an interview with
      Mohammed Taibi Larbi, Minister of Agriculture. See Item
      ALG-20a for individually cited article.

6a.   Anton, Günther Kurt. LE REGIME FONCIER AUX COLONIES; RAPPORTS
      PRESENTES A L'INSTITUT COLONIAL INTERNATIONAL. 1904.
                                                   Mem HD 588 A6

      See Item AFR-10 for citation and annotation.

7.    Ashford, D. E. "The Politics of rural mobilization in North
      Africa." 1969.                           Mem AP J83 M686

      See Item NE-4 for citation and annotation.

# LAND TENURE AND AGRARIAN REFORM

7a.    Bennoune, Mahfoud. "French counter-revolutionary doctrine and
the Algerian peasantry." (In MR, 25:7, 1973. p. 43-60)

8.    Berque, J. "Les Droits des terres au Maghreb." 1964.

Mem HD 1415 S2

See Item NE-6 for citation and annotation.

9.    Blair, Thomas Lucien. THE LAND TO THOSE WHO WORK IT;
ALGERIA'S EXPERIMENT IN WORKERS' MANAGEMENT. New York,
Doubleday, 1969. viii, 275 p. Bibl.      HD 5660 A4 B55

Sympathetic description of theoretical bases and actual operation of worker-managed autogestion farms. However, criticizes
their failure to benefit appreciably peasants in the traditional, non-socialized rural sector. In the absence of adequate agrarian reform, colonial socio-economic patterns
continue to prevail. Appendices include texts and summaries
of decrees concerning the status of vacated lands (biens
vacants), worker management, etc.

9a.    Bourdieu, Pierre; et Sayad, Abdel Malek. LE DERACINEMENT: LA
CRISE DE L'AGRICULTURE TRADITIONELLE EN ALGERIA. Grands
documents, 14. (Paris) Editions de Minuit (1964). 225 p.

HN 810 A4 B67

10.    Daoud, Z. "Algérie: réforme foncière ou révolution agraire?"
(In JA, 503, 1970. p. 42-49)      Mem AP J5929 A258

Enthusiastic review of agricultural development progress.
Endorses increased decentralization of decision-making authority in autogestion collectives. Presents elements of an
anticipated agrarian reform, introducing landownership ceilings, confiscation of absentee holdings, and their distribution and organization into cooperatives.

11.    d'Arcy, François; Krieger, Annie; et Marill, Alain. ESSAIS
SUR L'ECONOMIE DE L'ALGERIE NOUVELLE. Travaux et recherches
de la Faculté de Droit et des Sciences Economiques de Paris,
série "Afrique," no. 1. Paris, Presses Universitaires de
France, 1965. viii, 255 p. Bibl.      Mem Control B20300

A three-part study of Algerian rural collectives, agrarian
reform, and the Algerianization of industry. The first section
concentrates on administrative problems of collectives in
northeastern Algeria. The second section views Algerian
agrarian reform from an international perspective, emphasizing
areas whose programs have influenced the Algerian situation.
Includes historical, ideological, and practical assessments.

# LAND TENURE AND AGRARIAN REFORM

12. Doxsee, Gifford B. ASPECTS OF LAND USE AND AGRARIAN REFORM
    IN ALGERIA. Papers in international studies, no. 6. Athens,
    Center for International Studies, Ohio University, 1967.
    16 1. Bibl.                                      Files Alg 3 D69

    Focuses on worker-managed autogestion farms. These units are
    plagued by a lack of trained personnel, as well as politically
    motivated administrative and policy conflicts. Peasants out-
    side such farms have remained largely untouched by the polit-
    ical, social, and economic effects of independence.

13. Dumont, René. "Des Conditions de la réussite de la réforme
    agraire en Algérie." 1963. (In Item ALG-34, p. 79-123)
                                               Mem HC 547 A4 T5

    Sets forth proposals for agrarian reform, comprising measures
    to reorganize and more closely direct autogestion farms to
    enhance their productivity. Also suggests removing the
    institutional underpinnings of the sharecropping system.
    Peasants are to be incorporated into the mainstream of economy
    and society through "committees of working peasants." Out-
    lines initiatives for the long-term improvement of productive
    resources (irrigation, etc.).

14. Foster, Phillips W. LAND REFORM IN ALGERIA. SR/LR/C-13.
    (Washington) USAID, 1970. vi, 81 p. Country paper for Spring
    Review of Land Reform.                         Files Alg 3 F67

    Describes the evolution of land tenure and rural socio-economic
    conditions during precolonial and colonial periods. Devotes
    primary attention to land reform measures since independence.
    Finds little substantial change or improvement in the equality
    of income distribution, availability of employment, or agri-
    cultural productivity. Overemphasis on socialized agriculture
    (autogestion) has resulted in neglect of the peasant farmer
    majority. Attributes these shortcomings to inconsistent
    policy goals. Appendix includes texts of decrees regulating
    vacated properties (biens vacants), the operation of worker
    control on these properties, and formation of the National
    Office for Agrarian Reform.

15. _____; and Steiner, Herbert. THE STRUCTURE OF ALGERIAN
    SOCIALIZED AGRICULTURE. Miscellaneous publication no. 527.
    College Park, Dept. of Agricultural Economics, College of
    Agriculture, University of Maryland, 1964. xviii, 171 p.
    No. 3603 of the Maryland Agricultural Experiment Station.
                                               Files Alg 7 F67

    More detailed version of Item ALG-14.

# Land Tenure and Agrarian Reform

15a.  Goussarov, Vladilen. LE ROLE DE L'AUTOGESTION AGRICOLE DANS
      LA SOLUTION DU PROBLEME DU DUALISME RURAL EN ALGERIA.
      IDEP/ET/CS/2379-16. Dakar, Nations Unies, Institut Africain
      de Développement Economique et de Planification, 1972. 23 p.
      Paper for Séminaire-Cours sur le Dualisme Rural au Maghreb:
      Problèmes et Politiques, Alger, 1972.      Files Alg 55.5 G68

16.   Goussault, Yves. "Education des masses et encadrement dans la
      réforme agraire." 1963. (In Item ALG-34, p. 53-78)
                                          Mem HC 547 A4 T5

      Emphasizes the efficacy of rural educational campaigns to
      mobilize peasants for agrarian reform and development efforts.
      Sees this as a way to broaden the impact of agrarian reform
      to the hitherto neglected traditional sector. Cites positive
      experiences in other nations, particularly China.

17.   Holm, Henrietta M. THE AGRICULTURAL ECONOMY OF ALGERIA.
      FAS-M-38. (Washington) Foreign Agricultural Service, USDA,
      1956. iv, 52 p.                         Files Alg 7 H65

      Considers limited land resources, demographic pressure, and
      traditional farming practices as the major development con-
      straints. Claims that disruptions by Algerian nationalists
      were sabotaging French land reform efforts. Projections for
      the future assume continued French rule. Includes statistics
      on the division of land by tenure categories.

18.   Jaulin, R. "Les Problèmes de l'autogestion dans les grandes
      fermes algériennes en 1963." (In AUTO, 2, 1967. p. 3-44)
                                          Mem AP A9396

      Attempts to analyze peasant perceptions of the link between
      their assemblies (on autogestion farms) and the government
      agents who supervise operations on each farm. Strongly
      advocates self-government in these agricultural enterprises,
      regarding government interference as detrimental and unneces-
      sary. Additional comments by an agricultural technician and
      a rural sociologist support this view.

18a.  Koulytchizky, Serge. "Dynamiques de l'autogestion genèse et
      ambivalence de l'expérience algérienne." (In CAIS, 31, 1972.
      p. 131-183)

19.   Lazarev, Grigori. "Remarques sur l'autogestion en Algérie."
      (In INSTITUTIONS ET DEVELOPPEMENT AGRICOLE AU MAGHREB. Paris,
      Presses Universitaires de France, 1965. p. 5-74)   HD 996 I57

ALG 19-23

(Lazarev, Grigori)
Concludes that agrarian reform, consisting essentially of the
socialization of large ex-colonial estates (autogestion), had
little impact on changing the basic agrarian structure. It
actually widened the gap between the socialized and traditional sectors. Despite this assessment, Lazarev sees
national policies followed as optimal in view of particular
historical conditions. Emphasizes the need to extend benefits
to the peasant masses through distribution of lands organized
on a cooperative basis.

19a.   Lucas, Philippe. "Réforme agraire en Algérie." (In HOMS, 27,
       1973. p. 131-142)                      Mem AP H7681 E84
       Also available as a separate.           Files Alg 3 L81

20.    Marthelot, Pierre. "Les Poids des traditions communautaires
       dans l'agriculture au Maghreb." 1971.

       See Item NE-27 for citation and annotation.

20a.   Mergui, Raphaël. "Donner la terre sans paysans aux paysans
       sans terre." 1972. (In Item ALG-6, p. 58-62) Mem AP J5929 A258

21.    Miette, R. "Une Formule pour la réforme agraire en Algérie:
       la coopérative ouvrière agricole." (In AFAS, 60, 1962.
       p. 45-48)                              Mem AP A2585 E83
       Also available as a separate.           Files Alg 3 M42

       In place of a precipitous expropriation and distribution of
       lands into uneconomical units, and to avoid the incentive
       problems of cooperativization, Miette proposes establishment
       of "agricultural worker cooperatives." Already expropriated
       lands would be leased to individuals with the possibility of
       ownership later.

22.    Muralt, Jürgen von. "Die Selbstverwaltung in der algerischen
       Landwirtschaft." (In ZAL, 5:3, 1966. p. 231-242)

       Examines the character of collective land use, which has
       developed from former foreign-owned estates. These were not
       subdivided, but became the focus for the socialist sector of
       agriculture.

23.    Ollivier, Marc. "The Decolonization of agriculture." (In
       CERES, 6:1, 1973. p. 24-28)

       Terms agrarian reform efforts since independence as "global"
       in their attention to both agricultural production as well as

(Ollivier, Marc)
social institutional changes. Describes initiatives to trans-
form the rural economy to meet internal national priorities
rather than those of foreign markets.

24.   Ouzegane, Amar. "Perspectives de la réforme agraire en
      Algérie." 1963. (In Item ALG-34, p. 9-14)   Mem HC 547 A4 T5

      A brief outline of the problems facing agrarian reform in
      Algeria, concentrating on the need for reconstruction after
      the war years and the need for reorientation of traditional
      agricultural methods.

24a.  Planhol, X. de. NOUVEAUX VILLAGES ALGEROIS:  ATLAS BLIDEEN,
      CHENOUA, MITIDIJA OCCIDENTALE.  Publications de la Faculté
      des Sciences Humaines d'Algérie, 39.  Paris, Presses Univer-
      sitaires de France, 1961.  120 p.        Mem HT 148 A4 P55

25.   Poncet, Jean. "Vers une nouvelle structuration de l'agricul-
      ture en Algérie." (In PENSEE, 113, 1964.  p. 23-40)
                                                      Mem AP P4183

      Misguided diagnoses of rural underdevelopment have ignored
      basic socio-economic issues of skewed distribution of land
      and the means to effect agricultural modernization.  Instead,
      development programs have accentuated differences in a dual
      modern-traditional agrarian structure.  Considers autogestion
      as too limited in scope and advocates a broader approach to
      agrarian reform to specifically meet the needs of the vast
      majority of peasants.

26.   Reggam, Z. "Agrarian reform in Algeria." (In Item NE-10,
      p. 235-246)                       HD 850.8 Z63 D46 1965
      Also available as a separate.            Files Alg 3 R23

      An official's description of the organization and operation
      of autogestion farms and advances attained in marketing and
      production.  Considers tasks remaining to be the diversifica-
      tion of agricultural production and the extension of self-
      managed cooperatives to the traditional peasant sector.

27.   Rosciszewski, Marcin M. "Traditional sector of Maghreb
      agriculture:  character and development trends." 1970.

      See Item NE-31 for citation and annotation.

28.   Ruedy, John. LAND POLICY IN COLONIAL ALGERIA:  THE ORIGINS OF
      THE RURAL PUBLIC DOMAIN. Near Eastern studies, 10.  Berkeley,

# Land Tenure and Agrarian Reform

ALG 28-32

(Ruedy, John)
University of California Press, 1967. xiii, 115 p. Bibl.
HD 999 A4 R82

Scholarly analysis of the precolonial tenure status of various categories of land and the means used to aggregate them into the colonial state domain during 1830-1852. Notes that private French seizures of native lands were representative of a continuing split between official French policy and actions of the settlers (or <u>colons</u>).

28a.  Sari, Djilali. "Le Démantèlement de la propriété foncière."
(In RH, 249, 1973. p. 47-76)   Mem AP R452 H6
Also available as a separate.   Files Alg 58 S17

29.  Schliephapke, Konrad. "Changing the traditional sector of Algeria's agriculture." (In LRLSC, 1973:1. p. 19-28)
REF HD 1261 A1 L1 1973 v. 1

Describes the establishment of the National Agrarian Revolution Fund to redistribute land to landless peasants. The author maintains that postindependence land policy recalls traditional Islamic land categories. He asserts that to raise rural living standards and to keep traditional sector peasants in agriculture will require improved production inputs and the extension of cultivable areas.

30.  Séreni, J. P. "Peut-on révolutionner l'agriculture?" (In JA, 586, 1972. p. 40-43)   Mem AP J5929 A258

Description of agrarian reform policy enunciated in 1971 extending benefits to the impoverished traditional sector. Redistribution of land and modernization of agricultural techniques are envisaged as part of this "agrarian revolution."

31.  Shelepin, V. "Algeria: new phase." (In NT, 23, 1973. p. 23-24)

Describes positive progress made in extending the national cooperative agrarian structure. Advocates the organizational harnessing of revolutionary energies embodied in peasants and laboring masses to overcome obstacles presented by private landowners to the extension of this structure.

32.  Sicard, H. "Problèmes fonciers au Maghreb." 1965.
Mem AP A2585 E83

See Item NE-33 for citation and annotation.

LAND TENURE AND AGRARIAN REFORM

32a.   Sutton, K.  "Agrarian reform in Algeria:  the conversion of
projects into action."  (In AFSPEC, 9:1, 1974.  p. 50-68)
                                           Mem AP A25811 S747

32b.   Temmar, Hamid.  "Notre dossier; l'organisation de l'autogestion dans l'agriculture algérienne."  (In DCI, 43, 1971.
p. 56-96)

33.    Tidafi, T.  L'AGRICULTURE ALGERIENNE:  CONDITIONS ET PERSPEC-
TIVES D'UN DEVELOPPEMENT REEL.  Documents, études, recherches,
no. 2.  Paris, François Maspero, 1969.  223 p.  Bibl.
                                           S 473 A5 T42

Analyzes institutional and structural barriers to progress in
both the modern socialized and the impoverished traditional
agricultural sectors.  Insists on the necessity of radical
agrarian reform, delimiting maximum landholding and income
levels.  Cites the colonial heritage and continued dependence
on industrialized countries as the principal causes of
Algerian underdevelopment, and argues that real development
must comprise coordinated efforts in industry as well as in
agriculture.

34.    Tiers Monde.  PROBLEMES DE L'ALGERIE INDEPENDANTE.  Etude
présentée par François Perroux.  (1. ed.)  Paris, Presses
Universitaires de France, 1963.  vii, 207 p.  Mem HC 547 A4 T5

A collection of essays on various socio-economic problems in
postcolonial Algeria.  See Items ALG-13; ALG-16; and ALG-24
for individually annotated articles.

35.    Verdier, Jean M.; Desanti, Pierre; et Karila, Juliana.
STRUCTURES FONCIERS ET DEVELOPPEMENT RURAL AU MAGHREB.  1969.
                                           Mem HD 1169 V4

See Item NE-37 for citation and annotation.

35a.   Waterbury, John.  LAND, MAN, AND DEVELOPMENT IN ALGERIA.
North Africa series, 17:1/3.  (Hanover, N. H.)  American
Universities Field Staff, 1973.  (55) p.        Files Alg 30 W18

LAND TENURE AND AGRARIAN REFORM

ARAB 1-7

## ARABIAN PENINSULA

1.  Addad, Hani Abdul-Hameed. "The Nomad problem and the imple-
    mentation of a nomadic settlement scheme in Saudi Arabia."
    (In Item NE-10, p. 296-305)            HD 850.8 Z63 D46 1965

2.  Dequin, Horst. DIE LANDWIRTSCHAFT SAUDISCH-ARABIENS UND IHRE
    ENTWICKLUNGSMOGLICHKEITEN. Zeitschrift für Ausländische
    Landwirtschaft, sonderheft nr. 1. Frankfurt, DLG-Verlag-GMBH,
    n.d. xii, 259 p.                        HD 2111 S3 D26

3.  Issawi, Charles P., ed. THE ECONOMIC HISTORY OF THE MIDDLE
    EAST. 1966.                            Mem HC 412 I787

    See Item NE-19 for citation and annotation.

4.  Saudi Arabia. THE AGRICULTURAL LAND SITUATION IN SOUTH
    ARABIA. RU:WLR-C/66/38. (Rome) FAO, 1966. 5 p. Paper for
    World Land Reform Conference, Rome, 1966.   Files Arab 58 S18

    Describes the differential impact of physical and customary
    influences on forms of land tenure, pointing to the inter-
    dependence of land and water rights. Delineates agricultural
    development schemes noting the lack of radical land reform.
    Some cooperativization has occurred, consolidating small plots.

5.  ____. Ministry of Information. THE KINGDOM OF SAUDI ARABIA:
    FACTS AND FIGURES; LAND DISTRIBUTION AND SETTLEMENT. n.p.,
    1971. 45 p.                            Files Arab 17 S18

6.  Tannous, Afif F. "Land ownership in the Middle East." 1950.
                                           Ag Docs

    See Item NE-34 for citation and annotation.

7.  Walpole, Norman C. AREA HANDBOOK FOR SAUDI ARABIA. 2nd. enl.
    ed. DA Pam 550-51. Washington, American University; for
    sale by the U.S. Govt. Print. Off., 1971. 373 p.   DS 204 W16

    Short, descriptive section (p. 218-225) on land tenure, ten-
    ancy, and water rights.

LAND TENURE AND AGRARIAN REFORM

## CYPRUS

1.  Christodoulou, P. "The Tenure and inheritance of immovable
    property in Cyprus and the 1946 reform." 1947. (In Item
    CYP-2, p. 19-23)                                    Ag REWH C76

    Describes the influence of the Ottoman land laws on Cypriot
    land tenure. The practice of dividing property into fixed
    shares upon the owner's death has resulted in tremendous
    fragmentation of land, complicated by the problem of dual
    ownership--that is, land and the trees and buildings on it may
    be inherited separately, so that while one individual may own
    a piece of land, others may own the barn or the olive trees on
    it. The Land Law of 1946 abolished the separate categories
    of immovable property and required that when land was sold,
    all immovable property must go with it, and adjustments and
    compensation must be arranged accordingly. In addition, sub-
    division of holdings below a certain size will not be
    permitted.

2.  Conference on Land Use in a Mediterranean Environment,
    Nicosia, Cyprus, 1946. PROCEEDINGS. Nicosia, Govt. Print.
    Off., 1947. 55 p.                                   Ag REWH C76

    Includes brief papers on various agricultural, land tenure,
    land use, and health-related problems in the Cypriot rural
    sector. See Item CYP-1 for an individually cited and anno-
    tated article.

3.  Cyprus. Land Consolidation Authority. CYPRUS BIBLIOGRAPHY
    ON LAND TENURE AND SETTLEMENT. Nicosia, 1972. 5 1.
                                                    Files Cyp 58 C87

    Items in Greek and English concerned with land consolidation,
    registration, and land legislation. Also cites sources deal-
    ing with sociological and administrative aspects of tenure
    and settlement issues.

4.  _____. Laws, statutes, etc. THE LAND CONSOLIDATION LAW (24
    of 1969). Nicosia, Land Consolidation Service, Dept. of Agri-
    culture, Ministry of Agriculture and Natural Resources, 1970.
    38 1. Translated by G. Karouzis, N. Georgiades, and
    G. Camelaris.                                   Files Cyp 58 C91

    Sets up administrative machinery, notably the Land Consolida-
    tion Authority. Delineates procedures for consolidation and

# LAND TENURE AND AGRARIAN REFORM

CYP 4-8

(Cyprus. Laws, statutes, etc.)
includes provisions for infrastructural improvements (water
supply, transport, etc.).

5. Karouzis, George. "Land tenure in Cyprus: a powerful typo-
logical criterion." n.p., 1971. 13 1. Bibl. Originally
published in the "Symposium of Agricultural Typology and
Agricultural Settlements," European Regional Conference,
International Geographical Union, Szeged, Pecs, 1971.

Files Cyp 58 K17

Examines the impact of particular land tenure forms on farm
size, labor and land utilization, and production and productivity. Concludes that the existing land tenure structure
"impedes full, efficient use of the land, labor force, etc."
A table summarizes the distribution of the various categories
of tenure.

6. _____. "An Outline of the land tenure structure of Cyprus."
(In CGA/GC, 2/3:5/6, 1974. 24 p.)
Also available as a separate. Files Cyp 58 K173

Discusses land use, categories of land tenure, size and frag-
mentatation of holdings, water rights, and land consolidation.
Suggests various measures for the improvement of the tenure
situation, including new land-leasing legislation, the imposition of maximum and minimum size limits on holdings, regulation of water rights, the introduction of group farming, the
prohibition of the sale of agricultural lands to non-farmers,
and the early retirement of elderly landowners.

7. _____. REPORT ON ASPECTS OF LAND TENURE IN CYPRUS. Nicosia,
Ministry of Agriculture and Natural Resources, Dept. of
Agriculture, 1970. ii, 193 p. HD 951 C9 K3

Emphasizes the phenomenon of fragmentary land ownership and
assesses the effects of the Land Consolidation Law
(Item Cyp-4). Though Karouzis expects this law to alleviate
conditions, he advocates: (1) additional measures to regulate leasing; (2) establishment of ownership maxima and
minima; and (3) state purchase of uncultivated ecclesiastical
and absentee lands. Replete with tables, maps, and diagrams
depicting the overall land tenure structure and changes in it.

8. Karouzis, George; and Ioannides, P. BIBLIOGRAPHY ON LAND
TENURE IN CYPRUS. Nicosia, Land Consolidation Authority,
1974. 26 1. Text in English and Greek. Files Cyp 58 K165

# LAND TENURE AND AGRARIAN REFORM

CYP 8–EGY 1

(Karouzis, George; and Ioannides, P.)
Includes 116 items, many from 1969 and 1970. About half are
in Greek.

9.    Meek, Charles Kingsley. "Cyprus." 1949. (In Item AFR-91,
      p. 62-71)                                        HD 599 Z5 M4

Provides a description of the land tenure situation in Cyprus
with its basis of Ottoman land laws promulgated up to 1878.
Major problems in the system's operation (e.g., fragmentation
of holdings and lack of credit) are discussed.

10.   Tornaritis, Criton G. EXPROPRIATION AND NATIONALIZATION OF
      PRIVATE PROPERTY UNDER THE LAW OF THE REPUBLIC OF CYPRUS.
      Nicosia (Public Information Office) 1970.  23 p.
                                            Files Cyp 36 T67

The Cypriot Attorney General examines the broad notion of
"Property" and its conception in Cyprus as defined in the
Constitution.  Argues that the strict guarantee of individual
property rights has sometimes hindered development efforts.
Advocates limits to these rights so that the state can act to
expropriate or nationalize property for the public good.

11.   Zaken, Denis van der. REPORT TO THE GOVERNMENT OF CYPRUS ON
      LAND CONSOLIDATION. Expanded Technical Assistance Program
      report no. 1617.  Rome, FAO, 1963.  ii, 37 p.  Bibl.
                                            Files Cyp 58 Z14

Analyzes implications of the prevalence of small-sized, fragmented holdings.  Applies cost-benefit criteria in discussing
implementation of the consolidation program proposed to
alleviate this situation.


## EGYPT


1.    Abdel-Malek, Anouar. "La Réforme agraire en Egypte (R.A.U.):
      problèmes et perspectives." (In DCI, 22, 1965.  p. 19-27)
      Also available as a separate.          Files UAR 3 A1

Views Egypt's land reform programs between 1952 and 1964
according to a theoretical typology of agrarian reform in
general.  Analyzes the background and effects of the reform
on social structure, economy, and the political life of
Egypt.

# LAND TENURE AND AGRARIAN REFORM

1a. Abussooud, Hassan. GENERAL ASPECTS OF LAND REFORM IN EGYPT. (Cairo, Press Dept., H.C.A.R., 1954). 19 p.   Files UAR 3 A18

2. Adamawicz, Mieczyslaw. "Transformation of agricultural structure in the United Arab Republic." (In AB, 13, 1970. p. 75-88)

   Calls for a policy approach sensitive to the needs of national economic and social development as a whole. Regards land reform as the main instrument of social transformation in agriculture. The author discusses the progress of socialization especially as regards cooperativization. Suggests that although central direction had been necessary initially, future success will depend on farmers' active participation in changes affecting them.

2a. Adbel-Rasoul, Ragaa. THE ROLE OF THE PUBLIC SECTOR IN AGRICULTURE, WITH SPECIAL REFERENCE TO EGYPTIAN AGRICULTURE. IDEP/ET/CS/2365-23. Dakar, United Nations, African Institute for Economic Development and Planning, 1972. 21 p. Bibl. Paper for Seminar on the Role of Public Sector in the Economic Development of Africa, Cairo, 1972.   Files UAR 4 A21

2b. Afifi, Hani. "The Egyptian experience of agrarian reform." (In EAJRD, 5:1/2, 1972. p. 193-200)   Ag Per

3. "Agricultural cooperation in the U.A.R." (In NBE/EB, 19:4, 1966. p. 351-361)

   A brief history focusing on the Agrarian Reform Law of 1952, which provided for the formation of agricultural cooperatives to meet credit, production, and marketing needs. Discusses role of the General Agricultural Cooperative Organization in formulating policy and supervising various types of cooperatives.

4. Ahmad, M. S.; and Roy, E. P. "Cooperation and land reform in the Middle East." 1963.   Files Asia 3 A35

   See Item NE-2 for citation and annotation.

4a. Ahmed, S. M. Sayed. "Land reform in Egypt." n.p. (1973). 4 p. Paper for Study Seminar 35: Land Tenure, Distribution and Reform, Institute of Development Studies, University of Sussex, 1973.   Files UAR 3 A35

5. Albaum, Melvin. "Cooperative agricultural settlement in Egypt and Israel." (In LE, 42:2, 1966. p. 221-225)

(Albaum, Melvin)
Concludes that aims and principles are similar, but different
means are used to achieve the goals in each case.

6.  Andrawos, Naim Michel. EGYPTE. Bruxelles, Institut Inter-
    national des Civilisations Différentes, 1973. 15 1. Paper
    for INCIDI Study Session on Obstacles and Restraints Impeding
    the Success of Land Reform in Developing Countries, Brussels,
    1973.                                          Files UAR 3 A52

7.  Ayrout, Henry Habib. THE EGYPTIAN PEASANT. Translated from
    the French by John Alden Williams. Foreword by Chester Bowles.
    Introduction by Morroe Berger. Boston, Beacon Press (1963).
    167 p. Bibl. Translation of MOEURS ET COUTUMES DES FELLAHS,
    first published in 1938.              Ag HD 1538 E3 A952 2

The chapter on "Landowners and government" makes the connection between the daily life of the peasant and the potential
impact of governmental agrarian policy. Berger's introduction
gives more up-to-date information on changes in rural Egypt,
including a discussion of the 1952 land reform.

8.  Baer, Gabriel. A HISTORY OF LANDOWNERSHIP IN MODERN EGYPT,
    1800-1950. Middle Eastern monographs, 4. London, New York,
    Oxford University Press, 1962. xii, 252 p. Bibl.
                                          Ag HD 975 B233

Excellent historical discussion of the development of private
land ownership. Also discusses land distribution, waqf (religious endowment) lands, and various opinions of the modern
land reform. Includes tables on land distribution and private,
foreign, and state landholdings. The bibliography lists Arab
as well as European and American sources.

9.  _____. "New data on Egypt's land reform." (In NO, 10:3 (87),
    1967. p. 26-29)                       Mem AP N523 0941

Examines the ramifications of Egypt's agrarian reform, con-
cluding that although the reform has changed Egyptian society
considerably, it has not solved the problem of the landless
peasants.

10. _____. STUDIES IN THE SOCIAL HISTORY OF MODERN EGYPT.
    Chicago, University of Chicago Press, 1969. xx, 259 p.
                                          Mem HN 783 B32

Analyzes Egypt's socio-economic and institutional transformation in the nineteenth and first half of the twentieth

(Baer, Gabriel)
centuries. Describes the detribalization of the bedouins and the emergence of their leaders as large landowners; the dissolution of village communities as communal landowners with the development of private land rights (to which a full chapter is devoted); and the status of religious endowments (waqf). Reference is make to other countries in the area, particularly Turkey, and nations of the Fertile Crescent.

11.    Barrāwī, Rashid al-. "The Agrarian problem in Egypt." (In MEA, 2:3, 1951. p. 75-84)     Mem AP M6275

Analyzes the emergence of a polarized agrarian structure with concentration of landownership in a few hands opposed to a mass of poor and landless peasants. Argues that curtailing the power of the skeikhs and large landowners is a precondition for the large-scale, redistributive land reform that is needed.

11a.    _____. ECONOMIC DEVELOPMENT IN THE UNITED ARAB REPUBLIC, EGYPT. 2nd ed. Cairo, Anglo-Egyptian Bookshop, 1972. xiii, 376 p. Bibl.     HC 535 B17

12.    Boeckx, Cecile. "Réforme agraire et structures sociales en Egypte Nassérienne." (In CIV, 21:4, 1971. p. 373-393)

Outlines land reform measures enacted under Nasser and concludes that the class structure of the Egyptian countryside remains unchanged from that before 1952.

13.    Chanbour, Mohamed-Issam. "La Politique agricole en Egypte Nassérienne." Poitiers, Faculté de Droit et des Sciences Economiques, Université de Poitiers, 1968. 276 1. Thesis, Université de Poitiers.     HD 2123 1968 C32

Studies various aspects of agrarian reform, including the distribution of land, credit and finance, cooperatives, and the rights of agricultural workers. An appendix contains legal texts pertaining to agrarian reform.

14.    Dawood, Hassan Aly. "Farm land acquisition problems in Egypt." (In LE, 26:3, 1950. p. 305-307)     Ag Per
Also available in Item EGY-15.     HD 105 C67 1951b

Attributes to high rents and low agricultural wages the inability of tenants and agricultural laborers to acquire land.

15.    _____. "Landownership and tenancy systems in Egypt" [and]
"Farm land acquisition problems in Egypt." 1951. (In Conference on World Land Tenure Problems, University of Wisconsin,
1951. PAPERS, 4. Madison, 1951. 10 p.)    HD 105 C67 1951b

    Includes Item EGY-14 plus a survey of tenure relationships,
    particularly various rental and leasing practices. Evils of
    the tenancy system include oral contracts, lack of occupant
    security, and the activities of intermediaries who rent land
    and sublet it at inflated prices.

15a.   Dresch, Jean. "Réforme agraire et sous-développement; Moyen-
Orient Muselman." 1964.                     Mem HD 1415 S2

    See Item NE-11 for citation and annotation.

15b.   Dumont, René. "The Effects of the rising tide of population
on the modest progress of 'bureaucratic-military socialism'
in Egypt." (In Dumont, René; and Mazoyer, Marcel. SOCIALISMS
AND DEVELOPMENT. Translated by Rupert Cunningham. New York,
Praeger, 1973. p. 185-207)                  HC 59.7 D813 1973b

15c.   Egypt. "Agrarian reform, El-Faroukia." n.p., n.d.  8 1.
                                            Files UAR 3 E37

15d.   _____. Higher Committee for Agrarian Reform. AGRARIAN REFORM
IN EGYPT; RELEASE NO. 10. Cairo (195-). 14 1.
                                            Files UAR 3 E372

15e.   _____. _____. THE FIRST PROCEDURE OF LAND DISTRIBUTION IN
UPPER EGYPT. (Cairo) Press Dept., H.C.A.R., 1954. 31 p.
                                            Files UAR 3 E385

15f.   _____. _____. LAND TENURE IN EGYPT BEFORE THE START OF THE
AGRARIAN REFORM. Cairo, 1955. 4 1.          Files UAR 58 E39

15g.   _____. _____. STEPS TAKEN IN THE IMPLEMENTATION OF EGYPTIAN
AGRARIAN REFORM. Cairo, 1955. 7 1.          Files UAR 3 E386

15h.   _____. _____. TWO YEARS OF AGRARIAN REFORM. Cairo (195-).
       35 p.                                Files UAR 3 E387

16.    _____. Laws, statutes, etc. LAND REFORM LAW. Full text.
Cairo, Press Dept., H.C.A.R., 1954. 22 p.   Files UAR 3 E39

    Text of Decree-Law no. 178 of 1952 on land reform. Deals with
    limits on agricultural holdings and provisions for expropriat-
    ing certain land for distribution among small farmers;

EGY 16-20

(Egypt. Laws, statutes, etc.)
agricultural cooperative societies; supplementary taxes; and
the rights of the agricultural worker.  See Item EGY-34 for
summary of provisions.

16a.  El Abd, Mohamed.  EGYPTIAN AGRARIAN REFORM SYSTEM OF LAND
      REQUISITION.  Cairo, H.C.A.R., 1955.  9 l.      Files UAR 3 E51
      Also available as a Background document for Center on Land
      Problems in the Near East, Salahuddin, Iraq, 1955.  Rome, FAO,
      1955.  8 p.                                     Files UAR 3 E51

17.   El-Beblaoui, H.  "La Réforme agraire et les coopératives
      agricoles en Egypt."  (In CAIS, 24, 1968.  p. 137-156)

      Characterizes Egyptian agricultural cooperatives as highly
      bureaucratic--a necessary evil during the initial phases of a
      centrally directed economic reconstruction.  Though aiming at
      a more egalitarian land distribution, the primary thrust
      appears to be toward changing the technology of and increasing
      production in agriculture.

18.   El-Gabaly, Mostafa M.  "New trends in land policy in the
      U.A.R."  (In Item NE-10, p. 205-218)      HD 850.8 Z63 D46 1965

      Overview of schemes to increase productivity and extend the
      impact of agrarian reforms.  Measures discussed include better
      soil management and land settlement programs.  Regards land
      reform in terms of its setting the institutional stage for
      such efforts.

19.   El-Kammash, Magdi M.  ECONOMIC DEVELOPMENT AND PLANNING IN
      EGYPT.  New York, Praeger, 1968.  xxvi, 408 p.  Bibl.
                                                      HC 535 E42

      A multi-faceted analysis of social, religious, and political
      factors in the process of development.  Traces the evolution
      of Egypt's land tenure system and the changing land distribu-
      tion picture with an evaluation of the changes subsequent to
      the 1952 agrarian reform.

20.   El Serafy, Salah.  "Egyptian land taxation and land reform."
      n.p., n.d.  17 l.                             Files UAR 3 E57

      Describes the replacement of indirect fiscal policy approaches
      by the more direct manipulation of the economy through land
      reform.  Traces the evolution since the nineteenth century of
      conditions--concentration of landownership and sky-rocketing
      rents--which produced the need for land reform.

## Land Tenure and Agrarian Reform

21. El-Shagi, El-Shagi. NEUORDNUNG DER BODENNUTZUNG IN ÄGYPTEN:
DREI FALLSTUDIEN. Afrika-studien, nr. 36. München, Weltforum
Verlag (1969). 175 p. Bibl.                   Mem HC 501 A32/36

    Analyzes the process of socialization in the agriculture sec-
    tor, discussing measures related to cooperatives and the pro-
    vision of credit. Illustrates the socio-economic repercussions
    of cooperativization on three communities. The author also
    considers agrarian politics, weaknesses in the agrarian sys-
    tem, and the reform program of 1952.

22. El-Zoghby, Salah. "Approaches to community development in
rural Egypt (U.A.R.) with special reference to land reform."
Madison, 1966. 182 1. M. S. thesis, University of Wisconsin.
                                              Mem AWO Z853 S159

    Deals with the extent to which land reform and governmental
    agencies can aid in community development. Concludes that
    there is a complementary relationship between community devel-
    opment and these elements.

22a. Ezzat, Abd El Wahab. LAND REFORM IN EGYPT. Country project
no. CP-4. (Rome) FAO, 1955. 10 p. Paper for Center on Land
Problems in the Near East, Salahuddin, Iraq, 1955.
                                              Files UAR 3 E99

23. _____. "The Land tenure system of Egypt." 1951. (In Conference on World Land Tenure Problems, University of Wisconsin,
1951. LAND TENURE: PROCEEDINGS OF THE INTERNATIONAL CONFER-
ENCE. Madison, University of Wisconsin Press, 1956. p. 100-
103)                                          HD 105 C67 1951

    Outlines the historical evolution and problems of the present
    agrarian situation. Sees improvement either through "direct"
    measures (extending cultivable areas and redistributing land)
    or "indirect" measures (education, migration, birth control,
    or industrialization).

24. Gadalla, Saad M. LAND REFORM IN RELATION TO SOCIAL DEVELOP-
MENT, EGYPT. University of Missouri studies, no. 39. Columbia, University of Missouri Press (1962). 139 p. Bibl.
                                              HD 976 G3

    Maintains that in Egypt, with a 70 percent rural population,
    the land tenure system determines not only the basic economic
    laws, but also those of the social system. Describes the pro-
    visions of the 1952 reform, its social effects between 1952

EGY 24-26e

(Gadalla, Saad M.)
and 1956, and a projection for future impact. Makes recommendations for further measures for social development of the
farm population.

25. Garzouzi, Eva. OLD ILLS AND NEW REMEDIES IN EGYPT; A COMPRE-
HENSIVE REVIEW OF THE DIFFERENT MEASURES ADOPTED IN RECENT
YEARS TO DEAL WITH THE PROBLEMS RESULTING FROM OVERPOPULATION.
Cairo, D. al Maaref, 1958? 159 p. Bibl.     Mem HN 783 G3

Action in such spheres as education and social welfare are
mentioned as necessary initiatives to deal with Egypt's major
problems, but the main emphasis is placed on agrarian reform.

26. Grienig, H. "Landreform verändert Klassenstruktur in der
V.A.R." (In DA, 12:19, 1967. p. 1110-1116)  Mem AP D491 A932

Discusses changes in class structure produced by the agrarian
reform laws of 1952 and 1961. Grienig observes that class
lines have been sharpened, and a new class--that of reform
beneficiaries--has been created. Agriculture on the whole
remains a stronghold of private ownership.

26a. Guirguis, Malak. AGRARIAN REFORM IN THE ARAB REPUBLIC OF
EGYPT; A SOCIO-ECONOMIC EVALUATION. Bruxelles, Institut International des Civilisations Différentes, 1973. 16 1. Paper
for INCIDI Study Session on Obstacles and Restraints Impeding
the Success of Land Reform in Developing Countries, Brussels,
1973.                                           Files UAR 3 G84

26b. _____. SOME OF THE CAUSES OF SUCCESS OF AGRARIAN REFORM IN
THE ARAB REPUBLIC OF EGYPT; A COMPLEMENTARY REPORT. Bruxelles,
Institut International des Civilisations Différentes, 1973.
9 1. Paper for INCIDI Study Session on Obstacles and Re-
straints Impeding the Success of Land Reform in Developing
Countries, Brussels, 1973.                     Files UAR 3 G843

26c. Hagrass, Saad. "Agrarian reform in the U.A.R." n.p., n.d.
9 1.                                           Files UAR 3 H128

26d. _____. EGYPTIAN AGRARIAN REFORM SYSTEM OF LAND DISTRIBUTION.
Cairo, H.C.A.R., 1955. 9 1.                    Files UAR 3 H129

26e. _____. FACTORS AFFECTING RETURN OF AGRARIAN REFORM LANDS;
SEPTEMBER 1955. Cairo, H.C.A.R., 1955. 5 1.
                                              Files UAR 3 H1295

# LAND TENURE AND AGRARIAN REFORM

26f.   _____.  "Land distribution."  Training course document no. 46.
       n.p., n.d.  17 p.                              Files UAR 3 H13

27.    Hansen, Bent; and Marzouk, Girgis.  DEVELOPMENT AND ECONOMIC
       POLICY IN THE U.A.R.  Amsterdam, North Holland Publishing Co.,
       1965.  xv, 333 p.                              HC 535.2 H15

       Economic study of development policies undertaken in Egypt
       since 1959.  The chapter on "Agricultural policies" contains
       a section on land reforms up to those of 1961, with a discus-
       sion of redistribution of agricultural income and productivity.

28.    Harik, Iliya F.  "Mobilization policy and political change in
       rural Egypt."  1972.  (In Item NE-32, p. 287-314)    DS 57 R87

       Case study of the mechanisms of national bureaucratic inter-
       vention and its impact on the local level.  Notes the power of
       ideology and pragmatism when fused in policy-making, something
       reflected in the relatively successful redistribution of wealth
       achieved in this instance.

29.    Hilmy, Hussein.  SETTLEMENT OF NOMADS IN EGYPT.  (Rome) FAO,
       1971.  20 1.  Paper prepared for the Ad Hoc Consultation on
       the Settlement of Nomads in Africa and the Near East, Cairo,
       1971.                                          Files UAR 17 H45

       Depicts the problematic features of nomadic existence, includ-
       ing the insecurity posed by unwritten, customary land tenure
       arrangements and the diseconomies of land fragmentation.  Pro-
       poses settlement of coastal tribes in conjunction with a thor-
       ough agricultural development program.  Contains illustrative
       maps and tables.

30.    Issawi, Charles P., ed.  THE ECONOMIC HISTORY OF THE MIDDLE
       EAST.  1966.                                   Mem HC 412 I787

       See Item NE-19 for citation and annotation.

31.    _____.  EGYPT IN REVOLUTION: AN ECONOMIC ANALYSIS.  London,
       New York, Oxford University Press, 1963.  343 p.
                                                      Mem HC 535 I74

       Examines agrarian structure and impact of the 1952 reform
       within the framework of a changing Egyptian economy.

31a.   Johnson, V. Webster.  "Land reform and related programs in
       Egypt."  Beirut, 1956.  22 1.                  Files UAR 3 J63

299

# LAND TENURE AND AGRARIAN REFORM

32.  Kamal, Adel.  "Feudalism and land reform."     DS 44 A3 1971b

     See Item NE-20 for citation and annotation.

32a. Khadry, Aziz,  IMPROVING AGRICULTURAL PRODUCTION IN LAND RE-
     FORM AREAS IN EGYPT.  Background document no. B-24.  (Rome)
     FAO, 1955.  7 p.  Paper for Center on Land Problems in the
     Near East, Salahuddin, Iraq, 1955.          Files UAR 3 K12

32b. _____.  OBJECTIVES OF EGYPTIAN LAND REFORM.  Background docu-
     ment no. B-9.  (Rome) FAO, 1955.  3 p.  Paper for Center on
     Land Problems in the Near East, Salahuddin, Iraq, 1955.
                                                 Files UAR 3 K31

32c. Kuhnen, Frithjof.  "Fallstudie über Auswirkungen der syrischen
     Agrarreform:  ein Beitrag zur Ermittlung relevanter Faktoren
     und Prozesse."  1963.

     See Item SYRIA-11 for citation and annotation.

33.  "Land reform."  n.d.                         Files 3 L15

     See Item NE-23 for citation and annotation.

34.  "Legislation governing land redistribution in Italy and Egypt."
     (Rome, 197-).  7 l.                          Files 3 L23

     Contains summary of the provisions of "Legislative decree on
     agrarian reform No. 178, 9 September 1952, and subsequent
     revision on 1962 and on 1970."  See Item EGY-16 for full text.

35.  Mabro, Robert.  THE EGYPTIAN ECONOMY 1952-1972.  Oxford,
     Clarendon Press, 1974.  xii, 254 p.  Bibl.        HC 535 M17

     This summary review of Egyptian economic developments in the
     last 20 years contains a chapter on the agrarian reform which
     analyzes the land reform laws, their implementation, and their
     social and economic effects.  Includes statistics on land
     redistribution and holding and discusses the contribution of
     the cooperatives to increased agricultural production.

36.  Marei, Sayed.  AGRARIAN REFORM IN EGYPT.  1st ed.  Cairo,
     Imprimerie de l'Institut Français d'Archéologie Orientale,
     1957.  xii, 480 p.  Bibl.                         HD 972 M3

     Detailed account by the Minister of State for Agrarian Reform
     of the formulation and implementation of the 1952 agrarian
     reform law and an evaluation of its results up to 1957.

# LAND TENURE AND AGRARIAN REFORM

(Marei, Sayed)
Contends that the reform has been successful, not only in re-
distributing land, but also in maintaining and increasing
productivity. Contains texts of the 1952 law and subsequent
amendments and additions.

37. _____. "The Agrarian reform in Egypt." (In ILR, 69, 1954.
p. 140-150)                                      Mem AP I616 L135

Describes the conditions which created the need for the 1952
agrarian reform and outlines its main provisions. Stresses
the importance of redirecting capital through indemnities into
investment in commerce, industry, and agricultural production.
Sees the reform as the end of feudalism and the beginning of
a new era.

37a. _____. OUTLINE OF LAND REFORM IN EGYPT. (Cairo, Press Dept.,
H.C.A.R., 195-). 36 p.                           Files UAR 3 M169

38. _____. "An Outline of the Egyptian land reform." Rome (1971?)
16 1.                                            Files UAR 3 M17

Surveys the evolution of agrarian reform efforts and outlines
features emergent after 1969. Examines obstacles confronting
general improvement in the rural sector, including population
pressure, fragmentation of landholdings, inadequate credit,
and shortage of trained personnel to run cooperatives.

39. _____. "Overturning the pyramid (U.A.R.)." (In CERES, 2:6,
1969. p. 48-51)

Contends that narrowing the property-wealth gap by land reform
improved peasant living standards and provided incentives for
higher tenant and small landowner productivity. Other elements
in this increase in productivity are discussed.

39a. _____. U.A.R. AGRICULTURE ENTERS A NEW AGE; AN INTERPRETATIVE
SURVEY. Cairo, 1960. vii, 231 p.                 S 471 U5 M3

40. Mead, Donald C. GROWTH AND STRUCTURAL CHANGE IN THE EGYPTIAN
ECONOMY. Homewood, Ill., Irwin, 1967. xv, 414 p. Bibl.
HC 533 M4

Examines the agrarian structure and its influence on productivity and employment, income, etc. Includes tables on landownership, landholdings by size, distribution of holdings by type
of lease, and figures on fragmentation.

# LAND TENURE AND AGRARIAN REFORM

41. Nasharty, A. H. E. AGRARIAN REFORM IN THE UNITED ARAB REPUB-
    LIC. RU:WLR-C/66/17. (Rome) FAO, 1966. 15 p. Paper for
    World Land Reform Conference, Rome, 1966.    Files UAR 3 N17

    Review of agrarian reform efforts since 1952 and an assessment
    of their impact. Praises the greater equality in wealth dis-
    tribution and the growing contribution of agriculture to the
    national income resulting from land reform activities. In-
    cludes tables on landownership and cooperatives.

42. Oweis, Jiryis Sbetan. "The Impact of land reform on Egyptian
    agriculture 1952-1965." (Salt Lake City) 1970. 2 v. (xviii,
    533 1.). Bibl. Ph. D. dissertation, University of Utah.
    HD 976 092

    Analysis of "land reform as a catalyst to activate agricultural
    development." Oweis lauds governmental attention to the essen-
    tial components of credit and cooperative organization. He
    notes the pervasive political and social consequences of land
    reform, especially the improvement of the peasants' lot. Calls
    for further action in limiting population growth and increasing
    efficiency of agricultural organizations to assure continued
    progress.

43. _____. "The Impact of land reform on Egyptian agriculture;
    1952-1965." (In IER, 2:1, 1971. p. 45-72)
    Also available as LTC reprint no. 78. Madison, 1971.
    Files UAR 3 092

    Based on Item EGY-42.

44. Owen, Edward R. J. COTTON AND THE EGYPTIAN ECONOMY, 1820-
    1914; A STUDY IN TRADE AND DEVELOPMENT. Oxford, Clarendon
    Press, 1969. xxvi, 416 p. Bibl. Revision of thesis, Oxford
    University.    Mem HD 9087 E42 09

    Analyzes the process and effects of monoculture in Egypt. Owen
    traces the growth of large estates, especially in the Delta, as
    well as rising land prices, rents, and subsequent tax reforms.
    Effects on production, agricultural income, and income distri-
    bution are also examined. He feels that the disadvantages of
    extending cotton cultivation far outweighed any of the gains.

45. Parsons, Kenneth H. "Land reform in the United Arab Republic."
    (In LE, 35:4, 1959. p. 319-326)
    Also available as a separate.    Files UAR 3 P17

(Parsons, Kenneth H.)
Comparison of provisions and operation of land reform programs
in both regions of the U.A.R.--Syria and Egypt.  Discusses
adaptation of the Egyptian law to the very different conditions
in Syria as well as the legal and organizational provisions
themselves in both cases.

46.    _____.  "Land tenure in Asia."  1960.      Files Asia 58 P17

See Item NE-29 for citation and annotation.

47.   Platt, Kenneth B.  LAND REFORM IN THE UNITED ARAB REPUBLIC.
SR/LR/C-17.  Washington, USAID, 1970.  68 p.  Bibl.  Country
paper for Spring Review of Land Reform.      Files UAR 3 P52

Suggests that even though agrarian reforms had originally been
politically motivated, success in land redistribution and increasing productivity have been accomplished "to a creditable
degree."  Expects continued progress.

48.   Rivlin, Helen A. B.  THE AGRICULTURAL POLICY OF MUHAMMAD ALI
IN EGYPT.  Harvard Middle Eastern studies, 4.  Cambridge,
Mass., Harvard University Press, 1961.  xvii, 393 p.  Bibl.
                                        Mem HD 2123 1961 R5

Traces the evolution of land tenure under Ottoman rule, the
changes brought about under French influence in the early
nineteenth century, and the "revolution in Egyptian land
tenure" executed by Muhammad Ali.  Regards expropriation and
reorganization of land use and holding patterns to be primarily
aimed at meeting the fiscal needs of the state.  Includes
tables on land use and distribution by size of holding for
1820 and 1844.

49.   Rosciszewski, Marcin M.  "Agricultural geography of Egypt,
problems and perspectives."  (In AB, 5, 1966.  p. 33-51)

Emphasizes the dominance of natural and demographic forces in
shaping rural life.  The author analyzes the impact on and
interaction between these forces and elements of the agrarian
reform program.  Concludes that the gradual displacement of
family farming by a hired labor system will probably aggravate
unemployment problems.

50.   Saab, Gabriel S.  THE EGYPTIAN AGRARIAN REFORM:  1952-1962.
Middle Eastern monographs, no. 8.  New York, issued under the
auspices of the Royal Institute of International Affairs (by)
Oxford University Press, 1967.  xvi, 236 p.  Bibl.    HD 976 S2

(Saab, Gabriel S.)
Excellent review of agrarian reform from 1952 to 1962. Attempts to appraise the extent to which the various laws and
measures were effectively implemented and determines their
immediate effects. Concludes that the agrarian reform has
changed Egyptian rural life and has influenced the land tenure
policies of Arab countries of the Middle East and North Africa.
Includes tables, maps, and bibliography.

51.    _____. "Rationalization of agriculture and land tenure problems in Egypt." (In MEEP, 1960. p. 65-90)    Mem AP M62707

Outlines major problems faced in increasing productive efficiency and fostering links with the non-agricultural sectors.
Evaluating the 1952 agrarian reform, Saab points to shortfalls
in intensifying and diversifying production and the lack of
long-term security and protection for tenants. Does indicate
some improvement in peasant living conditions.

52.    Salumah, Hassan. "U.A.R. agricultural reform produces results."
Translations on Near East, no. 346, p. 95-100. (In JPRS,
7:10, 1968/1969. reel 107). Translated from AL-AHRAM, January
11, 1969. p. 9                                        Microfilm

Brief outline of progress in the activities of the Egyptian
General Organization of Agricultural and Cooperative Credit
and its associated banks.

53.    Schamp, H. "Vorläufiger Bericht über eine Ruse nach Ägypten."
(In ERDE, 96:3, 1965. p. 224-230)             Geol MC ER25

Considers the impact of the 1952 land reform as only sporadi-
cally visible though some change is evidenced by new schools,
social centers, and agricultural stations. Characterizes
technological advance in agriculture as slow.

54.    Schmidt, S. C. "The Egyptian agrarian reform: problems and
prospects." (In EP, 6:2, 1970. p. 7-9)

A look at Egyptian reforms of 1952 and 1961. Points out that
they have been successful in maintaining land productivity,
yet the real problem remaining is that of an acute land
shortage.

55.    Sheira, A. Z. "Credit aspects of land reform in Africa."
1965.                                       Mem JX 1977 +A22

See Item AFR-122 for citation and annotation.

56. Souza, João Gonçalves de. ALGUMAS EXPERIENCIAS EXTRACONTINEN-
TAIS DE REFORMA AGRARIA. Washington, PAU, 1964. ix, 254 p.
Bibl.
HD 156 S6

Includes a discussion of land reform, community development,
cooperation, and colonization in Egypt and Israel.

57. Stauffer, Thomas. "The Egyptian land reform law." (In EDCC,
4, 1952. p. 295-314)

Regards the land reform of 1952 as a means to rechannel investment away from land and into mining, industrial, and commercial
enterprises. Terms of the reform law are discussed with the
text of the law appended.

58. Tai, Hung-Chao. LAND REFORM IN COLOMBIA, INDIA, IRAN, MEXICO,
PAKISTAN, PHILIPPINES, TAIWAN, U.A.R.: A SELECTED BIBLIOGRA-
PHY. Cambridge, Mass., prepared and distributed by Center for
Rural Development, 1967. 107 1. Supplement: 10 1.
Files 3 T14

Contains 150 items ranging from general works to others of
more specific interest, covering statistical data, economic
development, community development, land tenure, and political
developments of Egypt and Iran.

59. Tannous, Afif F. "Land ownership in the Middle East." 1950.
Ag Per

See Item NE-34 for citation and annotation.

60. Thweatt, William. "The Egyptian agrarian reform." (In MEEP,
1956. p. 143-175)
Mem AP M62707

Maintains that land redistribution, though notable, was insufficient to cause a dramatic reduction in economic inequalities. Nevertheless, the greater equality in the distribution
of wealth achieved by the reform, combined with cooperativization, may enhance the amount of aggregate investments in agriculture and spur economic growth.

61. United Arab Republic. Laws, statutes, etc. "Act no. 15, pro-
hibiting foreigners from being owners of agricultural land;
Loi no. 15, interdisant aux étrangers agricoles - 14 January
1963." (In FAL, 12:4, V/1c. 4 p.) From LA GAZETTE FISCALE,
COMMERCIALE ET INDUSTRIELLE, 151/153, March/May 1963, p. 12.
Ag Docs
Also available as a separate.
Files UAR 58 U6

EGY 61-67

(United Arab Republic. Laws, statutes, etc.)
Prohibits foreign ownership of land in the U.A.R. and provides
for compensating present foreign owners.

62.  ＿＿. ＿＿. "Legislative decree no. 178 on agrarian
reform – 9 September 1952." (In FAL, 1:2, V.1/52.4. 10 p.)
From EGYPTIAN GOVERNMENT GAZETTE, no. 131 bis 9 September 1952.
p. 1.                                                    Ag Docs
Also available as a separate.                    Files UAR 3 U6

Places an upper limit of 200 feddan on individual holdings of
agricultural land. Also deals with expropriation of certain
land for distribution among small farmers.

63.  ＿＿. Ministry of Agrarian Reform and Land Reclamation.
AGRARIAN REFORM AND LAND RECLAMATION IN TEN YEARS. (Cairo?,
1962?). 168 p.                              Mem HD 2122 A47

Evaluation of the agrarian reform law enacted at the beginning
of the revolution in 1952 and its subsequent modifications.
Also lists the different land reform laws. Includes statistical data.

64.  ＿＿. ＿＿. AGRARIAN REFORM IN THE UNITED ARAB REPUBLIC.
n.p., 1965. 25 1.                               Files UAR 3 U7

Official summary of aspects of Egyptian agricultural and social
structure before the agrarian reform; fundamental aspects of
the reform; and economic and social effects of the reform.

65.  Warriner, Doreen. "Employment and income aspects of recent
agrarian reforms in the Middle East." 1970. Mem AP I616 L135

See Item NE-38 for citation and annotation.

66.  ＿＿. LAND REFORM AND DEVELOPMENT IN THE MIDDLE EAST; A
STUDY OF EGYPT, SYRIA AND IRAQ. 1962.        HD 850.8 W3 1962

See Item NE-39 for citation. Warriner finds only limited success in Egypt. Concludes that the "wider conception" of land
reform as part of a comprehensive development policy is a
better approach as long as the policy is not blunted by excessive broadening. Suggests that the agrarian reform in Egypt
gave more "social equality" to the peasants and produced a
more stable society.

67.  ＿＿. "Land reform in Egypt and its repercussions." (In IA/
L, 29:1, 1953. p. 1-10)                      Mem AP I616 A256

LAND TENURE AND AGRARIAN REFORM

(Warriner, Doreen)
A brief historical background of the land situation prior to
the 1952 coup d'etat. States that humanitarian and political
motives led to the present land reform policy. Suggests that
Egypt's land reform policy will serve as an example for agrarian reform programs of other Arab nations.

68.  _____. "Observations on land reform administration in Egypt."
(In JLAO, 2:2, 1963. p. 100-111)           Mem AP J83 L811

Maintains that implementation of the reform has fallen short
in its goals of redistribution of land and rent control.
Warriner attributes greater success to the cooperatives. Sees
future progress as dependent on more effective land redistribution in accordance with the 1961 reform law.

69.  Wilson, Rodney J. A. AGRICULTURAL DEVELOPMENT IN THE MIDDLE
EAST, 1950-1970. 1972.                      Files NE 4 W45

See Item NE-40 for citation and annotation.

70.  _____. RURAL EMPLOYMENT AND LAND TENURE: A PROPOSAL FOR RE-
SEARCH IN EGYPT. Economic research paper no. 2. Durham (Eng.)
University of Durham, Centre for Middle Eastern and Islamic
Studies, 1972. 14 l.                        Files UAR 35.4 W45

Proposes examining the relationship between labor utilization
and size of holding and type of land tenure. Posits five hy-
potheses to be tested. Provides some background information on
the Egyptian agrarian structure and land tenure situation.

71.  Wörz, J. G. F. "Genossenschaftliche Produktionsförderung in
der ägyptischen Landwirtschaft." (In ZAL, 5:2, 1966. p. 133-
142)

Relates how cooperatives, modern production techniques, and
supervised credits have been applied to minimize inefficien-
cies inherent in the postreform, small-farm agrarian structure.
Views the government's aim as the maintenance of private
initiative despite limitations on the range of decisions.

## IRAN

1.  Ajami, Ismali. "Land reform and modernisation of the farming
structure in Iran." (In OAS, 2:2, 1973. p. 120-131)

IRAN 1-5

(Ajami, Ismali)
Summarizes measures to reform the land tenure structure from
1927 to 1971. Among the efforts to modernize the farming
structure is the formation of rural cooperative societies
which are mostly small units without adequate financial resources and qualified personnel. As a complementary measure
to land reform, the government established Farm Corporations
whose success will depend on substantial government financial
assistance and the supply of managerial staff.

2.  Ajdari, Ahmad. "Les Conditions de la réforme agraire en Iran."
    (In DCI, 22, 1965. p. 37-46)
    Also available as a separate.                    Files Iran 3 A4

    Examines the underlying reasons behind the 1962 Land Reform
    Law and the political and organizational aspects (cooperatives,
    etc.) of implementation. Points to shortcomings in regard to
    the extent of land distribution and the goal of raising pro-
    ductivity. Includes tables on agrarian structure and changes
    in land distribution.

3.  Alam, Assadollah. "The Land tenure situation in Iran." (In
    Conference on World Land Tenure Problems, University of Wiscon-
    sin, 1951. PROCEEDINGS . . . . Madison, University of Wiscon-
    sin Press, 1956. p. 95-100)                     HD 105 C67 1951

    Description of Iran's landholding structure and past efforts at
    its reform. Stresses that land tenure cannot be considered
    in isolation from other components of agricultural development.
    Necessary supplements to tenure reform include cooperatives
    and management agencies, but the author notes the shortage of
    capital and leadership required for such supplemental
    activities.

4.  Alberts, Robert C. "Social structure and change in an Iranian
    village." Madison, 1963. 3 v. (xxii, 1094 p.) Ph. D. disser-
    tation, University of Wisconsin.              Mem AW AL14 R54

    Intensive community study of social structure and cultural
    change. Though implied in other sections, agrarian structure
    is focused upon in Part 4 on "Economic Organization."

5.  Ali Hekmat, Hassan. "Land reform law seen ineffectual."
    Translations on the Near East, no. 342. p. 4-9. (In JPRS,
    7:10, 1968/1969. reel 107) Translated from KHANDANIHA, Nov.
    30 - Dec. 3, 1968. p. 12.                        Microfilm

# LAND TENURE AND AGRARIAN REFORM

(Ali Hekmat, Hassan)
Criticizes as discriminatory and unjust proposals in 1968
entailing the confiscation of small landowners' holdings.
Especially critical of bases of land valuation and compensation
offered those facing expropriation.

6.  Avery, Peter. "The Shah's proclamation on reform." (Transla-
    tion). (In MEJ, 16:1, 1962. p. 86-92)
                                            Mem AP M6272

    Text of the Shah's statement of November 1961, announcing the
    temporary suspension of Parliament in conjunction with the
    proposed enactment of a sweeping program of reforms. Included
    are land reform and other schemes to modernize the rural sec-
    tor. Followed by the National Front attack against the Shah's
    program as "a return to despotism."

7.  _____. "Trends in Iran in the past five years." (In WT, 21,
    1965. p. 279-289)
                                            Mem AP W926 T633

    Places the initiation of land reform and other related govern-
    mental measures of the 1960s within the political context of
    Iran in that same period. Avery sees land reform moves,
    notably that in 1962, as an effort by the Shah to "create a
    new balance . . . by calling up the peasant reserve in the
    Shah's favor."

8.  Bank Omran, Teheran. THE PAHLAVI DOMAIN LAND DISTRIBUTION
    PROGRAM; OBJECTIVES, ACCOMPLISHMENTS, NEEDS. Teheran, n.d.
    17 p.
                                            Files Iran 3 B15

    Traces the historical, social, and economic background of the
    1951 land distribution program with discussion of its resulting
    impact on rural Iran. The role of Bank Omran, founded in con-
    junction with this program, is also described. Statistics
    related to these topics are included.

9.  Bank-i-Markazi-i Iran. "The Land Reform Law of Iran." (In
    BMIB, 2:10, 1963. p. 515-533)
                                            Mem HC 471 B28

    Text of the 1962 Land Reform Law and the amendment of January
    17, 1963.

10. Barth, Fredrik. "The Land use patterns of migratory tribes of
    South Persia." (In NGT, 17:1/4, 1959. p. 1-11)  Geol MC N795

    Examines the ecological and political interplay of factors in
    seasonally dynamic land use patterns of tribes in southern
    Persia. Analyzes the temporal and spatial aspects of usufruct
    rights.

LAND TENURE AND AGRARIAN REFORM

11. Bartsch, William; and Bharier, Julian. THE ECONOMY OF IRAN
1940-1970: A BIBLIOGRAPHY. Durham, Eng., Centre for Middle
Eastern and Islamic Studies, University of Durham, 1971.
114 p.                                   REF Z 7165 I66 B37

Includes sections with references to village and tribal studies, rural development and agriculture, and investigations of
land tenure and land reform.

12. Beckett, P. H. T.; and Gordon, F. D. "Land use and settlement
round Kerman in southern Iran." (In GJL, 132:12, 1966. p.
476-490)                                  Geol MC G273 J82

Considers water availability to be the decisive factor not
only in land use and settlement but in determining price and
wage structure as well. Sees the land tenure system as a
constraint on capital improvements and investment in
agriculture.

13. Bemont, Frédy. L'IRAN DEVANT LE PROGRES. Paris, Presses
Universitaires de France, Institut d'Etude du Développement
Economique et Social de l'Université de Paris, 1964. 243 p.
                                          HC 475.2 B25

The chapter on agriculture contains a brief history of agrarian
reform in Iran, together with a survey of various related
issues (irrigation, cultural practices, mechanization, etc.).

14. Bharier, Julian. ECONOMIC DEVELOPMENT IN IRAN 1900-1970.
London, New York, Oxford University Press, 1971. xviii, 314
p.                                        HC 497 P4 B32

Chapter 7 includes a concise section on "Land Tenure and Reform." Bharier concludes that, despite attempts to alter the
land tenure system and the status of sharecroppers prior to
1960, no substantial change occurred until after the 1962
reform drive. Provides demographic data and tables on agricultural production, mechanization, etc., and attempts to rate
the validity and accuracy of statistics used.

15. Bigdeli, M. "Iran's experience in land reform: part II, the
second phase of land reform law." n.p., n.d. 3 l.
                                          Files Iran 3 B43

Summarizes the results of the first phase of the law and outlines provisions of its second phase, which regulates areas already distributed. Also describes the three alternatives set
for landlords in the second phase, namely: lease, sale, or
distribution.

310

# LAND TENURE AND AGRARIAN REFORM

15a.  Boroumand, A. M.  IRAN.  Bruxelles, Institut International des Civilisations Différentes, 1973.  17 l.  Paper for INCIDI Study Session on Obstacles and Restraints Impeding the Success of Land Reform in Developing Countries, 1973.

Files Iran 3 B67

15b.  Center on Land Problems in the Near East, Salahuddin, Iraq, 1955.  COUNTRY INFORMATION REPORT:  IRAN.  CI-4.  (Rome) FAO, 1955.  8 p.

Files Iran 58 C25

16.  Central Treaty Organization.  SYMPOSIUM ON RURAL DEVELOPMENT. 1963?

HT 395 A77 C25

See Item NE-7 for citation.  See Items IRAN-17; IRAN-48; and IRAN-67 for individually cited and annotated articles dealing with Iran.

17.  Dehbod, Abolghassem.  "Land ownership and use conditions in Iran."  1963.  (In Item NE-7, p. 59-74)

HT 395 A77 C25

Surveys modes of land ownership and land use in Iran before and after the 1962 land reform.  Outlines components of village social structure and organization, methods of land exploitation, and the peasant-landlord relationship.  Defines terms related to the issues discussed.  The author considers the existing agrarian situation unsatisfactory and hopes it will be improved by implementation of the 1962 Law and the introduction of cooperatives.

18.  Denman, D. R.  "Land reform in Iran."  (In A/GB, 77:8, 1970. p. 384-386; and 77:9, 1970.  p. 436-438)
Also available as a separate.

Files Iran 3 D25

Traces land reform legislation since 1951, focusing on the 1962 Land Reform Law.  Also treats other aspects of land reform such as rural cooperatives and farm corporations.

19.  Ehlers, Eckhart.  "Bunvar Shami-Siah Mansour:  Methoden und Probleme der Landreforme en Khusistan Südiran."  (In ZAL, 12:2, 1973.  p. 183-200)

Depicts some problems of Iranian land reform by analyzing two neighboring villages in Khuzistan/Iran.

20.  English, Paul Ward.  CITY AND VILLAGE IN IRAN:  SETTLEMENT AND ECONOMY IN THE KIRMAN BASIN.  Madison, University of Wisconsin Press, 1966.  xx, 204 p.

HN 740 K5 E5

# LAND TENURE AND AGRARIAN REFORM

IRAN 20-23

(English, Paul Ward)
The author's "geographical" approach concentrates on the
interactions within a region rather than a single community.
Describes land tenure relationships and the dismal, precarious
existence of the region's sharecroppers. Discusses urban dominance over rural areas, particularly the changes in farming
organization produced by the flow of Western influence through
the urban centers. Argues that the region is more modernized
socially than economically. Includes appendices on agricultural production and land ownership.

21. Gharatchehdaghi, Cyrus. DISTRIBUTION OF LAND IN VARAMIN: AN
OPENING PHASE OF THE AGRARIAN REFORM IN IRAN. Publications of
the German Orient Institute, Documents and materials, DM-29.
Opladen, Germany, C. W. Leske Verlag, 1967. 179 p. Bibl.
HD 1265 P4 G32

Evaluates this distribution project (1951-1952) in light of
local socio-economic conditions as well as previous and subsequent nationwide initiatives, notably the land reform laws
of 1960 and 1962. Despite substantial investment, success was
undermined by inadequate planning of viable farm size and
especially by deficient credit and extension policies.

22. Hadary, Gideon. "The Agrarian reform problem in Iran." (In
MEJ, 5:2, 1951. p. 181-196)                          Mem AP M6272
Also available in Conference on World Land Tenure Problems,
University of Wisconsin, 1951. PAPERS, 4. Madison, 1951.
11 p.                                           HD 105 C67 1951b

Review of land tenure and agricultural conditions, tracing
attempts between 1937 and 1961 at improvement. Examines
deterrents to any far-reaching reform. Sees progress even
within constraints described, provided that the essential
ingredients of efficient extension and credit services plus
the organization of cooperatives are included.

23. Hanessian, John. "Iranian land reform; comments on recent
developments and the program's current status." (In American
Universities Field Staff. AUFS REPORTS: SOUTHWEST ASIA
SERIES, 12:10, 1963. p. 105-120)          REF DS 41 A6 1961/64

A nontechnical survey of Iran's land reform, including the
1962 land reform law. Covers the role of rural cooperatives
and gives attention to political development and some central
figures in the land reform movement, especially Dr. Arsanjani,
whose career is reviewed.

312

# Land Tenure and Agrarian Reform

23a.    _____. "Reform in Iran by decree and referendum:  problems
and prospects."  (In American Universities Field Staff.  AUFS
REPORTS:  SOUTHWEST ASIA SERIES, 12:9, 1963.  p. 89-104)
                                            REF DS 41 A6 1961/64

23b.    _____. "Yosouf-Abad, an Iranian village; parts 1-6."  (In
American Universities Field Staff.  AUFS REPORTS:  SOUTHWEST
ASIA SERIES, 12:1-6, 1963.  p. 1-66)      REF DS 41 A6 1961/64

24.  Hobbs, John A.  "Land reform in Iran."  (In ORBIS, 7:3, 1963.
p. 617-630)
                                            Mem AP 06356

Perceives the 1962 Land Reform Law as a governmentally initiated "revolution from above."  Analyzes economic and political forces behind the reform.  Expresses optimism about the
reform's ultimate success in both its political and economic
objectives and sees the Iranian experience as a relevant
example for other developing countries.

25.  Hottinger, A.  "Land reform in Iran."  (In SRWA, 13:8, 1963.
p. 7-10; and 13:9, 1963.  p. 17-18)
                                            Mem AP S9765

A journalist's observations on the impact of the 1962 land
reform and an outline of its main provisions.  Notes the deep
political repercussions of the reform and that future implementation depends largely on political forces.

26.  IMPLEMENTATION OF IRAN'S LAND REFORM PROGRAM.  (Teheran,
Offset Press) 1962.  23 p.            Files Iran 3 I56

A collection of speeches, messages, and articles published
on the occasion of the distribution by the Shah of the first
lot of title deeds to farmers affected by the land reform.
Includes descriptions of accomplishments and of economic and
social effects of land reform.

27.  Iran.  Laws, statutes, etc.  "Land reform law, approved
January 9, 1962."  Rev. unofficial translation.  n.p., 1962.
1 folder (various pagings)            Files Iran 3 I71

A full text of the 1962 Land Reform Law in Iran and a series
of decrees and regulations enacted thereafter to amend, clar-
ify, and help implement it.

28.    _____.  _____.  "Land reform law - 9 January 1962."  (In FAL,
11:2, 1962.  V/1b.  14 p.)
                                            Ag Docs

Unofficial translation of the full text of the law.  Main
provisions include definitions; ownership limits; land subject

313

# Land Tenure and Agrarian Reform

(Iran. Laws, statutes, etc.)
to distribution, assessment, and payment; landlord-peasant
relationships; and financial regulations.

29. _____. _____. "Regulations for the implementation of the
land reform law approved by the Joint Committee of the
Parliament. Date of approval: Mordad 3, 1343 (7-25-64)."
Unofficial translation. n.p., n.d. 15 1.   Files Iran 3 I717

A full text of the regulations designed to cover all intricacies, rights, obligations, etc., of parties involved in the
implementation of land reform in Iran.

30. _____. _____. REVISED LAND REFORM LAW, APPROVED BY THE
COUNCIL OF MINISTERS ON JANUARY 9, 1962. (Madison, Reproduced
by Land Tenure Center, University of Wisconsin, 1964). 12 p.
Files Iran 3 I719

A full text of the 1962 Land Reform Law.

31. _____. Ministry of Agriculture. Land Reform Organization.
"Iran's land reform program." (Teheran, 1962). 4 1.
Files Iran 3 I72

A brief summary of the 1962 Land Reform Law and some results
of its implementation. Includes statistics on number of
villages and farmers affected by the law. Also describes the
Cooperative Service and Technical Assistance established to
help implement the reform.

32. _____. Ministry of Cooperation and Rural Affairs. "Land
reform programme in Iran." (Teheran) n.d. 18 p.
Files Iran 3 I73

An official account of the merits and achievements of land
reform programs in Iran. Highlights the central role of the
Shah in the land reform and the vital roles of rural
cooperatives, farm corporations, rural cultural houses,
rural research centers, farmer social security, and the
agricultural cooperative bank.

33. _____. Ministry of Information. "Land reform." (In its
IRAN. 2nd ed. Teheran, 1971. p. 147-156)        DS 254.5 I7

An official account of land reform activities in Iran, divided
into a discussion of a first stage in 1962 and a second stage
extending between 1965 and 1969. Propagandistic in tone,
this chapter nevertheless provides a concise source of official statistics on Iranian land reform in the 1960s.

# LAND TENURE AND AGRARIAN REFORM

34.  Issawi, Charles P., ed. THE ECONOMIC HISTORY OF IRAN.
     Chicago, University of Chicago Press, 1971. xv, 405 p. Bibl.
                                           Mem HC 475 I85

     A general overview of changes undergone in the socio-economic
     structure of Iran between 1800 and 1914. Contains, in its
     extensive section on agriculture, comments on irrigation, land
     tenure, and rent and lease arrangements, accompanied by selec-
     tions from other authors' works. An important aid in under-
     standing more recent developments in Iran's agrarian situation.

35.  Johnson, Sherman E. "A.I.D. assistance on land reform pro-
     grams." n.p., 1963. 8 1.                Files Iran 29 J63

     Presents ideas on how USAID field operations concerned with
     the land reform program of 1962 could be most effectively
     organized. Strongly advocates the concentration of efforts
     and resources on production, credit, and cooperative activities.

36.  _____. "Rural development in Iran as affected by land reform."
     n.p., n.d. 22 1.                        Files Iran 3 J63

     Discusses measures needed to extend the effects of the land
     reform program beyond the mere distribution of land. Suggests
     as prerequisites literacy training, organization of coopera-
     tive societies, and ensuring the availability of credit to
     peasant farmers.

37.  Jones, Royal Maurice. "The Short-run economic impact of land
     reform on feudal village irrigated agriculture in Iran."
     (College Park) 1967. xiv, 145 1. Bibl. Ph. D. dissertation,
     University of Maryland. Photocopy. Ann Arbor, Mich., Uni-
     versity Microfilms, 1973.                HD 926 J65

     Finds little or no increase in commodity production. However,
     does note improvement in income distribution. Includes a
     description of the 1962 land reform with excerpts from arti-
     cles on land appraisal, expropriation and land distribution,
     and landlord-tenant relations.

38.  Katouzian, M. A. "Land reform in Iran: a case study in the
     political economy of social engineering." (In JPS, 1:2, 1974.
     p. 220-239)

     Critical view of Iranian land reform efforts up to 1972.
     Regards primary impact as the consolidation of state bureau-
     cratic power over all social classes and the sharpening of
     stratification in the rural social structure. Finds little

IRAN 38-42

(Katouzian, M. A.)
improvement in either peasant standards of living or agricultural production.

39.   Keddie, Nikki R.  "Stratification, social control and capitalism in Iranian villages:  before and after land reform."
1972.  (In Item NE-32, p. 364-402)                DS 57 R87

Historico-political analysis of the peasantry since the early
nineteenth century.  Compares the land tenure situation before
and after the 1962 reform law.  Considers peasant living conditions to have been better in the nineteenth century, before
the Western impact, the emergence of centralized government,
and the rise of landlords.

40.   Kermani, Taghi T.  ECONOMIC DEVELOPMENT IN ACTION:  THEORIES,
PROBLEMS AND PROCEDURES AS APPLIED TO THE MIDDLE EAST.  1967.
HC 410.7 K4

See Item NE-21 for citation and annotation.

40a.  Khademadam, Nasser; und Bergmann, Herbert.  "Sozio-ökonomische
Differenzierung im Gefolge der Bodenreform im Iran."  (In ZAL,
12:3/4, 1973.  p. 270-285)

41.   Khamsi, F.  "Land reform in Iran."  (In MR, 21:2, 1969.
p. 20-28)                              Mem AP M789 R452

Marxist analysis of Iran's land reforms of the 1960s.  Khamsi
maintains that "the beneficiaries have been not the impoverished masses, but the landlords and capitalists."  Forecasts
the spread of capitalist, large-scale commercial farming in
Iran.

41a.  Khatibi, Nosratollah.  "Land reform in Iran and its role in
rural development."  (In LRLSC, 1972:2.  p. 61-68)
REF HD 1261 A1 L1 1972 v. 2

42.   Khosrovi, Khosrov.  "La Réforme agraire et l'apparition d'une
nouvelle classe en Iran."  (In ETR, 34, 1969.  p. 122-126)
Ag Per

Maintains that, rather than being of primary benefit to the
peasants, the 1962 land reform merely replaced the large landowning classes who displayed some responsibility toward the
peasants with a strengthened money-lending class.  Sees an
accentuation of class tensions resulting from this state of
affairs.

# Land Tenure and Agrarian Reform

42a.   Klayman, Maxwell Irving. THE MOSHAV IN ISRAEL:   A CASE
       STUDY OF INSTITUTION-BUILDING FOR AGRICULTURAL DEVELOPMENT.
       1970.                                           HD 1491 P3 K5

       See Item ISRAEL-15 for citation and annotation.

43.    Kristajanson, Baldur H.   "The Agrarian-based development of
       Iran."   (In LE, 36:1, 1960.  p. 1-13)                Ag Per
       Also available as a separate.          Files Iran 3K74

       Stresses the close ties between rural development and land
       ownership and cultivation patterns.  Describes major features
       of land tenure organization; cites small farm unit size, lack
       of credit, and failure to mechanize sufficiently as the major
       limitations of the reforms of 1952 and 1959.  Formation of
       cooperatives is reviewed, but criticized as superficial.

44.    Lambton, Ann K. S.   "Land reform and rural cooperative soci-
       eties in Persia."   (In RCA/J, 56:11(2), 1969.  p. 142-155)
                                              Mem AP R888 C28

       Scrutinizes provisions of the 1962 law and amendments to it in
       1964 and 1968.  Lambton regards progress of the cooperative
       movement since 1962 as "very considerable," despite shortages
       of credit and trained personnel.

45.    _____.  LANDLORD AND PEASANT IN PERSIA.  London, Oxford Uni-
       versity Press, 1953.  459 p.                  Ag HD 923 L3

       Scholarly treatment of the historical development of land
       tenure and rural organization in Iran, outlined in Part 1 from
       Islamic times to 1906 and in Part 2 from the beginning of
       constitutional government to the mid-twentieth century.
       Stresses continuity in such matters as governmental attitudes
       toward rural administration and the landlord-peasant relation-
       ship.  Lambton concludes that the central problem is political
       or social, and that rural reform can only take place within
       the context of changes throughout the whole fabric of Iran's
       national life.

46.    _____.  "The New land decrees in Persia."   (In WT, 8, 1952.
       p. 532-536)                                  Mem AP W926 T633

       Analytical review of the main articles and provisions of
       Dr. Moussadek's land reform bill of 1952.  Criticizes the bill
       as badly drafted, ambiguous, and of little real substance.

47.    _____.  THE PERSIAN LAND REFORM, 1962-1966.  Oxford, Clarendon
       Press, 1969.  xii, 386 p.                     HD 926 L15

(Lambton, Ann K. S.)
The main body of the book deals with the Land Reform Law of 1962, its implementation, and consequences. A comprehensive survey of the land and people as well as the overall political, social, and economic climate of the country provides a rich context for clarifying the complex elements involved in the land reform question. Lambton devotes attention to the Iranian cooperative movement which she considers to be crucial to the ultimate success of the land reform effort. The author's assessment of the 1962 reform is largely positive, seeing it as the spur to a "movement of change" in the countryside.

48. _____. "Rural development and land reform in Iran." 1963. (In Item NE-7, p. 111-116)                    HT 395 A77 C25

A brief essay aimed at illustrating the fact that "rural development and land reform cannot ultimately be carried out in isolation...," being closely linked with other aspects of society. Basically a warning against generalization, stressing the historical uniqueness of Iran's experience and the sharp variations within the country which must be taken into account in formulating and assessing agrarian reform efforts. Rural development and land reform are thus presented as primarily a political and social rather than an economic problem.

49. "Land reform." n.d.                                    Files 3 L15

See Item NE-23 for citation and annotation.

50. "Land reform in Iran." n.p., Printed in England by Williams Lea, n.d. (3) 16 p.                              Files Iran 3 L14

A journalist's description and assessment of land reform efforts as an attempt "to halt the menace of communism...." Includes statistics on villages purchased and distributed under the reform.

51. "Land reform in Iran: a decade of progress." n.p., n.d. 23 1.                                              Files Iran 3 L142

An official evaluation of land reform and related efforts in the 1960s, including cooperatives, farm corporations, and cultural houses. Statistical data cover the period up to 1970.

LAND TENURE AND AGRARIAN REFORM

52.    "Land reform's second phase implemented." Teheran, 1963.
       4 1.  Clippings from TEHERAN JOURNAL, 9/24/63--11/18/63.
                                           Files Iran 3 L15

       A series of newspaper articles about the second phase of land
       reforms concerned mainly with fixing land ceilings per family.
       A table specifies such ceilings by province.  Includes offi-
       cial statements on this occasion and directives to landowners
       on alternatives open for their compliance with the new
       provisions.

53.    Mahdavy, Hossein.  "The Coming crisis in Iran."  (In FAF,
       44:1, 1965.  p. 134-146)

       Analyzes reforms initiated in 1962 and continued in 1964
       within their internal and external political contexts.  Sees
       little real change, especially in regard to the problem of
       landless laborers, and little benefit in merely replacing
       few large with many small landowners.  Also critical of the
       failure to improve the technological and organizational
       aspects of agricultural production.

53a.   Malek, Hocein.  "Iran after the agrarian reform."  (In AG,
       75:409, 1966.  p. 268-285)                Geol MC AN62

53b.   _____.  LA REFORME AGRAIRE IRANIENNE DANS SON CONTEXTE SOCIAL
       ET POLITIQUE.  Bruxelles, Institut International des Civilisa-
       tions Différentes, 1973.  15 1.  Paper for INCIDI Study Ses-
       sion on Obstacles and Restraints Impeding the Success of Land
       Reform in Developing Countries, 1973.        Files Iran 3 M15

54.    Mehrain, Fattaneh.  "Development programmes and stratification
       (a case study of Iran)."  Madison, 1972.  iii, 91 p.  M. S.
       thesis, University of Wisconsin.        Mem AWO M4984 F377

       Maintains that attempts at modernization and development, most
       notably the land reforms, did little in achieving any real
       structural, redistributive changes.  Rather, the results
       appeared to be a greater concentration of wealth for the land-
       holding elite.

54a.   Mendras, Henri.  "La Réforme agraire en Iran."  (In RTSS, 2,
       1965.  p. 9-30)
       Also available as a separate.             Files Iran 3 M25

54b.   Moarefi, Ali.  DISTRIBUTION OF PAHLAVI ESTATES.  Rev. Country
       project no. CP-3.  (Rome) FAO, 1955.  33 p.  Paper for Center
       on Land Problems in the Near East, Salahuddin, Iraq, 1955.
                                           Files Iran 17 M61

# LAND TENURE AND AGRARIAN REFORM

55. Moghaddam, Reza. "Land reform and rural development in Iran."
    (In LE, 48:2, 1972.  p. 160-168)

    Views favorably the two-stage agrarian reform effort of the
    government and discusses the third stage put into effect dur-
    ing the 1968-72 Plan period.  The author also examines the
    three types of rural cooperatives and governmental efforts
    outside these co-ops to improve credit availability, as well
    as the educational level and material well-being of the
    peasant population.

56. Mohammed Reza Pahlavi, Shah of Iran. MISSION FOR MY COUNTRY.
    (1st. ed.).  New York, McGraw-Hill (c1960).  336 p.
                                                    Mem DS 318 M6

    Briefly discusses the agrarian situation in Iran.  Outlines
    land reform and supporting infrastructural measures.

57. Motheral, Joe R.  "Land reform in Iran:  problems and possible
    solutions."  n.p., 1957.  40 1.  Mimeograph report prepared
    for the U.S. Operations Mission in Iran.      Files Iran 3 M68

    Discusses land reform in relation to the Crown Lands Distribu-
    tion Program.  Attributes great social, economic, and political
    benefit to land distribution in general and concludes that the
    Crown Lands Program is both feasible and necessary.  Makes
    various recommendations and specific proposals in regard to
    this and other possible programs.

58. "New deal for Persians."  (In ECON, 203:6194, 1962.
    p. 557-558)                                      Mem AP E216

    Newsman's brief report stressing the obstacles to the success-
    ful implementation of Iran's 1962 Land Reform Law.

59. Nomani, Farhad.  "The Origin and development of feudalism in
    Iran:  300-1600 A.D. (Part 1)."  (In QJER, 9:27, 1972.  p. 5-61)

    Though different in form, European and Iranian feudalism were
    similar in their essential qualities.  The article traces the
    evolution of the various categories of tenure, concluding that
    state ownership of land has not been predominant throughout
    most of Iran's history.

60. Okazaki, Shōkō. THE DEVELOPMENT OF LARGE-SCALE FARMING IN
    IRAN:  THE CASE OF THE PROVINCE OF GORGAN.  IAEA Occasional
    paper, series no. 3.  Tokyo, The Institute of Asian Economic
    Affairs, 1968.  51 p.                        Files Iran 4 041

(Okazaki, Shōkō)
Study of changes in traditional agriculture effected by innovations such as cotton cultivation and increased mechanization
introduced in the late 1950s. Notes "drastic modification in
land tenure" as a result. Views these developments favorably,
forecasting a dual agricultural structure in Iran and other
Mid-Eastern countries.

61.      _____. "Shīrang-Soflā: the economics of a northeast Iranian
village." (In DEC, 7:3, 1969. p. 261-283)

Case study of the impact of commercialization and mechanization
on traditional agriculture. Depicts subsequent changes in
agrarian economic structure, especially landholding patterns,
as well as in social class stratification.

61a.   Pahlavi Estates Information Service. DISTRIBUTION OF PAHLAVI
ESTATES AMONG PEASANTS. n.p. (1949). 1 v. (various pagings)
HD 1339 I7 P13

62.    Parham, B. "Land reform in Iran." (In STUDIES IN ASIAN
SOCIAL DEVELOPMENT, NO. 1. Bombay, Institute of Economic
Growth, 1971. p. 95-124)                          HN 663.5 S89

Surveys characteristics of Iranian society before and after
the land reform drives of the 1960s. Three stages of land
reform occurring successively in 1962, 1963, and 1969 are
discussed and outlined. The author describes these laws as
"the most important historical event" of the decade for Iran.
Appended by useful statistical information on Iranian society
in general as well as on the country's land distribution picture between 1956 and 1966.

63.    Parsons, Kenneth H. "Land tenure in Asia." 1960.
Files Asia 58 P17

See Item NE-29 for citation and annotation.

63a.   Pignatti, A. "La Riforma agraria in Iran." (In REA, 27:6,
1972. p. 115-133)
Ag Per

64.    Platt, Kenneth B. LAND REFORM IN IRAN. SR/LR/C-18.
(Washington) USAID, 1970. 101, 6 p. Bibl. Country paper
for Spring Review of Land Reform.                 Files Iran 3 P52

Broad analysis of political and economic conditions leading
up to and following land reform efforts in the period
1900-1969. Evaluates the initial stages of the reform

# LAND TENURE AND AGRARIAN REFORM

(Platt, Kenneth B.)
positively, but expresses reservation about the later emphasis
on large-scale mechanized farm corporations.

65.    Rad, Farhang; and Zarrinkafsh, A. R.   "Implementation of the
       land reform program in Iran."   (In Item NE-10, p. 273-295)
                                               HD 850.8 Z63 D46 1965

       A descriptive classification and analysis of forms of land
       ownership, methods of land exploitation, and peasant-landlord
       relationships.   Reviews the main provisions of the 1962 Land
       Reform Law and the activities of the Land Reform Organization
       created by the law.   Reform efforts prior and subsequent to
       the 1962 law are also discussed.   Describes the role of the
       Bank of Development and Rural Cooperatives (Bank Omran)
       within the agrarian reform framework.

66.    Ronaghy, Hassan A.   "Land tenure in Iran."   (Madison) 1963.
       26 1.   Paper for Agricultural Economics 226, University of
       Wisconsin.                                   Files Iran 58 R65

       Covers land utilization, necessity of the land reform, and
       the 1962 Land Reform Law.   The writer states that "administra-
       tion is one of the greatest reasons for Iranian misfortunes."
       Points out the weakness in the law and loopholes in its appli-
       cation, and is skeptical about its effectiveness.

67.    Salour, Abbas.   "Land reform activities in Iran."   1963?
       (In Item NE-7, p. 47-58)                       HT 395 A77 C25

       Another version of Item IRAN-68.

68.    _____.   "Report on the program of land reform activities in
       Iran, September 1963."   n.p., 1963.   17 1.    Files Iran 3 S15

       The Supervisor of the Iranian Land Reform Organization reports
       on land reform in Iran and the activities of his organization.
       Mentions attempts at land distribution in the 1930s, then
       points to the shortcomings of the 1955 law, which eventually
       was replaced by the 1962 law.   The main articles of the 1962
       law are outlined.

69.    Schowkatfard, Freidun Djazai; und Fardi, Mohsen.   "Sozial-
       ökonomische Auswirkungen der landwirtschaftlichen
       Aktiengesellschaft im Iran:   Fallstudie eines Dorfes der
       Provinz Fars."   (In ZAL, 11:2, 1972.   p. 120-137)

(Schowkatfard, Freidun Djazai; und Fardi, Mohsen)
Contends that social and economic problems are not being alle-
viated by the farm corporations provided for in the agrarian
reform program.

70.   Sefari, Mohammad Ali. "Land reform lacking in Kerman Province."
      Translations on the Near East, no. 318. p. 8-11. (In JPRS,
      7:7, 1968/1969. reel 101) Translated from KHANDANIHA,
      Sept. 5-8, 1968. p. 14.                              Microfilm

      A reporter's description of rural poverty in the Kerman region
      where reforms were apparently not implemented.

70a.  Seminaire sur l'Evaluation de Changements Sociaux Provoqués
      par des Programmes ou Projets de Développement. MATIERES.
      Consultant Charles Loomis. Edité par N. Afshar Naderi en
      Anglais. Traduction L. Ghaffary. Teheran, Institut d'Etudes
      et de Recherche Sociales, Université de Teheran, n.d. iii,
      170 1. Organisé par l'Institut d'Etudes et de Recherche
      Sociales avec l'aide de l'UNESCO.                 HN 733.5 S25

71.   Stephanides, C. S. "Iran rounds out the fifth year of its
      land reform program." (In FA, 5:37, 1967. p. 5, 11) Ag Docs
      Also available as a separate.                Files Iran 4 S8

      Summarizes land reform provisions and evaluates progress at
      implementation. Considers the reform effort to be successful
      but points to disappointment over cooperative and credit opera-
      tions, apparently due to a shortage of skilled manpower.

72.   Stickley, Thomas S.; and Najafi, Bahaoldin. "The Effective-
      ness of farm corporations in Iran." (In QJER, 8:21, 1971.
      p. 18-28)

      Concludes that farm corporations were successful in solving
      the economic problems of land fragmentation and in increasing
      productivity of land, labor, and capital. They were less
      successful in their social goals of developing more favorable
      attitudes towards group work and awareness of goals and impli-
      cations of the new organization.

73.   Tai, Hung-Chao. LAND REFORM IN COLOMBIA, INDIA, IRAN, MEXICO,
      PAKISTAN, PHILIPPINES, TAIWAN, U.A.R.: A SELECTED BIBLIOGRAPHY.
      1967.                                               Files 3 T14

      See Item EGY-58 for citation and annotation.

# LAND TENURE AND AGRARIAN REFORM

74. Teheran. University. Institute for Economic Research.
Research Group in Agricultural Economics. "An Analysis of
the law governing the first stage of land reform in Iran."
(In QJER, 7:17, 1970. p. 49-74)

Discusses changing emphases and interpretations of provisions
in the 1962 Land Reform Law. Highlights the ambiguities left
open to political resolution by the unstated aims of the
reform, namely the economic aim of increased production and
the social justice aim of more equitable distribution of
wealth.

75. U.S. Consulate, Tabriz. "The Progress of land distribution
in Maraqeh." Drafted by Archie M. Bolster. Tabriz, 1961-1963.
1 v. (various pagings). Photocopies of unclassified Foreign
Service Despatches and airgrams from Amconsul TABRIZ to Dept.
of State, Washington, Nov. 1961-May 1963.     Files Iran 3 U54

These Foreign Service Despatches, based on first-hand observations, provide insight into the socio-political structure
surrounding implementation of the law. Includes a sample of
Land Transfer Deeds.

76. Vieille, Paul. "Les Paysans, la petite bourgeoisie rurale
et l'Etat après la réforme agraire en Iran." (In ANNALES,
27:2, 1972. p. 347-372)                      Mem AP A605
Also available as a separate.              Files Iran 3 V42

Discussion centers on the rising prominence of petty bourgeois
elements, enhanced by the virtual elimination of the feudal
landlords, whom the former replaced as intermediaries between
the state and the mass of small farmers.

77. Ward, Gordon H. "Farmers' cooperatives under land reform in
Iran." (In ICR, 3:2, 1966. p. 868-872)              Ag Per

Points to the dramatic growth of rural cooperatives since the
1962 land reform. Success of these co-ops is contingent upon
improved member education. Provides statistics on membership
and capital available to co-ops.

78. Warriner, Doreen. "Employment and income aspects of recent
agrarian reforms in the Middle East." 1971.      HD 111 I57

See Item NE-38 for citation and annotation.

79. _____. "Persia's original strategy." (In her LAND REFORM IN
PRINCIPLE AND PRACTICE. Oxford, Clarendon Press, 1969.
p. 109-135)                                      HD 111 W36

IRAN 79-IRAQ 2

(Warriner, Doreen)
Concentrates on the 1962 Land Reform Law and its results. The
author emphasizes the political objective of the land reform
and also the political reality as being the most formidable
obstacle. Highlights the central role of Dr. Arsanjani, Minister of Agriculture, in conceiving and implementing the reform. Regards the first stage (Feb. 1962 to Jan. 1963) as
successful, but casts doubt on the official claims about the
success in the following years.

80. Whetham, Edith H.  CO-OPERATION, LAND REFORM AND LAND SETTLE-
MENT. 1968.                                    Ag HD 1491 A52 W4

See Item AFR-140 for citation. A very brief, descriptive, and
nonanalytical exposition on land reforms of the 1950s and
1960s, emphasizing the spread of cooperatives as integral parts
of these reforms. Official statistics are presented on the
development and activities of cooperatives in Iran.

81. Wilson, Rodney J. A.  AGRICULTURAL DEVELOPMENT IN THE MIDDLE
EAST, 1950-1970. 1972.                         Files NE 4 W45

See Item NE-40 for citation and annotation.

81a. Zad, Akbar.  "Land reform in Iran."  Training course document
no. 53.  n.p., n.d.  24 p.  Extracts from M. A. thesis, University of Denver, 1954.                          Files Iran 3 Z12


## IRAQ


1. Adams, Martin E.  "Lessons from agrarian reform in Iraq."  (In
LRLSC, 1972:1.  p. 56-64)        REF HD 1261 A1 L1 1972 v. 1

Attributes insignificant improvements in land use patterns and
production levels in the Diyala region since the 1958 Agrarian
Reform Law to unfavorable agronomic conditions and shortcomings
of management. Does point, however, to improved peasant living
conditions.

2. Adams, Warren E.  "The Pre-revolutionary decade of land reform
in Iraq."  (In EDCC, 11:3, 1963.  p. 267-288)

Depicts administrative, technical, political, social, and
cultural problems encountered on state (Miri Sirf) lands.
Blames disappointing results in raising productivity and

(Adams, Warren E.)
farmers' incomes on inadequate governmental support and deficient coordination efforts. Concludes that attention to only
the technical aspects of settlement does not insure success.

3.   Ahmad, M. S.; and Roy, E. P.  "Cooperation and land reform in
the Middle East." 1963.                    Files Asia 3 A35

See Item NE-2 for citation and annotation.

4.   Ahmed, Mohammed M. A.; and Al-Ezzy, Jasim M.  "The Role of
supervised credit in land settlement; case studies of Mikdadiya
and Kanaan, Iraq." (In LRLSC, 1971:2.  p. 21-28)
                                 REF HD 1261 A1 L1 1971 v.2

Finds that farmers, most of whom deserted the credit program,
did so largely out of impatience with red tape and because of
inflexible lending and collection procedures.  Recommends
greater flexibility in loan practices and organizing teams of
qualified personnel as necessary supports for land reform
efforts.

4a.  Al-Hilali, Abdal-Razzag.  NADHARAT FI ISLAH IL-RIF: REFLECTIONS
ON RURAL REFORM.  Baghdad, Dal Al-Kashaff Press, 1954.  156 p.
Bibl.  Text in Arabic.                     HD 951 I7 A5

5.   Ali, Hassan Mohammad.  LAND RECLAMATION AND SETTLEMENT IN IRAQ.
Baghdad, Baghdad Printing Press, 1955.  xiii, 210 p.
                                           HD 1741 I7 A7

Chapter 4 describes the evolution of Iraq's land tenure system,
which is characterized as still essentially feudal.  Advocates
land reform as a necessary measure to confront widespread rural
poverty.  Appendices include texts of the Miri-Sirf Land (State
Land) Development Law No. 43,52 for 1951 and its amendment in
1952.

6.   Alitovski, Sergei N.  AGRARNYI VOPROS V SOVREMENNOM IRAKE,
1958-65 (AGRARIAN CHANGES IN THE REPUBLIC OF IRAQ, 1958-65).
Text in Russian.  Moscow, Nauka Publishing House, 1966.  174 p.
                                           Mem HD 951 I7 A73

Discusses land tenure and agrarian reforms in Iraq.

7.   Al-Soze, Abdul Amir.  "Land tenure and size of holding in the
United States of America and Iraq." n.p., n.d.  14 l.  Paper
for Rural Sociology 195.                   Files Iraq 58 A57

# LAND TENURE AND AGRARIAN REFORM

(Al-Soze, Abdul Amir)
A rather superficial study of land tenure in the U.S. and Iraq.

8. Alwan, Abdul Sahib H. "The Process of economic development in
Iraq with special reference to land problems and policies."
Madison, 1957. x, 572 p. Ph. D. dissertation, University of
Wisconsin. Mem AW AL925

In discussing stimulants to and constraints on Iraq's economic
development, emphasis is placed on land tenure as the major
barrier in this regard.

9. Baali, Fuad. "Agrarian reform in Iraq: some socio-economic
aspects." (In AJES, 28:1, 1969. p. 61-76) Mem AP A506 E19
Also available as a separate. Files Iraq 3 B12

Evaluates the success of the 1958 Land Reform Law and its
amendments of 1964 and 1965. Effective implementation was hampered by inadequate personnel, the small size of holdings
distributed, and lack of technical and institutional supports.
Concludes that mere redistribution of land is not enough, and
that political stability is essential to permit continuous and
consistent policy execution.

10. _____. RELATION OF THE PEOPLE TO THE LAND IN SOUTHERN IRAQ.
Monographs: Social Sciences no. 31. Gainesville, University
of Florida Press, 1966. 64 p. HD 951 I7 B3

Emphasizes the social problems arising out of land ownership
patterns. Discusses the background and impact of the 1958 land
reform and relates land tenure to availability and type of education, health services, social stratification, and rural-urban
migration.

11. _____. "Relationship of man to the land in Iraq." (In RURS,
31:2, 1966. p. 171-182) Ag Per

Contrasts conditions before and after the 1958 Agrarian Reform
Law. Despite this reform, Baali foresees little improvement
in the agrarian situation if political instability persists.

12. Baer, Gabriel. "The Agrarian problem in Iraq." (In MEA, 3:
12, 1952. p. 381-391) Mem AP M6276

Traces the evolution of the predominance of state-owned lands
and the growth of the extreme polarity between the few large
landowners and the masses of nearly landless peasants. Argues
that curtailing the power of the large landowners is a prerequisite for the extensive land reform which is needed.

# LAND TENURE AND AGRARIAN REFORM

13.   Boardman, Francis. "Iraq moves toward land reform." (In FA,
      15:9, 1951. p. 193-195)                              Ag Per
      Also available in Conference on World Land Tenure Problems,
      University of Wisconsin, 1951. PAPERS, 4. Madison, 1951.
      3 p.                                          HD 105 C67 1951b

      Outlines administrative and organizational aspects of the
      Dujaylah reclamation and resettlement scheme. Sees potential
      benefits resulting from this and similar projects, noting the
      financial, political, and technical problems associated with
      such efforts.

14.   Burns, Norman. "The Dujaylah land settlement in Iraq." (In
      MEJ, 5:3, 1951. p. 362-366)                      Mem AP M6272
      Also available in Conference on World Land Tenure Problems,
      University of Wisconsin, 1951. PAPERS, 4. Madison, 1951.
      7 p.                                          HD 105 C67 1951b

      Description of the project's legal and administrative frame-
      work and a generally favorable assessment of its actual
      accomplishments.

15.   Center on Land Problems in the Near East, Salahuddin, Iraq,
      1955. COUNTRY INFORMATION REPORT: IRAQ. CI-9. (Rome) FAO,
      1955. 22 p.                                  Files Iraq 58 C25

      Contains tables on land use, land tenure, size of landholdings,
      and brief sections on renting, agricultural taxation, and land
      laws.

16.   Dahiri, Abdul Wahab Mutar al-. THE INTRODUCTION OF TECHNOLOGY
      INTO TRADITIONAL SOCIETIES AND ECONOMIES (USING IRAQ AS A CASE
      STUDY). Baghdad, Al-Ani Press, 1969. vi, 253 p.
                                                   Mem HC 497 I7 D34

      Focuses on the agrarian structure as the relevant context in
      which to view the introduction of technology. Concludes that
      the major barrier to national economic development is a gen-
      eral lack of security, particularly in landholding. Views the
      1958 land reform as meeting this need by introducting a more
      equitable distribution of economic opportunity on a firm legal
      basis.

16a.  Dowson, Sir Ernest M. "Extracts from an Enquiry into Land
      Tenure and Related Questions." Training course document
      no. 18. n.p., n.d. 16 p. "A Report to the government of
      el 'Iraq, December 1931."                    Files Iraq 58 D69

      Extracts from Item IRAQ-17.

# LAND TENURE AND AGRARIAN REFORM

17. _____. AN ENQUIRY INTO LAND TENURE AND RELATED QUESTIONS. PROPOSALS FOR THE INITIATION OF REFORM. Letchworth, Eng., printed for the 'Iraqi Government by the Garden City Press, Ltd. (1932). 1, 78 p.                  Mem HX 633 D76 Cutter

     Classic report to the Iraqi Government stressing recommenda-
     tions to establish security of tenure "on a clear and legal
     basis of both statutory and equitable rights to land." Empha-
     sizes the need to conduct detailed cadastral surveys and
     suggests organizational and administrative reforms designed to
     achieve a more coordinated policy approach. Includes tables
     and maps illustrating the classification and distribution of
     lands.

17a. Efrat, M. "Agrarian reform in Iraq." (In NO, 10:5(89), 1967. p. 25-30)                  Mem AP N532 0941

18. El Shishtawy, S. A.; Agrawal, B. L.; and Ragheb, F. M. INSTI-
    TUTE OF COOPERATION AND AGRICULTURAL EXTENSION, IRAQ; STUDY OF
    SELECTED AGRARIAN REFORM PROBLEMS. UNDP technical report no.
    1. Rome, FAO, 1970. v, 136 p.                  Files Iraq 3 E5

     Analyzes the degree of effectiveness and farmer reaction to
     certain programs associated with agrarian reform. Recommends
     a reorganization of agricultural extension on the national and
     regional levels. Appendices contain survey data collected on
     "agro-socio-economic" aspects of the study with maps and tables
     on such matters as progress of land distribution, etc.

19. Fernea, Robert A. "Land reform and ecology in postrevolution-
    ary Iraq." (In EDCC, 17:3, 1969. p. 356-381)

     In this investigation of the insubstantial improvement of con-
     ditions in Southern Iraq after a decade of agrarian reform,
     Fernea challenges assumptions underlying the faith in agrarian
     reform. Maintains that aping of foreign institutional models
     must be replaced by an evaluation of traditional practice--
     both social and ecological--as bases for future programs.

20. _____. SHAYKH AND EFFENDI; CHANGING PATTERNS OF AUTHORITY
    AMONG THE SHABANA OF SOUTHERN IRAQ. Harvard Middle Eastern
    Studies, 14. Cambridge, Mass., Harvard University Press, 1970.
    xi, 224 p.                  HN 764 I7 F46

     Examines changes in patterns of local political authority,
     focusing on variations of land tenure and land use. Contains
     appendices on landownership by socio-economic categories,
     irrigation, and the state-controlled irrigation administration.

# LAND TENURE AND AGRARIAN REFORM

20a.     Haider, Saleh. THE LAND AND THE TRIBE IN IRAQ. Paper no.
         P-12. Rome, FAO, 1955. 15 p. Paper for Center on Land Prob-
         lems in the Near East, Salahuddin, Iraq, 1955.
                                              Files Iraq 95.13 H14

20b.     Haider, Saleh; and Hartley, B. J. PROBLEMS OF TRIBAL AND CUS-
         TOMARY RIGHTS, CADASTRAL SURVEYS AND TITLE REGISTRATION. Workshop
         report no. WR-8. (Rome) FAO, 1955. (14) p. Paper for Center
         on Land Problems in the Near East, Salahuddin, Iraq, 1955.
                                              Files NE 59 H14

20c.     Haider, Shakir Nasir. "The Iraq agricultural development law."
         Baghdad, 1959. 34 1.                 Files Iraq 3 H14

20d.     _____. "Land policy and the development of agriculture in
         Iraq." Madison, 1955. 108 1. M. S. thesis, University of
         Wisconsin.                           Mem AWM H1248

20e.     _____. LAND TENURE CLASSIFICATION IN IRAQ. Background docu-
         ment no. B-15. (Rome) FAO, 1955. 12, 6 p. Paper for Center
         on Land Problems in the Near East, Salahuddin, Iraq, 1955.
                                              Files Iraq 58 H136

20f.     _____. "Types of tenancy in various parts of Iraq." Training
         course document no. 49. n.p., n.d. 6 p.   Files Iraq 58 H14

21.      Hashimi, Rasool M. H. "Land reform in Iraq: economic and
         social implications." (In LE, 37:1, 1961. p. 68-81)

         Concentrates on changes introduced by the 1958 Land Reform Law.
         Critically analyzes the distribution measures, rigidities in-
         troduced by the reform, and the gaps to be filled to accomplish
         greater productivity along with more equitable apportionment
         of landholding rights.

21a.     Hüwe, Rudolf. AGRARSTRUKTUR UND AGRARREFORMEN IN DER REPUBLIK
         IRAK. Mitteilungen für Agrargeographie, landwirtschaftliche
         Regionalplanung und ausländische Landwirtschaft, nr. 49.
         (Wittenberg) Universität Halle, 1970. 6 1.   Files Iraq 3 H89

22.      Iraq. Laws, statutes, etc. "Agrarian reform law no. 30 - 30
         September 1958." (In FAL, 8:1, V1/58.5) From the WEEKLY
         GAZETTE OF THE REPUBLIC OF IRAQ, 20, 1958. p. 206.   Ag Docs
         Also available as a separate.          Files Iraq 3 I81
         Also available in Item IRAQ-30, p. 267-305.   HD 954 I7 K41

         Complete text of the 1958 Agrarian Reform Law. Covers land-
         holding ceilings, procedures for land distribution, guidelines

# Land Tenure and Agrarian Reform

(Iraq. Laws, statutes, etc.)
for the organization of cooperatives, and the rights of agricultural workers.

23. _____. _____. "Law no. 38 of 1961, concerning the ownership
of immovable property by foreigners in Iraq - 31 May 1961."
(In FAL, 16:1, V/1C) From the WEEKLY GAZETTE OF THE REPUBLIC
OF IRAQ, 37, 1961. p. 733. Text as amended by Law no. 82
of 1964.                                                  Ag Docs
Also available as a separate.              Files Iraq 58 I8

Regulations governing the acquisition and disposition of immovable property. Based on the principle of reciprocal rights
(i.e., of the legal status given to Iraqis in any country).

24. _____. _____. "Law no. 81 of 1964, amending the agrarian reform law no. 30 of 1958 - 4 June 1964." (In FAL, 14:1, V/1b)
From the WEEKLY GAZETTE OF THE REPUBLIC OF IRAQ, 48, 1964.
p. 7.                                                     Ag Docs
Also available as a separate.              Files Iraq 3 I82

Three amending articles regulating the establishment of agricultural cooperatives in the distributed lands.

25. _____. _____. "Law no. 117 of 1970. The Agrarian reform -
21 May 1970. Summary." (In FAL, 21:1, 1972. p. 44-45)
Complete text appears in the WEEKLY GAZETTE OF THE REPUBLIC OF
IRAQ, 14, 1971. p. 3.                                     Ag Docs
Also available as a separate.            Files Iraq 3 I824

Deals with the criteria and conditions under which land distribution and other aspects of agrarian relations are to be
conducted.

26. _____. _____. "Law no. 153 for right of Lazma in Miri lands -
26 September 1959." (In FAL, 9:4, V.1/59.14) From the
WEEKLY GAZETTE OF THE REPUBLIC OF IRAQ, 16, 1960. p. 450.
                                                          Ag Docs
Also available as a separate.              Files Iraq 58 I82

Defines the right of Lazma, i.e., the holding of Miri lands
(state lands). The law specifies conditions for granting of
ownership, mortgage, and transference of land by sale or gift,
and obligations for cultivation and planting of land affected
by the law.

# Land Tenure and Agrarian Reform

26a.   Iraq. Ministry of Agriculture. AGRARIAN REFORM IN IRAQ.
       Bruxelles, Institut International des Civilisations Différ-
       entes, 1973.   13 1.   Paper for INCIDI Study Session on Obsta-
       cles and Restraints Impeding the Success of Land Reform in
       Developing Countries, 1973.                     Files Iraq 3 I88

27.    Issawi, Charles P., ed.  THE ECONOMIC HISTORY OF THE MIDDLE
       EAST.  1966.                                Mem HC 412 I787

       See Item NE-19 for citation and annotation.

28.    Kamal, Adel.  "Feudalism and land reform."  1971.
                                                    DS 44 A3 1971b

       See Item NE-20 for citation and annotation.

29.    Kermani, Taghi T.  ECONOMIC DEVELOPMENT IN ACTION:  THEORIES,
       PROBLEMS AND PROCEDURES AS APPLIED TO THE MIDDLE EAST.  1967.
                                                    HC 410.7 K4

       See Item NE-21 for citation and annotation.

30.    Khadhiri, Riadh K.  "A Case study in agricultural reform:  the
       Iraqi experience."  State College, Miss., 1970.  viii, 314 1.
       Bibl.  Ph. D.  dissertation, Mississippi State University.
       Photocopy.  Ann Arbor, Mich., University Microfilms, 1973.
                                                    HD 951 I7 K41

       Concerned mainly with conditions related to agricultural policy
       before and after the land reform of 1958.  Political instabil-
       ity and insufficient attention to credit and marketing matters,
       etc., have hampered production as well as improvement of peas-
       ant living standards.  Nevertheless, Khadhiri points favorably
       to the new patterns of production and socio-economic organiza-
       tion established by the reform as a basis for future progress.
       Tables on agricultural development plans between 1951 and 1966,
       the text of the 1958 Land Reform Law (Item IRAQ-22), and an
       extensive bibliography are appended.

31.    "Land reform in Iraq:  an economic evaluation of the Al-Wahda
       Irrigation Project."  By Mohammed M. A. Ahmed, Abdul Nabi K.
       Radha, Abdul Wahab M. al-Dahiri (and) Jasim M. Al-Ezzy.  (In
       LRLSC, 1970:1.  p. 62-77)         REF HD 1261 A1 L1 1970 v.1

       Examines the obstacles to bringing about increases in agricul-
       tural production, expected but not achieved, after the 1958
       agrarian reform.  After evaluating various aspects of the pro-
       ject under consideration, action is recommended to develop
       physical and administrative elements of the rural infrastructure.

32. Meliczek, Hans. DIE WIRTSCHAFTLICHEN UND SOZIALPOLITISCHEN VERHALTNISSE IM IRAK UNTER BESONDERER BERUCKSICHTIGUNG VON AGRARVERFASSUNG UND AGRARREFORM. Zeitschrift für Ausländische Landwirtschaft; Materialsammlunger, heft 6. Frankfurt/Main, DLG-Verlag, 1966. xvi, 309 p.          HD 3060.5 M25

Examines Iraq's Islamic and Ottoman legal heritage and more recent factors (within the last 50 years) leading to the development of semi-feudal conditions. Analyzes problems encountered in implementing agrarian reform. Suggests that the example of Iraq throws light on the general impact of agrarian reform on a country's political, social, and economic structures.

32a. Palmer, Monte. AGRARIAN REFORM IN IRAQ. Bruxelles, Institut International des Civilisations Différentes, 1973. 17 1. Paper for INCIDI Study Session on Obstacles and Restraints Impeding the Success of Land Reform in Developing Countries, 1973.          Files Iraq 3 P145

33. _____. "Some political determinants of economic reform: agrarian reform in Iraq." n.p., n.d. 24, (3) 1.
          Files Iraq 3 P15

Maintains that the "primacy of political choices" over economic considerations in formulating the 1958 agrarian reform entailed extensive economic and social disruptions in Iraq.

34. Parsons, Kenneth H. "Land tenure in Asia." 1960.
          Files Asia 58 P17

See Item NE-29 for citation and annotation.

35. Pouros, T. L. "Agrarian reform and the development of agricultural cooperative societies within the agrarian reform regions." (In ILRLSC, 1965:1. p. 32-37)     REF HD 1261 A1 I5 1965 v.1

Attributes reduced production after the 1958 Iraqi agrarian reform to the lack of supporting cooperative, credit, and extension facilities. Describes governmental actions to fill these gaps.

36. Qubain, Fahim I. RECONSTRUCTION OF IRAQ: 1950-1957. New York, Praeger, 1958. xxi, 277 p.          Mem HC 497 I7 Q4

Discusses land tenure and agrarian reform (Chapter 8) within the general context of national development efforts. Regards redistribution of large holdings to landless peasants as

(Qubain, Fahim I.)
economically unsound.  Instead, the author advocates distribution and settlement of state lands.  Reviews and evaluates
settlement projects already in effect.

36a.  Radha, Abdul Nabi K.  "The Agrarian reform in Iraq and the
need for a new agricultural credit policy."  Madison, 1961.
123 (2) 1.  Bibl.  M. S. thesis, University of Wisconsin.
Mem AWM R1182

37.  Rephaeli, Nimrod.  "Agrarian reform in Iraq:  some political
and administrative problems."  (In JLAO, 5:2, 1966.  p. 102-
111)                                              Mem AP J83 L811

Attributes the lack of land reforms up to 1958 and the relative
failure of initiatives since then to political rather than
economic causes.  Lack of trained manpower to implement programs of land expropriation and cooperativization has also
limited progress.

38.  Simmons, John L.  "Agricultural development in Iraq:  planning
and management failures."  (In REP, 2:2, 1965.  p. 59-74)

Discusses the shortcomings of land reform and related initiatives (cooperatives, etc.) since 1958.  Blames ineffectual
administration and management as primarily responsible for the
failure in formulating and implementing adequate agricultural
policy.

39.  Tannous, Afif F.  "Land ownership in the Middle East."
HD 105 C67 1951b

See Item NE-34 for citation and annotation.

40.  Treakle, H. Charles.  LAND REFORM IN IRAQ.  SR/LR/C-19.
(Washington) USAID, 1970.  68 p.  Bibl.  Country paper for
Spring Review of Land Reform.                     Files Iraq 3 T72

Traces the evolution of land tenure patterns and the socio-
economic and political contexts in which agrarian reforms,
notably that of 1958, operated.  Though political objectives
of the 1958 reform have largely been achieved, economic and
social objectives, in terms of production, distribution, and
the management functions of co-ops, have fallen short of expec-
tations.  Bases future progress on governmental stability.

# LAND TENURE AND AGRARIAN REFORM

41. Ule, W. "Die Auswirkungen der Bodenreform auf Entwicklung
und Stand des ländlichen Genossenschaftswesens im Irak." (In
ZGG, 21:2, 1971. p. 190-200)                 Mem AP Z494 D226

Critical survey of agricultural cooperative activities, initiated in conjunction with the agrarian reforms of the 1950s
and 1960s. Though characterized by some success, future prospects depend on the eradication of traditional attitudes of
individuality, etc., which had limited past accomplishments
of Iraq's cooperatives.

42. Ward, Gordon H. FARMER COOPERATIVES IN IRAQ. Mimeo pamphlet
no. AES-2. Beirut, American University of Beirut, Agricultural
Economics and Sociology Division, 1967. 23 l.
                                            Files Iraq 20.1 W17

Assessment of the growth of cooperatives and their contribution
to agricultural development, particularly between 1958 and
1967. Describes the legal administrative framework of cooperative operations. Ward regards progress as having been slow
and analyzes factors supporting and hindering cooperative
effectiveness.

43. Warriner, Doreen. "Employment and income aspects of recent
agrarian reforms in the Middle East." 1971.         HD 111 I57

See Item NE-38 for citation and annotation.

44. _____. "Money in Iraq." (In Item NE-39, p. 113-183)
                                            HD 850.8 W3 1962

Presents an elaborate analysis of land tenure system in Iraq
and strong arguments for land reform. In the author's view,
"the real obstacle to reform in Iraq is not a shortage of experts, or money, or administrative inefficiency. . . . The root
of the trouble is simply that there is no new economic class
to rival the power of the landowners."

45. _____. "Revolutions in Iraq." 1969. (In her LAND REFORM IN
PRINCIPLE AND PRACTICE. Oxford, Clarendon Press, 1969. p.
77-108)                                            HD 111 W36

Views agrarian reform within an overall context of political
instability. The central dilemma described is that, "without
revolution there would be no effective reform; with a revolution, reform was likely to be inefficient." Warriner stresses
the shortage of trained personnel to implement and plan the
comprehensive programs needed for the development of Iraq's
agriculture.

# Land Tenure and Agrarian Reform

46.  Wilson, Rodney J. A. AGRICULTURAL DEVELOPMENT IN THE MIDDLE
     EAST, 1950-1970. 1972.                         Files NE 4 W45

     See Item NE-40 for citation and annotation.

47.  Yacoub, Salah M. THE ROLE OF LAND REFORM PROGRAMS IN COMMUNITY
     DEVELOPMENT AND OVERALL SOCIAL AND ECONOMIC DEVELOPMENT IN
     SELECTED NEAR EASTERN COUNTRIES. 1970.          Files NE 3 Y12

     See Item NE-41 for citation and annotation.


## ISRAEL

1.  Albaum, Melvin. "Cooperative agricultural settlement in
    Egypt and Israel," 1966.

    See Item EGY-5 for citation and annotation.

2.  Ben-Arieh, Yehoshua. "The Lakhish Settlement Project--planning
    and reality." (In TVESG, 61, 1970. p. 334-347)   Geol MC T44
    Also available as a separate.            Files Israel 17 B25

    Examines the interaction of geographical, social, and economic
    factors and their impact on the actual outcome of this settle-
    ment project. Maintains that the social element, involving
    ethnic and ideological background, is "the determining factor
    in the success of agricultural settlement today."

3.  Ben-David, Joseph. "The Kibbutz and the moshav." (In his
    AGRICULTURAL PLANNING AND VILLAGE COMMUNITY IN ISRAEL. Arid
    zone research, 23. Paris, UNESCO, 1964. p. 45-57)
                                                  HX 765 P3 B43

    Outlines organizational elements of moshav and kibbutz rural
    settlement forms. Foresees little prospect for renewed expan-
    sion of the kibbutz movement.

4.  Bonné, Alfred. "Major aspects of land tenure and rural social
    structure in Israel." (In Conference on World Land Tenure
    Problems, University of Wisconsin, 1951. LAND TENURE; PRO-
    CEEDINGS. . . . Madison, University of Wisconsin Press, 1956.
    p. 111-117)                                HD 105 C67 1951

    Describes the operation of the Jewish National Fund as the
    primary landholder in Israel. Stresses the interaction between

# Land Tenure and Agrarian Reform

(Bonné, Alfred)
changing circumstances and institutional responses, as in the
various types of rural settlements that evolved.

5.   Cohen, Abner.  ARAB BORDER-VILLAGES IN ISRAEL:  A STUDY OF
CONTINUITY AND CHANGE IN SOCIAL ORGANIZATION.  Manchester,
Eng., Manchester University Press, 1965.  194 p.
Mem DS 113.7 C6

Analyzes shifts in landholding patterns through three main
stages--the Ottoman, Mandatory, and postindependence periods.
Depicts changing village power relations (as related to landholding and land use), emphasizing the reemergence of the extended family as Arabs have become involved in the Israeli
market economy.

6.   Costa, Frank J.  "A Comparative analysis of changes in land
tenure in Italy and Israel."  (Madison) 1970.  35 1.  Paper
for Seminar in Land Problems, University of Wisconsin.
Files Israel 17 C67

Though regarding Israel's experience as unique, Costa points
to the applicability elsewhere of her national and regional
commitment and coordination in rural development efforts.  Also
underlines institutional flexibility and variability of agricultural settlement as crucial to Israel's success.

7.   Firestone, Ya'akov.  "Crop-sharing economics in mandatory
Palestine."  n.p. (197-).  (79) 1.          Files Israel 58 F47

Examines tenure arrangements as reflections of social, political, and economic dependence and mutual obligation.  Focuses
on changes introduced with the penetration of the monetized
economy, notably the spread of cash rents replacing precedent
systems of payment.

8.   Frank, Michael.  COOPERATIVE LAND SETTLEMENTS IN ISRAEL AND
THEIR RELEVANCE TO AFRICAN COUNTRIES.  1968.   HD 1491 P3 F72

See Item AFR-54 for citation and annotation.

9.   Granott, Abraham.  AGRARIAN REFORM AND THE RECORD OF ISRAEL.
London, Eyre and Spottiswoode, 1956.  301 p.  Mem HD 951 P3 G7

Depicts the process of Jewish land acquisition and settlement.
Emphasizes the role of the Jewish National Fund and its leasing
policies as a key factor in the success experienced.  Compares
agrarian structural change in other countries and concludes

337

ISRAEL 9-14

(Granott, Abraham)
that Israel enjoyed advantages (no handicapping traditions,
etc.) not shared elsewhere.

10.    _____.  LAND POLICY IN PALESTINE.  New York, Bloch Publishing
Company, 1940.  xv, 208 p.                    Ag REWJ G76 LAN

Probes the factors facilitating and impeding acquisition of
land in Palestine for Jewish national purposes.  Examines
issues of land reserves, irrigation, land prices, and dangers
of speculation, etc.  Provides background information on
national Jewish land policy as it developed in theory and then
in practice through the Jewish National Fund.

11.    _____.  THE LAND SYSTEM IN PALESTINE; HISTORY AND STRUCTURE.
1952.                                          HD 850.8 P1 G71

See Item NE-16 for citation and annotation.

11a.   Heysen Incháustegui, Luis E.  LA REFORMA AGRARIA:  SEMILLA DEL
MUNDO.  Lima, Universidad Nacional Federico Villarreal, Depto.
de Prensa y Publicaciones, 1967.  30 p.          Files 3 H29

12.    Kaddar, Gershon.  "The Israeli experience in mass settlement."
n.p., 1973.  16 1.  Paper for First National Land Reform Conference, San Francisco, 1973.          Files Israel 17 K12

Outlines background, types, management, and financing of
cooperative-based settlement, favorably assessing its achievements.  Notes predominance of public landownership and describes leasing arrangements.

13.    KARKA:  JOURNAL OF THE LAND USE RESEARCH INSTITUTE.  Tel Aviv,
Land Use Research Institute.  Library has:  no. 5, Spring 1974--
to date.  Text in English and Hebrew.

A quarterly journal devoted mainly to questions of land policy,
land use, and land development in Israel.

13a.   Kerem, Moshe.  THE KIBBUTZ.  Israel today, no. 27.  Jerusalem,
Israel Digest, 1973.  (64) p.  Bibl.     Files Israel 55.5 K27

14.    Klayman, Maxwell Irving.  "The Moshav in Israel."  (In LRLSC,
1971:1.  p. 52-67)              REF HD 1261 A1 L1 1971 v.1

Based on Item ISRAEL-15.

# Land Tenure and Agrarian Reform

15. _____. THE MOSHAV IN ISRAEL: A CASE STUDY OF INSTITUTION-
BUILDING FOR AGRICULTURAL DEVELOPMENT. New York, Praeger
(1970). xvi, 371 p. Bibl.                      HD 1491 P3 K5

    Analyzes the evolution and operation of family farm-based
    cooperatives (moshavs). Notes the importance of land national-
    ization as the foundation of these cooperatives. Discusses the
    relevance of this institution for other developing countries,
    rather favorably evaluating attempts to incorporate basic prin-
    ciples of moshav organization and comprehensive planning in
    relation to land reform and settlement efforts in Venezuela
    and Iran.

16. Landau, Y. H.; and Rokach, A. "Rural development in Israel."
    n.p., n.d.  23 l.                       Files Israel 82 L15

    Describes the background and rationale behind the differing
    forms of rural settlement. Underscores the powerful ideologi-
    cal orientation of the program, the land tenure arrangements
    which assure accrual of benefits to the farmer, and the decen-
    tralized yet coordinated settlement administration as notable
    strengths in Israel's development efforts.

17. Levy, Itzjak. "Observaciones sobre el sistema agrario en
    Israel." Campinas, 1963.  10 l.  Paper for Seminario Inter-
    americano sobre Problemas de la Reforma Agraria, Campinas,
    Brazil, 1963.                           Files Israel 7 L29

    Brief discussion of Israel's landholding system and principles
    of agricultural organization.

18. Madiman, S. G. "Report on land tenure in Palestine." n.p.,
    1947.  59 l.                          Files Israel 58 M12

19. Orni, Efraim. AGRARIAN REFORM AND SOCIAL PROGRESS IN ISRAEL.
    Jerusalem, Jewish National Fund (1972).  93 p.   HD 951 P3 075

    Describes the formulation of Jewish national land policy before
    and after the foundation of the state of Israel. Stresses the
    crucial role of the Jewish National Fund as the owner and
    administrator of 90 percent of Israel's land, and its role in
    encouraging rational planning and use of national and regional
    resources.

20. Shapiro, Avraham. THE KIBBUTZ: ISRAEL'S COLLECTIVE VILLAGE
    AND HOW IT WORKS. (Tel Aviv) Afro-Asian Institute for Coopera-
    tive and Labour Studies in Israel (1965).  30 p.  Bibl.
                                          Files Israel 55.5 S31

ISRAEL 20-24

(Shapiro, Avraham)
Concise description of kibbutz organization and daily life.
Notes that both land and capital are the possession of the
kibbutz.

21.   Solomonica, David. "The Israeli moshav ovdim: different
      types of adaptation to cooperative life." n.p. (1968). 22 1.
      Paper for the Second World Conference for Rural Sociology,
      The Netherlands-Enschede, 1968.           Files Israel 20.1 S65

      Stresses ethnic factors in settler adaptation and hopes that
      free development of moshavim will not be constrained by ideo-
      logical controversy or legal strictures.

21a.  Souza, João Gonçalves de. ALGUMAS EXPERIENCIAS EXTRACON-
      TINENTAIS DE REFORMA AGRARIA. 1964.                 HD 156 S6

      See Item EGY-56 for citation and annotation.

22.   Swann, Robert. "Trip to Israel, June 23 to July 17, 1968 (to
      study the operation and management of the Jewish National
      Fund)." n.p., 1968. 6, 7 1.              Files Israel 58 S91

      Reports on the relevance for sharecroppers in the southern
      United States of the activities of the Jewish National Fund
      in land leasing, reclamation, and settlement. Also examines
      the various settlement patterns, i.e., the moshav, the moshav-
      shitufi, and the kibbutz.

23.   Talmon-Garber, Y.; and Cohen, E. "Collective settlements in
      the Negev." (In Ben-David, Joseph, ed. AGRICULTURAL PLANNING
      AND VILLAGE COMMUNITY IN ISRAEL. Arid zone research, 23.
      Paris, UNESCO, 1964. p. 58-95)              HX 765 P3 B43

24.   Weintraub, Dov; Lissak, Moshe; and Azmon, Y. MOSHAVA, KIBBUTZ,
      AND MOSHAV; PATTERNS OF JEWISH RURAL SETTLEMENT AND DEVELOPMENT
      IN PALESTINE. Foreword by S. N. Eisenstadt. Ithaca (N.Y.)
      Cornell University Press (1969). xxiii, 360 p. Bibl.
                                                  HD 1491 P3 W38

      Analyzes the evolution of these cooperative/collective patterns
      of Jewish rural settlement. Investigates their ideological
      and social foundations as well as their relation and adaptation
      to the changing political, social, economic, and institutional
      environment. Places discussion of their relevance to Israel's
      development within the context of views on development in other
      countries.

# LAND TENURE AND AGRARIAN REFORM

25. Weitz, Raanan; Landau, Y. H.; and Marton, S. T. "Some development problems of family farms: experience of the Israeli 'Moshav' settlement." (In IJAE, 22:1, 1967. p. 53-65)

    Also available as a separate.

    Ag Per
    Files Israel 82.5 W24

    Focuses on the interaction between the forms of family-based cooperative settlements (moshavim) and the dynamic needs presented by demographic, socio-economic, and technological changes. Stress is placed throughout on the need for flexible settlement layout patterns which could meet such changing demands.


## JORDAN

1. Ahmed, Mohammed M. A. DRYLAND FARMING: JORDAN; A SOCIO-ECONOMIC STUDY WITH SPECIAL REFERENCE TO LAND TENURE PROBLEMS IN ABU-NASEIR AND MUBIS VILLAGES, BAQ'A VALLEY. UNDP, AGS:SF/JOR18, Technical report no. 1. Rome, FAO, 1970. v, 30 p.

    Files Jord 58 A35

    Preliminary, fact-finding study for an agricultural development project in this region. Survey results highlight the primacy of land tenure problems, particularly absenteeism and fragmentation of holdings. Proposes land consolidation, redistribution, and inheritance law reform to prevent refragmentation.

2. _____. DRYLAND FARMING: JORDAN; LAND TENURE PROBLEMS WITH SPECIAL REFERENCE TO CONSOLIDATION, BAQ'A VALLEY. AGS: project working paper no. 3. Rome, FAO, 1970. v, 11 l.

    Files Jord 58 A36

    Depicts the land tenure situation and relates it to farm family income levels and productivity. Considers measures to combat fragmentation and absentee ownership, suggesting provision of incentives to encourage land consolidation.

3. Baer, Gabriel. "Land tenure in the Hashemite Kingdom of Jordan." (In LE, 33:3, 1957, p. 187-197)

    Compares land tenure patterns in Jordan with the situation in other Arab states as well as that prevalent among Israeli Arabs. Notes the rather unique preponderance of small- to medium-sized farms in Jordan and the relatively small proportion of state-owned land.

# LAND TENURE AND AGRARIAN REFORM

4. Center on Land Problems in the Near East, Salahuddin, Iraq, 1955. COUNTRY INFORMATION REPORT: JORDAN. CI-1. (Rome) FAO, 1955. 10 p.         Files Jord 58 C25

   Summary report including statistics on crops, water supply, land use and tenure, and land taxation.

4a. Dajani, Nijmeddin. "Jordan Valley agricultural economic survey." n.p. (1954). 37 p.         Files Jord 77 D14

4b. _____. "Preliminary report--Yarmuk Jordan Valley agricultural economic survey." n.p., 1954. 54, 60, 27 1.         Files Jord 7 D14

5. International Bank for Reconstruction and Development. THE ECONOMIC DEVELOPMENT OF JORDAN. Baltimore, Johns Hopkins Press, 1957. xvi, 488 p.         Mem HC 497 J6 I5

   Comprehensive report, with proposals for development over the period 1955-1966. Contains an extensive section on land use and recommends changes in the agrarian structure. Land tenure reforms advocated include: establishment of clear title to lands; leasing of state lands by family farm units, rather than their outright sale; and the passage of legislation to regulate landlord-tenant relations.

6. Ismail, Mohammed. "Report on settlement operations and survey in the Hashemite Kingdom of Jordan with a brief note on property before and after settlement." n.p., 1955. 1 v. (various pagings). Bilingual edition.         Files Jord 17 L75

   Outlines the development of land tenure in Jordan from its core of Ottoman precedent to later provisions, notably the 1933 Fiscal Survey and Land Settlement Laws. Includes discussion and texts of laws passed between 1946 and 1955.

6a. _____. SETTLEMENT OPERATIONS AND SURVEY IN THE HASHEMITE KINGDOM OF JORDAN. Country project no. CP-8. (Rome) FAO, 1955. 35 p. Paper for Center on Land Problems in the Near East, Salahuddin, Iraq, 1955.         Files Jord 17 I753

6b. Jordan. Dept. of Lands and Surveys. ANNUAL REPORT. n.p., n.d. 2 v. Library has: 1953; 1954.         Files Jord 57.4 J67

6c. Kan'an, W. R. "Land tenure in Jordan." n.p. (1973). 4 1. Paper for Study Seminar 35: Land Tenure, Distribution, and Reform, Institute of Development Studies, University of Sussex, 1973.         Files Jord 58 K15

# LAND TENURE AND AGRARIAN REFORM

7. Kermani, Taghi T. ECONOMIC DEVELOPMENT IN ACTION: THEORIES, PROBLEMS AND PROCEDURES AS APPLIED TO THE MIDDLE EAST. 1967.
HC 410.7 K4

See Item NE-21 for citation and annotation.

7a. Qalyoubi, Taher Adib. JAFER PILOT PROJECT FOR THE SETTLEMENT OF BEDOUINS. Country project statement no. (2) Jordan. (Rome) FAO, 1965. 16 p. Paper for Development Center on Land Policy and Settlement for the Near East, Tripoli, 1965.
Files Jord 17 Q15
Also available in Item NE-10, p. 152-163.
HD 850.8 Z63 D46 1965

8. Stickley, Thomas S.; and Abu-Shaikha, Ahmad. "The Role of land tenure in agricultural development: the Bani-Hasan area of Jordan." (In OM, 11, 1972, p. 80-83)

This condensation of Abu-Shaikha's M. S. thesis outlines the major characteristics of tenure in the area studied. Problems related to the holding arrangements and productivity are discussed and certain remedies are proposed.

8a. United Nations. Relief and Works Agency for Palestine Refugees in the Near East. SPECIAL REPORTS ON JORDAN. Bulletin of Economic Development no. 14. Beirut, 1956. 208 p.     Files Jord 31 U53

8b. Walpole, G. F. "Land problems in Transjordan." Training course document no. 16. n.p., n.d. 12 p.     Files Jord 59 W15

9. Yacoub, Salah M. THE ROLE OF LAND REFORM PROGRAMS IN COMMUNITY DEVELOPMENT AND OVERALL SOCIAL AND ECONOMIC DEVELOPMENT IN SELECTED NEAR EASTERN COUNTRIES. 1970.     Files NE 3 Y12

See Item NE-41 for citation and annotation.

10. _____. A SOCIO-ECONOMIC SURVEY OF THE SETTLER-CANDIDATES IN THE QUATRANA IRRIGATED FARMING PILOT PROJECT IN EAST JORDAN. Mimeo pamphlet no. AES 11. Beirut, Faculty of Agricultural Science, American University of Beirut, 1972. (3) 34 1.
Files Jord 17 Y112

Investigation of project participants' attitudes on such matters as agricultural experience, family size, desired farm size, knowledge of cooperatives, preferred crops, etc.

LAND TENURE AND AGRARIAN REFORM

JORD 11-LEB 4

11.   Yacoub, Salah M.  SOCIOLOGICAL EVALUATION OF A PILOT PROJECT
      FOR BEDOUIN SETTLEMENT:  A CASE STUDY.  Publication no. 40.
      Beirut, Faculty of Agricultural Science, American University
      of Beirut, 1969.  69 p.  Arabic summary.    Files Jord 17 Y11

      Results of a survey conducted among bedouin project partici-
      pants.  Deals with changing consumption habits, dress, atti-
      tudes on kinship and authority, and male and female roles.
      Makes recommendations for this and future schemes.


## LEBANON


1.    Abdullah, Fawzi M.  "Comparative study of land tenure and
      size of holdings in Lebanon and U.S.A."  n.p., 1962.  17 1.
      Paper for Rural Sociology 195.            Files Leb 58 A12

      Emphasizes problems of comparing land tenure in the U.S. and
      Lebanon arising from different classification systems.  Sug-
      gests policies to alleviate Lebanese land fragmentation prob-
      lems and to make agricultural taxation more equitable.

2.    Alamuddin, Najib.  "Practical proposals for the solution of
      land tenure problems in Lebanon."  (In Conference on World
      Land Tenure Problems, University of Wisconsin, 1951.  LAND
      TENURE; PROCEEDINGS . . . . Madison, University of Wisconsin
      Press, 1956.  p. 103-108)                HD 105 C67 1951

      Highlights the need to deal with problems of absenteeism and
      land fragmentation and to improve credit terms for peasants.
      These actions should be combined with redistribution and con-
      solidation measures.  Proposes formulation of a model land
      code for Arab countries and stresses the importance of inter-
      national cooperation and U.S. aid.

3.    Cresswell, Robert.  "Parenté et propriété foncière dans la
      montagne libanaise."  (In ETR, 40, 1970.  p. 7-79)

      Shows how agricultural technical/economic needs have prevailed
      over religious rules on marriage and kinship regarding land
      tenure in a Maronite Christian village.

4.    Gabriel, Abbas.  ESTABLISHMENT OF LAND SURVEY AND REORGANIZA-
      TION OF RURAL PROPERTY IN LEBANON.  Country project no. CP-11.
      (Rome) FAO, 1955.  19 p.  Paper for Center on Land Problems in
      the Near East, Salahuddin, Iraq, 1955.    Files Leb 12.5 G12

344

# LAND TENURE AND AGRARIAN REFORM

5.  Gannage, Elias. "The Economy and agricultural development in
    Lebanon." n.d. (In Item NE-24, 2. p. 1-19)      HD 850.8 L21

    Focuses on Lebanon's problem in transferring capital from the
    commercial to the agricultural sector. Examines agrarian
    structure and infrastructural development, including educa-
    tional, technical, and institutional improvements. Contains
    statistics on land distribution.

6.  Kuhnen, Frithjof. "A Lebanese village in transition." n.d.
    (In Item NE-24, 1. p. 3-44)                     HD 850.8 L21

    Socio-economic analysis of a mountain village and its trans-
    formation from subsistence to a market orientation. Examines
    land ownership patterns, lamenting the miniscule size of hold-
    ings as a constraint to adequate living and production
    standards.

7.  Nasr, Joseph. "Government is blamed for 'Akkar problems."
    Translations on the Near East, no. 564. p. 54-61. (In JPRS,
    9:8, 1971. reel 151) Translated from AL-NAHR, November 29-30,
    1970.                                           Microfilm

    Describes the results of the failure to fully implement an
    agricultural development scheme. Depicts the subsequent con-
    fusion regarding land titles and the scattered revolts by
    peasants against landlords to appropriate land by force.

8.  Peters, Emrys L. "Shifts in power in a Lebanese village."
    1972. (In Item NE-32, p. 165-197)               DS 57 R87

    Analyzes factors in the displacement of traditional elites by
    emerging groups of professionals and peasants. Notes the ad-
    vantage of diversified bases of power afforded by land and
    modern education versus the almost total dependence of tradi-
    tional groups on land. Stresses the fluidity of social rela-
    tions as against the maintenance of discrete groupings and
    structural stability.

9.  Sadr, Kazem. "Land tenure and agricultural development in
    Lebanon." (In LRLSC, 1973:2. p. 24-30)
                                         REF HD 1261 A1 L1 1973 v.2

10. Touma, Toufic. PRESENTATION SOMMAIRE DES BLOCAGES ET FREINAGES
    S'OPPOSANT A LA REUSSITE DES REFORMES AGRAIRES AU LIBAN.
    Bruxelles, Institut International des Civilisations Différ-
    entes, 1973. 18 1. Paper for INCIDI Study Session on Obsta-
    cles and Restraints Impeding the Success of Land Reform in
    Developing Countries, Brussels, 1973.          Files Leb 4 T68

# Land Tenure and Agrarian Reform

11. Wilbrandt, Hans; and Kuhnen, Frithjof. "Some observations about the 'Green Plan' for the development of Lebanese agriculture." (In Item NE-24, 2. p. 20-39)      HD 850.8 L21

    Discusses landholding patterns in terms of topographically unique regions which provide differential capacities for absorbing technological improvements. Advocates a comprehensive rural development approach coordinated with non-agricultural sectors and deals with employment, marketing, and organizational aspects of such an approach.

## LIBYA

1. Al-Jawhary, Sayid Hamid. LAND SETTLEMENT PROGRAM IN LIBYA. RU:WLR-C/66/28. Rome, FAO, 1966. 3 p. Paper for World Land Reform Conference, Rome, 1966.      Files Liby 17 A53

    The Director-General of the National Agricultural Settlement Authority outlines the organization's goals of improved rural living standards and increased agricultural production. Also describes various settlement projects. Includes text of the law establishing the NASA.

2. _____. "Present land settlement policy and projects in Libya." 1967. (In Item NE-10, p. 137-151)      HD 850.8 Z63 D46 1965

    Similar to Item LIBY-1, but without the text of the law.

3. Alwan, Abdul Sahib. A BIBLIOGRAPHY ON LAND TENURE AND RELATED QUESTIONS IN LIBYA. Benghazi, Libya, FAO, 1963. 17 p. Microfiche, Zug, Switzerland, Inter Documentation Co.
                                        Microfiche NE 288 65
    Also available as a separate.      Files Liby 58 A59

    Includes approximately 200 references under the headings "Land Tenure and Water Rights," "Land Colonization and Settlement," "Agricultural Cooperatives, Credit, and Marketing," "General Agricultural Subjects," "Economic, Social, and Historical Aspects," and "Miscellaneous." The first two divisions contain about 30 items.

4. _____. A FIELD STUDY OF THE CUSTOMARY SYSTEM OF LAND TENURE AND RELATED PROBLEMS IN THE MUTASARRIFIA OF AGEDABIA, CYRENAICA, LIBYA. Benghazi, FAO Libya Mission, 1963. 27 l.
                                        Files Liby 58 A593

# LAND TENURE AND AGRARIAN REFORM

(Alwan, Abdul Sahib)
A survey of customary arrangements of land tenure and water use rights in a semi-desert area. Most of the population follows a semi-nomadic, pastoral way of life; agricultural production is concentrated around four oases. Land is held by the tribe and cannot be alienated without the consent of the tribe as a whole. Tribal lands are distributed so that each bait has access to water, grassland, and ploughland.

5.    _____. PLAN OF STUDY AND PROGRAM OF WORK TO INVESTIGATE THE LAND TENURE AND RELATED QUESTIONS IN THE LIBYAN PROJECT FOR THE DEVELOPMENT OF TRIBAL LANDS AND SETTLEMENTS. Benghazi, FAO Libya Mission, 1963.  11, 16 1.          Files Liby 58 A594

Outlines goals and procedures for an investigation of land tenure problems preliminary to the implementation of the Development of Tribal Lands and Settlement Project in Libya (Item LIBY-14).

6.    Bologna, Luigi M.  REPORT TO THE GOVERNMENT OF LIBYA ON SETTLEMENT PLANNING. Expanded Technical Assistance Program, report no. 732. Rome, FAO, 1957.  34 p.          Files Liby 17 B65

Considers land ownership, inheritance patterns, and other elements involved in existing agrarian problems. Proposes certain settlement schemes to alleviate these difficulties. Emphasizes the retarding influence of tradition and calls for a broad coordinated approach in planning and executing settlement projects.

7.    Bottomley, Anthony.  "The Effect of common ownership of land upon resource allocation in Tripolitania." (In LE, 39:1, 1963.  p. 91-95)          Ag Per

Maintains that communal land ownership patterns have encouraged the misallocation of capital investment into low-profit-yielding, marginal private plots. Advocates channelling investment into communal lands, in spite of the opposition such a change would engender among the peasant population.

8.    Clarke, John I.  "Studies of semi-nomadism in North Africa." (In EGEOG, 35:2, 1959.  p. 95-108)          Ag Per

Description of the migration and farming patterns of several semi-nomadic groups in Libya and Tunisia. Concludes that these people will be easier to sedentarize than true nomads. Points out difficulties due to problems of water supply, soil, land tenure, and socio-cultural attitudes.

LIBY 9-14

9.    Eldblom, Lars. LAND TENURE, SOCIAL ORGANIZATION AND STRUC-
TURE; A COMPARATIVE SAMPLE STUDY OF THE SOCIO-ECONOMIC LIFE
IN THE THREE LIBYAN CASES OF GHAT, MOURZOUK AND GHADAMES.
Research report no. 4. Uppsala, Scandinavian Institute of
African Studies, 1969. 17 1.       Files Liby 81.9 E52

English summary of Item LIBY-10.

10.      \_\_\_\_\_. STRUCTURE FONCIERE: ORGANISATION ET STRUCTURE SOCIALE,
UNE ETUDE COMPARATIVE SUR LA VIE SOCIOECONOMIQUE DANS LES
TROIS OASIS LIBYENNES DE GHAT, MOURZOUK ET PARTICULIEREMENT
GHADAMES. Lund, Sweden, Uniskol, 1968. 424 p. Bibl.
                                          HD 1265 L6 E52

Detailed, comparative study of three desert oases examining the
interrelations between the habitat; systems of land, water,
and tree ownership; and social organization. Suggests that
successful development initiatives depend on comprehensive
information of community structure.

11.    El Ghonemy, Mohammed Riad. "Development of tribal lands and
settlements in Libya." (In ILRLSC, 1965:1. p. 20-31)
                                  REF HD 1261 A1 I5 1963/7

Describes efforts between 1960 and 1965, including establishment of NASA and an FAO project concerned particularly with the
development and settlement of tribal lands.

12.      \_\_\_\_\_. "The Development of tribal lands and settlements in
Libya: report on a visit to Libya in March 1972." n.p., n.d.
19 p.                                   Files Liby 17 E53

Report of a week-long inspection of various Libyan settlement
projects. The author recommends a systematic investigation
of tribal land rights, carrying out of cadastral surveys and
water resource surveys, and training of land settlement personnel to be carried out by a team of experts in land tenure
and related fields.

13.      \_\_\_\_\_. "The Role of land policy in agricultural production
and income distribution in the Near East." 1965.
                                  Microfiche NE 288 31

See Item NE-13a for citation.

14.    Food and Agriculture Organization. REPORT TO THE GOVERNMENT
OF LIBYA ON DEVELOPMENT OF TRIBAL LANDS AND SETTLEMENTS PROJ-
ECT. FAO/LIB/TF 20. Rome, 1969. 4 v.        HD 1007 L5 F6

(Food and Agriculture Organization)
Detailed, systematic survey of agronomic, institutional, social, and economic conditions, with specific recommendations to develop the rural sector. The issue considered to be most crucial for settlement projects is the clarification of ownership and usage rights to land and water resources. Recommends preliminary tenure surveys, the promulgation of a land settlement law, and compulsory land registration to delineate land tenure relationships. Points out the need to utilize positive aspects of tribal organization rather than destroying it as a social institution.

15. Franzoni, Ausonio. COLONIZZAZIONE E PROPRIETA FONDIARI EN LIBIA CON SPECIALE RIGUARDO ALLA RELIGIONE, AL DIRITTO ED ALLE CONSUETUDINI LOCALI. Roma, Athenaeum, 1912. 370 p. Bibl.
Mem HC 568 T7 F7

16. International Bank for Reconstruction and Development. THE ECONOMIC DEVELOPMENT OF LIBYA. Report of a mission organized by the International Bank for Reconstruction and Development at the request of the Government of Libya. Baltimore, Johns Hopkins Press, 1960. 524 p.
HC 567 L5 I5

General appraisal of economic development efforts since independence followed by specific proposals for development over a projected five-year period. Stresses the economic disadvantages inherent in prevailing tribal communal tenure of the country and maintains that the most essential reform needed to extend settled agriculture is "a land law securing permanent individual rights in land."

17. Libya. National Organization for Agricultural Settling. "Agricultural settling in Libya 1963-1968." (Tripoli) n.d. 62 p.
Files Liby 17 L41

Outlines settlement schemes initiated before and after establishment of the NOAS in 1963. Also describes particular functions and activities of this organization's various administrative divisions. Appendices include the text of the law setting up the NOAS as well as a sample "temporary ownership certificate" given to settlement project participants.

18. Meliczek, Hans. SOCIO-ECONOMIC CONDITIONS OF A LIBYAN VILLAGE AND PROPOSALS FOR FUTURE DEVELOPMENT. Berlin, Institute of Foreign Agriculture, Technical University Berlin, 1964. 67 p.
Files Liby 81.9 M25

LIBY 18-MOR 1

      (Meliczek, Hans)
      Based on survey data on socio-economic conditions including
      land tenure, Meliczek makes preliminary recommendations for a
      development program.

18a.    Radha, Abdul Nabi K. "A Study in the land tenure system in
      Gurasha Mudirya, Mutassarifiah of Benghazi, a site for a pro-
      posed irrigation scheme receiving its water supply from
      Benghazi Sewage Disposal." n.p., FAO Libya Mission, 1965.
      12 1.                            Files Liby 58 R12

18b.    Rifaat, Hassan-Tabet. "Le Domaine public en droit libanaise:
      libéralisme ou formalisme?" 1970. (In Item AFR-112, p. 913-
      926)

18c.    Serrag, Mustapha. "Arab traditional farming and the need to
      reform." (Tripoli) 1954. 5 p. Microfiche, Zug, Switzerland,
      Inter Documentation Co.           Microfiche NE 288 46

18d.    Singh, Hakim. REPORT ON THE FARMING PROSPECTS IN THE PILOT
      AREA OF THE FAO TRIBAL LANDS AND SETTLEMENT PROJECTS TEAM,
      EASTERN REGION (CYRENAICA) OF LIBYA. Benghazi, FAO, 1966.
      53 p. Microfiche, Zug, Switzerland, Inter Documentation Co.
                            Microfiche NE 288 32/33

18e.    United Nations Tribunal in Libya. MEMORANDUM ON THE REGULA-
      TIONS GOVERNING POSSESSION AND OWNERSHIP UNDER THE ITALIAN
      REGIME IN LIBYA. A/AC.32/TRIB/R.1. n.p., 1951. 128 1.
                               Files Liby 58 U53

18f.    Wise, Harry. SUMMATION OF STUDIES MADE AND REPORTS SUBMITTED
      BY THE AGRICULTURAL ECONOMICS ADVISOR DURING THE YEAR 1960.
      Tripoli, United States Overseas Mission to Libya, 1961. 22 1.
                               Files Liby 58 W47

## MOROCCO

1.    Amor, Muhammed. "Le Domaine des collectivités publiques au
      Maroc." 1970. (In Item AFR-112, p. 815-822)

      Traces changes in law and usage affecting the relative posi-
      tions of public and private property domains on the state,
      provincial, and communal levels.

# Land Tenure and Agrarian Reform

2. Ashford, D. E. "The Politics of rural mobilization in North Africa." 1969.
   Mem AP J83 M686

   See Item NE-4 for citation and annotation.

2a. Beaudet, G. "Les Beni M'Guild du nord: étude géographique de l'évolution récente d'une confédération semi-nomade." (In RGM, 15, 1969. p. 3-80)
   Geol MC R32 G295

2b. Beguin, Hubert. FREINAGES ET BLOCAGES S'OPPOSANT A LA REFORME AGRAIRE DANS LES PAYS DU TIERS MONDE: LE MAROC. Bruxelles, Institut International des Civilisations Différentes, 1973. 9 l. Paper for INCIDI Study Session on Obstacles and Restraints Impeding the Success of Land Reform in Developing Countries, Brussels, 1973.
   Files Mor 58 B23

2c. Belal, Abdel Aziz; et Agourram, Abdel Jalil. LES PROBLEMES POSES PAR LA POLITIQUE AGRICOLE DANS UNE ECONOMIE "DUALISTE"; LES LEÇONS D'UNE EXPERIENCE: LA CAS MAROCAIN. IDEP/ET/CS/2379-20. Dakar, Nations Unies, Institut Africain de Développement Economique et de Planification, 1972. 55 p.
   Files Mor 6 B24

2d. Belbachir, Abdelatif. REPORT ON CADASTRAL SURVEYS IN MOROCCO. E/CN.14/CART/255. n.p., UNECA, 1970. 13 p. Paper for Seminar on Cadastre, Addis Ababa, Nov.-Dec. 1970.
   Files Mor 12.5 B25

3. Belkeziz, Abdelouahad. "L'Evolution du régime de la propriété immobilière au Maroc." 1970. (In Item AFR-112, p. 663-682)

   The coexistence of Moslem and French law has continued from the initiation of the Protectorate to the present. However, a definite tendency toward juridical uniformity since independence is noted.

4. Ben Barka, M. "Conditions de la réforme agraire au Maroc." (In Sachs, Ignacy, ed. AGRICULTURE, LAND REFORMS, AND ECONOMIC DEVELOPMENT. Warsaw, PWN, Polish Scientific Publishers, 1964. p. 245-284)
   Mem HD 1415 S2

   Characterizes real agrarian reform as necessarily encompassing political, agro-technical, social, and psychological aspects. Beyond mere redistribution of land, Ben Barka stresses the importance of peasant mobilization and organization. Imputes a crucial role to education in this effort. Statistics depict the land distribution picture.

MOR 5-9

5. Berque, J. "Les Droits des terres au Maghreb." 1964.
Mem HD 1415 S2

See Item NE-6 for citation and annotation.

6. Curie, Raymond. "Quelques aspects de la mise en valeur agricole dans la province de Casablanca depuis l'indépendance
(1956-1966)." (In BESM, 32:116, 1970? p. 63-89)
Also available as a separate.
Files Mor 5 C87

Describes land tenure, tax, and credit structures as the principal barriers to growth in the traditional sector of this
region. Though efforts to increase production through the
introduction of modern inputs (as in "Opération Labour") have
met with some success, Curie sees little subsequent improvement in peasant living conditions.

7. Dubois, Jacques. "Pour une réforme de l'administration agricole au Maroc." (In INSTITUTIONS ET DEVELOPPEMENT AGRICOLE
AU MAGHREB. Paris, Presses Universitaires de France, 1965.
p. 77-183)
HD 996 I57

Argues that administrative reform is a necessary precondition
for successful planning or agrarian reform efforts. This
point is illustrated by a case study of a large-scale viticul-
tural operation. Dubois suggests possible improvements in
administrative practice for greater coherence and coordination.

7a. El Ghorfi, N. LA REFORME AGRAIRE. (Rabat, Morocco) Sous-
Sécretariat d'Etat à l'Agriculture, 1964. (79) p.
Files Mor 3 E53

8. Fassi-Fehri, Boubker. NOTE ON THE SYSTEM OF LAND REGISTRATION
IN MOROCCO. E/CN.14/CART/254. n.p., UNECA, 1970. 9 p.
Paper for Seminar on Cadastre, Addis Ababa, Nov.-Dec. 1970.
Files Mor 59 F17

Describes purposes, procedures, and implications of land registration. Attributes success of registration efforts to the
broad support by both urban and rural landowners who appreciated the security of tenure this provided.

9. Fosset, R. "Quelques aspects de la vie rurale dans l'arrière-
pays de Mohammedia (Basse Chaoia)." (In RGM, 13, 1968. p.
103-119)
Geol MC R32 G295
Also available as a separate.
Files Mor 81.9 F67

(Fosset, R.)
Ecological analysis of geographical and social features of the
area and their impact on land utilization and agrarian structure. Explains that the region's large commercial estates
result from proximity to Casablanca.

10. Goussalt, Yves. "Diverses expériences tentées dans le domaine
rural après l'indépendance du Maroc." (In Sachs, Ignacy, ed.
AGRICULTURE, LAND REFORMS, AND ECONOMIC DEVELOPMENT. Warsaw,
PWN, Polish Scientific Publishers, 1964. p. 239-244)

Mem HD 1415 S2

Focuses criticism of rural development programs between 1956
and 1962 on the inordinate degree of state intervention.
Little was done to increase peasant participation in policy
formation. Specifically discusses "Opération Labour" and
"Promotion Nationale," programs which did not reflect the
desires or needs of the peasants.

11. Guillaume, Albert. LA PROPRIETE COLLECTIVE AU MAROC. Préface
de Ahmed Bahnini. L'Université du Maroc, Faculté de Droit,
collection d'études juridiques, politiques et économiques,
série de langue française, 8. Rabat, Editions La Porte, 1960.
177 p. Bibl.                                      HD 1021 M7 G8

Traces the evolution of the nature and status of collective
property. Emphasizes legal developments and problems arising
in the twentieth century. Insists that policy toward this
institution should take into account this long, complex evolution and avoid any sharp breaks with traditional practice.
Includes texts of laws dealing with collective lands passed in
the period 1912-1959.

12. Holm, Henrietta M. THE AGRICULTURE OF MOROCCO: PROGRAMS,
PROGRESS, PROSPECTS. ERS foreign 11. Washington, Regional
Analysis Division, Economic Research Service, USDA (1961).
35 p.                                          Files Mor 7 H65

Outlines some of the major problems and programs designed to
create a modern productive agricultural sector. Describes
"Operation Plow," concerned with land consolidation and application of improved techniques, as part of this effort. Sees
great potential for future growth, though shortage of trained
personnel, farmer traditionalism, and the "unwieldy" system of
land tenure remain as unresolved constraints.

13. Hutteball, Eugene E.; and Torbet, Grover B. REPORT ON LAND RECORDS, TITLING, AND CADASTRAL PROBLEMS OF MOROCCO. Washington, Dept. of the Interior, Bureau of Land Management, 1963. 1 v. (various pagings)      HD 1026 M6 H88

   USAID report assessing the feasibility of and presenting guidelines for a national cadastral survey. Appended are texts of documents on the cadastral survey, land reallocation, and definitions of certain categories of land, publicized mainly in 1960 and 1962. Also includes maps on the distribution of forest, titled, and collective lands.

13a. "Inequalities toward small fellahs deplored." Translations on Africa, no. 973. p. 68-77. (In JPRS, 9:6, 1970/1971. reel 147) Translated from AL'ALAM, October 15, 1970.
        Microfilm

13b. Isler, Rudolph M. LAND TENURE IN MOROCCO, SOUTHERN ZONE. Rabat, Agriculture Division, United States Operations Mission, 1960. 8 1.      Files Mor 58 I75

14. Kebbaj, Abdel-Khalek. "Certain aspects of the agrarian policy of the Moroccan Government." (In Item NE-10, p. 247-256)
        HD 850.8 Z63 D46 1965

   Defines objectives of agrarian policy as the aggregation of various categories of land under state control, its rational and just division, and maximizing productive exploitation of land. Outlines land reorganization and administrative reforms designed to attain these ends.

14a. Khattabi, Mustapha. "Les Particularités de la législation marocaine sur le domaine public de l'Etat et des collectivités locales." 1970. (In Item AFR-112, p. 823-832)

15. Lazarev, Grigori. "Les Concessions foncières au Maroc; contribution à l'étude de la formation des domaines personnels dans les campagnes marocaines." (In AMS, 1968. p. 99-135) Also available as a separate.      Files Mor 58 L18

   Attempts to show how, under changing historical conditions, the institution of sovereign land grants contributed to the rise of a private landowning class. Crystallizing under colonial rule, this development occurred despite strong inhibiting factors of tribal, communal landholding structures and the tradition of eminent domain of the ruler.

# LAND TENURE AND AGRARIAN REFORM

16.    _____. "Répartition de la propriété et organisation village-
oise dans le Prérif:  l'exemple des Hayaïna." (In RGM, 8,
1965.  p. 61-74)
Also available as a separate.                    Files Mor 58 L191

An effort to establish a typology of villages based on patterns
of land distribution and a discussion of the viability of the
village as an organizational framework for development.
Argues that distinctions elucidated demonstrate the need for
development and land policies cognizant of the complex differ-
entiated reality.  Contends that the village is a living institution, not necessarily detrimental to development.

17.    _____. "Structures agraires et grandes propriétés en pays
Hayaïna (Prérif)." (In RGM, 9, 1966.  p. 23-58)
Also available as a separate.                    Files Mor 58 L19

Sequel to Item MOR-16, concentrating on the large estates.
Examines the impact of recent economic forces in undermining
communal and family-based traditional patterns of agriculture.
Maintains that only a radical agrarian policy dealing with
structural as well as technical issues, and one sensitive to
diverse conditions, could alleviate the pauperization and disintegration which is occurring.

18.    Le Coz, Jean.  "Les Lotissements au Maroc:  du rapiéçage
agraire aux coopératives de production." (In RTSS, 5:15,
1968.  p. 139-156)                             Mem AP R454 T926

Analyzes the government policy of distributing lands on a cooperative organizational basis.  Perceives a fundamental con-
tradiction of state-directed rural development within a
liberal economy.  Concludes that this conflict has been re-
solved in favor of bourgeois peasant elements.

19.    _____. "Les Tribus guichs au Maroc; essai de géographie
agraire (1)." (In RGM, 7, 1965.  p. 1-51)    Geol MC R32 G295
Also available as a separate.                    Files Mor 58 L21

Examines the historical fortunes of guichs tribes, i.e., those
selected to perform military and security functions in return
for certain land rights.  Their changing status is used to
highlight forces generally affecting group integrity and collective landholding and the emergence of individualized landownership patterns.  Emphasizes the impact of French policy
geared to facilitate European settlement.

# LAND TENURE AND AGRARIAN REFORM

20. Le Coz, Jean. "Le Troisième âge agraire du Maroc." (In AG, 77:422, 1968. p. 385-413)                    Geol MC AN62
    Also available as a separate.              Files Mor 3 L21

    Critical discussion of agricultural development efforts since independence (1956-1966). Concludes that initiatives were rather timid and ineffectual compared with other Maghreb countries. Partial solutions must be replaced by more comprehensive designs to deal with basic agrarian structural defects.

21. Marthelot, Pierre. "Diverses expériences tentées dans le domaine rural avant l'indépendance du Maroc." (In Sachs, Ignacy, ed. AGRICULTURE, LAND REFORMS, AND ECONOMIC DEVELOPMENT. Warsaw, PWN, Polish Scientific Publishers, 1964. p. 233-237)                    Mem HD 1415 S2

    Describes the rapid agricultural development of the colonial European sector accompanied by stagnation in the native traditional sector before independence. Failure to incorporate peasants into the modern agricultural economy is blamed on peasant intransigence. Evaluates several development projects.

22. _____. "Les Poids des traditions communautaires dans l'agriculture au Maghreb." 1971.

    See Item NE-27 for citation and annotation.

23. Méot, Robert. "La Portée et l'organisation de la promotion nationale." (In CAIS, 24, 1968. p. 91-101)

    Evaluative study of the organization and functioning of the "Promotion Nationale" rural development program. Suggests that its failure in spurring a transformative grass roots development was due to the absence of land reform. This had originally been intended to be and remained a necessary component of any successful effort.

24. Moati, Paul; et Rainaut, P. LA REFORME AGRICOLE: CLE POUR LE DEVELOPPEMENT DU MAGHREB. Agronomie moderne, no. 2. Paris, Dunod, 1970. x, 336 p.                    HD 1021 M6 M62

    Views agriculture rather than industrialization as the key to development in Morocco. A highly theoretical approach in which the authors stress the importance of assimilating the peasant into the modern economy by inducing him to abandon traditional farming practices in favor of an efficient, market-oriented mode of production. Advocates voluntary production cooperatives incorporating a high degree of peasant decision-making.

25.    Morocco. LA REFORME DES STRUCTURES AGRAIRES ET L'INVESTISSE-
       MENT REGIONAL. STRUCTURE FONCIERE ET REFORME AGRAIRE. RU:
       WLR-C/66/48. Rome, FAO, 1966. 12 p. Paper for World Land
       Reform Conference, Rome, 1966.                 Files Mor 3 M17

       Argues the need to create structural conditions in the rural
       sector that facilitate the introduction of modern techniques
       and maximize production possibilities. Favorably describes
       main elements of the 1965-67 agrarian reform which apparently
       satisfy these economic as well as related social needs of the
       country.

26.    _____. Laws, statutes, etc. "Dahir no. 1-63-245 du 25
       joumada II 1383-13; novembre 1963 - relatif au recensement des
       propriétés agricoles. . . ." (In BO/M, 2666, November 29,
       1963; and 3150, March 14, 1973)
       Also available as a separate.                  Files Mor 36 M67

       Establishes procedures for registration of all agricultural lands.

26a.   _____. _____. GOVERNMENT BILL ON LAND REFORM; LAND REFORM,
       AL ISTIQLAL, 1963. Rabat, USAID Mission, 1963. 16 p.
                                                      Files Mor 3 M25

26b.   _____. Ministère de l'Agriculture. ALLOTISSEMENT DES TERRES
       CONFISQUEES, BUIDA ET MERS EL BGHAL; 1.175,80 HA., 115 BENEFI-
       CIAIRES. (Rabat?) 1959. (7) 1.                 Files Mor 3 M3

       _____. Ministère de l'Economie Nationale et des Finances.
       THE MOROCCAN FIVE-YEAR PLAN 1960-1964: AGRICULTURAL DEVELOP-
       MENT, PRESENT SITUATION AND PROSPECTS. Part two, chapter I
       of the official text appended to the Dahir of November 17,
       1960. Translation no. 4696 (61) from French by the Language
       Services Section, United States Operations Mission. Rabat,
       1961. vl, 82 p.              REF HC 591 M8 A4 1960/4 pt. 2 Ch.1

27.    Naciri, M. "Expérience de modernisation en milieu rural
       marocain." (In RTSS, 5:15, 1968. p. 121-138)
                                                      Mem AP R454 T926

       Sees growing disequilibrium between traditional and modern
       sectors resulting from agricultural modernization efforts.
       Illustrates this by a review of government programs over a
       20-year period.

28.    _____. "Les Expériences de modernisation de l'agriculture au
       Maroc." (In RGM, 11, 1967. p. 102-114)        Geol MC R32 G295
       Also available as a separate.                  Files Mor 82 E96

MOR 28-32

(Naciri, M.)
Traces rural modernization initiatives since World War I and
the concurrent evolution of development thinking. Program
shortcomings are analyzed, emphasizing the communication gap
between the administrative source of programs and the peasantry.
Criticizes the partial nature of development efforts.

29. Pascon, Paul. "La Modernisation rurale au Maroc: sociologie
d'un programme." (In RTSS, 5:15, 1968. p. 157-171)
Mem AP R454 T926
Also available as a separate.     Files Mor 82 P17

Warns against introducing foreign technologies and programs
unsuited for Morocco's socio-economic conditions. Sees an
indivisible tie between technological innovation and the social
and political structure and its reform. Suggests reviving
traditional peasant organizations as the medium through which
new technologies might be introduced.

30. Ponkiewski, Augustyn. "Social and agrarian relations in
Moroccan agriculture." (In AB, 18, 1973. p. 127-141)

Compares the differential impact of agricultural innovations
and development plans between Arab and Berber socio-economic
systems. Attributes failure to adopt innovations to the system of social relations which resists threats to its continued
existence, a serious problem in view of static production and
rising population.

31. "La Question de la réforme agraire au Maroc." (In NRI, 8:11,
1965. p. 213-227)     Mem AP N935 R4542
Also available as a separate.     Files Mor 3 Q82

Characterizes postindependence agriculture as stagnant and
regressive. Castigates agrarian reform efforts as serving the
interests of the upper classes rather than the peasants. Calls
for more bold initiatives involving a sweeping program of land
redistribution and the socialization of former foreign estates.

31a. "A Real revolution: agrarian reform." n.p., 1963. 9 l.
Translation from LA NATION AFRICAINE, April 3/4/5, 1963, by
Kopieff, Agriculture Division, USAID.     Files Mor 3 R21

32. REFORME AGRAIRE AU MAGHREB: SEMINAIRE SUR LES CONDITIONS
D'UNE VERITABLE REFORME AGRAIRE AU MAROC. (Par) Jean Dresch
(et al.). Paris, Maspero, 1963. (73) l.     HD 2147 M6 R4

# Land Tenure and Agrarian Reform

33. Rhares, Tayeb. "La Réforme agraire du Maroc." Paris, 1969.
    460 p. Bibl. Thesis (Doctorat d'Etat Sciences Economiques)
    Université de Paris, Faculté de Droit et Sciences Economiques.
    Microfilm

34. Rosciszewski, Marcin M. "Traditional sector of Maghreb agri-
    culture: character and development trends." 1969.

    See Item NE-31 for citation and annotation.

35. Sicard, H. "Problèmes fonciers au Maghreb." 1965.
    Mem AP A2585 E83

    See Item NE-33 for citation and annotation.

35a. Skadberg, J. Marvin. "Agrarian reform in Morocco." (Ames,
     Iowa) 1962. 14 1. Bibl. Paper for Economics 512, Iowa State
     University, May 1962.                        Files Mor 3 S42

36. Ulsaker, Norman. "Land and agrarian reform in Morocco."
    (Rabat) n.d. 19 1.                            Files Mor 3 U57

    Criticizes policy emphases on the technical aspects of modern-
    izing agriculture which have benefited mainly the large farmers.
    To deal with the problems of the predominant small-scale tra-
    ditional sector, comprehensive agrarian reform is needed.
    Reviews and evaluates government efforts and suggests further
    steps to be taken (training, tax policies, employment
    creation).

37. Verdier, Jean M.; Desanti, Pierre; et Karila, Juliana. STRUC-
    TURES FONCIERS ET DEVELOPPEMENT RURAL AU MAGHREB. 1969.
    Mem HD 1169 V4

    See Item NE-37 for citation and annotation.

37a. Vitanyl, C. von. "Die ländliche Sozialordnung im Marokko."
     (In AFH, 15 April 1975. p. 96-100)          Mem AP A25811 H596
     Also available as a separate.                Files Mor 81.9 V48

38. Zartman, William. "Farming and land ownership in Morocco."
    (In LE, 39:2, 1963. p. 187-198)
    Also available as a separate.                 Files Mor 58 Z17

    Delineates the various systems of landownership and land use
    in prerevolution Morocco. Regards changes introduced since
    independence as insufficient. Concludes that agricultural
    development has been stymied by the antiquated land tenure

MOR 38-SYRIA 4

(Zartman, William)
system and failure to launch a coordinated attack against
traditionalism.


## SYRIA


1.  Ahmad, M. S.; and Roy, E. P.  "Cooperation and land reform in
    the Middle East."  1963.                    Files Asia 3 A35

    See Item NE-2 for citation and annotation.

2.  Akhras, Chafik.  "The Coordination of economic and social
    criteria in the organization of agricultural property, with
    special reference to Syria."  n.d.  (In Item NE-24, 2.  p. 40-
    85)                                            HD 850.8 L21

    Attempts to clarify the conflict inherent in efforts to simul-
    taneously maximize productive efficiency and enhance social
    justice.  Suggests resolution of this dilemma through estab-
    lishment of large units of agricultural exploitation within
    which ownership would be divided among a large number of
    people.  Includes tables on mechanization, land distribution,
    and agricultural production.  Remarks by Charles Issawi follow,
    illustrating the social and economic advantages of small,
    individually owned agricultural units.

2a. Al Zoobi, Ahmad.  "Role of agrarian reform in development of
    animal wealth."  (In Item NE-10, p. 257-266)
                                        HD 850.8 Z63 D46 1965

3.  Ayoub, Antoine.  "Réforme agraire et propriété rurale:  le
    cas de la Syrie."  (In OM, 8, 1971.  p. 55-61)

    Warns that only radical progress in land distribution and co-
    operativization could assure any future development.  Finds
    little evidence of such change ten years after the 1958 land
    reform.  Tables illustrate the extent of expropriation, dis-
    tribution, etc.

3a. Center on Land Problems in the Near East, Salahuddin, Iraq,
    1955.  COUNTRY INFORMATION REPORT:  SYRIA.  CI-3.  (Rome) FAO,
    1955.  8 p.                              Files Syria 58 C25

4.  Dabbagh, Salah M.  "Agrarian reform in Syria."  (In MEEP, 1962.
    p. 1-15)                                    Mem AP M62707

(Dabbagh, Salah M.)
Traces land reform initiatives between 1926 and 1962.  Focuses
on reforms since the union with Egypt (1958-1962) which introduced expropriation and distribution of landholdings above
designated ceilings.  Notes that although implementation of
distribution has lagged, positive social and economic benefits
have accrued to peasants.

4a.    El-Ricaby, Akram.  "Land tenure in Syria."  (In Conference on
       World Land Tenure Problems, University of Wisconsin, 1951.
       LAND TENURE; PROCEEDINGS . . . . Madison, University of Wiscon-
       sin Press, 1956.  p. 84-94)                    HD 105 C67 1951

4b.    _____.  LAND TENURE PROBLEMS AND THE ECONOMIC DEVELOPMENT OF
       SYRIA.  Country project no. CP-2.  Rome, FAO, 1955.  37 p.
       Country paper for Center on Land Problems in the Near East,
       Salahuddin, Iraq, 1955.                        Files Syria 58 E57

       Another version of Item SYRIA-4a.

4c.    Gataullin, Maliuta Fazleevitch.  AGRARNYE OTNOSHENIIA V SIRII
       (AGRARIAN RELATIONS IN SYRAA.)  Moscow, Izd-vo Academiia Nauk,
       SSSR, 1957.  132 p.                             Mem HD 951 S9 G3

5.     Granott, Abraham.  THE LAND SYSTEM IN PALESTINE; HISTORY AND
       STRUCTURE.  1952.                               HD 850.8 P1 G71

       See Item NE-16 for citation and annotation.

6.     Hammadi, Sadoon.  COMMENTS ON THE RESULTS OF AGRARIAN REFORM
       IN SYRIA.  Research paper no. 1.  Damascus, Planning Institute
       for Economic and Social Development, 1966.  46 1.
                                                       Files Syria 3 H15

       Findings based on a survey of peasant reaction to agrarian
       reform measures.  Generally positive assessment of the results
       in increasing production and of the adequacy of the structural/
       institutional framework (cooperatives, etc.) set up.  Supports
       imposition of programs from above, particularly where tradi-
       tional attitudes present obstacles to progress.  Appendices
       include excerpts from the Agrarian Reform Law.

7.     Issawi, Charles P., ed.  THE ECONOMIC HISTORY OF THE MIDDLE
       EAST.  1966.                                    Mem HC 412 I787

       See Item NE-19 for citation and annotation.

# Land Tenure and Agrarian Reform

8. Kamal, Adel. "Feudalism and land reform." 1971.

    DS 44 A3 1971b

    See Item NE-20 for citation and annotation.

8a. Khader, Bichara. STRUCTURES ET REFORME AGRAIRE EN SYRIE. Bruxelles, Institut International des Civilisations Différentes, 1973. 20 1. Paper for INCIDI Study Session on Obstacles and Restraints Impeding the Success of Land Reform in Developing Countries, 1973.

    Files Syria 3 K31

9. Klat, Paul J. "Musha holdings and land fragmentation in Syria." (In MEEP, 1957. p. 12-23)

    Mem AP M62707

    Discusses the evolution of musha (collective holdings, individual use) toward a more individualized, less communal character. Attributes low productivity to this form of tenure, resulting mainly from its encouragement of over-fragmentation. Advocates the setting of minima for plot sizes or incentives to consolidate family-holdings by individual heirs. The ultimate solution lies in expanding alternative economic opportunities for peasants.

10. _____. "The Origins of land ownership in Syria." (In MEEP, 1958. p. 51-66)

    Mem AP M62707

    Outlines Islamic/Ottoman and French influences on the land tenure system that emerged after Syrian independence. Notes the overwhelming proportion of state-owned land and describes the categories within this class of lands.

11. Kuhnen, Frithjof. "Fallstudie über Auswirkungen der syrischen Agrarreform: ein Beitrag zur Ermittlung relevanter Faktoren und Prozesse." (In ZAL, 2:3, 1963. p. 63-82)

    Compares Syria's 1962 Agrarian Reform Law with measures enacted in Egypt. Considers the amount of land distributed to new landowners in Syria to be insufficient. Former landowners to whom additional properties were distributed are in a more favorable situation.

11a. Parsons, Kenneth H. "Land reform in the United Arab Republic." 1959.

    See Item EGY-45 for citation and annotation.

12. _____. "Land tenure in Asia." 1960.

    Files Asia 58 P17

    See Item NE-29 for citation and annotation.

# LAND TENURE AND AGRARIAN REFORM

13.   Syria. Laws, statutes, etc. "Consolidated text of legislative order no. 161 of 27 September 1958, on agrarian reform
in the Syrian Arab Republic in force as of 15 May 1962."
(In FAL, 11:2, 1962. V/1b)                          Ag Docs
Also available as a separate.            Files Syria 3 S92

Contains revisions and additions to Legislative Order no. 161
(Item SYRIA-14) through Act no. 193 of November 1958; Legislative
Order no. 266 of December 1959; and Legislative Decree no. 2
of May 1962. These deal with compensation provisions, landholding ceilings, and the role of special tribunals to settle
disputes.

14.   _____. _____. "Legislative order no. 161 on agrarian reform
in the province of Syria - 27 September 1958." (In FAL, 7:4,
1958. V.1/58.1) From JOURNAL OFFICIEL, 29-bis A, Special
number.                                             Ag Docs
Also available as a separate.            Files Syria 3 S95

Establishes guidelines for expropriation and distribution of
lands above a maximum landholding ceiling. Sets up administrative machinery, notably the Agrarian Reform Institute, and
outlines organizational and operational features of agricultural cooperatives.

14a.  _____. Ministry of Agrarian Reform. "The Role of land reform
in developing agriculture." n.p. (1965). 11 1. "A study by
the delegation of the Syrian Arab Republic to FAO Development
Center on Lands Policy and Settlement, Tripoli, 1965."
                                         Files Syria 3 S97

15.   Tannous, Afif F. "Land ownership in the Middle East." 1950.
                                                    Ag Docs

See Item NE-34 for citation and annotation.

16.   Vanzetti, C. "Impressions of a Syrian agrarian reform cooperative." n.d. (In Item NE-24, 2. p. 86-94)        HD 850.8 L21

Critical description, pointing to the inadequate investment
capital and credit. Also laments the absence of livestock and
crop rotation. Hints that innovative, efficient large landowners might have been displaced only to make way for uneconom-
ical fragmentation of redistributed lands. Urges the establishment of an efficient extension service. Paul Klat's
follow-up discussion reiterates the problem of insufficient
credit.

# Land Tenure and Agrarian Reform

17. Warriner, Doreen. LAND REFORM AND DEVELOPMENT IN THE MIDDLE
    EAST; A STUDY OF EGYPT, SYRIA AND IRAQ.      HD 850.8 W3 1962

    See Item NE-39 for citation and annotation.

18. Weulersse, Jacques. PAYSANS DE SYRIE ET DU PROCHE-ORIENT.
    Paris, Gallimard, 1946. 329 p.            Mem HD 951 S9 W4

    Discusses the various categories of landholding, their geo-
    graphical distribution, and the social consequences of evolving
    land tenure patterns. Points out the variation between written
    law and customary practice, a condition largely detrimental
    to the peasant masses. Lauds efforts under the French Mandate
    to clarify the situation through registration, etc. Stresses
    the central importance of the peasantry to the future of the
    region.

19. Wilson, Rodney J. A. AGRICULTURAL DEVELOPMENT IN THE MIDDLE
    EAST, 1950-1970. 1972.                      Files NE 4 W45

    See Item NE-40 for citation and annotation.

20. Yacoub, Salah M. THE ROLE OF LAND REFORM PROGRAMS IN COMMUNITY
    DEVELOPMENT AND OVERALL SOCIAL AND ECONOMIC DEVELOPMENT IN
    SELECTED NEAR EASTERN COUNTRIES. 1970.      Files NE 3 Y12

    See Item NE-41 for citation and annotation.


## TUNISIA

1. Abillama, R. "Land reform in Tunisia." (In MEF, 36:2, 1960.
   p. 30-33)                                    Mem AP M62708

   Brief description of land reform and supplemental measures
   (i.e., irrigation, credit, education, etc.) undertaken since
   independence in 1956.

1a. Accolti Gil, F. "Recent evolution of ownership and land ten-
    ure in Tunisia." (In PU/MP, 1, 1972. p. 89-106)

2. Anton, Günther Kurt. LE REGIME FONCIER AUX COLONIES; RAPPORTS
   PRESENTES A L'INSTITUT COLONIAL INTERNATIONAL. 1904.
                                                Mem HD 588 A6

   See Item AFR-10 for citation and annotation.

# LAND TENURE AND AGRARIAN REFORM

3.  Ashford, D. E.  "The Politics of rural mobilization in North
    Africa."  1969.                          Mem AP J83 M686

    See Item NE-4 for citation and annotation.

4.  Attia, Habib.  "L'Evolution des structures agraires en Tunisie
    depuis 1962."  (In RTSS, 3:7, 1966.  p. 33-58)
                                              Mem AP R454 T926
    Also available as a separate.            Files Tunis 58 A88

    An appraisal of the growth of Tunisian agriculture, based on
    the census of 1951 and the FAO study of 1961-62.  Interprets
    the statistics from these two sources and discusses various
    government agencies and their role in agricultural development.

5.  Berque, J.  "Les Droits des terres au Maghreb."  1964.
                                              Mem HD 1415 S2

    See Item NE-6 for citation and annotation.

6.  Bouslama, Abdelmajid.  "L'Evolution du régime de la propriété
    immobilière en Tunisie."  1970.  (In Item AFR-112, p. 683-698)

    Traces the legal foundations of land registration initiated
    under French rule and extended after independence.  Considers
    this as the crucial means of facilitating state authority and
    efforts at structural reform so necessary to meet pressing
    social and economic problems.

7.  _____.  "La Réforme du régime des Habous en Tunisie."  1970.
    (In Item AFR-112, p. 1113-1118)

    Outlines history of the habous landholdings system (usufruct
    rights granted in perpetuity for religious purposes), describ-
    ing legal steps since independence eventually eliminating it.
    Behind this abolition was the desire to free lands from rigid-
    ified ownership into productive use.

8.  Chabert, J. P.; et Lochard, Y.  LA POLITIQUE AGRICOLE DU
    GOUVERNEMENT TUNISIEN EN 1971; DOCUMENTS COMMENTES:  ANALYSE
    CRITIQUE, ELEMENTS DE SYNTHESE.  Série travaux de recherche
    no. 16.  Paris, Institut National de la Recherche Agronomique,
    1972.  vi, 129 1.                         HD 2135 T83 C32

9.  Chebil, M. Mohsen.  "Evolution of land tenure in Tunisia in
    relation to agricultural development programs."  (In ILRLSC,
    1965:2.  p. 12-24)              REF HD 1261 A1 I5 1965 v.2
    Also available in Item NE-10, p. 189-204.
                                     HD 850.8 Z63 D46 1965

TUNIS 9-14

(Chebil, M. Mohsen)
Briefly outlines Tunisian land tenure conditions, discusses
the actions taken by the government to change the tenure structure, and describes structural reforms which it is hoped will
increase agricultural production, principally the introduction
of cooperative and collective farming.

10.  Clarke, John I.  "Studies of semi-nomadism in North Africa."
     1959.
                                                          Ag Per

     See Item LIBY-8 for citation and annotation.

11.  Dahl, Reynold P.  AGRICULTURAL DEVELOPMENT STRATEGIES IN A
     SMALL ECONOMY; THE CASE OF TUNISIA.  Staff paper P71-28.  St.
     Paul, University of Minnesota, Dept. of Agricultural Economics,
     1971.  61 1.                              Files Tunis 6 D13

     Discussion centers on agriculture development policies and
     their impact on production.  Depicts structural reform of land
     tenure and farm reorganization (into production cooperatives)
     "as the principal means of transforming Tunisian agriculture
     and implementing agricultural diversification and intensifica-
     tion plans."  Failure in reaching production goals is blamed
     on problems of policy implementation.

12.  Donner, Wolf.  "Die agrarische Entwicklung des Medjerda-Tals
     in Tunesien."  (In ZAL, 2:3, 1963.  p. 96-111)

     Discusses technical, social, and economic aspects of the
     Medjerda Valley project as well as the history and organization
     of land reform and new settlements.  Also analyzes changes in
     production.

13.  Dooren, P. J. van.  "State controlled changes in Tunisia's
     agrarian structure."  (In TROPM, 1, 1968.  50 p.)
                                                     Mem GN 1 T75

     Distinguishes between land tenure reform, affecting only the
     legal framework of landholding, versus land operation reform,
     i.e., financial and technical changes affecting the productiv-
     ity of farm units.  Reviews governmental actions in these
     spheres, regarded as jointly necessary for any degree of eco-
     nomic development.

14.  Dufour, Jean.  "The Problem of collectively owned land in
     Tunisia."  (In LRLSC, 1971:1.  p. 38-51)
                                     REF HD 1261 A1 L1 1971 v.1

# LAND TENURE AND AGRARIAN REFORM

(Dufour, Jean)
Examines the nature of social and land tenure organizations as
they interacted to produce the existing agrarian situation.
Concludes that the fit between social and tenurial realities
within the new legal and institutional framework is satisfac-
tory, though certain persistent problems remain.

15.  Dufour, M. J.  "Réformes agraires en Tunisie:  chapitre V,
réforme des structures de production et des services d'appui."
n.p., n.d.  30 p.                          Files Tunis 20.1 D83

Critical evaluation of the Tunisian development plan for 1962-
1971.  Attributes deficiencies of cooperatives to the overly
rapid introduction of new forms insufficiently grounded in
traditional social structures.

16.  Duwaji, G.  "Land ownership in Tunisia:  an obstacle to agricultural development."  (In LE, 44:1, 1968.  p. 129-132)
                                                          Ag Per

Stresses that the complex land laws have greatly hampered
agricultural development.  Other factors such as soil erosion,
lack of technical skills, and limited access to credit have
also contributed to low agricultural productivity.

17.  El Aouani, Mohamed.  "Les Lotissements de réforme agraire de
la Basse Vallé de la Medjerda."  (In RTSS, 5, 1968.  p. 75-
92)                                       Mem AP R454 T926
Also available as a separate.             Files Tunis 3 E51

Describes land parcelization measures and support systems set
up under the Tunisian land reform in the Medjerda Valley.
Stresses technical and agronomic aspects of this regional
project.

18.  Haraguichi, Takehiko.  "Réforme agraire en Tunisie; quelques
aspects socio-économiques de l'unité de production."  (In RTSS,
5, 1968.  p. 89-120)                      Mem AP R454 T926
Also available as a separate.             Files Tunis 3 H17

A case study illustrating the interplay between Tunisia's
national socialist ideology and the outstanding concrete
embodiment of this ideology--the production cooperatives.
Presents administrative and operational features of these cooperatives accompanied by charts and tables.

# Land Tenure and Agrarian Reform

19.   Haupert, John S. "The Medjerda land reform scheme in
      Tunisia." n.p. (1972) 10 1. Paper presented at the annual
      meeting of the Middle East Studies Association, Binghamton,
      N.Y., 1972.                                        Files Tunis 3 H18

      Regards this scheme as part of the effort to transfer large
      numbers of peasants from the traditional into the modern agri-
      cultural sector. Notes gains in per capita income, though
      costs have exceeded anticipated ceilings. Ultimate success
      depends on continued foreign financial and technical aid.

20.   Karabenick, Edward. "The Medjerda plan: a precedent to
      agrarian reform in Tunisia." (In PG, 19:1, 1967. p. 17-22)
                                                        Geol MC P943 G29
      Also available as a separate.                     Files Tunis 3 K17

      Discusses various features of the scheme, particularly the
      restructuring of land tenure patterns into a new framework of
      small- to medium-sized holdings cooperatively organized.
      Despite problems encountered, Karabenick notes the improved
      living standards of participants and stresses the importance
      of experience gained for future agricultural development
      projects.

21.   Ladhari, Noe. "Aspects of agrarian law analyzed." Transla-
      tions on Africa, no. 850. p. 74-84. (In JPRS, 8:7, 1969/1970.
      reel 125) Translated from LA PRESSE, October 1, 1969. p. 2.
                                                        Microfilm

      Examines the methods by which the state, private persons, or
      cooperatives exercise their right of land exploitation.

22.   Makhlouf, Ezzedine. STRUCTURES AGRAIRES ET MODERNISATION DE
      L'AGRICULTURE DANS LES PLAINES DU KEF; LES UNITES COOPERATIVES
      DE PRODUCTION. Cahiers du C.E.R.E.S., série géographique, 1.
      Tunis, Université de Tunis, Centre d'Etudes et de Recherches
      Economiques et Sociales, 1968. v, 261 p. Bibl.
                                                        HD 2135 T8 M13

      Study of the interaction between agrarian structure and agri-
      cultural production under precolonial, colonial, and post-
      independence conditions. Examines the nature of production
      cooperatives and considers their advantage in facilitating the
      modernization and diversification of agricultural production.
      Makhlouf is critical, however, of the failure to deal with the
      problems of the landless and smallholder. Also questions
      rapid mechanization with insufficient regard to costs and
      impact on rural employment.

LAND TENURE AND AGRARIAN REFORM

TUNIS 23-27

23. Marthelot, Pierre. "Les Poids des traditions communautaires dans l'agriculture au Maghreb." 1971.

See Item NE-27 for citation and annotation.

24. Mensching, H. "Das Medjerda-Projekt in Tunesien: agrarwirtschaftlicher und sozial-geographischer Wandel in der Kulturlandschaft des Medjerda-Tales." (In ERDE, 93:2, 1962. p. 117-135)                                      Geol MC ER25

Discusses geographical, historical, and cultural factors associated with the planning and execution of this irrigation scheme.

25. "New law will promote reclamation of communal lands." Translations on Africa, no. 995. p. 42-47. (In JPRS, 9:8, 1970/ 1971. reel 151) Translated from AL'AMAL, January 14, 1971. p. 3.                                             Microfilm

Report on parliamentary debates concerned with extending authority to issue land deeds to private persons as well as to production cooperatives in accordance with the three-sector concept of public, cooperative, and private ownership.

26. Parsons, Kenneth H. "The Tunisian program for cooperative farming." (In LE, 41:4, 1965. p. 303-316)          Ag Per

Focuses discussion on production cooperatives against the backdrop of a dichotomous modern and traditional agrarian structure. States the central purpose of cooperatives to be the grouping of small farmers into units providing the efficiencies of scale and allowing the introduction of modernized farming. Expresses concern about problems of labor absorption in these production units.

27. Poncet, Jean. LA COLONIZATION ET L'AGRICULTURE EUROPEENNES EN TUNISIE DEPUIS 1881: ETUDE DE GEOGRAPHIE HISTORIQUE ET ECONOMIQUE. Recherches méditerranéennes, études 2. Paris, Mouton, 1962 (i.e., 1961). 700 p. Bibl.    Mem HD 1516 T6 P6

Traces the rise, under French colonization, of a dual agricultural structure composed of a dominant, modern commercial sector and an overpopulated, poor traditional sector. Deals extensively with modifications of land tenure and farm organization resulting from colonization. Argues for a replacement of exploitative capitalist development by approaches more conducive to long-term preservation of natural resources and the broadening of the social base to which benefits accrue.

369

# LAND TENURE AND AGRARIAN REFORM

28. Poncet, Jean. PAYSAGES ET PROBLEMES RURAUX EN TUNISIE.
    Memoires du Centre d'études de sciences humaines, 8. Paris,
    Presses Universitaires de France (1963). 374 p.
                                              Mem HD 2135 T85 P6

    Regional analysis of the colonial impact on rural life and the
    evolution of agricultural policy since independence. Supports
    governmental efforts of comprehensive rural development, par-
    ticularly its actions through cooperatives and associated
    institutional changes, geared to raise the level of life for
    the rural masses.

29. Rosciszewski, Marcin M. "Traditional sector of Maghreb agri-
    culture: character and development trends." 1969.

    See Item NE-31 for citation and annotation.

30. Schiller, Otto. "Die landwirtschaftlichen Produktionsgenossen-
    schaften Tunesiens." (In ZGG, 18:2/3, 1968. p. 204-208)
                                              Mem AP Z494 D226

    Examines the establishment and operation of agricultural pro-
    duction cooperatives. Schiller notes the diversity of socio-
    economic backgrounds of co-op members ranging from large
    landowners to agricultural laborers. Views increased pro-
    duction as a question yet to be answered.

31. Sicard, H. "Problèmes fonciers au Maghreb." 1965.
                                              Mem AP A2585 E83

    See Item NE-33 for citation and annotation.

32. Simmons, John L. LAND REFORM IN TUNISIA. SR/LR/C-14.
    (Washington) USAID, 1970. 92, (16) p. Bibl. Country paper
    for Spring Review of Land Reform.        Files Tunis 3 S45

    Attributes "the meager results of land reform efforts . . ."
    between 1956 and 1970 to their lack of focus. Illustrative is
    the sharp turn-about of policy emphasis in 1969, away from
    large state farms to private landownership patterns. Includes
    bibliography and tables on agricultural production, credit,
    distribution of farms by size, etc.

33. _____. "The Political economy of land use: Tunisian private
    farms." n.p., 1970. 41 1. Paper presented at the conference
    "Rural Politics and Social Change in the Middle East," Indiana
    University, Bloomington, Oct. 23-25, 1969.
                                              Files Tunis 57.5 S45

# Land Tenure and Agrarian Reform

(Simmons, John L.)
Study on the interplay of international economic and political forces, governmental policy inclinations, and changes in land tenure and use. Illustrates this interaction as it occurred in the development of citrus agriculture. Analyzing the influences before 1969 to widen the scope of state involvement in agricultural production and after 1969 to reduce it, Simmons predicts higher levels of production and well-being resulting from this turn to greater private control.

34. Thierry, H. "La Cession à la Tunisie des terres des agriculteurs français." (In ANFRIDI, 9, 1963. p. 933-948)
Law JX 21 A63

A discussion of the background and effects of the Tunisian-French protocols relating to the nationalization of farm land formerly owned and cultivated by French nationals.

35. Tunisia. Laws, statutes, etc. "Act no. 58-63 on agrarian reform in the lower valley of the Medjerda - 11 June 1958." (In FAL, 7:4, 1958. V.1/58.2) From JO/RT, 47, 13 June 1958. p. 649.
Ag Docs
Also available as a separate.
Files Tunis 3 T85

Provisions deal with differential liabilities for investment in irrigation facilities; property holding size limits; conditions governing expropriation; and land reform (largely consolidation).

36. _____. _____. "Act no. 58-63 of 11 June 1958 on agrarian reform in the lower valley of the Medjerda as amended by the Act no. 60-6 - 26 July 1960." (In FAL, 9:4, 1960. V.1/60.4) From JO/RT, 36, 29 July 1960. p. 1002.
Ag Docs
Also available as a separate.
Files Tunis 3 T84

Amended text of Item TUNIS-35. Amendments concern payments to finance the irrigation scheme, curtailment of leases, expropriation and expropriation indemnities, and size of landholding subject to division.

36a. _____. Office de Mise en Valeur de Sidi Bou Zid. "Office de Mise en Valeur de Sidi Bou Zid." n.p., n.d. (19) 1.
Files Tunis 7.5 T85

37. "Tunisia: agricultural reform act." (In ILR, 101:4, 1970. p. 401-402)

TUNIS 37–41

> ("Tunisia: agricultural reform act)
> A summary of the chief provisions of the 1969 Agricultural
> Reform Act, especially the Unités Coopératives de Production
> Agricole (UCPAs).

37a.   "Tunisia re-makes a river basin." (In TOWARD FREEDOM, Jan.
       1963.  5 p.)  At head of title:  Background material:
       Medjerda Valley Development.
       Also available as a separate.            Files Tunis 78 T9

38.    Verdier, Jean M.  "Les Principales tendances du droit foncier
       tunisien depuis l'indépendance." (In RJPOM, 15:2, 1961.
       p. 204–224)                              Mem AP R454 J986

       Outlines the evolution of land tenure from the beginning of
       French hegemony, assessing the direction and extent of change
       since independence.  Indicates continuity in the aims of land
       law policy, though emphasis has shifted toward the more social
       aspects of the issue.  Argues for policies more directly
       grounded in the Tunisian reality rather than the outright
       importation of foreign institutional models.

39.    Verdier, Jean M.; Desanti, Pierre; et Karila, Juliana.
       STRUCTURES FONCIERS ET DEVELOPPEMENT RURAL AU MAGHREB.  1969.
                                                Mem HD 1169 V4

       See Item NE-37 for citation and annotation.

39a.   Yaiche, Bechir.  "Vers une réforme agraire tunisienne." n.p.
       (1963).  11 p.                           Files Tunis 3 Y14

40.    Younès, Henry.  "Les Réformes agraires dans le monde
       contemporain:  l'expérience tunisienne." (In DCI, 22, 1965.
       p. 28–34)
       Also available as a separate.            Files Tunis 3 Y6

       Brief presentation of the history and administrative features
       of Tunisian land reform.  Evaluates results and calls for a
       less ad hoc, more coherent agrarian policy.

41.    Zamiti, K.  "Les Obstacles matériels et ideologiques à
       l'évolution sociale des campagnes tunisiennes: l'expérience
       de mise en coopératives dans le gouvernorat de Béja." (In
       RTSS, 7:21, 1970.  p. 9–55)              Mem AP R454 T926

       Regards production cooperatives as the "most advanced stage of
       structural reform."  Contends that while cooperatives upset
       the equilibrium of traditional subsistence agriculture, they
       are potentially able to modernize the Tunisian economy.

# Land Tenure and Agrarian Reform

42.     Zghal, Abdelkader.  "Changement de systèmes politiques et
        réformes des structures agraires en Tunisie."  (In RTSS, 12,
        1968.  p. 9-32)
        Also available as a separate.          Files Tunis 58 Z33

        Traces the interaction of political systems and agricultural
        development from earliest colonial days (1881) through the
        colonial period and nationalist liberation movements to the
        attempts at agrarian reform by postindependence planning
        agencies.


## TURKEY


1.     Aktan, Resat.  "Analysis and evaluation of land reform
       activities in Turkey."  (In AUSBFD, 26:3, 1971.  p. 85-136)
                                             Mem AP A6016 S625

       Surveys land reform since independence, focusing on the series
       of draft proposals formulated between 1960 and 1970.  Charac-
       terizes these proposals as capitalist-oriented measures con-
       cerned with production efficiency rather than equitable land
       distribution.  Perceives a greater concern for social justice
       in the proposals of 1971 and regards the situation at the
       time of writing as favorable for the enactment of a far-
       reaching land reform.

2.     _____.  "Problems of land reform in Turkey."  (In MEJ, 20:3,
       1966.  p. 317-334)                          Mem AP M6272
       Also available as a separate.          Files Turk 3 A48

       Discusses the historical background of Turkish land tenure,
       the defects of Turkey's agrarian structure, and land reform
       legislation since 1960.  Sees an urgent need for reform to
       widen the scope of income redistribution, reduce poverty
       among the peasants, lessen the power of the landlords, and
       reduce land fragmentation.

2a.    Arkun, E. F.  "Turkey."  (In REPORT OF WORKING GROUP C.  By
       K. Obayya and others.  n.p., 1973.  p. 20-24).  Paper for
       Study Seminar 35:  Land Tenure, Distribution and Reform,
       Institute of Development Studies, University of Sussex, 1973.
                                                   Files 3 R26

3.     Balaban, Ali.  "Land reform basic to usefulness of irrigation
       system."  Translations on the Near East, no. 618.  p. 24-27.

# LAND TENURE AND AGRARIAN REFORM

(Balaban, Ali)
(In JPRS, 9:12, 1970/1971.  reel 161).  Translated from
CUMHURIYET, May 25, 1971.  p. 2.                    Microfilm

Emphasizes the need for irrigation in conjunction with land
reform to establish a family-based agrarian structure.  Criticizes development plans founded on temporary increases in
productivity and speculative exploitation of land resources.

4.  Barkan, Omer Lûtfi.  "Çiftçiyi topraklandirma kanunu.  (The
    Land reform law)."  (In IUR, 6:1/2, 1945.  p. 54-145)
                                            Mem AP I871 I24

    The discussion of the 1945 Land Reform Law concentrates on the
    impact of Ottoman and Swiss legal influences.  Labels the law
    as a "land distribution law" rather than an "agrarian reform"
    in the more comprehensive sense.  Regards this narrowness as
    its central deficiency, pointing to the economic inefficien-
    cies involved in the division of large productive estates to
    create a small farm rural structure.

5.  Besikçi, Ismail.  DOGU ANADOLU'NUN DUZENI; SOSYO-EKONOMIK VE
    ETNIK TEMELLER.  (SOCIAL, ECONOMIC, AND ETHNIC BASES OF THE
    EASTERN ANATOLIAN ORDER).  Istanbul, E. Yayinlari, 1970.
    519 p.  Bibl.                            Mem HC 405 B43 1970

    Describes historical and contemporary patterns of interaction
    between economic structure and specific ethnic, religious,
    and socio-organizational features of the region.  Maintains
    that discussion of economic "backwardness" in Eastern Turkey
    requires analysis of ethnic and class factors.  Characterizes
    the overall situation as feudal.  Includes tables on land
    distribution, farm mechanization, migration, etc.

5a. Center on Land Problems in the Near East, Salahuddin, Iraq,
    1955.  COUNTRY INFORMATION REPORT: TURKEY.  CI-2.  (Rome)
    FAO, 1955.  11 p.                         Files Turk 58 C25

6.  Central Treaty Organization.  SYMPOSIUM ON RURAL DEVELOPMENT.
    1963?                                     HT 395 A77 C25

    See Item NE-7 for citation and annotation.

7.  Cohn, Edward J.  "Land reform in Turkey."  (In U.S. Agency for
    International Development.  LAND REFORM IN TURKEY, PAKISTAN,
    AND INDONESIA.  SR/LR/C-30.  Washington, 1970.  13 p.).  Paper
    for Spring Review of Land Reform.         Files Asia 3 U54
    Also available as a separate.            Files Turk 3 C63

# LAND TENURE AND AGRARIAN REFORM

(Cohn, Edward J.)
Traces land reform initiatives, notably the law of 1945. Concludes that the modest amount of land redistributed up to 1967 has engendered political pressures to reduce gross landholding inequalities.

8.  Dooren, P. J. van. "Structural and institutional obstacles facing Turkey's peasant-farmers." (In TROPM, 2, 1961. p. 107-161)                                    Mem GN 1 T75
    Also available as a separate.          Files Turk 7 D66

    Suggests that agricultural development requires radical changes in land tenure as well as improved extension, credit, and other supportive services. Land reform alone is not a panacea.

9.  Frey, Frederick W.; and Sertel, Ayse. LAND OWNERSHIP AND PEASANT ORIENTATIONS IN RURAL TURKEY. Rural Development Research Project, report no. 6. Cambridge, Center for International Studies, M.I.T., 1967. 27 1.          Files Turk 58 F72

    Survey-based study of peasant attitudinal, socio-economic, and educational correlates with the variable of landownership. Landownership emerges as a weak predictor of peasant attitudes, innovativeness, stake in the community, etc.

10. Frey, Frederick W.; and Roos, Leslie L. THE PROPENSITY TO INNOVATE AMONG TURKISH PEASANTS. Rural Development Research Project, report no. 7. Cambridge, Center for International Studies, M.I.T., 1967. 15 1.          Files Turk 83 F72

    Attempts to arrive at an index of the propensity to innovate. Maintains that propensity to innovate depends more on psychic measures than on "such concrete things as landownership."

11. Geray, Cevat. "Toplum kalkinmasi ve toprak reformu. (Community development and land reform)." (In AUSBFD, 21:3, 1971. p. 51-68)                                    Mem AP A6016 S625

    Regards land reform and community development as mutually interdependent. Community development efforts can succeed only on the basis of an equitable land tenure system.

12. Gibb, H. A. R.; and Bowen, Harold. ISLAMIC SOCIETY AND THE WEST: A STUDY OF THE IMPACT OF WESTERN CIVILIZATION ON MOSLEM CULTURE IN THE NEAR EAST. 1957.          Mem DS 38 G485

    See Item NE-15 for citation and annotation.

# LAND TENURE AND AGRARIAN REFORM

13. Granott, Abraham. THE LAND SYSTEM IN PALESTINE; HISTORY AND
    STRUCTURE. 1952.                                    HD 850.8 P1 G71

    See Item NE-16 for citation and annotation.

13a. Hamitogullari, B. "Türkiye'de toprak, toprak reformu ve
     iktisadi kalkinma. (Land, land reform, and economic develop-
     ment in Turkey)." (In AUSBFD, 21:1, 1966. p. 21-46)
                                                   Mem AP A6016 S625

14. Hershlag, Zvi Yehbda. TURKEY: THE CHALLENGE OF GROWTH.
    2nd ed. Leiden, E. J. Brill, 1968. xvii, 406 p. Bibl.
    Second, revised ed. of TURKEY, AN ECONOMY IN TRANSITION.
                                                        HC 492.9 H27

    Chapter 17, "Beginnings of structural change in agriculture,"
    and chapter 22, "The Enigma of agriculture," deal directly
    with land reform initiatives--particularly the law of 1945 and
    generally ineffectual efforts to more vigorously implement the
    law during the 1960s. Simultaneous displacement of labor by
    mechanization and the inability to absorb this labor in indus-
    try make "genuine land reform unavoidable." Includes tables
    on landownership, distribution, and utilization.

15. Hiltner, J. "Land accumulation in the Turkish Çukurova."
    (In JFE, 42:3, 1960. p. 615-628)                          Ag Per

    Discusses the evolution, operation, and prospects for large-
    scale commercially oriented (çiftçi) agriculture in this
    cotton-growing region. Concludes that future expansion
    depends largely on the government's inclination to enforce
    land tenure laws limiting farm size. Foresees such action
    only when economic disadvantages of land accumulation exceed
    advantages in production.

16. Hinderink, Jan; and Kiray, Mübeccel B. SOCIAL STRATIFICATION
    AS AN OBSTACLE TO DEVELOPMENT: A STUDY OF FOUR TURKISH VIL-
    LAGES. New York, Praeger (1970). xxviii, 248 p.
                                                     HD 2037 H55 1970

    Analyzes the interdependence between agro-technical innovations
    and changes in the social structure. Stratifies four villages
    according to stage of agro-economic development. Concludes
    that the continuum of villages studied represents an ascending
    order of technological sophistication though not necessarily
    of human well-being.

# LAND TENURE AND AGRARIAN REFORM

17.  Hirsch, Eva. POVERTY AND PLENTY ON THE TURKISH FARM:  A
     STUDY OF INCOME DISTRIBUTION IN TURKISH AGRICULTURE. Modern
     Middle East series, no. 1.  New York, Columbia University
     Press, 1970.  xv, 313 p.  Bibl.                HD 2037 H57 1970

     Assessment of the distribution of income, first by functional
     shares, i.e., by shares to each factor of production, and then
     by measures based on the distribution of land.  Finds that
     the main equalizing factor is income from animal husbandry.
     Appendices contain statistical analyses of incomes, costs,
     and investment returns by landholding size.

18.  Inalcik, Halil.  "Land problems in Turkish history."  (In
     MW, 45:2, 1955.  p. 221-228)                  Mem AP M9915

     Traces the evolution of predominant state control up to the
     mid-nineteenth century, the emergence of de facto private own-
     ership at that time, and the reassertion of state prerogatives
     in Turkey, notably through the 1945 Land Reform Law.  Argues
     that policy emphasis should be placed on distributing state
     and uncultivated lands rather than breaking up existing farms.

19.  Issawi, Charles P., ed.  THE ECONOMIC HISTORY OF THE MIDDLE
     EAST.  1966.                                  Mem HC 412 I787

     See Item NE-19 for citation and annotation.

20.  Kiray, Mübeccel Belik.  "Esodo agricolo e ristructturazione
     fondiaria in Turchia."  (In REA, 23:3, 1968.  p. 121-145)
                                                          Ag Per

     Attributes rural-urban migration to inadequate employment
     opportunities for a growing rural population.  Proposes land
     reform to stem this movement by widening the scope of rural
     opportunities.

21.  Kodolbas, Kadri Sencer.  "Land settlement policy in Turkey."
     (In Item NE-10, p. 164-174)        HD 850.8 Z63 D46 1965

     Discusses economic, physical, and political motivations for
     land settlement in Turkey.  Social factors such as matching
     ethnic groups are also considered.

22.  Koksal, Osman.  "Land reform is only answer to farmers' ills."
     Translations on the Near East, no. 318.  p. 42-47.  (In JPRS,
     7:7, 1968/1969.  reel 101)  Translated from AKSAN (Istanbul),
     December 7, 1968.  p. 2.                       Microfilm

TURK 22-26

(Koksal, Osman)
Criticizes inadequate government attention to the inequality
of land distribution. Argues that this situation is inconsis-
tent with constitutional provisions and guarantees. Presents
statistics illustrating the extent of inequality.

23. Kolars, John F. TRADITION, SEASON AND CHANGE IN A TURKISH
VILLAGE. Chicago, University of Chicago Press, 1968. xv,
205 p.                                              Geol MC C433 82

Land tenure is one of the factors discussed in this study
based on data from three villages, representing three different types of agricultural systems: subsistence, mixed, and
commercial.

24. Kubali, Ali Nail. "Agriculture: the choice of a development
strategy for Turkey." St. Louis, 1970. viii, 285 1. Ph. D.
dissertation, St. Louis University. Bibl. Photocopy. Ann
Arbor, Mich., University Microfilms, 1973.          HD 2038 K81

Maintains that the optimum development policy would emphasize
major reforms in agriculture. This is "impossible without the
accomplishment of an effective land reform" in conjunction
with resettlement and rural education efforts. Includes statistics on landownership, distribution, etc.

25. Meyer, Albert J. "Turkish land reform; an experiment in
moderation." (In his MIDDLE EASTERN CAPITALISM; NINE ESSAYS.
Cambridge, Harvard University Press, 1959. p. 65-79)
                                                    Mem HC 412 M4

Characterizes the 1945 Land Reform Law as deficient in the
extent of redistribution, although some degree of land title
clarification and improvement in the lot of small farmers was
achieved. Indicates that the traditional mental outlook of
peasants is the main barrier to progress. Calls for more
sectorally balanced investment.

25a. Miller, Duncan; and Çetin, Ihsan. LAND AND MAN IN RURAL
TURKEY: A CONCISE VIEW OF REGIONAL LAND TENURE, LAND USE AND
LAND CAPABILITY. A.I.D. discussion paper no. 20. Ankara,
USAID, 1974. 23 1.                                  Files Turk 58 M45

26. Öztrak, Ilhan. "Toprak reformu ve hukuk politikasi. (Land
reform and legal policy)." (In AUSBFD, 22:1, 1967. p. 67-96)
                                                    Mem AP A6016 S625

378

(Öztrak, Ilhan)
Views land reform as a precondition for agricultural development. Stresses the importance of land registration as an aid
to agrarian reform. Commenting on the Land Registration Act
of 1962 and the Land Consolidation Law of 1966, the author
criticizes the former for its arbitrary land ceilings and the
latter for its failure to protect the integrity of small farms.
Includes tables illustrating land fragmentation in 1950 and
1962.

27. Padel, W.; et Steeg, Louis. DE LA LEGISLATION FONCIERE
OTTOMANE. Paris, 1904. 350 p.  Mem HX 29 P13 Cutter

Begins with a general introduction to the types and sources of
law in the Ottoman Empire. Includes provisions classifying
and regulating various categories of State or miri lands.
Also covers law of persons, their rights over private and
state lands, transactions, inheritance, religious endowments
(i.e., waqfs), judicial procedure, and taxation.

28. Pine, Wilfred H. "Some land problems in Turkey." (In JFE,
34:2, 1952. p. 263-267)  Ag Per

Problems noted include limited farmland area, fragmentation of
landholdings, and lack of reliable cadastral surveys and
registration. Advocates a comprehensive approach to rural
development (including land tenure and infrastructural reforms)
to alleviate these difficulties.

28a. Posada F., Antonio J. "Different systems of land reform
relevant to the Turkish experience." (In LRLSC, 1971:2.
p. 9-13). Paper presented at the Land Reform and Economic
Development Seminar, Istanbul, 18-20 October 1971.
REF HD 1261 A1 L1 1971 v. 2

29. Robinson, Richard D. "Tractors in the village; a study in
Turkey." (In JFE, 34:4, 1952. p. 451-462)  Ag Per
Also available as a separate.  Files Turk 82 R62

Suggests that results of mechanization depend on a community's
particular historical and socio-economic features. Generally
observes an alteration of the land tenure situation, decrease
in labor requirements, fall in village income, and weakening
of village morale.

30. Sadiklar, C. Tayyar. "Land tenure and agrarian reform in
Turkey." (Madison) 1963. 18 1. Paper for Agricultural
Economics 226, University of Wisconsin.  Files Turk 58 S12

# LAND TENURE AND AGRARIAN REFORM

(Sadiklar, C. Tayyar)
Discusses land reform attempts since 1923. States that in
addition to land reform, other structural and institutional
changes are also necessary for rural development.

31. Sanda, Hüseyin Avni. REAYA VE KOLU. (PEASANT AND VILLAGER).
    Istanbul, Habora Kitabevi, 1970. 159 p.  Mem HD 1537 T8 S27

    Discusses the evolving status of peasants within the Ottoman
    Empire's feudal framework. Examines the nature of peasant-
    landlord relations and analyzes changes wrought under the
    impact of Western European economic influence, including
    monetization and capitalization.

32. Sargut, Ibrahim Atif. "The Program of agricultural develop-
    ment in Turkey." (In Conference on World Land Tenure Problems,
    University of Wisconsin, 1951. PAPERS, 2. Madison, 1951.
    7 p.)                                    HD 105 C67 1951b

    Describes overall agrarian make-up of the country and efforts
    to develop the agricultural sector by means of settlement,
    land distribution, and land registration.

33. Savci, Bahri. "Toprak reformu üzerine. (On the land reform)."
    (In AUSBFD, 20:1, 1965. p. 375-418)     Mem AP A6016 S625

    Maintains that real land reform involves drastic social,
    political, and economic changes, a fact that hindered such
    reform until 1965. Summarizes the opposing arguments of
    economic efficiency versus social justice presented by oppo-
    nents and supporters of the reform. Outlines the main features
    of the Turkish reform. The author advocates comprehensive
    agrarian reform which must be based on placing land tenure
    relations on more equitable foundations.

34. Sonmez, Necmi. "Techniques for facilitating land purchase
    in ownership dispersion program in Turkey." 1963? (In Item
    NE-7, p. 99-104)                           HT 395 A77 C25

    Describes the legal framework within which land distribution
    and settlement are being conducted. Outlines features of a
    new land reform law to deal with redistribution and regulation
    of sharecropping and tenancy.

35. Sonmez, Necmi; and Uner, Naki. "Existing land ownership and
    use in Turkey." 1963. (In Item NE-7, p. 81-97)
                                               HT 395 A77 C25

# Land Tenure and Agrarian Reform

(Sonmez, Necmi; and Uner, Naki)
Places the need for agrarian reform within the context of
limitations on potential extension of arable land for distribution to peasants. Outlines land reform initiatives dealing
with land distribution and consolidation as well as technological measures and price policies. Provides statistics on
landownership, distribution, and use.

36. Steeg, Louis. "Land tenure." (In Mears, Eliot G. MODERN
TURKEY. New York, Macmillan, 1924. p. 238-264)

Mem DR 587 M4

A summary of legal provisions for land tenure as they developed
until 1913.

37. Suzuki, Peter T. SOCIAL CHANGE IN TURKEY SINCE 1950--A
BIBLIOGRAPHY OF 886 PUBLICATIONS. College Park, University
of Maryland, 1969. 108 p. Mem Z 716 T9 S9

Contains references on rural life in general and land tenure
in particular.

37a. Turgay, Soliman Necati. LAND DISTRIBUTION AND SETTLEMENT
PROJECTS IN TURKEY. Country project no. CP-7. (Rome) FAO,
1955. 6 p. Paper for Center on Land Problems in the Near
East, Salahuddin, Iraq, 1955.

38. Turkey. Laws, statutes, etc. "Agrarian reform law." Final
draft. Ankara, 1972. 90 (9) 1. Files Turk 3 T87

Full text of the law. Its stated purpose and scope include
"regulating the distribution of landownership, the type of
use of land and structure concerning this use in accordance
with the principles of social justice and productivity."
Gives priority to heads of families with little or no land
as the main recipients of distributed lands. Tables illustrate
the maximum family holdings by district.

39. _____. _____. "The Law of preliminary measures for agrarian
reform; Law no. 1617." n.p., n.d. (10) 1. Published in the
OFFICIAL GAZETTE, 14257, July 26, 1972. Files Turk 3 T875

Restricts land transfer and allotment and sets landholding
limits. Chief among administrative and organizational provisions is the establishment of the Agrarian Reform Secretar-
iat to enforce the law and maintain supportive services.

# LAND TENURE AND AGRARIAN REFORM

40.   Turkey. Laws, statutes, etc. THE OTTOMAN LAND CODE. Trans-
      lated from the Turkish by F. Ongley... Rev., and the marginal
      notes and index added, by Horace E. Miller... London,
      W. Clowes and Sons, 1892. xii, 396 p.   Mem HX 29 T84 Cutter

      Consists of laws enacted between 1858 and 1876. Concerned
      mainly with codifying, definitions of the classes of land and
      regulation of purchase, use, inheritance, adjustment of
      claims, mortgage, and purchase by aliens of miri or state
      lands.

40a.  Tveritinova, Anna Stepanovna. AGRARNYI STROI OSMANSKOI
      IMPERII, XV-XVII V. V.: DOCUMENTII I MATERIALII. (AGRARIAN
      FOUNDATIONS OF THE OSMAN EMPIRE, XV-XVII CENTURIES: DOCU-
      MENTS AND MATERIALS). Moscow, Ist-vo vostochnoi lit-ri,
      1963. 222 p.                              Mem HD 804 T9

40b.  Willson, Clifford H. "A Settlement plan for Turkey." n.p.,
      Economic Cooperation Administration, Special Mission to
      Turkey, 1951. 32 1.                        Files Turk 17 W45

41.   Wilson, Rodney J. A. AGRICULTURAL DEVELOPMENT IN THE MIDDLE
      EAST, 1950-1970. 1972.                     Files NE 4 W45

      See Item NE-40 for citation and annotation.

42.   Yasa, Ibrahim. YIRMIBES YIL SONRA HASANOGLAN KÖYÜ. (THE
      VILLAGE OF HASANOGLAN AFTER TWENTY-FIVE YEARS). Ankara,
      1969. 381 p.                              Mem HN 620 H3 Y35

      Sets forth the contextual framework for landownership struc-
      ture and use in the village of Hasanoglan over a twenty-five
      year period.

43.   Yavuz, Fehmi. "Toprak ya da tarim reformu. (Land as well as
      agricultural reform)." (In AUSBFD, 22:2, 1967. p. 29-42)
                                                Mem AP A6016 S625

      Contends that emulation of developed countries' emphasis on
      "agrarian reform" (i.e., technologically and economically
      oriented measures) is misplaced in Turkey, where a basically
      feudal rural structure still persists. Instead, primary focus
      should be on "land reform" designed to infuse greater social
      justice and order into the land tenure system, according to
      guarantees included in the 1965 Constitution. Advocates
      incorporation of both agrarian and land reform elements in
      rural development efforts.

# Personal Author Index

# Author Index

# Author Index

Landau, Y. H., ISRAEL-16, 25
Langlands, B. W., UGA-34
Langley, Michael, KEN-85;
    RHOD-13
Larbi, Mohammed Taibi, ALG-6
Lawrance, J. C. D., AFR-77, 78;
    ETH-39; KEN-86, 87; UGA-11,
    35, 36
Lawson, Rowena, GHA-35
Lazarev, Grigori, ALG-19; MOR-15,
    16, 17
Leake, Hugh Martin, AFR-79, 80;
    GHA-36; KEN-88, 89;
    MAURITI-3; NIG-72, 73;
    SL-9; SUD-14, 15; TANZ-40;
    UGA-37
Le Coz, Jean, MOR-18, 19, 20
Leonard, H., ZAI-21
Lericollais, André, SEN-12
Le Roy, Etienne, SEN-12a
Letnev, A. B., AFR-81
Leupolt, M., CAM-10
Leurquin, Phillippe P., RWA-5
Levy, Itzjak, ISRAEL-17
Lexander, Arne, ETH-40, 41
Ley, Albert, IC-5, 6, 7
Linington, P. A., SA-14
Link, Heinrich, KEN-89a
Lippens, Philippe, CAM-4, 5
Lissak, Moshe, ISRAEL-24
Little, Kenneth, SL-10
Lloyd, Peter Cutt, NIG-74, 75
Lochard, Y., TUNIS-8
Loomis, Charles, IRAN-70a
Lord, R. F., TANZ-8
Loudon, J. B., SA-11
Louzoun, G., MR-12
Loveridge, A. J., GHA-37
Low, Graeme Campbell, UGA-38
Lucas, Philippe, ALG-19a
Luedtke, Roger Alfred, AFR-82;
    NIG-76
Lugard, Frederick D., AFR-83;
    NIG-77; TANZ-41
Lulseged Asfaw, ETH-41a, 61
Luning, H. A., NIG-78, 79
Luswata, F. J., UGA-39
Mabogunje, A. L., NIG-80
Mabro, Robert, EGY-35
MacArthur, J. D., ETH-42, 43;
    KEN-6, 90, 91, 92, 93

McAuslan, J. P. W. B., KEN-94;
    94a; TANZ-42, 42a; UGA-39a
McBorrough, M. W. J., LIBE-3
MacBride, D. F. H., NIG-81
McDonald, A. S., UGA-40
McDowell, Charles M., NIG-82, 83,
    84
McEntee, P. D., KEN-95
McGlashen, N. D., KEN-96, 97
Machyo, B. Chango, AFR-83a, 84
McIntyre, Paula, UGA-41
McKay, John, TANZ-38, 43
McKenzie, B. R., KEN-98
McLoughlin, Peter F. M., AFR-85
MacMillan, William Miller, SA-12
McNaughton, J. H. M., ZAM-1
Madiman, S. G., ISRAEL-18; KEN-99;
    NE-25, 26; TANZ-44; UGA-42
Mafeje, Archie, UGA-43, 44
Magnes, B., DAHOM-8
Mahdavy, Hossein, IRAN-53
Mahgoub, Sayed Mirghani, SUD-16
Mahteme Sellasie Wolde Maskal,
    ETH-44
Maina, J. W., KEN-24, 100
Maini, Krishan M., KEN-101, 102,
    103; TANZ-45; UGA-45
Mair, Lucy P., AFR-86, 87;
    GHA-37a; KEN-104, 105, 106,
    106a; MALAW-6a; NIG-85, 86;
    SL-11; TANZ-46, UGA-46, 47,
    48, 49; ZAM-12
Makhlouf, Ezzedine, TUNIS-22
Makings, S. M., AFR-88; ZAM-13
Malek, Hocein, IRAN-53a, 53b
Mann, H. S., ETH-39, 45, 46, 47
Manners, R. A., KEN-107
Manshard, Walther, GHA-38
Maquet, Jacques, RWA-6
Marchal, J. Y., MR-13
Marciniak, Louis, NIGER-3
Marei, Sayed, EGY-36, 37, 37a,
    38, 39, 39a
Marill, Alain, ALG-11
Marnay, P., CHAD-4
Maro, M. A. M., TANZ-47
Marthelot, Pierre, ALG-20; MOR-21,
    22; NE-27; TUNIS-23
Marton, S. T., ISRAEL-25
Marzouk, Girgis, EGY-27
Masefield, B. G., AFR-89
Massitu, M. Jean Albert, ZAI-24

May-Parker, I. I., SL-12
Mayer, I., KEN-108
Mayer, P., KEN-108
Mead, Donald C., EGY-40
Meadows, S. J., KEN-109
Meek, Charles Kingsley, AFR-90,
    91, 92; CAM-11; CYP-9;
    GHA-39; KEN-110; MALAW-14;
    MAURITI-5; NIG-87, 88; SL-13;
    TANZ-48, 49; UGA-50; ZAM-14
Mehrain, Fattaneh, IRAN-54
Meillassoux, Claude, IC-8
Meliczek, Hans, IRAQ-32; LIBY-18
Mendras, Henri, IRAN-54a
Mensah, M., DAHOM-9
Mensching, H., TUNIS-24
Méot, Robert, MOR-23
Mergui, Raphaël, ALG-20a
Mesfin Kassu, ETH-47a
Mesfin Kinfu, ETH-48, 49, 50,
    51
Messavussu-Akue, H., TOGO-3
Meyer, Albert J., TURK-25
Middleton, John F. M., TANZ-50,
    51
Miette, R., ALG-21
Mifsud, Frank M., AFR-93, 94;
    GHA-40; NIG-89
Miller, Duncan, TURK-25a
Minko, Henri, GAB-3, 4
Miracle, Marvin P., GHA-41;
    ZAI-25
Missiaen, Edmond, MOZ-2a
Mitchell, Nicolas P., AFR-95;
    CAM-12; TANZ-52; TOGO-4
Moarefi, Ali, IRAN-54b
Moati, Paul, MOR-24
Moghaddam, Reza, IRAN-55
Mohamed Fall, Ould Ahmed,
    MAURITA-1, 2
Mohamed, I., SA-4
Mohammed Reza Pahlavi, Shah of
    Iran, IRAN-56
Moody, R. W., KEN-111; UGA-51
Moore, Franklin C., GHA-42
Morel, Edmund Dene, ZAI-26
Morgan, W. T. W., KEN-112, 113
Moris, Jon, KEN-23
Mortimore, M. J., NIG-90
Motheral, Joe R., IRAN-57
Mouity, Albert, GAB-5

M'Tukudzi, Bonet, RHOD-14, 15
Mueller, James V., LIBE-5
Mueller, Peter, SUD-17
Mugerwa, E. B., UGA-51a
Mugerwa, P. J. Nkambo, KEN-114;
    TANZ-53; UGA-52
Mukwaya, A. B., UGA-53, 53a
Müller, Ernst W., ZAI-27
Müller, Peter, AFR-96
Müller-Praefke, Dieter, AFR-97;
    KEN-115; TANZ-53a; UGA-54
Mulugeta Taye, ETH-52
Munro, Ann P., KEN-116
Murage, B. C., AFR-77
Muralt, Jürgen von, AFR-98;
    ALG-22; NE-28
Murphy, M. C., GHA-42a
Murray, J. S., AFR-99
Mutahaba, Gelase R., TANZ-53b
Mutsau, R. J., ZAM-14a
Muyangana, G. M., ZAM-14b
Naciri, M., MOR-27, 28
Nadel, S. F., ETH-53
Nadel, Siegfried F., NIG-91
Naderi, N. Afshar, IRAN-70a
Najafi, Bahaoldin, IRAN-72
Nasharty, A. H. E., EGY-41
Nasr, Joseph, LEB-7
Nasser, S. F., TANZ-54
N'Dongala, E., ZAI-28
Nelson, Anton, TANZ-55
Netting, Robert McC., NIG-92
Neustadt, I., GHA-14
Newiger, Nikolaus J., KEN-117;
    TANZ-56
Newitt, M. D. D., MOZ-3, 4
Nguema, Isaac, GAB-6
Nguyo, Wilson, KEN-118
Nicolas, Gildad, ETH-53a
Niemeier, G., ANG-2; MOZ-5
Nisbet, James, AFR-100
Njao, Njuguna, KEN-119
Njoku, Athanasius Onwusaka, SL-14
Noble, B. P., GAM-4; SEN-13
Nomani, Farhad, IRAN-59
Noor, Hassan Adan, SOM-3
Norman, D. W., NIG-49
Nottidge, C. P. R., KEN-120
Ntirukigwa, Esperius N., TANZ-57
Nukunya, G. K., GHA-43, 44
Nwabara, Samuel Nwankwo, NIG-94

# Corporate Author Index

Algeria. Laws, Statutes, etc.,
    ALG-3, 4
Algeria. Ministère de l'Agri-
    culture et de la Réforme
    Agraire, ALG-5
Algeria. Ministère de l'Infor-
    mation, ALG-5a
Bank Omran, Teheran, IRAN-8
Bank-i-Markazi-i Iran, IRAN-9
Barclay's Bank (Dominion, Colo-
    nial and Overseas),
    MAURITI-1
Center on Land Problems in the
    Near East, Salahuddin, Iraq,
    1955, IRAN-15b; IRAQ-15;
    JORD-4; SUD-5a; SYRIA-3a;
    TURK-5a
Central Treaty Organization,
    IRAN-16; NE-7; TURK-6
Chilalo Agricultural Develop-
    ment Unit. Asella,
    Ethiopia, ETH-8
Colonial Office Summer Confer-
    ence on African Adminis-
    tration. 7th, King's
    College, Cambridge, 1956,
    AFR-36
Conference on Land Use in a
    Mediterranean Environment,
    Nicosia, Cyprus, 1946,
    CYP-1
Congo (Democratic Republic).
    Ministère de l'Agriculture,
    ZAI-10
Congres de l'Institut Inter-
    national de Droit d'Expres-
    sion Française, Libreville,
    1970, AFR-16

Consortium for the Study of
    Nigerian Rural Development,
    NIG-28
Cyprus. Land Consolidation
    Authority, CYP-3
Cyprus. Laws, Statutes, etc.,
    CYP-4
Development Center on Land Policy
    and Settlement for the Near
    East, Tripoli, 1965, NE-10,
    10a
Development Center on Land Policy
    for West African Countries,
    Fourah Bay College, Freetown,
    Sierra Leone, 1964. AFR-43
East African Institute of Social
    Research Conference, Kampala,
    Uganda, 1963, KEN-37
Egypt, EGY-15c
Egypt. Higher Committee for
    Agrarian Reform, EGY-15d,
    15e, 15f, 15g, 15h
Egypt. Laws, Statutes, etc.,
    EGY-16
Ethiopia, ETH-16, 17, 18
Ethiopia. Central Statistical
    Office, ETH-19
Ethiopia. Livestock and Meat
    Board, ETH-20
Ethiopia. Ministry of Agricul-
    ture. Extension and Project
    Implementation Dept., ETH-20a
Ethiopia. Ministry of Land
    Reform and Administration,
    ETH-21, 22, 61
Ethiopia. Ministry of Land Re-
    form and Administration.
    Dept. of Land Tenure, ETH-23,
    24

# Classified Outline of Subject Index

# Subject Index

SUBJECT INDEX

Uganda, UGA-4, 17, 24, 25,
33, 41, 42, 50, 51, 53,
53a, 54, 56, 60, 65, 71,
75
Upper Volta, UV-1, 3, 4a,
5
Zaire, ZAI-3, 4, 5, 6, 19,
27, 32, 35, 36, 40
Zambia, ZAM-1, 5, 6, 15a,
16, 19

101.  Indigenous Tenure Systems
Africa, AFR-1, 4, 5, 7, 8,
10, 14, 15, 16, 18, 21,
22, 28, 30, 31, 34, 35,
42, 45, 47, 55, 57, 58,
61, 62, 67, 70, 72, 73,
77, 78, 82, 83, 87, 88,
90, 91, 93, 99, 101, 103,
104, 107, 108, 109, 111a,
119, 124, 132, 133, 135,
138, 141, 143
Algeria, ALG-6a, 28a
Botswana, BOTS-3, 4, 5
Burundi, BURU-2, 3, 4, 8,
9
Cameroon, CAM-1, 3, 4, 5, 8,
9, 13, 15
Central African Republic,
CAF-1
Congo, CONGO-3
Dahomey, DAHOM-3, 4, 7, 8,
12
Egypt, EGY-29, 30
Ethiopia, ETH-2, 2a, 2b,
2c, 3, 26, 27, 29, 30,
31, 38a, 40, 44, 46, 53,
57, 59
Gabon, GAB-1, 6
Gambia, GAM-1, 3, 4
Ghana, GHA-2, 3, 4, 5, 6, 9,
13, 14, 15, 19, 20, 21,
31, 38, 40, 42, 42a, 43,
44, 48, 52, 53, 55, 57,
60, 61, 63, 64
Guinea, GUIN-2, 3
Iran, IRAN-10, 34
Iraq, IRAQ-5, 16a, 17, 20,
20a, 20b, 27, 32
Israel, ISRAEL-11
Ivory Coast, IC-1, 2, 4, 5,
8

Kenya, KEN-1, 8, 9, 10, 13a,
13b, 14, 35a, 41, 51, 64,
65, 77, 81, 82, 84, 93,
94, 106, 111, 114, 129, 131,
138, 145, 160
Lesotho, LESO-2, 3a, 7
Liberia, LIBE-5
Libya, LIBY-4, 5, 11, 12, 14
Malagasy Republic, MR-2
Malawi, MALAW-1, 2, 3, 6,
7, 10, 14
Mali, MALI-2
Morocco, MOR-3, 11
Mozambique, MOZ-2, 6
Near East, NE-15, 16
Niger, NIGER-3a
Nigeria, NIG-8, 14, 24, 25,
26, 29, 32, 40, 41, 42, 43,
44, 57, 58, 59, 64, 66, 74,
75, 76, 80, 82, 83, 86, 87,
88, 89, 91, 92, 94, 96,
105, 107, 110, 118, 128
Rwanda, RWA-1, 6, 8
Senegal, SEN-1, 3, 4, 5, 6,
7, 10, 11, 12a, 13, 17, 20
Sierra Leone, SL-1, 2, 2a, 7,
10, 13, 15
South Africa, SA-3, 10
Sudan, SUD-11
Swaziland, SWAZ-2, 3, 4, 7
Syria, SYRIA-5, 7
Tanzania, TANZ-4, 7, 13, 16,
19, 26, 35, 41, 42, 51, 53,
54, 57, 59a, 60, 64, 72, 79,
80, 82, 83
Togo, TOGO-1, 2, 3
Turkey, TURK-12, 13, 19, 27,
42
Uganda, UGA-1, 6, 7, 11, 12,
16, 21, 24, 25, 47, 48, 49,
52, 55, 59, 65, 74
Upper Volta, UP-1, 2, 3, 5, 8,
10, 11
Zaire, ZAI-2, 3, 4, 5, 6, 7,
12, 13, 14, 17, 17a, 18,
22, 26, 27, 32, 35, 36, 37,
38, 40
Zambia, ZAM-1, 4, 5, 6, 7,
14b, 19, 21, 22

403

Morocco, MOR-2a, 19, 33
Mozambique, MOZ-5
Niger, NIGER-1, 2
Nigeria, NIG-1, 17, 43, 46,
53, 69, 70, 98, 101, 115,
121
Rhodesia, RHOD-10, 17, 20
Sierra Leone, SL-18
Somalia, SOM-2
South Africa, SA-3, 3a, 4,
7, 15, 16, 20
Sudan, SUD-17
Tanzania, TANZ-14, 19, 21,
27, 29, 32, 43, 50, 56,
57, 59, 72, 74, 75, 76
Tunisia, TUNIS-10
Turkey, TURK-16
Uganda, UGA-14, 19, 30, 51,
57
Upper Volta, UV-6, 9
Zaire, ZAI-1, 9, 17, 18, 19,
29, 38
Zambia, ZAM-8, 10, 11a

104. Communal Ownership of Land
Africa, AFR-33, 66, 88, 97,
103, 110, 137, 143
Algeria, ALG-2, 20
Botswana, BOTS-4
Cameroon, CAM-2, 15
Egypt, EGY-10
Ethiopia, ETH-2, 2a, 7, 20,
24a, 32, 35, 63
Ghana, GHA-15, 23, 24, 39
Iraq, IRAQ-20a, 20b
Israel, ISRAEL-11
Kenya, KEN-12, 41, 51, 62,
107, 135
Lebanon, LEB-3
Libya, LIBY-5, 7, 16
Malagasy Republic, MR-2, 3,
14
Malawi, MALAW-5
Morocco, MOR-11, 15, 17, 19,
22
Near East, NE-15, 16, 19,
26, 27, 30
Nigeria, NIG-4, 12, 13, 16,
27, 30, 32, 33, 48, 55,
64, 66, 73, 74, 90, 94,
114, 117, 121

Senegal, SEN-3, 22
Sierra Leone, SL-12, 16
Sudan, SUD-1, 5
Syria, SYRIA-5, 9, 18
Tanzania, TANZ-2, 6, 35, 38,
47
Togo, TOGO-2
Tunisia, TUNIS-8, 14, 23, 25
Turkey, TURK-12, 13, 17
Uganda, UGA-10, 39, 54, 55
Zaire, ZAI-7, 32
Zambia, ZAM-6

105. State or Public Ownership
Africa, AFR-29, 48, 92, 101,
120
Algeria, ALG-28, 28a, 35
Botswana, BOTS-4, 5
Burundi, BURU-3
Cameroon, CAM-1, 4, 5, 8, 15
Chad, CHAD-1, 2, 3
Cyprus, CYPRUS-10
Dahomey, DAHOM-5
Egypt, EGY-8, 48
Ethiopia, ETH-6, 9, 11, 14,
22, 23, 24, 32, 41a, 50,
54, 55
Ghana, GHA-18, 23, 24, 39,
51, 53, 56
Iran, IRAN-8, 54b, 57, 59,
61a
Iraq, IRAQ-2, 5, 12, 20a,
20e, 26, 36
Israel, ISRAEL-4, 9, 10, 12,
15, 19, 22
Ivory Coast, IC-5, 10
Jordan, JORD-3, 8a
Kenya, KEN-78, 81
Libya, LIBY-18b
Malagasy Republic, MR-9, 14
Malawi, MALAW-5, 10, 14, 15
Morocco, MOR-1, 13, 14, 14a,
15, 37
Near East, NE-15, 19, 37
Niger, NIGER-3a, 8
Nigeria, NIG-104, 114
Senegal, SEN-3, 7, 11, 13,
19, 22
South Africa, SA-14, 19
Sudan, SUD-5
Swaziland, SWAZ-7

# SUBJECT INDEX

Iran, IRAN-20, 34, 39, 41,
 60, 61
Iraq, IRAQ-27, 28
Israel, ISRAEL-5, 7, 11
Ivory Coast, IC-9, 11
Kenya, KEN-13, 25, 27, 33,
 43, 65, 69, 136, 146
Lebanon, LEB-6
Liberia, LIBE-1
Malagasy Republic, MR-10,
 11, 17
Malawi, MALAW-4, 5
Mauritius, MAURITI-1, 2, 3,
 5
Morocco, MOR-2c, 7, 9, 17,
 21, 24 38
Mozambique, MOZ-9
Near East, NE-15, 16, 18,
 19, 20, 32
Niger, NIGER-5
Nigeria, NIG-11, 20, 55, 80,
 90, 93, 98, 123
Rhodesia, RHOD-4
Sudan, SUD-3, 3a, 9, 12, 14,
 15, 16
Swaziland, SWAZ-1
Syria, SYRIA-5, 7, 8
Tanzania, TANZ-12, 23, 25,
 26, 49, 50, 51, 71, 72
Tunisia, TUNIS-27, 33
Turkey, TURK-12, 13, 15, 16,
 19, 23, 31
Uganda, UGA-20, 61
Zaire, ZAI-17a, 26, 33, 39
Zambia, ZAM-2a, 16

204. Influence of Colonial
 Administrations
Africa, AFR-2, 7, 8, 10, 14,
 23, 28, 29, 30, 31, 37,
 42, 45, 55, 56, 63, 72,
 80, 83, 86, 87, 90, 91,
 92, 95, 106, 109, 110,
 111, 121, 136
Algeria, ALG-6a, 8, 14, 15,
 18a, 22, 23, 27, 28, 28a,
 32, 33, 34, 35
Angola, ANG-2, 3, 4
Botswana, BOTS-2, 4
Burundi, BURU-4, 7
Cameroon, CAM-3, 11, 12, 15

Egypt, EGY-48
Gabon, GAB-1
Gambia, GAM-4
Ghana, GHA-2, 23, 24, 33, 36,
 39, 42, 52, 53
Iraq, IRAQ-16a, 17
Ivory Coast, IC-5, 10
Kenya, KEN-2, 13, 17, 20, 34,
 36, 39, 41, 47, 48, 49, 50,
 67, 75, 76, 77, 88, 89,
 104, 107, 108, 113, 114,
 116, 134, 145, 147, 148,
 156, 157
Libya, LIBY-15, 18e
Malagasy Republic, MR-6, 7,
 11, 14
Malawi, MALAW-14
Morocco, MOR-3, 5, 15, 19,
 21, 28, 34, 35, 37
Mozambique, MOZ-4, 5, 6, 7
Near East, NE-6, 31, 33, 37
Niger, NIGER-2
Nigeria, NIG-24, 27, 31, 46
 58, 64, 72, 73, 74, 77, 82,
 83, 85, 86, 87, 94, 106,
 107, 118, 123, 128
Rhodesia, RHOD-1, 3, 4, 15,
 15a, 16, 18, 20
Rwanda, RWA-7, 18
Senegal, SEN-3, 6, 14a
Sierra Leone, SL-9, 11, 17
South Africa, SA-3, 5, 13,
 14, 20
Sudan, SUD-4, 14, 21, 26
Syria, SYRIA-10, 18
Tanzania, TANZ-7, 40, 41,
 46, 52, 64, 83
Togo, TOGO-3, 4
Tunisia, TUNIS-2, 5, 6, 27,
 28, 29, 31, 38, 39, 42
Uganda, UGA-16, 29, 37, 43,
 46, 47, 49, 50, 52, 64, 72,
 77
Zaire, ZAI-7, 12, 14, 15, 16,
 17, 17a, 19, 23, 26, 30, 33
Zambia, ZAM-8, 12, 14

205. Influence of Colonial
 Settlement
Africa, AFR-110

410

# SUBJECT INDEX

Algeria, ALG-1, 6a, 9, 14,
15, 17, 18a, 19, 22, 23,
28, 28a, 33, 34
Angola, ANG-2, 3, 4
Botswana, BOTS-2
Kenya, KEN-6, 21, 39, 47,
50, 53, 54, 55, 67, 68,
75, 76, 77, 88, 89, 110,
113, 145, 147, 159
Malagasy Republic, MR-10
Malawi, MALAW-4
Morocco, MOR-19, 21, 32
Mozambique, MOZ-3, 4, 5, 7
Rhodesia, RHOD-1, 3, 4, 5, 6,
15, 17, 20
South Africa, SA-3, 13, 20
Tanzania, TANZ-36, 55, 69
Tunisia, TUNIS-33, 34
Zaire, ZAI-7
Zambia, ZAM-8

206. French Influences
Africa, AFR-10, 14, 28, 29,
30, 31, 38, 42, 45, 56,
109, 136
Algeria, ALG-1, 2, 6a, 7a,
8, 9, 11, 14, 15, 17, 18a,
19, 22, 27, 28, 28a, 29,
32, 33, 34, 35
Cameroon, CAM-15
Chad, CHAD-1
Egypt, EGY-8, 10, 30, 48
Iraq, IRAQ-27
Ivory Coast, IC-5, 10
Mauritius, MAURITI-3
Morocco, MOR-3, 5, 15, 19,
21, 28, 34, 35, 37
Near East, NE-6, 18, 19, 31,
33, 37
Senegal, SEN-14a, 22
Syria, SYRIA-7, 10, 18
Togo, TOGO-3
Tunisia, TUNIS-2, 5, 6, 27,
28, 29, 31, 33, 34, 38, 39,
42
Turkey, TURK-19

207. English Influences
Africa, AFR-2, 10, 14, 23,
63, 70, 80, 83, 86, 87, 90,
91, 92, 95, 106, 121

Arabian Peninsula, ARAB-3
Botswana, BOTS-4
Cameroon, CAM-11, 12
Egypt, EGY-8, 10, 30, 44
Gambia, GAM-4
Ghana, GHA-2, 23, 24, 33, 36,
39, 42, 52, 53, 60, 64
Iraq, IRAQ-16a, 17, 27
Israel, ISRAEL-5, 7
Jordan, JORD-6
Kenya, KEN-2, 17, 20, 21, 34,
36, 41, 47, 48, 49, 50,
75, 76, 77, 88, 104, 107,
108, 113, 114, 116, 134,
147, 148, 157
Malawi, MALAW-14
Near East, NE-18, 19
Nigeria, NIG-24, 27, 31, 64,
72, 73, 74, 77, 82, 83,
85, 86, 87, 94, 106, 107,
118, 128
Sierra Leone, SL-9, 11, 17
South Africa, SA-5
Sudan, SUD-4, 14, 21, 26
Tanzania, TANZ-7, 40, 41,
46, 52, 64, 83
Togo, TOGO-4
Tunisia, TUNIS-2
Turkey, TURK-19
Uganda, UGA-9, 16, 29, 37,
46, 47, 49, 50, 52, 64,
72, 74, 77
Zambia, ZAM-8, 12, 14, 15

208. Belgian Influences
Africa, AFR-14
Burundi, BURU-4, 7
Rwanda, RWA-7, 8
Zaire, ZAI-7, 12, 15, 16, 17,
17a, 19, 23, 26, 30, 33

209. Portuguese Influences
Africa, AFR-14, 55
Angola, ANG-2, 3, 4
Mozambique, MOZ-2, 3, 4, 5,
6, 7

210. German Influences
Africa, AFR-14
Cameroon, CAM-3, 11
Tanzania, TANZ-40, 64

411

# Subject Index

# Subject Index

304. Land Taxation

305. Land Redistribution

# Subject Index

Syria, SYRIA-2, 5, 8, 17, 18, 20

Tanzania, TANZ-8, 13, 24, 25, 26, 27, 35, 47, 53, 63, 77, 78, 81, 83

Togo, TOGO-2

Tunisia, TUNIS-10, 14, 15, 23, 24, 27, 29, 30, 41

Turkey, TURK-1, 5, 9, 10, 12, 13, 16, 19, 23, 25, 29, 31, 33, 37, 42, 43

Uganda, UGA-4, 5, 7, 12, 26, 31, 43, 47, 48, 53, 55, 56, 59, 63a, 67, 78

Upper Volta, UV-1, 2, 5, 7, 10

Zaire, ZAI-2, 3, 4, 5, 8, 9, 11, 12, 13, 17, 17a, 20, 22, 37, 38, 39, 40

Zambia, ZAM-5a, 7, 11a, 19, 20, 21

316. **Political Aspects of Agrarian Reform**

Africa, AFR-26, 67, 71

Algeria, ALG-7, 7a, 11, 12, 17, 18a, 25, 28, 31, 33, 34, 35, 35a

Botswana, BOTS-6

Burundi, BURU-4

Egypt, EGY-1, 11, 12, 15b, 19, 28, 31, 42, 46, 47, 58, 65, 66

Ethiopia, ETH-9, 9a, 10, 13, 53a, 55, 60

Ghana, GHA-13, 20, 22

Iran, IRAN-2, 6, 7, 10, 23, 23a, 24, 25, 38, 39, 41, 45, 47, 48, 50, 53, 53b, 57, 58, 59, 61, 63, 64, 70a, 75, 76, 79

Iraq, IRAQ-2, 9, 11, 12, 20, 30, 32, 33, 34, 36, 37, 40, 43, 44, 45

Israel, ISRAEL-11, 16, 18, 24

Ivory Coast, IC-9

Kenya, KEN-5, 20, 52, 53, 54, 67, 70, 75, 76, 77, 78, 81, 94, 121, 138, 141, 156

Lebanon, LEB-8

Lesotho, LESO-6, 7

Malawi, MALAW-2

Morocco, MOR-2, 4, 10, 29, 31, 32

Near East, NE-4, 16, 22, 29, 32, 35, 37, 38

Niger, NIGER-2

Nigeria, NIG-29, 96, 99

Rhodesia, RHOD-11, 13, 16a, 20

Rwanda, RWA-1, 4, 10

Sudan, SUD-11

Syria, SYRIA-5, 12

Tanzania, TANZ-9, 13, 14, 24, 26, 27, 35, 60, 65, 78, 81, 83

Tunisia, TUNIS-3, 8, 18, 25, 27, 32, 39, 42

Turkey, TURK-1, 2, 4, 7, 13, 33, 43

Uganda, UGA-9, 12, 16, 21, 43, 53, 61, 62, 63a, 79a

Upper Volta, UV-3

Zaire, ZAI-3, 11, 22, 37, 39, 40

Zambia, ZAM-19

317. **Economic Aspects of Agrarian Reform**

Africa, AFR-3, 7, 12, 13, 15, 27, 32, 48, 64, 65, 67, 68, 71, 74, 75, 79, 84, 93, 94, 100, 104, 108, 119, 120, 131, 139, 144

Algeria, ALG-13, 14, 15, 15a, 16, 17, 19, 23, 25, 26, 32b, 33, 34, 35, 35a

Arabian Peninsula, ARAB-3, 6

Botswana, BOTS-6

Burundi, BURU-6

Cameroon, CAM-16

Cyprus, CYP-5

Dahomey, DAHOM-1, 5

Egypt, EGY-1, 2, 2a, 3, 7, 9, 11, 11a, 14, 15a, 15b, 17, 18, 19, 20, 21, 24, 26a, 26e, 27, 29, 30, 31, 32, 35, 36, 37, 39, 40, 41, 42, 43, 47, 49, 51, 53, 54, 57, 58, 59, 60, 64, 65, 66, 67, 69, 70, 71

SUBJECT INDEX

## Subject Index

400. Bibliographies
Africa, AFR-52, 65, 90, 97
Burundi, BURU-5
Cyprus, CYP-3, 8
Egypt, EGY-58
Ethiopia, ETH-5, 59
Iran, IRAN-11, 73
Kenya, KEN-115, 134, 159
Libya, LIBY-3
Nigeria, NIG-111
Rwanda, RWA-2, 3
Turkey, TURK-37
Uganda, UGA-48, 54, 71
Zaire, ZAI-20